THE UNIVERSITY OF CHICAGO
ORIENTAL INSTITUTE PUBLICATIONS
VOLUME 104

Thomas A. Holland • *Editor*
with the assistance of *Thomas G. Urban*

THE UNIVERSITY OF CHICAGO
ORIENTAL INSTITUTE PUBLICATIONS
VOLUME 104

EARLIEST LAND TENURE SYSTEMS IN THE NEAR EAST: ANCIENT KUDURRUS

Text

Ignace J. Gelb† • *Piotr Steinkeller*
Robert M. Whiting, Jr.

THE ORIENTAL INSTITUTE OF THE UNIVERSITY OF CHICAGO
CHICAGO • ILLINOIS

Library of Congress Catalog Card Number: 89-50396

ISBN 0-918986-56-7
ISSN: 0069-3367

To Hester, John, and Walter

TABLE OF CONTENTS

LIST OF FIGURES x
LIST OF GENERAL ABBREVIATIONS xi
LIST OF BIBLIOGRAPHIC ABBREVIATIONS xi
PREFACE xvii

1. INTRODUCTION: DOCUMENTARY SOURCES
   1.1. Ancient Kudurrus and Sale Documents 1
   1.2. Date and Provenience 3
   1.3. Material and Form 4
   1.4. Writing 5
   1.5. Language 11
   1.6. Objects of Sale 14
   1.7. Multiple and Single Transactions 14
   1.8. Buyers and Sellers 15
   1.9. Formulary 20
   1.10. Purpose and Function 21
   1.11. Landed Property in Light of the Kudurrus and Sale Documents 24

2. THE EARLIEST KUDURRUS: NOS. 1–12, 18, AND 19
   2.1. External Structure (Form) and Iconography 27
   2.2. Internal Structure (Text) 28
   2.3. Object of the Transaction 30
   2.4. Multiple and Single Transactions 31
   2.5. Function of the Earliest Kudurrus 31

3. ANCIENT KUDURRUS
   No. 1 Hoffman Tablet 33
   No. 2 Walters Tablet 34
   No. 3 Philadelphia Tablet 34
   No. 4 Louvre Tablet 34
   No. 5 Yale Tablet I 35
   No. 6 Yale Tablet II 36
   No. 7 Leiden Tablet 36
   No. 8 Sheep(?) Figurine 37
   No. 9 Khafajah Bird 38
   No. 10 Blau Obelisk 39
   No. 11 Blau Plaque 39
   No. 12 Ushumgal Stela 43
   No. 13 RA 6 p. 143 47
   No. 14 Chicago Stone 48
   No. 15 Baltimore Stone 55
   No. 16 Kish Stone Fragments I 64
   No. 17 Kish Stone Fragment II 66
   No. 18 Figure aux Plumes 66
   No. 19 Lagash Stela 67
      No. 19a DC II p. XXXV 3 68
      No. 19b Cros, NFT p. 222 69
   No. 20 Enḫegal Tablet 69
   No. 21 Lupad Statue 72
   No. 22 Lummatur Tablet I 74
   No. 23 Lummatur Tablet II 80
   No. 24 Stela of Victory 88
   No. 25 Nippur Statue 90
   No. 26 Enna-Il Statue 91

No. 27	10 NT 1	92
No. 28	PBS XV 3	92
No. 29	PBS XV 17	93
No. 30	PBS XV 20	93
	No. 30a Nippur Disk	93
	No. 30b IM 57944	94
	No. 30c A 33678	95
No. 31	Adab Stone Fragment	95
No. 32	Adab Clay Fragment I	96
	Appendix to no. 32 = *Mesopotamia* 8 pp. 68f.	99
No. 33	Adab Clay Fragment II	103
No. 34	BIN II 2	104
No. 35	DP 2	106
No. 36	CT V 3	107
No. 37	CT XXXII 7f.	110
No. 38	Dar-a-a Tablet	113
No. 39	YBC 2409	115
No. 40	Manishtushu Obelisk	116
No. 41	Sippar Stone	140
No. 42	Eshnuna Stone Fragment	151
No. 43	Eshnuna Clay Tablet	152
No. 44	Eshnuna Clay Fragments	156
No. 45	Assur Stone Fragment	159
No. 46	TIM IX 97	159
No. 47	UM 32-40-436	160
No. 48	BM 91068	160
No. 49	BM 90909	161
No. 50	BM 33429	161
No. 51	BM 45593	162
No. 52	BM 139507	162

4. INDEXES TO ANCIENT KUDURRUS
   4.1. Personal Names 163
   4.2. Divine Names 181
   4.3. Geographical Names 182
   4.4. Professions and Titles 184

5. LISTING OF ANCIENT KUDURRUS AND SALE DOCUMENTS
   5.1. Listing of Ancient Kudurrus 187
   5.2. Listing of Sale Documents 189
   5.3. Concordance of Ancient Kudurrus and Sale Documents 193

6. STRUCTURE AND TYPOLOGY OF ANCIENT KUDURRUS AND SALE DOCUMENTS
   6.1. Introductory Remarks 199
   6.2. Structure and Typology of Kudurrus 199
       Nos. 14 Chicago Stone and 15 Baltimore Stone 199
       No. 16   Kish Stone Fragments I 200
       Nos. 21 Lupad Statue, 22 Lummatur Tablet I, and 23 Lummatar Tablet II ... 200
       Nos. 32 Adab Clay Fragment I and 33 Adab Clay Fragment II 200
       No. 34   BIN II 2 200
       No. 35   DP 2 201
       No. 36   CT V 3 201
       No. 37   CT XXXII 7f. 201
       No. 38   Dar-a-a Tablet 201
       No. 40   Manishtushu Obelisk 202
       No. 41   Sippar Stone 203
       Nos. 42 Eshnuna Stone Fragment, 43 Eshnuna Clay Tablet, and 44 Eshnuna Clay Fragments ... 203
   6.3. Structure and Typology of Sale Documents 203
       Nos. 100–136   Fara Sale Documents 203
       Nos. 137–153   Pre-Sargonic Sale Documents from Lagash 205
       No. 156a   Pre-Sargonic Sale Document of Unknown Provenience .. 206

Nos. 157–246   Sargonic Sale Documents 206
        Nos. 247–370   Ur III Sale Documents 210

7. TERMS AND CLAUSES
    7.1.   Introductory Remarks 213
    7.2.   Objects of Sale and Their Description 213
    7.3.   Terms for Price 217
    7.4.   Statement of Rate 219
    7.5.   Terms for Additional Payments 219
    7.6.   Sellers 226
    7.7.   Buyers 228
    7.8.   Terms for Buying and Selling 229
    7.9.   Witnesses 232
    7.10. Guarantors 236
    7.11. Other Participants of the Transaction 237
    7.12. Final Clauses 239
    7.13. Place of the Transaction 249
    7.14. Date Notations 249
    7.15. Sealed Sale Documents 249

8. CHARTS OF PRICES, RATES, AND ADDITIONAL PAYMENTS
    8.1.   Introductory Remarks 251
    8.2.   Kudurrus: Fields 251
    8.3.   Sale Documents 265

9. RELATIONSHIPS AMONG ADDITIONAL PAYMENTS AND BETWEEN PRICES
   AND ADDITIONAL PAYMENTS
    No. 14   Chicago Stone and No. 15 Baltimore Stone 281
    No. 16   Kish Stone Fragments I 281
    No. 22   Lummatur Tablet I and No. 23 Lummatur Tablet II 281
    No. 36   CT V 3 282
    No. 37   CT XXXII 7f. 282
    No. 40   Manishtushu Obelisk 283
    No. 41   Sippar Stone 283
    No. 43   Eshnuna Clay Tablet and No. 44 Eshnuna Clay Fragments 284
    Nos. 100–136 Fara Sale Documents 285

10. RATES OF COMMODITIES
    Figure 19.   Rates of Barley 287
    Figure 20.   Rates of Dates 288
    Figure 21.   Rates of Oil 289
    Figure 22.   Rates of Copper 289
    Figure 23.   Rates of Wool 289
    Figure 24.   Rates of Cloths 289
    Figure 25.   Rates of Metal Objects 290
    Figure 26.   Rates of Animals 290
    Figure 27.   Rates of Human Beings 290

11. COMMODITIES
    11.1.   Introductory Remarks 291
    11.2.   Grains and Grain Products 291
    11.3.   Fruits and Vegetables 292
    11.4.   Liquids 293
    11.5.   Wool and Cloths (Garments) 294
    11.6.   Metals 295
    11.7.   Metal, Stone, and Wooden Objects 296
    11.8.   Animals 297
    11.9.   Human Beings 297
    11.10. Miscellaneous 298

12. LIST OF AKKADIAN AND SUMERIAN WORDS DISCUSSED
    1. Akkadian 299
    2. Sumerian 299

LIST OF FIGURES

1. Main Characteristics of Ancient Kudurrus and Sale Documents . . . 3
2. Distribution of Ancient Kudurrus by Period, Site, and Language . . . 5
3. Distribution of Sale Documents by Period, Site, and Language . . . 6
4. Map of Geographical Distribution of Ancient Kudurrus and Sale Documents . . . 7
5. Evolution of the Form and Orientation of Writing . . . 9
6. Distribution of Sale Documents by Object of Sale . . . 14
7. Distribution of Sales in Sale Documents by Object of Sale . . . 14
8. Sellers and Buyers Appearing in Ancient Kudurrus and Sale Documents . . . 18
9. Main Characteristics of Ancient Kudurrus and Kassite/Post-Kassite Kudurrus . . . 22
10. Structure of the Earliest Kudurrus . . . 29
11. Chart of the Fields of the Manishtushu Obelisk . . . 117
12. Map Showing the Four Main Cities of the Manishtushu Obelisk . . . 118
13. The Relationship between the Price and Additional Payment in Kudurrus nos. 14 and 15 . . . 285
14. The Values of the Additional Payment in Kudurrus nos. 14 and 15 . . . 286
15. The Proportions between the Commodities in Kudurrus nos. 22 and 23 . . . 286
16. The Relationship between the Price and Additional Payment in Kudurru no. 36 . . . 286
17. The Relationship between the Price and Additional Payment in Kudurru no. 37 . . . 286
18. The Price of the Field in Relation to Its Seeding Rate in Kudurru no. 41 . . . 286
19. Rates of Barley . . . 287
20. Rates of Dates . . . 288
21. Rates of Oil . . . 289
22. Rates of Copper . . . 289
23. Rates of Wool . . . 289
24. Rates of Cloths . . . 289
25. Rates of Metal Objects . . . 290
26. Rates of Animals . . . 290
27. Rates of Human Beings . . . 290

LIST OF GENERAL ABBREVIATIONS

A	Amount
Com.	Commodity
DN	Divine Name
env.	envelope
FN	Field Name
GN	Geographical Name
GSG (or: gsg)	GUR.SAG.GÁL (or: gur-sag-gál)
ha	hectare(s)
K.B. (or: k.b.)	KUG.BABBAR (or: kug-babbar)
MB	Middle Babylonian
NB	Neo-Babylonian
OB	Old Babylonian
OS	Object of Sale
P	Price
PN	Personal Name
S(s)	Seller(s)
SS(s)	Secondary Seller(s)

LIST OF BIBLIOGRAPHIC ABBREVIATIONS

A	Tablets in the collections of The Oriental Institute, The University of Chicago
AAS	See Grégoire, *AAS*
AHWB	Wolfram von Soden, *Akkadisches Handwörterbuch* (Wiesbaden, 1959–1981)
AJA	*American Journal of Archaeology*
AJSL	*American Journal of Semitic Literature*
AnOr	*Analecta Orientalia* (Rome)
AO	Tablets in the collections of the Musée du Louvre
AOF	*Archiv für Orientforschung*
AOr	*Archiv Orientální*
ARET	*Archivi reali di Ebla, Testi* (Rome)
ARM	*Archives royales de Mari* (Paris)
ARMT	*Archives royales de Mari* (texts in transliteration and translation) (Paris)
AS	*Assyriological Studies* (Chicago)
ASJ	*Acta Sumerologica*
ATU	Prefix of signs appearing in Falkenstein, *ATU*
AUAM	Tablets in the collections of Horn Archaeological Museum, Andrews University
AUCT	*Andrews University Cuneiform Texts* (Berrien Springs, Michigan)
AWL	See Bauer, *AWL*
BA	*Beiträge zur Assyriologie und semitischen Sprachwissenschaft* (Leipzig)
BAL	See Borger, *BAL*
Bauer, *AWL*	Josef Bauer, *Altsumerische Wirtschaftstexte aus Lagasch*, Studia Pohl 9 (Rome 1972)
BE	*The Babylonian Expedition of The University of Pennsylvania, Series A: Cuneiform Texts* (Philadelphia)
Bibl. Mes.	*Bibliotheca Mesopotamica* (Malibu, California)
BIN	*Babylonian Inscriptions in the Collection of J. B. Nies*
BiOr	*Bibliotheca Orientalis*
Birot, *Tablettes*	Maurice Birot, *Tablettes économiques et administratives d'époque babylonienne ancienne conservées au Musée d'Art et d'Histoire de Genève* (Paris, 1969)
BJRL	*Bulletin of the John Rylands Library* (Manchester)
BM	Tablets in the collections of the British Museum
Böhl Coll.	Tablets in the F. M. T. de Liagre Böhl Collection, Rijksmuseum van Oudheden, Leiden
Borger, *BAL*	Rykle Borger, *Babylonisch-assyrische Lesestücke* (Rome, 1963)
BTBC	See Pinches, *BTBC*
Buccellati, *Amorites*	Giorgio Buccellati, *The Amorites of the Ur III Period*, Istituto Orientale di Napoli, Ricerche 1 (Naples, 1966)
BWL	See Lambert, *BWL*

CAD — *The Assyrian Dictionary of The Oriental Institute of The University of Chicago*, ed. by I. J. Gelb, et al. (Chicago and Gluckstadt, 1956–)

CBS — Tablets in the collections of the Babylonian Section of The University Museum, Philadelphia

Chiera, *CBTC* — Edward Chiera, *Catalogue of the Babylonian Cuneiform Tablets in the Princeton University Library* (Princeton, 1921)

CIRPL — See Sollberger, *CIRPL*

Coll. de Clerq — *Collections de Clerq* (Paris, 1888–1913)

CRAI — *Comptes rendus . . . Académie des Inscriptions et Belles-Lettres*

Cros, *NFT* — Gaston Cros, *Nouvelles fouilles de Tello, publiées avec le concours de Léon Heuzey, Fçois Thureau-Dangin* (Paris, 1910)

CST — See Fish, *CST*

CT — *Cuneiform Texts from Babylonian Tablets in the British Museum* (London)

DC — Ernest de Sarzec, *Découvertes en Chaldée . . .* (Paris, 1884–1912)

De Genouillac, *FT* — Henri de Genouillac, *Fouilles de Telloh*, 1–2 (Paris, 1934–1936)

De Genouillac, *TSA* — Henri de Genouillac, *Tablettes sumériennes archaïques . . .* (Paris, 1909)

Deimel, *Pantheon babylonicum* — Anton Deimel, *Pantheon babylonicum: Nomina deorum e textibus cuneiformibus excerpta . . .* (Rome, 1914)

Deimel, *ŠL* — Anton Deimel, ed., *Šumerisches Lexikon* (Rome)

Dok. — M. V. Nikolski, *Dokumenty khoziaistvennoj otčetnosti . . .*, 1–2 (St. Petersburg, 1908—Moscow, 1915)

Donbaz-Foster, *STTI* — Veysel Donbaz and Benjamin R. Foster, *Sargonic Texts from Telloh in the Istanbul Archaeological Museums*, Occasional Publications of the Babylonian Fund, 5, American Research Institute in Turkey Monographs, 2 (Philadelphia, 1982)

DP — M. Allotte de la Fuÿe, *Documents présargoniques* (Paris, 1908–1920)

ECTJ — See Westenholz, *ECTJ*

Edzard, *SRU* — Dietz O. Edzard, *Sumerische Rechtsurkunden des III. Jahrtausends aus der Zeit vor der III. Dynastie von Ur*, Abhandlungen der Bayerischen Akademie der Wissenschaften, philosophisch-historische Klasse, n.F. 67 (Munich, 1968)

Edzard, *Tell ed-Dēr* — Dietz O. Edzard, *Altbabylonische Rechts- und Wirtschaftsurkunden aus Tell ed-Dēr im Iraq Museum, Baghdad*, Abhandlungen der Bayerischen Akademie der Wissenschaften, philosophisch-historische Klasse, n.F. 72 (Munich, 1970)

EŞEM — Tablets in the collections of the Archaeological Museum of Istanbul (Eski Şark Eserleri Müzesi)

Falkenstein, *ATU* — Adam Falkenstein, *Archaische Texte aus Uruk*, Ausgrabungen der Deutschen Forschungsgemeinschaft in Uruk-Warka 2 (Berlin-Leipzig, 1936)

Falkenstein, *NSGU* — Adam Falkenstein, *Die neusumerischen Gerichtsurkunden*, 1–3, Abhandlungen der Bayerischen Akademie der Wissenschaften, philosophisch-historische Klasse, n.F. 39, 40, 44 (Munich, 1956–1957)

FAOS — *Freiburger altorientalische Studien* (Stuttgart)

Fara — Anton Deimel, *Die Inschriften von Fara*, 1–3, Wissenschaftliche Veröffentlichungen der Deutschen Orient-Gesellschaft 40, 43, 45 (Leipzig, 1922–1924)

Fish, *CST* — Thomas Fish, *Catalogue of the Sumerian Tablets in the John Rylands Library* (Manchester, 1932)

FM — See Gelb, *FM*

Forde, *NCT* — Nels W. Forde, *Nebraska Cuneiform Texts of the Sumerian Ur III Dynasty* (Lawrence, Kansas, 1967)

FT — See De Genouillac, *FT*

Gelb AV — *Approaches to the Study of the Ancient Near East: A Volume of Studies Offered to Ignace Jay Gelb*, ed. by G. Buccellati (Rome, 1973)

Gelb, *FM* — Ignace J. Gelb, *Old Akkadian Inscriptions in Chicago Natural History Museum*, Fieldiana: Anthropology 44/2 (Chicago, 1955)

Gordon, *Smith College* — Cyrus Gordon, *Smith College Tablets* (Northhampton, Massachusetts, 1952)

Grégoire, *AAS* — Jean-Pierre Grégoire, *Archives administratives sumériennes* (Paris, 1970)

Hallo, *Royal Titles* — William W. Hallo, *Early Mesopotamian Royal Titles: A Philologic and Historical Analysis*, American Oriental Series 43 (New Haven, 1957)

Heimpel, *Tierbilder* — Wolfgang Heimpel, *Tierbilder in der sumerischen Literatur*, Studia Pohl 2 (Rome, 1968)

Hoffner, *Alimenta* — H. A. Hoffner, Jr., *Alimenta Hethaeorum*, American Oriental Series 55 (New Haven, 1974)

Hrozný, *Getreide* — F. Hrozný, *Das Getreide im alten Babylonien*, 1 (Vienna, 1913)

HSS — *Harvard Semitic Series* (Cambridge, Massachusetts)

IM — Tablets in the collections of the Iraq Museum, Baghdad

Ist. Mus. Adab	Tablets in the Adab collection of the Archaeological Museum of Istanbul
Ist. Mus. L.	Tablets in the Lagash collection of the Archaeological Museum of Istanbul
Ist. Mus. Nippur	Tablets in the Nippur collection of the Archaeological Museum of Istanbul
ITT	François Thureau-Dangin et al., *Inventaire des tablettes de Tello conservées au Musée Impérial Ottoman*, 1–5 (Paris, 1910–1921)
JAOS	*Journal of the American Oriental Society*
JCS	*Journal of Cuneiform Studies*
Jean, *Tell Sifr*	Charles-François Jean, *Tell Sifr: Textes cunéiformes conservées au British Museum, réédités* (Paris, 1931)
JEN	*Joint Expedition with the Iraq Museum at Nuzi*, American Schools of Oriental Research, Publications of the Baghdad School, Texts, 1–6 (Paris, 1927—New Haven, 1939)
JEOL	*Jaarbericht van het Vooraziatisch-Egyptisch Genootschap "Ex Oriente Lux"*
JMEOS	*Journal of the Manchester Egyptian and Oriental Society*
JN	Prefix of signs appearing in S. Langdon, *The Herbert Weld Collection in the Ashmolean Museum: Pictographic Inscriptions from Jemdet Nasr Excavated by the Oxford and Field Museum Expedition*, Oxford Editions of Cuneiform Texts, Vol. 7 (Oxford, 1928)
JNES	*Journal of Near Eastern Studies*
JRAS	*Journal of the Royal Asiatic Society*
Kish	Tablets in the Kish collection of the Ashmolean Museum
Kraus AV	*Zikir Šumim: Assyriological Studies Presented to F. R. Kraus on the Occasion of his Seventieth Birthday*, ed. by G. van Driel, Th. J. H. Krispijn, M. Stol, and K. R. Veenhof (Leiden, 1982)
Krebernik, *Beschwörungen*	Manfred Krebernik, *Die Beschwörungen aus Fara und Ebla*, Texte und Studien zur Orientalistik, Band 2 (Hildesheim, 1984)
Krecher, *Kultlyrik*	Joachim Krecher, *Sumerische Kultlyrik* (Wiesbaden, 1966)
LAK	Prefix of signs appearing in Anton Deimel, *Die Inschriften von Fara* 1, Wissenschaftliche Veröffentlichungen der Deutschen Orient-Gesellschaft 40 (Leipzig, 1922)
Lambert, *BWL*	W. G. Lambert, *Babylonian Wisdom Literature* (Oxford, 1960)
LB	Tablets in the F. M. T. de Liagre Böhl Collection, Rijksmuseum van Oudheden, Leiden
Limet, *Anthroponymie*	Henri Limet, *L'anthroponymie sumérienne dans les documents de la* 3e *dynastie d'Ur*, Bibliothèque de la Faculté de Philosophie et Lettres de l'Université de Liège 180 (Paris, 1968)
Limet, *Documents*	Henri Limet, *Étude de documents de la période d'Agadé appartenant à l'Université de Liège* (Paris, 1973)
Limet, *Métal*	Henri Limet, *Le travail du métal au pays de Sumer au temps de la* IIIe *dynastie d'Ur* (Paris, 1960)
Limet, *TSDU*	Henri Limet, *Textes sumériens de la* 3e *dynastie d'Ur*, Documents du Proche-Oriente, Épigraphie 1 (Brussels, 1973?)
L'Oeil	*L'Oeil: Revue d'Art Mensuelle* (Lausanne)
MAD	*Materials for the Assyrian Dictionary* (Chicago)
MAH	Musée d'Art et d'Histoire, Genève
MAOG	*Mitteilungen der Altorientalischen Gesellschaft* (Leipzig)
M.A.R.I.	*Mari, Annales de Recherches Interdisciplinaires*
MDP	*Délégation en Perse: Mémoires* (Paris)
MEE	*Materiali epigrafici di Ebla* (Naples)
Mesopotamia	*Mesopotamia: Copenhagen Studies in Assyriology* (Copenhagen)
MJ	*The Museum Journal*
MLC	Tablets in the collections of the J. Pierpont Morgan Library
MM	Tablets in the collections of the Montserrat Museum
MSL	*Materialen zum sumerischen Lexikon; Materials for the Sumerian Lexicon* (Rome, 1937–)
MVNS	*Materiali per il vocabolario neo-sumerico* (Rome)
N.A.B.U.	*Nouvelles Assyriologiques Brèves et Utilitaires* (Paris)
NBC	Tablets in the J. B. Nies Collection, Yale University
NCT	See Forde, *NCT*
Ni.	Tablets in the Nippur collection of the Archaeological Museum of Istanbul
NRVN	M. Çiğ and H. Kizilyay, *Neusumerische Rechts- und Verwaltungsurkunden aus Nippur* 1, Türk tarih kurumu yayinlarindan, 6 seri, no. 7 (Ankara, 1965)
NSATN	David I. Owen, *Neo-Sumerian Archival Texts Primarily from Nippur* (Winona Lake, Indiana, 1982)
NSGU	See Falkenstein, *NSGU*
NT	Field numbers of tablets excavated at Nippur by The Oriental Institute and other institutions
NTSŠ	Raymond R. Jestin, *Nouvelles tablettes sumériennes de Šuruppak au Musée d'Istanbul*, Bibliothèque archéologique

	et historique de l'Institut français d'archéologie d'Istanbul 2 (Paris, 1957)
OA	*Oriens Antiquus*
OECT	*Oxford Editions of Cuneiform Texts* (Oxford)
OIC	*Oriental Institute Communications* (Chicago)
OIP	*Oriental Institute Publications* (Chicago)
OLZ	*Orientalische Literaturzeitung*
Oppenheim, *Eames Coll.*	A. Leo Oppenheim, *Catalogue of the Cuneiform Tablets of the Wilberforce Eames Babylonian Collection in the New York Public Library*, American Oriental Series 32 (New Haven, 1948)
Or.	*Orientalia*
OSP	Aage Westenholz, *Old Sumerian and Old Akkadian Texts in Philadelphia, 1: Literary and Lexical Texts and the Earliest Administrative Documents from Nippur*, Bibliotheca Mesopotamica 1 (Malibu, California, 1975)
PBS	*Publications of the Babylonian Section* (Philadelphia)
Pettinato, *UNL*	Giovanni Pettinato, *Untersuchungen zur neusumerischen Landwirtschaft*, 1–2, Istituto Orientale di Napoli, Ricerche 2–3 (Naples, 1967)
Pinches, *BTBC*	Theophilus G. Pinches, *The Babylonian Tablets of the Berens Collection*, Asiatic Society Monographs 16 (London, 1915)
PSBA	*Proceedings of the Society of Biblical Archaeology* (London)
PSD	*The Sumerian Dictionary of The University Museum of The University of Pennsylvania*, ed. by. Åke W. Sjöberg et al. (Philadelphia, 1984–)
RA	*Revue d'assyriologie et d'archéologie orientale*
RAI	*Compte rendu de la . . . Recontre Assyriologique Internationale*
RÉC	Prefix of signs appearing in François Thureau-Dangin, *Reserches sur l'origine de l'écriture cunéiforme* (Paris, 1898)
RGTC	*Répertoire géographique des textes cunéiformes* (Wiesbaden, 1974)
RLA	*Reallexikon der Assyriologie* (Leipzig and Berlin, 1932–)
Rosengarten, *Répertoire*	Yvonne Rosengarten, *Répertoire commenté des signes présargoniques sumériens de Lagaš* (Paris, 1967)
RS	*Revue sémitique d'épigraphie et d'histoire ancienne(s)* (Paris 1893–1914)
RSO	*Rivista degli studi orientali*
RT	*Recueil de travaux relatifs à la philologie et à l'archéologie égyptiennes et assyriennes* (Paris)
RTC	François Thureau-Dangin, *Recueil de tablettes chaldéennes* (Paris, 1903)
SAKI	See Thureau-Dangin, *SAKI*
San Nicolò, *Schlussklauseln*	Marian San Nicolò, *Die Schlussklauseln der altbabylonischen Kauf- und Tauschverträge. Ein Beitrag zur Geschichte des Barkaufes*, Münchener Beiträge zur Papyrusforschung und antiken Rechtsgeschichte 4 (Munich, 1922)
Schneider, *Götternamen*	Nikolaus Schneider, *Die Götternamen von Ur III*, Analecta Orientalia 19 (Rome, 1936)
SEb	*Studi Eblaiti*
SEL	*Studi epigrafici e linguistici*
Serota Coll.	Tablets in the Serota Collection, The Oriental Institute, The University of Chicago
SET	T. B. Jones and J. W. Snyder, *Sumerian Economic Texts from the Third Ur Dynasty: A Catalogue and Discussion of Documents from Various Collections* (Minneapolis, 1960)
Sjöberg, *Mondgott*	Åke Sjöberg, *Der Mondgott Nanna-Suen in der sumerischen Uberlieferung*, 1 (Stockholm, 1960)
ŠL	See Deimel, *ŠL*
Sollberger, *CIRPL*	Edmond Sollberger, *Corpus des inscriptions "royales" présargoniques de Lagaš* (Geneva, 1956)
Sommer Festschrift	*Corolla linguistica: Festschrift Ferdinand Sommer zum 80. Geburstag am 4. Mai 1955* (Wiesbaden, 1955)
SRT	Edward Chiera, *Sumerian Religious Texts* (Upland, Pennsylvania, 1924)
SRU	See Edzard, *SRU*
Steinkeller, *Sale Documents*	Piotr Steinkeller, *Sale Documents of the Ur III Period*, Freiburger altorientalische Studien 17 (Stuttgart, 1989)
StOr	*Studia Orientalia* (Helsinki)
STTI	See Donbaz-Foster, *STTI*
Szlechter, *TJA*	Émile Szlechter, *Tablettes juridiques et administratives de la IIIe dynastie d'Ur et de la Ire dynastie de Babylone* . . . (Paris, 1963)
TA	Tablets in the Tell Asmar collection of The Oriental Institute of The University of Chicago
TCL	*Textes cunéiformes, Musée du Louvre, Département des Antiquités Orientales*
TCS	*Texts from Cuneiform Sources* (Locust Valley, New York)
TÉL	Charles Virolleaud and Maurice Lambert, *Tablettes économiques de Lagash (époque de la IIIe dynastie d'Ur)* . . . (Paris, 1968)
Thureau-Dangin, *SAKI*	François Thureau-Dangin, *Die sumerischen und akkadischen Königsinschriften*, Vorderasiatische Bibliothek (Leipzig, 1907)
TIM	*Texts in the Iraq Museum* (Baghdad and Wiesbaden)
TJA	See Szlechter, *TJA*

TLB	*Tabulae cuneiformes a F. M. Th. de Liagre Böhl collectae* (Leiden)
TMH	*Texte und Materialien der Frau Professor Hilprecht Collection of Babylonian Antiquities im Eigentum der Friedrich-Schiller-Universität Jena* (Berlin)
TSA	See De Genouillac, *TSA*
TSDU	See Limet, *TSDU*
TSŠ	Raymond R. Jestin, *Tablettes sumériennes de Šuruppak conservées au Musée de Stamboul*, Mémoires de l'Institut français d'archéologie de Stamboul 3 (Paris, 1937)
TUT	George A. Reisner, *Tempelurkunden aus Telloh*, Mittheilungen aus den orientalischen Sammlungen 16 (Berlin, 1901)
UCP	*University of California Publications in Semitic Philology* (Berkeley)
UE	*Ur Excavations* (London)
UET	*Ur Excavations, Texts* (London)
UM	Tablets in the collections of The University Museum of The University of Pennsylvania
Unger AV	*Beiträge zu Geschichte, Kultur und Religion des alten Orients: Im memoriam Eckhard Unger*, ed. by Manfred Lurker (Baden-Baden, 1971)
UNL	See Pettinato, *UNL*
UVB	*Vorläufiger Bericht über . . . die Ausgrabungen in Uruk-Warka* (Berlin)
VA	Tablets in the collections of the Vorderasiatisches Museum, East Berlin (Vorderasiatische Abteilung)
VAS	*Vorderasiatische Schriftdenkmäler* (Leipzig and Berlin)
VDI	*Vestnik drevnej istorii* (Moscow)
Waetzoldt, *UNT*	Hartmut Waetzoldt, *Untersuchungen zur neusumerischen Textilindustrie*, Studi economici e tecnologici 1 (Rome, 1972)
Westenholz, *ECTJ*	Aage Westenholz, *Early Cuneiform Texts in Jena*, Det Kongelige Danske Videnskabernes Selskab Historisk-Filosofiske Skrifter 7/3 (Copenhagen, 1975)
WO	*Die Welt des Orients*
WZKM	*Wiener Zeitschrift für die Kunde des Morgenlandes*
YBC	Tablets in the Yale Babylonian Collection, Yale University
YNER	*Yale Near Eastern Researches* (New Haven)
Yondorf Coll.	Tablets in the collection of the late Milton Yondorf of Chicago
YOS	*Yale Oriental Series*, Babylonian Texts (New Haven)
ZA	*Zeitschrift für Assyriologie und vorderasiatische Archäologie*
ZAW	*Zeitschrift für die alttestamentliche Wissenschaft*

PREFACE

This book is the culmination of a long effort which extends over a period of four decades. Its beginning can be traced back to 1952, when in his *Old Akkadian Writing and Grammar* Ignace J. Gelb listed seven stone inscriptions of the Pre-Sargonic date, all of which dealt with fields and contained a number of Akkadian words and personal names. These inscriptions and their Sumerian counterparts, Gelb promised, were to be discussed "soon in a separate study." Due to his preoccupation with editing Sargonic texts and other duties, the publication of the promised study unfortunately was long delayed. Throughout the fifties and sixties, however, Gelb continued to work on the "ancient kudurrus," in which he was assisted by Joyce Bartles. At that time the transliterations and synoptic charts of some thirty "kudurrus" were prepared.

In 1974 the "ancient kudurrus" project entered a new phase, when Gelb received a major grant from the National Endowment for the Humanities to write the promised work. At that time Gelb was joined by two research associates, Piotr Steinkeller and Robert M. Whiting, then Ph.D. candidates in Assyriology at the Oriental Institute. During 1974–1976 Gelb and Whiting revised or wrote new transliterations and commentaries to the "kudurrus" (chap. 3). During the same years Steinkeller made transliterations of all the sale documents dating from the Fara through the Ur III periods, prepared synoptic charts of the "kudurrus" and sale documents (either working on the basis of the older charts by Gelb or independently), and began writing chapters 6–11.

The association of Whiting with the project ended officially in 1976, but he continued making additions to the manuscript and offering advice in the following years. Steinkeller, while working primarily on the project "Source Book for the Social and Economic History of the Ancient Near East," completed chapters 6–11 and typed all the synoptic charts in the the years 1976–1981. He continued adding textual comments to the "kudurrus" and prepared, working in collaboration with Gelb, transliterations and commentaries to several new "kudurrus." During the same period Gelb and Steinkeller, with the assistance of Lawrence A. Smith and Howard Farber, compiled the indexes (chap. 4).

Although Steinkeller had left Chicago in the summer of 1981, his work on the project continued virtually uninterrupted. From 1981 to 1985 he wrote translations to the "kudurrus," revised large sections of chapters 6–11, drew several figures, and continued to provide new readings and commentaries to the "kudurrus."

During those years Gelb, who worked in collaboration with Maureen Gallery, wrote chapters 1, 2, and 5, and prepared new transliterations and commentaries to the earliest "kudurrus" (nos. 1–12). At that time a decision was made to exclude from the book several chapters, written entirely by Gelb, which addressed the questions of household organization, family structure, and land tenure conditions. In making this decision we had been motivated primarily by practical and financial considerations, since the enormous size of the manuscript made it impossible to publish as a single volume. The excluded chapters were to be published by Gelb separately, under the title "Oikos Economy."

The status of the book, already in hands of the editor, changed dramatically in December of 1985. After three months of brave battle Gelb succumbed to leukemia, leaving his beloved "ancient kudurrus" project unfinished and his collaborators grief-stricken and uncertain about the future of the book. Although painfully aware that Gelb's death had created a void in the project that could not be filled, they nevertheless decided to go on with the original plans, in the knowledge that that had been his parting wish, and in hope that by completing the book they would build a truly lasting monument to his memory as a great scholar.

In April of 1986 Steinkeller assumed responsibility for preparing the book for publication. It became obvious to him at that time that the manuscript, due to its long period of gestation and the collective nature of its authorship, required major revisions and adjustments. This concerned especially the book's philological apparatus. Accordingly, in the fall of 1986 and during most of 1987 he revised systematically the whole manuscript. All the transliterations of the "kudurrus" (chap. 3) were checked against the photographs. This resulted in many new or improved readings and in changes in the evaluation of the meaning, origin, and date of some of these documents. Textual notes to the "kudurrus" were expanded and updated to reflect better the present state of cuneiform scholarship. Equally extensive revisions were made in chapters 1 and 2. Section 1.11, which discusses land tenure conditions, is completely new; for the views there expressed, which are somewhat at variance with Gelb's earlier writings, Steinkeller takes entire responsibility.

Due to the fact that the synoptic charts and figures had already been photographed in preparation for publication, it was impossible to make any major changes in them. Only two synoptic charts and some of the smaller figures were completely redone; in other synoptic charts only small alterations were made (primarily updated bibliographic information). Because of this, the reader will find some discrepancies between the transliterations of the "kudurrus" and the data in the synoptic charts; this affects primarily the readings. For the updated transliterations of the Ur III sale documents, consult Steinkeller's *Sale Documents of the Ur III Period* (Stuttgart, 1989).

Although the readings were improved and updated throughout the volume, the basic system of transliteration, which is characteristic of Gelb's publications, was left unchanged. In the case of the readings that Gelb favored and consistently defended (e.g., Innin against Inanna or en_5-si against énsi), no attempt was made to modify them. The numbering of homophones follows R. Borger, *Assyrisch-babylonische Zeichenliste* (Neukirchen-Vluyn, 1976), though their marking is in accordance with Thureau-Dangin's system.

So many persons contributed to the "ancient kudurrus" project over the years that it is almost impossible to list them all. We should mention here especially the names Joyce Bartels, Maureen Gallery, Lawrence A. Smith, and Howard Farber, whose valuable assistance is deeply appreciated. For advice we are particularly indebted to Miguel Civil and Robert D. Biggs. Among the contributors of copies, Margaret W. Green and Aage Westenholz deserve our special gratitude. Thanks are also due William W. Hallo, Åke W. Sjöberg, Edmond Sollberger, and Christopher B. F. Walker for granting us publication rights to the "kudurrus" and sale documents in their care and for other forms of assistance. For collations we are particularly grateful to Aage Westenholz. The assistance rendered by other persons and institutions is acknowledged in the respective commentaries to the "kudurrus."

We are grateful to Robert McC. Adams, the former director of the Oriental Institute, for agreeing to have this volume appear in this series. To him and to Janet H. Johnson, the present director of the Oriental Institute, go our deep thanks for the continuous and unwavering support of the project.

We were fortunate in being able to secure financial support over a five year period from the National Endowment for the Humanities. Lesser sums were provided by the National Science Foundation, The Oriental Institute of The University of Chicago, and an anonymous benefactor. To all of them goes our heartfelt gratitude.

Of special importance has been the assistance and extraordinary patience of Thomas A. Holland, the editor, and of Thomas G. Urban, the editor's assistant, in bringing this volume to print.

Our great regret is that Jay did not live to see the publication of this book, the work he so cherished, and to which he devoted several decades of his life. We may only hope that he would have graciously overlooked its imperfections.

Piotr Steinkeller
September 1989

CHAPTER 1

INTRODUCTION: DOCUMENTARY SOURCES

1.1. *Ancient Kudurrus and Sale Documents*

The area under investigation in this study is Mesopotamia, present-day Iraq, mainly its southern part, which extends from a line near Baghdad where the Tigris and the Euphrates come closest to each other, in the northwest, and down to the Persian Gulf, in the southeast. Within this area we distinguish Sumer in the south and Akkad in the north. The four provincial extensions of this central area of Sumer and Akkad consist of the Diyala region around the city Eshnuna on the Diyala River, of Assyria around Assur upriver on the Tigris, of the Mari region around Mari upriver on the Euphrates, and of Elam around Susa in southwestern Iran.

The time with which we are concerned in this study extends from the oldest periods of written history down to the end of the Third Dynasty of Ur. The following epigraphic periods are distinguished:

Uruk III period, about 3100–2900 B.C.
Early Dynastic I–II periods, about 2900–2600 B.C.
Early Dynastic IIIa, the Fara period, about 2600–2450 B.C.
Early Dynastic IIIb, the Pre-Sargonic period, about 2450–2340 B.C.
Sargonic period, about 2340–2159 B.C.
Ur III period, about 2117–2008 B.C.

There are no primary sources describing the structure of ancient Mesopotamian society and economy. We have no original studies of the ancient clan and family, the ruling and the working classes, agriculture, and other means of production. Because of that, our information can be reconstructed only on the basis of sources dealing indirectly with social and economic matters. While the laborious culling of information from such sources may be deemed less conducive to solid results than utilizing descriptive studies on the subject, the former has certain advantages in that it contains synchronic and objective information, while the latter contains (or may contain) diachronic and personal, and therefore, subjective information. Ancient Mesopotamia cannot boast of anything close to Aristotle's *Politeia*, but it has thousands of original documents approximating in type and value to the English *Doomsday Book*.

The number of original sources which can be utilized for the reconstruction of the structure of ancient Mesopotamian society and economy is virtually unlimited. It is much greater for Mesopotamia than for any other area of the ancient Near East, such as Egypt, Palestine, Anatolia, or Iran; it is even greater than that for classical Greece and Rome. And the number of sources published, and thus made available to scholars who can read cuneiform, forms only a part, often a very small part, of the collections of cuneiform texts which lie buried in the museums of the world.

By type, the ancient Mesopotamian sources can be divided into several classes, such as administrative texts, "ancient kudurrus," legal documents, letters, royal inscriptions, law codes, literary texts, rituals, omens, incantations, seals, school texts, and others. Of these, by far the largest is the class of administrative texts. In contrast, sources such as literary texts and incantations are scarce in number and of limited importance for our purpose.

The aim of the present volume is the elucidation of the ancient Mesopotamian land-tenure systems, as they may be reconstructed mainly from the "ancient kudurrus" on stone and sale documents on clay.

In the first edition of *Old Akkadian Writing and Grammar* (*MAD* 2, Chicago, 1952) pp. 3f., eight stone inscriptions of the Pre-Sargonic period were listed, all dealing with fields and containing a number of Akkadian words and personal names. At that time, our interest in these texts was primarily linguistic, since the Akkadian words and names occurring in them reflected the oldest attested stage of written Akkadian, and thus appeared to be of importance for the history of the Akkadian language and Semitics in general.

Since the stone inscriptions dealing with landed property in the third millennium B.C. had certain characteristics linking them with the kudurrus or "boundary stones" of the much later Kassite and post-Kassite periods, they were dubbed there "ancient kudurrus." The term has stuck and is now in general use among Assyriologists. The terms "ancient kudurru" or simply "kudurru" will be used for these documents throughout this volume.

The use of the term "kudurru" for these documents is somewhat anachronistic since the word *kudurru*, meaning "boundary stone," is not attested before the Middle

Babylonian period. Furthermore, the later kudurrus most frequently recorded a grant of land from the king to an individual and thus served a somewhat different purpose than the ancient kudurrus. On the other hand, both the later and ancient kudurrus served the ultimate purpose of describing the land owned by an individual and the manner by which it came into his possession.

Despite its inadequacy, the term "ancient kudurru" is brief and therefore useful. Over the years, several attempts have been made to replace it by long descriptive terminologies but without success. See now the full discussion in section 1.10.

In 1952, Gelb expressed the hope that he might "discuss these ancient 'kudurru's' and their Sumerian and Akkadian parallels soon, in a separate study" (*MAD* 2, p. 3f.). In working on ancient kudurrus, especially on the extent and sequence of their formulary, it soon became clear, however, that there were so many parallels between the kudurrus written on stone and sale documents written on clay that it would be impossible to understand the former without taking full account of the latter. The scope of the investigation thus grew from the original eight kudurrus to fifty-seven kudurrus and 282 sale documents, altogether 339 texts.

Similar optimistic forecasts about the forthcoming publication of the ancient kudurrus and related texts were made by Gelb in 1971, in his article "On the Alleged Temple and State Economies in Ancient Mesopotamia," *Studi in onore di Edoardo Volterra* 6 (Milan, 1971) pp. 137–54, which was devoted to a brief evaluation of these documents. In the same article Gelb also proposed the existence of private-family and private-individual ownership of land which occurred besides the public ownership by the state and temple.

The history of the study of ancient kudurrus begins with the Manishtushu Obelisk (no. 40), first published in 1900, which was treated independently by three scholars in the years 1906–7: E. Cuq, "La propriété foncière en Chaldée d'après les pierres-limites (Koudourrous)," *Nouvelle revue historique de droit français et d'étranger* 30 (1906) pp. 701–38 (republished with small changes in his *Études sur le droit babylonien, les lois assyriennes et les lois hittites* [Paris, 1929] pp. 77–112, expanded on pp. 112–49); J. Flach, "La propriété collective en Chaldée," *Revue historique* 95 (1907) pp. 309–36; and F. Hrozný, "Der Obelisk Maništusu's," *WZKM* 21 (1907) pp. 11–43, and "Das Problem der altbabylonischen Dynastien von Akkad und Kiš," *WZKM* 23 (1909) pp. 191–219. While Cuq and Flach discussed the Manishtushu Obelisk only cursorily, in connection with the Kassite kudurrus as providing evidence for the existence of private, tribal ownership of land, Hrozný treated it very extensively, both from the philological and the historical points of view.

At approximately the same time that Gelb first expressed interest in the study of ancient kudurrus, I. M. Diakonoff began his investigations which provided evidence favoring the existence of private, familial property contrasting with the state- and temple-owned land. His pertinent studies are: "O ploščadi i sostave naselenya šumerskogo 'goroda-gosudarstva,'" *VDI* 32 1952/2 pp. 77–93; "Sale of Land in Pre-Sargonic Sumer," *Papers Presented by the Soviet Delegation at the XXIII International Congress of Orientalists* (Moscow, 1954) pp. 19–29; "Kupla-prodaža zemli v drevneyšem Šumere i vopros o šumerskoy obščine," *VDI* 1955/4 pp. 10–40; and *Obščestvenny i gosudarstvenny stroy Drevnego Dvurečya. Šumer* (Moscow, 1959).

Fifteen Sumerian ancient kudurrus of the Uruk III and Early Dynastic II–III periods were provided with transliteration, translation, and a brief commentary by D. O. Edzard, *Sumerische Rechtsurkunden des III. Jahrtausends aus der Zeit vor der III. Dynastie von Ur* (= *SRU*) (Munich, 1968) pp. 106–98 nos. 106–20.

The fact that the ancient kudurrus were written on stone is significant in its own right. Stone was rare and expensive in Mesopotamia and its use for inscriptions was always limited. With a few exceptions, third millennium stone inscriptions can be narrowly circumscribed. There are votive inscriptions in the form of stelae, statues, tablets, vessels, maceheads, etc., either commemorating conquests or building activities and dedicated to some deity usually "for the life" of the votant; there are seal inscriptions, generally not meant to be read from the seal itself but cut in reverse to be read from the impression, and used for the identification of the seal owner and the security of property; there are weights in the form of ducks; and finally there are the ancient kudurrus.

The use of stone for the ancient kudurrus means that they were considered to have great significance at the time they were made and that they were intended to be a permanent and indestructible record.

The contribution of ancient kudurrus to our understanding of the social and economic structure of ancient Mesopotamia cannot be overestimated. Let it suffice to stress here two points only, land tenure and structure of clan and family.

As will be fully elaborated later on, ancient kudurrus deal with the acquisition of landed property by a single buyer from several sellers, the latter often being related to each other by blood. Thus, ancient kudurrus testify to the existence of a land tenure system based on family-owned property, contradicting the reconstructions of all those scholars who visualize land ownership as being limited to the state or the temple.

Ancient kudurrus enable us to see the structure of the ancient family and clan much better than at any other time of Mesopotamian history. Texts such as Manishtushu Obelisk (no. 40) describe the ancestry of sellers which is often as long as six generations. These long lists of generations provide us with evidence that there were also extended families besides nuclear families, which in turn were grouped into larger social configurations up to the level of "clans."

This volume as a whole is concerned with the records of purchase or sale of immovable and movable property in the third millennium B.C. in Mesopotamia and with their socio-economic and legal evaluation.

Two types of records are treated:

a) Ancient kudurrus on stone, which deal with the acquisition by purchase of multiple parcels of land by one individual. This type of document is peculiar to the third millennium B.C.

Figure 1. Main Characteristics of Ancient Kudurrus and Sale Documents

	Ancient Kudurrus	*Sale Documents*
Time:	From Uruk III to Sargonic	From Fara to Ur III
Place:	Sumer, Akkad, Diyala Region, Assyria	Sumer, Akkad, Diyala Region, Assyria, Elam
Material:	Stone	Clay
Form:	Tablet, stela, statuette, animal figurine	Tablet (very rarely brick or cone)
Language:	Sumerian, Akkadian	Sumerian, Akkadian
Contents:	Purchases of multiple parcels of land, each from one or more sellers by one buyer	Purchase of a single piece of property (field, orchard, house, slave, animal, etc.) from one or more sellers by one buyer
Purpose:	Publicity of the purchases	Record of the purchase, prepared for the buyer

b) Sale documents on clay, which deal with the purchase or sale of any kind of property, immovable and movable. This type of text is known from early, as well as from later Mesopotamian times.

This volume includes the edition of fifty-seven ancient kudurrus, about one-third of which are published here for the first time, and a treatment of 282 sale documents, about one-fourth of which have not been published previously. The texts are widely scattered in the various museums of Europe, Asia, and America. In size and state of preservation, they vary from small, broken, and insignificant fragments to the magnificent Manishtushu Obelisk, which is about one and one-half meters high and contains hundreds of lines of writing.

The fifty-seven kudurrus consist of fifty-two single plus five intercalated entries (nos. 19a and 19b, from Lagash, and nos. 30a, 30b, and 30c, from Nippur). The 282 sale documents consist of 271 single entries plus eleven intercalated entries (nos. 113a, 113b, 113c, 127a, 127b, 156a, 182a, 247a, 274a, 309a, and App. to no. 32).

Two texts are added to the transliterations of the kudurrus: App. to nos. 22 and 23 (= no. 144), from Lagash, and App. to no. 32, from Adab. Each is on clay, not stone, and each deals with a single purchase. The two appendices were added because they shed important light on the respective kudurrus.

There are eight entries under the kudurrus whose inclusion must be justified. Two texts from Lagash, namely nos. 19a and 19b, contain numerous sections, each with amounts of various commodities and personal names, but not fields or prices. Four texts, namely nos. 32, 33, 43, and 44, are written on clay, in contrast to the related nos. 31 and 42, which are written on stone. All these clay tablets are kudurrus in the sense that they record multiple purchases of land and in other respects parallel the structure of the kudurrus on stone. We take these documents to be either first drafts of the final copy or private copies destined for the personal use of the purchaser of land (see also section 1.3). The inclusion of two Lagash texts in this volume, namely nos. 19 and 24, is quite open to question. They both deal on the obverse with fields whose sizes are comparable to those of other kudurrus. On the reverse of no. 24, however, we are confronted with immense areas, possibly 67 kilometers by 67 kilometers or 21 kilometers by 21 kilometers, which have no parallels anywhere and can hardly be interpreted as purchases of fields. For some tentative interpretations, see the introductory comments to nos. 19 and 24.

Figure 1 contrasts the main characteristics of ancient kudurrus and sale documents. For details, see the following sections, especially section 1.10.

1.2. *Date and Provenience*

The sequence of the fifty-seven ancient kudurrus in this volume is generally chronological. However, nine texts of different periods are grouped together under Lagash and nine texts under Nippur.

The ancient kudurrus extend almost from the beginning of cuneiform writing in the Uruk III period (the so-called Jemdet Nasr period), through Early Dynastic I–II, Early Dynastic IIIa (Fara period), and Early Dynastic IIIb (Pre-Sargonic period), down to the Sargonic period. There are no examples of ancient kudurrus from the time of the Third Dynasty of Ur onward. The lack of kudurrus in the Ur III period can be easily interpreted as resulting from the prohibition of alienating landed property, which probably took place at that time.

Since there are no reliable paleographic charts showing the evolution of signs in terms of time, place of origin, and material used (stone as against clay), the dating of the earliest kudurrus is quite disputable. Generally, in determining the date of the early kudurrus we have been guided more by the degree of their legibility and understandability than by the form of the signs and other graphic criteria.

The place of origin of most ancient kudurrus can be determined with varying degrees of assurance, depending on the reliability of excavation reports. They have been found throughout the Akkadian area, namely, Akkad (Sippar, Kish, Babylon, and possibly Dilbat and Cuthah), the Diyala region (Eshnuna and Tutub), Assyria (Assur), and the Sumerian area (Lagash, Nippur, Adab, Ur, and possibly Umma and Shuruppak). The origin of over one-third of the kudurrus is unknown.

It is noteworthy that the ancient kudurrus come from the areas occupied by the Semites (Akkad, Diyala, and Assyria) and from the sites in the Sumerian area which were or might have been under Semitic influence. With the exception of a single text from Ur (no. 47), the Sumerian sites in the far South, such as Uruk, Eridu, and Larsa, have yielded no ancient kudurrus. For the linguistic distribution of the ancient kudurrus, see the extensive discussion in section 1.5.

Some typical examples of ancient kudurrus are listed below to enable the reader to visualize their distribution in terms of time and area. The oldest, Uruk III, group is represented by a group of texts of unknown geographic origin, including, among others, seven texts with a unique and characteristic tablet shape (nos. 1–7) and Blau Obelisk and Plaque (nos. 10 and 11). Although due to the difficulties in reading early cuneiform texts much of their content cannot be understood, the occurrence of the signs for fields and their measurements makes it safe to assume that the texts deal with large parcels of land. To the second group, Early Dynastic I–II, belong, e.g., no. 12 of unknown origin and no. 18 from Lagash. Typical examples of the next group, Early Dynastic IIIa and b (= Fara and Pre-Sargonic), are the two very large and important texts nos. 14 and 15, both of unknown origin, and the texts from Kish (nos. 16 and 17), Lagash (nos. 20–23) Adab (nos. 31–33), and a number of mostly fragmentary and ill-dated texts from Nippur (nos. 25–30c). The latest group consists of thirteen Sargonic inscriptions, almost all written in Akkadian and found in the Akkadian area of Babylonia. Among them are nos. 40, 41, and the texts from Eshnuna (nos. 42–44).

In terms of time, the fifty-seven ancient kudurrus are represented as follows:

11	kudurrus of the Uruk III period
3	kudurrus of the ED I–II periods
10	kudurrus of the Fara period
19	kudurrus of the Pre-Sargonic period
14	kudurrus of the Sargonic period
57	

Proceeding approximately from northwest to southeast, the geographical distribution of ancient kudurrus is:

Assur	1	
Tutub	1	
Eshnuna	3	
Sippar	7	including 6 uncertain
Cuthah	1	uncertain
Kish	3	including 1 uncertain
Babylon	1	
Dilbat	1	uncertain
Nippur	9	
Adab	3	
Shuruppak	1	uncertain
Umma	1	uncertain
Lagash/Girshu	9	including 1 uncertain
Ur	1	
Unknown Origin	15	
	57	30 of certain plus 27 of uncertain or unknown provenience

There are 282 sale documents on clay treated in this book. Their sequence is chronological. Period groupings are further subdivided, whenever necessary, by place of origin, contents, or type of transaction.

Sale documents begin in the Fara period, continue through the Pre-Sargonic, Sargonic, and Ur III periods, and then on to the end of cuneiform writing.

The temporal distribution of the sale documents is as follows:

42	Fara (nos. 101–136)
22	Pre-Sargonic (nos. 137–156a and App. to no. 32)
91	Sargonic (nos. 157–246)
127	Ur III (nos. 247–370)
282	sale documents (including 11 intercalated entries)

Proceeding approximately from northwest to southeast, the geographical distribution of these texts is:

Gasur	2	Sargonic
Eshnuna	10	8 Sargonic and 2 Ur III
Sippar	1	Sargonic
Umm-el-Jīr	1	Sargonic
Kish	2	Sargonic
Nippur	76	10 Sargonic and 66 Ur III
Adab	17	1 Pre-Sargonic, 7 Sargonic, and 9 Ur III
Isin	32	Sargonic
Shuruppak	42	Fara (including 1 excavated at Uruk)
Umma	12	1 Sargonic and 11 Ur III
Girshu	36	18 Pre-Sargonic, 9 Sargonic, and 9 Ur III
Lagash	2	Pre-Sargonic
Ur	10	Ur III
Susa	2	Ur III
Unknown Origin	37	1 Pre-Sargonic, 18 Sargonic, and 18 Ur III
	282	sale documents (including 11 intercalated entries)

Reorganizing this chart by regions, we have two texts from Assyria (Gasur), ten texts from the Diyala River region (Eshnuna), four texts from Akkad (Sippar, Kish, and Umm-el-Jīr), 227 texts from Sumer (Nippur, Isin, Shuruppak, Adab, Umma, Lagash, Girshu, and Ur), two texts from Elam (Susa), and thirty-seven texts of unknown provenience.

The distribution of ancient kudurrus and sale documents by period, site, and language is shown in figures 2–4. Their linguistic distribution is discussed in section 1.5. The circumstances of their discovery are discussed in section 1.10.

1.3. *Material and Form*

The material and form of the ancient kudurrus are systematically registered below in section 5.1.

In about one half of the fifty-seven kudurrus, the material is generally described merely as "black stone tablet," "light brown stone," or even simply "stone tablet."

When the material is known, limestone appears in nineteen cases (nos. 13, 16, 18, 19, 20, 23, 24, 26, 28, 30a, 34, 36, 37, 38, 41, 47, 48, 49, and 52), and diorite in three (nos. 21, 40, and 42). One or two cases are represented by

Figure 2. Distribution of Ancient Kudurrus by Period, Site, and Language

	Uruk III	ED I–II	Fara		Pre-Sargonic		Sargonic		Totals			
									Language			
	S	S	S	A	S	A	S	A	S	A	Site	Region
Akkad												13
North												
Sippar	—	—	—	—	—	2[a]	—	1 + 4[a]	—	7	1 + 6[a]	
Cuthah	—	—	—	—	—	—	—	1[a]	—	1	1[a]	
Kish	—	—	—	1 + 1[b]	—	1[a]	—	—	—	2 + 1[b]	2 + 1[a]	
Babylon	—	—	—	—	—	—	—	1	—	1	1	
Dilbat	—	—	—	—	—	1[a]	—	—	—	1	1[a]	
Sumer												24
Near South												
Nippur	—	—	—	1 + 2[b]	3[b]	2 + 1[b]	—	—	3[b]	3 + 3[b]	9	
Adab	—	—	—	—	1	1 + 1[b]	—	—	1	1 + 1[b]	3	
Shuruppak	—	—	1[a]	—	—	—	—	—	1	—	1[a]	
Umma	—	1[a]	—	—	—	—	—	—	1	—	1[a]	
Lagash/Girshu	—	2	2	—	4	—	1	—	9	—	9	
Far South												
Ur	—	—	—	—	—	1[b]	—	—	—	1[b]	1	
Assyria												1
Assur	—	—	—	—	—	—	—	1	—	1	1	
Diyala Region												4
Tutub	1	—	—	—	—	—	—	—	1	—	1	
Eshnuna	—	—	—	—	—	—	—	3	—	3	3	
Unknown Origin	10[a]	—	2[a]	—	—	1[a]	1[a]	1[a]	13	2	15[a]	15
Totals, Site	1 + 10[a]	2 + 1[a]	7 + 3[a]		14 + 5[a]		7 + 7[a]			—	31 + 26[a]	—
Totals, Language	11	3	5	2 + 3[b]	5 + 3[b]	8 + 3[b]	2	12	26 + 3[b]	22 + 6[b]	—	—
Totals, Period	11	3	10		19		14		57		57	57

a = Site uncertain b = Language uncertain S = Sumerian A = Akkadian

alabaster (nos. 31 and 51?), gypsum (nos. 12 and 25), onyx (no. 4), schist (nos. 9? and 30?), serpentine or shale (nos. 10 and 11), shale (no. 30c), slate (nos. 29 and 30b), and syenite (no. 35).

Apart from stone, four kudurrus are preserved on clay: nos. 32 and 33 (both from Adab), and nos. 43 and 44 (both from Eshnuna). We do not know the reason for the use of clay at Adab and Eshnuna. The broken condition in which the fragments making up no. 43 were found in the field suggests that the tablet was smashed after being used as a first draft, from which the scribe prepared the final copy on stone.

On the other hand, it should be noted that while the purpose of setting up a stone kudurru is public, the purpose of preparing a clay document is private. Thus, it is quite possible that the clay texts were written to serve either as a first draft or as a private copy for the personal use of the purchaser of land. A similar draft may be the Isin *Sammelurkunde* no. 182a (see section 1.7).

By far the most common form of ancient kudurrus is in the shape of tablets (square, rectangular, or round), slabs, or plaques. Other forms represented are: obelisks (nos. 10 and 40), stelae (nos. 12 and 19), a disk (no. 30a), a vessel (no. 46), and a cylinder (no. 51).

Still other forms, all of early periods, are statues or statuettes (nos. 21, 25, and 26, all Fara) and animal figurines (nos. 8 and 9, both Uruk III). Human figures are carved on nos. 10 and 11 of the Uruk III period, and nos. 12, 18 and 19 of the ED I–II periods.

The form of sale documents is regularly a tablet (rectangular, square, or round), occasionally a cone (nos. 139, 140, 141, 145, 147, and 148, all Pre-Sargonic Lagash, and no. 263, Ur III), or a brick (no. 146, Pre-Sargonic Lagash). The form, use, and function of the cones are discussed in section 1.10.

1.4. *Writing*

The writing of the ancient kudurrus begins with the pictorial stage, in which the signs generally represent pictures, and progresses steadily in its formal development to the cuneiform stage, in which the signs have the characteristic wedge-like form.

The ability to read and understand ancient kudurrus grows remarkably between the Uruk III period, the time of the earliest kudurrus, and the classical Sargonic period, to which our latest kudurrus are dated.

During these periods, important innovations took place in the graphotactical arrangement of writing. They affect 1) the vertical/horizontal orientation of the text, 2) the sequence of the sides, rows/columns, and cases/lines, and 3) the sequence of the signs within cases/lines.

Figure 5 shows the form and orientation of writing as it developed from pictorial to linear and from vertical to

Figure 3. Distribution of Sale Documents by Period, Site, and Language

	Fara	Pre-Sargonic		Sargonic		Ur III		Totals			
								Language			
	S	S	A	S	A	S	A	S	A	Site	Region
Akkad											4
Sippar	—	—	—	—	1	—	—	—	1	1	
Umm-el-Jīr	—	—	—	—	1	—	—	—	1	1	
Kish	—	—	—	—	2	—	—	—	2	2	
Sumer											227
Near South											
Nippur	—	—	—	10	—	64 + 2[a]	—	77	—	74 + 3[a]	
Adab	—	1	—	7	—	9	—	17	—	17	
Isin	—	—	—	32	—	—	—	32	—	32	
Shuruppak	42	—	—	—	—	—	—	42	—	42	
Umma	—	—	—	1	—	9 + 2[a]	—	12	—	10 + 2[a]	
Girshu	—	18	—	9	—	9	—	36	—	36	
Lagash	—	2	—	—	—	—	—	2	—	2	
Far South											
Ur	—	—	—	—	—	10	—	10	—	10	
Assyria											2
Gasur	—	—	—	—	2	—	—	—	2	2	
Diyala											10
Eshnuna	—	—	—	—	7 + 1[a]	2	—	2	8	9 + 1[a]	
Elam											2
Susa	—	—	—	—	—	2	—	2	—	2	
Unknown Origin	—	—	1[a]	12[a]	6[a]	13[a]	5[a]	25	11	37[a]	37
Totals, Site	42	21 + 1[a]		72 + 19[a]		105 + 22[a]		—		240 + 42[a]	—
Totals, Language	42	21	1	71	20	122	5	257	25	—	282
Totals, Period	42	22		91		127		282		282	282

a = Site uncertain S = Sumerian A = Akkadian

horizontal. The signs selected for the illustration show easily recognizable pictures of objects and living beings. The signs are GUD "bull" (here, its head), SAL "woman" (here, vulva), UR "dog" (here, its head), ŠE "barley," APIN "plow," DU "foot," and UD "sun."

In drawing A, which illustrates the older stage, the form of the signs is pictorial. They are grouped in small cases, which run in horizontal rows from right to left across the obverse and then the reverse. As in other types of writing, such as Egyptian, hieroglyphic Hittite, or the Phaistos Disk, certain signs that have a "front" and a "back," such as UR "dog," APIN "plow," or DU "foot," regularly face towards the beginning of a row of writing.

In drawing B, which illustrates the younger stage, the orientation of the text changed by 90° to the left and the forms of the pictures changed from a standing position to one that shows them lying on their backs. Accordingly, the right-to-left orientation of the cases within the rows changed to a top-to-bottom orientation of the cases within columns, and the right-to-left orientation of the signs within the cases changed to the left-to-right orientation. All that affected the sequence of the rows/columns on the obverse and reverse. While in the older stage the rows ran consecutively from top to bottom across the whole tablet, including obverse and reverse, in the younger stage the columns ran consecutively first from left to right across the obverse and then from right to left across the reverse, as in all later stages of cuneiform writing. Thus the three rows of the older stage in our illustration become six columns in the younger stage, three on the obverse and three on the reverse. By observing the two drawings, it is easy to see that the three-row number is self-imposed in the older stage by the easy flow of cases in one row from obverse to reverse, with the cases often overlapping the boundary between them. By contrast, there is a clean division between the obverse and reverse in the younger stage, and the six-column number is imposed by the fact that, while column iv of the reverse continues column iii of the obverse, column v does not continue column ii and column vi does not continue column i.

The formal evolution of the signs, from pictorial to linear to cuneiform, is a matter of paleography, which is of no concern to us here.

There is no doubt that the first drawing represents the older stage and the second drawing the younger stage of writing. All ancient pictographic writings such as the old Egyptian, hieroglyphic Hittite, or Aegean, as well as modern American Indian or African systems, represent the signs in their natural, vertical standing position, as in the first drawing; and this vertical orientation of the signs is the only one that is attested on stone inscriptions in all

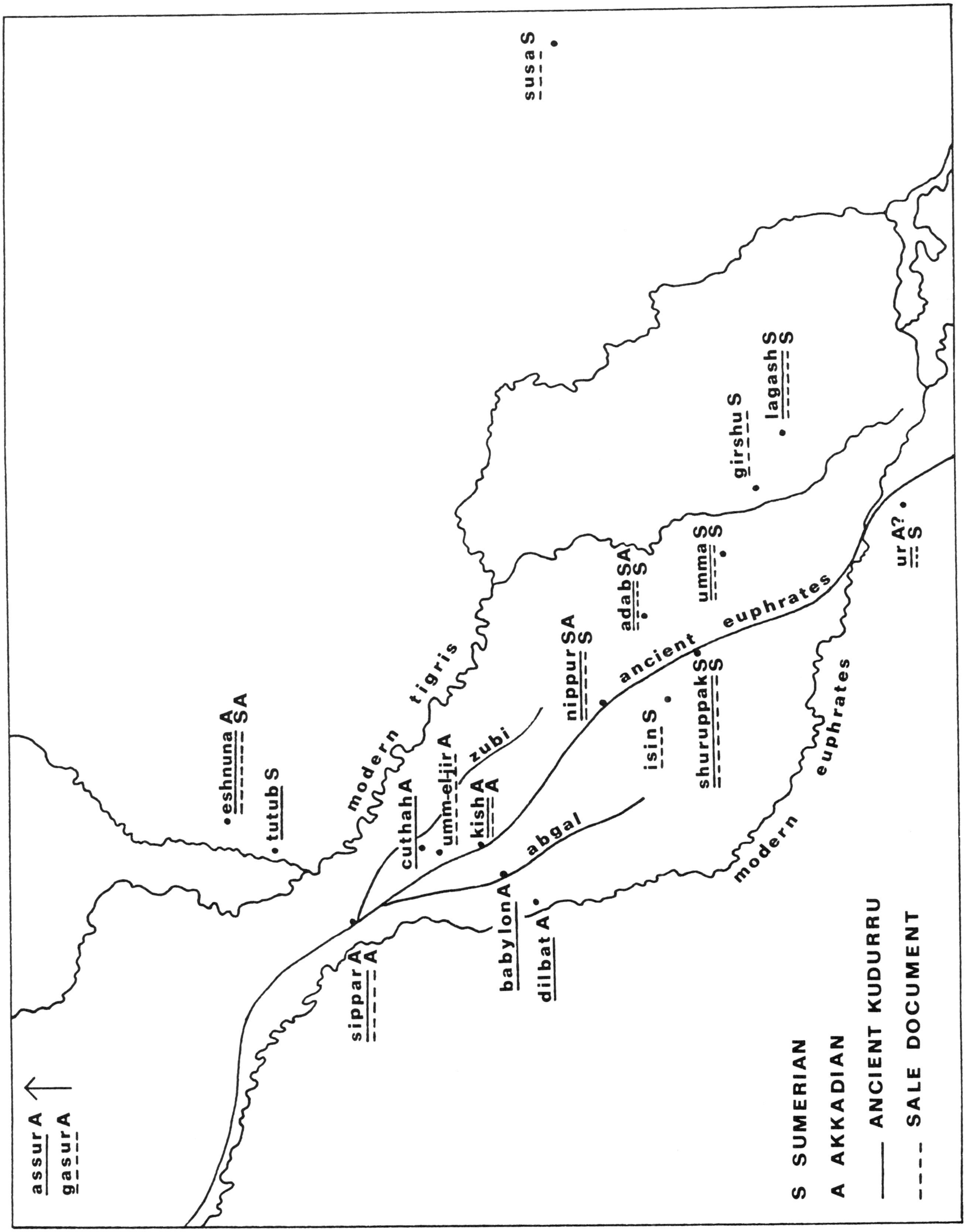

Figure 4. Map of Geographical Distribution of Ancient Kudurrus and Sale Documents.

stages of the cuneiform writing from the oldest pictographic to the Old Babylonian period. Consequently, the orientation of the signs in a horizontal, lying position, attested on clay tablets and illustrated in the second drawing, must be a later development, which took place in Mesopotamia and nowhere else. The reason for the development is a moot question. Our feeling is that it is connected with the use of writing on clay tablets and with the way the tablets were held in the hand by the scribe. When the tablets were small and only slightly elongated, the scribe could hold them by their two broader sides and write the signs vertically without difficulty. As the shape of the tablets became ever longer, it may have been difficult for the scribe to hold the tablet by its two broad sides, now wider apart, and he was forced to abandon holding the tablet by its two broad sides and to begin holding it by its two narrow sides. This in turn may have forced the change in the orientation of writing from the vertical to the horizontal position.

The exact time when the orientation of writing changed from vertical to horizontal is unknown. It could have taken place suddenly and systematically at one time and in one area and slowly and gradually at other times and in other areas. It is our firm judgment that the question of the vertical-horizontal orientation of writing on clay tablets cannot be resolved without a microscopic investigation of the imprints of the fingers of the scribes which were left at the time when the scribe held a soft clay tablet in his hand. The possibility also may be envisaged that the writing in a horizontal position may have been introduced on clay tablets at the same time that its reading in a vertical position may have been continued.

M. W. Green reported in Chicago in 1979 that the imprints preserved on archaic Uruk tablets clearly indicate that a scribe holding naturally a tablet in his hand could produce only signs lying in their horizontal orientation and not standing in their natural, vertical position. She offered a similar opinion at the international conference on the language of Ebla in Naples in 1980. H. Nissen, in his comments at the conference, agreed completely with her conclusions, which were also drawn, more than fifty years ago, by A. Falkenstein, *ATU* pp. 9ff., on the basis of the orientation of the wedges in signs of the Uruk III writing. For reasons unknown, Green chose not to discuss this important question in her paper "The Construction and Implementation of the Cuneiform Writing System," *Visible Language* 4 (1981) pp. 345–60.

The Falkenstein-Green-Nissen conclusion that the horizontal orientation of writing may be proven as far back as the Uruk III period is contrary to the conclusion reached recently on the basis of a study of the Pre-Sargonic texts from Ebla by S. A. Picchioni, "La direzione della scrittura cuneiforme e gli archivi di Tell Mardikh-Ebla," *Or.* n.s. 44 (1980) pp. 225–51, and by G. Pettinato, *Ebla* (Milan, 1979) p. 46, and *MEE* 1 p. xix and nn. 26 and 31. They both contend that the writing was vertical, not horizontal, but while Pettinato limits his observation to Ebla, Picchioni extends it widely to cover cuneiform writing, both on clay and stone, from its inception to and including the Old Babylonian period.

The new conclusion is explained in detail by Picchioni, *op. cit.* pp. 240–45. As found ordered in rows on the room floor, the Ebla tablets allowed immediately two important observations: the front or obverse of the tablet faced towards the center of the room, that is, towards a prospective reader, and its back or reverse faced towards the wall; each tablet was lying with one of its longer edges touching the ground of the room, allowing the text to be read in a vertical, but not horizontal, orientation of the writing. This led Picchioni to assume that the order and orientation of the tablets as they were found on the floor reflect exactly the order and orientation of the tablets as they were lying on the original shelves from which they had fallen to the ground. The vertical orientation would allow, according to Picchioni, easy consultation of the text by the scribes, especially of its most important part, the title or the colophon, by reading it in the top right corner of the reverse, which was abutting the first signs of the first column in the top right corner of the obverse.

Plausible as these observations and conclusions appear on the surface, we note that they affect the reading, not the writing, of the text and that the orientation of the tablets on the shelf allows easy reading of the vertical writing on the obverse, but not of the backward-running vertical writing on the reverse of the tablet.

We shall proceed in the following with the illustration of the various aspects of early cuneiform writing discussed above on the basis of ancient kudurrus and sale documents.

As is generally known, the vertical orientation of writing on stone monuments is attested from its beginning up to and including the Old Babylonian period. The standing position of the signs in their vertical orientation is easily provable in the early kudurrus which contain writing interspersed with iconographic representations. The oldest of these are nos. 10 and 11, of Uruk III time, in which the pictorial signs can still be clearly recognized, and nos. 12 and 18, of ED I–II time, which testify to a gradual evolution of the signs from pictorial to linear.

The earliest sale documents treated in this volume date from the Fara and Pre-Sargonic periods (ED IIIa and IIIb). While nothing clear about the vertical-horizontal orientation of the writing can be found—as far as we can see—in our Fara texts, Falkenstein, *ATU* p. 10 and n. 1, pointed out that the writing accompanying the pictorial representations in two Fara texts, *Fara* 2, 62, and E. Heinrich, *Fara* (Berlin, 1931) pls. 27f., can be read normally in their horizontal orientation. The decisive evidence in favor of the horizontal orientation is offered by the writing on clay cones (nails or pegs) of the Pre-Sargonic period. Six of these truncated cones, recording sale transactions, are discussed in section 1.10. Of these, only no. 140 *DP* 31 has an inscription running not only on the side of the cone, but also on its wider base. Since the purpose of the cones was to make the sale public, the wider base with the inscription must have faced the prospective reader, while the narrower base rested against the wall. Looking at the cone attached to the wall in this way, the writing can be read horizontally when standing to the left of the cone or vertically when standing in front of it. There are many truncated and tapering cones of the Pre-

Figure 5. Evolution of the Form and Orientation of Writing

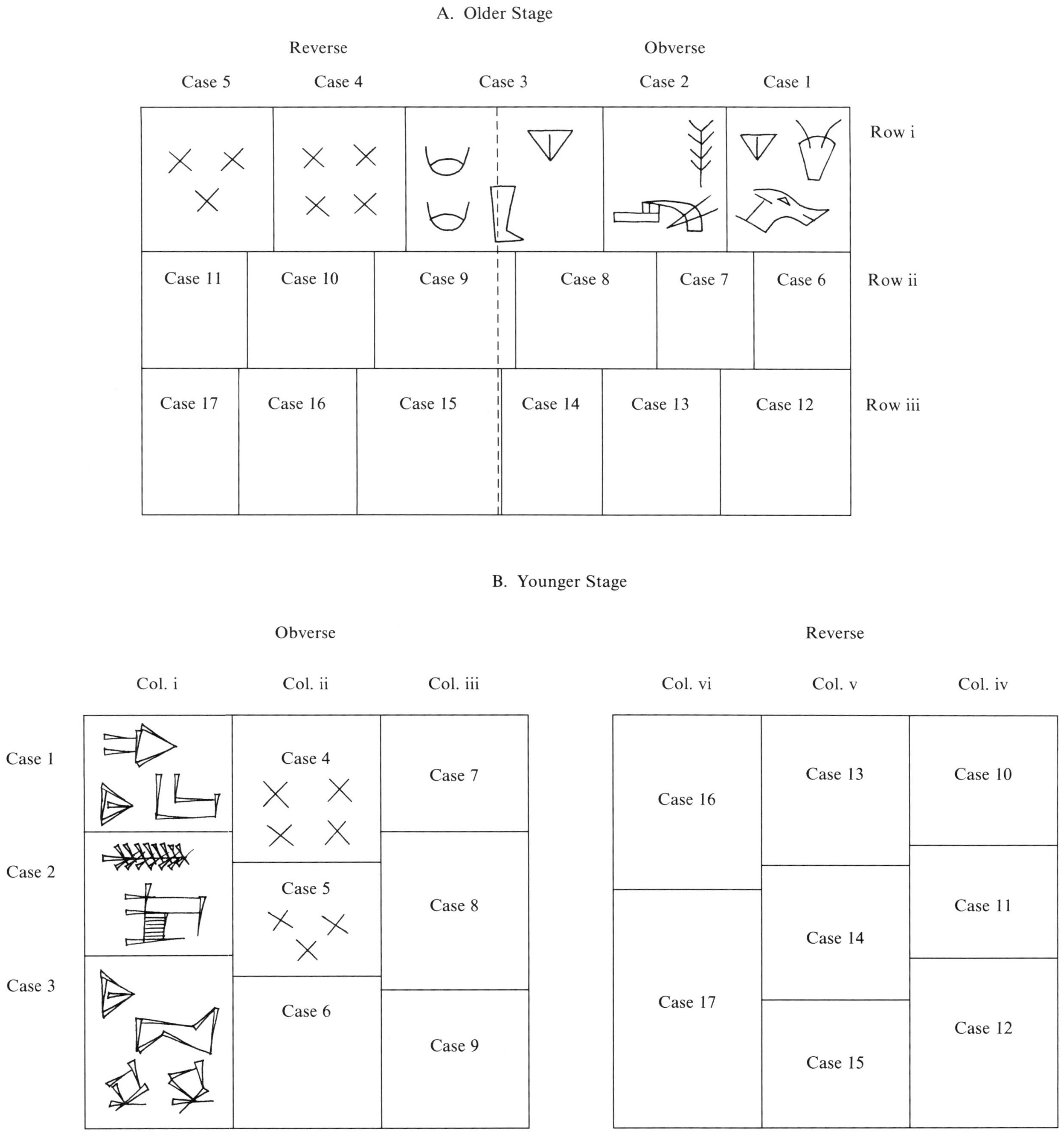

Sargonic rulers of Lagash, three of which are photographically reproduced in *DC* 2 pl. 32 bis, figs. 3–5; all of them are inscribed on the side, but not on the base. With the narrow side attached to the wall, the inscription of figures 4–5 (Urukagina) can be read horizontally when standing to the left of the cone and vertically when standing in front of it, exactly as on no. 140 *DP* 31, described above, or *BIN* 2 pl. LVII (Entemena). On the other hand, the inscription of figure 3 (Entemena) can be read horizontally when standing to the right of the cone, but cannot be read vertically at all, since the writing in the vertical orientation would appear upside down to the reader no matter where he stood. Thus, no matter how the cone was attached to the wall and whether the person stood in front or beside the inscription, he could always read it horizontally, but not vertically.

The following examples serve to illustrate the sequence of the sides and rows/columns of the ancient kudurrus in both the older and younger practice. We shall leave out of consideration the kudurrus with ill-defined sides, such as those on figurines or statuettes, because of their unpredictable sequence of text.

In considering the kudurrus with well-defined sides, we should distinguish: a) solids in the form of flattened tablets and b) solids with all sides more or less equal in size, such as a cube, obelisk, or stela. The tablets, in turn, can be separated into two types: a) tablets with all six sides clearly defined (obverse, lower edge, reverse, upper edge, left edge, and right edge) and b) tablets in which two sides, obverse and reverse, taper off gradually in all directions, leaving no or very little room for writing in the lower, upper, left, and right edges. On a tablet with six well-defined sides, the inscription may cover only obverse and reverse, or all six sides, or obverse, reverse, plus some other sides.

Here are some typical Uruk III examples of the older sequence on tablets in which each row (later, column) of writing runs across the obverse and reverse: nos. 3 and 4 run across the obverse, lower edge, reverse, and upper edge. No. 7 runs across the obverse, lower edge, and reverse, with the first row further subdivided by a line. No. 2, inscribed on the obverse only, contains a group of signs within a linear enclosure, which apparently stands for a personal name. The function of the enclosure resembles that of the Egyptian cartouche. In no. 9 the rows of signs run from the obverse to the reverse, with the upper and lower edges rounded off. The obverse-reverse sequence of writing is apparent in no. 11.

The same sequence continues in some kudurrus of the following Fara and Pre-Sargonic periods. Among them, the sequence obverse–lower edge–reverse–upper edge appears in no. 13 (Fara period), but in addition, small strokes are used to separate the individual entries for number plus commodities; the same sequence of the four sides persists in the Pre-Sargonic period in the two Lummatur tablets from Lagash (nos. 22 and 23) and possibly of the three preserved sides in no. 35.

The separate sequence of columns on the obverse and reverse first appears occasionally in the kudurrus of the ED I–II, Fara, and Pre-Sargonic periods and becomes standard in the Sargonic period. In between, a number of variations are attested. This sequence is well exemplified in no. 18 of the ED I–II periods and in no. 14 of the Fara period, the latter being a tablet without well-defined edges. In the related text no. 15, a slab with well-defined edges, the sequence of columns is first upper edge plus obverse, from left to right, and then lower edge plus reverse, from right to left. The same sequence is attested in no. 37 of the Pre-Sargonic period. This sequence of the sides, proposed here, is contrary to that followed in the original publication in *CT* 32, 7f.

In contrast to the standard, right-to-left sequence of the columns on the reverse, some kudurrus exhibit a sequence which may run from left to right. The context and formulary favor this sequence on the reverse of nos. 18 (ED I–II), 20 (Fara), and 32 (Pre-Sargonic). No. 34 (Pre-Sargonic) has only one column on the reverse, which is on the left side.

The standard sequence of the columns, left to right on the obverse and right to left on the reverse, is exemplified in no. 33 (Pre-Sargonic period) and in numerous kudurrus of the Sargonic period (nos. 41, 42, 43, 44, and 48).

Two of the kudurrus have the left side preserved. In no. 15 of the Fara period and no. 41 of the Sargonic period, the direction of writing on the left edge is consistent in relation to that of the reverse. The left edge begins near where the last line of the last column of the reverse ends and is, therefore, a continuation of the reverse. Only no. 37 has the right edge preserved; it must follow the left edge, now destroyed, which should begin on top on a line parallel to the last line on the left edge, now destroyed on the tablet.

The sequence of the sides on the kudurrus that have the form of a stela, cube, or obelisk, is, or should be, identical with that of tablets. On no. 12 (ED I–II), the sides run from right to left in the order (A-)B-C-D, with each row of signs running across several sides. Of the pieces now gathered under no. 16 (Fara) several have sides whose form suggests that the original object had some sort of cubical shape. Unfortunately, the sequence of the sides cannot be ascertained owing to the poor state of preservation of the fragments. The kudurru no. 40 Manishtushu Obelisk (Sargonic) exhibits the older sequence of sides and the younger sequence of columns. As in the earlier periods, the sides run from right to left in the order A-B-C-D, but the columns run not across the whole obelisk, but within each side, from left to right. The sequence of the sides here proposed is different from that given in the original publication of the Manishtushu Obelisk (no. 40) in *MDP* 2. See the introductory remarks to the Manishtushu Obelisk (no. 40) in chapter 3.

The second sequence, in which the columns of writing run consecutively first from left to right on the obverse and then from right to left on the reverse, attested already on the clay tablets of the Uruk III period, can be clearly recognized from Falkenstein, *ATU* 323, 324, and many others. Examples of texts with this sequence are given in J. Friberg, *The Early Roots of Babylonian Mathematics* 2

(Göteborg, 1979), where they are reproduced photomechanically on pp. 19 and 28 and analyzed on subsequent pages.

Thus, we are faced with the following situation: in one sequence each row of writing runs consecutively from the obverse to reverse as occurs on the stone kudurrus dated to the Uruk III and partially to the ED I–II, Fara, and Pre-Sargonic periods; in the other sequence the columns of writing run consecutively first on the obverse and then on the reverse as on clay tablets of the Uruk III and all subsequent periods. Two possible explanations may be envisioned. One possibility is that the two kinds of sequences co-existed side by side, one favored on stone monuments and the other on clay tablets. The second possibility is that the sequence on stone is older than the one on clay, and that it was preserved archaically up to and including the Pre-Sargonic period, just as the vertical orientation of the signs was preserved on stone up to and including the Old Babylonian period, when the horizontal orientation of the signs was fully enforced in writing on clay tablets. Of the two possibilities, the second is to be favored mainly because of the unnatural orientation of the columns of the reverse in which only the first column of the reverse continues directly the last column of the obverse, while the other columns of the reverse run backwards in relation to the obverse.

Discounting small and fragmentary texts, kudurrus in the form of tablets often exhibit distinctly different profiles of the obverse and reverse in that the former is flat and the latter is rounded or convex. The curvature of the reverse can vary from slight to prominent. Tablets with the characteristic curvature are found in the Fara period (nos. 13, 14, and 20), the Pre-Sargonic period (nos. 22, 23, 31, and 35), and the Sargonic period (no. 41), all on stone tablets; and in the Pre-Sargonic period (nos. 32 and 33) and the Sargonic period (no. 42), all on clay tablets.

The knowledge of the difference between the flat obverse and rounded reverse was of great help in ascertaining the correct sequence of the text in the case of nos. 31, 32, 33, 35, 41, and 42.

No discernible difference between the obverse and reverse was found in a number of stone tablets of various periods: nos. 1–7 (Uruk III), 15 (Fara), 23, 34 and 37 (Pre-Sargonic), and 45 (Sargonic).

One important question relating to early writing concerns the graphotactical arrangement and order of signs within a case or line. A case contains a small number of signs which normally express a linguistic unit, which corresponds to our word or a brief phrase, such as a noun with a preposition or postposition, a number plus the name of a commodity, etc. The formal development of a case to a line, in which all signs are ordered horizontally, one after another, is of no relevance here, since ancient kudurrus, being written on stone, employ exclusively the case arrangement.

The sequence of the signs within a case is quite irregular in early kudurrus, as it is in the hieroglyphic Hittite writing, for example. But even before the formal development of a case to a line, the orderly sequence of signs within a case, that is, the sequence of signs following the sequence of speech elements, comes into being, becoming mandatory in both Sumerian and Akkadian texts during the later phase of the Pre-Sargonic period (ED IIIb). However, there are great discrepancies in the just-preceding periods. More details on this question are given in section 1.5.

1.5. *Language*

As can be seen from the introductory sections to each ancient kudurru, those of the earliest date, Uruk III and ED I–II (nos. 1–12, 18, and 19), are hardly comprehensible. What we can read safely or interpret in them is no more than the sign-groups for areal measures and fields and for a few names and words. Their language could be either Sumerian or Akkadian.

Some general comment is necessary about how the linguistic affiliation of a text, Akkadian or Sumerian, was determined for this volume. The linguistic affiliation of a text is assured whenever it contains any clear linguistic, Akkadian or Sumerian, elements. In addition, some of the texts without any clearly definable linguistic elements were identified as Akkadian-written due to the occurrence of certain extra-linguistic, mainly graphic features which are otherwise found only in Akkadian sources. Among these Akkadian extra-linguistic features are: a) the use of certain logograms, such as AB + ÁŠ "witness," instead of Sumerian lú-ki-inim-ma, NÍG.KI.GAR "additional payment," instead of níg-dirig, DÙL "statue," instead of alam, and DUMU.DUMU "descendant," which are not used in Sumerian; b) the use of logograms without the verbal affixation, such as SAG.RIG$_7$ "he offered ex-voto," instead of Sumerian a-mu-ru or a-mu-na-ru; c) the use of certain syllabograms, such as *iš*$_{11}$(LAM+KUR) and *ʾà*(É), which are not used in Sumerian; and d) the use of the genealogical structures of the type PN DUMU.NITA PN$_2$ "PN son of PN$_2$," and PN DUMU.SAL PN$_2$ "PN daughter of PN$_2$," instead of PN dumu PN$_2$ "PN child (male or female) of PN$_2$" in Sumerian, and of PN LÚ (= Akkadian *šu*) PN$_2$ "PN of the household of PN$_2$," which are rarely used in Sumerian-written texts.

There is a difference in the graphotactical order of "measures plus things counted" between the Sumerian and Akkadian kudurrus. The specific measures are those of weight and liquid capacity. Not applicable in the present discussion are measures of length, area, and dry capacity.

The Sumerian kudurrus of the Fara, Pre-Sargonic, and Sargonic periods regularly have the sequence "thing counted plus measure," as in:

x kug gín	"x shekels of silver"	14 and 15, Fara
x kug ma-na	"x pounds of silver"	14 and 15, Fara
x síg ma-na	"x pounds of wool"	14, 15, and 21, Fara; 32 and 33, Pre-Sargonic
x urudu ma-na	"x pounds of copper"	20 and 21, Fara
x ì silà	"x quarts of oil"	14 and 15, Fara

x tu_7 silà	"x quarts of soup"	22, 23, and App. to nos. 22 and 23, Pre-Sargonic
x ì šagan	"x containers of oil"	22, 23, and App. to nos. 22 and 23, Pre-Sargonic

The Akkadian kudurrus of the Fara, Pre-Sargonic, and Sargonic periods regularly have the sequence "measure plus thing counted," that is, the reverse order from the Sumerian convention, as in:

x GÍN KUG. BABBAR	"x shekels of silver"	16, Fara; 40 and 41, Sargonic
x MA.NA KUG. BABBAR	"x pounds of silver"	40, Sargonic
x MA.NA SÍG	"x pounds of wool"	40 and 41, Sargonic
x MA.NA URUDU/ UD.KA.BAR	"x pounds of copper/bronze"	17, Fara; 31, Pre-Sargonic; 38, Sargonic
x DUG Ì.ŠÁḪ/ Ì.DÙG.GA	"x pots of lard/perfume"	38, Sargonic
x SILÀ Ì	"x quarts of oil"	41, Sargonic

The general conclusion that may be drawn is that the Sumerian kudurrus use the order "thing counted plus measure," while the Akkadian kudurrus use the order "measure plus thing counted." The exceptions are few and all are found in the Akkadian-written kudurrus of the later phase of the Pre-Sargonic period, which have the Sumerian order in x KUG.BABBAR MA.NA, x SÍG MA.NA, x Ì SILÀ, and x Ì.ŠÁḪ SILÀ (nos. 34, 36, and 37). Very few scattered exceptions are found even in the Akkadian kudurrus of the Sargonic period (nos. 40 and 41).

Unfortunately, the rather consistent use of the Sumerian graphotactical convention in writing "thing counted plus measure," observable in ancient kudurrus of the Fara and Pre-Sargonic periods, is not fully duplicated in the legal and administrative texts of the same periods.

The same applies, *pari passu*, to the graphotactical convention of writing the signs within a case, either in the free order of the linguistic elements, as in the spellings A-da-ma, A-ma-da, Ma-da-a, etc., or in the fixed order of the linguistic elements, as in the spelling A-da-ma. In section 1.4 above we noted that the free order of signs within a case was characteristic of early cuneiform writing. The development from the free to the fixed order of signs takes different lines in Akkadian and Sumerian kudurrus. While the order of signs is fixed in the Akkadian kudurrus of the Fara and Pre-Sargonic periods, there are some discrepancies in the Sumerian kudurrus of the same periods. Thus, the sequence of signs in nos. 13 and 20, both of the Fara period, is quite unpredictable, but the sequence in nos. 14 and 15, also of the Fara period (or perhaps of the earlier phase of the Pre-Sargonic period) is generally orderly. The same discrepancies are observable in the Sumerian legal and administrative texts of the Fara and Pre-Sargonic periods. And the fixed order of signs does not become mandatory in all phases and genres of cuneiform writing until the later phase of the Pre-Sargonic period.

All the features that help in distinguishing Akkadian-written from Sumerian-written texts apply also to the distinctions between Eblaic-written texts and Sumerian-written texts at Ebla. See Gelb, "Thoughts about Ibla," *Syro-Mesopotamian Studies* 1 (1977) pp. 6f., and "Ebla and the Kish Civilization" in L. Cagni, ed., *La lingua di Ebla* (Naples, 1981) pp. 11–18.

The gains obtained by utilizing the features discussed above in defining the linguistic affiliation of the kudurrus of the Fara and Pre-Sargonic periods, especially those preserved in a fragmentary state, are considerable. Nevertheless, a note of warning is necessary, as may be judged from a text such as *JCS* 31 (1979) p. 52. This text has features that are both Akkadian, such as ŠE.BA *šu* 1 ITI "barley rations of one month" (colophon), and Sumerian, such as ŠE.BA.BI "their rations" (*passim*). It is such misuse of Sumerian as shown in the writing of ossified ŠE.BA.BI, meaning "its rations" (= "their rations"), that leads to the conclusion that this text of the classical Sargonic period (not "Early Dynastic" as stated by M. de J. Ellis, *ibid.* p. 32) would presumably have been read in the Akkadian language. Similar problems are found in the areas of mixed Sumerian and Akkadian influences, as at Nippur or Adab (see below), where the occurrence of a Sumerian feature in a kudurru does not necessarily mean that it was written in Sumerian. There are three kudurrus (nos. 26 and 30a from Nippur, and no. 33 from Adab), each of which contains certain distinctive features that are Akkadian and others that are Sumerian. In such cases, the definition of the language of a kudurru must be governed by additional considerations, such as whether a certain feature is used exclusively and does not allow of any exceptions in groups of texts of ascertainable linguistic affiliation. Such considerations lead to the conclusion that kudurrus nos. 26, 30a, and 33 are to be identified as Akkadian, with or without question mark, in the listing of kudurrus given in section 5.1, despite their Sumerian features.

There are, in addition, some fragmentary kudurrus that contain no distinctive Sumerian or Akkadian features. In such cases, the language of a kudurru was generally marked as "unknown," unless other considerations led to a different conclusion. Thus, we concluded that the language of no. 51 (allegedly from Cuthah) must be Akkadian because the kudurru is Sargonic in date and comes from the north, which proffers only kudurrus composed in the Akkadian language.

In the past, it has been taken for granted that the Semitic language of the kudurrus and related sources of the Fara and Pre-Sargonic periods represents merely an earlier dialect of the Old Akkadian of the Sargonic period. A recent restudy of all these sources, both in relation to the contemporary material of Abu Salabikh, Ebla, and Mari and to the later Old Akkadian material of the Sargonic period, brought about some surprising results. In the earlier-cited article "Ebla and the Kish

Civilization," pp. 60ff. and 72, Gelb pointed out several features of the Sargonic dialect which cannot be derived from the dialect of the Fara and Pre-Sargonic periods, and suggested that the Fara and Pre-Sargonic dialect represents a linguistic entity that may have been different from the later Old Akkadian of the Sargonic period. He proposed tentatively to call this earliest Semitic dialect of Babylonia "Kishite" after the city Kish, the capital and the heart of the Kish Civilization.

The first understandable kudurrus come from the Fara period. Of these, five texts are written in Sumerian and four in Akkadian.

In three Sumerian-written texts, nos. 13 (from Shuruppak?), 20, and 21 (both from Lagash), the sequence of individual signs within a case is still free to a large extent, and as a result these texts teem with textual difficulties. In contrast, the texts nos. 14 and 15 (both of uncertain provenience, possibly Isin) are characterized by an orderly sequence of signs, and we have few difficulties in following the interpretation of the texts.

The four oldest Akkadian-written texts are dated to the Fara period and come from Kish (nos. 16) and Nippur (nos. 25, 26, and 30b). No. 16 can be recognized as Akkadian because of the occurrence of NÍG.KI.GAR "additional payment" (instead of the Sumerian níg-dirig), and of the writing KÚ "he/they ate," that is, "received (the price)" (instead of the Sumerian ì-kú or the like), whereas no. 26 betrays its Akkadian background by the writing of *in* GN "in GN," and by the occurrence of Enna-Il king of Kish. The Akkadian affiliation of the two other Nippur texts is less certain.

From the Pre-Sargonic period there are eight Sumerian kudurrus, from Lagash (nos. 19a?, 19b?, 22, and 23), Nippur (nos. 27?, 29?, and 30?), and Adab (no. 32), and eleven Akkadian kudurrus, from Nippur (nos. 28, 30a, and 30b?), Adab (nos. 31 and 33?), Kish (no. 34), Sippar (nos. 35 and 36), Dilbat (no. 37), Ur (no. 47?), and of unknown origin (no. 46).

From the Sargonic period there are only two Sumerian kudurrus, one from Lagash (no. 24) and one of unknown provenience (no. 39). There are twelve Akkadian texts: from Sippar (nos. 38, 40, 41, 48, and 49), Babylon (no. 50), Cuthah (no. 51), Eshnuna (nos. 42, 43, and 44), Assur (no. 45), and of unknown provenience (no. 52).

The linguistic distribution of sale documents presents a less varied picture than that of the kudurrus. All forty-two Fara sale documents from Shuruppak (including one found at Uruk), all twenty Pre-Sargonic sale documents from Lagash, and one sale document from Adab are written in Sumerian. The exception is the Pre-Sargonic text no. 156a, which is of unknown provenience and is written in Akkadian.

The ninety-one sale documents of the Sargonic period consist of seventy-one entries written in Sumerian: ten from Nippur, thirty-two from Isin, seven from Adab, one from Umma, nine from Lagash, and twelve of unknown provenience; and of twenty entries written in Akkadian: two from Gasur, eight from Eshnuna, two from Kish, one from Sippar, one from Umm-el-Jīr, and six of unknown provenience.

The great majority of the 127 sale documents of the Ur III period are written in Sumerian. Of the 122 Sumerian-written texts, two are from Eshnuna, sixty-six from Nippur, nine from Adab, eleven from Umma, nine from Lagash, ten from Ur, two from Susa, thirteen of unknown provenience. The five Akkadian-written texts are of unknown provenience.

Data concerning the linguistic distribution of ancient kudurrus and sale documents are given in figures 2 and 3. A map illustrating it is shown in figure 4.

In accordance with the standard Sumerian designation ki-en-gi ki-uri "the land of Sumer and Akkad" for Babylonia, we normally distinguish the Akkadian north from the Sumerian south. This bipartite division of Babylonia is not adequate for the purpose of the linguistic distribution of the kudurrus and sale documents, as the evidence forces us to distinguish not two but three areas: north, near south, and far south. The north designates the Akkadian Akkad, and the areas to the north, including the Diyala River region and Assyria. The south is divided into the near south, with Nippur, Isin, Adab, Shuruppak, Umma, and Lagash (Girshu), situated close to and potentially under the influence of the Akkadian north, and the far south, with Ur, Uruk and Larsa, with less likelihood of Akkadian influence.

The statistical evaluations of the linguistic distribution of ancient kudurrus and sale documents, given above, must be viewed with a certain amount of caution. This is imposed by the accident of archaeological discovery and the fact that the written attestations for the third millennium B.C. are much richer in the near south than either in the north or the far south.

With these reservations in mind, we may draw certain conclusions. Akkadian kudurrus are used in the north and near south, while Sumerian kudurrus dominate only in the near south. Sumerian sale documents of the Fara, Pre-Sargonic, and Sargonic periods are attested in the near south, while no sale documents are known from the far south. There is only one Akkadian sale document of Pre-Sargonic date (of unknown provenience), and the Sargonic-period sale documents are attested only in the north and from unknown sites. In the Ur III period, we can observe an almost complete Sumerization of the language of sale documents. Coming from the capital city of Ur in the far south, the Sumerian influence—ephemeral as it was—extends in the Ur III period from the far south, through the near south, to the north, with only a handful of sale documents (all from unknown sites) testifying to the use of Akkadian.

Some striking conclusions may be drawn from the geographical distribution of the ancient kudurrus. One is that the Akkadian-written kudurrus are at home not only in the Akkadian north, but also at Nippur and Adab in the near south, evidencing the influence emanating from the Akkadian north to the Sumerian near south. Much more striking is the fact that even the Sumerian-written kudurrus are attested only at Nippur, Adab, Lagash, Umma(?), and Shuruppak in the near south, but not at Ur, Uruk, Eridu, or Larsa in the far south. This may allow a tentative conclusion that the custom of selling

Figure 6. Distribution of Sale Documents by Object of Sale
(*Sammelurkunden* are counted only once, under main object of sale)

	Fields	*Orchards*	*Humans*	*Houses*	*Animals*	*Other*	*Total*
Fara	25	—	—	17	—	—	42
Pre-Sargonic	4	1	8	7	—	2 unidentified real estate	22
Sargonic	20	2	44	18	3	1 dates 2 gold 1 canal(?)	91
Ur III	—	9	80	19	10	9 unknown	127
Total	49	12	132	61	13	15	= 282

Figure 7. Distribution of Sales in Sale Documents by Object of Sale

	Fields	*Orchards*	*Humans*	*Houses*	*Animals*	*Other*	*Total*
Fara	25	—	—	18	—	—	43
Pre-Sargonic	5	1	10	8	—	2 unidentified real estate	26
Sargonic	47	17	56	25	4	1 dates 2 gold 1 canal(?)	153
Ur III	—	10	95+	18	12	9 unknown	144+
Total	77	28	161+	69	16	15	= 366+

(arable) land originated in the Akkadian north, from where it expanded southward to the Sumerians. See in detail section 1.11.

There is nothing radical about the assumption of the Akkadian influence in the near south between the Fara and Sargonic periods, as it can be corroborated by the use of the Akkadian language in letters and administrative documents at Adab and Lagash, of Akkadian personal names at Adab, Lagash, Nippur, Umma, and Shuruppak, and of Akkadian month names at Adab, Lagash, Nippur, and Umma. Compare the evidence collected by Gelb in *MAD* 2[2] pp. 1–13 (which has grown in the meantime), and discussed in "Thoughts about Ibla" pp. 6f., and "Ebla and the Kish Civilization" p. 66.

1.6. *Objects of Sale*

An ancient kudurru deals exclusively with land (fields), while a sale document deals with any kind of property, movable (humans, animals, also dates and gold) and immovable (fields, orchards, and houses).

Detailed information about the different kinds of objects of sale in sale documents is given in chapter 8; some general discussion is found in section 1.8.

The distribution of 282 sale documents by period and object of sale is shown in figure 6.

This does not reflect the actual number of sale transactions because some tablets record several purchases from different sellers by one or more buyers. A truer view of the frequency of sales results from counting the number of separate transactions, as shown in figure 7.

The most common object of sale over all periods is humans. Of the texts that deal with the sale of humans, nearly two thirds are of Ur III date, which may be correlated with the complete lack of field sales in this period. Sales of humans involve men, women, and children, either chattel slaves or debt slaves. Next in number are sales of houses and fields. A relatively small number of orchard sales are found; the size is given either in area (*passim*) or in number of palm trees grown on it (nos. 266–268). The most frequent animal sold is gud "bull" (nos. 317, 319, 321, 322, and 348) and GIR "heifer" (no. 316), followed by anše "donkey" (nos. 223, 318, 323, and 368), and also two kinds of equids with uncertain meaning, namely ANŠE.BAR.AN (nos. 225 and 235) and ANŠE.LIBIR (nos. 222 and 320). There are two sales of gold (nos. 226 and 236), one of dates (no. 224), and one of a canal(?) (no. 183).

Detailed information on the sizes, quantities, qualities, and prices of objects of sale is given in chapter 8.

1.7. *Multiple and Single Transactions*

An ancient kudurru records several purchases of arable land (fields), while a sale document usually records a single purchase of property, which can be immovables (fields, orchards, and houses) or movables (humans, animals, and commodities).

As may be seen from the synoptic charts of ancient kudurrus (pls. 87–115), the number of purchases per kudurru varies from two to as many as sixteen and seventeen. This number rises to at least twenty-seven in no. 41, and at least twenty-eight in no. 16, with the possibility that the total number of the transactions originally recorded in no. 41 may have been as high as one hundred.

The question of a single occurrence of one parcel of land in some of the earliest kudurrus, such as no. 2, is discussed in chapter 2.

Although the overwhelming majority of sale documents deals with single purchases, there are also examples of texts recording two or more purchases, made by the same buyer from different sellers. Such texts are especially common among the Sargonic material from Isin and Nippur, though they occasionally appear also in the Fara and Pre-Sargonic periods. The Isin and Nippur texts of this type may in addition include transactions other than sales. The following is a complete listing of the sale documents recording multiple purchases, showing the numbers and types of properties sold:

Fara period	
no. 107	2 houses
Pre-Sargonic period	
no. 143	2 houses
Sargonic period	
no. 166	3 houses and 2 fields
no. 167	1 house (and another transaction)
no. 172	2 fields
no. 179	2 fields
no. 181	4 orchards and 1 house
no. 182a	20 fields and 12 orchards
no. 189	2 persons (and 2 other transactions)
no. 191	1 house (and another transaction)
no. 204	3 houses
no. 210	3 fields and 4(?) houses (and another transaction)
no. 211	2 fields
no. 212	2 fields (and another transaction)
no. 232	2 persons

Since the documents of this type are extremely rare in the Fara and Pre-Sargonic periods, it is possible that nos. 107 and 143 deal with the sales that took place at the same time and involved related sellers. The same explanation may also apply to the Sargonic text no. 232, of unknown origin. In contrast, the Sargonic examples from Isin (nos. 166, 167, 172, 179, 181, 182a, 189, and 191) and Nippur (nos. 204, 210, 211, and 212) must be interpreted as the records of separate purchases, which involved unrelated sellers and took place independently of one another. This interpretation rests primarily on the fact that the Isin text no. 169, which deals with a single purchase of a field, reappears verbatim in no. 182a (as transaction F). This shows quite conclusively that no. 182a is a *Sammelurkunde* of separate purchases which involved the same buyer, whose name apparently is not spelled out in the text (in pls. 143–45 transactions D, E, H, I, J, and U, the persons identified as "buyers" should, in all likelihood, be reclassified as sellers).

The Isin and Nippur *Sammelurkunden* thus bear an uncanny resemblance to the stone kudurrus, since they both record (mostly) unrelated purchases, made, over a period of time, by one buyer. This comparison is particularly apt in the case of no. 182a, which, because of its huge size (thirty-two separate purchases), is virtually indistinguishable from the kudurrus. In fact, it cannot be excluded that no. 182a actually is the clay draft of a stone kudurru (for similar drafts, see nos. 32, 33, 43, and 44, discussed in section 1.3). It should be noted, however, that no. 182a deals, apart from fields, also with orchards, which otherwise do not appear in the kudurrus. An identical text is IM 11053/156, also stemming from Isin and dealing with the purchases of fields and orchards, which will be published by Steinkeller as no. 4 in his forthcoming book *Third Millennium Legal and Administrative Texts in the Iraq Museum, Baghdad.*

As concerns the other Isin and Nippur texts dealing with multiple (but fewer) transactions, we probably find here composite records of purchases (and sometimes of other transactions as well) that the buyer compiled periodically for his own records, based on the individual sale documents in his possession. It appears that once the buyer accumulated a considerable number of such records (either multiple or individual), he had them copied on a stone kudurru, which he then deposited in a temple, to serve as a permanent and public record of his purchases (see section 1.10).

A completely unique case is presented by the Pre-Sargonic sale document no. 156a, which records the sale of two fields by the same seller to different buyers. Unless this text was prepared for the seller (which is most unlikely, considering the complete absence of parallels for such a practice), we have to assume that the buyers were related and resided together, which made the preparation of two separate sale documents unnecessary.

1.8. *Buyers and Sellers*

Of primary importance for the evaluation of land tenure conditions in Mesopotamia during the third millennium B.C. is the question of the numbers of buyers and sellers appearing in sale transactions. We exclude here from consideration the earliest kudurrus nos. 1–12, as well as nos. 13, 18, 19, 19a, 19b, 24, and 38, whose interpretation as sale transactions is uncertain (see section 2.4 and the respective commentaries).

In all periods, both in the kudurrus and sale documents, there is regularly only one buyer named. Although due to the fragmentary state of the final portions of many kudurrus (where the name of the buyer is expected) the number of occurrences of buyers is exceedingly small, all the kudurrus whose final portions are preserved list only one buyer, as in nos. 20(?), 21, 22, 23, 37, and 40. A notable exception here are nos. 14 and 15 which, though fully preserved, do not name the buyer anywhere in their texts. A possible explanation is that these related pieces were followed by still another kudurru, which presumably listed the name of the buyer at the end of the inscription.

With four exceptions, nos. 124, 125, 156a, and 260, all of the sale documents from the Fara through the Ur III periods list a single buyer.

The situation pertaining to the numbers of sellers is considerably more complicated. In order to obtain a full and objective picture of this issue, we offer first a summary of the relevant data in chronological order.

In the sale documents from Shuruppak (Fara period), dealing with fields and houses, the numbers of sellers (including secondary sellers) range from one to nine. The most common number of sellers is between two and five (twenty-eight instances out of the thirty-nine texts where such a determination can be made). The figures of sellers may be actually lower, since some of the examples counted doubly may involve the construction PN PN_2 "PN Of PN_2."

In nos. 14 and 15, dating to the Fara or the earlier phase of the Pre-Sargonic period, and possibly stemming from Isin, in the overwhelming majority of instances there are either one or two sellers listed. There are six instances of three sellers, and one instance of four sellers. As in the case of the Shuruppak sale documents, the actual figures may be lower, due to the use of the construction PN PN_2 in these two kudurrus.

In the Pre-Sargonic kudurrus from Lagash and in the contemporaneous Lagash sale documents dealing with fields, orchards, and houses, the numbers of sellers (including secondary sellers) are generally high (up to twenty-seven in no. 137), though there are also cases of single sellers (as in nos. 142, 143, and 146). In the instances involving large numbers of sellers, these are generally related by blood (see especially nos. 22, 23, and 139). Both in the kudurrus and in the sale documents, secondary sellers regularly receive additional payments and gifts. A different situation exists in the Lagash sales of persons, which usually involve single sellers and as a rule list neither secondary sellers nor additional payments and gifts (the only exception here is no. 150, which records one secondary seller receiving a gift).

Two Pre-Sargonic kudurrus from Adab (nos. 31 and 32) yield conflicting data. No. 31 lists a single seller in each of its eleven transactions. In contrast, no. 32, which records two sale transactions, names eighteen sellers (including secondary sellers or primary witnesses) in the first transaction and four sellers in the second. It is significant that in each case the sellers were members of the same kinship grouping.

In the Pre-Sargonic kudurrus from northern Babylonia which are sufficiently preserved to make such a determination (nos. 34, 36, and 37), the numbers of sellers are generally small: one or two, occasionally three or more. Of special interest is the mention of the "sons/descendants of Ur-ma," who appear in addition to the two sellers, and who receive the additional payment, in no. 37 rev. i–ii. It is characteristic that the Pre-Sargonic kudurrus from northern Babylonia regularly list additional payments and gifts, which, we may assume, were always intended for secondary sellers (even though secondary sellers may not be named in the text).

In the Sargonic sale documents, which come primarily from southern Babylonia, there is generally only one seller listed. This applies equally to the transactions involving immovables (fields, orchards, and houses) and those concerning movables (persons, animals, and commodities). Occasionally, there are two sellers, and very rarely, three or four sellers. It is notable that secondary sellers virtually disappear in this period; the only occurrences of secondary sellers are found in no. 237 (which may actually belong to the Pre-Sargonic period) and possibly in no. 177. Concomitant with this development is the comparative rarity of additional payments and gifts in the sales of real property, which, as we have seen, were an indispensable element of the Fara and Pre-Sargonic sales.

The picture offered by the Sargonic kudurrus, which without exception come from northern Babylonia and places farther north such as Assur and Eshnuna, is considerably different. In the Manishtushu Obelisk (no. 40), the most representative Sargonic kudurru, the numbers of sellers, designated as "lords of the field" and "brother-lords of the field," are conspicuously large (up to twenty-six individuals). In the case of the three transactions recorded on side A (and, similarly, the transactions on side C), it can be demonstrated that all the sellers, as well as the witnesses of the sellers, were members of the same kinship grouping. See Gelb in E. Lipiński, ed., *State and Temple Economy in the Ancient Near East* 1 (Leuven, 1979) pp. 76–89. In other Sargonic kudurrus, the numbers of sellers are considerably lower. For example, in no. 41 there is usually only one seller listed in a transaction, though there are also single occurrences of two, three, and four sellers. In addition, some of the Sargonic kudurrus do not mention secondary sellers (e.g., nos. 42 and 43). It is notable, however, that all of these documents are consistent in listing additional payments and gifts, which, as noted above, become rare in the Sargonic sale documents.

While the documentation grows considerably in the Ur III period, there are no sales of fields, and the number of sellers in sales of orchards and houses varies from one to four, with the great majority of cases represented by one seller only. Single sellers predominate also in the Ur III sales of chattels.

In consideration of the above data, the following tentative conclusions may be reached. During the Fara and Pre-Sargonic periods, sales of real property (fields, orchards, and houses) generally involved multiple sellers, who comprised sellers proper, the actual "owners" of the sold property, and their kinsmen, who acted as "secondary sellers." The latter invariably received gifts and additional payments. As far as we can judge, humans (and probably other types of chattels) were sold freely by single individuals, without the participation (and, presumably, the consent) of their kinsmen (= secondary sellers). It appears that this picture obtained equally for southern and northern Babylonia.

In the Sargonic period, we can observe in southern Babylonia a clear transition toward sales involving single sellers, as evidenced in the disappearance of secondary sellers and the rarity of additional payments and gifts. In contrast, in northern Babylonia sales continued to involve multiple sellers. This is shown best by the Manishtushu Obelisk (no. 40), but equally well by the fact that the northern Babylonian kudurrus consistently list additional payments and gifts, which implies the attendance of sale transactions by secondary sellers (even though they may not be explicitly mentioned in texts).

This evolutionary process, from multiple to single sellers, beginning in southern Babylonia in the Sargonic period, culminated in Ur III times, with the practice of both secondary sellers and additional payments and gifts becoming completely extinct. The question whether the same was true of northern Babylonia in that period is difficult to evaluate, because of the great scarcity of written documentation coming from that region.

It is equally difficult to assess if, and to what extent, the described development reflects a transition from the "familial" to the "private" form of ownership (this affects only real property, since it is clear that chattels were privately/individually owned as early as the Fara and Pre-Sargonic periods and probably even much earlier). Here we must note that already in the earliest periods the actual "owners" (= primary sellers) of sold real property were either single individuals or, at best, nuclear families. This, in our view, precludes any possibility of the existence of a truly familial/communal ownership of land during the time-span with which this study is concerned.

This conclusion is consistent with the fact that throughout the second half of the third millennium buyers of real property were invariably single individuals. Obviously, if fields and other types of real property were owned by kinship groupings larger than nuclear families, we would expect to find multiple purchasers in at least some of the texts.

At the same time, it must be emphasized that the vesting of land tenure in an individual as distinct from a social group is a very modern notion (see C. Brinkman, "Land Tenure," in *Encyclopedia of the Social Science* [New York, 1937] p. 74), and thus one cannot talk of purely private/individual ownership in third millennium Mesopotamia either. Therefore, all that our evidence permits us to say is that during the Fara and Pre-Sargonic periods familial (or, more broadly, communal) consent was required to permit the alienation of real property by individuals or nuclear families. The importance of such a consent declined visibly in the Sargonic period, but only in southern Babylonia. In Ur III times, there is no evidence for any form of familial or communal consent in sales of orchards and houses (sales of fields apparently were prohibited), with such transactions now possibly being supervised and authorized by the state.

The above questions are taken up in greater detail in section 1.11, where it is also suggested that there may have existed significant differences between southern and northern Babylonian systems of land tenure.

From the socio-economic point of view, another important issue is the status of the buyers and sellers. Figure 8 offers a listing of the professions and titles of the buyers and sellers occurring in the kudurrus and sale documents, ordered by the object of sale.

As shown in figure 8, nos. 1–52 are kudurrus and nos. 100–370 are sale documents. The temporal distribution of the sale documents is as follows: nos. 100–136 (Fara), nos. 137–156a (Pre-Sargonic), nos. 157–246 (Sargonic), and nos. 247–370 (Ur III). The date of the kudurrus is reflected only approximately from the sequence since certain groups of kudurrus are ordered not by date but by provenience.

The first impression one gets from scanning the figure is that practically anyone could be either a seller or a buyer. This is especially important for the fields, since this evidence shows that landed property could be sold and consequently "owned" by private persons and not exclusively by the temples or state as claimed until quite recently.

Considering the accidents of discovery of texts in our limited sampling, any conclusion that might be drawn about the relative frequency of the occupations and titles of buyers and sellers must be viewed with a certain amount of suspicion. With this in mind, we note that the most common among both the buyers and sellers are various high administrative officials: lugal "king" (or, in the Pre-Sargonic Lagash, "governor"), en_5-si "governor," sanga "chief temple administrator," sabra or ugula é "chief temple steward." Also conspicuous in their frequency are dam-gàr "merchant," dub-sar "scribe," and sipa "shepherd." All other professions and titles occur fewer than five times.

Women participate very frequently in sale transactions, both as buyers and sellers (primary and secondary). Among them, we find gemé DN "servant of DN" (no. 150), GEMÉ.DINGIR "temple servant" (nos. 40 D iii 10–12, 41 i 13′–15′), SAL.BALAG.DI "lamenter" (nos. 43 viii 8–9, x 6–7, 44h ii 4′–5′), and wives of such people as lugal "king," here "governor" (no. 154), en_5-si "governor" (nos. 149, 151, 152, 153, and 155), sanga "chief temple administrator" (nos. 14 viii 6–10, 137, and 150), sag-du_5 "field recorder" (no. 22 iv 4–6), lú-udu "shepherd" (no. 109), ašgab "leather worker" (no. 155), and sagi, "cupbearer" (no. 159). A daughter of a simug "smith" occurs in no. 33 rev. iv 3–8. Wives, daughters, and sisters of men not identified by name, as well as mothers of sold individuals, appear in nos. 15 iii 9–10, v 28–30, 32 v 18–vi 2, rev. ii 12–13, 36 iii 7–9, 37 R. E. 9–12, 44h i 5′–6′, 125, 142, 145, 157, 159, 164, 168, 175, 182a B, M, T, Y, CC, DD, 184, 186, 187, 188, 205, 215, 216, 227, 234, 253, 263, 300, 304, 306, and 308. In other instances, either sellers or buyers may be identified as female on the basis of their names and the verbal form used (in Akkadian texts; see, e.g., nos. 41 v 22′–24′ and 235).

In evaluating the status of buyers, in the case of field sales a sharp distinction must be made between the buyers appearing in the kudurrus (and in the *Sammelurkunde* no. 182a) and those found in the sale documents. This follows from the simple fact that the kudurrus involve incomparably greater land areas, such as 770.5 iku (no. 14 plus no. 15), 144.3 iku (no. 22 plus no. 23), 206 iku (no. 32), 217 iku (no. 36), 9723 iku (no. 40), 628.6 iku (no. 41—only fourteen transactions out of the possible total of 100 transactions that were originally recorded in this document!), and 427 iku (no. 182a). Naturally, the purchasers of these huge tracts of land must have been important and exceedingly rich individuals. Although the

Figure 8. Sellers and Buyers Appearing in Ancient Kudurrus and Sale Documents

CIVIL AUTHORITY	*SELLERS*				*BUYERS*			
	Field	*House*	*Person*	*Other*	*Field*	*House*	*Person*	*Other*
lugal "king"	20 182a A	—	—	—	40	—	—	—
wife	—	—	—	—	—	—	154	—
en$_5$-si "governor"	30b 34 iv 40 C iii, vii	—	—	—	22 23 App. to 22–23 35 351	—	195 196 198 200 201 202	orchard: 146
wife	—	—	—	—	—	—	149 151 152 153 155	—
GAR-en$_5$-si	—	—	—	—	App. to 32	—	—	—

TEMPLE	*SELLERS*				*BUYERS*			
	Field	*House*	*Person*	*Other*	*Field*	*House*	*Person*	*Other*
en DN "en-priest of DN"	—	—	214	—	—	—	—	—
sanga (DN) "chief temple administrator"	App. to 32 40 A viii, ix 182a G	—	217	—	—	140 263	—	—
wife	14 viii	—	—	—	—	137	150	—
[SAN]GA?.GAR	30a	—	—	—	—	—	—	—
SABRA(.É) "chief temple steward"	44 i	—	—	—	—	—	341	—
ugula é "chief temple steward"	—	—	—	—	—	—	275 345 349 350 353	—
ugula É-sikil	—	—	208	—	—	—	—	—
arád DN "servant of DN"	—	—	—	—	—	—	310	—
gala "cantor"	—	—	149 154	—	—	—	—	—
gemé DN "servant of DN"	—	—	150	—	—	—	—	—
GEMÉ.DINGIR "temple servant"	40 D iii 41 i	—	—	—	—	—	—	—
gudá? (a type of priest)	—	—	315	—	—	—	—	—
išib DN "purification priest of DN"	—	—	350	—	20 rev. ii	—	—	—
nu-èš (a type of priest)	—	—	—	—	—	—	306	—
pab-šeš (DN) (a type of priest)	16d B iii 182a FF	—	—	—	—	—	—	—
SAL.BALAG.DI "lamenter"	43 viii, x 44h	—	—	—	—	—	—	—

OFFICIALS	*SELLERS*				*BUYERS*			
	Field	*House*	*Person*	*Other*	*Field*	*House*	*Person*	*Other*
AB+ÁŠ.URU GN "city elder"	40 A vi, vii, x	—	—	—	—	—	—	—
agà-uš lugal "royal constable"	—	—	286	—	—	—	—	—

OFFICIALS (continued)	*SELLERS*				*BUYERS*			
	Field	*House*	*Person*	*Other*	*Field*	*House*	*Person*	*Other*
agrig "manager"	15 L. E.	—	—	—	—	—	—	—
di-kud "judge"	—	—	201	—	—	—	—	—
dub-sar "scribe"	40 C xiv 40 D ii	206	309a 345	orchard: 182a N	—	247	—	equid: 318
dub-sar gud	—	—	—	—	—	—	—	—
dub-sar-maḫ	—	—	—	—	—	—	367	—
GÁ-dub-ba "archivist"	—	—	203	—	—	—	—	—
GAL.UKÙ "military commander"	40 A iv	—	—	—	—	—	—	—
GAL.URI "chief of the Akkadians"	—	—	—	—	127	—	—	—
GU.SUR.NUN "field assessor"	—	—	—	—	—	104	—	—
ḫa-za-núm GN "mayor"	—	—	—	equid: 368	—	—	—	—
IŠ "equerry"	40 A vi 182a U	—	—	—	—	—	—	—
ka-guru$_7$ "granary superintendent"	—	—	—	—	—	252	—	—
KUG.GÁL "canal inspector"	41 rev. ix	—	—	—	—	—	—	—
nu-banda "overseer"	—	—	190 341	—	—	—	314	bovid?: 348
sag-du$_5$ "field recorder"	40 B v	105	—	unknown: 327	21 i, ii	—	—	—
wife	22 iv	—	—	—	—	—	—	—
sagi "cupbearer"	—	—	216	—	—	—	365	—
wife	—	—	159	—	—	—	—	—
ugula "foreman"	—	—	188	—	—	—	—	—
ugula a-ru	—	—	—	—	117	—	—	—

OCCUPATIONS	*SELLERS*				*BUYERS*			
	Field	*House*	*Person*	*Other*	*Field*	*House*	*Person*	*Other*
a-zu$_5$ "physician"	131	—	—	—	—	—	—	—
[A]?.ZU	30a	—	—	—	—	—	—	—
arád "servant," "slave"	—	—	—	—	—	—	—	—
arád PN šidim-gal	—	—	—	—	—	—	—	bovid: 322
ašgab "leather worker"	179	—	—	—	—	—	271?	—
wife	—	—	155	—	—	—	—	—
ašlàg "bleacher," "fuller"	—	137	—	—	—	—	—	—
ašlàg-gada	—	—	215	—	—	—	—	—
baḫár "potter"	—	—	—	—	—	100	—	—
dam-gàr "merchant"	207 210	210 355	155 231 349	gold: 236	207 211?	138 262	277 295 311 333	equids: 323
dam-gàr é-SAL	—	—	156	—	—	—	—	—
engar "farmer"	166	—	357	—	—	—	—	—
ga-raš "seafaring merchant"	—	—	—	orchard: 146	—	—	—	—
galla-gal "policeman"	—	—	—	—	113c 122 123 124	106	—	—

OCCUPATIONS (continued)	*SELLERS*				*BUYERS*			
	Field	*House*	*Person*	*Other*	*Field*	*House*	*Person*	*Other*
ì-DU.DU "perfumer"	—	—	295	—	—	—	—	—
INNIN.ÙH̲ "undertaker"	30b	—	—	—	—	—	—	—
lú-má-gur$_8$ "boatman"	—	—	—	equid: 225	—	—	—	—
lú-SAR "vegetable-grower"	—	—	152	—	—	—	—	—
lú sukkal-maḫ "man of the chancellor"	—	—	275	—	—	—	—	—
lú-u$_5$ GN "courier"	182a A	—	—	—	—	—	—	—
lú-udu "shepherd"	—	—	—	—	—	—	—	—
wife	—	—	—	—	—	109	—	—
má-laḫ$_4$ "boatman"	40 D iv	—	155 311	—	—	—	—	—
MU "cook"	—	—	—	—	—	—	159	—
na-gada "shepherd"	—	—	—	—	—	—	363	—
nar "singer"	127	112	—	orchard: 182	—	—	—	—
nu-kiri$_6$ "gardener"	—	166	153 272	—	—	113a 113b	156	—
rá-gaba "courier"	—	—	—	—	—	—	281	—
simug "smith"	33 rev. iv	—	—	—	175 177 210	— —	— — —	— — —
sipa "shepherd"	40 A iv	—	—	—	136	—	—	—
sipa DN	—	—	—	equids: 222	130	—	—	—
sipa udu-síg-ka	—	—	—	—	—	—	156	—
šandan "chief gardener"	—	—	—	—	212	210	—	—
šidim "mason"	—	247	—	—	—	—	—	—
ŠIM "brewer"	129?	—	—	—	—	—	—	—
lú-ŠIM(-ma)	—	—	—	equid: 318	—	—	309	—
šu-ḫa "fisherman"	—	—	195 196	—	—	113c	209	—
unud$_x$ "cowherd"	—	—	—	—	—	108	—	—

MISCELLANEOUS	*SELLERS*				*BUYERS*			
	Field	*House*	*Person*	*Other*	*Field*	*House*	*Person*	*Other*
IB	—	—	—	—	133	—	—	—
KA-dug	—	—	—	—	—	—	—	gold: 226
MAR.TU "Amorite"	—	—	356	—	—	—	—	—
ni-is-ku	—	—	157	—	—	—	—	—
ZÍD.DA "miller?"	—	—	362	—	—	—	—	—

status of buyers is known only in four kudurrus (a son of the governor of Lagash [nos. 22 and 23], a son of a northern Babylonian governor [no. 35], and the king Manishtushu [no. 40]), it can be safely assumed that in all other cases the buyers were members of the highest social stratum (if not the ruling elite).

1.9. *Formulary*

In general, the formulary of the kudurrus closely resembles that of the sale documents. This is especially true of the Pre-Sargonic kudurrus from Lagash, which are clearly compilations of individual sale documents. Among the kudurrus, operative sections styled *ex latere venditoris* predominate. In contrast, the sale documents usually use operative sections styled *ex latere emptoris*.

The information contained in an individual transaction of a kudurru can be so terse as to furnish only the size of the sold field, the purchase price, and the names of the buyer and the seller. In its most complete form, the transaction also specifies additional payments and gifts, and the names of secondary sellers (= primary witnesses), witnesses, and various officials who authorized or witnessed the sale. Additional clauses, the so-called *Schlussklauseln*, are rare in the kudurrus.

The same basic information is given in the sale documents, with a difference that sale documents are generally longer and more informative than the individual transactions of the kudurrus. In particular, the sale documents use a large repertoire of *Schlussklauseln*. For a detailed discussion of the formulary of the kudurrus and sale documents, see chapters 6 and 7.

1.10. *Purpose and Function*

The discussion of the purpose and function of the ancient kudurrus may profitably proceed by comparing them with their Kassite/post-Kassite counterparts.

A Kassite or post-Kassite kudurru deals usually with a grant of land by the king (or official) to an individual (or temple), very rarely, with a gift of land by an individual to a member of his family or with a purchase or sale of land by one individual from another.

The main characteristics of the ancient kudurrus are shown in figure 1. These characteristics compared with those of the Kassite and post-Kassite kudurrus are charted in figure 9. This figure lists only the main characteristics of the grants of land preserved on conical stelae, which form the bulk of the Kassite and post-Kassite kudurrus, and not the many internal and external variations of the texts which are usually included under the overall class of these documents.

The brief description of the contents of the Kassite and post-Kassite and ancient kudurrus given in the chart shows several convergences and divergences.

The most apparent outward feature of the Kassite and post-Kassite and ancient kudurrus is that both are made of stone. As noted in section 1.1, stone was rare and expensive in Mesopotamia, and its use in writing was generally limited to votive-building-memorial inscriptions, seals, weights, and kudurrus. The use of stone for kudurrus means that they were intended to be a permanent and indestructible record. Because of that, kudurrus and stelae with votive-building-memorial inscriptions were considered sacred and inviolable. The Sumerian term for them is often deified (^{d}Na-dù-a), the dedicated stelae are to be anointed at regular intervals, and the inscriptions bear curses against potential violators. While Kassite and post-Kassite kudurrus contain curse formulas and extensive representational symbolism placing the kudurrus under the divine protection, ancient kudurrus have neither. Nevertheless, it is worth noting that a badly preserved ancient kudurru presumably from Sippar (no. 48), has a brief curse formula that was added at the end of the inscription in the Neo-Babylonian period.

Some ancient kudurrus at Adab and Eshnuna are written on either stone or clay. See section 1.3, where it is suggested that the clay tablets served either as first drafts written in preparation for the final edition on stone or as private copies destined for the personal use of the purchaser of land.

Since ancient kudurrus contain a collection of purchases of land, it is reasonable to assume that they were based on documents of clay, each recording a purchase of a single piece of land. For a good illustration of the latter, see App. to kudurrus nos. 22–23.

Since the Kassite and post-Kassite kudurrus regularly have the form of a more or less conical stela made of stone, parallel texts (but without the curse formulas) which were preserved on clay tablets may be—as in the case of ancient kudurrus on clay—either first drafts or private copies of the purchaser of landed property.

As is well known, the term kudurru, when applied to the Kassite and post-Kassite periods, means "boundary" or "boundary stone." It is this meaning, plus the form of the kudurrus, and some rather debatable textual evidence (see just below), which led scholars to argue that the kudurrus were actually set up on the boundary of the property with which they were concerned. See W. J. Hinke, *A New Boundary Stone of Nebuchadnezzar I* (Philadelphia, 1907) pp. 8ff.; L. W. King, *Babylonian Boundary-Stones and Memorial Tablets in the British Museum* (London, 1912) p. vii; F. X. Steinmetzer, *Die babylonischen Kudurru (Grenzsteine) als Urkundenform* (Padeborn, 1922) pp. 95, 97, and 101ff. Even V. Seidl, in an article published in *Bagh. Mitt.* 4 (1968) pp. 7–220, especially p. 73, still defended the proposition that at least all kudurrus of the early first millennium were set up in the field. Against this, several scholars have noted in the past that the phrase *ina muḫḫi eqlišu*, which occurs frequently in the kudurrus, could just as well be translated "concerning his field," rather than "on his field," and the passage *narâ ša ina eqli šâšu šaknu* "the monument that was set up in this field" (*MDP* 6 p. 45 v 9f.) is unique, and does not allow for generalizations. See J. A. Brinkman, *RLA* 6 (1982) p. 270a, for the latest statement on this matter.

As may be seen from the ensuing discussion, the Akkadian word kudurru lost its original meaning "boundary," "boundary stone," when the stones were no longer set up in the field, but were deposited in a temple. A good parallel is provided by the Greek *horos* that also originally meant "boundary," "boundary stone," but was deposited not in the field, but in a building (see below, p. 24).

New information concerning the setting up of the Kassite kudurru in the Ebabbar temple of Larsa gave rise to the publication of two articles, one by J.-C. Margueron, *RA* 66 (1972) pp. 147–61, and the other by D. Arnaud, *ibid.* pp. 163–76. The information indicates that the kudurrus of Nazi-maruttash (1307–1282 B.C.) and of Kudurri-Enlil (1254–1246 B.C.), and an uninscribed fragment were discovered in a disturbed context within the complex of the Ebabbar temple (pp. 147, 157, and 161). While the temple Ebabbar is cited, in inconclusive context, in both inscribed kudurrus (pp. 164 line 6, 172 lines 56 and 59), Nazi-maruttash writes of having placed the kudurru in the sanctuary of Gula (p. 167 lines 48–50), which must have formed a part of the Ebabbar temple complex at Larsa. Gula of Larsa is briefly mentioned by R. Frankena, *RLA* 3 p. 696a, with reference to F. R. Kraus, *JCS* 3 (1951) p. 85.

Certain conclusions about the topographic origin of the Kassite and post-Kassite kudurrus may be drawn from the fact that the great majority of these documents are housed today in two museums, the British Museum and the Louvre. Almost all Louvre kudurrus were excavated

Figure 9. Main Characteristics of Ancient Kudurrus and Kassite/Post-Kassite Kudurrus

	Ancient Kudurrus	*Kassite and Post-Kassite Kudurrus*
Time:	Uruk III–Sargonic	Kassite and Post-Kassite
Material:	Stone	Mainly stone
Form:	Mainly tablet	Mainly conical stela
Divine Symbol:	No	Normally yes
Curses:	No	Normally yes
Contents:	Multiple purchases of land by one individual from one or more, often related individuals	Grant of land by the king to an individual
Purpose:	Publicity of purchases of land	Publicity of a grant of land

in faraway Susa in Elam, where they had been brought as booty by the Elamite invaders of Babylonia in the early first millennium B.C., just as the Hammurapi Code and the Manishtushu Obelisk (no. 40) had been. The first question is, did the Elamite soldiers collect the individual stones as they found them lying in the fields as markers of property or did they find them together in one place in one of the cities of Babylonia? In answer to this question, we submit that the Elamites were much more likely to carry away the stones which they had found in one place rather than to hunt for them in fields. As for the identity of that place, the most likely candidate here is the temple of Shamash at Sippar. In our opinion, this suggestion is supported, despite doubts expressed by some scholars, by the Sippar origin of the Code of Hammurapi, which was dedicated to Shamash of Sippar and was also found at Susa, and by our assumed Sippar derivation of the Kassite and post-Kassite kudurrus now housed in the British Museum. The latter assumption is based on the results of the recent "rediscovery" of the Sippar archive in the British Museum, which has shown that many British Museum texts (not necessarily kudurrus) which were suspected as having originated at Sippar or were noted as being of unknown origin had actually been excavated at Sippar. See, for instance, Sollberger, *RAI* 11 pp. 6f., *RAI* 15 pp. 103–7, and *JEOL* 20 (1968) pp. 50–70, especially his observations on the Sippar origin of the Cruciform Monument of Manishtushu (dedicated to Shamash of Sippar) and its copies on clay tablets. On that basis, we venture to suggest that many, if not most, of the middle Babylonian kudurrus in the British Museum may have come from Sippar, presumably the Shamash temple.

In suggesting that the Kassite and post-Kassite kudurrus of the Louvre and the British Museum come mainly from the temple of Shamash in Sippar, we do not wish to imply that this was the only place where the kudurrus were deposited. As a matter of fact, Seidl, *op. cit.* pp. 69f., lists fifteen sites where kudurrus were excavated or allegedly found, among them Babylon, Nippur, and Warka, to name only the sites with a larger number of kudurrus. On pp. 72f., Seidl lists several sites which yielded information about the findspots of the kudurrus. Of the seven cases she discusses, five describe the location as a temple, unfortunately, in almost all cases, of the period following that of the post-Kassite kudurrus. Still, the fact that these kudurrus were excavated in a temple area supports our suggestion that the Louvre and British Museum kudurrus come mainly from the temple of Shamash in Sippar.

If it can be proven that a large number of the Kassite and post-Kassite kudurrus served not as boundary stones to be erected in the field but as records to be deposited in the temple, then the same point may be applied also to the ancient kudurrus. As can be seen from section 1.3, most of the latter have the form of tablets or slabs which were more likely to be deposited in a building than in a field. Others, in the form of human statuettes and animal figurines, suggest a display purpose and again favor the proposition that they were accessible for viewing in a public building, such as a temple.

A note by C. B. F. Walker and D. Collon, "Hormuzd Rassam's Excavations for the British Museum at Sippar in 1881–1882" in L. de Meyer, ed., *Tell ed-Der* 3 (Leuven, 1980) pp. 93–114, sheds very important light on the Shamash temple at Sippar as the place of origin of several ancient, Kassite, and post-Kassite kudurrus, and other types of texts now housed in the British Museum. While Walker and Collon could list only three ancient kudurrus (nos. 55, 58, and 66 on p. 111 under B, corresponding to our kudurrus nos. 36, 49, and 48) and eight Kassite and post-Kassite kudurrus (p. 112 under F) among the 108 mainly inscribed items as certainly or possibly found in the Shamash temple at Sippar, they pointed out on p. 96 that their listing "is certainly far from complete since many of the objects recorded in Rassam's inventories cannot be identified." The expectation that many more ancient and Kassite and post-Kassite kudurrus in the British Museum will be identified in the course of time as coming from the Shamash temple at Sippar derives from the information given on p. 111: "Rassam's brief account of the excavations and his plans show that most of his efforts were concentrated on the Shamash temple, Ebabbar, although he may have worked in official or private buildings on the periphery of the temple, and his workmen doubtless brought him objects picked up elsewhere at Abu Ḫabba. It seems reasonable to suppose that most of the objects listed above were found in the temple, which seems to have functioned also as a local treasury or museum (. . .). Some (. . .) of this material may have been brought into the temple as booty, for its historical or religious significance, or for the sake of permanent record."

The concrete evidence in favor of the Sippar origin of a number of ancient kudurrus is not conclusive but suggestive. Of the seven kudurrus marked as coming from Sippar, with or without a question mark in the listing in section 5.1, none was found in a controlled excavation: three are now in the British Museum (nos. 36, 48, and 49), two in the Louvre (nos. 35 and 40), one in the Istanbul Museum (no. 41), and one in the Ashmolean Museum in Oxford (no. 38). Of these, the most informative is the British Museum kudurru no. 48, which states at its end that this stone was NÍG.GA ^{d}UTU "property of Shamash (of Sippar)," and continues with a brief curse formula. Note that this addition was made in the Neo-Babylonian period, almost two thousand years after the date of the original stone inscription, testifying to a long continuity of the temple of Shamash at Sippar, which is reflected also in the Sippar origin of the Cruciform Monument, dedicated to Shamash of Sippar (see above) and probably of the Manishtushu Obelisk.

The information that the ancient kudurru no. 48 (and probably other kudurrus from Sippar) were deposited in a temple may be duplicated by kudurrus from other sites. Thus, no. 26, excavated at Nippur and dating to the Fara period, has at the end of the inscription a brief remark stating that "Enna-Il king of Kish set up (this statue) before Innin (in Nippur)." Confirming this ancient statement we find that the statue was excavated in a Parthian fill just above the temple of Innin. Similarly, kudurru no. 25 was found buried below a cella in a temple, and kudurru no. 9 was excavated in a room near the entrance to the Sin temple.

Additional information about the temple origin of ancient kudurrus may be obtained from nos. 18, 19, 19a, and 24, all of which were excavated from Tell K at Girshu (Telloh) which was identified as the temple of Ningirshu by A. Parrot, *Tello* (Paris, 1948) pp. 56ff.

An apparent discrepancy exists between kudurrus nos. 22 and 23, which were excavated in an unknown locus at Telloh (= Girshu), while the related sale document published as App. to nos. 22–23 was excavated in Al-Hiba (= Lagash) in Area C which yielded both private administrative and legal texts, as well as royal inscriptions. This discrepancy may be resolved by assuming that the two kudurrus, like the kudurrus discussed just above, were deposited in the temple of Ningirshu in Girshu, while the clay tablet was kept in the house of the buyer, in this case, the palace of Lummatur in Lagash.

The purpose of depositing kudurrus, ancient and later, in a temple was not to register them in a sort of record office, but to afford them the protection of gods and, at the same time, to make them accessible to public scrutiny, and, therefore, to publicize the deed of purchase or donation of land by or to an individual.

The act of publicity, "ius publicitatis" (French "publicité," German "Publizität"), connected with Kassite and post-Kassite kudurrus, had been noted previously by several legal historians, especially E. Cuq, *Études sur le droit babylonien* (Paris, 1929) pp. 85f.; and P. Koschaker, *Neue keilschriftliche Rechtsurkunden aus der El-Amarna-Zeit* (Leipzig, 1928) p. 178, and *idem, Über einige griechische Rechtsurkunden* . . . (Leipzig, 1931) pp. 101f.

Ample and direct evidence in favor of the act of publicity as part of sale transactions is found in the ancient kudurrus of the Pre-Sargonic period and in the sale documents of the Pre-Sargonic to Ur III periods. The first references to such an act are attested in the Pre-Sargonic kudurrus nos. 22 and 23, which contain the formula that the main seller kag-bi é-gar$_8$-ra bí-dù ì-bi zag-gí bi-ag "drove this cone into the wall and spread the oil on the side," that is, he performed certain actions to symbolize and legitimize the transfer of the title to the buyer. The exact meaning and form of Sumerian kag, Akkadian *sikkatum*, which is usually translated as "cone," "nail," or "peg," is clear from the six Pre-Sargonic and the Ur III sale documents which were written on clay cones (see below). The various forms of clay "cones" are described by F. R. Kraus, *Halil Edhem Hâtira Kurumu* 1 (Ankara, 1947) pp. 71–113, and R. S. Ellis, *Foundation Deposits in Ancient Mesopotamia* (New Haven, 1968) pp. 72–93. The act of attaching the clay cone to the wall with the help of a wooden peg that pierces the center of the cone and is driven into the wall is discussed in section 7.12.5.1.

Although not clearly drawn, an illustration of a cone driven into the wall of a tall structure, which is apparently a doorway, may be shown in kudurru no. 12 of Early Dynastic I-II times (see introduction to no. 12).

The six Pre-Sargonic contracts on cones dealing with the sale of houses (nos. 139, 140, and 141), a field (no. 145), and unknown properties (nos. 147 and 148) contain the same symbolic formula of driving the cone into the wall and pouring oil as kudurrus nos. 22–23, cited above. In addition to the six Pre-Sargonic cones, three Pre-Sargonic texts (App. to nos. 22–23, concerning a field, no. 142, a house, and no. 151, an individual) contain the same formula, but are preserved on tablets, and one Ur III text (no. 263, concerning a house) is written on a clay cone, but does not contain the formula in question.

It is notable that, whereas in the sales of fields the kag ceremony was performed by the (main) seller (nos. 22, 23, and 144), in the sales of houses (nos. 139, 140, 141, and 142) and persons (no. 151) the actor was a nigir(-uru), "(town) herald."

Thus, in the Pre-Sargonic period the publicity of sale transactions was achieved by driving the cone into the wall of a house in such a way that the exposed part of the cone containing the inscription would be accessible to private scrutiny.

Further illustration of the use of cones in legal transactions is furnished by several loans of barley from the Old Babylonian period at Susa (*MDP* 23, 179, 182, 184, 186, and 189). What we learn from them is that *sikkatum maḫṣat* "the cone was driven" by the creditor into the house, field, or orchard of the debtor, and stayed there until the debtor repaid his debt.

Three Sargonic examples of the use of the cone are inconclusive. Of these, *BIN* 8, 121 states that two persons apparently went to court and that the witnesses testified that the first of the two persons (the seller?) drove the cone into the wall under the oath of the king; a similar text, sale document no. 239, states at its conclusion that the cone was driven under the oath of Narâm-Sin. In addition to these two clay tablets, there is a text on a clay cone, *MAD* 4, 170, about the witnesses who testified that two individuals came to an agreement under the oath of the king and the temple administrator (sanga) of Isin.

Up to now, we have been considering primarily similarities between the ancient and later kudurrus. A crucial difference between the two lies in the following: ancient kudurrus deal almost exclusively with multiple purchases of land by a single buyer from several sellers, while the Kassite/post-Kassite kudurrus deal mainly with a single grant of land by the king to an individual (or temple) or rarely with a single purchase of land by a single buyer from a single seller. It is true, of course, that some of the later kudurrus contain multiple contractual arrangements that took place over a longer period of time, but in all cases they deal with *one and the same* landed property, while the ancient kudurrus deal regularly with several purchases of *different* properties.

Different field names and locations and different sets of sellers prove that ancient kudurrus deal with the acquisition of different pieces of landed property. This general statement is valid even though a kudurru may occasionally contain a few acquisitions of land that lay in the same location and/or were bought from the same sellers. The same applies to the question of the date of the acquisitions within a single kudurru. The occurrence of dozens of acquisitions listed in a kudurru obviously means that the many plots of land were acquired at different times. On the other hand, the acquisition of three parcels, of the same size of 9 ¼ iku "acres," at exactly the same price of 288 silà "quarts" of barley per 1 acre, from three families by the son of the ruler of Lagash (no. 22), implies that the land was acquired at one time.

Outside Mesopotamia, the only possible parallel to the ancient kudurrus, with their multiple purchases of land, are the Greek *horoi* stones which, contrary to ancient kudurrus, deal regularly with a single property, but on some points resemble both ancient and Kassite/post-Kassite kudurrus, as well as the clay cones. As we learn from M. I. Finley, *Studies in Land and Credit in Ancient Athens, 500–200 B.C.* (New Brunswick, 1952), "The basic meaning of the word *horos* in Greek is 'limit,' 'boundary,' 'definition'. By an easy figure of speech the same word was applied to the object that marked a boundary" (p. 3). The *horoi* were, Finley continues, "slabs of marble, limestone, volcanic rock, or other available stone driven into the ground at appropriate spots" (p. 4); "At some point, the Athenians found a second use for the *horoi* (. . .) a stone serving to make public the fact that a particular piece of property was legally encumbered and hence in a certain sense not fully at the disposal of the proprietor" (p. 4); "The owner-debtor remained in physical possession of his holding while it served as guaranty of a debt" (p. 10). A whole section on pp. 13–21 is devoted to the relation of *horoi* to such instruments of publicity as the "announcement by herald, consummation of the sale before a magistrate, payment of a token to three neighbors, or public sacrifice and an oath." According to Finley, the normal procedure at Athens "was the creation of an obligation by mutual agreement, the affixing of *horoi* in the presence of witnesses, eventually the payment of the debt on the agreed date and the removal of the *horoi*, again before witnesses" (p. 18). On pp. 26f. Finley states that *horoi* of land, houses, or orchards were sometimes deposited with officials or temples, mainly, however, with private individuals.

In section 1.1, we stated that the term "ancient kudurru" is somewhat anachronistic when applied to the stones of the third millennium B.C., mainly because the meaning of kudurru as "boundary stone" is not attested before the Middle Babylonian period. In spite of its inadequacy, we use the term "ancient kudurru" if for no other reason than because we know of no other term, brief and useful, that might adequately describe the function of these objects.

Diakonoff, *Oikumene* 3 (1982) pp. 15f. n. 21, objected to the use of this term by calling it "rather unfortunate," and pointed out that "the Kassite and post-Kassite *kudurrus* were usually grants of land and/or charters of immunity, while the *Sammelurkunden* of the third millennium B.C. are deeds of purchase." It is interesting to note that while Diakonoff calls the ancient kudurrus *Sammelurkunden*, elsewhere in the same article he describes them in a roundabout way and uses no term whatsoever.

Recently, Brinkman, *RLA* 6 p. 273b, discussed the terminology as applied both to the ancient kudurrus of the third millennium B.C. and the Kassite and post-Kassite kudurrus. He pointed out the important differences between these two types of documents and concluded that "on this evidence it seems unlikely that the later type descended from the earlier, despite the modern choice of nomenclature."

The characteristics of the ancient kudurrus, on the one hand, and the Kassite and post-Kassite kudurrus, on the other, are charted in figure 9. While no genetic relationship between them can be proven at the present time—because of the substantial gap in time separating them—it seems to us that the convergences and divergences of these two groups of texts are neither greater nor smaller than those characterizing the earliest ancient kudurrus and the classical ancient kudurrus or even the ancient kudurrus and the Kassite and post-Kassite kudurrus, on the one hand, and the Greek *horoi*, on the other.

Symbolic of the great discrepancy between meaning and function is that both the Akkadian term *kudurru* and the Greek *horos* lost their original meaning "boundary," "boundary stone" when they were no longer set up in the field, but were deposited in a building.

Until some more adequate term comes up, we shall continue using the term "ancient kudurru" for the stones of the third millennium B.C. that deal with the transfer of landed property.

1.11. *Landed Property in Light of the Kudurrus and Sale Documents*

One of the most important points which have emerged from this study is the uneven geographical and linguistic distribution of the ancient kudurrus. As already noted in sections 1.2 and 1.5, there are virtually no kudurrus stemming from the far south (Uruk, Ur, Eridu, and Larsa). The surviving kudurrus are distributed rather evenly in the north (northern Babylonia, Diyala region, and Assyria) and in the near south at Nippur, Isin, Adab,

Shuruppak, Umma, and Lagash (Girshu). It is notable, however, that many of the kudurrus coming from the near south, especially from the places situated closest to the Akkadian north and thus potentially under the Akkadian influence, are written in Akkadian.

A corollary to the above observation is the uneven geographical distribution of sizes of the fields sold. Summarized below is the information on field sizes, culled from the kudurrus and sale documents (with the exclusion of the earliest kudurrus nos. 1–12, 18, and 19).

1) Lagash. In the kudurrus nos. 22 and 23 the attested sizes of fields are 9¼ iku (3 times), 14½ iku (twice), 22⅓ iku (once), 29¼ iku (once), and 36 iku (once), with an average size being ca. 18 iku. The kudurru no. 21 records fields whose sizes range from 6 to 72 iku. In the contemporaneous sale documents from Lagash field sizes are 16½ iku (no. 144), 18 iku (no. 145), and 20 iku (no. 146). The last example involves an orchard. A drastically different picture is offered by no. 20, the Enḫegal Tablet, which records considerably larger fields, from 54 to 504 iku; the total of land listed in this document is 2700 iku.

2) Shuruppak. In the sample of twenty-two Shuruppak field sales, sizes of fields range from 60 sar to 41 iku, with the most common figures being between 2 and 8 iku. An average size of a sold field is ca. 8⅓ iku.

3) Adab. In the Adab kudurru no. 31 sizes of fields range from 8 to 24 iku. An average size is ca. 15.8 iku. In another Adab kudurru, no. 32, the sizes of the two fields sold are 84 iku and 122 iku.

4) Nos. 14 and 15 date to the Fara or the earlier phase of the Pre-Sargonic period, and possibly come from Isin. In these two documents sizes of fields range from 2.5 iku to 132 iku; the most common figures are between 6 and 30 iku. An average size of the field is ca. 23.3 iku.

5) Isin. In the Isin field sales, which date to the late Pre-Sargonic and Sargonic periods (nos. 169, 170, 173, 175, 176, 177, 178, and 179), sizes of fields range from 1½ to 18 iku. An average size of the field is 6 iku. In the Isin *Sammelurkunde* no. 182a, which dates to the late Pre-Sargonic period, sizes of the twenty fields range from 2 to 180 iku. An average size of the field is ca. 20 iku.

6) Nippur. In four Nippur field sales (nos. 207, 210, 211, and 212) field sizes range from 2 to 6 iku. An average size of the field is 5.3 iku.

7) No. 36, from northern Babylonia. Sizes of fields range from 4 to 96 iku. An average size of the field is ca. 31 iku.

8) No. 37, from northern Babylonia. Sizes of fields range from 6 to 48 iku. An average size of the field is ca. 12 iku.

9) No. 41, from Sippar. Sizes of fields range from 1⅓ to 118(?) iku. An average size of the field is ca. 45 iku.

10) No. 40, from northern Babylonia. Sizes of fields range from 73 to 3834 iku. An average size of the field is ca. 1215 iku.

Although the picture presented by the above data is far from uniform, it can be observed that the kudurrus stemming from the north generally involve larger fields than the southern kudurrus and sale documents. Moreover, among the southern kudurrus and sale documents, field sizes tend to become larger as one moves from Lagash to places situated farther north, such as Adab and Isin. The only document which is seriously dissonant with this distribution is the Lagash kudurru no. 20, which involves conspicuously large fields.

This general trend, by which the sizes of fields increase along the south-north axis, is paralleled by the corresponding increase in the total acreage of land sold: from 144.3 iku in the Lagash kudurrus nos. 22 and 23 and 300+ iku in the Lagash kudurru no. 21, to 427 iku in the Isin *Sammelurkunde* no. 182a and 770.5 iku in the Isin(?) kudurrus nos. 14 and 15, to 628.6 iku in the Sippar kudurru no. 41 (only fourteen out of the possible total of 100 transactions), to 9723 iku in no. 40. The case of the Lagash kudurru no. 20, which records a total of 2700 iku of land, presents the only anomaly here.

These facts seem to indicate that during the Fara, Pre-Sargonic, and Sargonic periods the "private" ownership of land was considerably more widespread in the north than in the south. As for the south, "private" land holdings appear to have been insignificant in the far south, their importance gradually increasing in the near south as one moves in the northern direction.

Coupled with the decreasing significance of "private" land holdings as one passes from northern Babylonia into the south, is the complementary phenomenon of the increasing importance of temple households and temple estates within the same geographical area. As is abundantly shown by the third millennium economic sources, temple households and temple domains were most prevalent in the far south and in the lower section of the near south, at Lagash and Umma. Their importance was markedly less in the places located farther north, such as Adab, Isin, and Nippur, decreasing even further in northern Babylonia, where the dominant forms of economic organization were the royal and private households.

On the basis of these data it can be tentatively suggested that the institution of "private"/alienable landed property originated in the north, from where it spread to the south. Conversely, the institution of the temple household and its peculiar system of land tenancy appears to have been originally a southern phenomenon, which was eventually transmitted to the north, though never superseding in importance the royal and private households.

It is significant that these deep-rooted differences between the southern and northern economies, though becoming progressively less and less distinct, survived well into the second millennium. The importance of temple households in the south, as contrasted with their comparative insignificance in the north, is still discernible in the Old Babylonian period. Even more telling is the fact that among the Old Babylonian sale documents dealing with (arable) land there is only a handful of texts that originated in the south (we owe this information to J. Renger).

The fact remains, however, that, in spite of its comparative rarity in the south, "private" landed property did exist in the region already in very early times. This raises the question as to the origin of that type of land. Two possible answers may be considered here: either the southern "private" land represented a survival of the familial or communal holdings, which may have theoretically existed there prior to the formation of temple estates, or it was a comparatively late innovation that came into being under the northern influence. Against the first solution is the fact that the sellers of fields who appear in the Fara and Pre-Sargonic kudurrus and sale documents from the south are generally either single individuals or nuclear families. It is equally significant that, in the cases when their status is known, the sellers invariably turn out to be high administrative or priestly officials, such as lugal "king" (no. 20), sag-du$_5$ "field recorder" (no. 22), and pab-šeš "anointing priest" (no. 23), and not, as one would expect, members of rural or tribal groupings. These facts favor the assumption that in the south alienable land represented a foreign and rather marginal addition to the temple-estate system, and that its possession was reserved to the city-state's ruling elite. Note that in Pre-Sargonic kudurrus and sale documents from Lagash the sold fields are described by the phrase éš šám-ma-ta "(measured) by the purchase(?) rope," which may refer to that category of holdings.

In the Sargonic period, especially during the reigns of Narâm-Sin and Shar-kali-sharri, the spread of northern institutions throughout the south greatly intensified. Perhaps the most significant innovation of that time was the creation in the south of a new category of land, the crown land, which was distributed in exchange for services among various types of royal dependents. It appears that the crown land was formed primarily through the confiscation of temple estates, though it is possible that the development of new tracks may have also played an important part in its creation. Temple estates, though severely diminished by the royal encroachments, retained much of their former importance and continued to be managed according to the old system.

An important source attesting to the creation of royal estates in southern Babylonia is no. 24, the Stela of Victory. This document records a total of 444,505¼ iku of land, comprising seventeen major towns and eight large villages, which was confiscated in the province of Lagash by an unnamed Sargonic king (probably Narâm-Sin) and distributed among his dependents.

The mode of management of southern royal estates can be studied in great detail on the example of the "Mesag Archive." This group of texts, probably stemming from Sagub on the border between the provinces of Lagash and Umma, illustrates the activities of a large royal estate managed by Mesag, the governor of Umma during the reigns of Narâm-Sin and Shar-kali-sharri. See provisionally S. J. Bridges, "The Mesag Archive: A Study of Sargonic Society and Economy" (unpubl. Ph.D. dissertation, Yale University, 1981); B. R. Foster, *Administration and Use of Institutional Land in Sargonic Sumer* (Copenhagen, 1982) pp. 52–84.

We have also strong indications that during the Sargonic period private landed property became more prevalent in the south. Although the only Sargonic sale documents stemming from the south that deal with fields are Isin and Nippur texts, and there is a total absence of southern kudurrus in this period, the existence of large private holdings in the south is proven by the administrative text *BIN* 8, 291 (collated by Foster, *op. cit.* p. 57), stemming from the "Mesag Archive." This text records the total of land held by Mesag in the province of Lagash. His holdings comprised 1176 iku of purchased land (gán ⌜šám-a⌝), as well as 2424 iku of prebend land (gán ŠUKU), granted to him on usufruct by the crown.

Another important Sargonic source attesting to the existence of private land holdings in southern Babylonia is the Lagash tablet *ITT* 1, 1091. This text lists five minas or pounds of purified silver, various silver objects and garments, and quantities of wool and oil, of the total value of over 937 shekels of silver, which are designated as the "price of the field" (níg-šám GÁN-kam). At the rate of 3.3 shekels of silver per 1 iku of land, used in kudurru no. 40, the Manishtushu Obelisk, 937 shekels of silver would purchase ca. 284 iku of land. Unfortunately, the text names neither the buyer nor the seller of the field.

Both in the case of the private holdings of Mesag and the field alluded to by *ITT* 1, 1091 the crucial question is what was the source of the purchased land. Given the very large sizes of the fields involved, it seems unlikely that these holdings could have been purchased from small landowners. In this connection, it is striking that the contemporaneous sale documents and administrative texts from Umma and Lagash offer no allusions to the sale of fields by private individuals. Therefore, a more probable answer is that the holdings in question were purchased directly from the crown.

The picture of land tenure conditions changed considerably in Ur III times. It appears that the kings of Ur became the de facto owners of the southern temple estates and possibly of all other categories of arable land as well. Although the temple estates continued to function, at least in theory, as the domains of individual gods, they were now managed and exploited directly by the state, through the medium of provincial governments. The category of crown land, first introduced by the Sargonic kings, was greatly expanded in the Ur III period, to support the vast numbers of state dependents, and equally, to provide the king with a strong power base.

The question of the existence of "private" land in Ur III times is difficult to evaluate. This is primarily due to the fact that our documentation comes almost exclusively from the south, where, as we stressed before, this type of land was always comparatively insignificant. As far as testimony of the Ur III sale documents is concerned, they attest only to the "private" ownership of orchards and houses. At any rate, the absence of any references to the sale of fields in Ur III times, though not precluding the existence of "private" land, suggests that the alienation of arable land was prohibited by the state in that period.

CHAPTER 2

THE EARLIEST KUDURRUS: NOS. 1–12, 18, AND 19

This chapter discusses the fourteen earliest kudurrus, dating to the Uruk III (nos. 1–11) and Early Dynastic I–II periods (nos. 12, 18, 19). Our decision to treat this group of documents separately from other ancient kudurrus is due partly to the overall difficulties involved in their interpretation, and partly to their unique characteristics, which set them apart from the later kudurrus.

2.1. *External Structure (Form) and Iconography*

a) *Nos. 1–7*

Tablets nos. 1–7 are all of stone and all share a characteristic shape. Both the obverse and reverse of the tablets are convex, tapering off more severely toward the corners than toward the edges, with the result that all the edges of the tablets have the shape of a pointed ellipse when viewed head on. All seven tablets have this same basic form, but the most extreme variation is found in no. 4, which has a thickness almost as great as its length and width, giving it a more nearly spherical or cubical shape than the other six. This peculiar shape, which is common to these seven tablets, is not found in any other group of documents, either of stone or clay, from any other period or area.

Despite the fact that the flat/rounded contrast which distinguishes obverse from reverse in later tablets is not present in our texts, it is quite easy to determine which side is the obverse and which is the reverse. One way is simply by concluding that the fully inscribed side constitutes the beginning of the text and therefore its obverse, while the partially inscribed side constitutes the end of the text and therefore its reverse. Confirming the determination of the obverse/reverse sequence of the text is the fact that each column of what must be taken as the reverse is the continuation of the same column from the obverse. In other words, a column was begun on the obverse and continued until completed, using the reverse if necessary. The next column was again begun on the obverse, continuing on the reverse, and so on.

The remarkable formal similarity of nos. 1–7 makes it immediately apparent that they all served the same purpose. Unfortunately for the assessment of the significance of the overall similarity of these tablets, not one of them was found in situ or can be directly associated with a definite site.

The seven tablets form a unique group and share several notable features:

a) All are of stone.
b) All have the same peculiar shape which is not found in any other group of tablets, either of stone or clay, from any other period or area.
c) All have the sign for field (GÁN) in the first row (column) in association with numbers of the type used for giving measurements of fields in later periods.
d) All have the signs symbolized here as "DUG.SILÀ," in association with the sign for field (GÁN).
e) All belong to the same stage of writing, roughly dated to the Uruk III (= "Jemdet Nasr") period.
f) In all cases, even though most of the signs can be identified, the texts cannot be read by extrapolation from our knowledge of later sale documents. Even personal and geographical names cannot be identified with certainty.

Since there is no possibility that these tablets are forgeries, the unique shape of the tablets rules out coincidence as a possible explanation of their similarity. Two broad situations are possible: the tablets have either a different or a single origin. In the former case, their existence may be explained as a widespread cultural phenomenon showing a uniform treatment of real estate transactions at a very early stage of Mesopotamian civilization. This possibility is unlikely in the light of our knowledge of the uneven development of the ancient kudurrus in later periods. For that reason, a single origin of the kudurrus nos. 1–7 should be favored, and it may be suggested that they all came from the same period, the same site, and possibly the same hand.

It is quite possible that these seven tablets could have come from the same site and reached the antiquities market at different times and different places. The possibility that they may have come from different sites does not necessarily imply that they had diverse origins. The tablets are stone, which is rare in Mesopotamia, and the antiquity of the inscriptions would have made them objects of interest even to the ancients themselves. As a consequence, they could have been dispersed in antiquity, carried off as booty or souvenirs from one locale.

b) *Nos. 8–12, 18, and 19*

In contrast to kudurrus nos. 1–7, which are written on tablets with a peculiar shape, other early kudurrus are either animal figurines (nos. 8 and 9) or solid forms covered by text and human representations (nos. 10–12, 18, and 19).

Of the two kudurrus written on animal figurines, one is possibly a sheep (no. 8) and the other is a lion-headed bird (no. 9). No relationship between the form of the animal figurines and the text can be detected.

Of the four kudurrus with human representations, nos. 18 and 19 show only one person, who cannot be connected unambiguously with any of the actors of the transactions. In contrast, the figures in nos. 10–11 and 12 are possibly those of the buyer and sellers. Additionally, nos. 10–11 and 12 may provide information about the feast and the rite of passage accompanying the transfer of property, both features known only from the kudurrus of later times. For specifics, see commentaries to the respective texts.

2.2. *Internal Structure (Text)*

a) *Nos. 1–7 (and 8, 9, and 19)*

The contents and sequence of the text show a strong coherence within the group nos. 1–7. All of these tablets obviously deal with fields because of the appearance of the signs for measures of area and field (GÁN) in each text.

An overall view of the formulary and sequence of nos. 1–7 is given in figure 10. Included there are nos. 8, 9, and 19 which, while of a different shape, share certain textual characteristics with nos. 1–7, especially the occurrence of the sign-group DUG.SILÀ.

Although there is some variation in the individual texts, all have the same general structure, which can be divided into two basic parts: a) the first part, always in column i of the text, giving the total amount of land involved in the transaction and possibly the name of the buyer, and b) the second part, listing the individual parcels making up the total, and possibly their sellers.

The first case (= line) always includes: a number giving the total size of the field, the sign for field (GÁN), a two-sign-group which can be analyzed as DUG.SILÀ (pictographically, "PITCHER"+"CUP"), and a number of signs which vary from one text to another.

The numbers occurring in these texts in conjunction with the sign GÁN for "field" are of the type used for field measurements in later periods, and it is easy to see that the size of field given in column i is always, that is, in ascertainable cases, the total of the individual parcels of land listed in the remainder of the text.

The sign-group DUG.SILÀ and its variants are in immediate juxtaposition to the sign GÁN. The reading of the two signs as DUG and SILÀ is based on the characteristic forms of these two signs found in the early texts. For DUG, which is a pictogram of a spouted jar or pitcher, compare ATU-139, RÉC-380 and Supplément p. 19, and LAK-636f.; for SILÀ, a pictogram of a cup or solid-footed goblet, compare ATU-132, RÉC-164, and LAK-269. The two signs were taken together and interpreted as GAN by Edzard, *SRU* p. 168, a reading which had earlier been suggested by Deimel, *Or.* 9 p. 93, and S. Langdon, *OECT* 7 no. 323, for one of the groups with a variant form of SILÀ. However, the characteristic form of the sign GAN is a jar or pitcher on a flat two-legged stand (cf. RÉC-382, LAK-644), while the second element of our sign-group can always be seen to be a cup even though the representation of the cup varies slightly in a few cases. Recently, J. Friberg, *The Early Roots of Babylonian Mathematics* 2 (Göteborg, 1979, photomechanical reproduction) p. 9, argued that our DUG.SILÀ is a compound sign, "dug × sila$_x$," and not GAN (or ḪÉ) of other scholars. Although Friberg's conclusion is very close to ours, the evidence he adduced in its favor, namely, "the fact that both signs, ḪÉ and 'dug × sila$_x$,' appear in Jemdet Nasr type texts," is not supported by the copies or photographs of the texts: *JRAS* 1931 p. 842 no. 6 has DUG.GAN, but no DUG.SILÀ, while *UVB* 25 p. 26, W.21864 and W.21866, have the signs DUG and a variant of DUG in DUG.SILÀ, but no ḪÉ (or GAN). It is interesting that this DUG.SILÀ is preceded by what apparently are measures of area, as in two other Uruk texts, discussed just below. Variations in the DUG.SILÀ group of signs appear in several texts.

The sign in no. 2 is probably a graphic variant of the standard DUG.SILÀ.

No. 3 has two variants, one in the standard form in ii 3 and two diverging forms in i 1 and iii 1. Edzard, *SRU* p. 168, read the diverging forms as GUD QA, but the first sign cannot be GUD (the two lines representing the horns should not be connected in the sign GUD), and Thureau-Dangin, *RA* 24 (1927) p. 25, unquestioningly saw this as the same sign which is in column i of our no. 4.

No. 6 has ŠA.DUG ("CUP+GUNU"+"PITCHER") instead of the sign-group DUG.SILÀ ("PITCHER"+"CUP"), which is three signs removed from the sign GAN. This sign-group may be analyzed as SILÀ-*gunû*.DUG, a reversed form of the standard DUG.SILÀ.

No. 19 has a variant sign combination of DIN.SILÀ.

All these variants may be due to the uneven development of the pictographic writing.

Outside of the ancient kudurrus, the sign-group DUG.SILÀ occurs very rarely, as in the Uruk texts cited just above and in two other Uruk texts of the Uruk III period, which are cited here courtesy M. W. Green. The first of these texts, W.20551.1, gives the total size of the fields expressed in measures of area, followed by DUG.SILÀ and a number of signs, in the colophon at the end of the text; the obverse of this text is either destroyed or unavailable. The second text, W.20552.8 + 20593.2, gives the sizes of two fields on the obverse and the sign-group DUG.SILÀ in the midst of unreadable signs in column ii of the reverse.

A compound word dug-silà is normally used for a vessel measuring one silà or about one quart in the Ur III

Figure 10. Structure of the Earliest Kudurrus

	First Part			Second Part	
Text	Total Field in bùr	DUG.SILÀ and Variants	Buyer (?)	Individual Fields + Sellers(?) + Qualifications + Gifts(?)	Notes
1	55	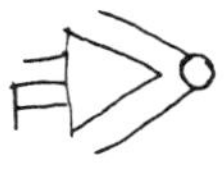	AN.ATU-912.KI sanga or sanga ^{d}ATU-912.KI	ii 1) 15(bùr) SELLER$_1$; ii 2) 15(bùr) SELLER$_2$ + signs; iii 1) 10(bùr) SELLER$_3$; iii 2–4) 15(bùr) SELLER$_4$ + signs	—
2	10	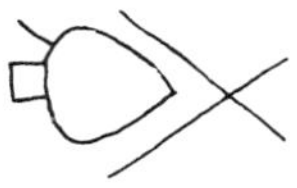	*AN.EN.SAR.NUN or ^{d}EN.SAR.NUN	SELLER	*Written within a "cartouche"
3	10	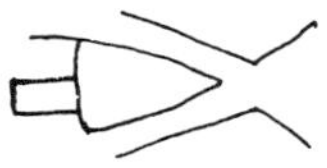	GI.ATU-329.AN.SAL or ^{d}GI.ATU-329.SAL	ii 1) 3(bùr) SELLER$_1$; ii 2) 2(bùr) SELLER$_2$; [= ii 3) 5(bùr) gán 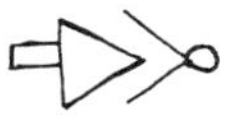]; ii 4–iii 2) signs include 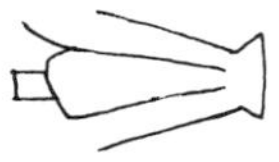 ; iii 3–5) 2(bùr) gán SELLER$_3$ + signs; iii 6) 3(bùr) gán SELLER$_4$ + signs	—
4	105	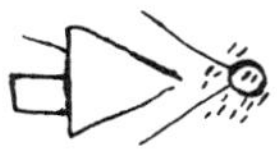	JN-67.NÀD.PAB.GÁ.IB	ii 1) 60(bùr) gán SELLER$_1$; ii 2–5) 45(bùr) SELLER$_2$ + signs	—
5	25	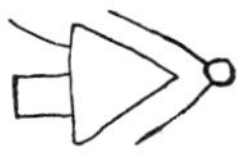	ŠIR.SIG/ÁB.KU.AN or ^{d}ŠIR.SIG/ÁB.KU	ii 1) 20(bùr) SELLER$_1$ + signs; ii 2) 5(bùr) SELLER$_2$ + signs	—
6	10	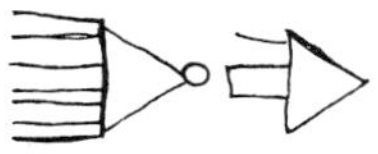	NIN.IŠ.X	SELLER engar + signs	—
7	*3	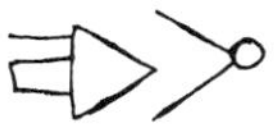	⌜KUG⌝.GIŠ+ŠÚ	ii–iii Rest very difficult; no sign for field and no signs for numbers or measures visible	*Preceded by 18 gemé-arád "18 slave women and slaves" plus name of seller and his qualification?
8	68	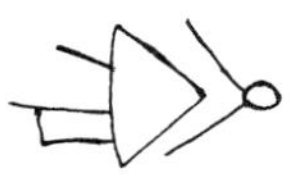	ÉN.ATU-328 é ^{d}Nin-gal or ^{d}Nin-é-gal	8 fields and sellers	—
9	5?		—	x fields, gifts(?), and sellers	—
10–11	5	—	ALAM.NE.PAB.KÍD?. GÍR.DU engar èš	gifts and sellers	—
12	25	—	Ušum-gal pab-šeš ^{d}Šará?	x fields, gifts, and sellers	—
18	—	—	AG.EN.NAM	x fields	—
19	72,001	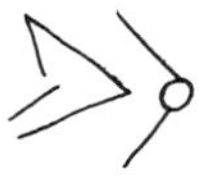	[. . .]	x fields	—

period. Different types of these one-quart vessels are listed in the administrative texts discussed by H. Waetzoldt, *WO* 6 (1971) pp. 13ff. and pl. opposite p. 12. Thousands of these vessels were produced (*ibid.* pp. 7–41, especially pp. 19ff.) and transported on boats (*TÉL* 16 and 18).

Still within the first line (case) of the obverse of the kudurrus nos. 1–7, the sign-group DUG.SILÀ and its variants are followed by three to five signs, which may provisionally be taken to stand for the name of the buyer of the property.

There are several points in favor of the assumption that the signs following the sign-group DUG.SILÀ are to be interpreted as the name of the buyer. From the structure of the ancient kudurrus of later times, we know that they regularly name only one buyer, usually of high status, and several sellers of several parcels of land, who are generally related to each other. In application to our case, this would mean that the name occurring with one large field in the first part should be that of the buyer of the land, in contrast to the several names occurring with several parcels of land in the second part of the text, who should be the sellers of the land.

Beginning with column ii, the second part of the text lists several fields representing a breakdown of the total given in the first part. Each field is usually allotted one case of writing, which gives the size of the individual parcel, with or without the sign GÁN, and several signs which may stand for the name of the seller.

Additional information associated with the total field, DUG.SILÀ, and the name of the buyer(?) in the first part, and with the individual parcels and their sellers(?) in the second part, is furnished by groups of signs that are generally difficult to interpret.

Relatively understood are the signs that denote the description of the field in the first part of kudurrus nos. 1–3. The groups of signs, intermingling with the size of the parcels and their sellers(?), which occur in the second part, as in nos. 1, 3, and 5, cannot be read, and we may only suggest that the groups of signs which occur in several cases at the end of nos. 1, 4, and 5 yield information about the family relationship of the sellers(?) of the property.

Clearly, the meaning of the sign-group DUG.SILÀ and its variants is crucial to our full understanding of the exact nature and significance of these texts. Unfortunately, the sphere of possibilities is too broad to allow any sure conclusions at the present time. As an educated guess, we may suggest that the sign-group DUG.SILÀ means something like "purchase"; or, if we wish to avoid confusion with the meaning šám "to buy," "to purchase," it may be suggested that the meaning of DUG.SILÀ revolves around the sphere of "to alienate," "alienated."

Still within the considerations of the exact meaning of DUG.SILÀ in the first part of the kudurrus nos. 1–7, one has to keep in mind the occurrence of this sign-group in other contexts, namely, in the second part of the kudurru no. 3 and in the administrative texts from Uruk (see above).

As a good example of the structure of the earliest kudurrus, we may cite no. 1. The first part lists first 55 bùr of land, followed by DUG.SILÀ and the name of the buyer(?), and ending with a few signs, which may represent a description of the field. The second part of the text lists four fields, 15, 15, 10, and 15 bùr in size (= 55 bùr of the first part), which were alienated(?) by four sellers(?) whose family relationship may be given in the few unreadable signs at the end of the text.

Variations to this structure are found in several texts, usually for readily apparent reasons. No. 2 evidently deals with only one field, making the second part of the formulary unnecessary, and hence contains a one-column inscription which presumably gives the size of the field and the names of the buyer(?) and seller(?). No. 3 has a subtotal in column ii, which gives the total of the two fields listed in that column. Significantly, the subtotal contains the sign GÁN and the sign-group DUG.SILÀ, but not in immediate juxtaposition to one another. Following the subtotal are several additional cases which continue into column iii before the listing of individual fields is resumed.

By far the most unusual variation among the first seven tablets is found in no. 7, which begins not with a total of fields, but with a total of 18 gemé-arád "18 slave women and slaves." This total is then broken down into 10 gemé "10 slave women" and 8 arád "8 slaves," and the total size of the field, DUG.SILÀ, and the name of the buyer(?) follow after this, still in column i. No individual fields can be discerned in columns ii and iii. For a possible interpretation, see the introductory comments to that text.

b) *Nos. 8–12*

Several characteristics pertaining to internal structure distinguish the first group (nos. 1–7) from the second (nos. 8–12).

While the texts of the first group are terse and contain limited information, the texts of the second group are larger and contain much more information.

Both groups of kudurrus agree in internal structure in that the first part of the text records the total of the alienated(?) land. But while the second part of the texts of the first group generally deals with the breakdown of the total land area into smaller parcels, there is a great variation in the contents of the second part in the second group. Already no. 7, which belongs by its physical form to the first group, gives in its second part not the breakdown of the fields, but presumably the names of the slaves. No. 8 of the second group follows the structure of the first group in giving the breakdown of the total fields into smaller parcels. The structure of no. 9 is controversial and it may concern both the fields and the commodities given to the sellers(?) in lieu of the price. In support, we note that no. 12 also treats of both the breakdown of the total field into parcels and of commodities. The structure of the related nos. 10 and 11 is more straightforward. No. 10 deals with only one field, while no. 11 contains a listing of commodities.

2.3. *Object of the Transaction*

Like the later kudurrus, their early counterparts deal with fields and only fields. The ascertainable sizes of the alienated fields are: 55 bùr (no. 1), 10 bùr (no. 2), 10 bùr (no. 3), 105 bùr (no. 4), 25 bùr (no. 5), 10 bùr (no. 6), 3 bùr (no. 7), 68 bùr (no. 8), 5? bùr (no. 9), and 5 bùr (nos. 10–11) in the Uruk III period; and 25 bùr (no. 12) in the Early Dynastic I–II periods. *Nota bene*: 1 bùr = 6.35 hectares = 15.7 acres.

Several important observations may be made on the basis of this listing.

First, all field dimensions are given in bùr (and higher area measures, here converted to bùr), and not in subdivisions of 1 bùr, such as 1 eše = ⅓ bùr and 1 iku = 1/18 bùr. As a matter of fact, subdivisions of 1 bùr are not utilized even when citing the sizes of the smaller parcels forming part of the alienated field in any of the kudurrus of the Uruk III period, and they do not appear until the time of the kudurrus nos. 12 and 18 in the Early Dynastic period.

Second, the recorded sizes of fields are generally large, in fact very large, in comparison with those recorded in the kudurrus of the later periods.

Third, the recorded sizes of fields are often given in round figures, such as 5 bùr (twice), 10 bùr (three times), or 25 bùr (twice). This characteristic of the earliest kudurrus is unmatched anywhere in later periods. For important implications of the last two observations, see section 2.5.

2.4. *Multiple and Single Transactions*

An ancient kudurru regularly deals with multiple purchases of land (fields), while a sale document generally deals with a single purchase of property (see section 1.7). This rule affects all kudurrus from the Fara to Sargonic periods, as best exemplified by the numerous purchases of smaller parcels of land recorded in nos. 14 and 15 of Fara date.

In contrast, the earliest kudurrus exhibit several exceptions to that rule. Of the thirteen kudurrus here discussed, at least two and possibly two more deal with one transaction only: nos. 2 and 10–11, and possibly no. 6 (unfinished) and no. 7 (mostly destroyed).

2.5. *Function of the Earliest Kudurrus*

Passing now to the question of the function of nos. 1–12, 18, and 19, it goes without saying that the simplest and most obvious solution to this problem is to assume that these documents are counterparts of the later ancient kudurrus, and, accordingly, to see in them records of the purchases of fields, each involving a single buyer and multiple sellers. This is, in principle, the position adopted in this volume, in which we follow the previous students of the earliest kudurrus. See, e.g., Edzard, *SRU* pp. 167–98 *Anhang*.

Based on the assumption that the earliest kudurrus record purchases of fields, in texts nos. 1–9, and perhaps in no. 19, the sign-group found after the total of land and after the signs DUG.SILÀ in column i could be identified as the name of the buyer, whereas the similar sign-groups appearing in connection with the individual parcels elsewhere in the inscription could be interpreted as the names of the sellers. In the same way, in texts nos. 10–11, 12, and 18, the personal name associated with the total of land could be interpreted as that of the buyer, whereas the names found elsewhere in the inscription, depending on the unique structure of each of these documents, could be taken as those of the sellers.

While this may be the easiest, and probably the most rational, way out of our dilemma, there are important reasons to question the validity of such a solution. It is noteworthy that the earliest kudurrus exhibit a number of unique characteristics that are not duplicated in the Fara and later kudurrus. To begin with, ten of the earliest kudurrus (nos. 1–9, 19) use, following the total of land, the sign-group DUG.SILÀ, which is found only in this group of texts and in a number of contemporaneous tablets from Uruk (see above section 2.2). It has been suggested earlier that the meaning of DUG.SILÀ may revolve around the sphere of "to alienate" or "alienation." It is equally possible, however, that DUG.SILÀ has a different, yet unknown, meaning, which may provide a key to the understanding of the function of the earliest kudurrus.

Another point that radically distinguishes the earliest kudurrus from their later counterparts is the absence in the former of any terminology for "buying," "selling," and "price." Even more striking is the fact that, with one or possibly two exceptions, these texts do not record any numerals and signs for commodities (such as silver, barley, oil, wool, etc.) which could be interpreted as the purchase price and/or additional payments, both of which are regularly recorded in the later kudurrus. The only early kudurru which clearly records commodities is no. 11. In addition, a list of commodities may also be included in no. 9, though this is far from certain, due to the overall difficulties involved in the interpretation of this document. Of course, one could attribute the absence of references to the price and additional payments in these documents to their small size and the extreme terseness of their texts. As the ancient kudurru is a record of the buyer's acquisitions of land, not a binding contract between the buyer and seller, the only three points that are absolutely necessary in such a record are the size of the alienated field and the names of the buyer and seller. Or, alternatively, we could speculate that the custom of recording the price and additional payments in kudurrus was not introduced until much later. Admittedly, however, neither of these explanations is fully satisfactory.

Also in contrast to the later texts, the earliest kudurrus involve surprisingly large areas of land. The highest figures attested in these documents are 55, 68, and 105 bùr (see section 2.3). These figures are considerably larger than those found in the later kudurrus, except for no. 40, which records areas as great as 62 bùr, 130 bùr, and 213 bùr. The figures found in other kudurrus are considerably smaller.

Finally, as already noted in section 2.4, two or possibly four of the fourteen earliest kudurrus deal not with multiple but with one land transaction only. This phenomenon is not attested in the kudurrus of later periods, which uniformly record multiple transactions.

All these facts caution against too-ready an assumption that the earliest kudurrus deal with the purchases of land. While considering alternative solutions, the possibility that comes first to mind is that these documents are records of land grants, comparable to those of the Kassite and post-Kassite periods. See section 1.10 and figure 9, which show the main characteristics of the earliest kudurrus as contrasted with the kudurrus of the Kassite and post-Kassite periods.

Partly favoring this possibility are several distinctive features which the earliest kudurrus share with later land grants. The first among them is the occurrence of a single transaction in several of the earliest kudurrus (see section 2.4), just as the Kassite and post-Kassite kudurrus record a single grant of land.

Another feature common to the earliest kudurrus and later land grants is that both groups of texts involve relatively large areas of land. It is noteworthy that the sizes of fields attested in the Kassite kudurrus are consistently large, such as 336 iku (= ca. 19 bùr), 500 iku (= ca. 28 bùr), and 1130 iku (= ca. 63 bùr).

With reference to section 2.3, it also may be noted that the earliest kudurrus frequently exhibit round figures, such as 10 bùr occurring three times and 25 bùr occurring twice, for the size of the field. This characteristic is unmatched anywhere in other ancient kudurrus. In contrast, among the eleven kudurrus of Kassite and post-Kassite date which specify the size of the granted field, we found 50 and 100 iku occurring twice and 200 and 500 iku occurring once.

Interesting as these similarities may be, it seems nevertheless quite certain that, even if the earliest kudurrus involve a type of grant, they cannot be merely analogues of the Kassite and post-Kassite kudurrus. This follows from the simple fact that the institution of royal grant, which is characteristic of the latter documents, seems to be completely out of place in the historical realities of the Uruk III period.

As we know from the archaeological record, the Uruk III period was a time of great upheavals and changes, constituting in many ways a completely unique stage in Mesopotamian history. There is all reason to believe that it was precisely then that the social and economic organization of Babylonia, as it is known from the later third millennium sources, acquired its basic shape. This formative and transitional character of the proto-historical age militates against the assumption that the earliest kudurrus are merely an earlier manifestation of the phenomenon known from the later periods. It could very well be that they are a phenomenon *sui generis*, which was characteristic of and unique to proto-historical times. If so, the internal differences between the earliest and the later kudurrus could find explanation in the unique purpose of the former.

Needless to say, any speculation as to what that hypothetical purpose of the earliest kudurrus might have been cannot be anything but pure guesswork. We may, however, consider at least two possibilities. The first of them is that these documents record the transfers or grants of family-owned land on behalf of temple households. Such transfers of familial property could have occurred, at least theoretically, when an extended family, attracted by a combination of economic and ideological incentives, joined the temple community of their own free will. The second possibility is that the earliest kudurrus are simply listings of the fields belonging to individual temple households. In either case, these documents would concern the holdings of temples, and this could account for the large sizes of the fields involved.

It should be stressed, however, that the above suggestions must be considered highly tentative, and that we lay no claims of having found the final answer. In view of all the uncertainties pertaining to the function of the earliest kudurrus, we feel it advisable to leave this question open for now. Clearly, its resolution will depend on the improved understanding of the archaic script and the discoveries of new inscriptions.

CHAPTER 3

ANCIENT KUDURRUS

No. 1 Hoffman Tablet

Photograph: Plate 1, Metropolitan Museum of Art, New York, negative no. L67161 A.
Copy: Plate 1, copied from the original by Gelb and redrawn by Steinkeller from copy and photograph.
Synopsis: Figure 10.
Provenience: Unknown (purchased).
Date: Uruk III.
Language: Sumerian(?).
Present location: E. A. Hoffman Collection of Babylonian Clay-Tablets, General Theological Seminary (New York).
Publications: E. S. Ogden, *JAOS* 23 (1902) pp. 19ff. (copy); G. A. Barton, *JAOS* 23 (1902) pp. 21–28; *idem*, *A Sketch of Semitic Origins* (New York, 1902) pp. 213ff.; *idem*, *The Origin and Development of Babylonian Writing* (= *BA* 9, Leipzig, 1913) p. VII (photograph); Deimel, *Fara* 1 p. 74 no. 5 (copy); Edzard, *SRU* no. 109.
Description: Smooth black stone tablet measuring 9.1 × 8.9 cm. Its thickness varies from 2.6 cm in the center to 1 cm on the edges.
Text: The Hoffman Tablet has beautifully preserved writing on the obverse; its reverse is uninscribed. Column i of the text deals with the acquisition(?) of a total of 5 burʾu (= 900 iku) and 5 bùr (= 90 iku), that is, 990 iku = 349.24 hectares of land by what is written, after the sign-group DUG.SILÀ, as AN.ATU-912.KI.SANGA, that is, either "AN.ATU-912.KI (= PN), the temple-administrator," or "the temple-administrator of the household of the deity ^{d}ATU-912.KI." For another example of a name or profession connected with a temple household, see no. 8. In columns ii and iii the total of 55 bùr of column i is broken up into four fields:

1 burʾu (= 180 iku) 5 bùr (= 90 iku)
1 burʾu (= 180 iku) 5 bùr (= 90 iku)
1 burʾu (= 180 iku)
1 burʾu (= 180 iku) 5 bùr (= 90 iku)

Each of the four field occurrences is followed by signs and cases that cannot be read safely. They could express the names of the sellers of the property, but see section 2.5.

Transliteration

i 1) 5(burʾu) 5(bùr) gán DUG.SILÀ AN.ATU-912.KI.SANGA
2) SAL.LÀL+vertical-GIŠ.TÙR
ii 1) 1(burʾu) 5(bùr) ŠAGA$_x$(LAK-175).NE.A. SIG.UR.A
2) 1(burʾu) 5(bùr) X.NUN.A.DA NÁM.vertical-GIŠ.TE.UD. NIN.A.LAK-131
iii 1) 1(burʾu) É.UD.SUKKAL.LAK-131. "NINDÁ"
2) 1(burʾu) 5(bùr) X.DU$_6$.ŠÀ
3) UR.A.PA.KUG.A
4) LUL.NAGA

Notes

i 2.—The compound sign transliterated here as LÀL+vertical-GIŠ is found five times in the ancient kudurrus in combination with other signs in the following contexts:
1) SAL.LÀL+vertical-GIŠ.TÙR (1 i 2), following the size of the field and the name of the buyer(?).
2) NIN.LÀL+vertical-GIŠ (5 ii 1), following the size of the field.
3) LÀL+vertical-GIŠ.NIN (8 iii 2), following the size of the field and followed by the name of a seller(?).
4) SAL.⌜X⌝.LÀL+[vertical-GIŠ]? (8 iv 2), following the size of the field.
5) [. . .] LÀL+vertical-GIŠ.X (9 ii 20), in difficult context.

In the third of these attestations (8 iii 2), the best meaning that can be assigned to LÀL+vertical-GIŠ is a field description. This meaning seems to fit the other occurrences as well.

The recurrent sign-group in these five examples is LÀL+vertical-GIŠ, that is, LÀL, written DUG "vessel" with an inscribed DÙG "sweet," plus a vertical GIŠ at the end. In four cases, the sign LÀL appears without the initial "spout," in one case (5 ii 1) with one. The function of the vertical GIŠ, written after LÀL, is not clear. In earlier pictographic writing, this sign is a long horizontal rectangle, which may depict the stand on which the vessel stood. Its reflexes may be detected in the vertical wedge that is found in the later forms of LÀL (as in Gudea Cyl. A xviii 20) and in other compounds with DUG.

Three parallels to these spellings should be noted: the initial "spout" found in the sign LÀL+vertical-GIŠ in no. 5 ii 1 occurs also in the writing of làl "honey" in no. 11:15. In place of the sign LÀL, written DUG+DÙG, occurring in all six examples, we find the sign-group DUG+Ì in 1 DUG+Ì "1 vessel of oil" (three times in no. 13) and in 2 DUG+Ì+vertical-GIŠ.X (no. 11:7c). In these cases, the sign-group DUG+Ì occurs with an initial "spout," and both occurrences clearly stand for a commodity. A variant of LÀL, written DUG+DÙG in no. 15 i 9, occurs as DUG+KAG in no. 14 ii 16 and iii 5, as it does in *ITT* 3, 5258:2, Ur III.

ii 1.—For the reading of LAK-175 as šaga$_x$, see note to no. 18 rev. i 2.

iii 1.—The sign transliterated here as "NINDÁ" has the form of NINDÁ plus a vertical wedge at the end. The same form is found in the writing of ŠÁM in "NINDÁ"+ŠE in no. 3 iii 5. This irregular form of "NINDÁ," with a vertical wedge, occurs also in the writing of ŠÁM at Ebla (e.g., *ARET* 2, 6 v 1, vi 1, and xi 6).

No. 2 Walters Tablet

Photograph: Plate 1, Walters Art Gallery, Baltimore, negative no. H 41.
Copy: Plate 1, V. Scheil, *MDP* 2 p. 130, collated by Gelb.
Synopsis: Figure 10.
Provenience: Unknown (purchased).
Date: Uruk III.
Language: Sumerian(?). *Present location*: Walters Art Gallery (Baltimore), 41.219.
Publications: Scheil, *RT* 22 (1900) pp. 149ff.; *idem*, *MDP* 2 pp. 129ff. (copy); F. Delitzsch, *Mehr Licht* (Leipzig, 1907) p. 24 (copy); Barton, *JAOS* 22 (1901) pp. 126ff. (copy); B. Meissner, *Die Keilschrift* (Berlin and Leipzig, 1913) p. 19 (copy); *idem*, *Die babylonisch-assyrische Literatur* (Wildpark-Potsdam, 1927) p. 14 (copy); Deimel, *Fara* 1 p. 73 no. 3 (copy); *idem*, *Or.* 9 (1924) pp. 93ff. (copy); Edzard, *SRU* no. 106.
Description: Rectangular stone tablet of reddish color, measuring 6.5 × 6.5 cm. Thickness varies from 2.3 cm in the center to 0.8 cm on edges.
Text: Obverse is inscribed, reverse rough, with no trace of a sign, probably never inscribed. The text deals with the acquisition(?) of 1 burᵓu = 180 iku = 63.51 hectares of land either by a person named AN.EN.SAR.NUN or by a temple household of the deity ^{d}EN.SAR.NUN, written within a "cartouche" after the sign-group DUG.SILÀ, from(?) a person(?) named MI.ŠAGAN(without *gunû*). EN.DU. The two signs following GÁN, read here as KI?.ZAG?, possibly are the description (location?) of the field.

Transliteration

MI.ŠAGAN(without *gunû*).EN.DU
1(burᵓu) gán KI?.ZAG?
DUG.SILÀ AN.EN.SAR.NUN

No. 3 Philadelphia Tablet

Photographs: Plate 2, University Museum, University of Pennsylvania, Philadelphia, negative nos. 7578, 7586, 7590, and 7591.
Copy: Plate 2, copied from the original by Gelb and redrawn by Steinkeller from copy and photographs.
Synopsis: Figure 10.
Provenience: Unknown (purchased at Nippur).
Date: Uruk III.
Language: Sumerian(?).
Present location: University Museum, University of Pennsylvania (Philadelphia), CBS 16105.
Publications: Barton, *The Museum Journal* 3 (1912) pp. 4–6 (copy); *idem*, *PBS* 9 (1915) pp. 9ff., no. 1, and Pl. LXV (copy and photographs); *idem*, *The Origin and Development of Babylonian Writing* (Leipzig, 1913) p. VIII (copy); *idem*, *OLZ* 16 (1913) pp. 6–12 (photograph); Deimel, *Fara* 1 p. 75 no. 4 (copy); Edzard, *SRU* no. 107.
Description: Greenish-black stone tablet measuring 7.2 × 7.4 cm. Its thickness, 1.8 cm at the center, tapers off towards the edges.
Text: The sequence of writing runs consecutively in each of the three columns from the obverse to the lower edge to the reverse to the upper edge (see section 1.4). Column i of the text deals with the acquisition(?) of a total of 1 burᵓu, that is 180 iku = 63.51 hectares of land, by a person(?) named, following the sign-group "DUG".SILÀ, as GI.ATU-329.AN.SAL or, possibly, by a temple household of the deity ^{d}GI.ATU-329.SAL, or by a combination of a name or profession plus a temple household. His further description may be given in the subsequent cases of column i. In columns ii and iii the total of 180 iku of column i is broken up into four fields:

3 bùr (= 54 iku)
2 bùr (= 36 iku)
(5 bùr subtotal)
2 bùr (= 36 iku)
3 bùr (= 54 iku)

Each of the four field occurrences is followed by signs and cases that cannot be interpreted safely. They could express the names of the sellers, but see section 2.5.

Transliteration

i	1)	1(burᵓu) gán "DUG".SILÀ GI.ATU-329.AN.SAL
	2)	X.UD.APIN
	3a)	[X].ŠU
	3b)	SA.DA.GI
	4)?	X.MUD
ii	1)	3(bùr) SAL.A.ATU-768
	2)	2(bùr) EZEN.KI.NUN.SA.BAR
	3)	5(bùr) gán UD.SAG.NITA DUG.SILÀ PAB
	4)	DU.PAB.X.⌜LAK-131⌝?
	5)?	KA?.I
iii	1)	UD.⌜X⌝ DUG."SILÀ"
	2)	A.X.RAD(ATU-850)
	3)	2(bùr) gán KUG.A
	4)?	EN.DU.DU
	5)?	ŠÁM KUG GI_4.KI.LAK-131
	6)?	3(bùr) ŠÀ gán DUMU.NUN.DU. DU.X.LAK-131

Notes

i 1 and iii 1.—For divergent forms of DUG and SILÀ, see section 2.2.

iii 5.—For the form of ŠÁM, see note to no. 1 iii 1.

No. 4 Louvre Tablet

Photographs: Plate 3, Louvre Museum, Paris.
Copy: Plate 3, Thureau-Dangin, *RA* 24 (1927) p. 23, collated by Gelb.

Synopsis: Figure 10.
Provenience: Unknown (purchased).
Date: Uruk III.
Language: Sumerian(?).
Present location: Louvre Museum (Paris), AO 8844.
Publication: Thureau-Dangin, *RA* 24 (1927) pp. 23–26 (copy); Edzard, *SRU* no. 111.
Description: Light-green onyx tablet measuring about 4 × 4 cm. Its thickness varies from 4 cm in the center to 2 cm on the edges. The Louvre Tablet is much thicker in relation to its height and width than the other tablets of this group, giving it a more nearly spherical shape.
Text: The sequence of writing runs consecutively in each of the two columns from the obverse to the lower edge to the reverse to the upper edge (see section 1.4). Column i of the text deals with the acquisition(?) of a total of 1 sár (= 1080 iku) 4 burʾu (= 720 iku) 5 bùr (= 90 iku), that is, 1890 iku = 666.86 hectares of land, by a person(?) named, after the sign-group DUG.SILÀ, in five signs. The total of 1890 iku of column i is broken up in column ii into two fields:

1 sár (= 1080 iku)
4 burʾu (= 720 iku) 5 bùr (= 90 iku)

Each of the two fields is followed by signs and cases that cannot be interpreted safely. They could express the names of the sellers, but see section 2.5.

Transliteration

i 1) 1(sár) 4(burʾu) 5(bùr) gán DUG.SILÀ
JN-67.NÀD.PAB.GÁ.IB
ii 1) 1(sár) gán SI.A.EN.X.SI.X.X.KA?
2) 4(burʾu) 5(bùr) A.⌜GI⌝?.UD.DU$_6$
3) GÁL.SI.A.KA/PÙ
4) LÁL.É
5) UNUG.A

Notes

i 1.—Against Thureau-Dangin's copy, the sign SILÀ in DUG.SILÀ has a small circle, as in other forms of SILÀ in the earliest kudurrus.
ii 5.—The personal(?) name UNUG.A occurs also in no. 8 ii 2.

No. 5 Yale Tablet I

Photographs: Plate 4, Babylonian Collection, Yale University, New Haven.
Copy: Plate 4, G. G. Hackman, *BIN* 8, 1, collated by Gelb.
Synopsis: Figure 10.
Provenience: Unknown (purchased).
Date: Uruk III.
Language: Sumerian(?).
Present location: Babylonian Collection, Yale University (New Haven), YBC 2245.
Publication: Hackman, *BIN* 8 p. 4 and no. 1 (copy); Edzard, *SRU* no. 108.
Description: Square black stone tablet measuring 7.7 × 7.7 cm. The thickness is 2.2 cm in the center, tapering off to 1 cm on the edges.
Text: Writing begins in column i of the obverse, then, instead of continuing in the same column on the reverse, goes on to column ii of the obverse to be continued in the same column on the reverse.
Column i of the text deals with the acquisition(?) of a total of 2 burʾu (= 360 iku) 5 bùr (= 90 iku), that is, 450 iku = 158.78 hectares of land, by what is written, after the sign-group DUG.SILÀ, as either the personal name ŠIR.SIG/ÁB.KU.AN or (temple household of the deity) ^{d}ŠIR.SIG/ÁB.KU. The total of 450 iku of column i is broken up in column ii into two fields:

2 burʾu (= 360 iku)
5 bùr (= 90 iku)

The difficulty with the interpretation of 5 bùr in the second part of column ii is that the circles read here as bùr are of the same size as the circles for 2 burʾu at the beginning of column ii. However, the interpretation of 5 burʾu plus 2 burʾu in column ii would force the interpretation of 7 burʾu in column i and the reading as 5 burʾu of the five circles that are clearly smaller than the two circles read as 2 burʾu. This interpretation, therefore, is hardly to be considered. Edzard, *SRU* p. 169, takes the unit in column i not as the total of the two units of column ii, but as one of three independent units. M. Lambert's reconstruction of the units, offered in *RA* 53 (1959) p. 219, is without parallels.
Each of the two field occurrences is followed by a large number of signs that cannot be safely interpreted. They could express the names of the sellers, but see section 2.5.

Transliteration

i 1) 2 (burʾu) 5(bùr) gán DUG.SILÀ
ŠIR.SIG/ÁB.KU.AN
ii 1) 2(burʾu) NIN.LÀL+vertical-GIŠ
SIG/ÁB.GÁ.SIKIL?
URU.TE?.A.
UKÙ.SAG?
LAK-131.UKÙ.A
2) 5(bùr) X.SAL.SI
X
KISAL.KI

Notes

i 1.—It may be tempting to break up the sign-group ŠIR.SIG/ÁB.KU.AN into a name ŠIR.AN or AN.ŠIR and his occupation ÁB.KU = unud$_x$ (for the reading, see Waetzoldt, *Kraus AV* p. 396).
ii 1.—In the compound sign transliterated here as LÀL+vertical-GIŠ, the sign LÀL has an initial horizontal wedge, as in no. 11:15. The vertical GIŠ appears to have small horizontal wedges inside as if it were the sign ÉŠ. Its reading as a vertical GIŠ is recommended by the case of a clear LÀL+vertical-GIŠ in no. 1 i 2. See note to no. 1 i 2.
ii 1 and ii 2.—The large number of signs in these cases suggests that they should be subdivided.
ii 1.—The sign transliterated here as TE? has a small circle in the middle, and not the small vertical wedge that is found in the standard form of TE, as in no. 1 ii 2.
ii 2.—The horizontal wedge in front of KISAL is part of the sign. Compare the forms of KISAL in E. Burrows, *UET* 2 pl. 28 no. 357.

No. 6 Yale Tablet II

Photograph: Plate 4, Babylonian Collection, Yale University, New Haven.
Copy: Plate 4, Hackman, *BIN* 8, no. 2, collated by Gelb.
Synopsis: Figure 10.
Provenience: Unknown (purchased).
Date: Uruk III.
Language: Sumerian(?).
Present location: Yale Babylonian Collection, Yale University (New Haven), YBC 2244.
Publication: Hackman, *BIN* 8 p. 4 and no. 2 (copy).
Description: Square light-brown stone tablet measuring 8.8 × 8.8 cm. The thickness is 2 cm in the center, tapering off to 0.5 cm on the edges.
Text: The text, inscribed only on the obverse, was left unfinished in ancient times, but there is no reason to suspect its genuineness, as was done by F. J. Stephens in *BIN* 8 p. 4. Column i of the text deals with the acquisition(?) of 1 burᵓu = 180 iku = 63.51 hectares of land by a person(?) named NIN.IŠ.X, whose name is followed by the sign-group ŠA.DUG, not preceded by the sign-group DUG.SILÀ as in the case of the kudurrus treated above. Column ii contains, in two cases, seven(?) signs, which may be interpreted as a personal name (the seller?) and the profession engar "farmer."

Transliteration

i	1)	1(burᵓu) gán NIN.IŠ.X ŠA.DUG
ii	1)	1? DARA$_4$?.UD?
	2)	KA!.ŠA.ŠE APIN

Notes

i 1.—For the spelling ŠA.DUG instead of the standard DUG.SILÀ, see section 2.2.

ii 1.—The interpretation of the first sign as 1(iku) is unlikely, since the lowest area measure attested in the earliest kudurrus is 1(bùr) (see section 2.2).

ii 2.—For the reading of the first sign as KA, see the photograph. The sign-group KA.ŠA could be interpreted as PUZUR$_4$.

No. 7 Leiden Tablet

Photographs: Plate 5, Rijksmuseum van Oudheden, Leiden.
Copy: Plate 5, copied from the original by Gelb and redrawn by Steinkeller from copy and photograph; collated by M. Stol.
Synopsis: Figure 10.
Provenience: Unknown (purchased).
Date: Uruk III.
Language: Sumerian(?).
Present location: F. M. Th. de Liagre Böhl Collection of Cuneiform Tablets, Rijksmuseum van Oudheden (Leiden), LB 1338.
Publication: Text briefly discussed by Stol in M. Heerma van Voss, ed., *Van beitel tot penseel* (Leiden, 1973) p. 5.
Description: Black stone, almost square in shape measuring 10 × 9.5 m. Its thickness is 3 cm in the center, tapering off to 0.5 cm on the edges.
Text: The individual columns of writing run consecutively from the obverse to the lower edge to the reverse (see section 1.4). Part of the obverse is effaced. Unlike all other tablets belonging to this group (nos. 1–6), the present text begins not with an area of land, but with a number of "slaves." The number 18 gemé(SAL+[KUR])-arád(NITA+[KUR]) "18 slave women and slaves," given in i 1a, represents the total of 10 gemé(SAL+[KUR]) "10 slave women" and 8 arád([NI]TA+KUR) "8 slaves," given in i 1b. The number of "slaves" is followed, still in case 1 of column i, by three groups of signs, each group separated by a vertical division mark. Case 2 of the same column deals with the acquisition(?) of 54 iku = 19.05 hectares of land by a person(?) whose name is expressed, after the sign-group DUG.SILÀ, in the signs ⌜KUG⌝.GIŠ+ŠÚ.

The rest of the text is badly eroded but enough remains to surmise that no measures or numbers were used. This conclusion is based on the observation that measures and numbers are normally so deeply incised that they are recognizable even when the surface of the signs is totally effaced. Since none are visible in our text, the obvious conclusion is that it contained no information about fields (measures of area) or commodities (numbers). This indicates that, as in no. 2, only one field was involved and no breakdown of fields was necessary.

Column ii probably contained eight cases; the original number of cases in column iii is unknown. If the number of cases in column iii could be reconstructed as ten, one could speculate that columns ii and iii record the names of the eighteen "slaves" totaled in column i.

Be that as it may, the occurrence of "slaves," with or without their names, is quite unusual, as the only other examples of "slaves" in the ancient kudurrus come from nos. 11:9 and 40 (Manishtushu Obelisk) Side C ix 4–13. Two possible interpretations come to mind for the present example. One is that the eighteen "slaves" represented the agricultural personnel that was attached to the landed property in question. The other would be to assume that they were given in lieu of the field's price/additional payment. The latter interpretation seems somewhat less likely, given that, with the exception of the two examples cited above, human beings are never included in prices and additional payments.

Transliteration

i	1a)	18 gemé(SAL+[KUR])-arád(NITA+[KUR])
	1b)	10 gemé(SAL+[KUR]) [2]+6 arád([NI]TA+KUR)
	1a$_1$)	GUD-inversum.GUD.ME
	1a$_2$)	X.SAL
	1b$_1$)	[nothing?]
	2)	3(bùr) gán DUG.SILÀ ⌜KUG⌝.GIŠ+ŠÚ
ii	1)	BA.GUD
	2)	[X].KI
	3)	[X.TU]R?
	4)	⌜X⌝.[X]
	5)	⌜ḪA⌝?.[X]
	6)	[X].⌜X⌝.[X].TAB.[A]N?
	7)	DA.DU.PAB

	8)	PAB.SUKKAL?
iii	1)	[X].⸢É⸣
	2)	[X].X.ŠÀ
		(break)
	1′)	AN.[X]
	2′)	vertical-GIŠ.UR_4?
	3′)	X.SAG.JN-127

No. 8 Sheep(?) Figurine

Photographs: Plate 6, Oriental Institute, The University of Chicago, negatives nos. N. 33713, 33714, 33714.

Copy: Plate 6, copied by M. W. Green from the original and photographs, assisted by Whiting.

Synopsis: Figure 10.

Provenience: Unknown (purchased)—note the possible occurrence of ^{d}Nin-gal in i 2, a deity who is at home at Ur.

Date: Uruk III.

Language: Sumerian(?).

Present location: Oriental Institute, The University of Chicago, A 3669.

Description: Inscribed stone figurine in the form of a recumbent animal, perhaps a sheep. Maximum measurements are 4 × 11 × 4 cm. The inscription covers the whole figurine, with the exception of the bottom, which is rough and erose. It is impossible to deduce from the shape of the bottom whether it was inscribed originally. Still, if the reconstruction of the eight parcels of land is correct (see below), the bottom must have been uninscribed. As only about 1.5 cm is broken off along the left side, perhaps no more than the beginnings and ends of some cases are missing.

Text: The signs are badly preserved and their sequence is difficult to reconstruct, especially at the beginning and the end of the inscription.

The inscription begins at the top of the head with the numbers 1(sár) 8(bùr) and continues over the left shoulder toward the bottom with the sign GÁN and the sign-group DUG.SILÀ, ending with the signs É.GAL.NIN.AN on the left side of the face. The second column begins near the bottom of the right shoulder to the right of the first column, and the third and fourth columns continue in this manner towards the tail. The sequence of the cases inscribed around the tail (column iv) is questionable since the writing in this area apparently goes from bottom to top. The inscription continues in the same orientation in column v on the right shoulder, in the space above the beginning of column i (which is on the left shoulder of the animal). The cases in this portion of the inscription apparently move toward the head, and the final case with the sign UNUG is found on the right side of the head.

Column i deals with the total of 1 sár (1,080 iku) 8 bùr (144 iku), that is, 1,224 iku = 431.87 hectares of land, which were acquired(?) by ÉN.ATU-328 É.GAL.NIN.AN, that is, a person(?) ÉN.ATU-328 or ATU-328.ÉN, who was connected with é ^{d}Nin-gal "(temple household of) the deity Ningal." A less likely possibility is to interpret the signs as ÉN.ATU-328 NIN.DINGIR é-gal "PN, the nin-dingir priestess of the palace." For another possible example of a name or profession connected with a temple household, see no. 1. The deity Ningal is at home at Ur, which may be of some importance for the question of the original provenience of our kudurru. The total of 1,224 iku of column i is broken up in columns ii–v into eight fields:

9 bùr (= 162 iku)
5 bùr (= 90 iku)
4 bùr (= 72 iku)
5 bùr (= 90 iku)
2 bùr (= 36 iku)
1+[1] burᵓu [5] bùr (= 450 iku)
1 burᵓu 4+[2] bùr (= 288 iku)
2 bùr (= 36 iku)

The sizes of the sixth and seventh fields in column iv were reconstructed in such a way as to fit the total given in column i.

The above interpretation assumes that no. 8, like nos. 1–6, consists of two parts, the first part recording the total of land and the second giving the breakdown of the total into smaller parcels. The fact is, however, that the word gán "field" is never given in the second part of the text, and thus, at least theoretically, the circle-like numerals in the second part could refer to commodities. Against this possibility are the two occurrences of the numeral shaped as a circle within a circle (iv 1 and 3), which cannot be interpreted in any other way but as an area measure burᵓu, making it necessary to interpret the ambivalent circle-like numerals as bùr.

Area measures in the second part of the inscription are followed by signs which, in some instances at least, may be interpreted as personal names and the descriptions of fields. For example, in ii 2 UNUG.A, attested also in no. 4 ii 5, may stand for a personal name (or, alternatively, a toponym), whereas in iii 2 the sign-group LÀL+vertical-GIŠ, which appears in combination with other signs in several kudurrus (see note to no. 1 i 2), could be the field's description.

Transliteration

i	1)	1(sár) 8(bùr) gán DUG.SILÀ ÉN.ATU-328
	2)	É.GAL.NIN.AN
ii	1)	9(bùr) SU.É.ŠAGAN.GI.⸢X⸣
	2)	UNUG.A
	3)	5(bùr) X.LÁL+SAR.ŠE.É/SA
	4)	4(bùr) ⸢X.X⸣
iii	1)	5(bùr) ÚR?.KUG.URU.X.⸢X.X⸣
	2)	2(bùr) LÀL+vertical-GIŠ.NIN
	3)	INNIN?.KI
iv	1)	1+[1](burᵓu) [5](bùr) ⸢X.X⸣
	2)	SAL.⸢X⸣.LÀL+[vertical-GIŠ]?
	3)	1(burᵓu) 4+[2](bùr) UMBIN?.ŠÀ?.ÉŠ?.X
v	1)	2(bùr) X.ŠÀ
	2)	UNUG

Notes

iii 3.—The sign transliterated here as INNIN? could alternatively be read ŠEŠ. Note, however, that the resulting combination ŠEŠ.KI cannot be interpreted as the divine name Nanna (or the PN Nanna

(-ak)), for in the archaic script Nanna's name is written ŠEŠ.NA, i.e., $Nanna_x$(ŠEŠ)[na]. See Burrows, *UET* 2 pl. 2 no. 12.

No. 9 Khafajah Bird

Photographs: Plates 7, 8, and 10, Oriental Institute, The University of Chicago, negatives nos. N. 13796, 13797.

Copy: Plates 9 and 10, copied by Green on the basis of photographs and casts, assisted by Whiting.

Synopsis: Figure 10.

Provenience: Khafajah, Field number Kh. V 68.

Date: Uruk III. The object was found in a room near the entrance to the Sin Temple (R 42:2) in level VIII, which was dated to Early Dynastic II by the excavators. The manner in which the pieces of the lion-headed bird were found in the field suggests that the object may already have been in a fragmentary condition when it came to the room where it was discovered. Furthermore, its archaeological context is apparently secondary since it is clearly several hundred years older than the level in which it was found.

Language: Sumerian(?).

Present location: Iraq Museum (Baghdad), IM 24341.

Publications: P. Delougaz and S. Lloyd, *OIP* 58 pp. 58, 145, and Th. Jacobsen *ibid.* pp. 289 (photograph) and 290; H. Frankfort, *OIC* 20 pp. 29 and 32 (photograph); A. Moortgat, *Die Kunst des alten Mesopotamien* (Cologne, 1967) p. 33 and figure 37.

Description: "An inscribed stone (schist?) object in the shape of a bird with a lion's head" (*OIP* 58 p. 58). "It represents, no doubt, the lion-headed eagle Imdugud, and is most carefully made, the tongue being cut separately from red jasper. Unfortunately the stone is a kind of schist which flakes easily, and one side with the inscription is entirely lost" (*OIC* 20 p. 29). Length from head to tail is 25 cm, width 9.5 cm, thickness 3.5 cm.

Text: The inscription begins in column i on the head near the eye and continues to the tail. The same column is presumably continued on the reverse around the tail and back towards the head. The inscription continues with column ii to the right (or below it) on the obverse, which also presumably continues around the tail on the reverse until the head is reached. The obverse of column iii also extends from the head to the tail, but, because of the crowded conditions on the corresponding parts of the reverse, it continues as column iv to the left of column i on the obverse, ending near the tail. The ways in which columns iii and iv are written on the statuette are similar in that the top (or left) sections of column iii are written on the obverse, while its lower (or right) sections are written on the bottom of the bird, just as the lower (or right) sections of column iv are written on the obverse, while its top (or left) sections are written on the back part of the bird. The approximate dividing line between the obverse and the bottom and between the obverse and the back part of the bird is marked by a dash line in our drawing.

The first case of the inscription contains a number, a rectangular sign which is presumably GÁN, the sign-group DUG.SILÀ, and several additional signs which can be read as KAR, LAGAB, and GI.

Five large circles, which are of the same size and form as the large circles in the rest of the inscription, should be read as 5(bùr). There is no circle within the circle in any of them and the measure cannot, therefore, be interpreted as burᵓu or sarᵓu (see also below).

The greatest problem lies with the sign which is presumably GÁN but which has two additional strokes attached to it. One can only note that the stone is soft and that the inscription was not cut with any great care so that there are numerous extraneous lines appearing on the tablet as well as a number of poorly made signs.

Accordingly, one can conclude that i 1 deals with the acquisition(?) of a field that was 5(bùr) or 90 iku = 31.76 hectares in size. The sign-group KAR.LAGAB.GI, which is clearly related to KAR.LAGAB.BAR in i 5 and KAR.LAGAB.[N]IN?.KUG.GIŠ? in i 6, possibly is a description (location?) of the field.

As can be seen at a glance, all cases (or lines) from i 2 on, except i 8, ii 1, 15–19, and iv 6–9, begin with a number, which is followed by one to three signs. A priori, it can be considered that the cases with a number express either the area measures of individual parcels or the amounts of commodities, while the cases without a number stand for the parties to the transaction.

To judge from nos. 1–8, what we expect to find after the introductory statement in i 1, discussed just above, is the breakdown of the total of 5(bùr) into sections dealing with the acreage of smaller fields. The following numbers are commonly used in the text:

A large circle, of the same size and shape as the sign bùr in i 1, a small circle, or a combination of large and small circles. If the circles are to be taken as area measures, then the small circle should stand for 1(bùr), and the large circle for 1(burᵓu) or 1(sár), or potentially, even 1(sarᵓu).

While, theoretically, it is possible to assign any of these measures to the large and small circles, there is no way to add up the occurring and reconstructed measures so that they would correspond to the total area of 5 large circles given in i 1, even if we interpret it not as 5(bùr), but as 5(burᵓu), 5(sár), or 5(sarᵓu).

From the fact that the area of land given in i 1 cannot represent a sum of the numbers appearing elsewhere in the inscription, we may conclude that the subsequent sections of the inscription deal with either additional fields or commodities. Clear attestations of fields seem to be found in i 5 (gán? KAR.LAGAB.BAR) and i 6 (KAR.LAGAB.[N]IN?.KUG.GIŠ?), where the sign-group KAR.LAGAB is probably a topographic description (as it appears to be the case in i 1). Note also the possible occurrences of the sign GÁN in ii 9 and iii 3, and the mentions of Lagash (BUR.LA.ŠIR) in iii 7, and of the "canebrake of Antum" (giš-gi An-tum) in iii 8. On the other hand, commodities may be sought in, e.g., 7 small circles UD.GÚG (i 14), 2 horizontal strokes UD.LU (i 17), and 4 large circles MA.GÍD (iv 1), which could respectively be interpreted as "7 white cakes" (gúg babbar), "2 white turnips/sheep" (lu/udu babbar), and "40 big figs" (pèš gíd). In light of this, it is possible that, following i 1, the inscription lists both fields and various commodities. The final resolution of this problem is not possible at present, due partly to the difficulties in understanding the archaic script and partly to the poor state of preservation of the inscription.

Transliteration

Obv. i	1)	5(bùr) gán? DUG.SILÀ KAR.LAGAB.GI
	2)	3 large circles + 2 small circles LÁL+SAR
	3)	2 large circles SÁR.KI.A
	4)	4 large circles + 4 small circles BAR.A
	5)	2 large circles gán? KAR.LAGAB.BAR
	6)	1 large circle + 5 small circles KAR.LAGAB.[N]IN?.KUG.GIŠ?
	7)	3 large circles KA.DUMU.UR$_4$
	8)	X.X.EN.GÚ?.GI?.GI?
Rev. i	9)	[. . .]
	10)	[. . .]
	11)	[. . .]
	12)	[. . .]
	13)	[. . .].⌜GI⌝?.GAR
	14)	7 small circles UD.GÚG
	15)	2 horizontal strokes "DUG"
	16)	2 horizontal strokes? SAG.NUN
	17)	2 horizontal strokes UD.LU
	18)	[x] BA.X.Ḫ̮A
	19)	[. . .].GI
	20)	[. . .]
	21)	[. . .]
	22)	[. . .]
Obv. ii	1)	⌜UD⌝.MUG.KI
	2)	4 large circles + 3 small circles UD.NIN.KUG
	3)	3 large circles X.A.LÁL+SAR
	4)	5 large circles GIŠ?.A.NUN
	5)	3 large circles NIN.KUG
	6)	5 large circles MAR?.NA.A.X.ŠU?
	7)	2 large circles SU.É.GABA.X
	8)	2 large circles + 8 small circles SIG.MAR.GAL
	9)	4 large circles GI.GÁN?
	10)	4 large circles AG?.NE.NAGAR
	11)	[. . .] É
Rev. ii	12)	[. . .]
	13)	[. . .]
	14)	[. . .]
	15)	⌜X⌝.[K]UG
	16)	UD.KUG
	17)	NI.NU.LU
	18)	X.X
	19)	GÍR.X.⌜X⌝
	20)	[. . .] LÀL+vertical-GIŠ.X
	21)	[. . .]
	22)	[. . .]
	23)	[. . .]
	24)	[. . .]
Obv. iii	1)	2 large circles AN?.LÁL+SAR
	2)	4 large circles vertical GIŠ.TE.BAR
	3)	4 large circles GI.GÁN?
	4)	4 large circles BAR.UD.ŠAGAN
	5)	4 large circles DU$_6$?.KI
	6)	4 large circles BA.⌜Ḫ̮A⌝?
	7)	1 large circle NIN[DÁ]?.⌜X⌝ BUR.LA.ŠIR
	8)	2 large circles AN.TUM.GIŠ.GI
	9)	1 large circle LÁL+SAR.Ḫ̮A?
Obv. iv	1)	4 large circles MA.GÍD
	2)	2 large circles SAR.NIN.TAB?.GÚG?. A.GI?
	3)	2 large circles + [x] X
	4)	[x]+1 X.A?.⌜X⌝
	5)	[x] Ú?.X.X
	6)	⌜ŠE/GI.A?.ŠE/GI⌝
	7)	⌜X⌝.LAGAB.X.⌜X⌝.MAR
	8)	KA?.X.⌜X⌝.LA.⌜X⌝.RU
	9)	KA?.SAG

Notes

iii 7.—If our reading of the last three signs as BUR.LA.ŠIR is correct, we would find here the earliest mention of the city of Lagash.

iii 8.—Probably to be interpreted as giš-gi An-tum "canebrake of Antum." For giš-gi "canebrake," see J. Bauer, *AWL* p. 175.

No. 10 Blau Obelisk and No. 11 Blau Plaque

Photographs: Plates 11 and 12, British Museum, London.

Copy: Plates 11 and 12, copied by Green from photographs and copy from the original by Gelb.

Synopsis: Figure 10.

Provenience: Unknown (purchased)—said to have been obtained by A. Blau near Warka. For a possibility that the Blau tablets come from Tell ^{c}Uqair, see below under *Iconography and Text* a) *Blau Obelisk*.

Date: Uruk III.

Language: Sumerian(?).

Present location: British Museum (London), BM 86261 and 86260; the two numbers are wrongly identified in Edzard and Fenzel (see the last two entries under *Publications*, just below), since BM 86261 is the obelisk and BM 86260 is the plaque.

Publications: The older bibliography is cited fully; the later bibliography, containing mostly secondary and tertiary reproductions, is cited selectively. W. H. Ward, *JAOS* 13 (1889 = Proceedings for 1885) pp. LVIIf. (provisional copy); *idem*, *AJA* 4 (1888) pp. 39ff. and pls. IV–V (photographs); J. Ménant, *Revue archéologique* IIIme série, T. XI (1888) pp. 360–66 (provisional copy); M. V. Nikolskiy, *Drevnosti Vostochniya* 3 (1889) pp. 118–26 (provisional drawings); Thureau-Dangin, *RA* 4 (1896) pp. 43–52 (copy); Barton, *JAOS* 22 (1901) pp. 118–25 (copy); *idem*, *JAOS* 24 (1903) pp. 388f.; Meissner, *Die babylonisch-assyrische Literatur* (Wildpark-Potsdam, 1927) p. 14 (photograph of plaque); L. W. King, *A History of Sumer and Akkad* (London, 1916) opposite p. 62 (photographs); Deimel, *Fara* 1 p. 74 nos. 8–9 (sketches); E. Unger, *RLA* 2 (1938) p. 54; M. E. L. Mallowan in S. Piggot, ed., *The Dawn of Civilization* (London, 1961) pp. 72f. (photographs); E. Strommenger, *The Art of Mesopotamia* (London, 1962) pl. 15 (photographs) and pp. 382 f.; Edzard, *SRU* nos. 110–111;

K. Fenzel, *Überlegungen zu den "Blauʾschen Steinen"* (Eigenverlag, Berlin, 1975).

Description: The Blau Obelisk is a small obelisk with a pointed top and a flat bottom. It is made of the same material as the Blau Plaque. Maximum measurements are 18 × 4.3 × 1.3 cm. Both sides are flat.

The Blau Plaque is a small plaque with a rounded top and a flat bottom. The material is "greenish stone" or "jade-like green stone, perhaps a variety of serpentine," according to Ward, and "dark shale," according to Mallowan. Maximum measurements are 15.9 × 7.2 × 1.5 cm. Both obverse and reverse are flat.

Both Blau tablets contain writing and iconography. Although the inscriptions on both are oriented in the same manner with respect to the long axis of the tablets, the iconography of the plaque is horizontal while that of the obelisk has a vertical format. Since both sides of the plaque are inscribed, it is easy to see from the writing that one side is continued on the other side and that, therefore, the former is the obverse and the latter is the reverse. Since only one side of the obelisk is inscribed and the other side contains only pictorial representations, we arbitrarily designated the inscribed side as the obverse, although it cannot be determined whether the inscription was written first or as a sequel to the representations.

The occurrence of 5(bùr) gán "5 bùr of land" on the obelisk places it in the class of ancient kudurrus dealing with landed property. Although the plaque does not contain any references to fields, the identity of material and the stylistic and epigraphic similarity between the two tablets, especially in respect to the representations of the kneeling figures, indicate that they were fashioned at the same time and by the same hand. From the fact that the obelisk records a field, whereas the plaque lists what appear to be the price and/or additional payments, we can infer that the obelisk constitutes the beginning of the transaction and that the plaque is its conclusion.

Both the iconography and the writing appearing on the Blau tablets were considered so unusual at the time of their publication that their authenticity was seriously questioned by a number of scholars. Note the arguments brought forth in favor of the spurious character of the two pieces by Ménant, *op. cit.* pp. 360–66, and by W. St. Chad (and Ward's answer) in *The Athenaeum* 1 (1900) pp. 312, 440, 535f., and 696. Since that time, however, a large number of stylistic parallels have become available (cf. Strommenger, *op. cit.* pls. 16–22 and 32–33), and today the authenticity of the Blau tablets can no longer be questioned.

Iconography and Text: The interpretation of both the inscriptions and the scenes depicted on the Blau tablets abounds with difficulties. Therefore, the following discussion and the resulting conclusions are highly tentative, and we offer them with the utmost caution. This applies particularly to our analysis of the iconography of the two tablets.

a) *Blau Obelisk*

One side of the obelisk contains representations of two humans, the other a five-line cuneiform inscription.

The first side of the obelisk shows two male figures in two registers, upper and lower. The standing man in the upper register is represented with a beard, a skirt with a border, and a bulky band around his hair; he holds in his hands a four-legged animal, probably a goat. This man shows all the features of the central figure on the obverse of the plaque, with a difference that the latter holds instead an elongated object. In the lower register, there is visible a kneeling figure of a naked man, with a pestle and mortar, exactly paralleling the two kneeling figures depicted on the reverse of the plaque.

Given the similarity between the kneeling man in the lower register and the kneeling figures on the reverse of the plaque, it is possible that the scene depicted on the obelisk finds its continuation on the reverse of the plaque (or vice versa). The combined evidence of the two pieces suggests the preparation of food in connection with a feast (the goat[?] in the hands of the bearded man, the kneeling figures working with pestles and mortars). This point will be elaborated on below.

Of the five-line inscription on the other side of the obelisk easiest to understand are the first and the last lines. Line 1 reads 5(bùr) gán U_8.SAL Nin-GÍR.ḪA.RAD "5 bùr of land," that is 90 iku or 31.76 hectares, "(located? in) the meadow(?) of(?) Nin-GÍR.ḪA.RAD." Nin-GÍR.ḪA.RAD appears to be a divine name (for the reading, see below), here probably standing for a temple household.

The last line has two signs, AB.APIN or APIN.AB, which almost certainly are to be interpreted as the profession or title engar èš. The term engar seems to denote here a high official in charge of the agricultural sector in a household, comparable to the Greek *agronomos*. The combination engar èš "*agronomos* of the temple household" occurs also in Jemdet Nasr tablets (*OECT* 7, 5, 15, 52 twice, 102, 139, 144, and 164) and in a tablet from Tell ʿUqair (*JNES* 2 [1943] pl. XXI no. 117 rev.), always at the end or near the end of the text. A similar term is sanga èš "administrator of the temple household," which appears in several tablets from Jemdet Nasr (*OECT* 7, 11 ii 2, 31 rev. i 4, 110 i 2′). For èš as the archaic term for "temple household" (later é), see Burrows, *UET* 2 pp. 13f.; H. T. Wright, *The Administration of Rural Production in an Early Mesopotamian Town* (Ann Arbor, 1969) pp. 41f. The "temple household" of the present example is possibly that of Nin-GÍR.ḪA.RAD in line 1.

In all probability, the "*agronomos* of the temple household" referred to in our inscription is to be identified with the bearded man depicted on the other side of the obelisk. His name may be recorded in the preceding line (see below).

Line 4, which has the signs ALAM.NE.PAB.KÍD?.GÍR.DU, possibly gives the name of the official engar èš in line 5. This leaves us with lines 2 and 3, which read GI_4.RAD and ḪA.ÚR.LAK-131 respectively. The sign-group ḪA.ÚR in line 3 is almost certainly to be connected with ḪA.RAD.ÚR, the archaic writing of the city of Urum, for which see M. W. Green, *ASJ* 8 (1986) pp. 77ff. Note that the latter logogram can be optionally abbreviated as RAD.ÚR or even as ÚR (*ibid.* p. 78). At the same time, it cannot be excluded that lines 2–3 are in fact to be read together; in that case, we would arrive at the combination ḪA.RAD.ÚR, the full spelling of the name of Urum.

The assumption that lines 2–3 contain the name of Urum finds support in the occurrence of the divine(?) name Nin-GÍR.ḪA.RAD in line 1. The sign-group ḪA. RAD appears also in the Uruk name En-ḪA.RAD-dùg, where, as Green proposes (*ibid.* p. 79), ḪA.RAD may be the archaic spelling of the city of A.ḪA, a neighbor of Urum. [Given that the pair Urum and A.ḪA is replaced in *RA* 70 (1976) p. 112 G 24, M 13, by the pair *Ú-ru-mu-um*^{KI}/ *Wu-ru-mu*^{KI} and *Ti*-WA^{KI}, A.ḪA is probably to be read Tiwa or Tuwa and equated with Tuba(A.ḪA) of lexical texts; cf. Steinkeller, *JCS* 32 (1980) p. 28.] Accordingly, Nin-GÍR.ḪA.RAD of our text could very well be a goddess of A.ḪA.

Naturally, if the above identifications are correct, they would be of great importance for the question of the provenience of the Blau tablets. As Green convincingly argues, ḪA.RAD.ÚR = Urum is very likely to be identified with the site of Tell ᶜUqair in northern Babylonia (*op. cit.* pp. 78ff.). In favor of this interpretation, note that the title engar èš also occurs, at the very end of the text, in a tablet from Tell ᶜUqair (see above). In this connection, it also may be significant that all other examples of this title come from the tablets from Jemdet Nasr (none in the texts from Uruk!), which too is located in northern Babylonia, less than 15 miles from Tell ᶜUqair. And finally, it is noteworthy that three of the items listed on the obverse of the plaque, namely, šen, uri, and gada, routinely appear in the tablets from Tell ᶜUqair. For šen, see Falkenstein, *ATU* 629 i 5, 644 i 1, and 649 ii 1; for uri, see *ibid.* 631 i 1, 644 i 2, and 649 ii 2; for gada, see *ibid.* 624 ii 4, 625 i 2, 629 i 2, 643 i 1′, and 649 i 2.

On the basis of the occurrences of the toponyms ḪA(.RAD).ÚR (= Tell ᶜUqair) and ḪA.RAD (location unknown—possibly Jemdet Nasr) on the obelisk, we should thus consider that the Blau tablets come from either Tell ᶜUqair or the unknown site of A.ḪA. Of these two possibilities, the choice of Tell ᶜUqair is probably to be favored, given the fact that Tell ᶜUqair had produced a number of illicitly-excavated archaic tablets, which were purchased in 1903 by the Berlin Museum (see Green, *op. cit.* p. 78).

Disregarding whether the provenience of the Blau tablets is Tell ᶜUqair or A.ḪA, the point, if proven, that they stem from northern Babylonia, would have important implications for the question of the language of their inscriptions. Assuming, as it seems quite likely, that in the Jemdet Nasr (= Uruk III) period northern Babylonia already supported a Semitic population, the Blau tablets could very well be written in Akkadian. In this connection, note the possible occurrence of the word ba-dar, a loan from the Akkadian *patarrum*, among the commodities listed in the plaque (see below).

Let us now return to the iconography of the obelisk. As we have suggested above, the bearded man depicted on the obelisk is to be identified with the engar èš official (line 5), whose name may be ALAM.NE.PAB.KÍD?. GÍR.DU (line 4). Assuming that the Blau tablets record a sale transaction, he could, accordingly, be seen as either the buyer or the seller. In favor of interpreting him as the buyer is the fact that the scene shown on the obelisk may represent the preparation of the feast that, in the later periods, was customarily offered by the buyer in his house at the conclusion of the transaction (see section 7.12.5.7).

b) *Blau Plaque*

The Blau Plaque contains the representations of two humans on the obverse and four humans on the reverse plus the text running from obverse to reverse. The obverse-reverse designation is easily established from the iconography depicting the major scene on one side, which must, therefore, be the obverse, and the minor scene on the other side, which, consequently, is the reverse; and from the writing, which runs smoothly from the end (left side) of the obverse to the beginning (right side) of the reverse.

The obverse of the plaque shows two standing figures facing each other near the center. The larger figure (on the left) is a bearded man wearing a skirt of a net-like material. The man wears a cap which rolls up to form a bulky band around his head, and holds with both hands an elongated object which may represent a phallic symbol or a vessel. The smaller figure, apparently a woman, wears a skirt of solid material and stands with both hands raised and clasped in front of her body.

The reverse bears the representations of one standing, two kneeling, and one sitting male figures. The standing male is beardless and hairless, with no headdress, and wears the same kind of "net-skirt" as the man on the obverse. His hands are uplifted in the manner of the female figure on the obverse. In front of him there are figures of two persons kneeling on one knee, naked, without beard or headdress, and working with a pestle and mortar. The man behind the standing figure has all the features of the kneeling figures, except that he is slightly larger and that he sits on a stool.

The bearded man on the obverse is clearly the most important person represented on the plaque. Since the major figure shown on the obelisk should probably be identified as the buyer (see above), the bearded man on the plaque may be the seller. If so, the woman facing him could represent his wife or daughter, and thus a co-seller of the field. This assumption seems to find support in the fact that the commodities recorded on the obverse of the plaque are subdivided into two groups, each group followed by a personal name (see below). Because of their position in relation to the two figures, these two names, ḪAŠḪUR.LÀL and KA-GÍR-gal, can respectively be interpreted as the names of the bearded man and his female companion. The implication is that ḪAŠḪUR.LÀL and KA-GÍR-gal were the recipients of the itemized goods, thus corroborating the hypothesis that the two figures shown on the obverse of the plaque are the sellers. Further, it is possible that the enigmatic object held by the bearded man should be interpreted as a phallic symbol, comparable to the cone (kag) that was driven by the seller into the wall (of a public building?) as part of the rite symbolizing the transfer of the sold field to the buyer. See section 7.12.5.1 and discussion of no. 12 for a possible depiction of this rite on that piece.

The two kneeling and one sitting figures shown on the reverse of the plaque probably represent, like the lower figure on the obelisk, the personnel involved in the preparation of the feast celebrating the conclusion of the transaction. For a possible parallel, see the register of the Uruk Vase showing naked servants carrying baskets with food (Strommenger, *op. cit.* pls. 19–22).

The interpretation of the standing male figure on the reverse of the plaque is more problematic. Given his position within the scene, it would be tempting to see in this man the supervisor of the working personnel. Against this solution is the fact that he is identified by name (AN.GÍR.JN-312.NUNUZ.SAG, written immediately to his right), which indicates that he must have been a major party to the transaction. Excluding the unlikely possibility that he is another co-seller, he could be either a relative (son?) of the buyer or an official authorizing the transaction.

The inscribed portions of the Blau Plaque are found both on the obverse and reverse, partly independently, partly interwoven with the human figures. The beginning and the end of the text is clear: it begins with 2 BA.DAR in the top right corner of the obverse and ends with the signs AN.GÍR.JN-312.NUNUZ.SAG on the reverse, following the right to left direction in the earlier, vertical orientation of signs, or top to bottom in the later, horizontal orientation of signs (this question is fully discussed in section 1.4).

Because of the difficulties in citing the various portions of the text, we have decided to number the cases or lines consecutively from 1 to 16.

As can be seen at a glance, all entries, with the exception of lines 6, 15, and 16, begin with signs for numbers and measures and are followed by signs that can be interpreted as standing for commodities. The interpretation of some items is easy and self-evident, of others difficult and even completely unknown at the present stage of our knowledge of the archaic script.

The following numbers and measures occur in the text:

A small horizontal stroke is used for units (1–9), as in 1 arád "1 slave" in line 9.

A small circle is used for tens (10–50), as in 10 máš "10 goats" in line 12. The same circle also appears before kaš in line 14, where it should stand for 10 (dug) kaš "10 (pots) of beer."

Two longer horizontal strokes are used before síg "wool" in line 8. They should stand for a measure of weight, probably meaning 2 (ma-na) síg "2 (pounds) of wool."

One longer horizontal stroke and one longer vertical stroke appear before UŠ.BUR.TÚG in line 11. They should stand for a measure of weight, meaning 1½ (ma-na) UŠ.BUR.TÚG, "an UŠ.BUR cloth/garment (weighing) 1½ (pounds)." A close parallel to fractions in our text is provided by 1½ (ma-na) NÍG.LÁM.TÚG, meaning "a *lamaḫuššûm* garment (weighing) 1½ (pounds)" in no. 13 *passim*. This interpretation is based on such fully-written examples as 1½ síg ma-na túg "a cloth/garment (weighing) 1½ pounds of wool" (*Fara* 3, 33 ii 1–2 = our no. 115). For the occurrences of fractions with túg in later periods, see Waetzoldt, *UNT* pp. 237 and 242. It is tempting to identify our UŠ.BUR.TÚG with the later túg uš-bar "weaver cloth."

Two vertical strokes with circles on their top and bottom occur before ninda "bread" in line 13. They cannot be simple numbers, meaning "2 (or 20) (loaves) of bread," since the numbers for units and tens are expressed by different shapes in this inscription. They should, therefore, stand for a measure of dry capacity, either 2(ul) or 2(bán) (of bread).

The following commodities occur:

2 BA.DAR and 2 BA.NAM in lines 1 and 2. The first item should probably be identified with ba-da-ra "prod" or the like (see *PSD* B pp. 18f.), a loan from the Akkadian *patarrum* (see Steinkeller, *JNES* 46 [1987] p. 58). The same spelling is attested in 1 *ba-dar* UD.KA.BAR (*PBS* 9, 132:3, Akkadian, Sargonic). This identification is somewhat weakened by the fact that BA can alternatively be read IGI; the resulting form IGI.DAR could then be interpreted as igi-gùn, possibly a piece of jewelry. The meaning of BA.NAM (or IGI.NAM) is unknown.

2 šen in line 3. Šen is a large metal container, weighing as much as twenty-five pounds. For a recent discussion of šen, see Steinkeller, *OA* 20 (1981) pp. 243–49.

30 EN.ŠÀ and 30 EN.A in lines 4 and 5. Both items are not understandable.

2 uri in line 7a. Uri is a large metal container.

2 gada "2 linen cloths/garments" in line 7b.

2 DUG+Ì+vertical-GIŠ.X in line 7c is probably "2 vessels of . . . oil." For a similar compound sign, see note to no. 1 i 2.

"2" síg "2 (pounds) of wool" in line 8.

1 arád "1 slave" in line 9. For the occurrence of "slave" among commodities, compare no. 7 i.

2 KUG.NA in line 10. KUG.NA looks like an object na and kug "silver." Alternatively, one could interpret it as 2 kug ⟨ma-⟩na "2 pounds of silver."

"1½" UŠ.BUR.TÚG "1½ (pounds) of UŠ.BUR cloth/garment" in line 11 (see above).

10 máš "10 goats" in line 12.

2(ul) or 2(bán) ninda "120 (or 20) quarts of bread" in line 13 (see above).

10 kaš "10 (pots) of beer" in line 14.

Following the first five commodities, one finds the PN KA-GÍR-gal, which seems to identify the female figure represented on the obverse of the plaque. Accordingly, it can be assumed that the items listed in the preceding lines represent her share of the commodities.

By analogy, the signs ḪAŠḪUR.LÀL (15), which appear at the very end of the second group of the commodities, can be interpreted as the name of the bearded man, with the preceding items constituting his share of the proceeds.

The inscription ends with the signs AN.GÍR.JN-312.NUNUZ.SAG (16), which are written to the right of the beardless man on the reverse of the plaque. Because of their position in relation of the beardless man, they can be interpreted as his name.

In summary of our discussion of the texts and iconography of the Blau tablets, it may be suggested that they deal with a sale transaction, whose object was a single field, measuring 90 iku in size. The buyer of the field presumably was an "*agronomos* of the temple household," named ALAM.NE.PAB.KÍD?.GÍR.DU. The sellers were a certain ḪAŠḪUR.LÀL and his wife or daughter named KA-GÍR-gal. The price received by the two sellers consisted of the commodities that are listed on the obverse of the plaque. The parties to the transaction also included a man named AN.GÍR.JN-312.NUNUZ.SAG, who was either a relative of the buyer or an authorizing official.

It needs to be stressed, however, that the above interpretation is by no means certain. To begin with, the absence of any terminology for "buying" and "selling" in either text raises the question as to whether the transaction recorded in the Blau tablets is in fact a sale. Moreover, the analysis of their iconography is open to other explanations. For example, it cannot be excluded that the bearded man shown on the obelisk is actually the same person as the main figure on the obverse of the plaque. These and other questions will, however, have to wait for the recovery of similar contemporaneous material that should provide our speculations with a sounder footing.

Transliteration

No. 10 Blau Obelisk

Obv.	1)	5(bùr) gán U_8.SAL Nin-GÍR.ḪA.RAD(ATU-850)
	2)	GI_4.RAD
	3)	ḪA.ÚR.LAK-131
	4)	ALAM.NE.PAB.KÍD?.GÍR.DU
	5)	engar èš
Rev.		Figure of a bearded man holding a goat(?). Figure of an attendant.

No. 11 Blau Plaque

Obv.	i	1)	2 BA.DAR
		2)	2 BA.NAM
		3)	2 šen
	ii	4)	30 EN.ŠÀ
		5)	30 EN.A
		6)	KA-GÍR-gal
			Figure of a woman.
		7a)	2 uri
		7b)	2 gada
		7c)	2 DUG+Ì+vertical-GIŠ.X
			Figure of a bearded man holding a phallus-like object.
	i	8)	"2" (ma-na) síg
		9)	1 arád(NITA+KUR)
		10)	2 KUG.NA
Rev.		11)	"1½" (ma-na) UŠ.BUR.TÚG
Obv.	ii	12)	10 máš
		13)	2(ul)/2(bán) ninda
		14)	10 (dug) kaš
Rev.		15)	ḪAŠḪUR.LÀL
			Figure of an attendant.
		16)	AN.GÍR.JN-312.NUNUZ.SAG
			Figure of a beardless man.
			Figures of two attendants.

Notes

No. 10:1.—The word U_8.SAL is possibly to be connected with the toponym/topographical feature SAL.U_8.DI, which appears in a number of Pre-Sargonic texts from Nippur and Isin(?): gán SAL.U_8.DI (*TMH* 5, 72:1), gú U_8.DI.UD.SAL.ME (*OSP* 1, 114 ii 1), gán gú SAL.U_8.DI (*ibid.* 119:3′), and gán da SAL.U_8.DI ki íl-la (*MVNS* 3, 14 ii 2, 3, Isin?). SAL.U_8.DI should perhaps be read u_8-$sal^{sá}$ (read, accordingly, U_8.DI.UD.SAL.ME in *OSP* 1, 114 ii 1, as u_8-$sal^{u_4\text{-}sá}$-me?) and interpreted as a variant spelling of ú-sal(-la), Akk. *ušallum*, "meadow." In favor of this interpretation, note the following passage: 15(gur) še gur ud SAL.U_8.DI-a (= u_8-$sal^{sá}$-a?) dun-na PN PN_2-ra ur_5-šè mu-na-ta-gub "PN gave (lit.: put out) 15 bushels of barley as a loan to PN_2, when he excavated the meadow(?)" (*MVNS* 3, 29 i 1–ii 1, Isin?). In this connection, note also GIŠ.UB.U_8.SAL(.A) = *nu-ba-du/tum* in Pettinato, *MEE* 4 p. 254 line 487, for which compare *nubattu* "bivouac" and *nubattu*, a topographical term (*CAD* N/2 pp. 307ff.). Alternatively, U_8.SAL could simply be SAL-u_8 "ewe," for which see Pettinato, *MEE* 3 p. 66 line 27; Bauer, *AWL* p. 295.

No. 11:6.—For the element GÍR-gal, in later periods written GÍR-*gunû*-gal, see note to no. 14 vi 4. For another archaic occurrence of GÍR-gal, where GÍR likewise lacks the *gunû* wedges, see the PN A-GÍR-gal in no. 12 Side D.

No. 12 Ushumgal Stela

Photographs: Plates 14–17, Metropolitan Museum of Art, New York, negative nos. 165353–165358.

Copy: Plates 13, 16, and 17, copied in 1960 and 1963 by Gelb from the original—redrawn from copies and photographs by Green, assisted by Whiting.

Synopsis: Figure 10.

Provenience: Unknown (purchased), from Larsa (Senkereh) according to Parrot; perhaps from Umma, according to Crawford (see refs. below). The Umma origin of the stela is supported by the occurrence of Shara(?), the chief deity of Umma on side A, the personal name ^{d}Šará?-igi-zi-ZU.AB on side D, and the toponym Guedina in the personal name Ur-gú-edin?-na on side E.

Date: Early Dynastic I–II.

Language: Sumerian(?).

Present location: Metropolitan Museum of Art (New York), 58.29.

Publications: A. Parrot, *AOF* 12 (1937–39) pp. 319–24 (photographs); V. E. Crawford, *Bulletin of the Metropolitan Museum of Art* 1960 pp. 245f. (photographs); Parrot, *Syria* 38 (1961) pp. 348f. (photographs); Moortgat, *Die Kunst des alten Mesopotamien* (Cologne, 1967) p. 33 and figures 31–34 (photographs).

Description: Stela of light to dark-brown gypsum measuring 22 × 14 × 9.5 cm. Only the front (A) and the base (F) of the stela are flat, while the back (B, C, D) and the top (E) are rounded.

Iconography and Text: Four sides of the stela are covered by pictorial representations of men and women, which are accompanied by adscriptions (names and titles) written over or very close to them. In addition, writing appears on sides A, B, C, D above the figures, occasionally across them, and on the top (E) and bottom (F) of the stela. The antiquity of the writing and the necessity of squeezing in the writing wherever space was available make the interpretation of the written parts very difficult.

The three main terms used below are: "iconography" for the figures represented on sides A–D; "adscriptions" for the text accompanying the figures on sides A–D; and "inscriptions" for other text appearing on sides A–F.

The sequence of the sides may be established tolerably well. Side A is flat and marks, therefore, the beginning of the stela. From there on, the flow of the writing progresses normally from right to left, following the sequence from A to B to C to D, as, for instance, in no. 40.

Taking into consideration the iconography plus the adscriptions, the sequence of the four sides is different from that given above on the basis of the inscriptions. The images on the four sides of the stela form a continuous frieze, composed of two central panels (A and D) and two accessory panels (B and C). As will be seen below, sides A and D are linked together because the two figures represented on them face each other and are, due to their large size, the most important actors of the transaction. Since the "small" woman on side C follows the "large" woman on side D, side C should be considered an extension of side D. Analogically, since the three "small" men on side B follow the "large" man on side A, side B must be considered an extension of side A. In this way the scene depicted on the stela can be analyzed as two processions, meeting one another at the gate(?) of a building, with the men proceeding from left to right, and with the women proceeding from right to left.

In the following, iconography plus adscriptions will be taken up first, to be followed by inscriptions without the accompanying iconography.

Iconography Plus Adscriptions on Sides A–D

Side A. The flat front of the stela shows a man, with a beard and long hair, facing a tall, narrow structure. He wears a long skirt and holds in his hands close to his chest an object which was interpreted as a cup by Crawford. For parallels, see Strommenger, *The Art of Mesopotamia* figs. 50–55 and especially 73. The signs written across the figure read ^{d}ŠARÁ?.PAB.ŠEŠ GAL.UŠUM, to be interpreted as Ušum-gal pab-šeš ^{d}Šará? "Ushumgal, the pab-šeš priest of Shara(?)." The divine name read here as ^{d}Šará? (also in the personal name ^{d}Šará?-igi-zi-ZU.AB on side D) has the *Gestalt* of ŠARÁ but does not resemble in detail the sign ŠARÁ (= LAK-782) as it appears in the Fara and later periods.

There is little doubt that Ushumgal is the major figure in the transaction and, assuming that a sale is meant here, he is probably the buyer. Note that the same Ushumgal is named in conjunction with the total acreage of land in the inscription of side C.

There are several features on side A that illuminate further the nature of the scene depicted on the stela. First, we note that the stonecutter has taken pains to indicate what is apparently a cone or peg that has been driven into the wall (doorway?) of the building. This is very likely the "cone" (kag) that was customarily driven into the wall, either by the main seller or by the town herald, according to the sources from the Pre-Sargonic period onwards (see section 7.12.5.1). The structure from which the cone is protruding is quite elaborate, very much like the three-towered building of the Proto-literate period reproduced in Frankfort, *OIP* 72 pl. 6 no. 34. In all probability, it represents a public building, either the gate/doorway of a temple or a city gate. This interpretation agrees with our conclusion that the cones employed in the transfers of property at Pre-Sargonic Lagash were displayed on the wall of some public building (see section 7.12.5.1). In this connection, note that temple and city gates were the customary location of legal transactions and oath-taking in ancient Mesopotamia (see, e.g., the examples cited in *CAD* A/1 p. 84 under *abullu*, B pp. 19f. under *bābu*).

Side D. This side stands to the right of the front side A. It is occupied by a figure of a woman dressed in a long cloak, and, although larger, not much different from the figure represented on side C. She holds in her right hand a jar, and there is possibly a container or basket at her feet. The woman faces Ushumgal (on side A), apparently offering him a drink. The signs drawn across her figure identify her as ^{d}Šará?-igi-zi(wr. GI)-ZU.AB dumu Ušum-gal ÉŠ.A "Shara(?)-igizi-Abzu, the daughter of Ushumgal, the . . ." The meaning of ÉŠ.A (also side C) is unclear. The fact that Shara(?)-igizi-Abzu is represented with a jar, and possibly a basket, may indicate that she, as the daughter of the buyer, was in charge of the preparation of the feast that regularly took place in the house of the buyer (see section 7.12.5.7).

Side C. The back of the stela, to the right of side D, is occupied by a figure of a woman, dressed in a long cloak, and, though considerably smaller, very similar to the daughter of Ushumgal (side D), whom she is clearly following. The signs in front of the figure read: dumu Me-si pab-šeš É-nun. On the cloak of the figure appear three signs, IGI.ÉŠ.A, preceded by two signs which look like RU? and NUN. If the signs on the cloak should be connected with the signs in front of the figure, then the whole could be interpreted as "IGI.RU?.NUN, the . . . (ÉŠ.A), the daughter of Mesi, the pab-šeš priest of (the temple) Enun." The meaning of ÉŠ.A (also side D) is obscure. The role of IGI.RU?.NUN in the transaction is unclear.

Side B. Side B, to the right of side C, is divided into two registers, with the figures of one man in the upper register and of two men in the lower register. The latter two are of the same size as Mesi on side C; the man in the upper register is considerably smaller, due, apparently, to the restrictions of space. All three men are depicted with arms crossed over their chests and with kilts looped up into the belt baring one leg. Their position within the frieze makes it clear that they are following Ushumgal (side A). The man in the upper register, without hair and beard, is identified by the adscription a) Ag gal-ukkin "Ag, chief of the assembly." For the form of UKKIN in the present text (also in ugula-ukkin in adscription b), compare UKKIN in the Abu Salabikh and Ebla mss. of ED Lu A line 16 (*MSL* 12 pl. II i 16; *MEE* 3/A pl. I no. 1 ii 4). The first man in the lower register, shown with a beard, bears over his body the adscription b) ŠEŠ.KI/NA ugula-ukkin "Nanna, the foreman of the assembly." As far as we know, the title ugula-ukkin is a *hapax legomenon.* Written over the figure of the second man, without hair and beard, is the name X.KU.EN and, just next to his head, the title gal-nigir "chief herald."

In view of the fact that the last line of column i on sides B–C records 1(bùr) gán Ag "18 iku of land (of?) Ag," where Ag could be the same person as the "chief of the assembly" of adscription a), it would be tempting to interpret the three men depicted on side B as co-sellers. However, their titles (note especially gal-nigir "chief herald," who frequently appears in later sale documents) make it fairly certain that these three men were the officials who either authorized or witnessed the transaction.

Inscriptions on Sides A–E

Inscriptions without associated iconography appear on all six sides. The sequence of the inscriptions cannot be fully established, although certain sides obviously go together:

Side A standing alone.
Side B followed by C, continuing with one line on D behind the figure.
Side E continuing with one line on D above the figure.
Side D with the inscription in front of the figure.
Side C with the inscription behind the figure.
Side F standing alone.

Side A. Above the central figure on side A there are five lines of writing listing three houses (é-dù). The three houses are those of ⌜AN⌝.DAM.ŠE.DU.[A]? in line 1 (also in line 5 of the inscription on sides E–D), É.TÙR. ḪÚB?.⌜X⌝ in line 2, and ⌜É?.KI?.SÁR?.X⌝ in line 4.

Sides B–C. A two-column inscription begins on side B and continues on side C, with one line continuing on side D. This inscription is discussed together with that on sides E–D, just below.

Sides E–D. Of the five-line inscription, four lines are preserved on side E (top of the stela) and one line above the figure on side D.

The inscriptions on sides B–C and E–D obviously go together since both record measures/numbers, fields, animals, and personal names.

We may begin with the small round circles which are followed by gán "field" and, therefore, are to be interpreted as the area-measure bùr (B–C i 3, 6, ii 5, E–D 1). To be interpreted similarly are the subdivisions of bùr, written as semi-circles, as in 1(bùr) 3(iku) gán (B–C ii 3), or a combination of a circle plus a semi-circle, as in 1(eše) gán (E–D 5). What follows the measures of area and the sign gán are personal names and/or descriptions of fields. Clear examples of personal names are Ag (B–C i 6), which recurs in adscription a) on side B, AN.DAM. ŠE.DU.A (E–D 5), also attested in line 1 of the inscription of side A, ŠAG$_5$.TUR nig[ir]? (B–C ii 3), and possibly ⌜X⌝.EZEN (B–C ii 6). A field description may be found in E–D lines 1 and 3, which have the same sign-group GÚ.GÚ.SIG$_4$?.

Scattered throughout the inscription B–C and probably once in E–D 2, we find small squares which greatly resemble the semi-circles used for the area measure iku. The squares are regularly followed by the name of an animal, and must therefore be interpreted as standing for units. Thus we read: [x]+2 [g]ud-anše "[x]+2 bulls and donkeys" (B–C i 1); 2 udu "2 sheep" (ii 2); 1 gud "1 bull" (ii 4); and 3!(wr. as semi-circles) gud "3 bulls" (E–D 2). Alternatively, the squares could stand for tens, as is suggested by the spelling 4 vertical strokes gud-nita "4(?) bulls" in the inscription on side D (see below). The interpretation of 6 še PÚ? in B–C ii 1 is unknown.

In three instances, the numbers and the terms for animals are followed by personal names: sanga LÚ.Á. GAL.GÚ (B–C i 2), KUR pab-šeš (B–C ii 4), and LÚ.TIL?.PA Ur-gú-edin?-na (E–D 2). The name Ur-gú-edin?-na of the last example contains the toponym Guedina, which, by virtue of its proximity to Umma, corroborates the assumption that the Ushumgal Stela comes from Umma (see above under *Provenience*).

Side D. In front of the figure there are twenty-five signs, the first eighteen of which, ordered in two columns, may be reconstructed as yielding a similar structure:

nam-kud INNIN.TAB.AMAR "the oath of INNIN. TAB.AMAR"
6 vertical strokes gán GI.LAGAB " . . ."
nam-kud A-GÍR-gal "the oath of A-GÍR-gal"
3 vertical strokes gán GI.LAGAB " . . ."

What we find here, apparently, is a record of two separate oaths, made by a certain INNIN.TAB.AMAR (= Amar-INNIN.TAB?) and A-GÍR-gal concerning the field GI.LAGAB. The role of these two persons in our transaction is unclear. Since the numbers in front of gán cannot be area measures, we should probably interpret them as simple numbers. We may speculate that, perhaps, they denote the numbers of the kinsmen of INNIN.TAB. AMAR and A-GÍR-gal. This would result in the translation: "the oath of six (members of the family of) INNIN. TAB.AMAR (concerning) the field GI.LAGAB; the oath of three (members of the family of) A-GÍR-gal (concerning) the field GI.LAGAB."

The inscription then reads: 4 vertical strokes gud-nita. Theoretically, it is possible that this line is a continuation of the inscription on side E (top), which continues with one line on side D. If so, the present line (to be assigned number 6) could be interpreted as 4 gud-nita "four bulls." The problem with this interpretation, however, is that, as we have argued earlier, elsewhere in the stela the units of animals are written with squares and not with vertical strokes, as in the present example. This discrepancy could only be resolved by assuming that the squares actually stand for tens.

Finally, over the basket(?) in front of the woman, there are written the signs BUR, SI, EN, and LU. The first two signs should probably be interpreted as a PN Bur-si, for which see Burrows, *UET* 2 p. 30. Note also bur-si, a type of bowl, in Falkenstein, *ATU* 644 ii 1. The following two signs could possibly be analyzed as en udu "owner of the sheep," but we lack any parallels for it. The relationship of Bursi (if in fact it is a person) to other parties to the transaction is unknown.

Side C. In back of the female figure are nine signs arranged in two columns. The signs, which clearly go together, read 2(burʾu) 5(bùr) gán GÚ.AN, to be interpreted as gú-an⟨-šè⟩ 2(burʾu) 5(bùr) gán "grand total of 450 iku (or 158.75 hectares) of land." As now preserved, the first number is a large double circle, which is 1 burʾu = 10 bùr, the second number is a large circle, which in normal circumstances should be read as 1 sár = 60 bùr, and the third number is written as five small circles or 5 bùr. Since a larger number cannot be written below or after a smaller number, the large circle cannot be interpreted as 1 šár, but must be explained as 1 burʾu with the inner circle destroyed. Unfortunately, the reading of the total given here cannot be verified by adding up the various fields listed in sections B–C–D and E–D because of the poor state of preservation of the latter. Nevertheless, what is preserved in these two sections suffices to make the interpretation of the large circle as 1 šár = 60 bùr too high for serious consideration. Following a vertical line, we read GAL, UŠUM, ŠID, TA?, and NAM, of which only the name of Ushumgal (also in the adscription on side A) is clear.

Side F. The lower side of the stela contains two lines of writing, reading: 1) En-ḫé-gál DÍM 2) ⌜A⌝?, SAR, RA?. We can interpret the first line as En-ḫé-gal dím "Enḫegal, the maker (of the stela)," as in a later parallel on the Samarra tablet reading Sá-um-si-en DÍM "S., the maker (of the tablet)" (*RA* 9 [1912] p. 2 bottom). The three signs of the second line could then be interpreted as a tall, narrow sign, very dimly preserved, which could be A, then a clear SAR, and finally a possible RA. One would like to find in ⌜A⌝?.SAR.RA? a word for "stela" or "inscription," comparable to na-dù-a, mu-sar(-ra), or maš-darà. However, none of the possible readings of the first sign yields anything familiar.

The order in which the inscriptions on sides A–F were presented above can be justified by several considerations.

The inscription on side A, listing three houses, stands alone, but it is given on the stela in the same order, that is, from right to left, as the two-column inscription on sides B–C, listing fields and livestock. The section on sides E–D also lists fields and livestock. This section is probably followed by the inscription in front of the figure on side D, which deals with two oaths. The total of the fields is given in the inscription on side C. The subscription or colophon on side F giving the name of the maker of the stela completes the text.

The interpretation of the transaction recorded on the Ushumgal Stela is exceedingly difficult. The only point that can be determined with assurance is the object of the transaction. That object was 450 iku of land, located in several separate fields, plus various livestock and three houses. The personal names associated with the fields and livestock should probably be interpreted as the names of the tenants of the fields and of the renters of the animals. Accordingly, the names associated with the houses probably identify the occupants/tenants of the respective houses.

Turning now to the question of the nature of the transaction, it is clear that the main actor of the transaction was Ushumgal, who, therefore, must have stood in some proprietary relationship to the estate in question. Assuming that, as we have speculated earlier, Ushumgal is to be identified as the buyer, the most likely candidates for the sellers would be either IGI.RU?.NUN, daughter of Mesi (side C), or INNIN.TAB.AMAR and KA-GÍR-gal, whose oaths are recorded on side D. Accordingly, the three men represented on side B could be interpreted as the officials who authorized or witnessed the transaction.

However, the validity of this interpretation can be questioned for several reasons. First and the most important argument against analyzing the Ushumgal Stela as a sale is the fact that it records neither the price nor any terminology for "buying" and "selling." Second, one is troubled by the conspicuous role that is assigned to Shara(?)-igizi-Abzu, Ushumgal's daughter, in the stela. The fact that the inscription makes no mention of Ushumgal's sons implies that he had no male progeny, and it may be this particular circumstance that is crucial for the understanding of the transaction. And third, the use of the description ÉŠ.A in reference to both Shara(?)-igizi-Abzu and IGI.RU?.NUN, and the fact that IGI.RU?.NUN is represented as following Shara(?)-igizi-Abzu, makes one think that there was some sort of connection between these two women.

Among alternative interpretations one could consider the possibility that, as was suggested to us orally by I. Winter, the Ushumgal Stela records the grant of an estate, made by Ushumgal on behalf of Shara(?)-igizi-Abzu. The need for such a grant may have been occasioned by the fact that Ushumgal had no male descendants. Yet another solution would be to see in this inscription a record of the real estate owned by a temple household, whose chief administrator was Ushumgal.

Transliteration

Adscriptions

Side A
Adscription over the figure of a bearded man holding a cone:

Ušum-gal pab-šeš ^{d}Šará?

Side D
Adscription over the figure of a woman holding a vase:

^{d}Šará?-igi-zi(wr. GI)-ZU.AB dumu Ušum-gal ÉŠ.A

Side C
Adscriptions over and below the figure of a woman:

IGI.RU?.NUN ÉŠ.A dumu Me-si pab-šeš É-nun

Side B
Top register
Adscription a) next to the figure of a beardless man:

Ag gal-ukkin

Lower register
Adscription b) over the figure of a bearded man:

ŠEŠ.KI/NA ugula-ukkin

Adscription c) over the figure of a beardless man:

X.KU.EN gal-nigir

Inscriptions

Side A
1) ⌜AN⌝.DAM.ŠE.DU.[A]? é-dù
2) É.TÙR.ḪÚB?.⌜X⌝
3) é-dù

4) ⸢É?.KI?.SÁR?.X⸣
5) é-⸢dù⸣

Sides B–C, continuing with one line on side D

i 1) [x]+2 (or 20) [g]ud-anše
2) sanga LÚ.Á.GAL.GÚ
3) 1(bùr) gán [X]
4) 1 ⸢X.X⸣
5) [x] ⸢X.X⸣
6) 1(bùr) gán Ag

ii 1) 6 še PÚ?
2) 2 (or 20) udu
3) 1(bùr) 3(iku) gán ŠAG$_5$.TUR nig[ir]?
4) 1 (or 10) gud KUR pab-šeš
5) 4(bùr) gán ⸢A?.DÍM⸣?
6) 2(iku) gán ⸢X⸣.EZEN (on Side D)

Side E (Top), continuing with one line on side D

1) 4(bùr) gán GÚ.⸢GÚ⸣.SIG$_4$?
2) 3 (or 30) gud LÚ.TIL?.PA Ur-gú-edin?-na
3) 1(bùr) GÚ.GÚ.SIG$_4$?
4) gán BAL.LAGAB?.MUD.AB?.GIŠ.GÍR.A
5) 1(eše) gán AN.DAM.ŠE.DU.A (on Side D)

Side D

Inscription in front of the figure of a woman:

nam-kud INNIN.TAB.AMAR
6 vertical strokes gán GI.LAGAB
nam-kud A-GÍR-gal
3 vertical strokes gán GI.LAGAB
4 vertical strokes gud-nita (possibly the continuation of side E)

Inscription over the basket(?) before the woman:

Bur-si EN.LU

Side C

Inscription behind the figure of a woman:

gú-an⟨-šè⟩ 2(burʾu) 5(bùr) gán
Ušum-gal ŠID.TA?.NAM

Side F (Base)

1) En-ḫé-gál dím
2) ⸢A⸣?.SAR.RA?

No. 13 RA 6 p. 143

Photographs: Plate 18, Louvre, Paris.
Copy: Plate 19, Thureau-Dangin, *RA* 6 (1907) p. 143, collated by Gelb.
Provenience: Unknown (purchased), possibly from Shuruppak/Fara (see note to rev. i 7).
Date: Fara or earlier.
Language: Sumerian(?).
Present location: Louvre Museum (Paris), AO 2753.
Publications: Thureau-Dangin, *RA* 6 (1907) pp. 143–46; Edzard, *SRU* no. 113.
Description: Rectangular tablet of light-buff limestone, measuring 10.5 × 10 × 4 cm. Obverse flat, reverse slightly rounded.
Text: With the exception of the sign GÁN and signs denoting numbers for measures of area for fields and a few signs near the bottom, the obverse is almost totally destroyed. The sequence of the inscription is quite clear. The obverse runs from column i to ii to iii. The last column of the obverse continues, directly under it, with signs on the lower edge, and then with column i of the reverse and upper edge. As the rest of the lower edge is uninscribed, the sequence follows, from right to left, with column ii of the reverse and upper edge and with column iii on the reverse only.

A noteworthy and unusual feature of the inscription is the use of vertical lines to mark off one commodity from another within a case. This feature, standard in Uruk III tablets, and attested once in the archaic material from Ur (see Burrows, *UET* 2 p. 4), suggests a pre-Fara date.

In contrast to the reverse, the obverse is badly preserved. From the surviving traces we can see that it deals with several fields and their sellers(?). The long portion from the end of column iii on the obverse to the end of column ii on the reverse records various commodities offered by the buyer(?) to the sellers(?). The inscription ends in column iii of the reverse with the name and profession of the buyer(?), written MUL?.MUD um-me ^{d}TIR "MUL?.MUD, the master scribe(?) of (the temple household of) ^{d}TIR."

To judge from the preserved portions, the inscription is rather crudely cut, and the sloppy execution of the signs and lines does not allow much praise for the stonecutter.

Transliteration

Obv. i 1) 5(burʾu)? [. . .] gán
2) [. . .]
3) 2(burʾu)? [. . .]
4) [. . .]
5) [. . .]
6) 4(burʾu) [. . .]
7) ⸢x⸣.IM.KI

ii 1) ⸢x field⸣
2) ⸢x field⸣
3) ⸢x field⸣
4) ⸢x field⸣
5) ⸢x field⸣
6) [. . .]
7) INNIN?.ZI?

iii 1) 1(burʾu)? [. . .]
2) [. . .]
3) [. . .]
4) [. . .]
5) [x X] / [x] gud
6) 1 síg? / 1 dug+ì
7) 1½ NÍG.LÁM.TÚG

Lo. E. iii 1) UD.NUN.GUR?.NÁM
2) 2 gud / 1½ [NÍG].LÁM.[TÚG]
3) SIG?.GÍN?.[X]?

Rev. i 1) ÁŠ?.UR?.[X]?
2) gud / 1 dug+ì
3) 1½ NÍG.LÁM.TÚG
4) KI.⸢NA⸣?.LUGAL.ŠIR.UR?
5) 1 gud / 1 dug+ì
6) 30 síg / 1½ NÍG.LÁM.TÚG
7) SU.KUR.RU

U. E.	i	1)	1 gud / 1½ NÍG.LÁM.TÚG
		2)	PA.UR.NIGIR?.⌜X⌝
Rev.	ii	1)	30 síg
		2)	1½ NÍG.LÁM.TÚG
		3)	ḪU.É?.⌜X⌝
		4)	1 gud
		5)	1½ [NÍG].LÁM.TÚG
		6)	SAR.KI
		7)	1 gud
U. E.	ii	1)	1½ NÍG.LÁM.TÚG
		2)	PA [. . .]
Rev.	iii	1)	MUL?.MUD
		2)	um-me ^{d}TIR

Notes

The following commodities occur in the text:

gud "bull"; 1 or 2 are given.

síg "wool" is preceded by the numbers 30 or 60 which should refer to ma-na "mina." The older texts frequently give high numbers of minas disregarding the use of gú "talent." In this volume, compare e.g., 720, 180, 300 ma-na, etc. in no. 20.

ì "(animal) oil/fat" is given in the amount of 1 dug. The dug is a variable measure which normally consists of 20 or 30 sìla "quarts." The two words dug ì are written here with the sign Ì inscribed inside DUG, as in no. 11:7c discussed in the note to no. 1:2.

NÍG.LÁM.TÚG, the *lamaḫuššûm* garment, is given in each instance in the amount of 1½, which should be interpreted as a NÍG.LÁM garment weighing 1½ ma-na of wool, as, for instance, in no. 115 = *Fara* 3, 33 ii 1–2. The same usage is found in 1½ (ma-na) UŠ.BUR.TÚG i in no. 11:11. For the difference between the sign TÚG and NÁM see R. D. Biggs, *JCS* 20 (1966) p. 77 figure 1 and p. 81 n. 59. The sign NÁM in Lo. E. iii 1 is clearly differentiated from TÚG in NÍG.LÁM.TÚG.

Rev. i 7.—It is on the basis of the occurrence of SU.KUR.RU that Thureau-Dangin, *op. cit.* p. 145, drew the conclusion that our tablet came originally from Fara (Shuruppak).

Rev. iii 1.—Since the "star" in this line has about 15–17 rays, in contrast to the "star" in DINGIR of ^{d}TIR, which has the normal number of rays, Thureau-Dangin, *op. cit.* p. 145, assumed that the form with many rays stands for mul or nab.

Rev. iii 2.—The profession or occupation UM.ME "wet nurse" is borne by women in the Pre-Sargonic texts from Lagash, as can best be seen from Deimel, *AnOr* 2 pp. 41 iii 4, 42 ii 6. Compare also Steinkeller, *ASJ* 3 (1981) pp. 88ff. The other possibility is to consider, with Edzard, *SRU* p. 176, that the spelling um-me is a variant of um-mi-a "master," usually "master scribe" in the texts of early periods. The latter possibility appears more plausible considering the lowly social position of a wet nurse, who could hardly be in a position to acquire the large-size fields recorded in the kudurru (assuming that the buyer is meant here). The divine name ^{d}TIR is found also in *RTC* 8 iii 1, and at Shuruppak (*TSŠ* 629 vi 5).

No. 14 Chicago Stone

Photographs: Plates 20 and 22, Oriental Institute, The University of Chicago—negatives—plate 20: N. 26289, 26296, N. 26290, 33716; plate 22: N. 33717, 26292, N. 26293, 26294.

Copy: Plates 21 and 23, copied by Green from the original and photographs, assisted by Whiting and Gelb.

Synopsis: Plates 87, 88, and 91.

Provenience: Unknown; purchased from a private individual in 1943. The dealer had claimed that it came from Telloh. The origin of this kudurru (and of the related piece no. 15) is possibly Isin. This is suggested by the following evidence: 1) the occurrences of the PN Isin$_{x}$(IN)^{KI}-dùg in no. 14 ii 15, xvii 9; 2) the fact that the field name É-gud, attested in no. 14 xviii 13 and in no. 15 i 2, iv 27, occurs also in the Isin *Sammelurkunde* no. 182a transactions A, D, E, and F; 3) the attestations of the PN Lugal-níg-BE-dùg in no. 14 iii 4 and in no. 182a ii 20 (this name is also common at Nippur, with whom Isin traditionally had close political and cultural ties; for the examples of Lugal-níg-BE-dùg in Nippur sources, see Westenholz, *OSP* 1, p. 90); 4) the attestations of the container umbin?, used for sheep oil (ì-udu), in no. 14 i 7 and *passim* and in no. 182a transactions I and J; and 5) the fact that "Abhari in Southern Babylonia," the alleged find-spot of no. 15 (see no. 15 under *Provenience*) may very well be a garbled (Ishān) Baḫriyāt.

Date: Fara or the earlier phase of the Pre-Sargonic period.

Language: Sumerian.

Present location: Oriental Institute, The University of Chicago, A 25412.

Description: Black basalt tablet measuring 25 × 32 cm; rectangular in outline, with thin rounded edges. Thickness varies from 5.5 cm in the center tapering off to 2.5 cm at the edges. Obverse flat, reverse rounded.

Text: The writing is found in nine columns of the obverse and nine columns of the reverse. The state of preservation of the text is very good. In fact, with the exception of a few signs in the first two columns of the reverse, all signs are perfectly preserved. The sequence of the writing is from left to right in columns i to ix of the obverse, and from right to left in columns x to xviii of the reverse, following the order of columns known from later periods. There is no dividing line nor any space between the last lines of the columns of the obverse and the first lines of the columns of the reverse, so that—at first glance—the writing appears to be consecutive from the obverse to the reverse. The difficulties disappear, however, after a more thorough study of the different sections of the inscription based on the formulary.

The text of no. 14 must be studied together with that of no. 15, since there is no doubt that the two inscriptions were written in the same place, in the same period, and perhaps by the same scribe. This can be proved by the following points:

1) The forms of the signs in the two inscriptions are identical.
2) The formulary, including the list of commodities, is identical in the two inscriptions and found nowhere else.
3) The following field names appear in both inscriptions:
   gán DUN (14 i 2, ii 7, viii 3, xvi 5, xviii 4, and 15 ii 2, 29, iii 27, xiii 17, L. E. 22)
   (gán) É-gud (14 xviii 13 and 15 i 2, iv 27)
4) The following personal names appear in both inscriptions:

Kum-tuš-šè	(14 i 12 and 15 xiii 3)
Ur-Ab-ra	(14 i 13 and 15 ix 9, 17)
Zur-Zur	(14 i 15 and 15 xiv 29)

Lugal-ezen	(14 iii 8, xv 12, and 15 i 23, ii 22 and *passim*)
Ur-^{d}En-ki	(14 iv 4 and 15 x 9, xi 10, xiii 1, L. E. 14)
Ur-^{d}Gu-nu-ra	(14 v 5, xiv 9, xv 10, xvii 13, and 15 vi 12, viii 26)
Šeš-GÍR-*gunû*-gal	(14 vi 4, vii 9, viii 6, 10, and 15 x 12, xi 9)
Ur-^{d}En-líl	(14 x 11, xii 15, xiii 14, and 15 xiii 19)
Nam-maḫ	(14 x 14 and 15 i 4)
Lugal-da-gur-ra	(14 xvii 4, xviii 1, 10, 16, and 15 L. E. 24)

The sequence of two signs within each line is free. As a consequence, the reading and interpretation of many personal and field names in both the Chicago and Baltimore inscriptions, whether indicated by capitalization or not, cannot be safely established.

The two inscriptions list sixteen and seventeen transactions, respectively, pertaining to the acquisition of land from different sellers by a single(?) buyer. It is disconcerting that the name of the buyer, which normally should be listed at the end of the inscription, can be found nowhere on the Chicago and Baltimore Stones. This leads us to suspect that the two inscriptions were followed by still another inscription (or perhaps even more than one), now lost, which listed additional pieces of acquired land and ended with the name of the buyer.

For the structure of individual transactions, see section 6.2.

Transliteration and Translation

Obv. i	1)	1(eše) gán	6 iku of land,
	2)	gán DUN	the field DUN;
	3)	10 kug gín	10 shekels of silver (as its price)
	4)	Nin-dalla	(to) 2(?) PNs
	5)	Sum-ti	
	6)	an-na-lal	were weighed out.
	7)	1 ì-udu umbin?	1 umbin?-container of sheep oil,
	8)	2 síg ma-na	2 pounds of wool,
	9)	1 iš-gán NI-ga	1 NI-ga of . . . ,
	10)	10 ninda-bappir	10 beer-breads,
	11)	3 ninda-banšur	(and) 3 table-breads (is the additional payment).
	12)	Kum-tuš-šè	5(?) PNs
	13)	Ur-Ab-ra	
	14)	Iš-dup-Il	
	15)	Zur-zur	
	16)	LAK-483-TAR	
Obv. ii	1)	lú-ki-inim-ma	are the witnesses.
	2)	ì-bi	The oil
	3)	zag ag	was spread on the side (of the field?).
	4)	inim-bi	This transaction
	5)	é-ta ab-è	"left the house" (i.e., was completed).
	6)	1(eše) 1(iku) gán	7 iku of land,
	7)	gán DUN	the field DUN;
	8)	12 kug gín	12 shekels of silver
	9)	1 ì-udu umbin?	(and) Additional Payment
	10)	2 síg ma-na	
	11)	1 iš-gán NI-ga	
	12)	10 ninda-bappir	
	13)	3 ninda-banšur!	
	14)	Lugal-geštúg-gíd	(to) 3(?) PNs
	15)	Isin$_{x}$(IN)^{KI}-dùg	
	16)	Engur-làl	
	17)	an-na-sum	were given.
	18)	ì-bi	The oil
Obv. iii	1)	zag ag	was spread on the side.
	2)	inim-bi	This transaction "left the
	3)	é-ta ab-è(DU+⸢UD⸣)	house."
	4)	Lugal-níg-BE-dùg	3(?) PNs
	5)	Engur-làl	
	6)	Maš-lugal	

	7)	dumu	
	8)	Lugal-ezen	
	9)	lú-ki-inim-ma	are the witnesses.

---

	10)	2(eše) 3(iku) gán	15 iku of land,
	11)	gán Gúg	the field Gúg,
	12)	dumu	(the former? property) of the son(s) of
	13)	Ur-sag-a-me-nàd	Ur-sag-a-me-nàd;
	14)	½ kug ma-na	30 shekels of silver
	15)	Á-kal-li	(to) 1 PN
	16)	an-šè-lal	were weighed out.
	17)	3 ì-udu umbin?	Additional Payment.
	18)	6 síg ma-na	
Obv. iv	1)	2(NI-ga) 2(UL) iš-gán NI-ga	
	2)	30 ninda-bappir	
	3)	4 ninda-ban⟨šur⟩	
	4)	Ur-^{d}En-ki	5(?) PNs
	5)	GIŠ.BU	
	6)	NI-su-NI	
	7)	Lú-barag-si	
	8)	SIG$_7$	
	9)	Gúg-bar-rúm(NE.RU)^{KI}	
	10)	lú-ki-inim-ma	are the witnesses.
	11)	ì-bi	The oil
	12)	zag ag	was spread on the side.
	13)	inim-bi	This transaction
	14)	é-ta ab-è(wr. DU)	"left the house."

---

	15)	4(eše) 2(iku) gán	26 iku of land,
	16)	gán É-ad-KID	the field É-ad-KID;
Obv. v	1)	2/3 (ma-na) 3 gín	43⅓ shekels of silver
		1 šám-ma-na	(is its price);
	2)	1(bùr) 2(eše) gán	30 iku of land,
	3)	gán É-Ì-la-lum	the field É-Ì-la-lum;
	4)	1 kug ma-na lal 10 gín	50 shekels of silver (is its price);
	5)	Ur-^{d}Gu-nu-ra	(the silver to) 2(?) PNs
	6)	Lú-barag!-si	
	7)	an-na-sum	was given.
	8)	20 lal 2 síg ma-na	Additional Payment.
	9)	9 iš-gán NI-ga	
	10)	9 ì-udu umbin?	
	11)	90 ninda bappir	
Obv. vi	1)	Ur-^{d}En-líl	5(?) PNs
	2)	Lú-barag-si	
	3)	Im-ta-è-e	
	4)	Šeš-GÍR-*gunû*-gal	
	5)	Lú-dingir-mu	
	6)	lú-ki-inim-ma	are the witnesses.
	7)	En-ZU.AB	3(?) PNs,
	8)	É-zi	
	9)	Gala	
	10)	engar	the "farmers,"
	11)	zag durun-durun	sat on the side (of the field?).

---

	12)	1(bùr) 4(iku) gán	22 iku of land,
	13)	gán É!-ad-KID	the field É!-ad-KID;
	14)	½ kug ma-na 6 gín	36 shekels of silver
	15)	Ur-DUN	(to) 2 PNs
	16)	dumu X(erasure?)	
	17)	ŠEŠ.KI-na	

Obv. vii	1)	an-na-lal	were weighed out.
	2)	4 ì-udu umbin?	Additional Payment.
	3)	8 síg ma-na	
	4)	4 iš-gán še NI-ga	
	5)	Me-^{d}Tud	3 PNs
	6)	Ḫar-tu	
	7)	dumu	
	8)	Pab-geštin	
	9)	Šeš-GÍR-*gunû*-gal	
	10)	dumu	
	11)	Lú-dingir-mu	
	12)	lú-ki-inim-ma	are the witnesses.
	13)	ì-bi	The oil
	14)	zag ag	was spread on the side.
	15)	inim-bi	This transaction
Obv. viii	1)	é-ta ab-è	"left the house."
	2)	6(bùr) gán	108 iku of land,
	3)	gán DUN	the field DUN,
	4)	1(bùr) 1(eše) gán	(and) 24 iku of land,
	5)	gán É-udu-ninda-kú	the field É-udu-ninda-kú,
	6)	Šeš-GÍR-*gunû*-gal	(the property of) Š.,
	7)	sanga	the temple administrator;
	8)	4½ kug ma-na 5 gín	275 shekels of silver (as their price)
	9)	dam	(to) the wife of
	10)	Šeš-GÍR-*gunû*-gal	Š.
	11)	Edin-ri	(and?) E.
	12)	an-na-túm	were brought.
	13)	21 iš-gán še NI-ga	Additional Payment.
		(blank)	
Obv. ix	1)	42 síg ma-na	
	2)	21 ì-udu umbin?	
	3)	Edin-ri	5(?) PNs,
	4)	Pab-da-maḫ	
	5)	Ur-sag-Utu	
	6)	dumu	
	7)	Edin-ri	
	8)	Inim-ma-zi	
	9)	dumu	
	10)	Edin-ri	
	11)	Ur-PA	
	12)	dumu	
	13)	Ur-AN.U+É	
	14)	lú-ki-inim-ma	the witnesses,
Rev. x	1)	ki ⸢gán?-šám⸣?	in the place where the ⸢field? was sold?⸣,
	2)	ì-durun-durun	they sat.
	3)	1(bùr) 3(iku) gán	21 iku of land,
	4)	gán É-udu-ninda-⸢kú⸣	the field É-udu-ninda-⸢kú⸣;
	5)	½ kug ma-na 5 ⸢gín⸣	35 shekels of silver
	6)	7 ⸢síg⸣ ma-na	(and) Additional Payment
	7)	4 ⸢ì⸣-udu um[bin?]	
	8)	3(NI-ga) 2(UL) iš-gán še NI-ga	
	9)	⸢ŠEŠ.KI⸣-na	(to) 2 PNs
	10)	dumu	
	11)	Ur-^{d}En-líl	
	12)	Engur-ušum	
	13)	an-na-sum	were given.
	14)	Nam-maḫ	1 PN
	15)	dumu	

Rev. xi	1)	Lugal-GÁR.KAG	
	2)	é-ta íb-è(wr. DU)	"removed it (i.e., the price and additional payment?) from the house."
	3)	X-si-ga	2 PNs
	4)	Nin-SAL-zi	
	5)	dumu	
	6)	Kun?-LAGAB?	
	7)	lú-ki-inim-ma	are the witnesses.
	8)	ì-bi	The oil
	9)	zag ag	was spread on the side.
	10)	inim-bi	This transaction
	11)	é-ta ab-è	"left the house."

---

	12)	2(bùr) 3(iku) gán	39 iku of land;
	13)	1 kug ma-na 5 gín	65 shekels of silver
	14)	13 síg ma-na	(and) Additional Payment
Rev. xii	1)	6(NI-ga) 2(UL) iš-gán NI-ga	
	2)	7 ì-udu umbin?	
	3)	Mes-ZU.AB	1 PN
	4)	é-ta íb-è	"removed from the house" (i.e., received).
	5)	Ḫur-sag	2(?) PNs
	6)	GAM.GAM	
	7)	lú-ki-inim-ma	are the witnesses.

---

	8)	2(bùr) 3(iku) gán	39 iku of land,
	9)	gán X.PAB.ÚŠ	the field X.PAB.ÚŠ;
	10)	1 kug ma-na 5 gín	65 shekels of silver
	11)	13 síg ma-na	(and) Additional Payment
	12)	6(NI-ga) 2(UL) iš-gán NI-ga	
	13)	7 ì-udu umbin?	
	14)	Ri-ti	3(?) PNs
	15)	Ur-^{d}En-líl	
	16)	Amar-aš?-è	
Rev. xiii	1)	é-ta íb-è	"removed from the house."

---

	2)	2(bùr) 3(iku) gán	39 iku of land,
	3)	gán X.PAB!.ÚŠ	the field X.PAB!.ÚŠ;
	4)	1 kug ma-na 5 gín	65 shekels of silver
	5)	13 síg ma-na	(and) Additional Payment
	6)	6(NI-ga) 2(UL) iš-gán NI-ga	
	7)	7 ì-udu umbin?	
	8)	Ur-AN.UR.GÁN?.GA.IGI?	1 PN
	9)	é-ta íb-è	"removed from the house."

---

	10)	3(bùr) gán	54 iku of land,
	11)	gán Pab-rúm	the field Pab-rúm;
	12)	1½ kug ma-na	90 shekels of silver
	13)	Ri-ti	3(?) PNs
	14)	Ur-^{d}En-líl	
	15)	Amar-aš?-è	
	16)	é-ta íb-è	"removed from the house."
	17)	10 lal 1 iš-gán NI-ga	Additional Payment
Rev. xiv	1)	10 lal 1 ì-udu umbin?	
	2)	20 ⸢lal 2⸣ síg ma-na	
	3)	Ur-PA dumu	1 PN
	4)	Ur-NE-ra	
	5)	é-ta íb-è	"removed from the house."
	6)	Lugal-ki-ni	L.
	7)	iš-gán	did not give (lit.: make)
	8)	nu-ag	the additional payment;
	9)	Ur-^{d}Gu-nu-ra	U.

	10)	ì-ag	gave (it).
	11)	inim-bi é-ta ab-è	This transaction "left the house."
	12)	Ḫar-tu	5(?) PNs,
	13)	Mes-U+É	
	14)	Ur-^{d}Gu-nu-ra	
	15)	Lugal-i-mu	
	16)	En-ZU.AB	
	17)	engar!	the "farmers,"
	18)	ki durun-durun	sat in (this) place.
		(space)	
Rev. xv	1)	ì-bi	The oil
	2)	zag ag	was spread on the side.
	3)	Lum-ma	6(?) PNs
	4)	AN.MAŠ.LU.UŠ	
	5)	Lugal-á-zi-da	
	6)	Lugal-na-nam	
	7)	Lugal-⸢x-x⸣	
	8)	Barag?-me?-⸢x⸣-GAR	
	9)	lú-ki-inim-ma	are the witnesses;
	10)	Ur-^{d}Gu-nu-ra	12 PNs, the . . .
	11)	É-Ma-ma	
	12)	Lugal-ezen(sic)	
	13)	Mes-ZU.AB	
	14)	Lugal-ù-ma	
	15)	Ur-PA	
	16)	Úr-ni	
	17)	É-kur-rí	
	18)	Me-kar-si	
	19)	IGI.ZA	
	20)	Ú-da-ur$_4$	
Rev. xvi	1)	≪d≫Ur-dingir-ra	

---

	2)	1(bùr) 2(iku) gán	20 iku of land,
	3)	É-sag-ki-ti	(the field) É-sag-ki-ti;
	4)	1(bùr) 1(eše) 1(iku) gán	25 iku of land,
	5)	gán DUN	the field DUN;
	6)	1(bùr) 4(iku) gán	22 iku of land,
	7)	gán Mu-ni-gár	the field (of) Mu-ni-gár;
	8)	2 kug ma-na lal 7 ⸢gín⸣	113 shekels of silver
	9)	11 iš-gán še NI-ga	(and) Additional Payment
	10)	22 síg ma-na	
	11)	11 ì-udu umbin?	
	12)	Lugal-maš-usu(Á.KAL)	(to) 2 PNs
	13)	Lugal-kar-si	
	14)	an-ne-túm?	were brought.

Rev. xvii	1)	2(eše) gán	12 iku of land,
	2)	gán Kug-gál^{KI}	the field (located in) Kug-gál;
	3)	⅓ kug (ma-na)	20 shekels of silver
	4)	Lugal-da-gur!-ra	(to) 1 PN
	5)	an-na⟨-lal⟩	were ⟨weighed out⟩.
	6)	2 iš-gán NI-ga	Additional Payment
	7)	2 ì-udu umbin?	
	8)	4 síg ma-na	
	9)	Isin$_x$(IN)^{KI}-dùg	(to) 2(?) PNs
	10)	En-na-Il	
	11)	an-na-sum	was given.

---

	12)	2(eše) gán	12 iku of land,
	13)	gán Ur-^{d}Gu-nu-ra	the field (of) Ur-^{d}Gu-nu-ra,
	14)	ENGUR! da im-ru	the . . . ;

15)	⅓ kug ma-na	20 shekels of silver
16)	2 iš-gán NI-ga	(and) Additional Payment
17)	2 ì-udu umbin?	
18)	4 síg ma-na	
19)	3?	
Rev. xviii 1)	Lugal-da-gur-ra	(to) 1 PN
2)	an-na-sum	were given.
3)	1(eše) 3(iku) gán	9 iku of land,
4)	gán DUN	the field DUN,
5)	Ur-sag-gur?-ra?!	(the former? property of) U.;
6)	15 kug gín	15 shekels of silver
7)	1(NI-ga) 2(UL) iš-gán ⟨NI-⟩ga	(and) Additional Payment
8)	3 síg ma-na	
9)	3 ì silà	
10)	Lugal-da-gur!-ra	(to) 1 PN
11)	an-na-sum	were given.
12)	2(eše) 3(iku) gán	15 iku of land,
13)	É-gud	(the field) É-gud,
14)	X-kar	(the former? property of) X.;
15)	⅓ kug (ma-na) 5 gín	25 shekels of silver
16)	Lugal-da-gur!-ra	(to) 1 PN
17)	an-gi_4	were . . .
18)	5 ì silà	Additional Payment?

Notes

i 4.—For the PN Nin-dalla, see *THM* 5 p. 20 (*passim*).

i 7 and *passim*.—The sign which we tentatively read as umbin? is composed of the ÚR sign crossed in the middle with three or four parallel vertical wedges (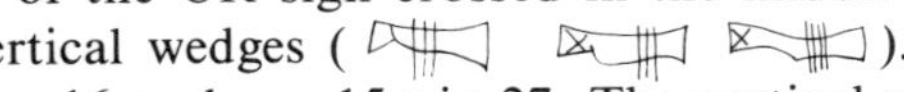). For the sign ÚR, compare xv 16 and no. 15 xiv 27. The vertical wedges crossing the sign seem to represent the *gunû* but, given the difficulties the stonecutter had in reproducing many of the signs appearing in these two inscriptions, they may stand as well for TAG_4. The sign appears to be the same as LAK-289 (= ÚR+TAG_4) of the Fara texts, which was identified by Deimel as the later UMBIN (≐ GADA+ÚR+TAG_4). The same sign, preceded by the word bur "bowl," appears in a Fara/Pre-Sargonic votive inscription (M. Lambert, *RA* 70 [1976] p. 191 i 1), clearly demonstrating that umbin? was a type of container. The same container, likewise serving as a capacity measure of sheep oil/fat, is found in no. 182a transactions I and J, which stems from Isin and dates to the late Pre-Sargonic or early Sargonic period. Further, note the occurrence of 15 umbin? ì-šáḫ in the Pre-Sargonic tablet Fish, *CST* 22 i 3 (the reading "emeda" of the sign, given by Westenholz *apud* B. R. Foster, *BJRL* 64 [1982] p. 475, is obscure to us). Our umbin? is possibly related to the container ÚR+GAR, which appears in an OB text from Tell ed-Dēr (*TIM* 7, 198:2 and *passim*). For a discussion of the latter container, see Edzard, *Tell ed-Dēr* pp. 192f.

The examination of the commodities listed in nos. 14 and 15 shows that ì-udu "sheep oil," which is measured in umbin?, alternates with the ì "oil," which is measured in silà. Furthermore, given the constant nature of the relationships between the amounts of the commodities in these two inscriptions, one can establish that one umbin? corresponds to two silà. Accordingly, the umbin? must have had the capacity of two silà.

i 9 and *passim*.—The interpretation of this commodity, which is also written iš-gán še (vii 4, x 8, xvi 9, and *passim* in no. 15), presents serious difficulties. In view of the variant spelling with še, the simplest explanation, of course, would be to assume that the commodity in question is simply še "barley," and that iš-gán is the well-known term for "additional payment" (see section 7.5.2). This interpretation, however, leaves open the question as to why the term iš-gán should in each case describe only barley and not, as is the usual practice, all of the commodities included in the additional payment. As an alternative solution one could speculate that iš-gán (še) is a type of commodity (but note the occurrence of iš-gán, clearly "additional payment," in xiv 6–10), but this appears even less likely, considering the complete absence of references to such a commodity. Further, the latter explanation would require us to assume that še in iš-gán (še) is a phonetic or semantic indicator, which too is a most unlikely proposition. Because of this, the question of the meaning of iš-gán (še) must be left unanswered for the time being.

i 12.—For the reading of this PN, see Steinkeller, *WZKM* 77 (1987) p. 191.

i 15.—This PN could alternatively be read Már-már.

i 16.—The reading of LAK-483 remains unknown.

ii 2–3 and *passim*.—For the meaning of this clause, see section 7.12.5.2.

ii 4–5 and *passim*.—For this clause, which seems to signify the completion of the transaction, see section 7.12.3.2.

ii 15.—The same(?) person appears, also as a seller, in xvii 9. For the reading $isin_x$ of IN, see J. N. Postgate, *Sumer* 30 (1974) pp. 207ff.; Steinkeller, *JCS* 30 (1978) pp. 168f.

ii 16 and iii 5.—The sign LÀL has a KAG inside, as in the Ur III text *ITT* 3, 5258:2, in contrast to no. 15 i 9, which has the expected SÁR.

iii 4.—This PN is very common in the Pre-Sargonic and Sargonic texts from Nippur. See Westenholz, *OSP* 1 p. 90.

iii 6.—Read probably Lugal-maš, and compare with Lugal-maš-usu(Á.KAL) in xvi 12 and Lugal-maš-su (e.g., *BIN* 8, 102 i 4).

iii 11.—The identification of the second sign as GÚG is not beyond all doubt, but compare the forms of LAK-790 and RÉC-463. The same sign occurs also in the toponym Gúg-bar-rum^{KI} in iv 9.

iii 13.—As the sign ME in Ur-sag-a-me-nàd is clear, it is impossible to correct it to DU, as in Ur-sag-a-DU-nàd in *TMH* 5, 134 i 5 (= Westenholz, *ECTJ* p. 69).

iv 7, v 6, and vi 2.—The sign read here as BARAG (in Lú-barag-si) occurs also in several different names in this inscription and in no. 15 (see, e.g., Barag-ga-ni in no. 15 i 25, ii 24, etc., and Barag-$^{sá}sag_7$-nu-di in no. 15 xii 1, 9). In form, our sign is identical with $DARA_4$ (= LAK-670), for which see the equation $DARA_4$ = *dè-rí-ḫum* in

Pettinato, *MEE* 3 p. 198 line 58, and the syllabic spelling da-ra for $DARA_4$ in the "Animal List A" (Th. J. H. Krispijn, *JEOL* 27 [1981–82] p. 50; J. Krecher, *OA* 22 [1983] p. 184f.). This form of BARAG, in which the sign lacks the small wedges that are attached to the four sides of the standard BARAG (see Y. Rosengarten, *Répertoire* p. 48 no. 267), is also found in the Pre-Sargonic texts from Nippur; see, e.g., the PN Nin-barag-gi in *OSP* 1, 23 vi 16, viii 20, 24 iv 11, 138 ii 3.

v 5.—For the DN ^{d}Gu-nu-ra, appearing in this name (found also in xiv 9, 14, xv 10, xvii 13 and in no. 15 vi 12 and viii 26), see Deimel, *Pantheon Babylonicum* p. 89 no. 549; N. Schneider, *Götternamen* p. 32 no. 179. Note the spelling ^{d}Gu-nir-ra in the Ur III PN Ur-^{d}Gu-nir-ra (*TUT* 258:4), as contrasted with Ur-^{d}Gu-nu-ra in other sources (H. Limet, *Anthroponymie* p. 547).

vi 3.—For this PN, cf. Im-ta-e_{11} in *OSP* 1, 45 vii′ 7′.

vi 4.—In the element GÍR-*gunû*-gal, found in this and various other names (see A-GÍR-*gunû*-gal and Lugal-GÍR-*gunû*-gal in Burrows, *UET* 2 pp. 27, 34, and Westenholz, *OSP* 1 pp. 75, 89, and the examples cited in Limet, *Anthroponymie* p. 332), the first sign is regularly GÍR-*gunû*, i.e., LAK-7. See Biggs, *OIP* 99 pp. 69f., who also suggests that GÍR-*gunû*-gal, probably to be read ul_4-gal, is to be connected with GÍR-gal = *šarḫu*. Note, however, that in the archaic texts the first sign in GÍR-*gunû*-gal is GÍR, as in the names KA-GÍR-gal in no. 11 ii 6 and A-GÍR-gal in no. 12 side D.

vi 7–11.—For this clause, see section 7.11.1.

vi 9.—Note that the second sign of Gala is clear DÚR/TUŠ. This is in agreement with the observation of Biggs, *JCS* 20 (1966) p. 78 n. 37, that the archaic spelling of gala was UŠ.DÚR (later UŠ.KU). Cf. also Gelb, *StOr* 46 (1975) p. 64.

vi 11.—The verb durun-durun, found also in xiv 18 and *passim* in no. 15, is an abbreviation of ì-durun-durun, the latter attested in x 2 and no. 15 xii 15. As suggested by Steinkeller, *Or.* n.s. 48 (1979) p. 56 n. 6, durun-durun is almost certainly to be read $durun_x$(TUŠ.TUŠ). Compare M. Krebernik, *BiOr* 41 (1984) p. 643. In favor of this reading, see also M. Civil's suggestion, *OA* 21 (1982) p. 10 n. 9, that the bread ninda-KU.KU-na of the Pre-Sargonic texts from Lagash (see section 11.2) is to be read ninda-$durun_x$(TUŠ.TUŠ)-na "oven(-baked) bread," where $durun_x$ would be a variant spelling of duruna(TUŠ), durúna(LAGAB+IM), durùna(ŠU.LAGAB.NA), and tu-ru-na, all meaning "oven."

vi 17.—This person is probably identical with ŠEŠ.KI-na, son of Ur-^{d}En-líl, who is the seller in x 9–11.

viii 6–7, 9–10.—Šeš-GÍR-*gunû*-gal may be the same person as one of the sellers in no. 15 x 12 and the witness in no. 14 vi 4, vii 9, and no. 15 xi 9.

viii 11, ix 3, and 10.—In spite of the divergent forms, the first sign of Edin-ri is assuredly EDIN (= LAK-747). This precludes any possibility of reading the name as Baḫár-ri. For a clear BAḪÁR (= LAK-742), see no. 15 xii 17.

ix 13.—The sign U+É (= LAK-397, RÉC-265) occurs also in the names Mes-U+É (xiv 13), É-U+É-X (no. 15 ii 4), and U+É-šum (no. 15 xiv 15). It may be identical with the later sign U+KÍD, i.e., $šita_4$.

xi 1.—For the reading of the second sign as GÁR (see the photograph), compare the form of GÁR in xvi 7 and no. 15 iii 30, iv 7 and 10.

xi 3.—The sign read here as X is possibly an erased NIN (note the name Nin-SAL-zi in the following line), with GAN? written over it. See the form of GAN in En-ḫé-gál in no. 12 side F.

xii 4 and *passim*.—The construction é-ta . . . è, lit.: "to leave the house" or "to remove (something) from the house," probably means here simply "to take out." For this sense of é-ta . . . è, see *BIN* 8, 124:10–11 (two expenditures of barley é-ta im-ta-è), 206:7 (two expenditures of barley é-ta im-ta-è), 271:22–23 (various goods é-ta im-ta-è gá-nun-na ba-ku_4 "were taken out / received (and) brought into the storehouse").

xii 6.—The PN GAM.GAM is attested also in *UET* 2, 203 i 5′, Suppl. 14 iv 2, *Fara* 3, 71 xiii 2, and *TSŠ* 532 i 4. For the observation that GAM.GAM is different from BAN (= LAK-180), see Biggs, *Or.* n.s. 36 (1967) p. 65 n. 4. Assuming that GAM.GAM is a ligature of two GAMs, the signs would have the reading gam-gam or gurum-gurum. Note the syllabic spelling gi-gi-ru-ma-ni, giving the pronunciation of GAM.GAM-ma-ni = /gu(rum)-gurum-ani/, which was discussed by J. Krecher, *Kultlyrik* p. 197.

xii 9 and xiii 3.—The sign read as X is possibly GÚ.

xii 14–16.—The same three(?) persons appear as sellers in xiii 13–15. Further, note Ur-^{d}En-líl, father of ŠEŠ.KI-na, in x 9–11, and Ur-^{d}En-líl, a seller, in no. 15 xiii 19.

xiii 8.—The reading of the name is unclear. The signs GÁN?.GA could be interpreted as $ašag_x$(GÁN)-ga.

xv 7.—Possibly to be reconstructed as Lugal-⌜ki-ni⌝. Cf. xiv 6.

xv 12.—The PN Lugal-ezen is written in two separate lines.

xv 19.—Read probably Ba-za. Cf. the PN Ba-za in *TMH* 5, 69 i 2.

xv 20.—This PN could alternatively be read É-da-ur_4. Cf. the sign É, written Ú, in vi 13.

xvii 4.—The same person acts as a seller in xviii 1, 10, and 16, and no. 15 L. E. 24.

xvii 14.—Possibly to be interpreted as da im-ru-ENGUR! "(located) at the (holdings? of the) ENGUR-clan(?)."

xvii 18–19.—These two lines are actually written at the very end of column xvi. That the 4 pounds of wool of line 18 belong to the additional payment listed in the preceding three lines is demonstrated by the comparison with xvii 6–8. The identity (and placement in the text) of the commodity recorded in line 19 is uncertain.

xviii 16.—There is a large circle in front of the name Lugal-da-gur!-ra, which does not occur anywhere else, and is probably a scribal error.

xviii 17–18.—The meaning of an-gi_4 in this context is unclear. The 5 quarts of oil listed following the verb possibly do not belong here.

No. 15 Baltimore Stone

Photographs: Plates 24 and 26, Walters Art Gallery, Baltimore, negative nos. H 63 (1), (2), and (3).

Copy: Plates 25 and 27, copied by Green from photographs, assisted by Whiting and Gelb.

Synopsis: Plates 89–91.

Provenience: Unknown—purchased (possibly Isin, see under *Provenience* of no. 14). According to the information from the dealer, the stone "was found at a ruin called Abhari in Southern Babylonia." Abhari or Ab Huri is situated between Sunkara (Larsa) and Warka (Uruk), according to information gathered by A. Poebel, *JAOS* 57 (1937) p. 362.

Date: Fara or the earlier phase of the Pre-Sargonic period.

Language: Sumerian.

Present location: Walters Art Gallery (Baltimore), 41.107.

Description: Square tablet of reddish-brown stone measuring 25 × 26 × 4.4 cm.

Text: In contrast to no. 14, which is a rectangular tablet with all edges rounded, no. 15 is a regular square slab, with its six sides fully delineated. The writing is preserved on all sides with the exception of the right edge. The sequence of writing can be established without difficulty on the basis of the formulary. The text begins with column i on the obverse and so on to column vii, the last one of the obverse. The text then follows the same way from the lower edge to the reverse, until the end of the seventh column on the reverse. The text then continues on the left edge of the tablet.

The writing is generally well preserved and easy to read. Certain parts of the reverse, which had chipped off, were incorrectly pasted on by the dealer in whatever empty space on the inscription he felt needed filling. Subsequently, the fragments have been placed in correct positions by the museum staff with the help of our reconstructed text.

For the relationship of no. 15 to no. 14, see no. 14 under *Text*.

Transliteration and Translation

U. E. i	1)	1(bùr) gán	18 iku of land,
	2)	gán É-gud	the field É-gud;
	3)	½ kug ma-na	30 shekels of silver (as its price)
	4)	Nam?-maḫ	(to) 1 PN
Obv. i	5)	dumu	
	6)	Sum-du-du	
	7)	an-na-lal	were weighed out.
	8)	Ur-ur	2 PNs
	9)	Làl-ad-da-na	
	10)	é-t[a] íb-è	"removed it (i.e., the additional payment?) from the house."
	11)	2 iš-gán še NI-ga	Additional Payment.
	12)	6 síg ma-na	
	13)	3 ì-udu umbin?	
	14)	30 ninda-bappir	
	15)	Ur-sag-ki-gal-la	1 PN
	16)	dumu	
	17)	Edin-ni-si	
	18)	lú-ki-inim-ma	is the witness.
	19)	ì-bi	The oil
	20)	zag ab-ag	was spread on the side.
	21)	inim-bi	This transaction
	22)	é-ta ab-è	"left the house."
	23)	Lugal-ezen	4 PNs,
	24)	Iš-me-ì-lum	
	25)	Barag-gan-ni	
	26)	É-Anzud$_{x}$(AN.MI.MUŠEN)	
	27)	engar	the "farmers,"
	28)	zag durun-durun	sat on the side.

U. E. ii	1)	2(eše) gán	12 iku of land,
	2)	gán DUN	the field DUN;
	3)	⅓ (ma-na) kug	20 shekels of silver
	4)	É-U+É-X	to E.
Obv. ii	5)	an-na-lal	were weighed out.
	6)	2 iš-gán še NI-ga	Additional Payment.
	7)	4 síg ma-na	
	8)	4 ì silà	
	9)	20 ninda-bappir	
	10)	4 ninda-banšur	
	11)	Igi-⌜gùn⌝	6(?) PNs
	12)	Lugal-bí-túm	
	13)	Ad-da	
	14)	En-ra-rúm	
	15)	MU-ì-lí	
	16)	Lugal-bí-túm	
	17)	lú-ki-inim-ma	are the witnesses.
	18)	ì-bi	The oil
	19)	zag ab-ag	was spread on the side.
	20)	inim-bi	This transaction
	21)	é-ta ab-è	"left the house."
	22)	Lugal-ezen	4 PNs,
	23)	Iš-me-ì-lum	
	24)	Barag-gan-ni	
	25)	É-Anzud$_{x}$	
	26)	engar	the "farmers,"
	27)	zag durun-durun	sat on the side.

	28)	2(eše) gán	12 iku of land,
	29)	gán DUN	the field DUN;
	30)	⅓ kug (ma-na)	20 shekels of silver
U. E. iii	1)	Mes-níg-b[ur-LUL]	(to) 2(?) PNs
	2)	A-bu-bu	
	3)	an-n[a-la]l	were weighed out.
	4)	⸢2⸣ iš-gán [še] N[I-g]a	Additional Payment.
Obv. iii	5)	4 síg ma-na	
	6)	4 ì silà	
	7)	20 ninda-bappir	
	8)	4 ninda-banšur	
	9)	dam	5(?) PNs
	10)	Mes-níg-bur-LUL	
	11)	Lugal-mu-dù	
	12)	A-bu-bu	
	13)	Ki-lí-lí	
	14)	Mes-níg-bur-LUL	
	15)	lú-ki-inim-ma	are the witnesses.
	16)	ì-bi	The oil
	17)	zag ab-ag	was spread on the side.
	18)	inim-bi	This transaction
	19)	é-ta ab-è	"left the house."
	20)	Lugal-ezen	4 PNs,
	21)	Iš-me-ì-lum	
	22)	Barag-gan-ni	
	23)	É-Anzud$_x$	
	24)	engar	the "farmers,"
	25)	zag durun-durun	sat on the side.

---

	26)	1(eše) gán	6 iku of land,
	27)	gán DUN	the field DUN;
	28)	10 kug gín	10 shekels of silver
	29)	Ad-da	(to) 2(?) PNs
	30)	Mu-ni-gár	
	31)	an-na-lal	were weighed out.
U. E. iv	1)	1 iš-[gán še N]I-g[a]	Additional Payment.
	2)	2 síg m[a-na]	
	3)	2 ì [silà]	
	4)	10 ninda-bap[pir]	
	5)	5 ninda-ban[šur]	
Obv. iv	6)	Lugal-šà-sud(wr. BU)	9(?) PNs
	7)	Mu-ni-gár	
	8)	Za-la	
	9)	NI-X	
	10)	Mu-ni-gár	
	11)	Si-gar	
	12)	UD.A	
	13)	Ušum-ma	
	14)	È-du	
	15)	lú-ki-inim-ma	are the witnesses.
	16)	ì-bi	The oil
	17)	zag ab-ag	was spread on the side.
	18)	inim-bi	This transaction
	19)	é-ta ab-è	"left the house."
	20)	Lugal-ezen	4 PNs,
	21)	Iš-me-ì-lum	
	22)	Barag-gan-ni	
	23)	É-Anzud$_x$	
	24)	engar	the "farmers,"
	25)	zag durun-durun	sat on the side.

---

	26)	2(eše) 3(iku) gán	15 iku of land,
	27)	gán É-gud	the field É-gud;
	28)	⅓ kug (ma-na) 5 gín	25 shekels of silver
	29)	Ad-da	(to) 2(?) PNs
	30)	Amar-^{d}EN.ZU	
	31)	an-na-lal	were weighed out.
U. E. v	1)	[2(NI-ga)] ⸢2(UL)⸣ [iš]-⸢gán⸣ [še NI-ga]	Additional Payment.
	2)	[5 síg ma-na]	
	3)	[5 ì silà]	
	4)	[23]+2 ninda-ba[ppir]	
Obv. v	5)	[2]+4 ninda-banš[ur]	
	6)	A-mu-m[i]	5(?) PNs
	7)	É-ZU.AB	
	8)	Bàd-si-du	
	9)	Šà-gú-ba	
	10)	dumu	
	11)	Bàd⟨-si⟩-du	
	12)	Šag$_5$-šag$_5$	
	13)	nar?	
	14)	lú-ki-inim-ma	are the witnesses.
	15)	ì-bi	The oil
	16)	zag ab-ag	was spread on the side.
	17)	inim-bi	This transaction
	18)	é-ta ab-è(wr. DU)	"left the house."
	19)	Lugal-ezen	4 PNs,
	20)	Iš-me-ì-lum	
	21)	Barag-gan-ni	
	22)	É-Anzud$_x$	
	23)	engar	the "farmers,"
	24)	zag durun-durun	sat on the side.

---

	25)	1(eše) 1(iku) gán	7 iku of land,
	26)	gán É-GAM.GAM-maḫ-zu-zu	the field É-GAM.GAM-maḫ-zu-zu;
	27)	1(bùr) 5(iku) gán	23 iku of land,
	28)	BU.TUŠ.ḪU-da	(the field of) B.
	29)	dam	wife of
	30)	É-ZU.AB	E.;
	31)	⟨1 kug ma-na lal 10 gín⟩	⟨50 shekels of silver⟩
U. E. vi	1)	Ba-b[i?-. . . .]	(to) 1 P[N]
	2)	⸢an⸣-[na-lal]	were weighed out.
	3)	[x iš-gán še NI-ga]	[Additional Payment].
	4)	[x síg ma-na]	
Obv. vi	5)	[x ì silà]	
	6)	[x ninda-bappir]	
	7)	[x ninda-banšur]	
	8)	Ur-ḪAR	11(?) PNs
	9)	É-GÁN	
	10)	Igi-gùn	
	11)	Ur-^{d}Sud(wr. BU)-da	
	12)	Ur-^{d}Gu-nu-ra	
	13)	Si-gar	
	14)	BU.TUŠ.ḪU	
	15)	A-ki-gal	
	16)	Ad-da	
	17)	ugula anše	
	18)	Lugal-bí-túm	
	19)	I-gu-ì-lí	
	20)	lú-ki-inim-ma	are the witnesses.

	21)	ì-bi	The oil
	22)	zag ab-ag	was spread on the side.
	23)	inim-bi	This transaction
	24)	é-ta ab-è	"left the house."
	25)	Lugal-ezen	4 PNs,
	26)	Iš-me-ì-lum	
	27)	Barag-gan-ni	
	28)	É-Anzud$_x$	
	29)	engar	the "farmers,"
	30)	zag durun-durun	sat on the side.

---

	31)	1(bùr) 2(eše) gán	30 iku of land,
U. E. vii	1)	gán D[UN]	the field DUN;
	2)	⸢1 kug (ma-na) lal 10⸣ [gín]	⸢50 shekels of silver⸣
	3)	[PN]	[(to) 1 PN]
	4)	[an-na-lal]	[were weighed out].
	5)	[x iš-gán še NI-ga]	[Additional Payment].
Obv. vii	6)	[x síg ma-na]	
	7)	[x ì silà]	
	7a)	[x ninda-bappir]	
	7b)	[x ninda-banšur]	
	8)	A[N-. . .]	9(?) PNs
	9)	AN-⸢x⸣-[. . .]	
	10)	Maḫ?-[. . .]	
	11)	É-GÁN	
	12)	Ad-da《-da》	
	13)	ugula anše	
	14)	Mu-ni-ḫur-sag	
	15)	Ur-^{d}Sud-da	
	16)	IGI.UR	
	17)	É-GÁN	
	18)	lú-ki-inim-ma	are the witnesses.
	19)	ì-bi	The oil
	20)	zag ag	was spread on the side.
	21)	inim-bi	This transaction
	22)	é-ta ab-è	"left the house."
	23)	Lugal-ezen	4 PNs,
	24)	Iš-me-ì-lum	
	25)	Barag-gan-ni	
	26)	É-Anzud$_x$	
	27)	engar	the "farmers,"
	28)	zag durun-durun	sat on the side.

---

	29)	1(eše)(wr. 2(iku)) gán	6(?) iku of land,
	30)	gán É-dúr-BAḪÁR!.A.DU.GÍN	the field É-dúr-BAḪÁR!.A.DU.GÍN;
	31)	10 kug gín	10 shekels of silver
Lo. E. viii	1)	SÍG.BU-šè	(to) 1 PN
	2)	an-na-lal	were weighed out.
	3)	1(eše) gán	6 iku of land,
	4)	gán SAG.A	the field SAG.A;
Rev. viii	5)	10 kug gín	10 shekels of silver
	6)	[X-d]a?	[(to) 1 P]N
	7)	[an-na-lal]	[were weighed out].
	8)	[1(eše) gá]n	[6 iku of land],
	9)	[gán X]	[the field X];
	10)	[. . .]-⸢x⸣	⸢. . .⸣
	11)	⸢É⸣.TU[M]	⸢. . .⸣
	12)	BÀD [. . .]	⸢. . .⸣
	13)	10 kug gí[n]	10 shekels of silver

	14)	Na-n[a]	3(?) PNs
	15)	Me-é-mug!-si	
	16)	SÍG.BU-šè	
	17)	an-⸢kú⸣	received (lit.: ate).
	18)	U[r-. . .]	11(?) PNs
	19)	⸢É⸣?-[. . .]	
	20)	Ú-[. . .]	
	21)	Me-é-[mug-si]	
	22)	Igi-g[ùn]	
	23)	Ur-^{d}[S]ud-da	
	24)	⸢BU⸣.TUŠ.⸢ḪU⸣	
	25)	[A]-⸢ki⸣-[ga]l	
	26)	Ur-^{d}⸢Gu⸣-nu-ra	
	27)	⸢Si⸣?-[gar]	
	28)	⸢Ad⸣-[da]	
Lo. E. ix	1)	ugula anše	
	2)	lú-ki-inim-ma	are the witnesses.
	3)	ì-bi	The oil
	4)	zag ab-ag	was spread on the side.
Rev. ix	5)	inim-bi	This transaction
	6)	é-ta ab-è	"left the house."

---

	7)	1(eše) gán	6 iku of land;
	8)	10 kug gí[n]	10 shekels of silver
	9)	Ur-Ab-[ra]	to U.
	10)	an-n[a-lal]	were weighed out.
	11)	1 [iš-gán še NI-ga]	Additional Payment.
	12)	⸢2⸣ síg [ma]-n[a]	
	13)	2 [ì silà]	
	14)	[10 ninda-bap]pir	
	15)	[x ninda-ban]šur	
	16)	[Ad?-d]a	3(?) PNs
	17)	Ur-Ab-ra	
	18)	⸢UD⸣-la	
	19)	lú-ki-inim-ma	are the witnesses.
	20)	[ì-b]i	[The oi]l
	21)	[zag ab-a]g	was spre[ad on the side].
	22)	[inim-b]i	Th[is transaction]
	23)	[é-ta ab-è]	["left the house"].
	24)	[Lugal-ez]en	4 ⸢PNs⸣,
	25)	[Iš-me-ì]-lum	
	26)	[Barag-gan-n]i	
	27)	[É]-A[nzud$_{x}$]	
	28)	engar	the "farmers,"
Lo. E. x	1)	zag durun-durun	sat on the side.

---

	2)	1(eše) 3(iku) gán	9 iku of land,
	3)	gán É-dúr-BAḪÁR!.ZA.NUN.DU	the field É-dúr-BAḪÁR!.ZA.NUN.DU;
Rev. x	4)	15 gín	15 shekels (of silver is its price);
	5)	5 gín	(out of it:) 5 shekels
	6)	Lugal-gal-zu	1 PN
	7)	an-kú	received;
	8)	5 gín	5 shekels
	9)	Ur-^{d}En-ki	1 PN
	10)	an-kú	received;
	11)	5 gín	5 shekels
	12)	[Š]eš-GÍR-*gunû*-gal [an-k]ú	1 PN received.
	13)	2(NI-ga) 2(UL) iš-[gán še NI]-g[a]	Additional Payment.
	14)	3 síg ma-na	
	15)	3 ì si[là]	

	16)	⌜15⌝ ninda-⌜bappir⌝	
	17)	3 ninda-banšur	
	18)	A-ki-gal	1 PN ⟨witness?⟩.
	19)	⌜ì⌝-bi	⌜The oil⌝
	20)	[zag ab-ag]	[was spread on the side].
	21)	[inim-bi]	[This transaction]
	22)	[é-ta ab-è]	["left the house"].
	23)	[Lugal-ezen]	4 PNs,
	24)	[Iš-me-ì-lum]	
	25)	Barag-ga[n-ni]	
	26)	É-Anz[ud$_x$]	
	27)	[eng]ar	[the "far]mers,"
	28)	⟨zag durun-durun⟩	⟨sat on the side⟩.

Lo. E. xi	1)	3(iku) gán	3 iku of land;
	2)	5 kug gín	5 shekels of silver
	3)	2(UL) iš-gán še NI-ga	(and) Additional Payment
	4)	1 síg ma-na	
Rev. xi	5)	1 ì silà	
	6)	A-ki-gal	(to) 2(?) PNs
	7)	Lugal-gal-zu	
	8)	an-na!(wr. KI)-sum	were given.
	9)	Šeš-GÍR-*gunû*-gal	2(?) PNs
	10)	Ur-^{d}En-ki	
	11)	lú-[ki-in]im-ma	are the witnesses.

---

	12)	2(eše) ⌜3⌝(iku) gán	15 iku of land;
	13)	É-gud	(the field) É-gud;
	14)	½ kug [ma]-⌜na⌝ lal 2 gín	28 shekels of silver (is its price);
	15)	2(NI-ga) 2(UL) iš-gán [še] NI-g[a]	Additional Payment;
	16)	5 síg ma-na	
	17)	5 ì silà	
	18)	25 ninda-bappir	
	19)	2(eše) 3(iku) gán	15 iku of land,
	20)	gú-⌜nu⌝-[. . .]	⌜. . .⌝;
	21)	⅓ ku[g] (ma-na) 5 [gín]	25 shekels of silver (is its price);
	22)	[x iš-gán še NI-ga]	[Additional Payment];
	23)	[x síg ma-na]	
	24)	[x ì silà]	
	25)	[x ninda-bappir]	
	26)	[PN]	[(to) 3?]+1 PNs
	27)	[PN]	
	28)	[PN]	
Lo. E. xii	1)	Barag-^{sá}sag$_7$-nu-di!	
	2)	an-na!(wr. KI)-sum	were given.
	3)	ì-bi	The oil
Rev. xii	4)	zag ab⟨-ag⟩	was spread on the side.
	5)	inim-bi	This transaction
	6)	é-ta ab-è	"left the house."
	7)	Pab-ki-gal	3 PNs,
	8)	dumu	
	9)	Barag-$^{sá!}$sag$_7$-nu-di!	
	10)	Amar-^{d}Ezínu(ŠE.TIR)	
	11)	Igi-gùn	
	12)	dumu	
	13)	É-ki-tuš	
	14)	šeš gán	the "brothers of the field,"
	15)	ki-ba ì-durun-durun	sat in this place (i.e., of the transaction).

---

16)	2½(iku) gán	2½ iku of land,
17)	gán! É-dúr-BAḪÁR.ZA.NUN	the field É-dúr-BAḪÁR.ZA.NUN;
18)	4(wr. 40) kug gín	4 shekels of silver:
19)	2(wr. 20) gín	(out of it:) 2 shekels
20)	Bi-li-li	1 PN
21)	an-kú	received;
22)	2 gín	2 shekels
23)	DINGIR-en-ni	1 PN
24)	an-kú	received.
25)	iš-[gán še] NI-g[a]	Additional Payment.
26)	2 síg m[a-na]	
27)	2 ⸢ì⸣ [silà]	
28)	10 ninda-bap[pir]	
Lo. E. xiii 1)	Ur-^{d}En-ki	4(?) PNs
2)	DINGIR-en-ni	
3)	Kum-tuš-šè	
Rev. xiii 4)	Bi-li-li	
5)	lú-ki-inim-ma	are the witnesses.
6)	ì-bi	The oil
7)	zag ag	was spread on the side.
8)	inim-bi	This transaction
9)	é-ta ab-è	"left the house."
10)	Lugal-ezen	4 PNs,
11)	Iš-me-ì-lum	
12)	Barag-gan-ni	
13)	É-Anzud$_{x}$	
14)	engar	the "farmers,"
15)	zag durun-durun	sat on the side.

---

16)	1(eše) 1(iku) gán	7 iku of land,
17)	gán DUN	the field DUN;
18)	12 kug gín	12 shekels of silver
19)	Ur-^{d}En-líl	(to) 2(?) PNs
20)	X	
21)	an-na-lal	were weighed out.
22)	1(NI-ga) 2(UL) iš-gán NI-ga	Additional Payment.
23)	3 síg ma-na	
24)	3 ì silà	
25)	⸢15 nin]da-bappir	
26)	[x nin]da-banšur	
27)	Nin-⸢PA?-PI⸣	3(?) PNs
28)	Pab-ur-sag	
29)	Dingir-⸢azu⸣?-šè	
Lo. E. xiv 1)	lú-ki-inim-ma	are the witnesses.
2)	ì-bi	The oil
3)	zag ag	was spread on the side.
4)	inim-bi	This transaction
Rev. xiv 5)	é-ta ab-è	"left the house."
6)	Lugal-ezen	4 PNs,
7)	Iš-me-ì-lum	
8)	⸢Barag⸣-gan-ni	
9)	⸢É⸣-Anzud$_{x}$	
10)	engar	the "farmers,"
11)	zag durun-durun	sat on the side.

---

12)	1(eše) 4(iku) gán	10 iku of land,
13)	gán Da-da	the field (of?) Da-da;
14)	5(iku) gán	5 iku of land,
15)	U+É-šum	(the former? property of) U.,
16)	kug-gál	the canal-inspector;
17)	½ kug ma-na lal 2 gín	28 shekels of silver (as its price)

	18)	Igi-gùn	2(?) PNs
	19)	Ur-nin	
	20)	an-kú	received.
	21)	3 iš-gán NI-ga	Additional Payment.
	22)	6 síg ma-na	
	23)	3 ì-udu umbin?	
	24)	30 ninda-bappir	
	25)	4 ninda-banšur	
	26)	⌜A⌝-nu-GÁN	5(?) PNs
	27)	[É]-úr-bi-dùg!	
	28)	⌜X⌝-nigir	
	29)	⌜Zur⌝-zur	
	30)	D[a]?-ti?	
	31)	lú-ki-inim-[ma]	are the witnesses.
	32)	ì-bi	The oil
L. E.	1)	zag ag	was spread on the side.
	2)	inim-bi	This transaction
	3)	é-ta ab-è	"left the house."
	4)	Lugal-ezen	4 PNs,
	5)	Iš-me-ì-lum	
	6)	Barag-gan-ni	
	7)	É-Anzud$_x$	
	8)	engar	the "farmers,"
	9)	zag durun-durun	sat on the side.

---

	10)	1(eše) gán	6 iku of land
	11)	É-dúr-BAḪÁR!.DU	(the field) É-dúr-BAḪÁR!.DU
	12)	Kun?-si	the . . . ;
	13)	10 kug gín	10 shekels of silver
	14)	Ur-^{d}En-ki	(to) 1 PN
	15)	agrig	
	16)	an-na⟨-lal⟩	were weighed out.
	17)	ì-bi	The oil
	18)	⌜zag ag⌝	⌜was spread on the side⌝.
	19)	inim-b[i]	This transaction
	20)	é-ta ab-è	"left the house."

---

	21)	1(eše) gán	6 iku of land,
	22)	gán DUN	the field DUN;
	23)	10 kug gín	10 shekels of silver
	24)	Lugal-da-gur-r[a]	(to) 1 PN
	25)	an-na-lal	were weighed out.
	26)	ì-bi	The oil
	27)	zag ag	was spread on the side.
	28)	inim-bi	This transaction
	29)	é-ta ab-è	"left the house."

Notes

i 26 and passim in the list of engar's "farmers"—For the reading of the DN AN.IM.MI.MUŠEN as Anzud$_x$, see most recently Pettinato, *JCS* 31 (1979) pp. 116f. The abbreviated (or archaic) spelling AN.MI.MUŠEN, occurring in the present text, is found also in the Abu Salabikh ms. of the ED Names and Professions List line 231, in the PN Anzud$_x$(AN.MI.MUŠEN)-Me-ru; the corresponding Ebla ms. offers in its place a syllabic spelling An-zu-Me-ru (A. Archi, *SEb* 4 [1981] p. 187; cf. also *ibid.* p. 185 line 140).

ii 4.—For the sign U+É (= LAK-397), see note to no. 14 ix 13. The sign read as X is illegible.

ii 15.—For the PN MU-ì-lí, with the signs ì-lí written one upon the other, see *BIN* 8, 84 iii 2.

iii 29.—The same person is the seller in iv 29.

iv 9.—The second sign cannot be identified.

iv 12.—The signs could alternatively be interpreted as KAR.

v 26.—For the reading of GAM.GAM, see note to no. 14 xii 6.

vi 11, vii 15, and viii 23.—For the DN ^{d}Sud-da (probably different from ^{d}Sùd, the titulary goddess of Shuruppak), compare the parallels discussed by Gelb, *FM* pp. 198f., and Steinkeller, *ZA* 72 (1982) p. 242 n. to line 14.

vii 30, x 3, xii 17, and L. E. 11.—The GN in these four lines consists of the signs:

x 3	gán	É-dúr-BAḪÁR!.ZA.NUN.DU
xii 17	gán!	É-dúr-BAḪÁR.ZA.NUN

vii 30	gán	É-dúr-BAḪÁR!.A.DU.GÍN
L. E. 11		É-dúr-BAḪÁR!.DU

The form of BAḪÁR becomes progressively more schematic, from the clear form in xii 17, to L. E. 11, vii 30, and lastly x 3. The spelling é-dúr seems to correspond to the later é-dur_5(A). The geographical name is surely to be identified with the city É.BAḪÁR.NUNUZ in an Uruk III geographical list, cited in M. W. Green and H. J. Nissen, *Zeichenliste der archaischen Texte aus Uruk* (Berlin, 1987) p. 261 no. 423, in turn identical with the ED É-dúr-BAḪÁR.NUN.ZA (*Fara* 2 23 iv 9). The same sign-group occurs also in Pettinato, *MEE* 4 p. 236 line 326: É.ZA.NUN.BAḪÁR = *zi-lu-lu/ru*$_{12}$*-um*. Unfortunately, the meaning of the Semitic gloss (*Zilurum* or *Zir(u)rum*) is unknown. In these various spellings, ZA.NUN and NUN.ZA evidently represent ^{nun}nunuz$_x$(ZA).

viii 1 and 16.—The signs SÍG.BU, forming part of this name, are probably to be read as suluḫu. Another PN using the same word in Lugal-SÍG.BU/SUD, for which see Limet, *Anthroponymie* p. 472. For suluḫu, Akk. *sulumḫû* (*suluḫḫû*, etc.), a long-fleeced breed of sheep, see *CAD* S p. 371f.; W. Heimpel, *Tierbilder* p. 227.

x 2–28.—The sellers and witnesses appearing in this transaction recur in the following transaction (xi 1–11). Thus Lugal-gal-zu is a seller in both instances; Ur-^{d}En-ki, a seller in the first transaction, is a witness in the second transaction; Šeš-GÍR-*gunû*-gal, a seller in the first transaction, is a witness in the second transaction; and A-ki-gal, a witness in the first transaction, is a seller in the second transaction. Further, note that Šeš-GÍR-*gunû*-gal may be identical with Šeš-GÍR-*gunû*-gal, the temple administrator, husband of NN, in no. 14 viii 6–7, 9–10. For Ur-^{d}En-ki, cf. Ur-^{d}En-ki agrig in L. E. 14–15.

xii 1 and 9.—For the reading of this name, written also -sag_7-nu-di, -^{sa}sag_7-nu-di, and -sàg(PA)-nu-di, see H. Steible, *FAOS* 5 p. 5. The verb involved is the later ság(PA.GAN) . . . dug_4/di, Akk. *sapāḫum* (see *CAD* S p. 151) and *nasākum* (see *CAD* N/2 p. 15). Note here the equation SAG_7.DI = *nu-du-um*, *na-za-gúm* in Pettinato, *MEE* 4 p. 293 line 828 (cf. also line 829), where the second gloss is clearly *nasākum*.

xiii 19.—The same(?) Ur-^{d}En-líl appears as a seller in no. 14 xii 15 and xiii 14.

No. 16 Kish Stone Fragments I

Photographs: Plates 28 and 30, Ashmolean Museum, Oxford.

Copies: Plates 29 and 31, copied by Green from photographs and copy of originals by Gelb.

Synopsis: Plate 92.

Provenience: Kish, found by excavators during the 1930–31 and 1931–32 seasons.

Date: Fara.

Language: Akkadian—the texts are written in Akkadian, not Sumerian, because of the occurrence of NÍG.KI.GAR "additional payment," the absence of Sumerian affixes, as in KÚ "to eat," and the graphotactical sequence of "measure plus thing counted," as in x GÍN KUG.BABBAR "x shekels of silver," against the Sumerian sequence x kug gín.

Present location: Ashmolean Museum (Oxford).

Publication: Copies by J.-P. Grégoire published in microfiche in P. R. S. Moorey, *Kish Excavations 1928–1933* (Oxford, 1978) microfiche card 3, pp. D 12 and E 3 (description) and D 9, 13, 14 and E 2 (copy).

Description: All ten fragments are of whitish limestone. Although it cannot be proven that all or some of these fragments belong to the same tablet, their overall similarity in coloring, content, and writing makes it probable that they do.

Since none of the preserved fragments extend from edge to edge, it is impossible to determine the original shape and size of the pieces. The two edges preserved in fragment b suggest that the object may have had some sort of cubical shape about 12 cm^3 in size. It was probably not a rectangular slab such as no. 15, but was rather a free-standing piece such as no. 12. Owing to the fragmentary state of preservation of the texts, the sequence of the sides and columns of the fragments with more than one side (16a, 16b, 16c, and 16d) cannot be determined. Data concerning the fragments are presented below in tabular form. The measurements given below differ slightly from those offered by Grégoire.

Fragment	*Grégoire No.*	*Museum No.*	*Field No.*	*Locus*	*Measurements (cm)*
a	8	1930, 153	KM 13	C5 at plain level	8.9 × 9.0 × 6.8
b	6	1930, 154	KM 125	YWN 1 m below plain level	Side A: 7.7 × 9 × 12.5 Side B: 10.4 × 11 × 8 Side C: 4.8 × 5.7 × 12
c	9	1930, 155	(?)		Side A: 3 × 4.2 × 2.2 Side B: 2 × 4.7 × 2.8
d	7	1930, 156	V 337	C2 at 5 m	Side A: 9.5 × 12.3 × 5.7 Side B: 5 × 12 × 9.5 Side C: 9 × 4.7 × 12.2
e	10	1930, 178a	KM 196	YWN	5.5 × 3.5 × 2.5
f	11	1930, 178b	KM 260	YWM	4.5 × 3.8 × 2
g	12	1930, 179a	KM 101	C6	4.2 × 4.9 × 1.7
h	13	1930, 179b	KM 102	C6	2 × 3.4 × 3.2
i	15	1930, 180	KM 239	YW	11 × 9 × 3.8
j	14	1931, 162	K 838	YW	3.4 × 3.4 × 2.5

Transliteration

No. 16a (Kish 1930, 153)

i (beg. destr.)
1′) [. . .] ⌜x⌝
2′) [NÍG.KI.GAR x]+1 GÍN [KUG.BABBAR]
3′) [. . .A]N? EN
4′) [. . .] ⌜x⌝
(rest destr.)
ii (beg. destr.)
1′) NÍG.KI.G[AR]
2′) 8 GÍN(without *gunû*) KUG.BABBAR
3′) *A-pù-lum*
4′) *Ur-Utu*
5′) KA.GAR

6′) 1(EŠE) 2(IKU) GÁN
7′) ŠÁM
8′) ⌜1⌝? ŠA.P[I KUG.BABBAR]
(rest destr.)
iii (beg. destr.)
1′) DUM[U] *U*[*r*- . . .]
2′) K[A.GAR]

3′) 2(EŠE)+[x?(IKU) GÁN]
4′) Š[ÁM]
(rest destr.)

No. 16b (Kish 1930, 154)

A i 1) 3(IKU) GÁN
2) ŠÁM
3) 15 GÍN KUG.BABBAR
4) NÍG.KI.GAR 1 GÍN KUG.BABBAR
(rest destr.)
ii 1) 2(EŠE) ⌜GÁN⌝?
2) ½ (MA.NA) 4+[x GÍN] KU[G.BABBAR]
3) NÍG.KI.⌜GAR⌝ 1+[x] GÍN [KUG.BABBAR]
(rest destr.)
B i (blank)
ii (beg. destr.)
1′) 1 (MA.NA) ⌜x ŠÁM⌝ [. . .] GÍN KUG.BABBAR
2′) NÍG.KI.GAR 3 GÍN KUG.BABBAR
3′) *Im-li*[*k*?-X]
4′) *I-b*[*í*-. . .]
iii (destr.)
C i 1) 2(EŠE) 1(IKU) GÁN
2) ŠÁM
3) 1 ŠA.PI KUG.BABBAR
(rest destr.)
ii (destr.)

No. 16c (Kish 1930, 155)

A i (beg. destr.)
1′) [x GÍN KUG.BAB]BAR
2′) [NÍG.KI.G]AR [x GÍN KUG.BABBAR]
ii (beg. destr.)
1′) DUMU.DUM[U]
2′) *Ìr*-DU?-[. . .]
B ii 1) [x]+1(EŠE) 1(IKU) [GÁN]
(rest destr.)

No. 16d (Kish 1930, 156)

A i (beg. destr.)
1) NÍG.KI.GAR
2) ⌜1⌝+[x] GÍN [KUG.BABBAR]
3) A-NI-NI/GAR
4) *Ù-mes*
5) KA.GAR
ii (beg. destr.)
1′) [. . .] ⌜x⌝
2′) [K]A.GAR

3′) [x]+2(IKU) GÁN
4′) 7 GÍN KUG.BABBAR
5′) *I-bí*-DINGIR
iii (beg. destr.)
1′) [. . .]-⌜*x*⌝-[L]UM
2′) ⌜X⌝-*na-ma-nu*^{KI}
3′) LÚ
4′) *A-a*-[. . .]
5′) UK[Ù.GAL]
B i 1) 1(EŠE) 2(IKU) GÁN
2) ŠÁM
3) [x]+4 [GÍN KUG.BABBAR]
(rest destr.)
ii 1) KIL-*da*-DINGIR
2) DUMU *I-mu-mu*
(rest destr.)
iii 1) PAB.ŠEŠ
2) ^{d}*Innin*
3) 1(IKU) ⌜x⌝ GÁN
(rest destr.)

No. 16e (Kish 1930, 178a)

(beg. destr.)
1′) [x]+1 GÍ[N KUG.BABBAR]
2′) [X]-*la-m*[*u*(-*x*)]
3′) ⌜. . .⌝
(rest destr.)

No. 16f (Kish 1930, 178b)

i (beg. destr.)
1′) [. . .] KUG.[BABBAR]
(rest destr.)
ii (beg. destr.)
1′) *Ì-l*[*um*]?-[. . .]
2′) *I-b*[*í*]-*bí*
(rest destr.)

No. 16g (Kish 1930, 179a)

i (almost destr.)
ii (beg. destr.)

1′) DUMU ⸢*Šu?-x*⸣-[. . .]
2′) 2(EŠE) 1(IKU)+[x(IKU) GÁN]
3′) ŠÁM 1 Š[A.PI] K[UG.BABBAR]
(rest destr.)

No. 16h (Kish 1930, 179b)

(beg. destr.)
1′) [x]?+1 MA.N[A] KUG.BAB[BAR]
(rest destr.)

No. 16i (Kish 1930, 180)

i (destr.)
ii (beg. destr.)
1′) 20+[x GÍN KUG.BABBAR]
2′) NÍG.KI.GAR
3′) *Ur-mes*
4′) [K]A.[GAR]
(rest destr.)

No. 16j (Kish 1930, 162)

(beg. destr.)
1′) 1 ŠA.PI KUG.BABBAR
(rest destr.)

Notes

16a ii 5′ and *passim*.—The Kish texts regularly write KA.GAR, side by side, for KÚ (= KA+GAR) "to eat." The occurrence of the forms KA.GAR instead of KA+GAR for KÚ, and KA.ME instead of KA+ME for EME at Ebla was noted by Edzard, *ARET* 2 p. 131. The spelling KA.GAR appears also in an unusual text of the Fara period, which shows various features characteristic of Ebla texts. See M. Lambert, *RA* 67 (1973) p. 96 iii 3 and F. Pomponio, *OA* 19 (1980) pp. 172 and 175f.

16b A ii 2.—Note the very unusual way of writing ½ (MA.NA).

No. 17 Kish Stone Fragment II

Photograph: Plate 30, Ashmolean Museum, Oxford, courtesy Westenholz.
Copy: Plate 31, copied by Green from photograph and copy of original by Gelb.
Provenience: Kish, Field no. Y 222, locus V—found in debris at the extreme south of trench Y (Grégoire, see below); "from mound Z . . . above red-stone level" (Langdon, see below).
Date: Fara or earlier.
Language: Akkadian(?).
Present location: Ashmolean Museum (Oxford), Kish 1928–423.
Publications: Langdon, *OECT* 7, 149 (copy); Grégoire in Moorey, *Kish Excavations 1928–1933* (Oxford, 1978) microfiche card no. 3, p. D 11 no. 2 (copy).
Description: Fragment of a red stone slab measuring 9.2 × 6.9 × 3 cm.

Transliteration

i (beg. destr.)
1′) [. . .] URUDU [M]A.NA [x]+47
2′) [. . . U]RUDU.URUDU
(rest destr.)
ii (beg. destr.)
1′) Ù-*Aš-dar* (or *Aš-dar*-Ù)
2′) *Aš-dar*-BALA?
3′) 1(EŠE) 1½ (IKU) GÁN KI
(rest destr.)

Notes

ii 1′–2′.—The sign DAR in both lines is preceded by a short horizontal line which does not quite join the longer horizontal line extending from the back of the bird. If this short horizontal line is not part of the sign DAR, the sign should be read *Aš-dar*. This reading may yield two personal names in these two lines: *Aš-dar*-Ù and BALA?-*Aš-dar*. These two names appear in the Abu Salabikh texts as Ù-*Aš-dar* (*OIP* 99, 506 ii′ 3′) and *Aš-dar*-BALA (*OIP* 99 p. 66 line 146).

No. 18 Figure aux Plumes

Photographs: Plate 32, Louvre Museum, Paris.
Copy: Plate 33, Thureau-Dangin, *DC* 2 p. XXXIV.
Synopsis: Figure 10.
Provenience: Girshu (Telloh)—found (not in situ) in Tell K, identified as a temple of Ningirsu by Parrot, *Tello* pp. 56ff.
Date: ED I–II.
Language: Sumerian.
Present location: Louvre Museum (Paris), AO 221.
Publications: E. de Sarzec, *DC* 1 pp. 164ff. and 414; *idem*, *DC* 2 p. XXXIV (copy by Thureau-Dangin) and pl. 1bis 1 (photograph); L. Heuzey, *Une villa royale chaldéenne* (Paris, 1900) p. 53 (free drawing); *idem*, *RA* 5 (1903) p. 41 (free drawing); *idem*, *Musée National du Louvre, Catalogue des antiquités chaldéennes* (Paris, 1902) pp. 76–79 (free drawing); *Encyclopédie photographique de l'art* 1 (Paris, 1935) p. 175 (photograph of the side with figure); Parrot, *Tello* (Paris, 1948) p. 56; p. 57, fig. f; p. 70; p. 71, fig. a (free drawing); and p. 103, fig. g (free drawing); *idem*, *Sumer, The Dawn of Art* (New York, 1961) fig. 158 A–B (photographs of the side with figure); Moortgat, *Die Kunst des alten Mesopotamien* (Cologne, 1967) p. 33 and figure 30 (photograph of the side with figure); Edzard, *SRU* no. 112.
Description: Rectangular stone tablet measuring 15.7 × 13.4 × 3.5 cm—"Calcaire blanc à patine orangée." The obverse bears the representation of a male(?) figure with a two-plume headdress, holding in his left hand an elongated pole marked by several circular hatchings just below the knob near the top of the pole. Two more such poles are shown to the right.
Text: Langdon, *OECT* 7 p. IV, and Edzard, *SRU* no. 112, proposed—without giving any reason—to reverse the obverse-reverse designation given in the original publication in *DC* 2. Since the side with the figure appears to portray the main actor of the text and should, therefore, be the obverse, and since the older sequence of columns from left to right, as on the side without figure, is mandatory for the obverse, but optional for the reverse, we see no reason for changing the older designation.

If there is anything certain that can be said about this text, it is that we understand nothing about it. Even the earliest texts in this volume, nos. 1–7, for example, yield more information than the Figure aux Plumes. We can no more than guess that the AG.EN.NAM group of signs, which occurs five times on the obverse of this text, stands for a name, and that it is the name of the person who acquired(?) the field that is described on the reverse.

Transliteration

Between the second and third poles:
Obv. 1) AG.EN.NAM ŠÀ.Ú.DU (cf. line 8)
X.TU (cf. line 7) MAŠ.KAG

Between the first pole and the figure:
2) ŠITA KUR.ZA$_x$(LAK-813) GÁL.TI
3) ME.TE.TI.X.DU
4) IGI.ÉŠ.GÍD X.X.DU DA NUN

Behind the figure:
5) NU.GIŠ.KAG NU.GI.KAG
AG.EN.NAM
6) NU.SAG.ḪÚB NU.PA.ḪÚB
AG.EN.NAM
7) ⸢X⸣?.TU (cf. line 1) IGI.⸢X⸣.TU
A[G].EN.NAM
8) ŠÀ.Ú.D[U] (cf. line 1) AG.EN.NAM
Rev. i 1) 4(bùr) gán NI.SUM
2) 1(bùr-*gunû*) SAR.LAK-175
3) 5(bùr) ME.NAM?.⸢X⸣
4) 3(bùr) X.A
5) 3(burʾu) NI.DU$_6$
6) ⸢1(bùr)⸣? BE.SUG
ii 1) ^{d}Nin-Gír-su
2) Gír-su-me (cf. vi 5)
3) NISABA.ḪU.Ú.ME.TAB.É
4) Nin-Gír-su ⸢X.X.X⸣
5) GÁN.GAR (cf. iii 3) SAR.LAK-175
iii 1) TAB.SUD.É.ḪU.ME.NISABA.Ú
2) ^{d}Nin-Gír-su IM/SUD.X.X
3) GÁN.GAR (cf. ii 5) ⸢X.X.ZI⸣?
4) é Nin-G[ír-su]?
iv 1) AG.EN.NAM
2) UD.TU.⸢X.X⸣
3) ⸢X.X⸣.IGI?.É?.TI
4) ⸢X.IGI.GÁL⸣
5) AN.X
v 1) BARAG.É? 1(eše) 5(iku) ⸢IGI.GÁL?⸣
2) ⸢X.X.GÁL⸣
3) 3(bùr)? [. . .]
4) [. . .]
vi 1) NU.⸢X⸣.LAL?.ŠU?.ENGAR
2) ME.KA-zà-me
3) Nin-Gír-su-⸢zà-me⸣
4) EN.SAG?.SIG.X.GÁL
5) [Nin]?-Gír-su-me

Notes

Obv. 1.—The combination of three signs AG.EN.NAM occurs five times on the obverse. The sequence of these signs cannot be ascertained. They may stand for a PN or a PN plus a title or profession. PN Ag is found in the adscription of side B of no. 12. The Sumerian nam-en is Akkadian *bêlūtum* "lordship," and EN.NAM corresponds to *bêl pīḫati* "governor" of much later times.

Obv. 2.—The sign-sequence ŠITA KUR.ZA$_x$(LAK-813) corresponds to ŠITA KUR.ZA(LAK-798) found in the temple hymns from Abu Salabikh (Biggs, *OIP* 99 p. 52 line 226 and commentary on p. 56), and to šita za-gìn "lapis lazuli mace" of later texts (e.g., *SRT* 14:12; *CT* 36, 34:13). For LAK-813 as a graphic variant of LAK-798, see Biggs, *RA* 60 (1966) p. 175 and n. 5.

Obv. 3.—The sign transliterated here as X is a number, as in no. 11 line 13.

Rev. i 1–6.—These lines list six fields, each with measurements of area along with some information as to the quality or location of the land. The three measurements in lines 1, 3, and 4, given in the form of circles, read: 4(bùr), 5(bùr), and 3(bùr), equal to 72 iku, 90 iku, and 54 iku. The measurements in line 5, given in the form of double circles in the drawing, are not clearly recognizable on the photo. As double circles, the measurements should be read as 3(burʾu) or 540 iku.

The measurement in line 2 has the form of a double circle plus *gunû* markings in the copy, but of a single circle plus *gunû* markings in the photo. The former sign is known from the numerical system, where it expresses 216,000; the latter is known from no. 20, where it clearly stands for 1(burʾu). Thus, in accordance with the discussion under no. 20 note to i 1, we must assume that both the *gunû* circle of rev. i 2 and the double circle of rev. i 5 stand for 1(burʾu). The measure in line 6 cannot be identified either in the copy or in the photo.

Rev. i 2, 6, ii 5.—BE.SUG and SAR.LAK-175 occur together in Pettinato, *MEE* 3 p. 163 lines 96–97, an ED lexical text. The reading of LAK-175 is given as ša-ga-um in Pettinato, *MEE* 3 p. 197 line 27. See also Civil in L. Cagni, ed., *Il bilinguismo a Ebla* (Naples, 1984) p. 95.

Rev. ii 1 etc.—In contrast to rev. ii 1 and iii 2, where the divine name Ningirshu is written ^{d}Nin-Gír-su, with the semantic indicator ^{d}, other occurrences in ii 4, iii 4, and vi 3 and 5 either omit the indicator or the indicator is hidden among the signs that are preserved in traces after the name.

Rev. ii 2 and vi 5.—The combination of the signs GÍR.SU.ME and [Nin]?-GÍR.SU.ME may be interpreted as Gír-su-me "they are of Girshu" or Nin-Gír-su-me "they are of Ningirshu." Note the omission of the indicator KI in Gír-su-me, as regularly in the inscriptions of Ur-Nanshe.

Rev. vi 3.—The signs in this case look suspiciously like Nin-Gír-su ⸢zà-me⸣ "praise be to Ningirshu" (cf. Sollberger, *CIRPL* Urn. 49 iii 8–9 and Biggs, *OIP* 99 pp. 45–56), but such a doxology would be unlikely in a text of this nature. The simplest solution may be, therefore, to take this group of signs as a personal name Nin-Gír-su-zà-me, identical with ^{d}Nin-Gír-su-za-me in a Sargonic text, Limet, *Documents* no. 44:7, for which see C. Wilcke *apud* W. Farber, *WO* 8 (1975) p. 122. In the name ME.KA-zà-me in vi 2, there is no way of interpreting ME.KA as a divine name.

No. 19 Lagash Stela

Photographs: Plate 34, from *DC* 2 pl. 1ter 6.
Copy: Plate 35, Thureau-Dangin, *DC* 2 p. XXXV 2 A and B.
Synopsis: Figure 10.
Provenience: Girshu (Telloh)—found in Tell K, identified as a temple of Ningirshu by Parrot, *Tello* pp. 56ff.
Date: ED I–II.
Language: Sumerian(?).
Present location: Louvre Museum (Paris); not found.
Publications: De Sarzec, *DC* 1 p. 414, *DC* 2 p. XXXV 2 A and B (copy by Thureau-Dangin), and Plate 1ter 6 (photograph); Heuzey, *Une villa royale chaldéenne* (Paris, 1900) p. 53 (free drawing); *idem*, *RA* 5 (1903)

p. 41 (free drawing); Parrot, *Tello* (Paris, 1948) p. 56, p. 57 figure c (free drawing), and p. 74.

Description: Fragment of a small stela of gray limestone, measuring 21 cm wide with traces of a human head on the obverse.

Text: Nothing is clearly recognizable on this little fragment but the numbers for the areas of different fields. The occurrence of the grand total on the obverse and of smaller-size fields on the reverse speaks strongly in favor of the obverse-reverse sequence proposed by Thureau-Dangin.

Beginning with the obverse, we can recognize the following signs in the copy: GÁN, GAL, measures of area expressed in two large double circles (preceded by GAL) and a smaller single circle, and the DIN.SILÀ group of signs, which appears as DUG.SILÀ in the total of fields in the very early kudurrus discussed in section 2.2. The reading of this number is 2(sarʾu)-gal 1(bùr). At 1 sarʾu-gal = 36,000 bùr, this total yields 72,001 bùr or 45.73 km^2 or an area of about 6.7 km by about 6.7 km.

The copy of the reverse has a variety of larger double and single circles and once, in ii 3, two smaller circles following upon one larger circle, none of which can be confirmed by the photograph. Since all larger circles are shaded in the copy and one of them appears in the midst of true double circles, we assume that all larger circles, whether clear or not, probably stand for burʾu.

The only other kudurru which has high figures that are comparable to those of the obverse of our text is the reverse of no. 24, which concerns a territory of 24,694 bùr and 13¼ iku or about 15,684 km^2 or an area of about 40 km by 40 km.

The purpose of the present text is unclear. Given the great area of land involved, it is doubtful that it recorded a sale transaction. See the discussion in section 2.5.

Transliteration

Obv.			2(sarʾu)-gal 1(bùr) gán DIN.SILÀ [PN]?
Rev.	i	1)	4(burʾu)? gán ŠÀ.GIBIL
		2)	2(burʾu)? AN.GÁN
		3)	3(burʾu)? ŠÀ nigir-gal
		4)	2(burʾu)? GÍR.ŠÀ
		5)	4(burʾu)? A.[?]
			(rest destr.)
	ii	1)	2(burʾu)? [. . .]
		2)	1(burʾu)? A-⌜x⌝-[. . .]
		3)	1(burʾu)? 2(bùr)? [. . .]
		4)	2(burʾu)? [. . .]
		5)	2(burʾu)? [. . .]
			(rest destr.)

No. 19a DC II p. XXXV 3

Photographs: Plate 34, Istanbul Archaeological Museum.

Copy: Plate 35, Thureau-Dangin, *DC* 2 p. XXXV A and B; collated by Gelb in 1963.

Provenience: Girshu (Telloh).

Date: Pre-Sargonic or earlier.

Language: Sumerian(?).

Present location: Istanbul Archaeological Museum, EŞEM 424.

Publications: De Sarzec, *DC* 2 p. XXXV 3 A and B (copy by Thureau-Dangin), and plate 1ter 5 (photograph of obv. only); Parrot, *Tello* (Paris, 1948) p. 74.

Description: Tablet of black stone ("matière noire")—obverse is flat, reverse rounded. The upper left corner is preserved 7.8 cm high and 11.5 cm wide; as the outer, left corner is 2 cm thick but the inner, right corner is still increasing at 5.3 cm thick, and has thus not yet reached the middle of the tablet, the original width should have been at least twice the preserved.

Text: The obverse has six columns; the reverse is unruled and uninscribed except for one column on the bottom left with a two-line subscription. Though there is no mention of fields or prices, the listing of commodities resembles the listings of commodities given to sellers or officials participating in kudurrus. There are several commodities listed, among them oil (ì, ì-nun), dates (zú-lum), and garments (gada and NÍG.LÁM). Among the recipients(?) of commodities are three occurrences of Gatumdug, the chief goddess of Lagash. The final subscription names Lu-lu sanga ⌜X⌝.GAR/KAG IGI.GAR?, where IGI.GAR? is possibly to be interpreted as gurûm "inspection."

Even though no. 19a is written on stone, the fact that it mentions neither fields nor prices makes it highly unlikely that it deals with a sale transaction. Rather, one thinks of a list of offerings assigned in perpetuity to a temple or temples. For a similar text, compare no. 19b.

Transliteration

Obv.	i	1)	[2 dug] ì
		2)	⌜2⌝? šakan [x]
		3)	[1 NUN.IR].LAL.⌜A⌝
		4)	1 GAM.ERIN?
		5)	1 zú-lum gur
		6)	Bu-pum
		7)	2 dug ì
		8)	[2 šakan] ⌜x⌝
			(rest destr.)
	ii	1)	⌜1⌝ dug ì
		2)	2 šakan X
		3)	1 NUN.IR.LAL.A
		4)	1 zú-lum gur
		5)	⌜è⌝?-a
		6)	É-amar-si
		7)	1 dug ì
		8)	2 šak[an x]
			(rest destr.)
	iii	1)	[. . .]
		2)	[1 GAM.ER]IN?
		3)	1 dug ì-nun
		4)	še DU
		5)	1 zú-lum gur
		6)	1 GAM.ERIN?
		7)	še ^{d}Gá-tùm-dùg kú
		8)	1 dug ì
			(rest destr.)

iv 1) 1 GAM.ERIN?
2) É?/SANGA?-ta
3) ^{d}Gá-tùm-dùg
4) 1 dug ì
5) 4 gada
6) 1 NÍG.LAM
7) 1 AN.SÁR+AŠ
8) TAG_4.ALAM
9) 2 [šak]an X
(rest destr.)
v 1) 1 [dug ì]
2) 6 šak[an x]
3) 1 NUN.IR.LAL.A
4) 1 GAM.ERIN?
5) 1 zú-lum gur
6) ŠE.BAR.GI_4.TA
7) ^{d}Gá-tùm-dùg
8) 2 [dug ì]
(rest destr.)
vi 1) [. . .]
2) [. . .]
3) [. . .]
4) gal [. . .]
5) gal [. . .]
6) 10 [. . .]
7) 1 du[g ì]-nu[n]
8) 1 [. . .]
(rest destr.)
Rev. i 1) Lu-lu sanga ⸢X⸣.GAR/KAG
2) IGI.GAR?
(rest blank)

Notes

ii 2 and *passim*.—The sign read here as X looks like a ligature of KAG and NI.

iv 8.—For TAG_4.ALAM "statue," also an occupation ("statue-maker?"), see most recently Pettinato, *MEE* 3 p. 42 n. to line 20.

v 6.—Possibly to be interpreted as še bar-ta gi_4 "grain/food returned from the outside." Compare še DU "assigned/deposited (gub?) grain" in iii 4 and še ^{d}Gá-tùm-dùg kú "grain consumed by Gatumdug" in iii 7.

No. 19b Cros, NFT p. 222

Photograph: Plate 34, Louvre Museum, Paris.
Copy: Plate 35, Thureau-Dangin in G. Cros, *NFT* p. 222.
Provenience: Girshu (Telloh).
Date: Pre-Sargonic or earlier.
Language: Sumerian(?).
Present location: Louvre Museum (Paris), AO 4397.
Publication: Cros, *NFT* p. 222 (copy by Thureau-Dangin); Edzard, *SRU* no. 116; Civil, *N.A.B.U.* 1989/3 pp. 39f.
Description: Fragment of a black stone slab measuring 8 × 9.3 × 2.3 cm (all maximum measurements). The inscribed part is flat, the reverse is completely effaced. All sides are destroyed with the exception of the right side.
Text: The preserved portion of the inscription lists commodities and personal names, but no fields. For a similar text, compare 19a. Certain commodities are preceded by numbers or measures, others are preceded by an empty space. Some of the lines with signs which do not express commodities and which were drawn without an empty space at the beginning of the line may be taken as expressing personal names, such as GÚ.GIŠ or MÁ?.LI, even though we cannot find any parallels.

Transliteration

i′ (beg. destr.)
1′) [x] SUM.[X].KI
2′) [20]+30 SUM.[T]I.KI
3′) 30 ga dug
4′) [x] gará
(rest destr.)
ii′ (beg. destr.)
1′) ⟨x⟩ ÉŠ MÁ?
2′) 30 GI.GIŠ.INNIN
3′) 30 X
4′) GÚ.GIŠ
5′) ⟨x⟩ ÉŠ MÁ?.GÍD
6′) ⟨x⟩ GIŠ.LAL.LU
7′) ⟨x⟩ ÉŠ
8′) [x]-mar-[. . .]
(rest destr.)
iii′ (beg. destr.)
1′) ⟨x⟩ ⸢x⸣
2′) ⟨x⟩ dug še
3′) 30 ninda
4′) MÁ?.LI
5′) ⟨x⟩ dug
6′) ⟨x⟩ ninda
7′) ⟨x⟩ udu
8′) ⟨x⟩ dug geštin
9′) MÁ?.GUR_8 GÚ
10′) 1 dug [. . .]
(rest destr.)
(col. iv and rest blank)

Notes

ii′ 1′, ii′ 5′, iii′ 4′ and 9′.—The reading of the sign transliterated here as MÁ? in ⟨x⟩ ÉŠ MÁ.GÍD, MÁ?.LI, and MÁ?.GUR_8 GÚ cannot be safely established, since the form of the sign MÁ can be easily confused with the forms of the signs SI and GUR. See note to no. 20 i 3. For ÉŠ MÁ?.GÍD, compare éš má-gíd cited in A. Salonen, *Die Wasserfahrzeuge in Babylonien* (Helsinki, 1939) p. 118.

No. 20 Enḫegal Tablet

Photographs: Plate 36, University Museum, University of Pennsylvania, negative nos. 56142, 56143, 6548.
Copy: Plate 37, Barton, *PBS* 9 plates II and III; collated by Gelb.
Synopsis: Plates 93 and 94.
Provenience: Unknown (purchased, allegedly from Telloh/Girshu).
Date: Fara.
Language: Sumerian.
Present location: University Museum, University of Pennsylvania (Philadelphia), CBS 10000.

Publications: Barton, *PBS* 9 (1915) pp. 11–16 no. 2, and pls. LXVIf. (copy and photographs); *idem*, "The Tablet of Enkhegal," *MJ* 4 (1913) pp. 50–54 (photograph). Compare also Hilprecht *ZA* 11 (1896) pp. 330f; Barton, *AJA* 17 (1913) pp. 84f.; Deimel, *Or.* 9 (1924) pp. 282f.; Diakonoff, "Sale of Land in Pre-Sargonic Sumer," *Papers Presented by the Soviet Delegation at the XXIII International Congress of Orientalists* (Moscow, 1954) pp. 22ff.; *idem*, *VDI* 1954/4 pp. 15ff.; *idem*, *Obščestvenny i gosudarstvenny stroy Drevnego Dvurečya. Šumer* (Moscow, 1959) pp. 47–51; Edzard, *SRU* no. 114; Bauer, *ZA* 61 (1971) pp. 323f.

Description: A square stone tablet of light-buff limestone, measuring 12.4 × 12.8 × 3.8. Obverse flat, reverse rounded.

Text: The inscription consists of seven columns on the obverse, with some signs extending to the lower edge, and of two columns on the reverse. The sequence of the two columns of the reverse cannot be ascertained; however, this is immaterial for the context since each column consists of a self-contained unit. The five preserved signs appearing on the lower edge were incised with much thinner lines than the signs in the main part of the inscription.

As here provisionally interpreted, the inscription deals with eight acquisitions of eleven parcels of land by Lugal-kigala from Enḫegal, the king of Lagash, and a certain Sidu.

The Enḫegal Tablet is very well preserved, but the reading of many signs is difficult due to sloppy execution.

For over seventy years now, the Enḫegal Tablet has been challenging the interpretational skills of scholars. For the widely diverging views of its meaning and purpose, compare Diakonoff, *op. cit.* and Edzard, *op. cit.* Unfortunately, we too have failed to arrive at a fully satisfactory explanation of this inscription.

The crux of the inscription is the role of Enḫegal, king of Lagash, in the transaction and, with it, the question of the buyer and sellers. In all normal circumstances, we would expect Enḫegal to be the buyer of the fields. As a general rule, it is the rich and powerful who acquire landed property in third millennium sources. Still, two points can be raised against this assumption.

In three instances, Enḫegal's name and title are followed by the sign ÉŠ (i 6, ii 9, iv 10; lacking in iii 5), which should probably be interpreted as the terminative postposition -šè. Assuming that the phrase En-ḫé-gál lugal Lagaš-šè stands for the construction x (Buyer-e) Seller-šè e-šè-šám "(Buyer) bought x from Seller," which is frequent in the Pre-Sargonic kudurrus and sale documents from Lagash (see section 6.3), Enḫegal would have to be interpreted as a seller. On the other hand, one notes the absence of ÉŠ following the name and title of Sidu, who, as argued below, should too be considered a seller.

The term lugal, occurring after Sidu's name in five(?) transactions (ii 3, 10, v 12?, vi 6, 10?), appears to be the same as lugal gán "owner of the field," and must therefore denote a seller.

If neither Enḫegal nor Sidu can be the buyer, we must look for him elsewhere in the inscription. The most plausible candidate for this role is Lugal-ki-gal-la išib ^{d}Nin-Gír-su "Lugal-kigala, the išib priest of Ningirshu," in rev. ii 1–2. In the following line, one finds the signs GÁN GAR, where GAR is possibly a defective spelling of kú, i.e., KA+GAR (cf. Edzard, *SRU* p. 178). If so, this line could be translated "(Lugal-kigala) received (lit.: consumed) the fields."

Returning to the question of the sellers, we can tentatively identify them as Enḫegal and Sidu. Enḫegal appears in three transactions, Sidu in certainly three and possibly five transactions, and both Enḫegal and Sidu occur in one transaction.

In addition, in several transactions there appear other persons, with or without titles. The titled individuals are ŠEŠ.IB-geštin engar "farmer" (v 3–4, 10), Lugal-nim-du sag-du$_5$ "field recorder" (iii 8, v 11), Maš GU.SUR.NUN "field assessor" (iii 9, v 9), and Maš engar "farmer" (vii 4, 7), the last two possibly being one and the same person. Since the engar, sag-du$_5$, and GU.SUR.NUN routinely occur as authorizing/witnessing officials in the later kudurrus and sale documents (see section 7.11), we may assume that their presence in the Enḫegal Tablet is to be explained in the same way. The role of the untitled persons (Lugal-ki in iv 5, Lugal-kur-geštin?^{KI} in iv 6, Bar-sag?-šag$_5$ in iv 7, and É-muš-si? in vii 5) is unclear.

All eight transactions show basically the same pattern (the order of component parts varies):

1) Size of the field
2) Price (in copper, barley, emmer, goats, and pigs)
3) Location/name of the field
4) Names of the authorizing/witnessing officials
5) Name of the seller(?)

Following the last transaction, one finds the statement gán BUR.⌜ŠIR.LA⌝ šá[m] "the purchased fields in/of Lagash," plus the totals of the fields and prices paid. Contrary to Barton's copy, the reading 1(sár) + 1(sár) + 1(bùr-*gunû*) + 1(bùr-*gunû*) + 1(bùr-*gunû*), that is 150 bùr, is clear on the stone, as it is on the photograph. In order to obtain that total, we were forced to reconstruct [9(bùr) gán . . .] in vi 11. The totals of prices agree with the prices given in individual transactions, with the following qualifications: the 21½ še gur "21½ bushels of grain" of the total corresponds to the sum of 20½ še gur "20½ bushels of barley" and 1 zíz gur "1 bushel of emmer" of the individual transactions; for reasons unknown, the eleven pigs paid in the price of one field (iii 3) have been omitted in the totals. The items given in lieu of the prices are labeled as šám gán "price of the fields."

The line with the name of Lugal-kigala and the signs GÁN GAR (see above) then follows. And finally, on the lower edge there is scratched the name Lugal-šùd(SAG+ŠU)-dè plus a few illegible signs. This line does not seem to form an intrinsic part of the inscription; it may have been added later. Several points indicate that we are dealing here with a later addition. Unlike the rest of the inscription, the signs are not written in cases, but in a long continuous line which runs from the left to the right side of the stone. The signs are not carved in, but superficially scratched on the surface. The line is placed below the obverse, not at the end of the reverse, where it would properly belong if it were part of the text. Possibly, the person mentioned in this line is identical with Lugal-šùd-dè dub-sar-maḫ "chief scribe," who appears in *CT* 50, 44 vi 2–3, a Lagash economic tablet dating to the reign of Urukagina.

Transliteration

Obv. i 1) ⸢2⸣(bùr-*gunû*) 3(bùr) gán
2) 720 urudu ma-na
3) 2 še gur
4) 1 zíz gur
5) gán ⸢DU⸣?
6) [En-ḫé-gál] ⸢lugal⸣ Lagaš-šè

---

7) 7(bùr) gán
8) ⸢180⸣ urudu [ma-n]a
ii 1) 20 Ur-ú
2) 2 še gur
3) Si-dù lugal
4) gán ganun(GÁ+NUN)-dù

---

5) 1(bùr-*gunû*) 1(bùr) gán ki
6) 300 urudu ma-na
7) 2½ še gur
8) gán Ú.PAD.ME
9) En-ḫé-gál lugal Lagaš-šè
10) Si-dù lugal

---

iii 1) 8(bùr) gán
2) 20 BAL+U
3) 11 šáḫ-niga
4) 1½ še gur
5) En-ḫé-gál lugal
6) E+PAB.KAS^{KI}
7) LAL?.KI
8) Lugal-nim-du sag-du$_5$
9) Maš GU.SUR.NUN

---

10) 3(bùr-*gunû*) lal 2(bùr) gán
11) 720! urudu ma-na
iv 1) 4 še gur
2) 2(bùr-*gunû*) lal 1(bùr) gán
3) 420 urudu ma-na
4) 1½ še gur
5) 40 Lugal-ki
6) 30 Lugal-kur-geštin?^{KI}
7) Bar-sag?-šag$_5$
8) Gú-KALAM?
9) En-ḫé-gál
10) lugal Lagaš-šè

---

11) 1(bùr-*gunû*) 4(bùr) gán
12) 720 urudu ma-na
v 1) 2 še gur
2) Bàd-giš-gi$_4$
3) ŠEŠ+IB-geštin
4) engar!
5) 1(bùr-*gunû*) gán
6) 200 urudu ma-na
7) 2 še gur
8) gán A.UŠ
9) Maš GU.SUR.NUN
10) ŠEŠ+IB-geštin engar
11) Lugal-nim-du sag-du$_5$
12) [Si]?-dù? [lu]gal?

---

vi 1) 8(bùr) gán
2) 3 še gur
3) gán A+X-a-X-è?/sag?
4) Innin-sar engar
5) Maš GU.SUR.NUN
6) Si-dù lugal

---

7) 3(bùr) gán níg-è
8) gán gud
9) 80 urudu [ma-na]
10) [Si-dù lugal]?
11) [9(bùr) gán. . .]?
vii 1) 1(bùr-*gunû*) gá[n]
2) A.Ḫ[A. . .]
3) 360 urudu ma-na
4) Maš engar
5) 30 É-muš-si?
6) 120 urudu ma-na
7) Maš engar

---

8) gán BUR.⸢ŠIR.LA⸣ šá[m]

Rev. i 1) GÚ.AN.ŠÈ
2) 2(šár) 3(bùr-*gunû*) gán
3) 3820 urudu ma-na
4) 21½ še gur
5) 20 BAL+U
6) gán šám

---

ii 1) Lugal-ki-gal-la
2) išib ^{d}Nin-Gír-su
3) GÁN.GAR

Lo. E. 1) Lugal-šùd(SAG+ŠU)-dè BA/IGI.NU [. . .]

Notes

i 1.—In the present text bùr-*gunû* stands for 10 bùr and thereby corresponds in form to what is known as bur᾽u = 10 bùr. The archaic texts regularly use the bur᾽u form, that is a small circle inscribed within a larger circle, as best shown by the total in no. 1, and, without the total, in other archaic texts of the same type. The Jemdet Nasr texts also regularly use the bur᾽u form for 10 bùr, as pointed out by Langdon, *OECT* 7 pp. 66f. no. 461. The change from bur᾽u to bùr-*gunû* is first attested in the Early Dynastic I–II periods, as can be seen from the discussion under no. 18, note to rev. i 1–6, and both are still found in Fara texts, as can be seen from the interchange of the two forms in *Fara* 3, 53 end and 55 end to indicate the same total (cf. Langdon, *op. cit.*). Apparently, the change was made because of the difficulty of incising the smaller circle within the larger circle, especially on stone where the danger of damage in the inner or outer circle could easily result in a confusion between bùr and burʾu. On the other hand, increasing the size of the outer circle to accommodate an inner circle could result in a confusion with sár and sarʾu. For such possibilities, compare nos. 12 and 18.

i 2.—Against Barton's copy, the text reads 600+120 urudu ma-na, as clearly visible in the photograph.

i 3, 4 and *passim*.—The sign read here as GUR has the same form as SI (in Si-dù in ii 3 and *passim*). For similar cases, see Cros, *NFT* p. 222 ii 1 and *OIP* 99, 492 i 2′ as compared with *OIP* 99, 491 i 2.

i 5.—There is only one sign, partly preserved, after gán. The reading ⌜DU⌝ is preferable to ⌜URU⌝.

ii 3, 10, and vi 6.—Despite the consistency of the spelling KAG.SI, this PN must be interpreted as Si-dù because of the many occurrences of Si-dù in the Sargonic texts from Lagash (e.g., Donbaz-Foster, *STTI* 62:4).

ii 7, iii 4, iv 4, and rev. i 4.—The sign ⊽ is used for ½ gur(-maḫ) in the Fara texts, as pointed out by Deimel, *Or.* 9 pp. 190f., and as can be seen from calculation in *Fara* 3, 61. As the totals show, the sign in question is used for ½ gur in our text. Since the measure occurs only with the gur-maḫ (which had 8 ul) in Fara texts, it is possible that the gur of our text is also the gur-maḫ. The measure gur-maḫ is often written simply gur in the Abu Salabikh texts, as in *OIP* 99, 494, 495, and 503.

ii 8.—Edzard, *SRU* p. 177, reads the toponym as ú-gudá, i.e., ú-UḪ.ME. However, the second sign is clearly PAD and not UḪ.

iii 2 and rev. i 5.—The sign symbolized here as BAL+U is LAK-20. It is frequent in Fara texts, where it denotes a type of animal. See, e.g., *TSŠ* 453, 536, and 548, which list BAL+U together with udu-nita. In another Fara text (*Fara* 3, 126), one finds a total of 15 udu-nita and 23 BAL+U described as udu. In the Sargonic period, *HSS* 10, 171 lists sila$_4$, udu-kur, BAL+U (or MÁŠ+U), ùz, and udu, all identified in the total as udu "sheep." For variants of the sign form, see also *HSS* 10, 178:4 and 180:5′. The same animal also appears in *MDP* 14, 27 together with udu. For the identification of BAL+U as "male goat," see Steinkeller, *Third Millennium Legal and Administrative Texts in the Iraq Museum, Baghdad* (forthcoming). Compare also Pomponio, *RA* 80 (1986) pp. 187f., who translates it "she-goat."

iii 9, v 9, and vi 5.—The occupation GU.SUR.NUN, "field assessor" or the like, was the subject of an exhaustive study by W. Farber, *AOr* 45 (1977) pp. 148–56. The following observations may be added to it. The alternative spelling GAR.GU.SUR(.NUN) (with SUR being occasionally replaced by NUN), which is attested at Fara (for examples, see Farber, *op. cit.* pp. 148f.), Abu Salabikh (GAR. GU.SUR(.NUN) in ED Names and Professions List line 27, replaced by GAR.GU.GAR in the Ebla ms.—Archi, *SEb* 4 [1981] p. 181), and Nippur (*TMH* 5, 164 i 3, 168 i 4), is to be interpreted as níg-GU.SUR(.NUN), as is demonstrated by the lexical entry NÍG.GU. SUR = *ne-gú-su-ru*$_{12}$*-um* in Pettinato, *MEE* 4 p. 365 line 0254. Compare also SUR.TÚG = *ne-gú-su-ru*$_{12}$*-um*, *su-ra-um*, *gú-zi-ru*$_{12}$*-um* (*ibid.* p. 216 line 165), where the relationship between SUR.TÚG and NÍG.GU.SUR is unclear. It appears, therefore, that the occupation in question had originally two forms, GU.SUR(.NUN) and níg-GU.SUR(.NUN). As is shown by the fact that the same occupation is later written gu-sur (for examples, see Farber *op. cit.*, pp. 150ff.), in the combination GU.SUR.NUN the sign NUN is either a logogram, to be read gusur$_x$, or a phonetic indicator, to be read either gu$_x$ or sur$_x$. Given that neither the reading gusur$_x$ nor gu$_x$ nor sur$_x$ of NUN finds corroboration in the outside evidence, this question cannot be resolved at this time.

iv 6.—The reading of the sign GEŠTIN? in the PN Lugal-kur-geštin?[KI] is based on the comparison with GEŠTIN in v 10, whose reading, in turn, is assured by v 3.

v 3 and 10.—For the name ŠES+IB-geštin, see *UET* 2, 81A i 1. The element ŠEŠ+IB frequently occurs in the archaic texts from Ur (Burrows, *UET* 2 pl. 2 no. 13). See also Sollberger, *CIRPL* Urn. 49 iii 4, É-ŠEŠ+IB[KI] at Abu Salabikh (*OIP* 99, p. 73 line 99), and two Ebla lexical entries where IB.ŠEŠ plus other signs is identified with *gamārum* "to please," "to save," and *raʾāmum* "to love" (Pettinato, *MEE* 4 p. 225 lines 236–237; cf. Krebernik, *ZA* 73 [1983] p. 11).

v 8.—With the FN gán A.UŠ compare [gán]? A.UŠ [. . .] in no. 21 v 14 and gán A.UŠ.TA in *DP* 352, 353, 354, etc. (all discussed by Deimel, *Or.* 5, pp. 37ff.).

No. 21 Lupad Statue

Photographs: Plate 38, Louvre Museum, Paris.

Copy: Plate 39, Thureau-Dangin, *DC* 2 pp. LIVf.

Provenience: Girshu (Telloh). Found in the "tell des tablettes," see *DC* 1 p. 448.

Date: Fara.

Language: Sumerian.

Present location: Louvre Museum (Paris), AO 3279–3280, 4494.

Publications: De Sarzec, *DC* 2 pp. LIVf. (copy by Thureau-Dangin), and pls. 6ter 1 a+b and pl. 47,2 (photographs); Heuzey, *CRAI* 1907 pp. 769–71 (photograph) and a note by Thureau-Dangin, *ibid.*, p. 772; Thureau-Dangin, *CRAI* 1908 pl. opp. p. 205 (copy); P. Toscanne, *RT* 30 (1908) pp. 123–25; *idem*, *RA* 7 (1910) p. 57; King, *A History of Sumer and Akkad* (London, 1916) p. 96 (drawing showing position of inscription on the statue); Parrot, *Tello* (Paris, 1948) p. 78 and p. 79 fig. a (free drawing); Diakonoff, *Obščestvenny i gosudarstvenny stroy Drevnego Dvurečya. Šumer* (Moscow, 1959) pp. 60ff.; G. Garbini, *Le origini della statuaria sumerica* (Rome, 1962) pl. XXII (photograph); Edzard, *SRU* no. 115.

Description: Statue of dark-gray diorite measuring about 42 × 30 × 20 cm.

Text: In spite of certain difficulties, we follow here the sequence of columns and lines as proposed by Thureau-Dangin. The inscription begins with the name of Lú-pàd, written in line one of column i on the right shoulder (= obverse), and continues, after a long break, with the five-line fragment mentioning zag É-ti on the back (= reverse). This fragment continues on the left arm and across the chest of the statue. In normal circumstances the beginnings of column ii and the following columns should be aligned with the beginning of column i. This is impossible, as shown clearly by the preserved portions of column iii. The relationship of the two fragments of columns iv–vi to the rest of the inscription cannot be established. In addition, there is a small unnumbered and an unattached fragment, 3 × 4 cm, in the Louvre Museum, on which a few signs can be read, such as bi/kaš, engar, and 5 síg [ma-na].

It is exceedingly difficult to reconstruct the sequence of the formulary of the Lupad Statue, partly because its individual parts appear to be unequal in length, partly because of the poor state of preservation of the inscription. For these reasons, the following reconstruction must be considered very tentative.

Lines i 1–7, reading "Lupad, the field recorder of Umma, the son of Nadu, the field recorder, the father(?) of [. . .]-⌜x⌝," plus a few lines now destroyed, probably gave the total area acquired by Lupad and constituted a general résumé prefacing the rest of the inscription. For a possible parallel, compare the introductory lines on side A of no. 40.

The acquisition of the first group of fields begins around i 11 and should end around ii 12. As tentatively reconstructed, it consists of the following parts:

1) Size and location of the individual parcels, as indicated by the structure: x field located at the side (zag) of PN (i 11–39)
2) Lupad, the field recorder of Umma, bought [a total of x iku of land from P]N (ii 1–6)
3) Price paid in še "barley," síg "wool," and níg-urudu-babbar "'white' . . . copper" (ii 7–8)
4) [Additional Payment] (ii 9–12)

The acquisition of the second group of fields begins around ii 13 and should end around iii 12. It consists of the following parts:

1) [Size and location of the individual parcels] (ii 13–24)
2) [Lupad bought a total of x land from PN$_2$] (ii 25–28)
3) [Price] (ii 29–30)
4) Additional Payment, including commodities in various amounts, paid to the main seller, and five pounds of wool each to the secondary sellers and officials (ii 31– iii 8)

The acquisition of the third group of fields should begin around iii 13, but it is too much destroyed to allow any safe reconstruction. The rest yields fragmentary information.

In summary, the inscription deals with the acquisition of at least three groups of fields by Lupad, the field recorder of Umma, the son of Nadu, who was also a field recorder, presumably also at Umma.

Transliteration

i 1) Lú-pàd
2) sag-du$_5$
3) Umma^{KI}
4) dumu Na-dù
5) sag-du$_5$
6) [a]d-da
7) [. . .]-⌈x⌉
8–17) [. . .]
18) [x(iku)] ⌈. . .⌉
19) zag É-ti
20) 1(bùr) 3+[x]?(iku)
21) zag É-NI
22) 1(bùr) 3(iku) da lu[gal]
23) [zag . . .]-⌈x⌉
24) [x(iku) . . .]
25) [zag . . .]
26) 1(eše) [. . .]
27) zag [. . .]
28) 1(eše) [. . .]
29) zag [. . .]
30) 1(eše) [. . .]-gal-[. . .]
31) zag A-geštin simug
32) 3(bùr) LÁL.È
33) zag Amar-tùr
34) 1(bùr) 4(iku) UŠ-gal
35) zag Ur-PA ašgab?
36) É-ní-nu-DU
37) zag Dug$_4$-ga-ni
38) TE.GAL
39) UŠ-gal

ii 1) [šu-nigín x(iku) gán]
2) [. . .]-⌈GÍN?-zi?⌉-[šè]?
3) Lú-pàd
4) sag-du$_5$
5) Umma^{KI}
6) e-šè-šám

---

7) 15 še gur-sag-gál 10 lal 1 síg ma-na
8) 6? níg-urudu-babbar ma-na
9) [x]-bi 3? [. . .] SAG? [. . .] NE
10–18) [. . .]
19) 2+[x(iku) . . .]
20) zag [. . .] AN [. . .]
21) 4(bùr) [. . .]
22–29) [. . .]
30) [níg]-šám-bi
31) 20 síg ma-na
32) 10 še? gur-sag-gál
33) 3 TÚG.SU.A
34) 1 níg-lal-sag
35) 1 túg [. . .]
36–37) [. . .]
38) 10 [. . .]
39–40) [. . .]

iii 1) [. . .]
2) [5] síg ma-na Di-Utu
3) ^{d}Nanše-nu-me-a
4) 5 síg ma-na Dingir-pa-è
5) dub-sar
6) 5 síg ma-na Lagaš^{KI}
7) nigir
8) 5 síg m[a-na] Lugal-Giríd$^{K[I]}$
9) ud ì zag [. . .] KAG [. . .]
10) KA-[. . .] ki [. . .]
11–29) [. . .]
30) [a-šà ḪU.TUŠ.BU]-rú[m](NE.⌈RU⌉)
31) ZI/GI-[. . .]
32) 5 síg ma-na
33) Amar-^{d}Samàn(NUN.ŠE.ÉŠ.BU)
34) dub-sar
35) 5 síg ma-na DUN-tur
36–39) [. . .]

iv (beg. destr.)
1′) [. . .-S]AR?
2′) [níg-š]ám-bi
3′) [. . .] ⌈x⌉
(rest destr.)

v (beg. destr.)
1′) [a-šà] ḪU.TUŠ.BU-rúm
2′) É-[x]-DUN-⌈GÍN⌉?-[z]i
3′) [a-šà?] E-ga-rin

4′) zag Amar-tùr
5′) ⌜a⌝-šà ḪU.TUŠ.BU-rúm
6′) 4(bùr) [. . .]
7′–12′) [. . .]
13′) [. . .] sag [. . .]-šè
14′) [gán]? A.UŠ [. . .] KI?
(rest destr.)
vi (beg. destr.)
1′) lú-[. . .] ⌜gal⌝? [. . .]
2′–4′) [. . .]
5′) 5 ma-[na] Pab-⌜x⌝-[. . .]
6′) 5 síg m[a-na] Lugal-[é]?-mes-[lam]?
7′) 5 síg [ma-na] Nagar?-[. . .]
8′–10′) [. . .]
11′) [G]IŠ?ka[g? . . .]
12′) [x] TÚG [. . .] GIŠ.BIL Á [. . .]
13′) l[ú . . .]
(rest destr., only traces)

Notes

i 31.—For the PN A-geštin, see *UET* 2, 2 and *TMH* 5, 159 ix 15 and compare also ŠEŠ+IB-geštin in no. 20 v 3 and 10, and Pab-geštin in no. 14 vii 8.

i 38.—The occupation or profession read here as TE.GAL can stand for GAL.TE (Sumerian tiru, Akkadian *tīrum*), which denotes some kind of service personnel. It could also stand for galla(TE.LAL)-gal, a type of official, possibly a policeman.

ii 2.—For the name of the seller, cf. v 2′.

iii 9.—Possibly to be reconstructed ud ì zag [(bi-)ag] kag [é-gar$_8$ (bi-)dù] "at that time oil [was spread] on the side (and) the nail [was driven into the wall]." For this clause, found *passim* in the Pre-Sargonic kudurrus and sale documents from Lagash, see sections 7.12.5.1 and 7.12.5.2.

iii 30.—For this toponym, also in v 1 and 5, compare GIŠtir gán ḪU.TUŠ.BU-rúm-ma-kam (*DP* 446 v 1) and other occurrences in Lagash texts.

iii 33.—For the reading of the DN, note the personal name spelled Ur-dŠE.ÉŠ.NUN.BU on the seals of the Ur III documents *MVNS* 3, 361 and Grégoire, *AAS* 112, and Ur-dŠagan-na, in the respective texts.

v 2′.—This line possibly records the name of the seller mentioned in ii 2 ([. . .]-⌜GÍN?-zi?⌝).

v 3′.—For the GN E-ga-rin, compare the occurrences listed in *MAD* 2^2 p. 213 additions to p. 109 no. 280.

v 14′.—For the field gán A.UŠ, see note to no. 20 v 8.

No. 22 Lummatur Tablet I

Photographs: Plates 40 and 41, courtesy Westenholz.
Copy: Plates 40 and 41, Thureau-Dangin, *DC* 2 p. XLIX (obverse and reverse are exchanged here).
Synopsis: Plates 95, 96, and 100.
Provenience: Girshu (Telloh).
Date: Pre-Sargonic.
Language: Sumerian.
Present location: Istanbul Museum, EŞEM 1600.
Publications: De Sarzec, *DC* 2, p. XLI (copy by Thureau-Dangin). Compare also Diakonoff, "Sale of Land in Pre-Sargonic Sumer," *Papers Presented by the Soviet Delegation at the XXIII International Congress of Orientalists* (Moscow, 1954) pp. 25ff.; *idem*, *Obščestvenny i gosudarstvenny stroy Drevnego Dvurečya. Šumer* (Moscow, 1959) pp. 62–67; M. Lambert, *AOr* 23 (1955) pp. 558–61; Edzard, *SRU* no. 117.
Description: Black stone tablet measuring 32.5 × 23 cm (maximum). Thickness varies from 3 to 8.6 cm, increasing from left to right and from top to bottom. One side is flat, the other rounded. The roundness is clear on top, bottom, left side; the right side is cut off roughly.
Text: The sequence of obverse-reverse given in *DC* 2 p. XLIX is certainly wrong, as is the suggestion of Thureau-Dangin, *SAKI* p. 30 d) n. 1, proposing to reverse the obverse-reverse order of *DC* 2 p. XLIX. The context shows quite clearly that the sequence of each column runs from the obverse (the old reverse of *DC* 2 p. XLIX) to the lower edge, to the reverse, to the upper edge, and so on for other columns to the end. This is also the order found in no. 23. Gelb reconstructed this sequence of Lummatur I, as did Diakonoff and Edzard, long before he had a chance to inspect the stone tablet in the Istanbul Museum and to note that one side of it is flat and the other rounded, confirming the new reconstruction. Lambert, *op. cit.*, gives a transliteration and translation of the text following the old order of *DC* 2 p. XLIX. Except for the reconstruction of broken sections, the sequence, followed by Edzard, *SRU* no. 117, corresponds to ours.

The inscription consists of four columns of writing. To the right of the four inscribed columns the stone is uninscribed, although there are definite traces of a vertical ruling on both the obverse and the reverse, which must have been drawn in anticipation of a fifth column of writing, never written. For a similar case compare no. 36 under *Text*.

Apparently neither the stone tablet nor the inscription were completed. That the tablet is unfinished can be seen from the fact that the right side of the stone was not adjusted to the intended rectangular form but left rough. That the inscription is unfinished can be deduced from the fact that the expected list of witnesses is not given in the preserved parts of the inscription and may have been intended, therefore, for the fifth column. It may very well be that the irregular form of the tablet, rising abnormally in thickness from top to bottom and from left to right, as well as some space difficulties on the right side of the tablet, induced the ancient scribe to abandon his work before its completion and to try to erase the whole inscription. He succeeded rather well—to our detriment—in erasing the major part of the obverse. The reverse, upper and lower edges, show some traces of erasure.

The text deals with the acquisition of four parcels of land by Lummatur, son of Enanatum, the governor of Lagash, from different families. Three of the parcels are 9¼ iku in size, while the fourth measures 29¼ iku. For Lummatur, son of Enanatum I, compare Sollberger, *CIRPL* En. I 10.

We thank Dr. Sollberger for the collations of the text he kindly provided to us.

No. 22 is related to no. 23 and to the clay tablet here published as App. to nos. 22–23 by identical structure and the fact that all of them deal with the land acquired by Lummatur son of Enanatum, the governor of Lagash. In addition, the following individuals recur in two or three of these sources:

Ur-^{d}Dumu-zi-da, father of two "sons of the field" in no. 22 iv 54, may correspond to Ur-^{d}Dumu-zi-da, father of the "lord of the field" in no. 23 obv. vii 8.

Inim-ma-ni-zi, a "lord of the field" in no. 22 iv 43, may correspond to [In]im-ma-⸢ni⸣-zi, the "lord of the field" in no. 23 obv. ix 8.

[Lu]gal-šà-pàd, a "son of the field" and son of É-me-nam-nun, a "lord of the field" in no. 22 ii 36, may correspond to Lugal-šà-pàd-da, a "lord of the field" and a "son" of É-ib-zi in App. to nos. 22–23 iii 9. Accordingly, Lugal-šà-pàd-da may not be a son of É-ib-zi, but his grandson or descendent.

The same two men, Lugal-ḫé-gál-sir, the chief scribe, and É-nam-zu-šè, the chief of the servants of the "Inner-quarters," are named among the witnesses in no. 23 obv. x 3–7 and App. to nos. 22–23 v 8–vi 2.

For the commodities included in the additional payment in nos. 22, 23, and App. to nos. 22–23, see chapter 11.

Sample Interpretation

i 1–10: Lummatur, son of Enanatum, the governor of Lagash, bought 9¼ iku of land, (measured?) by the "purchase rope," from PN_1 and PN_2 sons of PN_x, the "lords of the field" (= primary sellers).

i 11–12: The rate is 1 iku of land at 2 gursaggal of barley.

i 13–30: PN_1 (= first primary seller) received 18½ gursaggal of barley as the price of the field and x commodities as the gift.

i 31–56: PN_2, the "lord of the field" (= second primary seller), and PN_3, PN_4, PN_5, PN_6, (4) sons of PN_1 (= first primary seller), and PN_7, PN_8, PN_9, PN_{10}, PN_{11}, PN_{12}, PN_{13}, (7) children of PN_2 (= second primary seller), the "sons of the field," received x commodities per person as the gift.

i 57–59: PN_1 (= first primary seller) drove this nail into the wall and spread the oil on the side.

Transliteration and Translation

Obv. i	1)	[1(eše) 3¼ (iku) gán éš šám-ma-ta]	[9¼ iku of land, (measured?) by the "purchase-rope"],
	2)	[X-pirig] (= i 57)	[from PN_1]
	3)	[X-x] (= i 46)	[(and) PN_2]
	4)	[dumu PN_x-me]	[sons of PN_x],
	5)	[lugal gán-š]è!	[the "lords of the field"],
	6)	Lum-ma-tur	L.
	7)	dumu En-an-na-túm	son of E.,
	8)	en$_5$-si	the governor of
	9)	Lagaš^{KI}-ka-ke$_4$	Lagash,
	10)	⸢e-ne⸣-šè-⸢šám⸣	⸢bought⸣.
	11)	iku 1-a!	Of 1 iku of land
	12)	še 2 gur-sag-gál-ta	(its) barley (equivalent) is 2. gsg;
	13)	še-bi 20 lal 1(gur) 2(ul) gur-sag-gál	the (corresponding) 18.2. gsg of barley,
	14)	níg-šám gán-kam	the price of the field,
	15)	šu-ba-ti	(the sellers) received.
	16)	5 síg-bar-udu-bar	Commodities
	17)	1 [ì] šakan	
	18)	1 ⸢ninda⸣-sag	
	19)	1 ŠU.KEŠDA	
	20)	40 ninda-še	
	21)	10 ninda-kalag	
	22)	40 ku$_6$-dar-ra	
	23)	10 tu$_7$ silà	
	24)	[1] sa [ga-raš]^{SAR}	
	25)	[1 s]a [lu]^{SAR}	
	26)	[1 sa sum-si]kil!	
	27)	[X-pirig]	[PN_1]
Lo. E. i	28)	[dumu PN_x]	[son of PN_x],
	29)	[níg-ba-šè]	[as the gift],
	30)	[šu-ba-ti]	[received].
	31)	[X-x]	[PN_2]
Rev. i	32)	[dumu PN_x]	[son of PN_x]
	33)	[lugal gán-kam]	[the "lord of the field"],
	34)	[1 PN_3]	[4 PNs]

	35)	[1 PN_4]	
	36)	[1 PN_5]	
	37)	[1 PN_6]	
	38)	[dumu X-pirig-ka-me]	[sons of PN_1],
	39)	[1] Ušùr(LÁL+LAGAB)-r[a-ni]?	7 PNs
	40)	1 Mes-ZU.A[B]	
	41)	1 Ur-^{d}Nin-Gír-su	
	42)	1 Tur-tur	
	43)	1 Úr-kug	
	44)	1 Ḫul-KAL-igi	
	45)	1 SAL-tur	
	46)	dumu ⌜X⌝-[x-m]e (= i 3)	children of ⌜PN_2⌝,
	47)	dumu gán-me	the "sons of the field,"
	48)	lú 1-šè	per each person
	49)	5 ninda-še	Commodities,
	50)	1 ninda-kalag	
	51)	3 tu_7 silà	
	52)	3 ku_6-dar-ra	
	53)	1 sa ga-raš^{SAR}	
	54)	1 silà še-sa	
	55)	níg-ba-šè	as the gift,
	56)	šu-ba-ti	received.
	57)	⌜X⌝-pirig-ke_4 (= i 2)	⌜PN_1⌝
	58)	kag-bi é-gar_8-ra ⌜bi⌝-dù	drove this nail into the wall
U. E. i	59)	ì-b[i] zag-[gi] ⌜bi-ag⌝	(and) spread the oil on the side.
	60)	⌜1(eše)⌝ 3¼ (iku) gán [éš] šám-m[a-ta]	⌜9⌝¼ iku of land, (measured?) [by the "purchase-rope"],
Obv. ii	1)	[É-me-nam-nun]	[from E.]
	2)	[dumu Luga]l?-[z]i?-dè	[son of L.],
	3)	É-geštin-sir	E.,
	4)	1 Da-d[a]	D.,
	5)	⌜1⌝ Gu-ni-du	(and) G.,
	6)	dumu UD.MÁ.NINA.ŠUM-pa-⌜è⌝-[me]	sons of U.,
	7)	⌜lugal gán⌝!-[šè]	the ⌜"lords of the field"⌝,
	8)	Lum-m[a-tur]	L.
	9)	dumu En-an-[na-túm]	son of E.,
	10)	en_5-[si]	the governor of
	11)	Lagaš$^{[KI]}$-ka-ke_4	L.,
	12)	e-n[e]-š[è-šám]	⌜bought⌝.
	13)	[iku 1-a]	[Of 1 iku of land]
	14)	[še 2 gur-sag-gál-ta]	[(its) barley (equivalent) is 2 gsg];
	15)	[še-bi] 20 [lá 1(gur)] 2(ul) [gur-sag-gál]	[the (corresponding)] ⌜18.2⌝ [gsg of barley],
	16)	níg-[šám gán-kam]	the ⌜price⌝ [of the field],
	17)	[šu-ba-ti]	[(the sellers) received].
	18)	2½? [síg-bar-udu-bar]	Commodities
	19)	1! [ì šakan]	
	20)	1 [ŠU.KEŠDA]	
	21)	20 ninda-[še]	
	22)	5 ni[nda]-kalag	
	23)	20 ku_6-dar-ra	
	24)	5 tu_7 silà	
	25)	1 sa lu^{SAR}	
	26)	1 sa ga-raš$^{[SAR]}$	
Lo. E. ii	27)	[É-me-nam-nun]	[E.]
	28)	[dumu Lugal-zi?-dè]	[son of L.],
	29)	[níg-ba-šè]	[as the gift],
	30)	[šu-ba-ti]	[received].

Rev.	ii	31)	[É-geštin-sir]	[3 PNs]
		32)	[1 Da-da]	
		33)	[1 Gu-ni-du]	
		34)	[dumu UD.MÁ.NINA.ŠUM-pa]-⸢è⸣-[me]	[sons of U.],
		35)	[lu]gal ⸢gán-me⸣	the ⸢"lords of the field"⸣,
		36)	[Lu]gal-šà-pàd	4 PNs,
		37)	[dumu] É-me-nam-nun-ka	
		38)	Sag?-šu-du$_7$	
		39)	dumu É-geštin-sir	
		40)	UD.MÁ.NINA.ŠUM-pa-è	
		41)	dumu Da-da	
		42)	Lugal-Anzud$_x$(AN.IM.MI.MUŠEN)	
		43)	dumu Gu-ni-du	
		44)	dumu gán-me	the "sons of the field,"
		45)	lú 1-šè	per each person
		46)	5 ninda-še	Commodities,
		47)	1 ninda-kalag	
		48)	3 tu$_7$ silà	
		49)	3 ku$_6$-dar-ra	
		50)	1 sa ga-raš^{SAR}	
		51)	1 silà še-sa	
		52)	níg-ba-šè	as the gift,
		53)	šu-ba-ti	received.
		54)	É-me-nam-nun-ke$_4$	E.
U. E.	ii	55)	kag-bi é-gar$_8$-ra bí-dù	drove this nail into the wall
		56)	ì-bi zag-[gi b]i-ag	(and) spread the oil on the side.

Obv.	iii	1)	[1(eše) 3]¼ (iku) ⸢gán⸣ éš šám-ma-ta	[9]¼ iku of land, (measured?) by the "purchase-rope,"
		2)	Ba-ni	from B.
		3)	Ba-lum	(and) B.
		4)	[dum]u [A]d-da-[tur]	[so]ns of ⸢A.⸣,
		5)	[p]ab-⸢šeš⸣	the ⸢pab-šeš⸣-priest,
		6)	Ú-[ti]	⸢U.⸣
		7)	KA+[IM-ti]?	(and) ⸢K.⸣
		8)	DUMU M[u-ni]-kala[m-ma-m]e	sons of [M.],
		9)	[Mes-sa]	[M.]
		10)	[dumu A-ZU.AB-si]	[son of A.],
		11)	[É-zi]	[(and) E.]
		12)	[dumu TAR.ḪU]	[son of T.],
		13)	[lugal gán-šè]	[the "lords of the field"],
		14)	[Lum-ma-tur]	[L.]
		15)	[dumu En-an-na-túm]	[son of E.],
		16)	[en$_5$-si]	[the governor of]
		17)	[Lagaš^{KI}-ka-ke$_4$]	[L.],
		18)	[e-ne-šè-šám]	[bought].
		19)	[iku] 1!-[a]	[Of] 1 [iku of land]
		20)	[še] 2! [gur-sag-gál]-ta	[(its) barley (equivalent) is] 2 [gsg];
		21)	[še]-⸢bi⸣ 20 lal 1(gur) 2(ul) gur-sag-gál	the (corresponding) 18.2. gsg of [barley],
		22)	[ní]g!-šám gán-kam	the price of the field,
		23)	šu-ba-ti	(the sellers) received.
		24)	3+[x] síg-bar-udu-[bar]	Commodities
		25)	[1] ì šakan	
		26)	[1] ⸢ŠU.KEŠDA⸣	
Lo. E.	iii	27)	[x] ninda-še	
		28)	[x ninda-kalag]	

		29)	[x ku$_6$-dar-ra]	
		30)	[x tu$_7$ si]là	
		31)	[1 sa lu^{SAR}]	
Rev.	iii	32)	[1 sa ga-raš^{SAR}]	
		33)	[1 Ba-ni]	[B.]
		34)	[dumu Ad-da-tur]	[son of A.],
		35)	[níg-ba-šè]	[as the gift],
		36)	[šu-ba]-ti	[received].
		37)	1 Ba-[lum]	B.
		38)	dumu Ad-da-tur	son of A.,
		39)	1 Ú-ti	U.
		40)	1 KA+IM-t[i]?	(and) K.
		41)	dumu Mu-ni-kalam-m[a-m]e	sons of M.,
		42)	1 Mes-sa	M.
		43)	dumu A-ZU.AB-si	son of A.,
		44)	1 É-zi	E.
		45)	dumu TAR.ḪU	son of T.,
		46)	lugal gán-me	the "lords of the field,"
		47)	1 GIŠGAL-ir-nun	G.
		48)	1 Lum-ma-ki-gal-la	(and) L.
		49)	dumu Ú-ti-me	sons of U.,
		50)	1 DUG.RU-ma-da-ág	D.,
		51)	1 Di-Utu	D.,
		52)	1 A-šu-El	(and) A.
		53)	dumu Ba-ni-me	sons of B.,
		54)	dumu gán-me	the "sons of the field,"
		55)	lú 1-šè	per each person
		56)	5 ninda-še	Commodities,
		57)	1 ninda-kalag	
		58)	3 tu$_7$ silà	
		59)	3 ku$_6$-dar-ra	
		60)	1 sa ga-raš^{SAR}	
		61)	1 silà še-sa	
		62)	níg-ba-šè	as the gift,
		63)	šu-ba-ti	received.
		64)	Ba-ni	B.
		65)	kag-bi é-gar$_8$ bi-dù	drove this nail into the wall
U. E.	iii	66)	ì-bi zag-gi bi-a[g]	(and) spread the oil on the side.

---

		67)	1(eše) [2]¼ (iku) gán	⸢8⸣¼ iku of land,
Obv.	iv	1)	[gán . . .]	[the field . . .];
		2)	1(bùr) 3(iku) g[án]	21 iku of land,
		3)	gán sag-[du$_5$-ka]	the field of the field recorder;
		4)	É-barag-šu-du$_7$	from E.
		5)	⸢dam⸣ Amar-tùr	⸢wife⸣ of A.,
		6)	s[ag]-[du$_5$]-⸢ka⸣	the field recorder,
		7)	[Ama-barag-si]	[A.]
		8)	[dam Ur-^{d}Dumu-zi-da]?	[wife of U.?],
		9)	[En-SAL.UŠ.DI-zi]	[E.],
		10)	[Inim-ma-ni-zi]	[I.],
		11)	[Nin-kal-SI.A]	[N.],
		12)	[Lugal-x-ni-x]	[L.],
		13)	[Me-kisal-si?]	[M.],
		14)	[A- . . .]	[A.],
		15)	[Lú-. . .]	[(and) L.]
		16)	[dumu Amar-tùr]	[children of A.],
		16a)	[sag-du$_5$-ka-me]	[the field recorder],
		17)	[lugal gán-šè]	[the "lords of the field"],
		18)	[Lum-ma-tur]	[L.]
		19)	[dumu En-an-na-túm]	[son of E.],

		20)	[en$_5$-si]	[the governor of]
		21)	[Lagaš^{KI}-ka-ke$_4$]	[L.],
		22)	[e-ne-šè-šám]	[bought].
		23)	⌈iku 1-a⌉	⌈Of 1 iku of land⌉
		24)	še 2 gur-sag-gál-ta	(its) barley (equivalent) is 2 gsg;
		25)	še-bi 60 lal 1(gur) 2(ul) gur-sag-gál	the (corresponding) 58.2. gsg of barley,
		26)	níg-šám gán-⌈kam⌉	the price of the field,
		27)	[šu-ba-ti]	[(the sellers) received].
		28)	[x síg-bar-udu-bar]	Commodities
		29)	[1] ⌈ì⌉ ša[kan]	
Lo. E.	iv	30)	1 ŠU.[KEŠDA]	
		31)	[x ninda-še]	
		32)	[x ninda-kalag]	
		33)	[x ku$_6$-dar-ra)	
		34)	[x tu$_7$ silà]	
Rev.	iv	35)	[. . .]-⌈x⌉	
		36)	[. . .]-⌈x⌉-ra	
		37)	2 ⌈x(-x)⌉-KEŠDA	
		38)	⌈É⌉-[ba]rag-šu-du$_7$	⌈E.⌉
		39)	Ama-barag-si	(and) A.,
		40)	níg-ba-šè	as the gift,
		41)	šu-ba-ti	received.
		42)	⌈En-SAL⌉.UŠ.⌈DI-zi⌉	7 PNs
		43)	Inim-ma-ni-zi	
		44)	Nin-⌈kal-SI.A⌉	
		45)	Lugal-⌈x⌉-ni-[x]	
		46)	Me-kisal-[si]?	
		47)	A-⌈. . .⌉	
		48)	Lú-[. . .]	
		49)	dumu Amar-[tùr]	children of A.,
		50)	sag-⌈du$_5$-ka⌉-me	the field recorder,
		51)	⟨lugal gán-me⟩	⟨the "lords of the field"⟩,
		52)	Làl?-li-l[i]?	8 PNs
		53)	Barag-ul-tu	
		54)	dumu Ur-^{d}Dumu-zi-da-me	
		55)	Nin-uru-ni-šè-ḫi-li	
		56)	dam Inim-ma-ni-zi	
		57)	Igi-zi-barag-gi	
		58)	Ur-^{d}Nin-PA	
		59)	Ur-^{d}GUR$_8$-⌈x⌉	
		60)	Barag-ga-[ni]	
		61)	dumu In[im-ma]-ni-[zi-me]	
		62)	Dug?-[. . .]	
		63)	d[umu . . .]	
U. E.	iv	64)	[dumu gán-me]	[the "sons of the field"],
		65)	[lú 1-šè]	[per each person]
		66)	[5 ninda še]	[Commodities]
		67)	1 n[inda kalag]	
		68)	[3 tu$_7$ silà]	
		69)	[3 ku$_6$-dar-ra]	
			(beg. of cols. v and vi destr.)	
			(rest of cols. v and vi blank)	

Notes

i 1, 60, iii 1, 67, and iv 2.—Although nowhere fully and clearly written, it can be safely assumed that the first three fields (i 1, 60, iii 1) were of the same size, namely 9¼ iku. This can be reconstructed from i 12–14 (and elsewhere), which indicate that the price was 18 gur-sag-gál and 2 ul of barley, at the rate of 2 gur-sag-gál of barley for 1 iku of land. Thus:

18 gur-sag-gál še = 9 iku
2 ul še = ¼ iku
(N.B.: 1 gur-sag-gál = 4 ul = 144 silà)

By the same reckoning of 2 gur-sag-gál of barley for one iku of land, we learn that the fourth field, comprising two parcels (iii 67, iv 2), was 29¼ iku in size and cost 58½ gur-sag-gál of barley.

The area of the field is followed by éš šám-ma-ta in three cases in no. 22 (all partially preserved), in several cases in no. 23 (all reconstructed), and in App. to nos. 22–23 (fully preserved). The interpretation of x gán éš šam-ma-ta "x land (measured?) by the 'purchase rope'" is uncertain. If this tentative translation is correct, the term éš šám would denote a certified measuring rope that was used in purchases of land. There are no occurrences of éš šám outside Lagash. However, a parallel case of the usage of such a term may be found in x GÁN ÉŠ.GÍD SI.SÁ "x field (measured) by the standard(?) measuring rope" in nos. 30a ii 1′ and 37 rev. iii 14, iv 16.

i 2 and 57.—The reading [X-pirig] in i 2 is reconstructed on the basis of i 57, which can be read as ⌜X⌝-pirig-ke$_4$. The preserved traces of the first sign show the lower portion of a tall and narrow sign in the shape of KU or ÉŠ. The reading É (or NIN), in partial agreement with É-pirig-sír of no. 32 rev. i 12, is impossible.

i 39.—For the reading ušùr of LÁL+LAGAB and for various PNs using this element, see Powell, *Or.* n.s. 43 (1974) pp. 399–402. The reconstruction of our name as [Lugal]-ušùr-r[a-nàd] (for the name, see *ibid.* p. 401) is theoretically also possible.

ii 3.—With the PN É-geštin-sir, compare É-geštin-sír in *BIN* 8, 16 ii 2. [Read better É-geštin-sug$_4$.]

ii 36.—The PN Lugal-šà-pàd occurs in the administrative text *Fara* 3, 35 xii and, under the form Lugal-šà-pàd-da, in App. to nos. 22–23 iii 9, making the interpretation of our Lugal-šà-pàd as "an elected representative of the family community" (Diakonoff, *Structure of Society and State in Early Dynastic Sumer* [Los Angeles, 1974] pp. 8 and 15 n. 13) impossible.

ii 42.—For the reading Anzud$_x$ of AN.IM.MI.MUŠEN, see note to no. 15 i 26.

iii 2, 3 and *passim*.—Since the signs BA and IGI are not clearly distinguished in our inscription, we may read Igi-ni and Igi-lum, instead of Ba-ni and Ba-lum. Compare, e.g., the middle sign in šu-ba-ti (i 15), clearly written in the form of IGI. Also in iii 62–64 the sign-form IGI is used in níg-ba-šè, šu-ba-ti, and Ba-ni.

iii 50.—The element DUG.RU appearing in this name was a sanctuary in Girshu/Lagash. See Bauer, *AWL* p. 242; H. Behrens and H. Steible, *FAOS* 6 p. 409.

iii 52.—For this PN, compare A-šu-^{d}El, the name of the wife of A-kalam-dùg king of Ur in the Early Dynastic period (*UE* 2 pls. 191 and 198, seal).

iv 5 and 49.—For the PN Amar-tùr, see also no. 21 i 33, v 4′.

iv 36–37.—The first commodity could be [ku$_6$]-⌜dar⌝-ra (reconstructed above in iv 33). Although it would be tempting to reconstruct the second commodity as ⌜ŠU⌝.KEŠDA, the reading of the first sign(s) as ŠU is not supported by the photograph.

iv 52–54.—In place of the sons of Ur-^{d}Dumu-zi-da, one would expect to find here the sons of Ama-barag-si, in accordance with ii 37 and other transactions in no. 22. The case allows an interesting suggestion. If Ama-barag-si is a feminine name, as indicated by the presence of the element ama "mother," then Ur-^{d}Dumu-zi-da could be taken as her deceased husband and the father of the two men in question. An identical situation is found in the same transaction in the case of É-barag-šu-du$_7$, the wife of the deceased(?) Amar-tùr and the mother of his seven sons, who acts in his place as one of the two "lords of the field."

iv 60.—For the reconstruction of the PN Barag-ga-[ni], see *BIN* 8, 76 ii 4, 86 ii 8 and *TMH* 5, 102 i 7.

No. 23 Lummatur Tablet II

Photographs: Plates 43 and 44. Fragments a and c from the Istanbul Archaeological Museum, fragment b from the Louvre Museum, Paris.

Copy: Plates 42–44, copied by Green from photographs and copies of originals by Gelb.

Synopsis: Plates 97–100.

Provenience: Girshu (Telloh).

Date: Pre-Sargonic.

Language: Sumerian.

Present location: a) Istanbul Museum, EŞEM 4808
b) Louvre Museum (Paris), AO 4464
c) Istanbul Museum, EŞEM 2517

Publication: a) Unpublished
b) Unpublished
c) Cros, *NFT* pp. 246 and 262ff. (copy by Thureau-Dangin); Edzard, *SRU* no. 118

Description of a): Fragment of light-buff limestone. Measurements of the inscribed surface of the obverse are 15.1 × 13.8 cm; of the reverse 17 × 18.2 cm. Thickness is about 8.2 cm. All edges are broken away and both sides are flat. Viewed from the side, the grain of the stone varies in color: the upper half, near the obverse, is darker than the lower half, near the reverse.

Description of b): This fragment, acquired in 1906 from Géjou, a dealer of antiquities, is of light-buff limestone, measuring 10 × 17.7 cm and roughly triangular in shape. Thickness varies from 5.5 to 7.7 cm. Only the obverse, which is flat, is preserved; the reverse and all edges are broken away. Viewed from the side, the grain of the stone varies in color: the upper half, near the obverse, is darker than the lower half, near the reverse. We acknowledge with thanks the kind cooperation of the late J. Nougayrol, who offered us this stone fragment for publication.

Description of c): Fragment of light-buff limestone, measuring 16 × 18 × 7.5 cm. The fragment is the upper right corner of the tablet and has the obverse, upper edge, and right edge preserved. The reverse is completely broken away. Viewed from the side, the grain of the stone varies in color: the upper half, near the obverse, is darker than the lower half, near the reverse.

Composite description: Since all three fragments share the same characteristic variation in the grain of the stone, there is no doubt that they form part of the same inscription. In the summer of 1963, Miss Lucienne Laroche of the Louvre Museum staff prepared a plaster cast of AO 4464 (= fragment b), which Gelb subsequently took to Istanbul to see whether the Louvre fragment would join the corner piece published by Cros, *NFT* p. 263 (= fragment c), in the Istanbul Museum. When he discovered that Istanbul Museum 4808 (= fragment a) belonged to the same tablet, he tried all three fragments for possible "joins." The only possible "join" is between fragments b) and c), where the right side of b) fits along the left side of c). At that point the two fragments fit more or less together, but not tightly. Considering the fact that a plaster cast of the Louvre fragment was used in place of the original for this test, it is not surprising that the two pieces did not fit snugly. The correct positioning of these two pieces is shown by the fact that the beginnings of lines in three separate columns preserved in fragment b) are continued in fragment c).

Knowledge of the structure of the inscription, coupled with the physical characteristics of the fragments, allows all three pieces to be placed in their proper positions relative to one another. See plate 42 and below under *Text*. On the basis of the assumptions made in the reconstruction of the text, the original inscription was a tablet that measured approximately 52 × 40 × 8.2 cm.

Text: The original tablet bore at least eleven columns. It is possible that there were more columns at the beginning of the inscription since the left edge of the tablet is not preserved. However, the last three preserved columns of the obverse of fragment a) are the continuation, after a gap of four or five lines, of the first three preserved columns of fragments b) and c), which have the right edge preserved. The tablet was originally inscribed on the obverse, lower edge, reverse, and upper edge, and the sequence of the inscription followed the same order as that of no. 22. This sequence is clearly demonstrated by fragment c), which has the upper edge and obverse preserved. In each case where the end of a column is preserved on the upper edge, the text continues in the next column over on the obverse. This same sequence for the text is also found in no. 22.

For relationships between nos. 23 and 22, as well as between these two kudurrus and the sale document here published as App. to nos. 22–23, see the introductory remarks to no. 22, under *Text*.

The tablet originally recorded at least nine individual purchases of land by Lummatur, son of Enanatum, the governor of Lagash. The missing text of the individual transactions is restored freely with the constraints of the preserved portions of the inscriptions, the fixed sequence of the formulary, and an assumption of approximately equal length for each column. The first two factors force the numerical value for the third, which, to fit the required text into the gaps, requires a column length of approximately thirty-five lines for both obverse and reverse. In this calculation, the lower edge is included with the obverse while the upper edge is included with the reverse. Where the upper edge is actually preserved, it is indicated but still counted with the reverse. The assumed number of thirty-five lines per column is actually the number of cases per column and does not count the number of lines of writing in each case. It can be seen from the preserved portions of the tablet that the cases vary in height. However, because of the repetitive nature of the transactions, the differences in case height tend to average out over the length of the columns giving each column approximately the same number of cases. As a check on this, the amount of space taken up by a number of consecutive cases was measured at six places in the preserved parts of the inscription and a value of 1.72 cm per case was obtained, with the greatest variations being 1.48 and 2.09 cm per case. This value of 1.72 cm per case was used to reconstruct the vertical dimension of the tablet as approximately 52 cm, by multiplying it by the assumed column length of 35 cases and allowing 8 cm for the upper and lower edges.

The only real variation in the length of each transaction is caused by the number of personal names included in it, since the number of lines required for the formulary is more or less fixed. Large numbers of personal names may occur in two places in the transaction: near the beginning in the description of the field where the names of the owners of the field are given (including the primary owners); and near the end of the transaction before the list of commodities given to the secondary owners of the field and to the children of the owners. Because of that fact, the reconstructed amount of space allowed for personal names near the end of the transaction is larger than the amount of space allowed for personal names near the beginning.

The reconstruction of the text assumes that the inscription begins with two transactions of average length, with the first preserved column of fragment a) being the first column of the inscription. Next, a very short transaction begins in obv. iii 6, which continues only to the end of the column on the obverse (actually lower edge). This reconstruction is required by the preserved portions of the text, which do not leave room for even the required formulary without considering personal names. This can only be accommodated by assuming that there is only a primary owner and no secondary owners or children of the owner and that the portion of the inscription which normally deals with these latter two is not included in the text. Note that the gap which forces this reconstruction is between the obverse and reverse of the same fragment, and so the problem cannot be resolved by assuming the incorrect positioning of two fragments relative to one another.

The text continues with five transactions of normal length to obv. vii 31. At this point begins what is either two fairly short transactions or one lengthy one. The present reconstruction favors the latter possibility because it is easier to fit to the preserved portions of the inscription and, moreover, a transaction of this length also occurs in no. 22. Following the final transaction, there begins in obv. ix 11 a list of witnesses who are not marked with a *Personenkeil*, and who receive gifts. Here the reconstructed number of lines is probably misleading, since this section consists almost entirely of personal names which tend to have more lines of writing per case and hence fewer cases per column. For this reason, the reconstructed line total should not be taken to indicate the number of witnesses listed. Following the list of commodities received by these witnesses, there begins in obv. x 1 a list of witnesses who are marked with a *Personenkeil* and who do not receive gifts. This list continues to obv. xi 1. In obv. xi 2 begin the names of the surveyors. It cannot be determined how much more of col. xi was inscribed since it breaks off after the names of the surveyors, and col. xi of the upper edge is not inscribed.

No. 23 has the same formulary as no. 22, except that it gives the rate and the price in še "barley" and síg "wool" (i 13–18). For the translation, see no. 22.

Transliteration

Obv. i 1) [x(iku) gán éš šám-ma-ta]
2) [PN]
3) [PN_2]
4) [PN_3]
5) [PN_4]
6) [dumu PN_x-me]

7) [lugal gán-šè]
8) [Lum-ma-tur]
9) [dumu En-an-na-túm]
10) [en$_5$-si]
11) [Lagaš^{KI}-ka-ke$_4$]
12) [e-ne-šè-šám]
13) [iku 1-a]
14) [še gur-2-ul 2-ta]
15) [iku 1-a]
16) [síg-ŠÀ.ŠÈ 3 ma-na-ta]
17) [še-bi x gur-2-ul]
Fragt. a) 18) [síg-bi x ma-n]a?
19) [níg-šá]m? [gán-kam]
20) [šu-ba-ti]
21) [x síg-bar-udu]
22) [1 ì šakan]
23) [1 ŠU.KEŠDA]
24) [x ninda-še]
25) [x ninda-kalag]
26) [x ku$_6$-dar-ra]
27) [x tu$_7$ silà]
28) [x silà še-sa]
29) [x sa ga-raš^{SAR}]
30) [PN]
31) [dumu PN$_x$]
32) [níg-ba-šè]
33) [šu-ba-ti]
34) [PN$_2$]
35) [PN$_3$]
Rev. i 1) [PN$_4$]
2) [dumu PN$_x$-me]
3) [lugal gán-me]
4) [PN$_5$]
5) [dumu PN]
6) [PN$_6$]
7) [dumu PN$_2$]
8) [PN$_7$]
9) [dumu PN$_3$]
10) [PN$_8$]
11) [dumu PN$_4$]
12) [dumu gán-me]
13) [lú 1-šè]
14) [x ninda-še]
15) [1 ninda-kalag]
16) [x ku$_6$-dar-ra]
17) [x tu$_7$ silà]
18) [1 udu]
19) [1 silà še-sa]
20) [1 sa ga-raš^{SAR}]
21) [níg-ba-šè]
22) [šu-ba-ti]
23) [PN]
24) [kag-bi é-gar$_8$ bí-dù]
25) [ì-bi zag-gi bí-ag]

---

26) [x(iku) gán éš šám-ma-ta]
27) [PN]
28) [dumu PN$_x$]
29) [PN$_2$]
30) [PN$_3$]
31) [PN$_4$]
32) [PN$_5$]
33) [dumu PN$_y$-me]
34) [PN$_6$]
35) [PN$_7$]
Obv. ii 1) [dumu PN$_z$-me]
2) [PN$_8$]
3) [PN$_9$]
4) [dumu PN$_{z1}$-me]
5) [lugal gán-šè]
6) [Lum-ma-tur]
7) [dumu En-an-na-túm]
8) [en$_5$-si]
9) [Lagaš^{KI}-ka-ke$_4$]
10) [e-ne-šè-šám]
11) [iku 1-a]
12) [še gur-2-ul 2-ta]
13) [iku 1-a]
14) [síg-ŠÀ.ŠÈ 3 ma-na-ta]
15) [še-bi x gur-2-ul]
Fragt. a) 16) [síg-b]i? [x]+15 [m]a-n[a]
17) [níg]-šám gán-kam
18) šu-ba-ti
19) 43+[2]? síg-bar-udu
20) [1 ì šakan]
21) [1 ŠU.KEŠDA]
22) [x ninda-še]
23) [x ninda-kalag]
24) [x ku$_6$-dar-ra]
25) [x tu$_7$ silà]
26) [x silà še-sa]
27) [x sa ga-raš^{SAR}]
28) [PN]
29) [dumu PN$_x$]
30) [níg-ba-šè]
31) [šu-ba-ti]
32) [PN$_2$]
33) [PN$_3$]
34) [PN$_4$]
35) [PN$_5$]
Rev. ii 1) [dumu PN$_y$-me]
2) [PN$_6$]
3) [PN$_7$]
4) [dumu PN$_z$-me]
5) [PN$_8$]
6) [PN$_9$]
7) [dumu PN$_{z1}$-me]
8) [lugal gán-me]
9) [PN$_{10}$]
10) [dumu PN]
11) [PN$_{11}$]
12) [dumu PN$_2$]
13) [PN$_{12}$]
14) [dumu PN$_3$]
15) [PN$_{13}$]
16) [dumu PN$_4$]
17) [PN$_{14}$]
18) [dumu PN$_5$]
19) [PN$_{15}$]
20) [dumu PN$_6$]
21) [PN$_{16}$]

22) [dumu PN$_7$]
23) [PN$_{17}$]
24) [dumu PN$_8$]
25) [PN$_{18}$]
26) [dumu PN$_9$]
27) [dumu gán-me]
28) [lú 1-šè]
29) [x ninda-še]
30) [1 ninda-kalag]
31) [x ku$_6$-dar-ra]
32) [x tu$_7$ silà]
33) [1 udu]
34) [1 silà še-sa]
35) [1 sa ga-raš^{SAR}]
Obv. iii 1) [níg-ba-šè]
2) [šu-ba-ti]
3) [PN]
4) [kag-bi é-gar$_8$ bí-dù]
5) [ì-bi zag-gi bí-ag]

---

6) [22⅓ (iku) gán eš šám-ma-ta]
7) [PN]
8) [dumu PN$_x$]
9) [lugal gán-šè]
10) [Lum-ma-tur]
11) [dumu En-an-na-túm]
12) [en$_5$-si]
13) [Lagaš^{KI}-ka-ke$_4$]
Fragt. a) 14) [e-šè]-šám
15) [iku] 1-a
16) [síg-Š]À.ŠÈ ⸢3⸣ ma-na-⸢ta⸣
17) síg-bi 67 ma-na
18) níg-šám gán-kam
19) šu-ba-ti
20) 33 síg-bar-udu
21) [1 ì šakan]
22) [1 ŠU.KEŠDA]
23) [x ninda-še]
24) [x ninda-kalag]
25) [x ku$_6$-dar-ra]
26) [x tu$_7$ silà]
27) [x silà še-sa]
28) [x sa ga-raš^{SAR}]
29) [PN]
30) [dumu PN$_x$]
31) [níg-ba-šè]
32) [šu-ba-ti]
33) [PN]
34) [kag-bi é-gar$_8$ bí-dù]
35) [ì-bi zag-gi bí-ag]

Rev. iii 1) [x(iku) gán éš šám-ma-ta]
2) [Dug$_4$-ga-ni] (= obv. iv 21)
3) [PN$_2$] (= [X]-⸢barag-si⸣ of obv. iv 7)
4) [PN$_3$]
5) [dumu PN$_x$]
6) [lugal gán-šè]
7) [Lum-ma-tur]
8) [dumu En-an-na-túm]
9) [en$_5$-si]
Fragt. a) 10) [Lagaš^{KI}-ka]-⸢ke$_4$⸣
11) [e]-⸢ne⸣-[šè-šám]
12) [ik]u 1-a
13) [še g]ur-2-[ul 2]-ta
14) [iku 1]-a
15) [síg-ŠÀ.ŠÈ 3 ma-na-t]a
16) [še-bi x gur-2-ul]
17) [síg-bi x ma-na]
18) [níg-šám gán-kam]
19) [šu-ba-ti]
20) [x síg-bar-udu]
21) [1 ì šakan]
22) [1 ŠU.KEŠDA]
23) [x ninda-še]
24) [x ninda-kalag]
25) [x ku$_6$-dar-ra]
26) [x tu$_7$ silà]
27) [x silà še-sa]
28) [x sa ga-raš^{SAR}]
29) [Dug$_4$-ga-ni]
30) [dumu PN$_x$]
31) [níg-ba-šè]
32) [šu-ba-ti]
33) [PN$_2$] (= [X]-⸢barag-si⸣ of obv. iv 7)
Obv. iv 1) [PN$_3$]
2) [dumu PN$_x$-me]
3) [lugal gán-me]
4) [PN$_4$]
5) [dumu Dug$_4$-ga-ni]
Fragt. b) 6) [. . .]-⸢ma⸣?
7) [dumu X]-⸢barag-si⸣
8) [PN$_5$]
9) [dumu PN$_3$]
10) [dumu gán-me]
11) [lú 1-šè]
12) [x udu]
Fragt. a) 13 5 ninda-še
14) 1 ninda-kalag
15) 3 tu$_7$ silà
16) 3 ku$_6$-dar-ra
17) 1 sa ga-raš^{SAR}
18) 1 silà še-⸢sa⸣
19) níg-ba-šè
20) šu-ba-ti
21) Dug$_4$-ga-ni (= rev. iii 2)
22) kag-bi é-gar$_8$ bí-dù
23) [ì-bi] ⸢zag⸣-[gi bí-ag]

---

24) [x(iku) gán éš šám-ma-ta]
25) [PN] (= [. . .]-⸢mu⸣-[. . .]-zu of obv. v 7)
26) [PN$_2$]
27) [dumu PN$_x$-me]
28) [lugal gán-šè]
29) [Lum-ma-tur]
30) [dumu En-an-na-túm]
31) [en$_5$-si]

32) [Lagaš^{KI}-ka-ke$_4$]
33) [e-ne-šè-šám]
34) [iku 1-a]
35) [še gur-2-ul 2-ta]
36) [iku 1-a]
Rev. iv 1) [síg-ŠÀ.ŠÈ 3 ma-na-ta]
2) [še-bi x gur-2-ul]
3) [síg-bi x ma-na]
4) [níg-šám gán-kam]
5) [šu-ba-ti]
6) [x síg-bar-udu]
7) [1 ì šakan]
8) [1 ŠU.KEŠDA]
Fragt. a) 9) [x ninda]-še
10) 1 ninda-kalag
11) 1 tu$_7$ silà
12) 20 ku$_6$-⌜dar-ra⌝
13) 1 ninda-ì
14) 3 silà [x]
15) 1 silà še-[sa]
16) 1 silà [x]
17) 1 sum-⌜gu⌝
18) 1 ⌜sa ga⌝-[raš^{SAR}]
19) [PN] (= obv. iv 25)
20) [dumu PN$_x$]
21) [níg-ba-šè]
22) [šu-ba-ti]
23) [PN$_2$]
24) [dumu PN$_x$]
25) [lugal gán-kam]
26) [PN$_3$]
27) [dumu PN]
28) [PN$_4$]
29) [dumu PN$_2$]
30) [dumu gán-me]
31) [lú 1-šè]
32) [x ninda-še]
33) [1 ninda-kalag]
34) [x ku$_6$-dar-ra]
Obv. v 1) [x tu$_7$ silà]
2) [1 udu]
3) [1 silà še-sa]
4) [1 sa ga-raš^{SAR}]
5) [níg-ba-šè]
6) [šu-ba-ti]
Fragt. b) 7) [. . .]-⌜mu⌝-[. . .]-zu (= obv. iv 25)
8) [kag]-bi é-gar$_8$ bí-dù
9) ì-bi zag-⌜gi⌝ [bí-ag]

---

10) [x(iku) gán éš šám-ma-ta]
11) [PN] (= [. . .]-a-nà[d-. . .] of rev. v 10)
12) [PN$_2$]
Fragt. a) 13) [dumu] ⌜PN$_x$⌝-[me]
14) ⟨lugal gán-šè⟩
15) Lum-ma-tur
16) dumu En-an-na-túm
17) en$_5$-si
18) Lagaš^{KI}-ka-ke$_4$
19) e-ne-šè-š[ám]
20) iku 1-[a]
21) še gu[r-2]-ul 2-t[a]
22) iku 1-[a]
23) [síg]-Š[À.ŠÈ 3 ma-na-ta]
24) [še-bi x gur-2-ul]
25) [síg-bi x ma-na]
26) [níg-šám gán-kam]
27) [šu-ba-ti]
28) [x síg-bar-udu]
29) [1 ì šakan]
30) [1 ŠU.KEŠDA]
31) [x ninda-še]
32) [x ninda-kalag]
33) [x ku$_6$-dar-ra]
34) [x tu$_7$ silà]
35) [x silà še-sa]
Rev. v 1) [x sa ga-raš^{SAR}]
2) [PN] (= obv. v 11)
3) [dumu PN$_x$]
4) [níg-ba-šè]
5) [šu-ba-ti]
6) [PN$_2$]
7) [dumu PN$_x$]
8) [lugal gán-kam]
9) [PN$_3$]
Fragt. a) 10) dumu [. . .]-a-nà[d-. . .] (= obv. v 11)
11) Ur?-[. . .]
12) dumu [PN$_2$]
13) [dumu gán-me]
14) lú 1-[šè]
15) 13+[x] ⌜ninda⌝-[še]
16) [1 ninda-kalag]
17) [x ku$_6$-dar-ra]
18) [x tu$_7$ silà]
19) [1 udu]
20) [1 silà še sa]
21) [x sa ga-raš^{SAR}]
22) [níg-ba-šè]
23) [šu-ba-ti]
24) [PN] (= obv. v 11)
25) [kag-bi é-gar$_8$ bí-dù]
26) [ì-bi zag-gi bí-ag]

---

27) [14½ or 14⅓(iku) gán éš šám-ma-ta]
28) [PN]
29) [PN$_2$]
30) [dumu PN$_x$-me]
31) [PN$_3$]
32) [PN$_4$]
33) [dumu PN$_y$-me]
34) [lugal gán-šè]
35) [Lum-ma-tur]
36) [dumu En-an-na-túm]
37) [en$_5$-si]
38) [Lagaš^{KI}-ka-ke$_4$]
Obv. vi 1) [e-ne-šè-šám]
2) [iku 1-a]

Fragt. b) 3) [še gu]r-2-[ul] ⸢2⸣-ta
4) [ik]u 1-a
5) síg-ŠÀ.ŠÈ 3 ma-na-ta
6) še-bi 30 lal 1 gur-2-ul
7) síg-bi 43 ma-[na]
8) [níg-šám gán-kam]
9) [šu-ba-ti]
10) [x síg-bar-udu]
11) [1 ì šakan]
12) [1 ŠU.KEŠDA]
13) [x ninda-še]
Fragt. a) 14) 1 [ninda-kalag]
15) 20 ku$_6$-[dar-ra]
16) 1 [tu$_7$ silà]
17) 2+[x silà še-sa]
18) 1 [sa ga-raš^{SAR}]
19) [PN]
20) [dumu PN$_x$]
21) [níg-ba-šè]
22) [šu-ba-ti]
23) [PN$_2$]
24) [dumu PN$_x$]
25) [PN$_3$]
26) [PN$_4$]
27) [dumu PN$_y$-me]
28) [lugal gán-me]
29) [PN$_5$]
30) [dumu PN]
31) [PN$_6$]
32) [dumu PN$_2$]
33) [PN$_7$]
34) [dumu PN$_3$]
35) [PN$_8$]
36) [dumu PN$_4$]
Rev. vi 1) [dumu gán-me]
2) [lú 1-šè]
3) [x ninda-še]
4) [1 ninda-kalag]
5) [x ku$_6$-dar-ra]
6) [x tu$_7$ silà]
7) [1 udu]
8) [1 silà še-sa]
9) [1 sa ga-raš^{SAR}]
10) [níg-ba-šè]
11) [šu-ba-ti]
12) [PN]
13) [kag-bi é-gar$_8$ bí-dù]
14) [ì-bi zag-gi bí-ag]

Fragt. a) 15) 2(bùr)? [x(iku) gán éš šám-ma-ta]
16) [UD.MÁ.NINA.KI.ŠUM-dùg] (= obv. vii 7)
17) [PN$_2$]?
18) [dumu Ur-^{d}Dumu-zi-da-šè] (= obv. vii 8)
19) [lugal gán-šè]
20) [Lum-ma-tur]
21) [dumu En-an-na-túm]
22) [en$_5$-si]

23) [Lagaš^{KI}-ka-ke$_4$]
24) [e-ne-šè-šám]
25) [iku 1-a]
26) [še gur-2-ul 2-ta]
27) [iku 1-a]
28) [síg-ŠÀ.ŠÈ 3 ma-na-ta]
29) [še-bi x gur-2-ul]
30) [síg-bi x ma-na]
31) [níg-šám gán-kam]
32) [šu-ba-ti]
33) [x síg-bar-udu]
34) [1 ì šakan]
35) [1 ŠU.KEŠDA]
36) [x ninda-še]
Fragt. c) Obv. vii 1) [x ninda]-kalag!
2) [x] ⸢ku$_6$⸣-dar-ra
Fragts. b+c) 3) 2 tu$_7$ silà
4) 1 ⸢udu⸣
Fragt. b) 5) 1 silà še-sa
6) 1 sa ga-raš$^{SAR!}$
7) UD.MÁ.NINA.KI.ŠUM-dùg (= rev. vi 16)
8) dumu Ur-^{d}Dumu-⸢zi-da⸣ (= rev. vi 18)
9) [níg-ba-šè]
10) [šu-ba-ti]
11) [PN$_2$]
12) [dumu Ur-^{d}Dumu-zi-da]
13) [lugal gán-kam]
14) [PN$_3$]
15) [dumu PN]
16) [PN$_4$]
17) [dumu PN$_2$]
18) [dumu gán-me]
19) [lú 1-šè]
20) [x ninda-še]
21) [1 ninda-kalag]
22) [x ku$_6$-dar-ra]
23) [x tu$_7$ silà]
24) [1 udu]
25) [1 silà še-sa]
26) [1 sa ga-raš^{SAR}]
27) [níg-ba-šè]
28) [šu-ba-ti]
29) [UD.MÁ.NINA.KI.ŠUM-dùg] (= rev. vi 16)
30) [kag-bi é-gar$_8$ bí-dù]
31) [ì-bi zag-gi bí-ag]

---

32) [14½ or 14⅓(iku) gán éš šám-ma-ta]
33) [Inim-ma-ni-zi] (= obv. ix 8)
34–35) [. . .]
Rev. vii 1-25) [. . .]
26) [lugal gán-šè]
27) [Lum-ma-tur]
28) [dumu En-an-na-túm]
29) [en$_5$-si]
30) [Lagaš^{KI}-ka-ke$_4$]

31) [e-ne-šè-šám]
32) [iku 1-a]
Fragt. c) U. E. vii 33) ⌜še gur⌝-[2]-ul 2-ta
34) iku 1-a
35) [sí]g ⌜ŠÀ⌝.ŠÈ [3] ma-na-ta
Obv. viii 1) še-bi 30 lal 1 gur-2-ul
2) síg-bi 43 ma-na
Fragts. b–c) 3) níg-šám gán-kam
4) šu-[b]a-ti
5) 20 síg-⌜bar⌝-udu
6) 1 ì šak[an]
Fragt. b) 7) 1 ŠU.KEŠDA
8) [x] ⌜ninda-še⌝
9) [x ninda-kalag]
10) [x ku$_6$-dar-ra]
11) [x tu$_7$ silà]
12) [x silà še-sa]
13) [x sa ga-raš^{SAR}]
14) [Inim-ma-ni-zi] (= obv. ix 8)
15) [dumu PN$_x$]
16) [níg-ba-šè]
17) [šu-ba-ti]
18–34) [. . .]
35) [lugal gán-me]
Rev. viii 1–31) [. . .]
32) [dumu gán-me]
Fragt. c) U. E. viii 33) lú 1-šè
34) 7 ninda-še
35) ⌜1⌝ ninda-kalag
Obv. ix 1) 5 ku$_6$-dar-ra
2) 1 tu$_7$ silà
3) 1 udu
4) 1 silà še-sa
5) 1 sa ga-raš^{SAR}
6) níg-ba-šè
7) [š]u-ba-ti
Fragts. b+c) 8) [In]im-ma-⌜ni⌝-zi
Fragt. c) 9) [kag-b]i [é-gar$_8$ bí-dù]
10) [ì-bi zag-gi bí-ag]

---

11) [PN]
12–35) [. . .]
Rev. ix 1–26) [. . .]
27) [lú-ki-inim-ma-bi-me]?
28) [lú 1-šè]
29–32) [. . .]
Fragt. c) U. E. ix 33) ⌜x⌝+3 silà ì-⌜sag⌝
34) níg-ba gán-kam
35) ⌜šu⌝-[ba-ti]
Obv. x 1) 1 Pù-la-lí
2) nu-banda é-gal
3) 1 Lugal-ḫé-gál-sir
4) dub-sar-maḫ
5) 1 É-nam-zu!-šè!
6) gal-ukù
7) ìr é-šà-ga
8–35) [. . .]
Rev. x 1–33) [. . .]
Fragt. c) U. E. x 34) [1] Lugal-níg-lu-lu
35) [1] ⌜X⌝-NI
Obv. xi 1) lú-ki-inim-ma-bi-me
2) Šà-tar
3) Lugal-nam-mu-šub-bi
4) dub-sar-me
5) lú-gá[n-gíd-da-me]
(rest destr.)

Notes

Obv. vi 2–7 and rev. vii 32—obv. viii 2.—The amounts of barley and wool listed in these two passages do not agree exactly with the reconstructed area of land. In both instances, the amount of barley is 29 gur-2-ul, which equals 14½ iku at the rate of 2 gur-2-ul for 1 iku of land, while the amount of wool is 43 ma-na, which equals 14⅓ iku at the rate of 3 ma-na for 1 iku. Since the size of the field is not preserved in either case, there is no way of resolving this discrepancy.

Obv. x 3–7.—The same two individuals appear in App. to nos. 22–23 v 8–vi 2.

Rev. x 34.—With the PN Lugal-níg-lu-lu, compare ^{d}Utu-níg-lu-lu in Ist. Mus. L. 30226, unpublished.

Appendix to nos. 22–23 = no. 144 *Bibl. Mes.* III 10

Synopsis: Plates 95, 96, and 100.

This sale document, which was excavated at Al-Hiba, is treated here because it closely parallels the two stone inscriptions of Lummatur (nos. 22–23) and thereby sheds important light on a number of controversial points in them.

For relationships between App. to nos. 22–23 and nos. 22 and 23, see the introductory remarks to no. 22 under *Text*.

The text concerns the acquisition of a single parcel of land by Lummatur, son of Enanatum, the governor of Lagash, from Ibmud, son of Anikura, of the family of E-ibzi. The size of the parcel is 16½ iku, and it was purchased for 83 ul or 498 silà of barley. This corresponds to just a little over 5 ul or 30 silà per 1 iku of land or about ten times cheaper than the price of land in no. 22.

Although a large portion of the tablet is missing, the reconstruction of the text presents no difficulty. As can be seen from notes to i 2, iii 6–8, and iv 7, the text is not free of mistakes.

Transliteration and Translation

Obv. i	1)	2(eše) 4½(iku) gán éš šám-ma-ta	16½ iku of land, (measured?) by the "purchase rope,"
	2)	gán Gi-lugal-la⟨-ka⟩	the field Gi-lugal,
	3)	Ib-mud	from Ibmud
	4)	dumu Á-ni-kur-ra	son of Anikura
	5)	⌜É⌝-ib-zi-ka-šè	of (the household of) E-ibzi
	6)	Lum-ma-tur	Lummatur

	7)	dumu En-an-na-túm	son of Enanatum,
	8)	en$_5$-si	the governor of
	9)	Lagaš^{KI}-ka-ke$_4$	Lagash,
ii	1)	e-šè-šám	bought.
	2)	20(gur) 3(ul) še gur-sag-gál	20¾ gsg of barley,
	3)	níg-šám gán-kam	as the price of the field,
	4)	šu-ba-ti	he (i.e., Ibmud) received.
	5)	10 síg-bar-udu	Commodities
	6)	1 ì šakan	
	7)	1 ŠU.KEŠDA	
	8)	5 ninda-kalag	
	9)	20 ninda-⸢še⸣	
	10)	20 ku$_6$-dar-ra	
	11)	5 ⸢tu$_7$ silà⸣	
	12)	1 sa lu^{SAR}	
iii	1)	[x silà še-sa]?	
	2)	[x ninda-ì]?	
	3)	[x ninda-sag]?	
	4)	[x sum-gu]?	
	5)	[1 sa ga-raš^{SAR}]	
	6)	[níg-ba]	as the gift
	7)	Ib-mud-šè!	Ibmud
	8)	šu-ba-ti	received.
	9)	1 Lugal-šà-pàd-da	Lugal-shapada
	10)	1 Lugal-⸢ù⸣-ma	(and) Lugal-uma
	11)	[d]umu É-[i]b-zi-me	sons of E-ibzi
iv	1)	[lugal gán-me]	[are the "lords of the field"].
	2)	[PN$_1$]	[PN$_1$]
	3)	[PN$_2$]	[(and) PN$_2$]
	4)	[dumu Lugal-šà-pàd-me]?	[sons of Lugal-shapada?],
	5)	[PN$_3$]	[(and) PN$_3$]
	6)	dumu [Lugal-ù]-⸢ma⸣?	son of ⸢Lugal-uma?⸣,
	7)	dumu gán《-kam》-me	are the "sons of the field";
	8)	lú 1-šè	per person
	9)	1 ninda-kalag	Commodities
	10)	5 ninda-še	
	11)	3 tu$_7$ silà	
	12)	3 ku$_6$-dar-ra	
v	1)	[1 silà še-sa]	
	2)	[1 sa ga-raš^{SAR}]	
	3)	[níg-ba-šè]	[as the gift]
	4)	[šu-ba-ti]	[they received].
	5)	[Ib-mud]	[Ibmud]
	6)	[kag-bi é-gar$_8$-ra bi-dù]	[drove this nail into the wall]
	7)	ì-bi zag-gi bi-ag	(and) spread the oil on the side.
	8)	1 Lugal-ḫé-gál-sir	x PNs
	9)	dub-sar-maḫ	
	10)	1 É-⸢nam-zu⸣-šè	
vi	1)	[gal-ukù]	
	2)	[ìr é-šà-ga]	
	3–5)	[. . .]	
	6)	[1] Lugal-uru-bar	
	7)	1 Lugal-^{d}En-líl	
	8)	lú-u$_5$	
	9)	Akšak^{KI}	
	10)	1 Mes-⸢ki⸣?-núm	
vii	1–6)	[. . .]	
	7)	1 [X-x-x]	
	8)	1 L[um-ma]-^{d}[X]	
	9)	⸢x x⸣ IR KÚ	
	10)	1 ⸢Šubur⸣?	

Rev.	viii	1)	ìr en$_5$-si-⸢GAR⸣	
		2)	1 [L]ugal-[t]ir?	
		3)	ugula e-me-a [(x)]	
		4)	1 Du-d[u]	
		5)	engar ki gu[b]	
		6)	1 Lú-[. . .]	
		7–11)	[. . .]	
	ix	1)	lú-gán-gíd-da-me	were the men who measured the field.
		2)	1 Mes-barag-si	x PNs
		3)	1 Lum-ma-en-TE.ME-na	
		4)	1 Lum-ma-EZEN+⸢X⸣-gal	
		5–8)	[. . .]	
	x	1)	1 Lugal-barag-ga-ni-dùg	
		2)	nu-banda é Lum-ma-tur-ka	
		3)	1 Nam-lugal-ni-dùg	
		4)	⸢lú⸣ [. . .]	
		5–8)	[. . .]	[are the witnesses].
			(2–3 cols. blank)	
	xi	1)	ud Šu-ni-al-dugud-dè	When Shuni-aldugud
		2)	dumu-ni	his son, bought
		3)	Lum-ma-tur-ra	for Lummatur
		4)	gán Gi-lugal-la-ka	the field Gi-lugal,
		5)	e-na-šám-a	
		6)	ki-^{GIŠ}ERÍN-ra-bi	its border
		7)	ba-ba 4	was divided. 4th (year).

Notes

i 2.—The reconstruction of gán Gi-lugal-la⟨-ka⟩ follows xi 4.

i 3–5.—For the structure PN PN$_2$ "PN of (the household/family of) PN$_2$," which is frequent in Fara and Pre-Sargonic sources, see in detail Gelb in E. Lipiński, ed., *State and Temple Economy in the Ancient Near East* 1 (Leuven, 1979) pp. 54ff.

Ib-mud occurs also in iii 7, and É-ib-zi in iii 11. The name Ib-mud apparently occurs in the form Ib-^{d}Mud in the Abu Salabikh text *OIP* 99, 254 rev. vi 3 and perhaps also in 124 rev. i 2 and 485.

iii 6–8.—The sign ÉŠ is clearly written between IB and MUD in line 7. Based on parallels in nos. 22 and 23, we expect níg-ba-šè Ib-mud šu-ba-ti "Ibmud received as a gift."

iv 7.—The writing dumu gán-kam-me stands for dumu gán-me.

v 8–vi 2.—Both Lugal-ḫé-gál-sir and É-nam-zu-šè, with the same titles, reappear in no. 23 obv. x 3–7.

vii 9.—We cannot offer any reconstruction for this line.

viii 3.—The term e-me-a [(x)]? is obscure.

viii 4–5.—For PN engar ki gu[b] "PN, the 'farmer,' who stood in (this) place," cf. PNs engar zag/ki durun$_x$(TUŠ.TUŠ) of nos. 14 and 15, discussed in section 7.11.1.

xi 1–3.—According to this passage, Shuni-aldugud was the son of Lummatur and therefore the grandson of Enanatum I. The same person occurs in another inscription from Al-Hiba, published by Biggs in *Bibl. Mes.* 3 p. 18 no. 2 and briefly discussed on p. 3. The latter text records the building of KIB by Shuni-aldugud, who is termed ìr-ra-ni "his (i.e., Enanatum's) servant." An exact parallel to the inscription published by Biggs is Sollberger, *CIRPL* En. I 10, except that it names Lummatur, son of Enanatum, governor of Lagash, in place of Shuni-aldugud and his attributes and titles.

xi 6.—The closest parallels to the term ki-^{GIŠ}ERÍN-ra are e-ki-ERÍN-ra-ka (*RTC* 47 i 2), a location, cited in *MAD* 2^2 p. 212 under no. 226, and e-ki-ER[ÍN-r]a (Sollberger, *CIRPL* Ukg 16 i 2), a building burned down by a ruler of Umma [see now Steinkeller, *N.A.B.U.* 1990/1 pp. 9f., who proposes the reading ki-^{GIŠ}sur$_x$-ra-bi].

The date "4th (year)" is written in the standard form of the Pre-Sargonic texts from Lagash.

No. 24 Stela of Victory

Photograph: Plate 45, from *DC* II pl. 5bis 3c.

Copy: Plate 46, Thureau-Dangin, *DC* 2 p. LVII; collated by Gelb.

Provenience: Girshu (Tello); found in Tell K (Parrot, *Tello* [Paris, 1948] p. 134).

Date: Sargonic.

Language: Sumerian.

Present location: Louvre Museum (Paris), AO 2679 (according to Parrot, *loc. cit.*).

Publications: L. Heuzey, *RA* 3 (1896) pp. 113–17, especially pp. 115ff. and pl. VI c (photo); Thureau-Dangin, *RS* 5 (1897) pp. 166–73 (copy); *idem*, *SAKI* p. 170 (transliteration and translation); *DC* 2 p. LVII (copy) and pl. 5bis 3c (photo of reverse only); B. R. Foster, *Iraq* 47 (1985) pp. 15–30 (transliteration, translation, and photograph).

Description: The inscribed fragment is of limestone measuring 9 cm high, 26 cm wide.

Another limestone fragment, AO 2678, 34 cm high, 28 cm wide, bearing a relief in three registers on each side of the fragment but no inscription, was published by Heuzey, *RA* 3 (1896) pls. VI A and B. The preserved portions of the fragment show battle scenes with the execution of prisoners of war.

The scholars referred to above have taken for granted that the two fragments, inscribed and sculptured, formed part of a large stela. Only Thureau-Dangin, *RS* 5 p. 166, expressed caution by adding the adverb "probablement."

Not to be confused with these two fragments is "stèla militaire" from Telloh discussed by Heuzey, *RA* 3 p. 113

and *DC* 1 pp. 195 f., and Parrot, *op. cit.* pp. 56 and 57 fig. a (free drawing). The very bulky block of limestone, 2 m wide, 85 cm high, and 20 cm thick, was covered by a partially preserved register of marching soldiers in relief, as shown in the excavation photo *DC* 2 pl. 56 fig. 2 and in the free drawing of Parrot, *op. cit.* p. 57 fig. a.

Foster, *Iraq* 47 pp. 15f., proposed that the Yale stone fragment YBC 2409, published in this volume as no. 39, formed part of the same inscription as no. 24. Foster also assumes, without providing any convincing evidence, that the sculptured fragment AO 2678 likewise belongs to the same stela (in fact, his own description of the physical characteristics of the latter piece, offered *ibid.* p. 15 n. 2, seems to contradict this conclusion).

The arguments in favor of connecting no. 39 with no. 24 are: 1) the fact that both pieces have a similar mineralogical appearance and composition (see the mineralogical analysis of nos. 24 and 39 by C. W. Skinner *apud* Foster, *op. cit.* pp. 29f.), and 2) that no. 39, like no. 24, stems from the general area of Girshu/Lagash. A strong argument against such an assumption is the fact that no. 39 was reused as a door socket, which necessarily means that, if nos. 24 and 39 are parts of the same stela, they were dispersed already in antiquity. In the circumstances, the probability of recovering two (or perhaps even three) fragments of the same object would be virtually nil. Further, if the first sign in no. 39 iii′ 3′ is KUG (as copied by Steinkeller—compare the photograph), then no. 39 would record a price, thus contrasting no. 24, whose preserved section lists neither prices nor additional payments.

In the same article, Foster proposes to date no. 24 to the reign of Rimush, basing this interpretation on the epigraphic evidence and his reconstruction of Rimush's name in rev. iv′ 12′ (incidentally, Foster's translation of the preceding line as "after he received kingship in Agade" is incorrect; the expected verbal form would have to be *šu-ba-an-ti-a-ta, and not šu-ba-ab-ti-a-ta). The sole epigraphic argument offered by Foster is the alleged "archaic" form of LUGAL in rev. iv′ 10′. This argument is simply untenable. On the other hand, Foster completely ignores other dating criteria of the script and language of the inscription, such as the form of ŠU with an upward vertical wedge (rev. iv′ 11′), the general appearance of the signs, and the presence of developed grammatical forms (as in šu-ba-ab-ti-a-ta), all of which point to the classical Sargonic period (Narâm-Sin and his followers) as the date of the inscription. As concerns Foster's interpretation of the traces of the last sign in iv′ 12′ as UŠ, this reading does not find sufficient support in the photograph of the inscription. In view of this, we see no reason to question the classical Sargonic date of no. 24, as determined already by Thureau-Dangin.

Text: The contents of the inscription should be divided into two parts: the part listing the assignment of individual fields, occupying the major part of the inscription, and the part listing totals, occupying the end of the inscription. This is the sequence followed by Thureau-Dangin in his transliteration, although he never tried to justify the discrepancy between his obverse-reverse designation and the sequence of columns i–iv on the reverse.

The preserved units in the major part of the inscription are given in a standard order: first, the size and the name of the individual field or fields; then, the total size of these fields; and finally, the name of the recipient (plus his paternity and title). The titles of the recipients are "senior(?) messenger," "captain of the Amorites," and "senior carpenter."

Almost all the names of the fields recur in the Lagash/Girshu area:

[g]án Ù-[dúg]-⌜KU$_4$ = gán Ù-dùg-KU$_4$ in *RTC* 142 iv 1, Sargonic;

gán ^{d}Nanše-gar-ra = a-šà ^{d}Nanše-gar-ra in Pettinato, *UNL* no. 610, Ur III;

gán Ù-a-dùg-ga = a-šà Ù-a-dùg-ga in Pettinato, *UNL* no. 785, Ur III;

gán sug Lagaš^{KI} = a-šà sug Lagaš^{KI} in Pettinato, *UNL* no. 84, Ur III;

gán Gír-gír-maḫ: Pettinato, *UNL* nos. 374–77 lists a-šà GÍR.GÍR and three other Ur III field names composed of GÍR.GÍR with a qualifier, but not with -maḫ.

We interpret the grand total in rev. iv 6′ as follows:

	bùr	bùr	iku
6(sár-gal)	= 6 × 3,600	= 21,600	= 388,800
5(sar$^{⌝}$u-*gunû*)	= 5 × 600	= 3,000	= 54,000
1(sár)	= 1 × 60	= 60	= 1,080
3(bùr-*gunû*)	= 3 × 10	= 30	= 540
4(bùr)		= 4	= 72
2(eše)		= ⅔	= 12
1(iku)		= $\frac{1}{18}$	= 1
¼(iku)		= $\frac{1}{72}$	= ¼
Total		24,694 53/72	= 444,505¼

The area of 444,505¼ iku (as counted here and earlier in *MAD* 3 p. 269) corresponds to 24,694 bùr and 13¼ iku or 156,837,450 m^2 (counted exactly) or slightly less than 40 km by 40 km. Counting differently, Thureau-Dangin, *RS* 5 p. 168 (and similarly in *idem, SAKI* p. 170) interpreted the total as 39,694 bùr and 13¼ iku by reading the first two numbers as 11(sár-gal) in place of our 6(sár-gal) and 5(sar$^{⌝}$u-*gunû*). Thureau-Dangin's reading is improbable, perhaps impossible, in the light of his own observation in *RS* 5 p. 168 n. 3 that "on ne distingue aucune trace de barres transversales" in the first six circles, as confirmed by Gelb's own collation.

There is a slight possibility of reading 5(sár-gal), instead of 6(sár-gal), according to Thureau-Dangin's transliteration and Gelb's collation.

Within this large territory there were 17 uru-sag "17 main towns" and 8 maš-ga-na-sag "8 main settlements." The term uru-sag must denote the major towns within the territory of the province of Lagash, such as Girshu, Urub$_x$(URU+KÁR), Sirara, Ki$^{⌝}$esh, Kinunir, and Guabba, all listed in BM 14618, which was discussed by Gelb, *StOr* 46 (1975) pp. 43–76. The exact definition of maš-ga-na-sag is not clear; it probably describes large villages or hamlets.

The rest of the inscription, reading A-ga-dè^{KI} nam-lugal šu-ba-ab-ti-a-ta [. . .] ⸢x⸣, is to be translated "after Akkadē received the kingship, ⸢. . .⸣." Due to the absence of parallels, there is no way of knowing what followed next. The reconstruction [nam-en$_5$-si Lagaš^{KI} . . . -ra mu-na-ta-sum], "[la patésitat de Shirpourla à . . . fut donné]," proposed by Thureau-Dangin, *RS* 5 p. 169 (also *idem, SAKI* p. 171), is only a guess.

As far as one can ascertain, the purpose of no. 24 was to record the distribution of land among various types of royal dependents. In this connection, note especially the presence among the fields' recipients of a nu-banda MAR.TU-ne, a high military commander in charge of Amorite troops. In all probability, the land was distributed according to the prebendal (ŠUKU) system, in lieu of services (ÍL, Akk. *ilkum*) provided by its recipients for the crown. It seems likely that most, if not all, of the land listed in no. 24 had been obtained through the confiscation of temple holdings. However, there is no reason to suppose, as does Foster, *op. cit.* pp. 27ff., that this event was necessarily the outcome of a punitive military operation that had been carried out by an Akkadian king against Girshu/Lagash. At any rate, even if the confiscation of the fields in question had a military prelude, it seems unthinkable that a document recording the land's redistribution, to be publicly displayed in Girshu/Lagash, would have been adorned with a scene of the slaughter of Lagashites. This, we believe, constitutes an important argument against assuming a connection between no. 24 and the sculptured fragment AO 2678.

Transliteration

Obv. (only traces at end of lines in last column)
1′) [x g]án Ù-[dùg]-⸢KU$_4$⸣
(rest destr.)

Rev. i′ (beg. destr.)
1′) [. . .] ⸢x⸣ é
(rest destr.)

ii′ (beg. destr.)
1′) [. . .] ⸢dirig(SI.A)⸣
2′) [2]+2(bùr-*gunû*) gán ^{d}Nanše-gar-ra
3′) 2(bùr-*gunû*) gán Ù-a-dùg-ga
4′) [. . .] ⸢x⸣
(rest destr.)

iii′ (beg. destr.)
1′) [šu-nigín x g]án
2′) [. . .]-sag
3′) [gal]?-sukkal
4′) [3]+2(bùr) gán sug Lagaš^{KI}
5′) 5(bùr) gán Gír-gír-maḫ
(blank)
6′) šu-nigín 1(bùr-*gunû*) gán
7′) U-zé-^{d}Ma-lik
8′) [nu]-banda Mar-tu-[n]e
9′) [. . .gá]n?
(rest destr.)

iv′ (beg. destr.)
1′) [x g]án $^{[GIŠ}$Š]E.DÙG
(double line)
2′) [šu-nigín? x] gán
3′) [. . .] ⸢x⸣
4′) [Na]-ba-lu$_5$
5′) [n]agar-gal
(blank)
6′) šu-nigín 6(sár-gal) 5(sarʾu-*gunû*) 1(sár) 3(bùr-*gunû*) 4(bùr) 2(eše) 1(iku) ¼(iku) gán
7′) šu-nigín 20 lal 3 uru-sag
8′) šu-nigín 8 maš-ga-na-sag
(double line)
9′) A-ga-dè^{KI}
10′) nam-lugal
11′) šu-ba-ab-ti-a-ta
12′) [. . .] ⸢x⸣
(rest destr.)

No. 25 Nippur Statue

Photographs: Plates 47 and 48, Oriental Institute, The University of Chicago, prints P. 47407, 47408 from field negatives of 3N-360, 3N-361.

Copy: Plate 48, new copy by Biggs, based on the copy in *OIP* 97 (Chicago, 1978) p. 78 no. 1; collated from photographs.

Provenience: Nippur, found in the Northern Temple in locus NT 99 III 1, field no. 3N 402. It was "among several [statues] found in a cache, apparently buried when the cella of the temple was extended in Level II" (see Biggs, *OIP* 97 p. 71). Compare also *ibid.* pp. 17, 21, 29, and pl. 32.

Date: Fara.

Language: Akkadian, because of the graphotactical sequence x MA.NA URUDU. For the discussion of the linguistic and extra-linguistic features which help in defining the linguistic affiliation, Sumerian or Akkadian, of the Nippur texts (nos. 25–30c), see section 1.5; for the discussion of the Akkadian influence in Sumerian Nippur, see section 1.5.

Present location: Iraq Museum (Baghdad), IM 56506.

Publication: The statue was first discussed by D. E. McCown, *Archaeology* 5/2 (Summer 1952) p. 75; the statue is reproduced on the cover of the issue, but the inscription is not shown. A photograph of the torso and head was published by Parrot, *Sumer* (Paris, 1961) fig. 132, where it was incorrectly identified as coming from the Diyala region. The statue and inscription were published by McCown, Haines, and Biggs, assisted by E. F. Carter, *OIP* 97 pp. 72 no. 1, p. 78 (copy of inscription), and pls. 67, 3 and 68, 1–2 (photographs).

Description: According to *OIP* 97 opposite pl. 67: "white gypsum; worn inscription on back; bitumen in eyes, two pieces of light green steatite inlay in left eyebrow; possibly vertical grooves on side locks; h. 75.8, at elbows w. 23.7, at skirt bottom w. 22.0, th. 23.5 cm." The inscription runs across the back between the neck and the waist band. It consists of three full columns and a fourth with only two lines. The surface is so badly worn that it is not certain where cols. i–iii begin; some of the dividing lines are carelessly and irregularly drawn.

Text: The text deals with the transfer of at least twelve fields, each of which is identified by the size of the field, the price in copper, and the name of the seller. Where both the size and price are adequately preserved the following ratios are found: 1 iku for 1.66 minas of copper (i 4–5, 7–8, 10–11, ii 9–10), 1 iku for 1.8 minas (iii 3–4), and 1 iku for 2.2 minas (iii 7–8). Apart from this, only one personal name in iii 5 and the term ⸢LÚ GÁN⸣ "owner(?) of the field" in iii 10 can be read. LÚ GÁN occurs also in no. 34 ii 9, from northern Babylonia.

Transliteration

i 1–3) [. . .]
4) 1(EŠE) [GÁN]
5) 10 [MA.NA URUDU]
6) [PN]

---

7) 2(EŠE) [GÁN]
8) 20 [MA.NA URUDU]
(blank)
9) P[N]

---

10) 1(EŠE) [GÁN]
11) 10 [MA.NA URUDU]
12) P[N]

---

13) 3(IKU) ⸢GÁN⸣
14) [x MA.NA URUDU]
15) P[N]

---

16) 2(BÙR) [GÁN]
17) [x MA.NA URUDU]
ii 1) [PN]

---

2) [x GÁN]
3) 40 MA.NA [URUDU]
4) ⸢PN⸣

5–8) [. . .]

---

9) 3(IKU) GÁN
10) 5 MA.NA [URUDU]
11) [PN]

12–14) [. . .]
15) ⸢X X⸣
iii 1–2) [. . .]

---

3) 5(IKU) GÁN
4) 10 LAL 1 MA.NA URUDU
5) *An-nu-me*
6) IM KUR LAGAB? KAG?

---

7) 1(BÙR) [G]ÁN
8) 40 MA.NA URUDU
9) ⸢UR? GAR⸣? [. . .]
10) ⸢LÚ GÁN⸣

---

11) ⸢X⸣ [. . .]
12) ⸢ŠÁM⸣ [. . .]
iv 1) ⸢X X⸣ [. . .]
(rest of col. blank)

No. 26 Enna-Il Statue

Photographs: Plates 49 and 50, Oriental Institute, The University of Chicago, print nos. P. 50175, 50176, and 50177 from field negatives of 6N-215, 6N-216, and 6N-217.

Copy: Plate 50, copied by Green from photographs and copy of the original by Gelb.

Provenience: Nippur, Field no. 6 N 271—found at SB 76 in fill of the Parthian platform under a temple, built over the Inanna Temple below level II. See McCown and Haines, *OIP* 78 p. 150 and Crawford, *Archaeology* 12 (1959) pp. 77ff.

Date: Fara.

Language: Akkadian, as indicated by the occurrence of *in* GN "in GN" in i 3′, as in the Akkadian-written Pre-Sargonic texts no. 37 U. E. iv′ 2′ and rev. iii 16, and no. 38 i 7 and 13, by the Akkadian graphotactical sequence x MA.NA URUDU, and by a possible occurrence of *áš-dè* "with," "from" in i 11′ (see below). On the other hand, the Sumerian usage of the logogram A[LAM]? "statue" in ii 3 is contrary to the Akkadian usage of DÙL "statue." See general remarks in section 1.5.

Present location: Iraq Museum (Baghdad), IM 61325.

Publication: A. Goetze, *JCS* 15 (1961) pp. 107f. (photograph).

Description: Part of a limestone statuette of a male figure—only the right half of the upper torso is preserved. The head of the statue, now missing, was probably made separately and was attached to the torso by means of a dowel passing into a hole, following the vertical axis of the statuette. Measurements are 10.2 × 10.7 × 8.8 cm.

Text: The two-column inscription is partially preserved on the front and back of the statuette. It is possible that the inscription did not continue around the arm of the statuette (where the curvature is the greatest) but stopped and then continued on the flat surface of the back. If this was the case, then the lines given as i 7′–8′ and ii 4–6 in the transliteration should be ignored.

The structure of the text in column i is difficult to determine. Three different fields occur in the preserved portions. The first two fields mentioned are followed by what appear to be personal names and field locations. At the end of the column we find the third field, followed immediately by GÁN ŠÁM and two lines of writing, which may be read as personal names Áš/Šu-bí/dè and Inim-ma-ni?-⸢zi⸣?. Thus, the end of the column could be interpreted as "2 bùr of land, the purchased field (GÁN ŠÁM) of PN and PN_2" or "2 bùr of land, the price of the field (ŠÁM GÁN), PN and PN_2 (received)." In either case, the two PNs would stand for the sellers of the field. No prices of the fields are apparent in the preserved portions of the inscription. Another interpretation of the end of column i results from interpreting Áš/Šu-bí/dè not as a name, but as the preposition *áš-dè* "with," "from," and of the whole passage as "2 bùr of land, the field purchased from Inimanizi." The occurrence of the form *áš-dè*, in place of the standard Old Akkadian *iš-dè*, is not so surprising as may appear at first glance. A possible graphic variant of *áš-dè* is *áš-ti* in no. 48 rev. iii 8 (from Sippar). Equally important are the occurrences of *áš-dè* PN in two unpublished texts from Kish, discussed by Gelb in L. Cagni, ed., *La lingua di Ebla* (Naples, 1981) p. 68. The attestations of *áš-dè* and *áš-da* at Kish, Sippar, and Adab are duplicated at Ebla in Syria, furnishing another important link between the language of the "Kish Civilization" in the east and that of Ebla in the west. See full discussion in *ibid.* pp. 57 and 66–70.

Both the beginning and end of column ii are preserved. If the arm of the statuette was not inscribed, then no full line of writing is missing and the column can be translated: "Enna-Il, king of Kish, set up [his stat]ue before Innin." The ruler *En-na-Il* LUGAL *Kiš*, occurring in ii 1–2, is possibly identical with *En-na-Il*, son of *A-Anzud*$_x$(AN.⌜IM⌝.MI.ḪU), who vanquished Elam and dedicated an object to Innin, as suggested by Goetze, *JCS* 15 p. 107. A king Enna-Il is also known from a literary text from Nippur which treats of his religious activities in Ur and Nippur(?) (*ECTJ* pl. XVIII no. 219.) Against Westenholz, *ECTJ* p. 100, who denies any connection between our Enna-Il and that of the literary text, it is tempting to speculate that in each instance the same ruler is meant. Compare J. S. Cooper, *Sumerian and Akkadian Royal Inscriptions* (New Haven, 1986) p. 21 commentary to Ki 7.

The buyer of the fields is apparently Enna-Il, king of Kish, who set up his statue in the temple of Innin on the occasion of his acquisition of three(?) fields.

Transliteration

i		(beg. destr.)
	1′)	[x]+4(BÙR) GÁN
	2′)	É? ḪA? GUD? X?
	3′)	*in Ur-šag*$_5$?^{KI}
	4′)	6(BÙR) GÁN
	5′)	⌜X X X⌝
	6′)	GÁN [. . .]
	7′–8′)	[. . .]?
	9′)	2(BÙR) GÁN
	10′)	GÁN ŠÁM (or ŠÁM GÁN)
	11′)	*áš-dè*
	12′)	*Inim-ma-ni?-*⌜*zi*⌝?
		(rest destr.)
ii	1)	*En-na-Il*
	2)	LUGAL *Kiš*
	3)	A[LAM?-*su*?]
	4–6)	[. . .]?
	7)	IGI ^{d}INNIN
	8)	MU.GUB

No. 27 10 NT 1

Photographs: Plate 51, University Museum, University of Pennsylvania, nos. 10 N 247+248.

Copy: Plate 51, copied by Westenholz from a cast and photographs.

Provenience: Nippur, Field No. 10 NT 1—found in a dump from the old Pennsylvania excavations on top of the Parthian fortress.

Date: Pre-Sargonic.

Language: Possibly Sumerian because of the graphotactical sequence of x kug gín. See general remarks in section 1.5.

Present location: Iraq Museum (Baghdad).

Description: Fragment of a red stone tablet measuring 6.2 × 4 × 5.5 cm. Part of the right edge is preserved.

Text: It is interesting, but perhaps no more than coincidental, that the preserved portions of the obverse of this tablet and no. 30 are parallel. This duplication is most striking in column i′, where all signs preserved in both pieces, including ⌜X⌝-KAG.KAG, are identical.

Transliteration

Obv.	i′		(beg. destr.)
		1′)	[x] kug m[a-n]a 4 gín
		2′)	⌜X⌝.KAG.KAG
		3′)	[x] kug gín
			(rest destr.)
	ii′		(beg. destr.)
		1′)	níg-šám
		2′)	⅔ kug ša-[na-pi]
			(rest destr.)
Rev.	i′		(beg. destr.)
		1′)	4 [. . .]
			(rest destr.)
	ii′		(beg. destr.)
		1′)	[níg-šá]m
		2′)	⌜⅔⌝ kug ša-na-pi
			(rest destr.)

No. 28 PBS XV 3

Photograph: Plate 51, University Museum, University of Pennsylvania.

Copy: Plate 51, copied by Westenholz.

Provenience: Nippur—in a letter A. Westenholz expresses his belief that *PBS* 15, 3 is in all likelihood identical with a stone fragment that was found by J. P. Peters on February 6, 1890, in the northwestern corner of Tablet Hill. In his field catalogue (unpublished) Peters describes the object as follows: "Two fragments of a piece of gypsum inscribed on one side, parts of three columns preserved, much effaced, very rude line characters. Length of two joined together 15 cm, breadth 11.5 cm. Found by the corner of mud brick wall, about 2.5 meters below surface, Fleyah's trench. V:1 [= Tablet Hill, trench 1]. Too much effaced to copy" (courtesy Westenholz). Westenholz's identification of this piece with *PBS* 15, 3 is "based on the general agreement of the description with the object, particularly the measurements. However, the two constituent fragments of *PBS* 15, 3 were entered by Hilprecht in the CBS catalogue with the information that one of them was excavated by Peters in 1890, the other by Haynes in 1893; but there are so many errors in Hilprecht's entries in the CBS catalogue that this disagreement is of little consequence."

Date: Pre-Sargonic.
Language: Akkadian because of the occurrence of AB+ÁŠ.AB+ÁŠ "witnesses" and of Akkadian personal names. See general remarks in section 1.5.
Present location: University Museum, University of Pennsylvania (Philadelphia), CBS 9569+9580.
Publication: L. Legrain, *PBS* 15 p. 7 and no. 3 (copy).
Description: Two fragments of a buff limestone tablet—part of the left and bottom edges are preserved but the reverse is broken away. Measurements are 15 × 11.5 × 2.8 cm.
Text: The inscription is badly preserved in three columns of writing. Clearly recognizable are: ⸢PÙ⸣.ŠA-⸢^{d}⸣[*A*]-*ba*$_4$, ⸢X⸣-*bí-bí*, AB+ÁŠ.AB+ÁŠ "witnesses," ⸢*Sá*⸣-*lim-a-lum*, and [X]-NI-*bí-zi*-⸢*x-x*⸣ in column i, and ⸢*E*⸣-*mi*-^{d}EN.ZU, *A-ku-ì-lum*, *A-za-šum*, and *Ur*-^{d}*Za-b*[*a*$_4$?-*ba*$_4$?] in column ii.

No. 29 PBS XV 17

Photograph: Plate 52, University Museum, University of Pennsylvania.
Copy: Plate 52, copied by Westenholz.
Provenience: Nippur—based on the Object Catalog no. 402, Westenholz believes that this text was found in a secondary context, probably the Parthian fill (personal communication).
Date: Pre-Sargonic.
Language: Probably Sumerian, because of the graphotactical sequence of x kug gín. See general remarks in section 1.5.
Present location: University Museum, University of Pennsylvania (Philadelphia), CBS 9568.
Publication: Legrain, *PBS* 15, 17.
Description: Small fragment of dark-gray slate or shale measuring 4.8 × 5.5 × 0.9 cm. All edges are broken away, with the exception of the bottom, which is smooth. The bottom may have been smoothed off for a secondary use, as in the case of no. 30. The reverse is broken away.
Text: The inscription is preserved in small portions of three columns.

Transliteration

i′ (beg. destr.)
1′) [. . .]
2′) [. . .]
3′) [. . .-t]um^{KI}
4′) [. . .] še
5′) [. . .-M]UD
ii′ (beg. destr.)
1′) ⸢x⸣ [. . .]
2′) 70 ⸢še⸣ [gur]
3′) níg-ŠID-ta è (or ì é-ta è)
4′) 2 kug gín
5′) 2(gur) 2(pi) še NI-ga
iii′ (beg. destr.)
1′) 10 [. . .]
2′) NI/NÍG ⸢x⸣ [. . .]

No. 30 PBS XV 20

Photograph: Plate 52, University Museum, University of Pennsylvania.
Copy: Plate 52, copied by Westenholz.
Provenience: Nippur.
Date: Pre-Sargonic.
Language: Possibly Sumerian, because of the graphotactical sequence of x kug gín. See general remarks in section 1.5.
Present location: University Museum, University of Pennsylvania (Philadelphia), CBS 14033.
Publication: Legrain, *PBS* 15, 20.
Description: A small fragment of buff "schist," cut and reused as a round lid in ancient times. Measurements are 4.5 × 4.5 × 1.3 cm. Reverse is broken away.
Text: Small portions of two columns are preserved. See comments to no. 27 for a discussion of the similarity between the contents of these two fragments.

Transliteration

i′ (beg. destr.)
1′) [x kug m]a-[na x g]ín
2′) [X.K]AG.KAG
3′) [x ku]g gín
4′) [. . .] ⸢x⸣
(rest. destr.)
ii′ (beg. destr.)
1′) ⸢x⸣ [. . .]
2′) 1(bùr) 3(iku) gán-maḫ
3′) níg-šám
4′) 10 kug gín
(rest destr.)

No. 30a Nippur Disk

Photograph: Plate 53, University Museum, University of Pennsylvania (negative no. 6442 = old no. 933).
Copy: Plate 54, copied by Westenholz from an old squeeze and photograph.
Provenience: Nippur—surface find on Mound X during the third campaign of the Nippur Expedition of the University of Pennsylvania (1893–1896).
Date: Pre-Sargonic.
Language: Akkadian, because of the occurrence of DUMU.DUMU(.ME) "descendant(s)" in i 7′ and iv 3′, of ÉŠ.GÍD [SI].SÁ in ii 1′ (which is attested only in the Akkadian kudurru no. 37 rev. iii 14, iv 16), and of Akkadian personal names. On the other hand, the Sumerian graphotactical sequence of "thing counted plus measure" is used throughout. See general remarks in section 1.5.
Present location: Unknown; a squeeze and photograph of the disk belong to the University Museum, University of Pennsylvania, but the disk itself cannot be located now. Westenholz suggests that this object may be the one described in the CBS catalogue as: "CBS 9326. Fr. [= fragmentary?] disk in limestone, restored from many frags., inscribed but largely destroyed. Pre-Sargonic. III Exp. excavated by Haynes 1893(?)."

Description: As the disk cannot now be located, this description is based on an old paper squeeze, photograph, and a letter written by J. H. Haynes to J. P. Peters, dated January 19, 1895. Haynes describes the stone as follows:

> (. . .) an inscribed block of broken and crumbling limestone (. . .). It was found near the surface of the ground in the bottom of a deep valley immediately below the outhouse of our second year's encampment. It has at some time been subjected to fire. Probably a fire was built upon it as upon a hearthstone, and a part of its inscription is entirely destroyed. From the fact that incised lines can be traced across the face of the stone, I judge its entire surface was inscribed (. . .). It is made from several fragments of the stone bound together to make the inscription continuous.

It is not known whether the paper squeeze and photograph were made in the field or when the stone was first transported to Philadelphia.

The photograph shows a flat slab with a curved edge, and parts of nine columns of inscription. The text is preserved only in a strip along the left and lower edge, the center being badly cracked and worn. A paper squeeze of part of the inscription along the curved edge is now somewhat distorted, but does allow one to calculate the size of the stone. The squeeze containing part of col. i 10′–col. vi seems to have its true shape, according to the photograph; from the top of NA in i 10′ to the bottom of the column, edge, the disk measures 7.5 cm; the corresponding section of the photograph is 3.5 cm. Thus, the photo is at a scale of 1:2.11 or slightly less than 1:2. As the total height of the preserved disk is 19.8 cm on the photograph, the extrapolation gives 39.6 cm as the actual height. The maximum width on the photograph is 17.3 cm, which gives 34.6 cm for the actual disk. The maximum curvature at the width appears to be at i 4′, while the maximum along the height seems to be a little beyond the preserved edge, perhaps at vii or viii. If so, the radius (on the photograph) would be 14.8 cm, which is (14.8 × 2.11 =) 31.2 cm to actual scale. The original diameter would have been ca. 62.5 cm. The present piece is about one-quarter to one-third of the original, though the inscribed surface is much less.

Text: The fragmentary state of the inscription does not allow one to draw any certain conclusions as to its structure. It is quite certain, however, that it recorded several purchases of fields, each section giving the size of the field, its price, and the name of the seller. The sizes and prices of fields are preserved in six instances (i, ii, iii, iv, v, and vi). In each case the price of one iku of land is five shekels of silver: 36 iku for 180 shekels in i, 25 iku for 125 shekels in ii, 6.5(?) iku for 32.5(?) shekels in iii, 7.5 iku for 37.5 shekels in iv, 2 iku for 10 shekels in v, and 2.5(?) iku for 12.5(?) shekels in vi.

The information, description, photograph, and copy of the text were kindly provided by Westenholz.

Transliteration

i (beg. destr.)
1′) [. . .] ⌜X⌝ [. . .]
2′) ⌜*I*⌝?-⌜x⌝-[. . .]
3′) TÚG N[I?. . .]
4′) KU? T[UM?. . .]
5′) ⌜X⌝ [. . .]
6′) ⌜MES⌝-*nàd*
7′) ⌜DUMU⌝.DUMU
8′) [SAN]GA?.GAR
9′) 2(BÙR) GÁN
10′) 3 KUG.BABBAR MA.NA
11′) [*T*]*i*-[*t*]*i* [A]?.ZU

ii (beg. destr.)
1′) ÉŠ.GÍD [SI].SÁ
2′) SAG GIŠ ⌜X⌝ GÁN
3′) 1(BÙR) 1(EŠE) 1(IKU) GÁN
4′) 2 KUG.BABBAR MA.NA ⌜5⌝ GÍN

iii (beg. destr.)
1′) ⌜*I*⌝-[*x*]-*lum*-[*x*]
2′) DUMU ⌜X-*x*⌝
3′) 1(EŠE) ⌜½?(IKU)⌝ GÁ[N]
4′) ½ (MA.NA) ⌜2½⌝? KUG.BABBAR GÍN

iv (beg. destr.)
1′) ⌜X⌝-[. . .]
2′) ⌜*Pù-Ma*⌝-[*ma*]?
3′) DUMU.DUMU.ME
4′) 1(EŠE) 1½(IKU) GÁN
5′) ⅔ (MA.NA) KUG.BABBAR LAL 2½ ŠA.NA GÍN

v (beg. destr.)
1′) 2(IKU) GÁN
2′) 10 KUG.⌜BABBAR GÍN⌝
3′) *Pù*-⌜*Ma?-ma?*⌝
4′) *Uru-mu*

vi (beg. destr.)
1′) [. . .] ⌜x⌝ [. . .]
2′) 2½?(IKU) ⌜GÁN⌝
3′) 12½? [KUG.BABBAR GÍN]
4′) ⌜X⌝ [. . .]
5′–7′) [. . .]
8′) ⌜*Lú*⌝?-⌜*x*⌝-*nàd-a* [. . .]

vii (beg. destr.)
1′) ⌜X⌝ [. . .]
2′) [. . .]-⌜*a*⌝?
3′) ⌜*Il*⌝-*su-ra-b*[*í*]
4′) ⌜*Ù*⌝-⌜*x*⌝-[. . .]
(rest. destr.)

Notes

i 6′.—The name ⌜MES⌝-*nàd* is probably identical with the one spelled MES-*na-at* in no. 40 C vi 15.

ii 1′.—For ÉŠ.GÍD [SI].SÁ "(measured with) the standard(?) measuring rope," see the full discussion in note to no. 22 i 1.

No. 30b IM 57944

Photograph: Plate 52, Oriental Institute, The University of Chicago, print P. 46758 from field negative of 2N/905. Fragment at top of column ii is upside down.

Copy: Plate 52, copied by Westenholz, from a cast and field photograph.
Provenience: Nippur, Field No. 2NT 328—found in TA level III locus 59, floor 2, which is a private house dated to the Assyrian period (see *OIP* 77 [1967] p. 70). Many dated tablets were found in chronologically remote strata due in large part to ancient construction activity (see *ibid.* p. 74).
Date: Fara.
Language: Akkadian(?), because of the graphotactical sequence of x SILÀ [X] "x quarts of [X]." See general remarks in section 1.5.
Present location: Iraq Museum (Baghdad), IM 57944.
Description: Fragment of a slate tablet measuring 7.2 × 7.5 cm. One edge is preserved; the reverse is broken away.
Text: The inscription is preserved in the lowest parts of two columns. The Fara date of the inscription is indicated by the occurrence in it of the personal name Ag-^{d}En-líl, since names employing the element Ag are not attested after the end of the Fara period. Compare the names Ag-^{d}Gibil$_4$ (e.g., *TSŠ* 1 vii 6′), Ag-^{d}Nu-muš-da (e.g., *Fara* 3, 13 iii), and Ag-^{d}Sùd (e.g., *TSŠ* 1 iv 16′).

The information, description, and copy of the text were kindly provided by Westenholz.

Transliteration

i′ (beg. destr.)
1′) DUMU ⸢PA.TE.SI⸣
2′) 1 TÚG ^{d}*En-líl*-IGI.SI.A
3′) [ŠE]Š PA.TE.SI
4′) [NÍG].ŠÁM
ii′ (beg. destr.)
1′) [x]+1 SILÀ [X]
2′) 1 ⸢NINDA⸣.SA[G]
3′) *Ag*-^{d}*En-líl*
4′) INNIN.ÙḪ

Notes

i′ 2′.—The sign SI in the PN is possibly ÉŠ. Compare the Fara name ^{d}En-líl-IGI.ÉŠ, attested in Edzard, *SRU* no. 6 iv 1.

ii′ 4′.—INNIN.ÙḪ, usually written ÙḪ.INNIN or ÙḪ.^{d}INNIN, is synonymous with ŠITA.^{d}INNIN. Both are equated in lexical texts with the Akk. *uruḫḫu*, and, apparently, both have the reading /uruḫ/. The /uruḫ/ was a type of funerary official, "undertaker," or the like. See now in detail Civil, *N.A.B.U.* 1987/1 pp. 4f.

No. 30c A 33678

Photograph: Plate 52, Oriental Institute, The University of Chicago, negative no. N. 43240.
Copy: Plate 52, copied by Westenholz.
Provenience: Nippur, Field No. 10 NT 2—found on the surface.
Date: Pre-Sargonic.
Language: Unknown.
Present location: Oriental Institute, The University of Chicago, A 33678.
Description: Fragment of a black shale tablet measuring 3.9 × 2.4 × 0.7 cm. Left edge preserved; reverse broken away.
Text: All that is preserved of the tablet are the initial portions of two lines: the number 20+[x] in one line and the sign PISAN+⸢AN?.NE?⸣ in the other.

The information and copy of the text were kindly provided by Westenholz.

No. 31 Adab Stone Fragment

Photographs: Plate 55, Oriental Institute, The University of Chicago, negatives N. 33707, 33708.
Copy: Plate 55, D. D. Luckenbill, *OIP* 14, 48 (obverse and reverse incorrectly identified); collated.
Synopsis: Plate 101.
Provenience: Adab.
Date: Pre-Sargonic.
Language: Akkadian, as indicated by the occurrence of *šu* "he of (the household)," the graphotactical sequence of x MA.NA URUDU "x pounds of copper," and Akkadian personal names. For the discussion of the linguistic and extra-linguistic features which help in defining the linguistic affiliation, Sumerian or Akkadian, of the Adab texts nos. 31–33, see section 1.5; for the discussion of the Akkadian influence in Sumerian Adab, see section 1.5.
Present location: Oriental Institute, The University of Chicago, A 265.
Publication: Luckenbill, *OIP* 14, 48.
Description: Part of an alabaster tablet measuring 11.6 × 8.2 × 2–3.7 cm with the two columns preserved on each side. The sides were misidentified in *OIP* 14, 48. The flat side (Luckenbill's reverse) must be the upper right corner of the obverse; the other side is slightly convex, and is the lower right corner of the reverse. As the thickness of the edge is still increasing down the edge, the midway point has not yet been reached; thus the fragment is less than twenty-five percent of the original.

Sample Interpretation

iii′ 5′–9′: PN (= Seller) of GN(?) (received) 45 (pounds) of copper for 9 iku of land.

Transliteration

Obv. i′ 1–2) [. . .]
3) [. . .] GÁN
4) [. . .].⸢X⸣.KI
5) [X].ME.RU^{KI}

---

6) [1(BÙR)]? 3(IKU) GÁN
7) ⅔ ŠA.NA.⸢PI⸣ 6 (MA.NA) URUDU
8) *Su*$_4$?-*ma*-⸢. . .⸣

---

9) 1(BÙR)? 1(EŠE) GÁN
10) [1]? (GÚ) [x]+2 (MA.NA) URUDU
(rest destr.)

---

ii′ 1) [. . .]
2) *Iš*-[. . .]
3) DUME *Ti-ti*
4) *šu* ^{d}ÁŠ?.TE?
5) GÁN TAR.⌈X⌉

---

6) 1(EŠE) 4(IKU) GÁN
7) ½ (GÚ) 2 (MA.NA) URUDU
8) *Mu-mu*
9) [*šu*]? ⌈*Um*⌉-*ma*-DÙG

---

10) 1(EŠE) 2(IKU) GÁN
11) [x MA.N]A [URUDU]
(rest destr.)

Rev. iii′ (beg. destr.)
1′) [x(IKU) GÁN]
2′) [x MA].N[A] URUDU
3′) *Pù-šu-tum*
4′) DUMU *Ib*-LUL-*Il*!

5′) 1(EŠE) 3(IKU) GÁN
6′) ⅔ ŠA.NA.PI 5 (MA.NA) URUDU
7′) *Ma-šum*
8′) *šu Ur-Ì-šum*
9′) ḪI.MA.KI?

10′) 1(BÙR) 1(EŠE) GÁN
11′) 1 (GÚ) LAL 10 MA.NA URUDU
12′) *Ìr-ì-pum*
13′) [*šu*] *Pù-šu-tum*

---

iv′ (beg. destr.)
1′) [x L]AL 1(IKU) GÁN
2′) [x]+4 (MA.NA) URUDU
3′) *Ú-bí-bí*
4′) *šu Da-tum*
5′) ⌈X⌉.GAL *A-tum*

6′) [1?(EŠE)]+1(EŠE) 3(IKU) GÁN
7′) [⅔] ŠA.NA.PI [UR]UDU
8′) [*Ad*]?-*da*
9′) [*šu*?. . .]-⌈X⌉
(rest destr.)

No. 32 Adab Clay Fragment I

Photographs: Plates 56 and 57, Oriental Institute, The University of Chicago, negatives N. 33709 and 33710.

Copy: Plates 56 and 57, Luckenbill, *OIP* 14, 49; collated.

Synopsis: Plate 102.

Provenience: Adab.

Date: Pre-Sargonic.

Language: Sumerian, as indicated by the words šám-bi "its price," lú-ki-inim-ma "witness," the Sumerian graphotactical order of x síg ma-na "x pounds of wool," and Sumerian personal names. See general remarks in section 1.5.

Present location: Oriental Institute, The University of Chicago, A 1118.

Publications: E. J. Banks, *Bismaya* (New York, 1912) pp. 322f. (photograph); Luckenbill, *OIP* 14, 49 (copy); Diakonoff, *Obščestvenny i gosudarstvenny stroy Drevnego Dvurečya. Šumer* (Moscow, 1959) pp. 657f.; Edzard, *SRU* no. 119.

Description: Fragment of clay tablet measuring 19.0 × 13.5 × 4.8 cm. The right and lower edges of the tablet are broken away, the left and upper are preserved. Obverse is flat, reverse is rounded. Judging from its thickness and the curvature of the reverse, the fragment represents slightly more than one-fourth of the original tablet. In other words, slightly more than half of the vertical and horizontal dimensions are preserved. The original tablet was approximately square, measuring about 24 × 23 cm and containing twelve columns of writing on the obverse with each column being approximately 18–20 lines (cases) in length. The number of columns on the reverse cannot be safely determined because of the variable spacing of the columns.

The size of the tablet is determined both by physical measurements and by the amount of text it must accommodate. The curvature of the reverse shows where the thickest part of the tablet must have been. Although this is not necessarily the exact center of the tablet, the measurements obtained from taking it as such should not be off by much more than a centimeter or two in each direction.

Text: Seven columns of writing are preserved on the obverse and two columns on the reverse. The reconstruction of the text is based on the reconstructed size of the tablet, the formulary, and the totals.

The text records the acquisition of two fields belonging to the families of Munsub$_x$(PA.USAN) (i–v) and É-sír-ág (v–vii) by an unknown buyer. Columns viii–xii of the obverse (destroyed), the preserved column i of the reverse, and the destroyed first lines of column ii probably contained a very long list of officials, scribes, surveyors, and witnesses of the buyer, such as is found in no. 33. The text concludes in rev. ii with the totals of commodities given to the families of Munsub$_x$ and É-sír-ág. The destroyed portion of the reverse probably contained the name of the buyer.

No. 32 is related to no. 33 by identical structure and by the fact that both documents deal with land acquired from two or three identical families. Also related is App. to no. 32, which involves several of the persons found in the other two texts. Note the following prosopographic links:

1) Bíl-làl-la, son of Munsub$_x$, one of the sellers appearing in no. 32 ii 6, is mentioned in App. to no. 32 i 6 and *passim* in this text;

2) Ur-^{d}En-líl, another son of Munsub$_x$ and a seller in no. 32 ii 9 and in no. 33 rev. iv 10, occurs as a witness in App. to no. 32 iv 7;

3) Ur-^{d}Šul-pa-è, another son of Munsub$_x$ and a secondary seller in no. 32 iii 6, occurs as a witness in App. to no. 32 iv 9;
4) Na-nar, another son of Munsub$_x$ and a secondary seller in no. 32 iii 12, occurs as a witness in no. 33 rev. i 1;
5) Ri-ti, another son of Munsub$_x$, occurs as a witness in no. 32 v 4 and no. 33 iii′ 1′;
6) Šà-gú-ba guruš-tab Lú-lum-ma, another son of Munsub$_x$, occurs as a witness in no. 32 v 7–9 and no. 33 i′ 3′–6′;
7) Gu-ni-du, one of the three "sons" (include one son-in-law) of É-sír-ág and a seller in no. 32 vi 8, occurs as a witness in no. 33 iv′ 6′.

Transliteration and Translation

Obv.	i	1)	6(bùr) 2(eše) 2(iku) gán É-kas	122 iku of land, the field É-kas;
		2)	šám-bi	its price is
		3)	1⅓ ma-na ˹kug gín˺ 2 šám-ma-na	80⅔ shekels of silver;
		4)	gán Munsub$_x$(PA.USAN)	the field of (the family of) Munsub$_x$;
		5)	[1 S]U.A.TÚG	9 PNs, each receiving
		6)	[5 síg ma-na]	1 SU.A.TÚG cloth and 5 pounds of wool,
		7)	[PN]	
		8)	[1 SU.A.TÚG]	
		9)	[5 síg ma-na]	
		10)	[PN]	
		11)	[1 SU.A.TÚG]	
		12)	[5 síg ma-na]	
		13)	[PN]	
		14)	[1 SU.A.TÚG]	
		15)	[5 síg ma-na]	
		16)	[PN]	
	ii	1)	1 SU.A.TÚG	
		2)	5 síg ma-na	
		3)	É-da-da	
		4)	1 SU.A.TÚG	
		5)	5 síg ma-na	
		6)	Bíl-làl-la(wr. -LA.LÀL)	
		7)	1 SU.A.TÚG	
		8)	5 síg ma-na	
		9)	Ur-^{d}En-líl	
		10)	[1 S]U.A.TÚG	
		11)	[5 s]íg [ma-na]	
		12)	[PN]	
		13)	[1 SU.A.TÚG]	
		14)	[5 síg ma-na]	
		15)	[PN]	
		16)	[dumu]	[the sons/children of]
	iii	1)	Munsub$_x$	Munsub$_x$,
		2)	lú-šám-kú	are the sellers.
		3)	1 SU.A.TÚG	4 PNs, each receiving 1 SU.A.TÚG cloth,
		4)	A-bí-bí	
		5)	1 SU.A.TÚG	
		6)	Ur-^{d}Šul-pa-è	
		7)	1 SU.A.TÚG	
		8)	Šeš-šeš	
		9)	1 SU.A.TÚG	
		10)	Ur-^{d}MUŠ	
		11)	5 síg ma-na	5 PNs, each receiving 5 pounds of wool,
		12)	[Na-n]ar	
		13)	[5 síg ma-na]	
		14)	[PN]	
		15)	[5 síg ma-na]	

	16)	[PN]	
	17)	[5 síg ma-na]	
	18)	[PN]	
	19)	[5 síg ma-na]	
	20)	[PN]	
iv	1)	[lú-k]i-inim-ma	are the secondary sellers (= primary witnesses).
	2)	1 Šà-gú-ba	22 PNs
	3)	1 Sag-an-tuku	
	4)	1 KA-ki-bi-šè	
	5)	1 Lugal-šag$_5$-ga	
	6)	1 Lugal-gal-zu	
	7)	1 Ur-igi-sag	
	8)	1 Barag-^{sá}sag$_7$(GAN)-nu-di	
	9)	1 Šà-gú-ba	
	10)	[P]A.URU	
	11–17)	[7 PNs]	
v	1–2)	[2 PNs]	
	3)	1 Ab-ba	
	4)	1 Ri-ti	
	5)	1 Šà-da-nu-NE	
	6)	1 Utu-mu-kúš	
	7)	1 Šà-gú-ba	
	8)	guruš-tab(wr. TAB.GURUŠ)	
	9)	Lú-lum-ma	
	10)	lú-ki-inim-ma	are the witnesses of
	11)	Munsub$_x$	(the family of) Munsub$_x$.
		---	
	12)	4(bùr) 2(eše) gán É-[kas]?	84 iku of land, the field É-[Kas]?;
	13)	[šám-bi]	[its price is]
	14)	[x kug ma-na]	[x shekels of silver];
	15)	[gán É-sír-ág]	[the field of (the family of) É-sír-ag];
	16)	[1 SU.A.TÚG]	[1 SU.A.TÚG cloth]
	17)	[5 síg ma-na]	[(and) 5 pounds of wool]
	18)	[PN]	[PN]
vi	1)	[dam]	[wife of]
	2)	⸢É-sír-ág⸣	⸢É-sír-ag (received)⸣;
	3)	1 SU.[A.TÚG]	1 SU.[A.TÚG] cloth
	4)	A-[. . .]	A.
	5)	SAL.DI.UŠ	son-in-law of
	6)	É-sír-ág	É-sír-ag (received);
	7)	5 síg ma-na	5 minas of wool
	8)	Gu-ni-du	G.
	9)	[dumu]?	[son? of]
	10)	[É-sír-ág]	[É-sír-ag (received)];
	11)	[1 SU.A.TÚG]	[1 SU.A.TÚG cloth]
	12)	[PN]	[PN]
	13)	[dumu]?	[son? of]
	14)	[É-sír-ág]	[É-sír-ag (received)];
	15)	[lú-šám-kú]	[(these are) the sellers].
	16–18)	[3 PNs]	19 PNs
vii	1–6)	[6 PNs]	
	7)	1 ⸢. . .⸣	
	8)	1 Bu-[x]-nu-[x]	
	9–16)	[8 PNs]	
	17)	[lú-ki-inim-ma]	[are the witnesses of]
	18)	[É-sír-ág]	[(the family of) É-sír-ag].
viii–xii		(destr.)	
Rev. i	1)	[1 PN]	14 PNs
	2–5)	[4 PNs]	

	6)	[1 . . .]-⸢ì-lí⸣	
	7)	[1 . . .]-⸢a⸣	
	8)	[1] Lugal-nir-gál	
	9)	1 É-zi	
	10)	1 Ur-é-maḫ	
	11)	1 Lugal-kur-da-kúš	
	12)	1 É-pirig-sír	
	13)	1 Maš	
	14)	dumu	
	15)	Šeš-a	
	16)	1 É-dam-si	
	17)	dumu	
	18)	Be-lí-iš-li	
		(blank space of 2 cols.)	
ii	1)	[lú-ki-inim-ma?]	[are the witnesses(?) of]
	2)	[PN]	[the buyer?].
	3)	[šu-nigín]	[Total]:
	4)	13 SU.A.TÚG	13 SU.A.TÚG cloths
	5)	70 síg ma-na	(and) 70 pounds of wool
	6)	níg-ba	is the gift of
	7)	dumu	the sons/children of
	8)	Munsub$_x$	Munsub$_x$;
	9)	3 SU.A.TÚG	3 SU.A.TÚG cloths
	10)	10 síg ma-na	(and) 10 pounds of wool
	11)	níg-ba	is the gift of
	12)	dam	the wife of
	13)	É-sír-ág	É-sír-ag
	14)	dumu	(and) the sons/children of
	15)	É-sír-ág	É-sír-ag.
		(blank space of at least 2 cols.)	

Notes

i 1 and v 12?.—In the field name, é-kas is evidently a variant spelling of é-kas$_4$ "road/runner-house," for which see, e.g., *YOS* 4, 189:3; *AUCT* 1, 349:2.

i 4, iii 1, v 11, and rev. ii 8.—The personal name or a profession meaning "shepherd," which is expressed by the signs PA.USAN, occurs frequently in the Sumerian administrative texts of the third millennium, as in the Fara period (Lambert, *Sumer* 10 [1954] p. 182; *TSŠ* 160 ii 5; *NTSŠ* 152 iii 2, 207 iii 2 and v 1; and our no. 123 = Unger *AV* pp. 37f. no. 3 vii 6); Pre-Sargonic at Lagash (*VAS* 14, 159 ii 13; *DP* 59 v 11 and 233 ii 5; and our no. 140 = *DP* 31 v 15); early Sargonic at Nippur (*OSP* 1, 125 i 2); and Ur III (*CT* 1, 6 i 11; *UCP* 9 p. 225 no. 100 rev. vi 5′). Since the lexical texts listed in *AHWB* p. 977, under *rēʾû* "shepherd," yield for USAN the readings munsùb, musùb, and sùb, it appears that PA.USAN is to be interpreted as ^{mu_6}munsùb or, with Å. Sjöberg, *Mondgott* p. 62, Krecher, *ZA* 63 (1974) p. 202, and Westenholz, *OSP* 1 p. 63, as mu$_6$-sùb. Of the two spellings, only PA.USAN is attested outside lexical texts, while USAN is not. Both USAN and PA.USAN correspond to the Akkadian *rēʾûm* "shepherd" according to lexical sources. The reading of ⸢*aš*⸣-*gi$_4$-du-um*, equated with PA.USAN in the Ebla lexical texts (Pettinato, *MEE* 4 p. 305 line 958), should be corrected to *na-gi-du-um*, with Krebernik, *ZA* 73 (1983) p. 35.

ii 6.—The sequence Bíl-làl-la, instead of Bíl-la-làl, is given in accordance with App. to no. 32 i 6 and *passim* in this text.

ii 16.—[dumu] Munsub$_x$ is reconstructed on the basis of rev. ii 7–8.

iii 10.—For the DN ^{d}MUŠ, see note to no. 41 obv. vii 17′–18′.

iv 8.—For the PN Barag-^{sá}sag$_7$-nu-di, see note to no. 15 xii 1.

iv 10.—For PA.URU "gang leader," also "recruiter (of workers/soldiers)," as an early graph of zilulu(PA.GIŠGAL), Akk. *zilul(l)û*, *sulilû*, and *saḫḫiru*, see Steinkeller, *ZA* 69 (1979) p. 182. This interpretation is now corroborated by the Ebla Vocabulary, which offers the equation PA.URU = *zu-ḫa-lum/lu-um* (Pettinato, *MEE* 4 p. 305 line 953, p. 377 line 0447), where the Semitic word is evidently a derivative of the verb *saḫārum*. Compare Steinkeller, *JCS* 35 (1983) p. 245.

iv 11–v 2, and in later sections.—Instead of single PNs, we can read, of course, PN + profession in some lines.

rev. i 18.—Although the sign LI is not fully preserved, the reading and interpretation of the name as Be-lí-iš-li is very probable.

ii 3–5 and 9–10.—The 13 SU.A cloths and 70 pounds of wool listed as the total in rev. ii 3–5 enables us to reconstruct the text of i 5 to iii 20, listing the numbers of cloths and amounts of wool given to the sellers and secondary sellers. The same may be said for the total of 3 SU.A cloths and 10 pounds of wool of rev. ii 9–10, which enables us to reconstruct v 16–vi 15.

Appendix to no. 32 = *Mesopotamia* 8 pp. 68f.

Synopsis: Plate 103.

This unique sale document on a clay tablet from Adab, which was published by D. A. Foxvog in *Mesopotamia: Copenhagen Studies in Assyriology* 8 = *RAI* 26 (Copenhagen, 1980) pp. 67–75, is presented here because it concerns Bíl-làl-la and his brothers, who appear in no. 32 as members of the family of Munsub$_x$(PA.USAN). For details, see the introductory remarks to no. 32 under *Text*. According to the information supplied by Foxvog, "a better enlarged photo of the obverse exists on p. 135 of the April 18, 1964 issue of *Business Week* magazine."

The time-span separating the two documents cannot be longer than one generation. This is demonstrated by the fact that several of Bíl-làl-la's brothers were still alive when the *Mesopotamia* 8 tablet was written. Bíl-làl-la himself appears to have been either dead or incapacitated at that time; the person who acted as the main seller in the transaction was his (presumably the oldest) son, Lugal-ezen.

Since the interpretation of this unusual document is exceedingly difficult, it will be useful to give first the outline of its structure and contents. The document may be divided into the following nine sections:

1) i 1–6: Two amounts of barley, totaling 300 bushels and provided by two different households, é Mug-si and é ^{d}Nin-mug, constituted the "price of the field of Bíl-làl-la."

2) i 7–iv 3: Two groups of commodities were given to Bíl-làl-la and Làl-la, his wife; the second group is followed by a statement explaining the purpose of these gifts. Two different interpretations of this statement are possible:

a) The second group of gifts was given to Làl-la, wife of Bíl-làl-la, to be used after "she dies and dwells buried together with him (i.e., Bíl-làl-la)." This interpretation assumes that Bíl-làl-la had already been dead when the transaction took place, and that his gifts, listed in the first group, were deposited in his grave. In contrast, Làl-la was still alive at that time, and her gifts were to be used for her future funeral.

b) The gifts were given to Làl-la when "she was living together with him (i. e., Bíl-làl-la), (to be used) when she is dead and buried." According to this interpretation, both Bíl-làl-la and Làl-la were still alive at the time of the transaction, and the gifts were meant for their future funerals. Since Bíl-làl-la does not act as the main seller in the text, we would have to assume that he had become incapacitated because of old age, and consequently, had been replaced as the head of the household by his oldest son.

3) iv 4–6: Statement that Lugal-ezen, son of Bíl-làl-la, was the (main) seller of the field in this transaction.

4) iv 7–v 10: List of eleven witnesses, seven of whom are Bíl-làl-la's brothers, two are his sons, and one is his brother's son; the identity of the last witness is unclear.

5) v 11–vi 5: Statement that 5 minas of silver, the "price" or "merchandise" of Làl-la, were obtained (du_8-a or a-du_8) in the land of Urua, apparently in exchange for the 300 bushels of barley listed in section 1.

6) vi 6–vii 14: List of fourteen witnesses, ten of whom are identified as "servants of Bíl-làl-la, the people who transported (lit.: carried) the barley"; the remaining four witnesses are called IB-me (meaning unknown).

7) viii 1–4: Statement that É-igi-nim-pa-è, the GAR-en_5-si of Adab, was the buyer of the property.

8) viii 5–8: Statement that Lugal-mu-da-kúš, the "major-domo" (ugula-é), was the man who weighed out the silver and measured out the barley.

9) ix 1–3: Statement that KA-ba-ni-maḫ, the master (scribe), wrote this tablet.

As can be seen from the above outline, key to the understanding this transaction is the relationship between the 300 bushels of barley which constitute the price of Bíl-làl-la's field (in section 1) and the 5 minas (= 300 shekels) of silver which are said to be the níg-šám of Làl-la (in section 5). As noted by Foxvog, *op. cit.* p. 72, these two amounts are clearly equivalent, since the standard ratio of barley to silver in this period is 1 bushel of barley = 1 shekel of silver. The question thus arises whether the sum of 5 minas of silver is simply the silver equivalent of the 300 bushels of barley, or whether the 300 bushels of barley and the 5 minas of silver are two equal halves of the total price.

The simplest explanation of the events described in the text would be that the field in question was sold jointly by Lugal-ezen and Làl-la, his mother, immediately after Bíl-làl-la's death. The buyer, the GAR-en_5-si of Adab (for this title, see note to viii 1–2), paid as the price 300 bushels of barley, which was supplied by two temple households of the Adab province. In addition, he provided funerary gifts for the interment of Bíl-làl-la, as well as a set of similar gifts for the future funeral of Làl-la. The barley of the price was then transported to Urua, where it was exchanged for silver.

According to another explanation, the sellers of the field would be likewise Lugal-ezen and Làl-la, but with the 300 bushels of barley and the 5 minas of silver representing two equal parts of the price, intended respectively for Lugal-ezen and Làl-la. In order to account for the episode with Urua in section 5, one would have to speculate that Làl-la resided in Urua at that time, and that her share of the price was paid/released to her in Urua.

In yet another scenario, the purpose of the sale was to obtain capital to ransom Làl-la from her captivity in Urua. Assuming that Bíl-làl-la was already dead at the time of the transaction, one could speculate that Làl-la's capture and Bíl-làl-la's death were connected with the same event, perhaps a raid of the army of Urua on Kesh. The amount of the ransom to be paid for Làl-la had been set at 5 minas of silver. In order to meet that demand, Lugal-ezen, the oldest(?) of Bíl-làl-la's sons, sold one of the family's fields to the GAR-en_5-si of Adab. The price was paid in grain, which was then transported to Urua.

Admittedly, neither of these three interpretations is fully satisfactory, and thus the question of the meaning of the present text cannot be resolved at this time.

Transliteration and Translation

Obv.	i	1)	180(gur) še gur	180 bushels of barley of
		2)	é Mug-si	the household of M.
		3)	120(gur) še gur	(and) 120 bushels of barley of
		4)	é ^{d}Nin-mug	the (temple) household of N.
		5)	níg-šám gán	are the price of the field of

	6)	Bíl-làl-la-kam$_4$	Bíl-làl-la;
	7)	1 erín anše	Commodities
	8)	1 ^{GIŠ}gigir gam-ma	
	9)	1 TÚG.DÙL.GARÁ?.SÁR+ DIŠ	
	10)	1 níg-lal-sag^{TÚG}	
	11)	1 níg-lal-gaba^{TÚG}	
	12)	1 A.SU.TÚG	
	13)	1 NI.TÚG	
ii	1)	1 íb-dù^{TÚG}	
	2)	1 nàd ^{GIŠ}taskarin	
	3)	1 IŠ.DÈ ^{GIŠ}taskarin	
	4)	1 ḫa-zi^{URUDU}	
	5)	1 esir$_x$(LAK-173) kug	
	6)	1 UD.KA.BAR kug-luḫ	
	7)	1 men kug	
	8)	1 ŠÀ.DAḪ	
	9)	1 gír kug	
	10)	1 gíd-da kug	
	11)	Bíl-làl-la	(for) Bíl-làl-la,
	12)	sanga Kèš	the temple-administrator of Kesh;
	13)	1 TÚG.A.AL	Commodities
	14)	1 níg-bar-3^{TÚG}	
	15)	1 A.SU.TÚG	
iii	1)	1 NI.TÚG	
	2)	1 níg-sag-kéš	
	3)	1 nàd ^{GIŠ}taskarin	
	4)	1 IŠ.DÈ ^{GIŠ}taskarin	
	5)	1 ad-tab za-gìn	
	6)	1 MAŠ.DA.LÚ kug	
	7)	1 gíd-da kug	
	8)	1 é-ba PI kug	
	9)	1 gi$_4$-gi$_4$-lum kug	
	10)	1 UD.KA.BAR kug	
	11)	Làl-la úš	were given to Làl-la
	12)	dam	wife
	13)	Bíl-làl-la	of Bíl-làl-la, (to be used after)
iv	1)	ki-túm-ma	she dies and lives
	2)	an-da-ti-li	buried together with
	3)	an-na-sum	him (i.e., Bíl-làl-la).
	4)	Lugal-ezen	Lugal-ezen
	5)	dumu Bíl-làl-la	son of Bíl-làl-la
	6)	lú-níg-šám-kú	is the seller.
	7)	1 Ur-^{d}En-líl	7 PNs,
	8)	1 X-ma-ni-dùg	
	9)	1 Ur-^{d}Šul-pa-è	
	10)	1 É-úr-bi-dùg	
	11)	1 Ú-ú-a	
	12)	1 É-me-me	
	13)	1 Ur-ur	
	14)	šeš Bíl-làl-la-me	brothers of Bíl-làl-la,
v	1)	1 Sag-kud	2 PNs,
	2)	1 Ur-sag-Kèš	
	3)	šeš-ni-me	his brothers,
	4)	1 An-na-bí-kúš	An-na-bí-kúš
	5)	dumu Ur-ur	son of Ur-ur,
	6)	šeš Bíl-làl-la	brother of Bíl-làl-la,
	7)	sanga Kèš	the temple-administrator of Kesh
	8)	1 Bí-zi-zi	(and) Bí-zi-zi,
	9)	RÉC-349.A.TU	the . . . ,
	10)	lú-ki-inim!-ma-me	are the witnesses.

		11)	5 kug ma-na	5 minas of silver,
		12)	níg-šám	the "price" of
	vi	1)	Làl-la	Làl-la
		2)	dam Bíl-làl-la	wife of Bíl-làl-la,
		3)	sanga Kèš	the temple-administrator of Kesh,
		4)	ma-ta Urua(URU+A)^{KI}	were obtained in the land of
		5)	du$_8$-a (or a-du$_8$)	Urua (in exchange for 300 bushels of barley).
		6)	1 Ma-síg-be-lí	10 PNs,
		7)	1 La-lí	
		8)	1 Im-ta-kas$_4$-e	
		9)	nagar	
		10)	1 Ú-tum-ma-ì-lum	
		11)	ašgab	
		12)	1 Šará-men	
		13)	1 Kèš-pa-è	
		14)	1 Dingir-gá-ab-⌜e⌝	
Rev.	vii	1)	1 Níg-šà	
		2)	1 Ùz-da-DU	
		3)	sipa	
		4)	arád-me	servants,
		5)	1 A-DU-nàd	(and) A.,
		6)	gemé	a female servant,
		7)	arád gemé Bíl-làl-la-me	the servants of Bíl-làl-la,
		8)	lú-še-íl-me	were the porters of barley.
		9)	1 Zi-rí-gúm	4 PNs,
		10)	1 Zi-lú-AŠ-da	
		11)	1 Zag-mu	
		12)	1 UŠ-ág-Kèš	
		13)	IB-me	the . . . ,
		14)	lú-ki-inim-ma-me	are the witnesses.
	viii	1)	É-igi-nim-pa-è	É-igi-nim-pa-è,
		2)	GAR-en$_5$-si	the . . . governor of
		3)	Adab^{KI}	Adab,
		4)	lú-níg-šám-ag	is the buyer.
		5)	Lugal-mu-da-kúš	L.,
		6)	ugula-é	the majordomo,
		7)	lú-kug-lal-a	was the weigher of silver
		8)	lú-še-ág	(and) measurer of barley.
	ix	1)	KA-ba-ni-maḫ	K.,
		2)	um-mi-a	the master scribe,
		3)	dub mu-sar	wrote the tablet.

Notes

i 2 and 4.—The barley given in the price of the field was provided by two households, é Mug-si "the household of Mug-si" and é ^{d}Nin-mug "the household of ^{d}Nin-mug." Of these, the household of Mug-si was apparently named after Mug-si, who is known as GAR-en$_5$-si Adab^{KI} "the . . . governor of Adab," (*OIP* 14, 52 rev. i 1–3) [but note the PN Me-é-mug-si in no. 15 viii 15, 21], whereas the second household was named after the goddess Ninmug, whose temple must have been located at Adab or its area.

i 7–ii 10 and ii 13–iii 10.—For the commodities listed in these two passages, see chapter 11.

ii 12.—For Kesh and its location in the area of Adab, see G. B. Gragg, *TCS* 3 pp. 159–64, *RGTC* 1 pp. 84f., and C. Wilcke, *ZA* 62 (1972) pp. 55–59. J. N. Postgate, *Sumer* 32 (1976) pp. 78–82, proposed to locate Kesh at Tell al-Wilaya. See also M. A. Powell, *JNES* 39 (1980) 51f., who supports Postgate's identification.

iv 8.—The first sign is possibly EZEN, but note the normal form and orientation of EZEN in iv 4.

v 9.—The reading and interpretation of RÉC-349.A.TU are unknown.

vi 4.—Note the spelling ma-ta in place of the expected ma-da. For the location of Urua in western Susiana and its contacts with Babylonia during the third millennium, see Steinkeller, *ZA* 72 (1982) pp. 244ff. and nn. 26–28.

vi 5.—The meaning of the verb du$_8$ (duḫ) in this context is obscure. For the meaning "to free," "to manumit," of du$_8$, see Gelb, *JNES* 32 (1973) p. 88.

vi 6.—The same name, spelled *Ma-si-gi-be-li*, occurs in *M.A.R.I.* 5 (1987) p. 113 no. 19 ii 5, a Pre-Sargonic Mari text. Compare also Ma-síg in *ECTJ* 28 ii 7 and 35 ii 4.

vi 10.—This PN apparently has no parallels.

vii 4, 6, and 7.—Here, the terms arád (probably to be read ìr or èr in this context) and gemé do not denote chattel slaves, but servants.

vii 13.—The meaning of the occupation/title IB is not known. It occurs at Fara (e.g., *Fara* 3, 3 ii), Pre-Sargonic (e.g., *OIP* 14, 62 i 6), and Sargonic sources (e.g., *FM* 9:11).

viii 1–2.—É-igi-nim-pa-è, with the same title, is mentioned in several inscriptions from Adab. For the occurrences, see W. W. Hallo, *Royal Titles* p. 37. The meaning of the title GAR-en$_5$-si (and of the related? term GAR-sanga) remains obscure. Steinkeller, *ASJ* 3 (1981) p. 83 n. 29, proposed the translation "former/retired (governor)." Compare Edzard in E. Lipiński, ed., *State and Temple Economy in the Ancient Near East* 1 (Leuven, 1979) pp. 163ff.

No. 33 Adab Clay Fragment II

Photograph: Plate 58, Oriental Institute, The University of Chicago, negatives N. 33711, and 33712.
Copy: Plate 58, Luckenbill, *OIP* 14, 51 (obverse and reverse incorrectly identified).
Provenience: Adab.
Date: Pre-Sargonic.
Language: Sumerian or Akkadian. Sumerian for the language of the text is suggested by the similarities with no. 32 (in texture of the clay tablet, style of writing, and Sumerian personal names), and by the occurrence of [l]ú-ki-[inim]-ma in i′ 7′. On the other hand, Akkadian as the language of no. 33 is suggested by the graphotactical sequence of 5 ma-na síg "5 pounds of wool" in rev. iv 5 and the genealogical structure PN dumu-SAL PN$_2$ "PN daughter of PN$_2$'" in rev. iv 6–8. See general remarks in section 1.5.
Present location: Oriental Institute, The University of Chicago, A 1131.
Publications: Luckenbill, *OIP* 14, 51 (copy); Edzard, *SRU* no. 120.
Description: Fragment of a clay tablet measuring 13.5 × 9.9 × 5.4 cm. One side is flat, the other rounded. Therefore, the obverse-reverse sequence of *OIP* 14, 51 should be reversed. Right and lower edges are preserved, left and upper edges are broken off, indicating that the fragment represents the lower right portion of the tablet. To judge from decreasing thickness from top to bottom and from left to right, the preserved portion corresponds to about one-fourth of the original.
Text: The text is preserved on four columns of the obverse and four columns of the reverse. Since the texture of the clay tablet and the style of writing are identical with those of no. 32, we may safely assume that the two texts were written by the same scribe.

Because only about one-fourth of the original is preserved, it is impossible to reconstruct the text. Col. i′ contains the end of a list of PNs, marked with a *Personenkeil*; they are witnesses of the seller [. . .]-KA-[. . .]-zi (i′ 8′). What follows is a long list of PNs, also marked with a *Personenkeil* (cols. ii′, iii′, iv′, rev. i, ii, iii). Finally, in rev. iv there is a list of unmarked PNs, who receive commodities. Several of the persons listed in this text also appear in no. 32. See discussion of no. 32 under *Text*.

Transliteration

Obv. i′ (beg. destr.)
1′–2′) [. . .]
3′) [1 Šà-gú]-ba
4′) [1 . . .]-si
5′) guruš-[tab](wr. [TAB].GURUŠ)
6′) [L]ú-[lum]-ma
7′) [l]ú-ki-[inim]-ma
8′) [. . .]-KA-[. . .]-zi
9′) [. . .]-⸢x⸣

ii′ (beg. destr.)
1′) 1 Sag-^{d}Aš$_7$(SÁR+DIŠ)-gi$_4$-da
2′) sagi
3′) 1 Šeš-pàd-da
4′) sagi
5′) 1 Ra-bí-Il
6′) 1 Pab-kalam-dùg
7′) 1 Gal-pum
8′) 1 Lugal-a-mu

iii′ (beg. destr.)
1′) 1 Ri-ti
2′) 1 Túl(LAGAB+TIL)-sag
3′) muḫaldim
4′) lú-banšur-íl
5′) 1 Amar-GUL
6′) šu-i
7′) 1 Sag-^{d}Aš$_7$-gi$_4$-da
8′) sukkal
9′) 1 Ur-DUN

iv′ (beg. destr.)
1′) 1 Ur-^{d}En-ki
2′) sukkal
3′) 1 Su-tu-ì-lum
4′) 1 ^{d}Maḫ-URUDU-e
5′) 1 É-gissu(GIŠ.MI)-bi
6′) 1 Gu-ni-du
7′) 1 Gu-da-ì-lí!

Rev. i
1) 1 Na-nar
2) lú-ašlág
3) 1 Túl(LAGAB+TIL)-li-li
4) kurušda
5) 1 Kur-mu-gam
6) 1 Ù-mu-ì-lí
7) 1 É-du-du
8) 1 DU$_6$.A
9) 1 ^{d}Ezínu(ŠE.TIR)-ur-sag
10) 1 ⸢Za-NI-NI⸣
(rest destr.)

ii
1) 1 Ur-^{d}Dumu-zi-da
2) 1 Á-ni-kur-ra
3) 1 Ur-^{d}Tud
4) 1 Lugal-mu-dùg
5) 1 ŠEŠ.KI-na
6) Uru!-⟨SAG.⟩ḪÚB.DU^{KI}
7) 1 Ur-⸢^{d}Aš$_7$⸣-[gi$_4$- . . .]
8) dumu
9) Di-Utu
10) [. . .]-⸢^{d}Aš$_7$⸣-[gi$_4$- . . .]
(rest destr.)

iii
1) [. . .]-⸢x⸣-dùg
2) 1 Utu-šeš-mu
3) 1 Ab-ba-ba
4) 1 Kum-tuš-šè
5) 1 La-ga-tum
6) sagi
7) 1 Gi-ni-šè
8) ì-du$_8$
9) 1 É-ti-la-dùg
10) [1] ⸢Ur⸣-^{d}⸢EN⸣.[X]
(rest destr.)

iv 1–2) [. . .]
3) Ud-da
4) simug
5) 5 ma-na síg
6) AN.RU.KÈŠ.TA
7) dumu-SAL
8) [U]d-da
9) 1 SU.A.TÚG
10) Ur-^{d}En-líl
11) šeš
(rest destr.)

Notes

ii′ 1′.—For the reading of ^{d}SÁR+DIŠ-gi$_4$ as ^{d}Aš$_7$-gi$_4$, see Biggs, *JCS* 24 (1971) pp. 1f. A detailed discussion of the values of SÁR+DIŠ and the related signs SÁR+AŠ and KAM will be offered by Steinkeller elsewhere.

rev. iv 6.—AN.RU is perhaps a defective spelling of ^{d}Sùd(SU.KUR.RU). Compare Edzard, *SRU* p. 196, who reads the signs as ^{d}sùd!?-x-ta. If so, the name could be interpreted as ^{d}Sùd!-Kèš-ta.

No. 34 BIN II 2

Photographs: Plate 59, Babylonian Collection, Yale University.

Copy: Plate 60, J. B. Nies, *BIN* 2, 2; collated by Gelb.

Synopsis: Plate 103.

Provenience: Unknown (purchased)—this text is alleged to have been found on the site of ancient Uruk. For its provenience from northern Babylonia, see the occurrence of Kish in ii 2. Further, note that if the governor *Il-su*-ERÍN+X, who is mentioned in iv 10–11, is identical with the governor of Matar of that name (see note to iv 10–11), the origin of the text could very well be Matar.

Date: Pre-Sargonic.

Language: Akkadian, because of the occurrence of ⌜*ù*⌝ "and" in i 2, for which compare IGI.3.GÁL *ù* 1 GÍN É "one-third sar and one shekel of a house," in the Akkadian sale document no. 227. Similarly, the writing of KÚ "to eat," without affixes (*passim*) and of DUMU. DUMU "descendant," point to Akkadian as the language of the text. On the other hand, the text uses consistently the Sumerian graphotactical order of x KUG.BABBAR MA.NA "x pounds of silver."
See general remarks in section 1.5.

Present location: Babylonian Collection, Yale University (New Haven), NBC 2515.

Publications: Nies, *JAOS* 38 (1918) pp. 188–96 (copy and photographs); Nies and C. E. Keiser, *BIN* 2 pp. 12ff. no. 2 and pl. LIX (copy and photographs); Diakonoff, *Obščestvenny i gosudarstvenny stroy Drevnego Dvurečya. Šumer* (Moscow, 1959) pp. 59f.

Description: Nearly rectangular slab of soft, gray limestone, measuring 15 × 12 × 3.5 cm. The right edge is rounded out 1.5 cm beyond the corners, and the bottom edge slopes down slightly toward the right corner.

Text: There are four inscribed columns on the obverse; on the reverse are found four and one-half ruler columns of which only the one on the left is inscribed. Two lines in obv. iv are erased; the signs belonging to the last line of obv. iv extend over onto the lower edge. The text is apparently not finished.

The preserved portion of the text records the sale of eight fields. The name of the buyer is not given.

Sample Interpretation

i 1–7: PN (= seller) son of PN$_2$ received 100 shekels of silver (as the price of) 15 iku of land.

Transliteration and Translation

Obv.	i	1)	1 KUG.BABBAR MA.NA	100 shekels of silver
		2)	⌜*ù*⌝ ⅔ (MA.NA) KUG.BABBAR *ša-[n]a*	(is the price of)
		3)	[2(EŠE) 3(IKU)] GÁN	[15] iku of land;
		4)	*Na-ni*	N.
		5)	[DUMU]? ⌜X⌝-*zu-zu*	[son of] ⌜X.⌝
		6)	ŠÁM GÁN	the price of the field
		7)	KÚ	received (lit.: ate).
		8)	⅔ (MA.NA) KUG.BABBAR *ša-na*	40 shekels of silver (is the price of)
		9)	⌜1(EŠE)⌝ GÁN	6 iku of land;
		10)	[*Ì*]?-⌜*lu-lu*⌝	⌜I.⌝
	ii	1)	DUMU *Pù-pù*	son of P., of
		2)	*Kiš*^{KI}	Kish,
		3)	ŠÁM GÁN	the price of the field
		4)	KÚ	received.
		5)	⅔(MA.NA) KUG.BABBAR *ša-na* 5(GÍN)	45 shekels of silver, (the price of)
		6)	1(EŠE) 1(IKU) GÁN	7 iku of land,
		7)	NE.USAN	N.,

	8)	LÚ ⸢*Su*⸣(wr. ⸢ZU⸣)-*ba-rí-um*	the Subarian,
	9)	*Il*-GIŠ.ERÍN LÚ GÁN	(and) I., the owners(?) of the field, (received).
	10)	⸢x x⸣ KUG.BABBAR [MA.NA]	x shekels of silver
iii	1)	5(GÍN) KUG.BABBAR	(and) 5 shekels of silver (is the price of)
	2)	2(EŠE) 1½(IKU) GÁN	13½ iku of land;
	3)	⸢*Pù-pù*⸣	P.
	4)	DUMU *Ag-a*	son of A.
	5)	⸢ŠÁM⸣ 〈GÁN〉 KÚ	received the ⸢price⸣ 〈of the field〉.
	6)	⅔(MA.NA) KUG.BABBAR *ša-na*	40 shekels of silver (is the price of)
	7)	1(EŠE) GÁN	6 iku of land;
	8)	A.SI	A.
	9)	*Lugal*-X-*nun*	(and) L.
	10)	⅔ (MA.NA) KUG.BABBAR *ša-na*	40 shekels of silver,
	11)	ŠÁM	the price of
	12)	[GÁN KÚ]	[the field, received].
iv	1)	1 [KUG.BABBAR (MA.NA)]	60 shekels of silver
	2)	⅔ (MA.NA) KUG.BABBAR [*š*]*a-na*	(and) 40 shekels of silver
	3–4)	(erasure)	(erasure)
	5)	32 SAR [GÁN]	32 sar of land;
	6)	4 KUG.BABBAR GÍN	4 shekels of silver (as its price)
	7)	*Zu-zu*	Z.
	8)	*Ra-bí-ì-lum*	(and) R.
	9)	DUMU.DUMU	sons of
	10)	*Il-su*(wr. ZU)-ERÍN+X	I.,
	11)	PA.TE.SI	the governor, (received).
Rev. i	1)	½(IKU) LAL 3 SAR GÁN	47 sar of land,
	2)	ZAG *Ḫur-rúm*	(located? at the) side(?) of Ḫ., (the property? of?),
	3)	*Ga-lí-su*(wr. ZU)-*ma*	G.
	4)	DUMU *Ur-é* (unfinished, several cols. blank)	son of U.

Notes

i 5.—The sign read as ⸢X⸣ looks like MA. Compare *Ma-z*[*u*?-*zu*] in no. 37 i 5′. The line could alternatively be read [X]-⸢*x*⸣-*zu-zu*.

i 8–9.—The reconstruction is based on iii 6–7.

ii 7.—The reading of the second sign as USAN is only tentative. Note that the sign is preceded by a small horizontal wedge (AŠ?), and that it has two extra vertical wedges, both features being unexpected in USAN. Assuming that the sign is USAN, the word could be interpreted as ne-sùb = *našāqum* "to kiss." For the value mùnsub (and hence sùb) of USAN, see already Ebla Syllabary line 35: USAN = en-ša-bù. See Archi in C. H. Gordon *et al.*, eds., *Eblaitica: Essays on the Ebla Archives and Eblaite Language* (Winona Lake, Indiana, 1987) p. 94.

ii 9.—The element GIŠ.ERÍN is common in Akkadian personal names of the Pre-Sargonic and Early Sargonic periods. See *A-ḫu*-GIŠ.ERÍN in no. 40 C xvii 3 and no. 41 ii 2′, *A-ša-su*-GIŠ.ERÍN in no. 41 rev. vi′ 6′, ᵈEN.ZU-GIŠ.ERÍN in no. 40 A x 5, and *Ì-lum*-GIŠ.ERÍN in no. 41 ii 19′ and iv 9′; for other examples, see *MAD* 3 p. 121. This element appears to be a graphic variant of IGI+LAK-527, the latter sign definitely being the ancestor of SIG$_5$ = Akk. *dam*(*i*)*qum*. See Steinkeller, *Vicino Oriente* 6 (1986) p. 36 and n. 44, and Krecher, *M.A.R.I.* 5 (1987) pp. 623f. The only obstacle in connecting GIŠ.ERÍN with SIG$_5$ is presented by the fact that no. 40, which contains several examples of the names with GIŠ.ERÍN (see above), has also an occurrence of the sign SIG$_5$ (in PN SIG$_5$-*ì-lum*, C xviii 26).

The term LÚ GÁN, possibly meaning "owner of the field" (cf. lugal gán and similar expressions discussed in section 7.6.2), also occurs in no. 25 iii 10, from Nippur.

ii 10.—Since the price is 6.6 and 6.4 shekels of silver for 1 iku in two preceding and one following transactions, we expect to find the price of about 80 (ii 10) + 5 (iii 1) shekels for the 13½ iku of land (iii 2). But the reading of ii 10 as 1(MA.NA) ⅓ KUG.BABBAR [*ša-na*] is very difficult. The first two wedges are drawn downwards as in the fraction ⅔; they are followed by a sign which can be PI or IGI, and a clear KUG.BABBAR. The rest of the line is destroyed.

iii 8.—Possibly to be read SI.A, i.e., DIRI. Compare *MAD* 3 p. 83 for various names with DIRI = *watrum*.

iii 9.—The second sign looks like URU with *gunû* marks inside and outside of the sign. We cannot offer any suggestion for its reading.

iii 10.—The price is given both here and in iii 6.

iv 5–6.—The price of 12+ shekels of silver for this small lot is about twice the price of other fields in this inscription.

iv 10–11.—The governor *Il-su*-ERÍN+X is very likely the same person as the governor of Matar mentioned in the seal *Coll. de*

Clercq 41 (Iš-má-ì-lum, dumu Il-su-ERÍN+X, en$_5$-si, Ma-tar^{KI}-ra!; Pre-Sargonic), which was discussed by Steinkeller, *Vicino Oriente* 6 (1986) pp. 27–31. For the sign ERÍN+X, see *ibid.* pp. 28f. For the city of Matar, possibly the place of origin of the present text, see *ibid.* pp. 29f.

rev. i 2.—The reading of the first sign as ZAG is only tentative. Perhaps, the line gives the location of the field: "(at) the side of Ḫur(r)um," where Ḫur(r)um could be connected with the toponym Ḫu-rúm^{KI} (*RGTC* 2 pp. 79f.) or with *ḫurrum* "hole, depression" (*CAD* Ḫ pp. 252f.). Alternatively, we could find here a PN.

No. 35 DP 2

Photographs: Plate 61, Louvre Museum, Paris.
Copy: Plate 61, Allotte de la Fuÿe, *DP* 2; collated by Gelb.
Provenience: Unknown—the occurrence of Sippar in i 2′ speaks in favor of a site in northern Babylonia.
Date: Pre-Sargonic.
Language: Akkadian.
Present location: Louvre Museum (Paris), AO 13210.
Publication: Allotte de la Fuÿe, *DP* 2 (copy and photograph).
Description: Fragment of a tablet of "syénite" of reddish color, measuring 6.7 × 9.0 × 3.1 cm. Obverse flat, reverse rounded; left and lower edges are preserved, upper and right edges are broken off.
Text: The preserved portion of the tablet is inscribed in two columns on the obverse, in two lines on the lower edge of column i, and in two columns on the reverse.

The sequence of the inscription is not fully assured. Two possible sequences, both discussed in section 1.4, may be considered. One sequence, traditional in the Sargonic and later periods, but used occasionally in the earlier periods, runs from left to right, from column i to column ii, etc., on the obverse and then from right to left, from column i to column ii, etc., on the reverse. In accordance with this sequence, column i of the obverse contains the names of the sellers of the property; column i of the reverse gives the total of 20 witnesses who receive bread/food and beer, and column ii lists names of persons who performed the Ì *šadādum* rite. The other sequence, traditional in Pre-Sargonic and earlier periods, runs from column i of the obverse, across the lower edge, below, to column i of the reverse and, accordingly, from column ii of the obverse, below, to column ii of the reverse, etc. In accordance with this sequence, the text probably began with the size of the property, its price, and the names of the sellers, all now lost. The preserved part of column i gives the names of several individuals, possibly sellers, who performed the Ì *šadādum* rite; column ii contains the location of the property and a total of twenty witnesses who received bread/food and beer in the house of the buyer.

Of the two sequences, the second one is definitely preferred, first, because this obverse-reverse sequence is well documented in the Pre-Sargonic period and, second, because the sequence of the formulary accords with parallels from the same period.

For sellers performing the Ì *šadādum* rite, parallel to the ì . . . ag rite in Sumerian, see section 7.12.5.2; for witnesses partaking in the feast in the house of the buyer, see section 7.12.5.7. The location of the field is given in the same terms (neighboring fields to the [north], south, west, and east) as in nos. 40 and 41.

Transliteration

Obv.	i		(beg. destr.)	
		1′)	[PA.TE].SI	governor
		2′)	[NUN.U]D.KIB^{KI}	of Sippar,
		3′)	*Ì-lum*-GÀR	I.,
		4′)	*Pù-su*-GI	P.,
		5′)	U_9(EZEN+AN)-*zi-um*	U.,
		6′)	*I*-GU-KU-DINGIR	I.
		7′)	DUMU U_9-*zi-um*	son of U.,
Lo. E.		8′)	*I-bí*-^{d}UTU	(and) I.
		9′)	[DUM]U *Na-ni*	son of N.,
Rev.	i	10′)	Ì *iš-du-du*	spread the oil;
		11′)	1 *Pù-za-um*	P.
		12′)	1 PÙ.ŠA-*be-lí*	(and) P.
		13′)	DUMU *Su-mu*-^{d}*A-a*	son of S.
		14′)	[*Ì*] *iš-du-du*	spread the oil;
		15′)	[*I*]*b*?-*lu*-DINGIR	⸢I.⸣
		16′)	[1 X]-⸢*x*⸣-*Eš*$_4$-*dar*	⸢(and) X.⸣
		17′)	[Ì *iš-du-d*]*u*!	spread the oil;
			(rest destr.)	
Obv.	ii		(beg. destr.)	
		1′)	[*è-d*]*a*-[*su*]	its (i.e., of the sold field) border
		2′)	⸢IM⸣.Ù	to the south is
		3′)	*A-rúm*	(the property of) A.
		4′)	*Na-mu-ra*-[*zu*]?	(and) N.;
		5′)	*è-da-s*[*u*]	its border

		6′)	IM.MAR.T[U]	to the west is
		7′)	*Kar-ki-rúm*	(the property of) K.;
		8′)	*è-da-su*	its border
		9′)	IM *sa-ti-um*	to the east is
		10′)	LÚ *I-nin-núm*	(the property of) the man of I.;
		11′)	⸢X⸣	
Lo. E.			(blank)	
Rev.	ii	12′)	ŠU.NIGÍN 20 AB+ÁŠ	Total of 20 witnesses
		13′)	*in* É!	in the house of
		14′)	*I-lu-*[*lu*]?	I. (i.e., the buyer)
		15′)	DUMU *Ì-lí-*⸢*x*⸣-[*x*]	son of I.,
		16′)	PA.TE.[SI]	the governor,
		17′)	NINDA KÚ(KA+⸢GAR⸣)	ate bread/food
		18′)	KAŠ Ì.NA[G](K[A+A])	(and) drank beer.
			(rest destr.)	

Notes

i 2′.—For the *gunû* form of KIB, cf. RÉC-171 and LAK-278. Instead of the crossed forms appearing there, our text has a form which is identical with that found in the PN Ur-sag-A.KIB.NUN^{KI} in *TMH* 5, 56 i 4.

i 5′ and 7′.—For the syllabic value u$_9$ of EZEN+AN, frequent in Ebla texts, see Krebernik, *ZA* 72 (1982) p. 186. Another example of this value in a text from Babylonia is found in the PN U$_9$-bar-tum (*TMH* 5, 67 i 3′; *OSP* 1, 120 iii′ 3′).

i 6′.—*I*-GU-KU-DINGIR, spelled *I*-KU-GU-*Il* in no. 37 iii′ 4 and in the colophons of *OIP* 99, 113, 268, and 479, should probably be interpreted as *I-*^{gu}*ku-Il*, i.e., Ikūn-Il.

i 15′—If the first sign of the name is IB, we could find here a variant spelling of the name *Ib*-LUL-DINGIR. As proposed by Steinkeller, *SEL* 1 (1984) pp. 16f. n. 30, *Ib*-LUL is to be read *Ip-lu*$_5$- (or perhaps even *Ip-lus*$_x$-) and interpreted as *Iplus*-. For this interpretation, see now the Ebla name *Ip-lu*$_5$*-zú* (*ARET* 3 p. 282; 4 p. 247; *MEE* 2 p. 344), which probably represents /*iplus-šu*/ "He-Looked-Upon-Him."

ii 4′.—For the PN *Na-mu-ra-zu*, see *MAD* 3 p. 193.

ii 11′.—There is apparently only one long sign in this line, which is possibly an erasure.

ii 13′.—Against the copy, the sign É is clear.

ii 17′.—The line could alternatively be read Ì.KÚ "they ate."

No. 36 CT V 3

Photograph: Plate 62, British Museum, London.
Copy: Plate 62, S. Smith, *CT* 5, 3; collated by Gelb.
Synopsis: Plate 104.
Provenience: Sippar—see C. B. F. Walker and D. Collon in L. de Meyer, ed., *Tell ed-Dēr* 3 (Leuven, 1980) p. 102 no. 55 and p. 111.
Date: Pre-Sargonic.
Language: Akkadian.
Present location: British Museum (London), BM 22506 (= 82-7-14, 1046).
Publications: H. Winckler, *Altorientalische Forschungen* 1 (Leipzig, 1893) p. 544 (copy); King, *CT* 5, 3 (copy).
Description: Large fragment of a limestone slab measuring 18.5 × 25 cm. Thickness varies from 3.5 to 5.7 cm. The obverse is flat, the reverse completely broken off. Traces of the upper edge are preserved above the first line of the first column of the obverse; also a large portion of the left edge is preserved; other edges are broken off.
Text: Five partially preserved columns can be counted on the obverse. The left edge is uninscribed, the reverse broken off. The inscription certainly begins with the signs 5 BUR GÁN in the first line of the first column. Since the deeply incised signs for numbers usually leave a trace even when much effaced, the lack of such a trace of a number in line 1 means that there was no sign either to the left or above the number 5; there is, however, a suggestion of a sign above GÁN, which should be interpreted as 1(EŠE), in accordance with the prices for fields given in other parts of the inscription. Following the five columns of the obverse there are two uninscribed columns, suggesting either that the inscription was left unfinished or that it had been finished, but that the stonecutter failed for one reason or another to cut off its unnecessary part. For a similar case compare no. 22 under *Text*.

The reconstruction of the length of the individual columns is tentative.

The reconstruction of the size and price of certain lots is based on their relationship to amounts given as the additional payment (NÍG.KI.GAR). See the full discussion in chapter 9.

The preserved portions of the inscription deal with the acquisition of about seven parcels of land by an unknown person.

Transliteration and Translation

Obv.	i	1)	5 BUR ⸢1(EŠE)⸣ GÁN	96 iku of land;
		2)	ŠÁM-*sù*	its price is
		3)	5⅓ KUG.BABBAR MA.NA GÍN	320 shekels of silver;
		4)	NÍG.KI.GAR	the additional payment is
		5)	5 TÚG.A.SU	5 TÚG.A.SU cloths,
		6)	26 Ì.ŠÁḪ SILÀ	26 quarts of pig oil,

	7)	15(GUR) 2(PI) ŠE GUR	(and) 4,620 quarts of barley;
	8)	[*Am*]*ar-Dilmun*-[*na?*^{K}]^{I}	A.
	9–20)	[. . .]	[(and) x PNs received (it)].
ii	1)	[. . .]	
	2)	DU[MU . . .]	
	3)	LÚ NI ⸢. . .⸣	
	4)	NAM.KUD	No-contest clause.
	5)	Ì.IR	
	6)	LÚ.NA.ME	
	7)	*i-na-kir*	
	8)	*ap-lu*	
	9)	GÍR	
	10)	^{d}*Lugal*-^{GIŠ}*asal*$_{x}$(RÉC-65.A)	
	11)	ḪI.ÚŠ	
	12)	[*A*]*mar-Dilmun-na?*^{KI}	
	13)	[. . .]-NE	
	14–20)	[. . .]	

---

iii	1)	[1 BUR GÁN]	[18 iku of land];
	2)	[ŠÁM-*sù*]	[its price is]
	3)	[1 KUG.BABBAR MA.NA]	[60 shekels of silver];
	4)	NÍG.KI.[GAR]	the additional payment is
	5)	6 KUG.BABBAR GÍN	6 shekels of silver
	6)	6 Ì SILÀ	(and) 6 quarts of oil;
	7)	*D*[*u*]-⸢*ba?-ba?*⸣	D.
	8)	DAM	wife of
	9)	*Šu-Eš*$_{4}$*-dar*	Š.
	10)	LÚ *Su*$_{4}$*-be-lí*	of S.
	11)	ŠU.BA.TI	received (it).

---

	12)	1 BUR GÁN	18 iku of land;
	13)	ŠÁM	(its) price is
	14)	⸢1⸣ KUG.BABBAR MA.NA	⸢60⸣ shekels of silver;
	15)	[NÍG.K]I.GAR	the additional payment is
	16)	[6 KUG.BABBAR GÍN]	[6 shekels of silver]
	17)	[6 Ì SILÀ]	[(and) 6 quarts of oil];
	18)	[PN]	[2? PNs]
	19)	[DUMU PN$_{2}$]	
	20)	[PN$_{3}$]	
	21)	[DUMU PN$_{4}$]	
	22)	[ŠU.BA.TI]	[received (it)].

---

iv	1)	[2 BUR 1(EŠE) 3(IKU) GÁN]	[45 iku of land];
	2)	[ŠÁM]	[(its) price is]
	3)	[2½ KUG.BABBAR MA.NA]	[150 shekels of silver];
	4)	[NÍG.KI.GAR]	the additional payment is
	5)	[15 KUG.BABBAR GÍN]	[15 shekels of silver]
	6)	15 [Ì SILÀ]	(and) 15 [quarts of oil];
	7)	*I-ku-tum*	2 PNs
	8)	DUMU *Ú-ḫúb*	
	9)	*Ib-ni*-DINGIR	
	10)	DUMU *I*-KA-*lum*	
	11)	ŠU.BA.TI	received (it).

---

	12)	4(IKU) GÁN	4 iku of land;
	13)	ŠÁM	(its) price is
	14)	13 KUG.BABBAR GÍN 1 MA.NA⟨.TUR⟩	13⅓ shekels of silver;
	15)	^{d}IM-[G]Ú?.GAL	[4? PNs]

	16)	[PN]	
	17)	[DUMU PN$_{2}$]	
	18)	[PN$_{3}$]	
	19)	[DUMU PN$_{4}$]	
	20)	[PN$_{5}$]	
v	1)	[DUMU PN$_{6}$]	
	2)	[ŠU.BA.TI]	[received (it)].

---

	3)	[2(EŠE) GÁN]	[12 iku of land];
	4)	[ŠÁM]	[(its) price is]
	5)	[⅔ KUG.BABBAR MA.NA]	[40 shekels of silver];
	6)	[NÍG.KI.GAR]	[the additional payment is]
	7)	⸢2⸣ [ŠE GUR]	⸢600⸣ [quarts of barley],
	8)	2 KUG.BAB[BAR GÍN]	2 [shekels] of silver,
	9)	4 Ì SILÀ	(and) 4 quarts of oil;
	10)	PÙ.ŠA-*ra-ra*	P.
	11)	DUMU *Ur-Ma-ma*	son of U.
	12)	ŠU.BA.TI	received (it).

---

	13)	1 BUR 1(EŠE) GÁN	24 iku of land;
	14)	1⅓ KUG.BABBAR MA.NA	(its price) is 80 shekels of silver;
	15)	NÍG.KI.GAR	the additional payment is
	16)	4 ŠE GUR	1,200 quarts of barley,
	17)	4 KUG.BABBAR GÍN	4 shekels of silver,
	18)	⸢8⸣ Ì SILÀ	(and) ⸢8⸣ quarts of oil;
	19)	[*Šu-Eš*$_{4}$]-*dar*	[2? PNs]
	20)	[PN]	
	21)	[DUMU PN$_{2}$]	
	22)	[ŠU.BA.TI]	[received (it)].

(cols. vi and viii are blank)

Rev. (destr.)

Notes

i 1 and *passim*.—For the writing 5 BUR in place of 5(BÙR), see note to no. 38 i 6.

i 8.—The reading of this PN is based on ii 12. The identification of the second sign as DILMUN (= LAK-514, ELLes 268 in Pettinato, *MEE* 3 p. 350) is not completely certain. Note that the sign lacks the final vertical wedge that is diagnostic for DILMUN.

ii 1–20.—Lines 4–11 record what appears to be a no-contest clause, in which the sellers promise under oath not to violate the conditions of the transaction (see below). The preceding three lines may have contained the beginning of the clause or dealt with a different clause altogether; it is possible that this section of the inscription actually began in column i. Lines 12–13, which follow immediately after the no-contest clause, could be the continuation of the clause; note that line 12 mentions *Amar-Dilmun-na*?^{KI}, who appears as a seller in i 8. Alternatively, we could find here the beginning of yet another clause.

Lines 4–11 can tentatively be translated as follows: "The oath by oil nobody should change/violate; (if somebody does change it), then the heirs(?) (of the sellers) with the dagger of Lugal-asal will kill him," or: "(the preceding persons) have sworn by oil that nobody should change/violate (the conditions of the transaction); (if somebody does change them), then etc." It is noteworthy that all of the logograms found in this passage are documented in the lexical and administrative texts from Ebla (see below). If the interpretation here proposed is correct, it would add new and very important information to the ever growing evidence for the close connections between the language and writing of northern Babylonia and those of Ebla and Mari in Pre-Sargonic times.

Specific comments to lines 4–11:

Line 4. For NAM.KUD, meaning both "oath" and "to take an oath," "to swear," see LUGAL.BÀD NAM.KUD KÁ ḪI.NA.SUM "the commander of the fortress took an oath at the gate" (Sollberger, *SEb* 3/9–10 [1980] p. 144 lines 480–483, cf. also p. 145 line 546); *wa* ÍL IGI.IGI EN *wa* NAM.KUD "the lord raised his eyes and swore" (Edzard, *SEb* 4 [1981] p. 38 iv 18–v 4); GIŠ? ŠIR+ZA NAM.KUD É ^{d}*Ku-ra* "I(?) swear . . . in the temple of Kura" (*ibid.* p. 43 xiii 5–8); *wa* NAM.KUD NAM.KUD AMA.GAL-*ga* NE.A NAM.KUD NI-*si-in* "you(?) swore an oath by(?) your 'Great Mother' . . ." (*ibid.* p. 43 xiii 14–xiv 2); NAM.KUD AMA.GAL LÚ *an-na* DUMU *I-ti-a an-na* LÚ NAM.KUD "I swear by(?) the 'Great Mother', that of I, son of Itiʾa, the one who swears" (*ibid.* p. 43 xiv 5–13); *wa* NAM.KUD EN GABA ^{d}*Ku-ra* "the lord swore before Kura" (*ibid.* p. 45 xvi 14–xvii 1); in UD NAM.KUD É ^{d}*ʾÀ-da* "when he swore in the temple of Hadad" (Pettinato, *MEE* 2, 19 rev. ii 1–4); UD DUG$_{4}$.GA NAM.KUD "when he took an oath" (*ibid.* 20 ii 6–7); *in* UD DU.DU NAM.KUD É ^{d}*Ku-ra* "when he came to swear in the temple of Kura" (Edzard, *ARET* 2, 13 x 6–10); BA.DAR DU *Iš*$_{11}$*-gi-ba-ìr* NAM.KUD "in the presence(?) of the dagger(?) (= ba-dar gub) I. swore" (Pettinato, *MEE* 3, 65 iv 1–3). See also the occurrences of nam-kud in the Stela of the Vultures, discussed by Edzard, *AS* 20 pp. 79ff. Further, note the possible examples of nam-kud in no. 12 Side D. For an oath taken before the god's dagger, see Falkenstein, *NSGU* 1 p. 65 n. 5, and compare the example from Pettinato, *MEE* 3, 65 iv 1–3, cited above.

Lines 6–7. For LÚ.NA.ME, corresponding to the negated *mamma* "somebody" in Akkadian (*CAD* M/1 p. 195), see Pettinato, *MEE* 3 p. 136 iv 9, p. 206 i 9. For LÚ.NA.ME *i-na-kir*, cf. lú-na-me inim-ma mu-un-ši-in-gá-ma = *mamma ul iraggum* in Ai. III iv 55 (*MSL* 1

p. 50), and see the examples of *nakārum*, with the meanings "to deny a statement, a fact, to contest an agreement, to refuse a request, to speak a falsehood," in *CAD* N/1 pp. 165f.

Line 8. The interpretation of *ap-lu* as a plural of *aplum* "heir" is only tentative.

Line 9. For GÍR, see GÍR.MAR.TU in Pettinato, *MEE* 4 p. 321 line 1127, and the occurrences of various GÍR in Edzard, *ARET* 2 p. 125.

Line 10. ^{d}Lugal-^{GIŠ}RÉC-65.A is a variant spelling of ^{d}Lugal-^{GIŠ}asál = *Bêl-ṣarbi* "Lord-of-Poplar," the god of Baz (see *CAD* Ṣ, pp. 109f.) and of BÀD ^{URU}*Ia-bu-šum*$^{\text{K[I]}}$ (R. Borger, *BAL* 2, p. 47 lines 50–51, reads *-bu-bi-n*[*i*^{ki}]). For this deity, see already *OIP* 99, 82 rev. iii′ 21. The sign RÉC-65 (since Ur III times generally written GABA.LIŠ), which represents a tree trunk, has the following forms in ED texts: 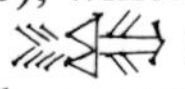 (*UET* 2, 241 i 1 and *passim* in this text);  (*TSŠ* 712:1; contrast with 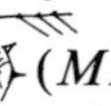 = GABA *ibid.* 715 ii 2′); (*OIP* 99, 82 rev. iii′ 21); 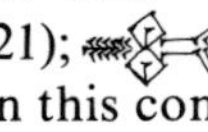 (*MEE* 4 pl. 3 vii 25, pl. 8 v 9);  (*VAS* 14, 98 iii 2). In this connection, note that RÉC-65 is also found in the sign GIŠIMMAR (= "tree trunk" + "date-palm crown"). The most common spelling of /asal/ "poplar" in ED sources is A."TU". RÉC-65, where A is a phonetic indicator, "TU" (written ŠE.NUNUZ at Ebla; see the examples from *MEE* 4 cited above) is "poplar crown," and RÉC-65 is "trunk." A, in fact, is often omitted, as in *UET* 2, 241, *OIP* 99, 82 rev. iii′ 21, and the Ebla examples.

Given the fact that the clause names Lugal-asal, who appears to have been primarily associated with the city of Baz, there is a strong possibility that the present text comes from Baz or its environs. The location of Baz, which was situated in the district of Dûr-Sin (see discussion of no. 40 under *Text*), is unknown. It is possibly identical with the Old Babylonian Bazum (*RGTC* 3 p. 39) and the Middle Babylonian (Bīt-)Bazi (J. A. Brinkman, *AnOr* 43 pp. 158ff.). Further, note the toponym KAR^{KI} (Abu Salabikh) = Ba-áš-zú^{KI} (Ebla) in the Abu Salabikh/Ebla Geographical List (Pettinato, *MEE* 3 p. 233 line 87).

Line 11. For ḪI.ÚŠ/TIL, see Pettinato, *MEE* 3 p. 208 v 19; *idem*, *MEE* 4 p. 334 line 1299′; Edzard, *SEb* 4 (1981) p. 42 xii 14.

iii 7.—The reading *D*[*u*]-⌜*zu-zu*⌝ is also possible.

No. 37 CT XXXII 7f.

Photographs: Plate 63, British Museum, London.
Copy: Plate 64, King, *CT* 32, 7f.
Synopsis: Plate 105.
Provenience: Found at Dailem (ancient Dilbat) according to *CT* 32 p. 3—no information as to the provenience of this text can be deduced from the occurrence of the three GNs, *Lugal-kalam-ma* (rev. iii 16), *É-dur*$_5$*-Me-me* (U. E. iv′ 2), and *Pù-sa-an*^{KI} (R. E. 12). The GN *É-dur*(sic)*-Me-me*^{KI} occurs in a text of unknown provenience (Fish, *CST* 20:2; cf. *MAD* 3, p. 20), while the other two GNs are *hapax legomena.*
Date: Pre-Sargonic.
Language: Akkadian.
Present location: British Museum (London), BM 22460 (= D. 82-3-23-2252).
Publications: King, *CT* 32, 7f. (copy); Diakonoff, *Obščestvenny i gosudarstvenny stroy Drevnego Dvurečya. Šumer* (Moscow, 1959) pp. 58f.
Description: Large fragment of a light-buff limestone tablet measuring 17 × 19.1 × 5.1 cm. Preserved are large portions of the obverse, reverse, upper and right edges. For the sequence, see below.
Text: The sequence of obverse-reverse given in *CT* 32, 7f. is very questionable. There is no doubt that what is called bottom edge and reverse on pl. 8 go together. This can be proved definitely by the fact that *Ì-lu-lu* and *Ma-z*[*u*?*-z*]*u* are added up as 2 DUMU in column iv (following the *CT* numeration) and that x ŠE GUR. SAG.GÁL is followed by NÍG.DÚR.GAR in column i, as elsewhere in the inscription. As the bottom edge goes with the reverse, so the now lost upper edge must go with the obverse, following the sequence found, e.g., in no. 15. Therefore, the upper edge-obverse of the present inscription becomes the lower edge-reverse, and its lower edge-reverse becomes the upper edge-obverse. The sequence favored by us is not beyond doubt, but it is supported by the occurrence of the buyer in the last two lines of the right edge, which certainly forms the end of the inscription, and should, therefore, be aligned with the reverse.

The inscription is preserved in four columns of the upper edge, obverse, and reverse, and in one column of the right edge.

The reconstruction of the length of the individual columns is tentative.

The preserved portions of the inscription deal with the acquisition of ten(?) parcels of land by a certain Tupšikka.

Sample Interpretation

Obv. iii′ 8–17: 6 iku of land; the price of the field is 15 gsg of barley, its additional payment is x commodities; 1 PN (= seller) (received it).

Transliteration and Translation

U. E. i′	1)	1 ŠE GUR.SAG.GÁL	1. gsg of barley,
	2)	2 SÍG MA.NA	2 pounds of wool,
	3)	2 Ì SILÀ	(and) 2 quarts of oil
	4)	*Ì-lu-lu*	I.
Obv. i′	5)	*Ma-z*[*u*?*-z*]*u*	(and) M.
	6)	2 DUMU	2 sons of
	7)	*I-ku-La-im*	I. (received).
	8)	[1(EŠE)] GÁN	[6 iku of land];
	9)	[GÁN ŠÁ]M	[the price of the field is]
	10)	[15 ŠE GUR.SAG.GÁL]	[15. gsg of barley];
	11)	[NÍG.DÚR.GAR]	[the additional payment is]

	12)	[1 ŠE GUR.SAG.GÁL]	[1. gsg of barley],
	13)	[2 SÍG MA.NA]	[2 pounds of wool],
	14)	[2 Ì SILÀ]	[(and) 2 quarts of oil];
	15)	[PN]	5 PNs
	16)	[PN_2]	
U. E. ii′	1)	*I-zi!-núm*	
	2)	*Iš-dup-Il*	
	3)	PÙ.ŠA-*sù*-DÙG	
Obv. ii′	4)	5 DUMU	5 sons of
	5)	*Su_4-ma-Ma-lik*	S. (received it).

	6)	1(EŠE) GÁN	6 iku of land;
	7)	GÁN ŠÁM	the price of the field is
	8)	15 ŠE GUR.SAG.GÁL	15. gsg of barley;
	9)	[NÍG.D]ÚR.GAR	the additional payment is
	10)	[1 ŠE GUR.SAG.GÁL]	[1. gsg of barley],
	11)	[2 SÍG MA.NA]	[2 pounds of wool],
	12)	[2 Ì SILÀ]	[(and) 2 quarts of oil];
U. E. iii′	1)	NÍG.BA	the gift is
	2)	1 TÚG.SU.A	1 TÚG.SU.A cloth;
	3)	*Il-sù*-LAK-647	3 PNs
Obv. iii′	4)	*I*-KU-GU-*Il*	
	5)	*Ur*-^{d}DUB-*an*	
	6)	DUMU.DUMU	sons of
	7)	*Ur*-PA	U. (received it).

	8)	1(EŠE) GÁN	6 iku of land;
	9)	GÁN ŠÁM	the price of the field is
	10)	15 ŠE GUR.SAG.GÁL	15. gsg of barley;
	11)	[NÍG].DÚR.GAR	the additional payment is
	12)	[1 ŠE GUR.SAG].GÁL	[1. gsg of barley],
	13)	[2 SÍG MA.N]A	[2 pounds of wool],
	14)	[2 Ì SILÀ]	[(and) 2 quarts of oil];
	15)	[PN]	[PN]
	16)	[DUMU]	[son of]
	17)	[PN_2]	[PN_2 (received it)].

U. E. iv′	1)	2(BÙR) 2(EŠE) GÁN	48 iku of land
	2)	*in É-dur_5-Me-me*	in E.;
	3)	GÁN ŠÁM	the price of the field is
	4)	90 ŠE GUR.SAG.GÁL	90. gsg of barley;
Obv. iv′	5)	NÍG.DÚR.GAR	the additional payment is
	6)	8 ŠE GUR.SAG.GÁL	8. gsg of barley,
	7)	16 SÍG MA.NA	16 pounds of wool,
	8)	16 Ì SILÀ	(and) 16 quarts of oil;
	9)	NÍG.BA	the gift is
	10)	1 TÚG.SU.A	1 TÚG.SU.A cloth;
	11)	*Ra-bí-ì-lum*	R.
	12)	DUMU	son of
	13)	*Iš-dup*-DINGIR.DINGIR	I. (received it).

	14)	⌜1(EŠE)⌝ GÁN	⌜6⌝ iku of land;
	15)	[GÁN Š]ÁM	the pri[ce of the field is]
	16)	[15 ŠE GUR.SAG.GÁL]	[15. gsg of barley];
	17)	[NÍG.DÚR.GAR]	[the additional payment is]
	18)	[1 ŠE.GUR.SAG.GÁL]	[1. gsg of barley],
	19)	[2 SÍG MA.NA]	[2 pounds of wool],
Lo. E. i	1)	[2 Ì SILÀ]	[(and) 2 quarts of oil];
	2)	[PN]	[PN]

	3)	[DUMU]	[son of]
	4)	[PN_2]	[PN_2 (received it)].

Rev. i	5)	[1(EŠE) GÁN]	[6 iku of land];
	6)	[GÁN ŠÁ]M	[the price of the field is]
	7)	[15 ŠE] GUR.SAG.GÁL	[15. gsg of barley];
	8)	*Pù-pù*	2 PNs (received it);
	9)	DUMU	
	10)	*Šeš*-ENGUR-*na*	
	11)	*Ur-Ab-ra*	
	12)	DUMU	
	13)	*A-lum*-DÙG	
	14)	NÍG.DÚR.GAR	the additional payment is
	15)	1 ŠE GUR.SAG.GÁL	1. gsg of barley,
	16)	2 SÍG MA.NA	2 pounds of wool,
	17)	2 Ì SILÀ	(and) 2 quarts of oil;
	18)	DUMU.DUMU *Ur-ma*	sons of U.
	19)	NÍG.DÚ[R.GAR]	received (lit.: ate) the
	20)	K[Ú]	additional payment.
Lo. E. ii	1–4)	[. . .]	
Rev. ii	5–8)	[. . .]	

---

	9)	[1(EŠE) GÁN]	[6 iku of land];
	10)	[GÁN ŠÁ]M	[the price of the field is]
	11)	[15 Š]E GUR.SAG.GÁL	[15. gsg of ba]rley;
	12)	NÍG.DÚR.GAR	the additional payment is
	13)	1 ŠE GUR.SAG.GÁL	1. gsg of barley,
	14)	2 SÍG MA.NA	2 pounds of wool,
	15)	2 Ì SILÀ	(and) 2 quarts of oil;
	16)	*Men-mu*	5(?) PNs,
	17)	DUMU	
	18)	*En-na-Il*	
	19)	*A*-NI-NI	
	20)	DUMU	
Lo. E. iii	1)	[PN]	
	2)	[PN_2]	
	3)	[DUMU]	
Rev. iii	4)	[PN_3]	
	5)	[PN_4]	
	6)	[DUMU]	
	7)	[PN_5]	
	8)	[PN_6]	
	9)	[DUMU]	
	10)	[PN_7]	
	11)	[DUMU.DUMU]	[descendants of]
	12)	[PN_8]	[PN (received it)].

---

	13)	[2(EŠE) GÁN]	[12 iku of land],
	14)	[É]Š.GÍD SI.SÁ	(measured with) the standard(?) rope,
	15)	GÁN *Ur-ma*	the field of U.
	16)	*in Lugal-kalam-ma*	(situated) in L.;
	17)	ŠÁM-*sù*	its price is
	18)	30 ŠE GUR.SAG.GÁL	30. gsg of barley;
Lo. E. iv	1)	[NÍG.DÚR.GAR]	[the additional payment is]
	2)	[2 ŠE GUR.SAG.GÁL]	[2. gsg of barley],
	3)	[4 SÍG MA.NA]	[4 pounds of wool],
	4)	[4 Ì SILÀ]	[(and) 4 quarts of oil];
Rev. iv	5–14)	[. . .]	

---

	15)	[GÚ].AN.ŠÈ 1(EŠE) GÁN 30 SAR	Total: 6 iku and 30 SAR of land,
	16)	ÉŠ.GÍD SI.SÁ	(measured with) the standard(?) rope;
	17)	DUMU.DUMU	sons/descendants of
		(1 or more cols. on lo.e. and rev. broken; l.e. broken)	
R. E.	1)	[1 ŠE GUR.SAG.GÁL]	[1. gsg of barley]
	2)	[ŠÁM 1 KUG.BABBAR GÍN]	[costs 1 shekel of silver];
	3)	[Ì . . . 1(PI)]	[60 quarts of oil]
	4)	ŠÁM 14+[1 KUG.BABBAR] G[ÍN]	costs 15 [shekels of silver];
	5)	SÍG.GI_6 1 GÚ	1 talent of black wool
	6)	ŠÁM 15 KUG.BABBAR GÍN	costs 15 shekels of silver;
	7)	NÍG.DÚR.GAR	(these are the rates of) the additional payment.
	8)	24 ŠE.NI.KID.NI GUR	24 gur of . . .
	9)	*Ì-a-ki-na-ni*	PN
	10)	DAM *Ur-*^{d}*Gú-gú*	wife of U.,
	11)	DUMU *Ur-túl-sag*	the son of U., of
	12)	*Pù-sa-an*^{KI}	Pusan,
	13)	ŠU.BA.TI	received.
	14)	NÍG.ŠÁM	The acquisitions of
	15)	*Dup-si-ga*	Tupšikka.

Notes

iii′ 3.—As is indicated by the interchange of LAK-647 with URI in the ED Names and Professions List line 114 (Archi, *SEb* 4 [1981] p. 184), LAK-647 is a graphic variant of URI. The name thus probably means "His-God-is-Uri (i.e., Warīum)." Compare *Il*-LAK-647 (*OIP* 99, 116 xiii, 283 rev.) and DINGIR-*Wa-ar* (*Himrin* 27:3, 31:2). The possibility that LAK-647 is identical with IGI+LAK-527 (see note to no. 34 ii 9), as suggested by Krecher, *M.A.R.I.* 5 (1987) pp. 623f., appears unlikely.

iii′ 4—For a discussion of the name *I*-KU-GU-*Il*, see note to no. 35 i 6′.

iii′ 5.—^{d}DUB-*an* is probably the deified Ṭabān-river/canal, for which see the Sargonic names KA-*Da-ba-an* (*MAD* 1, 163 viii 40), ⌜*Ki*⌝?-*nam-Da-ba-an*? (*ibid.* 72 rev. 5′), and possibly SÁR.AN-*mu-da* (*ibid.* 241:15), if SÁR.AN- is to be interpreted as *Ṭab-an-*. Further, note the name *A*-BAN-*Da-ba-an* in the Ebla text *ARET* 8, 522 vii 4. For the value dab_4 of DUB, see *MAD* 2^2 p. 69 no. 101. Physical occurrences of the Ṭabān in third millennium texts are infrequent. See *ù* ^{ÍD}*Da-ba-an iš-bi-ir-ma* (*CT* 44, 2 ii′ 1–2, an OB copy of Shulgi's? inscription); x su_7 . . . gú ^{ÍD}Da-ba-an (P. Michalowski, *OA* 16 [1977] p. 295 YBC 5612:1–3, Ur III); É-dur_5-Zu-za-núm gú ^{ÍD}Da-ba!-an (*NSATN* 320:8–9, Ur III). For the Ṭabān in OB sources, see *RGTC* 3 p. 312. The location of this watercourse was discussed most recently by Kh. Nashef, *Bagh. Mitt.* 13 (1982) pp. 117–41.

Rev. iii 14 and iv 16.—With our case of x GÁN ÉŠ.GÍD SI.SÁ "x land (measured with) the standard(?) measuring rope," which occurs also in no. 30a ii 1′, compare x gán éš šám-ma-ta "x land (measured) with the purchase(?) rope," discussed in note to no. 22 i 1.

R. E. 8.—The grain(?) called ŠE.NI.KID.NI is unknown elsewhere.

No. 38 Dar-a-a Tablet

Photographs: Plate 65, C. J. Ball, *Light from the East* p. 46.

Copy: Plate 65, J.-P. Grégoire, *MVNS* 10, 87.

Provenience: Allegedly found on the site of the Shamash temple in Sippar—the origin of the inscription is in all probability northern Babylonia. This is indicated by its language (Akkadian) and the occurrences of Ashnak (i 15) and the Akkadian toponyms *Ú-sá-la-tim* (Gen.) (i 7) and *Tu-la(l)-tim* (Gen.) (i 11). See also note to i 15.

Date: Sargonic.

Language: Akkadian, as can be judged from the following: the preposition *in* "in" occurring three times (i 7, 13, 15); the phrase GÁN *šu ba-la-ag Da-da-rí-im* "the field of the canal of D." (i 9); the logogram AB+ÁŠ occurring twice, in the meanings "elder" (ii 5) and "witness" (rev. i′ 1).

Present location: Originally in the possession of the Rev. C. J. Ball; now in the Ashmolean Museum (Oxford), 1971-408.

Publications: C. J. Ball, *PSBA* 20 (1898) pp. 19–23 and pls. If.; *idem*, *Light from the East* (London, 1899) pp. 46–50 (photograph, transliteration, and translation); J.-P. Grégoire, *MVNS* 10, 87 and plates 28f.

Description: A limestone tablet that appears to have been cut in half vertically so that the preserved piece, measuring 16 × 8.2 × 5.1 cm, is the left half of an originally square tablet. The thickness of the tablet is nearly one-third its height. The obverse is flat, the reverse rounded. There are two complete and inscribed columns on the obverse, but of the three ruled columns (two complete, one fragmentary) on the reverse only the middle of the last column is inscribed. Although rulings for four lines were drawn, only two were inscribed.

Text: The text contains a number of inconsistencies and misshapen signs. Note, for instance, among the former: 3 UDU.UDU (i 2), but 12 GUD 10 ÁB (i 4); LA in *Ú-sá-la-tim* (i 7) and *ba-la-ag* (i 9), but LAL in *Tu-la(l)-tim* (i 11), and KA+UD.BAR (ii 3), but UD.KA.[BAR] (ii 7). Among misshapen signs, note the second DA in *Da-da-rí-im* (i 9); the sign NIN with several horizontal wedges instead of two wedges in ^{d}*Nin-gal* (i 10); the sign GUR in GUR.SAG (ii 1); and the sign RA in *Eš*$_4$*-dar-ra* (ii 18). Also, the grammar of *šu ba-la-ag Da-da-rí-im* (i 9), instead of *šu ba-al-gi Da-da-rí-im*, is incorrect for the period.

The structure of the text resembles that of no other inscription in this volume. It can be divided into four sections:

1) A number of sheep and cattle, expended(?) by the palace(?) and received(?) by two shepherds (i 1–5).
2) Listing of six fields totaling 282 iku, together with their locations (i 6–15).
3) Listing of six commodities received by a city elder and two commodities received by at least nine persons, only one of whom is provided with a profession: "Edada, the gardener of the orchard of PAB.PAB (a PN)" (i 16–ii 19).
4) A long list of witnesses, of which only the end, reading "total of 25 witnesses of Darʾaʾa," now survives (rev. i′ 1–2).

Because the structure of this text is unique, the following suggestions must be considered very tentative.

1) The first section could be interpreted as the price given to the two shepherds who apparently functioned as primary sellers of the property. The value of the animals listed is very high, as it includes twenty-two head of cattle (which, at about ten shekels each, are valued at 220 shekels of silver) and three sheep. The high value of the animals would offer an indication that, in this context, the profession/title sipa does not denote a simple shepherd but a prosperous animal husbandman.

2) The six fields listed in the second section probably represent the sold property. Again, the high total of 282 iku of six fields in different locations would point to the high status and prosperity of the sellers.

3) The commodities listed in the third section might constitute the additional payment given to the secondary sellers.

4) The person Darʾaʾa, named at the very end of the inscription, was probably the buyer.

However, the interpretation of no. 38 as a sale transaction is complicated by the absence in it of any terminology for "selling" and "buying," and its failure to identify the livestock listed as "price." Equally disturbing is the reference to a "palace(?)" at the very beginning of the inscription. We are forced to consider, therefore, that no. 38 may concern some other type of legal transaction, such as a donation or bequest. If so, the animals listed in the first section could simply form part of the donated/inherited estate, with the two shepherds representing their respective caretakers.

Transliteration and Translation

Obv.	i	1)	⌜É(?)⌝.GAL	(From?) the palace(?)
		2)	3 UDU.UDU	3 sheep (were received? by)
		3)	*Be-lí*-BALA SIPA	B., the shepherd;
		4)	12 GUD 10 ÁB	12 bulls (and) 10 cows (were received? by)
		5)	*Pù-Nu-nu* SIPA	P., the shepherd.
		6)	1(BÙR.GUNU) BUR GÁN	180 iku of land
		7)	*in Ú-sá-la-tim*	(located) in Ushalatum;
		8)	1 BUR GÁN	18 iku of land
		9)	*šu ba-la-ag Da-da-rí-im*	of (= on) the canal of Dad(d)arum;
		10)	1(EŠE) GÁN ^{d}*Nin-gal*	6 iku of land (of?/at? the household) of the goddess Nin-gal;
		11)	1(EŠE) GÁN ⟨*in*⟩? *Tu-la(l)-tim*	6 iku of land (located in) Tula(l)tum;
		12)	3 BUR GÁN	54 iku of land
		13)	*in* X.EDIN^{KI}	(located) in X.EDIN;
		14)	1 BUR GÁN	18 iku of land
		15)	*in Áš-na-ak*^{KI}	(located) in Ashnak.
		16)	1 SI$_4$.SI$_4$	Commodities
		17)	20 DUG Ì.ŠÁḪ	
		18)	10 DUG Ì.DÙG.GA	
	ii	1)	2 ŠE GUR.SAG	
		2)	1 GÍN PI KUG.GI	
		3)	1 KA+UD.BAR [(X)]	
		4)	*Šu-ì-li*	(for) Š.,
		5)	AB+ÁŠ.URU^{KI}	the city elder.
		6)	1 GÍN PI KUG.GI	Commodities
		7)	½ MA.NA UD.KA.[BAR]	
		8)	KA-*Me-ir*	(for) 9+[x] PNs
		9)	*Túl*(LAGAB+TIL)*-ta*	
		10)	*Bìl-zum*	
		11)	*Be-lí*-GÚ	
		12)	*Rí-iṣ*-DINGIR	
		13)	*I-mu-tum*	

14) *E-da-da*
15) NU.SAR
16) GIŠ.SAR
17) PAB.PAB
18) *Eš$_4$-dar-ra*!
19) *Um-me*-DÙG
(1–2 cols. destr.)

Rev. (1–2 cols. destr.)

i′ 1) ŠU.NIGÍN 25 AB+ÁŠ — Total of 25 witnesses of

2) *Dar-a-a* — Darʾaʾa.

Notes

i 1.—The first sign could alternatively be interpreted as NIGIR. At any rate, since the beginning of the line definitely does not contain a numeral, the word in question cannot be a commodity.

i 6, 8, 12, and 14.—The spelling 1(circle) BUR GÁN for 1 bùr or 18 iku, and its multiples in small circles, instead of the standard spelling 1(BÙR) without BUR, has a number of parallels, as in 5 BUR ⌜1(EŠE)⌝ GÁN (no. 36 i 1 and *passim*); 1 BUR 3(IKU) GÁN (*MDP* 14, 33 rev. i, and similarly rev. ii); 1 BUR 1(IKU) 4 SAR GÁN (no. 246; correct to BUR in pl. 155); and 2 BUR GÁN (Montserrat MM 697 and similarly in other lines, unpublished). The only parallel to the spelling 1(BÙR.GUNU) BUR is possibly 1(BÙR.GUNU) LAL 2 BUR GÁN (*MVNS* 3, 27:1), where the reading 2 BUR is more plausible than 2(EŠE) BUR.

i 9.—The interpretation of *Da-da-rí-im* (not *Da-da rí-im*) is assured by the occurrence of *Da-da-rí-im* in the genitive in a Sargonic text recently excavated at Umm-al-Ḫafriyat (1 UmH 342, unpublished, courtesy McG. Gibson). For the meaning, compare the Akkadian word *daddarum* ("an ill-smelling plant, a thorny plant") in *CAD* D pp. 17f.

i 13.—*RGTC* 1 p. 5 reads this toponym as A.EDEN^{ki}. However, the first sign is not A (cf. A in rev. i′ 2) but a vertical wedge, identical with the capacity measure nigida. If the sign in question is in fact NIGIDA, one could interpret the toponym as *Pān*(NIGIDA)-*ṣērim*(EDIN), and compare it to the Middle Babylonian *Pa-an*-EDIN(.NA), IGI-EDIN(.NA), for which see *RGTC* 5 pp. 214f. For NIGIDA = *pānu*(*m*), see *AHWB* p. 822b. Alternatively, "NIGIDA" could simply be a redundant wedge, attributable to the stonecutter's error. Compare here the toponym EDIN, attested in various Sargonic sources (*RGTC* 1 pp. 38f.) and in the Abu Salabikh/Ebla geographical list (*MEE* 3 p. 235 line 171). In this connection, note the existence of several other third millennium toponyms that include the sign EDIN: *Ba-ra-az*-EDIN^{KI} (no. 40 Side D vi 16, xiv 17), É-gal-edin-na^{KI} (*RGTC* 1 p. 41), and [X].EDIN^{KI} (*ibid.* p. 198 under [X]$_{18}$.EDEN).

i 15.—The closest contemporary evidence for Ashnak comes from an inscription of Narâm-Sin, reading: *in ba-rí-ti* URU+UD^{KI} *ù Áš-na-ak^{KI} "between URU+*UD and Ashnak" (*PBS* 5, 36 iv 7–10, cited in *RGTC* 1 p. 199 under X$_{28}$-nak). Ashnak is also mentioned in the Abu Salabikh/Ebla geographical list: Áš-DI^{KI} (AbS), Áš-na-ak^{KI} (Ebla) (*MEE* 3 p. 232 line 82), and in an economic text from Abu Salabikh: Áš-DI^{KI} (*OIP* 99, 494 i 3); for the spelling Áš-DI^{KI}, see Steinkeller, *Vicino Oriente* 6 (1986) p. 34 and n. 31. The only later reference to this toponym is possibly found in an OB lexical text (*MSL* 11 p. 141 Forerunner 8 iii 6), which lists Aš-nik^{KI}. The above-cited occurrence of Ashnak in a tablet from Abu Salabikh may provide evidence that Ashnak was located in the vicinity of Abu Salabikh, i.e., in the border area between southern and northern Babylonia.

i 16.—With our SI$_4$.SI$_4$, cf. 1 SI$_4$.SI$_4$ KUG.GI, clearly an object of gold, which is attested in an Ebla text (*ARET* 2, 31 ii 1).

ii 18.—The reading of the name *Eš$_4$-dar-ra* is assured by a clear occurrence of this name in a Sargonic text published as *Himrin* 1 ii 3, vi 18. A rare form of RA in *Eš$_4$-dar-ra* appears also in *Ra-bí-ì-lum* in no. 34 iv 8.

No. 39 YBC 2409

Photograph: Plate 66, Babylonian Collection, Yale University, New Haven.

Copy: Plate 66, copied by Steinkeller in 1974.

Provenience: Unknown—the fact that the toponyms É-dur$_5$-sabra (i′ 1′) and [É-du]r$_5$-en$_5$-si (i′ 2′) are both documented in Lagash sources (see *RGTC* 1 p. 40) offers strong indication that the inscription comes from the province of Girshu/Lagash, possibly from the city of Girshu itself.

Date: Sargonic.

Language: Sumerian.

Present location: Yale Babylonian Collection, Yale University (New Haven), YBC 2409.

Publication: B. R. Foster, *Iraq* 47 (1985) pp. 15–30 (transliteration, translation, copy, and photograph).

Description: Large irregular light-buff stone fragment measuring 20 × 21 × 12 cm. A full perforation extends from the bottom to the top, with the largest diameter of 7.5 cm at the top. The stone must have been reused at one time for some secondary purpose, perhaps as a door socket.

Text: Ends of three columns are preserved on one surface. Column i lists only the sizes of four fields and their locations. Column ii must have contained other fields, which were then totaled as "the field of Mir-ki-ág, the (supervisor? of) perfumers" (ì-DU.DU-me).

The interesting feature of the fragmentary column iii is the sequence ⌜kug 14+x? gín? . . .⌝, which is paralleled in this corpus only by no. 47 ii′ 3′.

For the possibility that the present text may be part of no. 24, see no. 24 under *Text*.

Transliteration

i′ (beg. destr.)
1′) [x]+2(bùr) 2? ½(iku) ⌜gán⌝ É-dur$_5$-sabra
2′) [x]+3(bùr) lal 1? ½(iku) gán [É-du]r$_5$-en$_5$-si
3′) [x(bùr) x]+2½(iku) gán [. . .]-⌜x⌝-lú
4′) [x(bùr) x(iku) gá]n DÙG?

ii′ (beg. destr.)
1′) 4(bùr) gán SUG ⌜AB?.ZAG?⌝
(double line)
2′) šu-nigín 4(bùr) (wr. consecutively) gán
3′) Mir-ki-ág
4′) ì-DU.DU-me

iii′ (beg. destr.)
1′) ⌜. . .⌝

2′) Da-⌜x⌝-[. . .]
3′) ⌜kug 14+x? gín? . . .⌝
(rest. destr.)

No. 40 Manishtushu Obelisk

Photographs: Plates 67–72, courtesy J. Botteró.
Copy: None.
Synopsis: Plates 106–109.
Provenience: Unknown—the obelisk was excavated at Susa in Elam, to which the Elamites had carried it as booty from a site in northern Babylonia. Despite the fact that the obelisk deals with the fields of Dûr-Sin, Girtab, Marda, and Kish, it was probably deposited not in one of these four cities, but in Ebabbar, the temple of Shamash in Sippar. See section 1.10 for the evidence that the booty that was carried off by the Elamites to Susa had come mainly from the Ebabbar of Sippar. Note, however, that the transactions themselves seem to have taken place in Kazalu (Side C xix 19, D vii 4).
Date: Sargonic.
Language: Akkadian.
Present location: Louvre Museum (Paris), S^{B} 20 ("S" = Susiane).
Publications: Scheil, *MDP* 2 pp. 1–52 and pls. 1–10 (photographs); J. de Morgan, G. Jéquier, and G. Lampre, *MDP* 1 pp. 141f. and pl. IX (photograph); Ch. Zervos, *L'art de la Mésopotamie* (Paris, 1935) p. 160 (photograph). See also F. Hrozný, "Der Obelisk Maništusu's," *WZKM* 21 (1907) pp. 11–43; *idem*, "Das Problem der altbabylonischen Dynastien von Akkad und Kiš," *WZKM* 23 (1909) pp. 191–219; Diakonoff, *Obščestvenny i gosudarstvenny stroy Drevnego Dvurečya. Šumer* (Moscow, 1959) pp. 69f.
Description: Four-sided obelisk or pyramid of black diorite. The maximum height of the obelisk is at present 144 cm (measured along the side of the obelisk), including the 10–20 cm of plaster which was added in modern times at the bottom of the obelisk to ensure an even base. The original height of the obelisk is unknown.

The obelisk has four sides of uneven width (Side A, Side B, Side C, and Side D, henceforth abbreviated as A, B, C, and D). Measured at the bottom line of writing their width is: A-50 cm, B-45 cm, C-52 cm, and D-39 cm. The preserved top column of D is 12 cm wide. The top lines of other sides are broken away. While the top line of writing in column i of D is preserved, the very top of the obelisk is now destroyed, and we must assume that three columns of writing, now marked in transliteration as a, b, and c, preceded our column i.
Text: The inscription is preserved on four sides, with the number of columns and the number of lines in each column varying from one side to another:

Side	*Columns*	*Lines*
A	16	8–27
B	22	6–22
C	24	17–30
D	14	6–22

Although, with the exception of D, the top columns of individual sides are now destroyed, the missing columns and lines can be safely reconstructed on the basis of summations given in the preserved parts of the inscription.

The A, B, C, D sequence of the sides introduced by Scheil was accepted without question by Hrozný. However, Poebel, *JAOS* 57 (1937) p. 364, pointed out that this sequence is incorrect. As can be seen from the photographs published here as pls. 67–72, the end line of Scheil's B is followed by A, and the end line of Scheil's D is followed by C. The correct sequence of the sides is consequently not A, B, C, D, as proposed by Scheil, but A (= old A), B (= old D), C (= old C), D (= old B).

Structurally, the text may be analyzed as follows:

Side	A i	Introductory statement
	A ii 1–v 16	Transaction A_1
	A v 17–viii 4	Transaction A_2
	A viii 5–ix 8	Transaction A_3
	A ix 9–xvi 23	Details concerning transactions A_1, A_2, and A_3
Side	B	Transaction B
Side	C i 1–vii 17	Transaction C_1
	C vii 18–xii 5	Transaction C_2
	C xii 6–xiii 9	Transaction C_3
	C xiii 10–xxiv 29	Details concerning transactions C_1, C_2, and C_3
Side	D	Transaction D

The inscription deals with the acquisition of eight parcels of land, each from several sellers of the same kinship grouping, by the king Manishtushu. These eight parcels, totaling 9723 iku (= 3430 ha) of land, are situated in four areas around the cities Dûr-Sin, Girtab, Marda, and Kish, all in the land of Akkad.

Column i is separated from the beginning of transaction A_1 (in col. ii) by a full blank column. Only the last eight lines of column i are preserved. Of these, the first three lines and what preceded them are impossible to reconstruct. These lines are separated by a blank space from the last five lines, which read clearly that Manishtushu, king of Kish, bought 9723 iku of land.

The location of the four areas in which the eight parcels of land were purchased by Manishtushu is given in the text and is charted here in figure 11. The parcels acquired in each of the four areas are described by field names located near certain cities and abutting on four sides (north, west, east, and south) on the fields or households of neighbors and rivers or canals.

Locating the four areas on a modern map is relatively easy for B, C, and D, but difficult for A. Girtab of B lies on the Abgal Canal in the west, and the latter is a western branch of the Euphrates whose course passed through Sippar, Kish, and Nippur in ancient times. Marda of C is identified with the modern Wannat as-Saᶜdūn. Kish of D is Al-Uḫaimir of modern times. That leaves Baz in (the province of) Dûr-Sin of A to be discussed. At first glance, the location of Baz of Dûr-Sin offers no difficulties since the field of Baz is said to adjoin the Tigris River on its eastern border. However, several problems arise immedi-

Figure 11. Chart of the Fields of the Manishtushu Obelisk

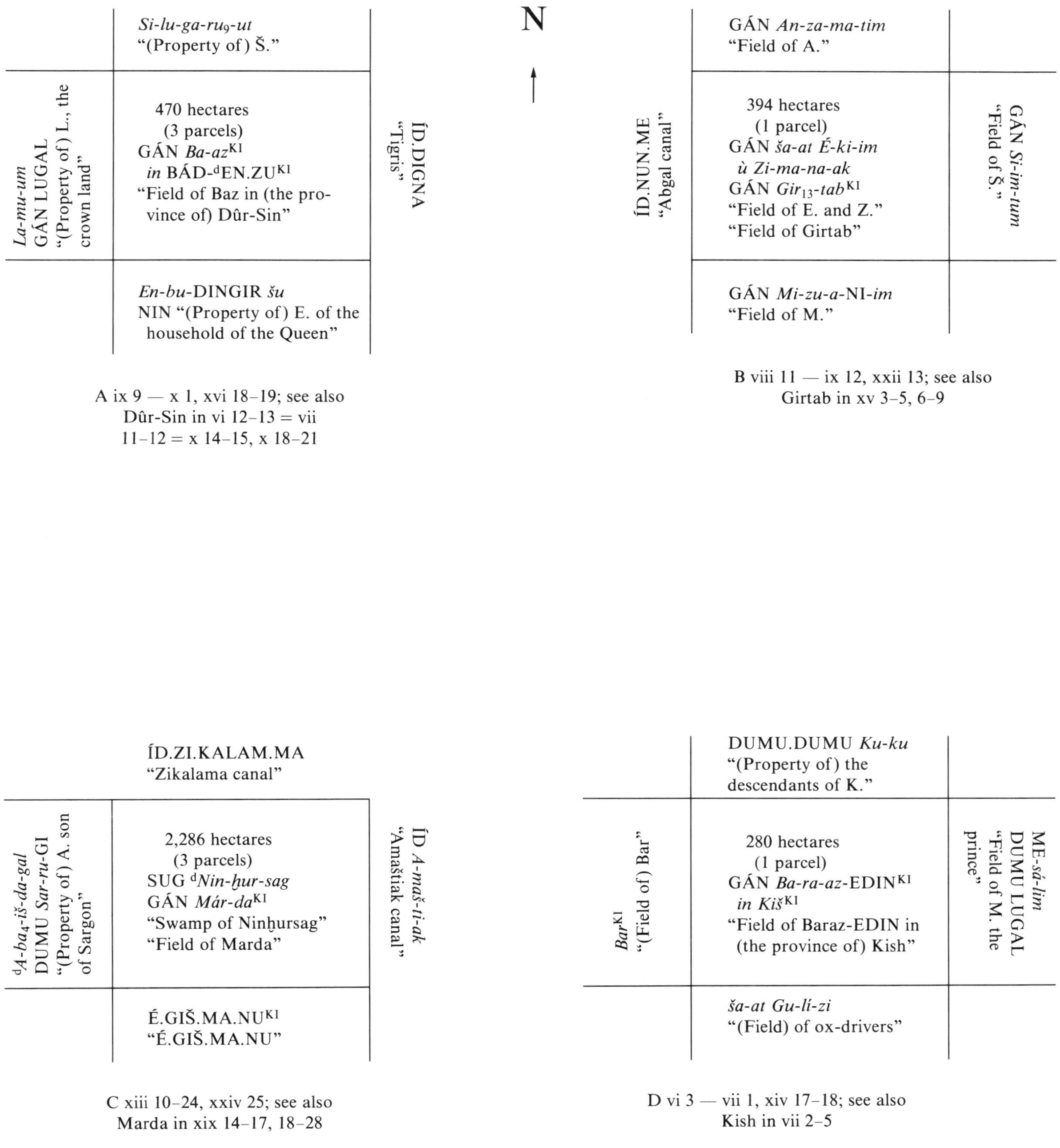
N
Si-lu-ga-ru9-ut
"(Property of) Š."
La-mu-um
GÁN LUGAL
"(Property of) L., the crown land"
470 hectares
(3 parcels)
GÁN Ba-az^{KI}
in BÁD-^{d}EN.ZU^{KI}
"Field of Baz in (the province of) Dûr-Sin"
ÍD.DIGNA
"Tigris"
En-bu-DINGIR šu
NIN "(Property of) E. of the household of the Queen"
A ix 9 — x 1, xvi 18–19; see also Dûr-Sin in vi 12–13 = vii 11–12 = x 14–15, x 18–21
GÁN An-za-ma-tim
"Field of A."
ÍD.NUN.ME
"Abgal canal"
394 hectares
(1 parcel)
GÁN ša-at É-ki-im
ù Zi-ma-na-ak
GÁN Gir$_{13}$-tab^{KI}
"Field of E. and Z."
"Field of Girtab"
GÁN Si-im-tum
"Field of Š."
GÁN Mi-zu-a-NI-im
"Field of M."
B viii 11 — ix 12, xxii 13; see also Girtab in xv 3–5, 6–9
ÍD.ZI.KALAM.MA
"Zikalama canal"
^{d}A-ba$_{4}$-iš-da-gal
DUMU Sar-ru-GI
"(Property of) A. son of Sargon"
2,286 hectares
(3 parcels)
SUG ^{d}Nin-ḫur-sag
GÁN Már-da^{KI}
"Swamp of Ninḫursag"
"Field of Marda"
ÍD A-maš-ti-ak
"Amaštiak canal"
É.GIŠ.MA.NU^{KI}
"É.GIŠ.MA.NU"
C xiii 10–24, xxiv 25; see also Marda in xix 14–17, 18–28
DUMU.DUMU Ku-ku
"(Property of) the descendants of K."
Bar^{KI}
"(Field of) Bar"
280 hectares
(1 parcel)
GÁN Ba-ra-az-EDIN^{KI}
in Kiš^{KI}
"Field of Baraz-EDIN in (the province of) Kish"
ME-sá-lim
DUMU LUGAL
"Field of M. the prince"
ša-at Gu-lí-zi
"(Field) of ox-drivers"
D vi 3 — vii 1, xiv 17–18; see also Kish in vii 2–5

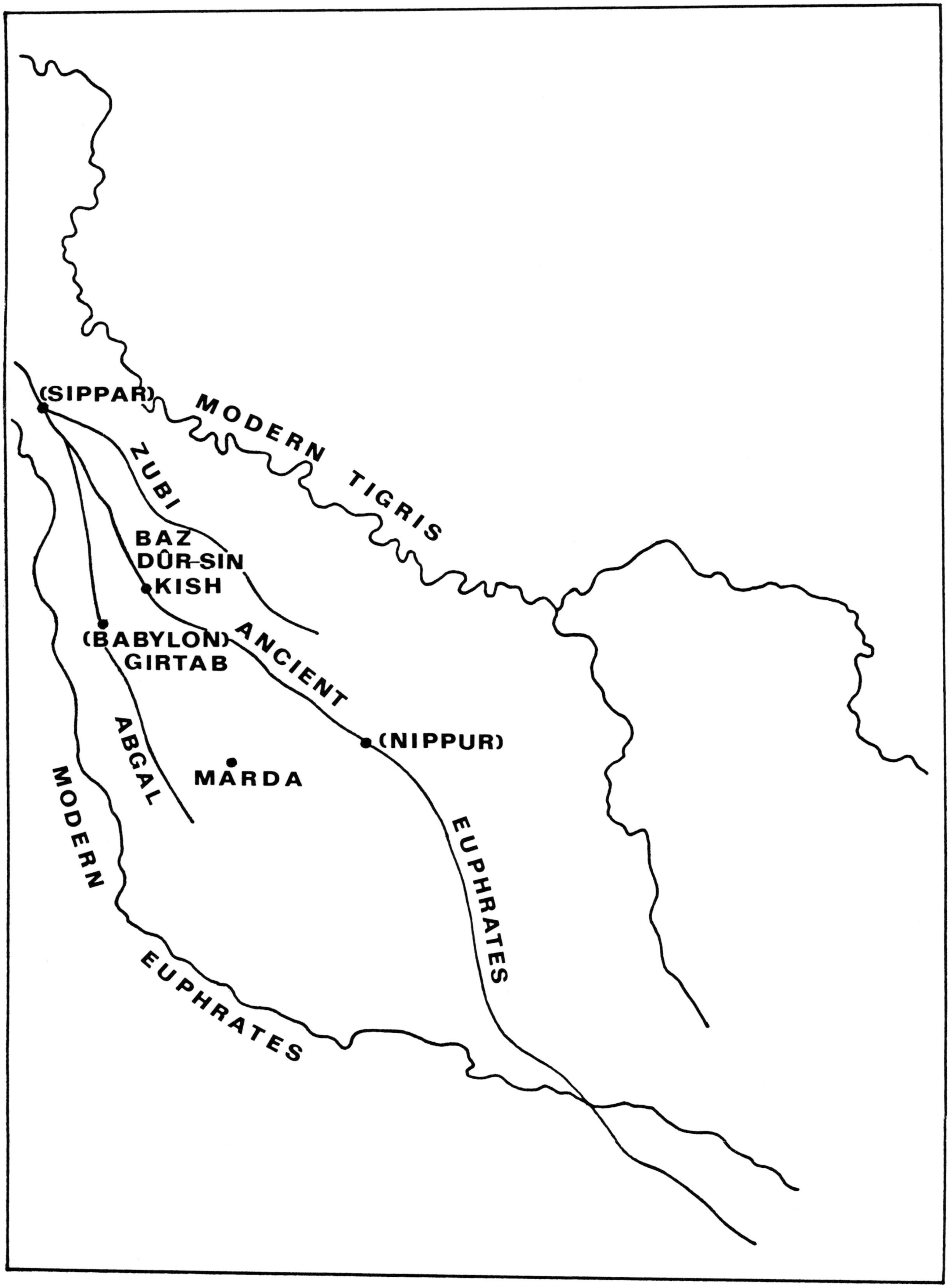

Figure 12. Map Showing the Four Main Cities of the Manishtushu Obelisk

ately. First, locating Dûr-Sin on or near the Tigris would force the conclusion that it was quite distant from the three other fields, which, while not adjoining, lay farther south in close proximity to each other. This assumption, while not impossible, is highly improbable. More serious is the second point, to wit, that all we know about Dûr-Sin is that it must have been located in the vicinity of Kish. This is indicated by several considerations, such as: 1) one of the sellers of the land located in area A is a certain Ilum-bānî, son of Rabî-ilum of the household of Lamum, the temple-administrator of Zababa, who is at home in Kish (A viii 17–20 = ix 7–8); 2) one of the witnesses to the sale of the land in area A, and, therefore, related to the sellers of that land, is a certain Imtallik, son of Ur-nin of Kish (A x 2–4); and 3) a place Dûr-Sin occurs together with Kish in a Sargonic text excavated at Kish (*MAD* 5, 10). This evidence strongly suggests that Dûr-Sin cannot be adjoining the Tigris if we take the bed of the ancient Tigris to correspond, more or less, to its modern bed. That means either that the bed of the Tigris lay much farther south than the present one, or more probably that the Tigris of the Manishtushu Obelisk and other texts of early times must be identified with the canal ÍD.ZUBI, Sumerian Izubi, Akkadian *Izubîtum*, which presumably was situated closer to Kish than to the present bed of the Tigris. Compare *RGTC* 1 p. 227; 2 p. 296; and 3 p. 316.

The four main cities of the obelisk are charted on the map reproduced in figure 12, based on McG. Gibson, *The City and Area of Kish* (Coconut Grove, Florida, 1972) fig. 69.

Genealogical tables of the main participants in the sales are fully discussed by Gelb in E. Lipiński, ed., *State and Temple Economy in the Ancient near East* 1 (Leuven, 1979) pp. 73–88.

Sample Interpretation

Transaction A_1: ii 1–v 16 (first field).
- ii 1–9: 439 iku of land, its price is 1463⅓ gsg of barley, at the ratio of 1 shekel of silver = 1 gsg of barley, its price is 1463⅓ shekels of silver. The price of the field.
- ii 10–11: 219½ (= 15 percent of price) shekels of silver is the additional payment.
- ii 12–v 16: 4 PNs who received x commodities as the "gift of the field" + 3 PNs (who received no commodities) = total of 7 men, "lords of the field" (= primary sellers), recipients of the silver. 10 PNs are "brother-lords of the field" (= secondary sellers). Total of 17 men, descendants of Mezizi.

Transaction A_2 v 17–viii 4 (second field) is similar to A_1.

Transaction A_3 viii 5–ix 8 (third field) is similar to A_1.
- ix 9–xvi 23 refers to all 3 transactions:
- ix 9–xvi 17: Total of 1333 iku of land ($A_1 + A_2 + A_3$). Location described by four cardinal points. Field of Baz. 5 PNs are witnesses of the field (= witnesses of the sellers). 190 men, inhabitants of Dûr-Sin, were "eaters of bread" (i. e., they participated in the feast celebrating the conclusion of the sale). 49 men, citizens of Akkadē, are witnesses of the field (= witnesses of the buyer).
- xvi 18–23: Manishtushu, king of the totality, bought the field of Baz, situated in Dûr-Sin.

Transliteration and Translation

Side A (= old Side A)

	i		(ca. 10 lines destr.)	
		1′)	[. . . -K]I	
		2′)	[. . .G]I	
		3′)	[X] ⌜X-GAL⌝?	
			[X] ⌜X⌝^{KI}	
			(blank)	
		4′)	[ŠU.NIGÍN] 9(ŠÁR) 3(IKU) GÁN	[Total of] 9723 iku of land
		5′)	[*M*]*a-an-iš-tu-su*	M.
		6′)	[L]UGAL	king of
		7′)	[K]IŠ	the totality
		8′)	⌜Ì⌝.ŠÁM	bought.
A_1	ii	1)	[2(BÙR.GUNU) 4(BÙR) 1(EŠE) 1(IKU) GÁN]	[439 iku of land];
		2)	[NÍG.ŠÁM-*su*]	[its price is]
		3)	[1463(GUR) 1(PI) 2(BÁN) ŠE GUR.SAG.GÁL]	[1463.1.2 gsg of barley];
		4)	[NÍG.ŠÁM]	[at the price of]
		5)	[1 GÍN K]UG.BABBAR	[1 shekel of si]lver for
		6)	[1] ŠE GUR.SAG.GÁL	[1.] gsg of barley,
		7)	KUG.BABBAR-*su*	its (i.e., of the barley) silver (equivalent) is

	8)	$24\frac{1}{3}$ ŠA MA.NA 3 GÍN 1 MA.NA.TUR KUG.BABBAR	$1463\frac{1}{3}$ shekels of silver;
	9)	NÍG.ŠÁM GÁN	(this is) the price of the field;
	10)	$3\frac{2}{3}$ ŠA MA.NA KUG.BABBAR LAL 1 TAR GÍN	$219\frac{1}{2}$ shekels of silver is
	11)	NÍG.KI.GAR GÁN	the additional payment of the field;
	12)	1 *su-ga-nu* KUG.BABBAR *maš-ga-na-at*	1 . . . overlaid with silver,
	13)	KI.LAL.BI 15 GÍN KUG.BABBAR	its weight is 15 shekels of silver,
	14)	1 TÚG.ŠU.DU$_7$.A.BAL	(and) 1 TÚG.ŠU.DU$_7$.A.BAL cloth
	15)	*I-ti*-DINGIR	(for) I.
	16)	DUMU *La-mu-sa*	son of L.
	17)	*ši* AGRIG	Of A.;
	18)	1 TÚG.ŠU.SÈ.GA	1 TÚG.ŠU.ŠÈ.GA cloth
iii	1)	[PN]	[(for) PN]
	2)	[DUMU . . . -*m*]*u*	[son of] ⌜PN$_2$⌝;
	3)	[1 TÚG].ŠU.[SÈ].GA	[1 TÚG]. ŠU.[SÈ].GA cloth
	4)	*Lam-gi-um*	(for) L.
	5)	DUMU *E-bi-ir-mu-bí*	son of E.;
	6)	1 TÚG.ŠU.SÈ.GA	1 TÚG.ŠU.SÈ.GA cloth
	7)	*E-bi-ir-ì-lum*	(for) E.
	8)	DUMU *Iš-dup*-^{d}EN.ZU (blank)	son of I.;
	9)	ŠU.NIGÍN 1 *su-ga-nu* KUG.BABBAR *maš-ga-na-at*	total of 1 . . . overlaid with silver,
	10)	ŠU.NIGÍN 1 TÚG.ŠU.DU$_7$.A.BAL	total of 1 TÚG.ŠU.DU$_7$.A.BAL cloth,
	11)	ŠU.NIGÍN 3 TÚG.ŠU.SÈ.GA	total of 3 TÚG.ŠU.SÈ.GA cloths;
	12)	NÍG.BA GÁN	(this is) the gift of the field;
	13)	1 *Su-ru-uš*-GI	3 PNs (who received no gifts);
	14)	DUMU *I-ti*-DINGIR	
	15)	*šu La-mu-sa*	
	16)	*ši* AGRIG	
	17)	1 *Iš-dup*-^{d}EN.ZU	
iv	1)	1 *I-bí*-^{d}EN.ZU	
	2)	2 DUMU GAL.ZU-DI.TAR	
	3)	DUMU.DUMU *Su-mu-núm* (blank)	
	4)	ŠU.NIGÍN 7 GURUŠ	total of 7 men,
	5)	*be-lu* GÁN	the "lords of the field,"
	6)	KÚ KUG.BABBAR	the recipients of the silver;
	7)	1 DINGIR-*a-ḫa*	10 PNs,
	8)	DUMU *Ì-lu-lu*	
	9)	GAL.UKÙ	
	10)	1 SI.A-*um*	
	11)	DUMU *La-mu-sa*	
	12)	*ši* AGRIG	
	13)	1 *A-ar*-DINGIR	
	14)	DUMU *Pù-ba-lum*	
	15)	SIPA	
	16)	1 ^{d}EN.ZU-*al-su*	
	17)	DUMU *A-ar*-DINGIR	
	18)	*ši Pù-ba-lum*	
	19)	1 UD.IŠ	
	20)	1 *Zu-zu*	
v	1)	2 DUMU *Iš-dup*-^{d}EN.ZU	
	2)	DUMU.DUMU *Ìr-ra-ra*	
	3)	1 *A-ma*-^{d}EN.ZU	

	4)	DUMU *Ga-zu-a-lum*	
	5)	*ši Ì-lu-lu*	
	6)	1 DINGIR-*a-zu*	
	7)	DUMU *A*-ŠI-*gu-ru-ud*	
	8)	1 *Pù-*^{d}*Da-gan*	
	9)	DUMU *Al-la-la*	
	10)	1 ARÁD-*zu-ni*	
	11)	DUMU *Me-zé-ì-lum*	
		(blank)	
	12)	ŠU.NIGÍN 10 GURUŠ	total of 10 men,
	13)	ŠEŠ *be-lu* GÁN	the "brother-lords of the field";
	14)	ŠU.NIGÍN.ŠU.NIGÍN	the grand total of
	15)	20 LAL 3 GURUŠ	17 men,
	16)	DUMU.DUMU *Me-zi-zi*	descendants of M.;

A$_2$	17)	4(BÙR.GUNU) 5(BÙR) 1(EŠE) 5(IKU) GÁN	821 iku of land;
	18)	NÍG.ŠÁM-*su*	its price is
	19)	2736(GUR) 2(PI) 4(BÁN) ŠE GUR.SAG.GÁL	2736.2.4 gsg of barley;
	20)	NÍG.ŠÁM	at the price of
vi	1)	1 GÍN KUG.BABBAR	1 shekel of silver (for)
	2)	1 ŠE GUR.SAG.GÁL	1. gsg of barley,
	3)	KUG.BABBAR-*su*	its silver (equivalent) is
	4)	45½ MA.NA 6 GÍN 2 MA.NA. TUR KUG.BABBAR	2736⅔ shekels of silver;
	5)	NÍG.ŠÁM GÁN	(this is) the price of the field;
	6)	7 MA.NA LAL 9 1 TAR GÍN KUG.BABBAR	410½ shekels of silver is
	7)	NÍG.KI.GAR GÁN	the additional payment of the field;
	8)	1 *su-ga-nu* KUG.BABBAR *maš-ga-na-at*	1 . . . overlaid with silver,
	9)	KI.LAL.BI 15 GÍN KUG.BABBAR	its weight is 15 shekels of silver,
	10)	1 TÚG.ŠU.DU$_{7}$.A.BAL	(and) 1 TÚG.ŠU.DU$_{7}$.A.BAL cloth
	11)	*En-na-núm*	(for) E.,
	12)	AB+ÁŠ.URU	the city-elder of
	13)	BÀD-^{d}EN.ZU^{KI}	Dûr-Sin,
	14)	DUMU *I-mi-*^{d}EN.ZU	son of I.;
	15)	1 TÚG.ŠU.SÈ.GA	1 TÚG.ŠU.SÈ.GA cloth
	16)	*Su*-NI-*um*	(for) S.
	17)	DUMU ARÁD-*zu-ni*	son of A.,
	18)	IŠ	the equerry;
	19)	1 TÚG.ŠU.SÈ.GA	1 TÚG.ŠU.SÈ.GA cloth
	20)	ARÁD-*zu-ni*	(for) A.
	21)	DUMU *Iš-dup*-DINGIR	son of I.;
vii	1)	1 TÚG.ŠU.SÈ.GA	1 TÚG.ŠU.SÈ.GA cloth
	2)	*Zu-zu*	(for) Z.
	3)	DUMU *A-ar-É-a*	son of A.;
		(blank)	
	4)	ŠU.NIGÍN 1 *su-ga-nu* KUG. BABBAR *maš-ga-na-at*	total of 1 . . . overlaid with silver;
	5)	ŠU.NIGÍN 1 TÚG.ŠU.DU$_{7}$.A. BAL	total of 1 TÚG.ŠU.DU$_{7}$.A.BAL cloth,
	6)	ŠU.NIGÍN 3 TÚG.ŠU.SÈ.GA	total of 3 TÚG.ŠU.SÈ GA cloths;
	7)	NÍG.BA GÁN	(this is) the gift of the field;
	8)	1 *Ì-lí-dan*	5 PNs;
	9)	1 *I-mi-*^{d}EN.ZU	
	10)	2 DUMU *En-na-núm*	

		11)	AB+ÁŠ.URU	
		12)	BÀD-^{d}EN.ZU^{KI}	
		13)	1 ^{d}EN.ZU-*a-ar*	
		14)	DUMU *A-ar-É-a*	
		15)	1 *Ì-lí-sa-lik*	
		16)	DUMU *Im*$_{4}$*-da-lik*	
		17)	1 *I-nin-me-šum*	
		18)	DUMU *Dam-ba-ba*	
			(blank)	
	viii	1)	ŠU.NIGÍN 10 LAL 1 GURUŠ	total of 9 men,
		2)	*be-lu* GÁN	the "lords of the field,"
		3)	KÚ KUG.BABBAR	the recipients of the silver,
		4)	DUMU.DUMU *Ši-ù-ni*	descendants of Š.
A$_{3}$		5)	4(BÙR) 1(IKU) GÁN	73 iku of land;
		6)	NÍG.ŠÁM-*su*	its price is
		7)	243(GUR) 1!(PI) 2(BÁN) ŠE GUR.SAG.GÁL	243.1.2 gsg of barley;
		8)	NÍG.ŠÁM	at the price of
		9)	1 GÍN KUG.BABBAR	1 shekel of silver (for)
		10)	1 ŠE GUR.SAG.GÁL	1. gsg of barley,
		11)	KUG.BABBAR-*su*	its silver (equivalent) is
		12)	4 MA.NA KUG.BABBAR 3 GÍN 1 MA.NA.TUR	243⅓ shekels of silver;
		13)	NÍG.ŠÁM GÁN	(this is) the price of the field;
		14)	½ MA.NA 6 1 TAR GÍN KUG.BABBAR	36½ shekels of silver is
		15)	NÍG.KI.GAR GÁN	the additional payment of the field;
		16)	1 TÚG.ŠU.SÈ.GA	1 TÚG.ŠU.SÈ.GA cloth
		17)	DINGIR-*ba-ni*	(for) I.
		18)	DUMU *Ra-bí*-DINGIR	son of R.
		19)	*ši La-mu-um*	Of L.,
		20)	SANGA ^{d}*Za-ba*$_{4}$*-ba*$_{4}$	the temple-administrator of Zababa;
		21)	1 TÚG.ŠU.SÈ.GA	1 TÚG.ŠU.SÈ.GA cloth
		22)	PÙ.ŠA-*Ma-ma*	(for) P.
	ix	1)	DUMU *Ur-*^{d}*Nin-kar*	son of U.;
			(blank)	
		2)	ŠU.NIGÍN 2 TÚG.ŠU.SÈ.GA	total of 2 TÚG.ŠU.SÈ.GA cloths;
		3)	NÍG.BA GÁN	(this is) the gift of the field;
		4)	ŠU.NIGÍN 2 GURUŠ	total of 2 men,
		5)	*be-lu* GÁN	the "lords of the field,"
		6)	KÚ KUG.BABBAR	the recipients of the silver,
		7)	DUMU.DUMU *La-mu-um*	descendants of L.,
		8)	SANGA ^{d}*Za-ba*$_{4}$*-ba*$_{4}$	the temple-administrator of Zababa.
			(blank)	
		9)	ŠU.NIGÍN 1(ŠÁR) 1(BÙR.GUNU) 4(BÙR) GÁN	Total of 1333 iku of land;
		10)	GÁN.NINDÁ	the field's border
		11)	IM.MIR	to the north is
		12)	*Si-lu-ga-ru*$_{9}$*-ut*	(the property of) S.;
		13)	GÁN.NINDÁ	the field's border
		14)	IM.MAR.TU	to the west is
		15)	*La-mu-um*	(the property of) L.,
		16)	GÁN LUGAL	the royal land;
		17)	GÁN.NINDÁ	the field's border
		18)	IM.KUR	to the east is
		19)	ÍD.IDIGNA (or ÍD.ZUBI)	the Tigris(?);
		20)	GÁN.NINDÁ	the field's border
		21)	IM.U$_{5}$	to the south is

	22)	*En-bu*-DINGIR	(the property of) E.
	23)	*šu* NIN	Of the queen;
x	1)	GÁN *Ba-az*^{KI}	(this is) the field of Baz.
		(blank)	
	2)	1 *Im*$_4$*-da-lik*	5 PNs,
	3)	DUMU *Ur-nin*	
	4)	*Kiš*^{KI}	
	5)	1 ^{d}EN.ZU-GIŠ.ERÍN	
	6)	1 *Ì-la-la*	
	7)	1 *Šu-ì-lí-su*	
	8)	3 DUMU *Zu-zu*	
	9)	*ši A-ar-É-a*	
	10)	1 *Im*$_4$*-da-lik*	
	11)	DUMU *Ì-la-la*	
	12)	MU	
	13)	*ši En-na-núm*	
	14)	AB+ÁŠ.URU	
	15)	BÀD-^{d}EN.ZU^{KI}	
		(blank)	
	16)	ŠU.NIGÍN 5 GURUŠ	total of 5 men,
	17)	AB+ÁŠ.AB+ÁŠ GÁN	are the witnesses of the field;
	18)	190 GURUŠ	190 men,
	19)	DUMU.DUMU	inhabitants of
	20)	BÀD-^{d}EN.ZU^{KI}	Dûr-Sin,
	21)	NINDA Ì.KÚ	ate bread,
		(blank)	
	22)	1 *A-li-a-ḫu*	49 PNs,
	23)	DUMU NI-*ba-rí-im*	
xi	1)	ŠEŠ LUGAL	
	2)	1 *Zu-zu*	
	3)	DUB.SAR	
	4)	*šu* KURUŠDA	
	5)	DUMU *La-mu-um*	
	6)	1 MES-*zi*	
	7)	UM.MI.A	
	8)	DUB.SAR	
	9)	1 ^{d}*Ma-lik-zi-in-su*	
	10)	DUMU *I-da*-DINGIR	
	11)	GAL.SUKKAL	
	12)	1 *Ma-ma-ḫir-su*	
	13)	DUMU *Na-ni*	
	14)	GÌR.NITA	
	15)	1 *Šu-*^{d}*Da-gan*	
	16)	DUMU *Be-lí-lí*	
	17)	*ši Na-zi-tim*	
	18)	SABRA.É	
	19)	1 *É-ga-lum*	
	20)	DUMU *Sa*-NI	
	21)	1 *Bí-su-šè-ib-nim*	
	22)	1 *É-a-ra-bí*	
	23)	2 DUMU *A-ḫu-ḫu*	
	24)	*ši Al-lu-lu*	
	25)	1 *In-su-mi-su-da-nu*	
xii	1)	DUMU *Iš-a-lum*	
	2)	*ši* TE.LAL.GAL	
	3)	1 PÙ.ŠA-*ì-li*	
	4)	DUMU *Be-lí*-GI	
	5)	GÌR.NITA	
	6)	LÚ.GIŠ.TI	
	7)	1 UD-*ti-ru*	

8) 1 *Sar-ru-*GI-*ì-lí*
9) 2 DUMU *Bala-ga*
10) *ši* NAR
11) 1 *Ì-lí-sar-ru*
12) DUMU *I-ti-sum*
13) GÌR.NITA
14) LÚ.GIŠ.GÍD.DA
15) 1 DINGIR-*su-su*
16) DUMU *Mu-mu*
17) ŠU.I
18) *ši Al-lu-lu*
19) 1 *A-bìl-dan*
20) 1 BÀD-*su-nu*
21) 2 DUMU *Su-ru-uš*-GI
22) *ši* PAB.ŠEŠ
23) PA.TE.SI
24) GIŠ.ÙḪ^{KI}
25) 1 *I-zi-ir-gul-la-zi-in*
xiii 1) DUMU *Šu-ì-li*
2) SILÀ.ŠU.DU$_8$
3) 1 *U-za-si-na-at*
4) DUMU *Ki-ti-ti*
5) 1 GIŠ.TUKUL-*ga-su-al-si-in*
6) DUMU UD-*ma*
7) 1 *Ur*-^{d}MUŠ
8) DUMU *Lugal-ku-li*
9) 1 *Zi-gur-mu-bí*
10) DUMU *Ì-lí-a-ḫi*
11) *ši* TE.LAL.GAL
12) 1 *Ma-ma-ḫir-su*
13) DUMU *Ra-bí*-DINGIR
14) *ši Ì-la-la*
15) 1 *Mu-mu*
16) DUMU *Ur-Már-da*
17) 1 *En-bu*-DINGIR
18) DUMU *Im$_4$-da-lik*
19) *ši* GAL.SUKKAL-*li*
20) 1 GAL.ZU-DI.TAR
21) DUMU *I-ti*-DINGIR.DINGIR
22) UD.KIB.NUN^{KI}
23) 1 *U-bìl-ga-zu*
24) DUMU *Ìr-ru-zum*
25) LÚ.IGI
xiv 1) 1 *Ù-na-gàr*
2) DUMU *Ì-ši-ši*
3) NU.BANDA *Ša-na-e*
4) 1 *Dan-ì-li*
5) DUMU *Ìr-e*-^{d}*Ma-lik*
6) *ši* MAŠKIM.GI$_4$
7) 1 *Uru*-KA-*gi-na*
8) DUMU *En-gil-sa*
9) PA.TE.SI
10) ŠIR.BUR.LA^{KI}
11) 1 *Da-núm*
12) DUMU *Iš-kùn*-DINGIR
13) GAL.UKÙ
14) 1 *I-pù-lum*
15) DUMU DINGIR-*su-ra-bí*
16) PA.TE.SI
17) *Ba-si-me*^{KI}

18) 1 *La-lí*
19) DUMU *Iš-má*-GÁR
20) *ši Ar-rí-im*
21) 1 *Ì-lu-lu*
22) DUMU *Ik-ru-ub*-DINGIR
23) *ši A-gu-tim*
24) 1 *Ga-lí-ì-li*
25) DUMU *La-mu-sa*
26) GÚ.DU$_8$.A^{KI}
27) 1 *Ì-lí-sa-lik*
xv 1) DUMU *Šu-da-ti*
2) 1 *Ik-su-zi-na-at*
3) DUMU *I-ši-me*
4) NU.BANDA AB+ÁŠ.AB+ÁŠ
5) 1 *U-bi-in*-LUGAL-*rí*
6) DUMU *Ur-ur*
7) *ši* GAL.SUKKAL-*li*
8) 1 *Ma-ma*-ḪU
9) DUMU *I-bí-bí*
10) NU.BANDA *Ša-na-e*
11) 1 *U-bi-in*-LUGAL-*rí*
12) DUMU BALA-*É-a*
13) ARÁD-*da-ni*^{KI}
14) 1 *A-ḫu*-DÙG
15) DUMU *Šu-Nu-nu*
16) *ši Ḫa-lum*
17) 1 *Šu-Nu-nu*
18) DUMU DINGIR-*dan*
19) SANGA ^{d}*A-ba*$_4$
20) *I-bí-rí*^{KI}
21) 1 *Im*$_4$*-da-lik*
22) DUMU *I-su*-DINGIR
23) DUMU.DUMU *A-ḫu-ḫu*
24) *Da-mi-gi*^{KI}
25) 1 *Sar-ru-ì-lí*
26) DUMU *Sar-ru*-BÀD
27) EN.ME.LI
xvi 1) 1 *Ì-lí-a-ḫi*
2) DUMU DINGIR-*a-ḫa*
3) 1 *Da-kum*
4) DUMU ARÁD-*zu-ni*
5) 1 *Mu-sa-ìr-su-nu*
6) DUMU *Da-da*-LUM
7) DUB.SAR
8) 1 *Na-bí-um*
9) DUMU *I-ti-ti*
10) *Da-mi-gi*^{KI}
11) *in Dan-ni-rí-iš-tim*
12) 1 *Tu-li-id-da-nam*
13) DUMU *Ì-lí-lí*
14) *ši Mu-na*
(blank)

15) ŠU.NIGÍN 50 LAL 1 DUMU.DUMU	total of 49 citizens of
16) *A-ga-dè*^{KI}	Akkadē are
17) AB+ÁŠ.AB+ÁŠ GÁN	the witnesses of the field.
(blank)	
18) GÁN *Ba-az*^{KI}	Field of Baz,
19) *in* BÀD-^{d}EN.ZU^{KI}	(located) in Dûr-Sin,
20) *Ma-an-iš-tu-su*	M.

	21)	LUGAL	king of
	22)	KIŠ	the totality
	23)	Ì.ŠÁM	bought.

Side B (= old Side D)

i	1)	6(BÙR.GUNU) 2(BÙR) GÁN	⸢1116⸣ iku of land;
	2)	[NÍ]G.ŠÁM-*su*	its price is
	3)	[1 ŠE] GUR$_7$ [120] GUR. [SAG].GÁL	⸢3720.⸣ gsg of barley;
	4)	[NÍG.Š]ÁM	at the price of
	5)	[1 GÍN] KUG.BABBAR	[1 shekel of] silver (for)
	6)	1 ŠE GUR.SAG.GÁL	1. gsg of barley,
ii	1)	KUG.BABBAR-*su*	its silver (equivalent) is
	2)	1 GÚ 2 MA.NA KUG. BABBAR	3720 shekels of silver;
	3)	NÍG.ŠÁM GÁN	(this is) the price of the field;
	4)	372 ŠE GUR.SAG.GÁL	372. gsg of barley,
	5)	KUG.BABBAR-*su*	its silver (equivalent) is
	6)	6 MA.NA 12 GÍN KUG. BABBAR	372 shekels of silver;
	7)	NÍG.KI.GAR GÁN	(this is) the additional payment of the field;
iii	1)	1 ERÍN ANŠE.BAR.AN	1 team of mules,
	2)	1 GIŠ.GIGIR.NÍG.ŠU	1 NÍG.ŠU chariot,
	3)	1 TÚG.ŠU.DU$_7$.A.BAL	1 TÚG.ŠU.DU$_7$.A.BAL cloth,
	4)	1 *ki-li-lum* KUG.BABBAR	(and) 1 silver wreath,
	5)	KI.LAL.BI 15 GÍN KUG. BABBAR	its weight is 15 shekels of silver,
	6)	*Iq-bí*-GI	(for) I.;
	7)	1 *ki-li-lum* KUG.BABBAR	1 silver wreath,
iv	1)	KI.LAL.BI 15 GÍN KUG. BABBAR	its weight is 15 shekels of silver,
	2)	1 TÚG.ŠU.DU$_7$.A.BAL	(and) 1 TÚG.ŠU.DU$_7$.A.BAL cloth
	3)	*Al-la*	(for) A.;
	4)	2 DUMU *Ab-ra-Il*	(these are) 2 sons of A.,
	5)	DUMU.DUMU *Iš-dup*-BE	descendants of I.;
	6)	1 TÚG.ŠU.ŠÈ.GA	1 TÚG.ŠU.ŠÈ.GA cloth
	7)	1 URUDU *maš-sa-tum* UD.KA.BAR	(and) 1 bronze . . .
	8)	*Pù-su*-GI	(for) P.,
v	1)	SAG.DU$_5$	the field recorder,
	2)	DUMU *Ír-a-mu*	son of I.,
	3)	DUMU.DUMU *Ab-ra-Il*	descendant of A.;
	4)	3 DUMU.DUMU *Ab-ra-Il*	(these are) 3 descendants of A.;
	5)	1 TÚG.ŠU.SÈ.GA	1 TÚG.ŠU.SÈ.GA cloth
	6)	*Su-mu*-GI	(for) S.;
	7)	1 TÚG.ŠU.SÈ.GA	1 TÚG.ŠU.SÈ.GA cloth
	8)	*U-li-id-ì-lum*	(for) U.;
	9)	2 DUMU BÀD-*Il*	(these are) 2 sons of D.,
vi	1)	DUMU.DUMU *Ib-bu-bu*	descendants of I.;
	2)	1 TÚG.ŠU.SÈ.GA	1 TÚG.ŠU.SÈ.GA cloth
	3)	PÙ.ŠA-PAB.PAB	(for) P.,
	4)	DUMU *Lugal-ezen*	son of L.;
	5)	1 TÚG.ŠU.SÈ.GA	1 TÚG.ŠU.SÈ.GA cloth
	6)	*Ti-da-nu*	(for) T.
	7)	DUMU DINGIR-*mu-da*	son of I.,
	8)	DUMU.DUMU Ur-^{d}SI.LU	descendant of U.;
	9)	1 TÚG.ŠU.SÈ.GA	1 TÚG.ŠU.SÈ.GA cloth
	10)	*Ku-ku*	(for) K.
vii	1)	DUMU *En-na-É-a*	son of E.,
	2)	DUMU.DUMU *Zi-zi*	descendant of Z.;

	3)	1 TÚG.ŠU.SÈ.GA	1 TÚG.ŠU.SÈ.GA cloth
	4)	DINGIR-*a-ḫa*	(for) I.
	5)	DUMU *I-ti-Eš*$_4$*-dar*	son of I.,
	6)	DUMU.DUMU LÚ.IGI	descendant of L.;
	7)	1 TÚG.ŠU.SÈ.GA	1 TÚG.ŠU.SÈ.GA cloth
	8)	ARÁD-*zu-ni*	(for) A.
	9)	DUMU *Iš-dup-pum*	son of I.,
	10)	DUMU.DUMU *Ši-na-na-tim*	descendant of Š.;
		(blank)	
viii	1)	ŠU.NIGÍN 1 ERÍN ANŠE. BAR.AN	total of 1 team of mules,
	2)	ŠU.NIGÍN 1 GIŠ.GIGIR. NÍG.ŠU	total of 1 NÍG.ŠU chariot,
	3)	ŠU.NIGÍN 2 *ki-li-lum* KUG. BABBAR	total of 2 silver wreaths,
	4)	ŠU.NIGÍN 1 URUDU *maš-sa-tum* UD.KA.BAR	total of 1 bronze . . . ,
	5)	ŠU.NIGÍN 2 TÚG.ŠU.DU$_7$.A. BAL	total of 2 TÚG.ŠU.DU$_7$.A.BAL cloths,
	6)	ŠU.NIGÍN 8 TÚG.ŠU.SÈ.GA	total of 8 TÚG.ŠU.SÈ.GA cloths;
	7)	NÍG.BA GÁN	(this is) the gift of the field;
	8)	ŠU.NIGÍN 10 GURUŠ	total of 10 men,
	9)	*be-lu* GÁN	the "lords of the field,"
	10)	KÚ KUG.BABBAR	the recipients of the silver.
	11)	GÁN *ša-at É-ki-im*	Field of É-kum
	12)	*ù Zi-ma-na-ak*	and Zimanak;
		(blank)	
ix	1)	GÁN.NINDÁ	the field's border
	2)	IM.MIR	to the north is
	3)	GÁN *An-za-ma-tim*	the field of A.;
	4)	GÁN.NINDÁ	the field's border
	5)	IM.MAR.TU	to the west is
	6)	ÍD.NUN.ME	the Abgal canal;
	7)	GÁN.NINDÁ	the field's border
	8)	IM.U$_5$	to the south is
	9)	GÁN *Mi-zu-a*-NI-*im*	the field of M.;
	10)	GÁN.NINDÁ	the field's border
	11)	IM.KUR	to the east is
	12)	GÁN *Si-im-tum*	the field of S.
		(blank)	
	13)	1 *I-zi-núm*	30 PNs,
	14)	1 *En-na-É-a*	
x	1)	2 DUMU *Ur-sa(g)-núm*	
	2)	DUMU.DUMU *Ti-ti*	
	3)	1 DINGIR-*a-ḫa*	
	4)	DUMU *Su*$_4$*-ma-ba-ni*	
	5)	UGULA	
	6)	1 *Lugal-ezen*	
	7)	UGULA	
	8)	DUMU *Iš-dup*-^{d}EN.ZU	
	9)	1 *Su-mu-núm*	
	10)	DUMU *Sa-tu-ni*	
	11)	1 PÙ.ŠA-^{d}*Nu-muš-da*	
	12)	*šu Dingir-nu-me-a*	
	13)	1 DINGIR-*a-ḫa*	
	14)	*šu Bi-e-tim*	
xi	1)	1 *Ìr-e-pum*	
	2)	DUMU DINGIR-*a-ḫa*	
	3)	*ši* DÉ.DÉ	
	4)	1 *Ga-la-ab-É-a*	
	5)	DUMU *I-ši-me*	

6) SIPA
7) 1 *Be-lí-mu-da*
8) DUMU *Su-mi-su*
9) 1 SI.A-*um*
10) DUMU *Gu-lí-zum*
11) 1 DINGIR-*ba-ni*
12) DUMU *A-ḫu-ba-lik*
13) DUMU.DUMU *Zi-im-tum*
14) 1 *Ur-ezen*
15) DUMU *Na-ʾà-šum*
xii 1) DAM.GÀR
2) 1 *Ik-ru-ub-É-a*
3) DUMU *I-ki-lum*
4) *a-bi* URU
5) *Elam*^{KI}
6) 1 PÙ.ŠA-^{d}IM
7) DUMU *I-dur-ma-at*
8) 1 *Ù-ì-lí*
9) DUMU PÙ.ŠA-*Ma-ma*
10) *ši Tu-gul-tim*
11) 1 *Su*$_{4}$*-ma-mu-tum*
12) DUMU *Ra-bí*-DINGIR
13) *ši* ^{d}*Nin-kar*
14) 1 ARÁD-*zu-ni*
15) DUMU *Gu-lí-zum*
xiii 1) *ši* SAL.ANŠE
2) 1 *En-na-É-a*
3) DUMU *A-ḫa-ar-ši*
4) NAGAR
5) 1 *La-a*-GUR
6) DUMU *Rí-pum*
7) *ši Wa-gi-rí*
8) 1 *Su-mi-su*
9) DUMU *Lu-da-na-at*
10) SIPA
11) 1 *La-gi-pum*
12) DUMU ARÁD-*zu-ni*
13) 1 *La-gi-pum*
14) DUMU *Pù-pù*
15) *ši* ŠU.I
16) 1 ARÁD-*zu-ni*
17) DUMU *Pù-pù*
xiv 1) LÚ.IGI
2) 1 *Su*-NI-*um*
3) DUMU *Bi-im*
4) *ši Zi-zi*
5) 1 *I-nin-sa-tu*
6) DUMU *En-na-É-a*
7) DAM.GÀR
8) 1 *Su-mi-su*
9) DUMU *Lu-zu-zum*
10) *ši* ^{d}*En-ki*
11) 1 *A-ku-ì-lum*
12) DUMU PÉŠ-*ì-lum*
13) *ši Ur*-^{d}AB
14) 1 *Zi-gàr-su*
15) DUMU *Ur*-^{d}*En-líl*
16) DUB.SAR
17) 1 *Im*$_{4}$*-da-lik*
18) DUMU *I-bí-ì-lum*

xv	1)	*šu* MES.BAR^{KI}	
	2)	2 DUB.SAR	
		(blank)	
	3)	ŠU.NIGÍN 30 GURUŠ	total of 30 men, are
	4)	AB+ÁŠ.AB+ÁŠ GÁN	the witnesses of the field of
	5)	*Gir*$_{13}$-*tab*^{KI}	Girtab.
	6)	94 GURUŠ	94 men,
	7)	DUMU.DUMU	citizens of
	8)	*Gir*$_{13}$-*tab*^{KI}	Girtab,
	9)	NINDA Ì.KÚ	ate bread.
		(blank)	
		(xv 10 to xxii 12 = A x 22 to xvi 17 = 49 citizens of Akkadē)	
		(blank)	
xxii	13)	GÁN *Gir*$_{13}$-*tab*^{KI}	Field of Girtab
	14)	*Ma-an-iš-tu-su*	M.
	15)	LUGAL	king of
	16)	KIŠ	the totality
	17)	Ì.ŠÁM	bought.

Side C (= old Side C)

C$_1$	i	1)	[2(ŠÁR) 1(BÙR.GUNU) G]ÁN	⸢2340⸣ iku of land;
		2)	[NÍG.ŠÁM]-*su*	its [price] (is)
		3)	[2 ŠE G]UR$_7$ [600 GUR.SAG].GÁL	⸢7800. gsg⸣ [of barley],
		4)	[NÍG.ŠÁ]M	[at the pri]ce of
		5)	[1 GÍN KUG].BABBAR	[1 shekel of sil]ver for
		6)	[1 ŠE GUR.SA]G.[G]ÁL	[1.] ⸢gsg⸣ [of barley],
		7)	[KUG.BABBAR-*su*]	[its silver (equivalent) is]
		8)	[2 GÚ 10 MA.NA KUG.BABBAR]	[7800 shekels of silver];
		9)	[NÍG.ŠÁM GÁN]	[(this is) the price of the field];
		10)	[31 GÚ SÍG]	[1860 pounds of wool];
		11)	[NÍG.ŠÁM]	[at the price of]
		12)	[1 GÍN KUG.BABBAR]	[1 shekel of silver for]
		13)	[4 MA.NA SÍG]	[4 pounds of wool],
		14)	[KUG.BABBAR-*si-in*]	[its silver (equivalent) is]
		15)	[7 MA.NA 45 GÍN KUG.BABBAR]	[465 shekels of silver];
		16)	[5? URUDU ḪA.ZI? UD.KA.BAR]	[5? bronze axes?],
		17)	[5? URUDU *na-ap-la-aq-tum*? UD.KA.BAR]	[5? bronze battle-axes?],
	ii	1)	1 URUDU *ba-da-ru-um* UD.KA.BAR	(and) 1 bronze prod(?);
		2)	NÍG.ŠÁM 1 GIŠ.TUKUL	at the price of 1 weapon for
		3)	5 GÍN KUG.BABBAR	5 shekels of silver,
		4)	KUG.BABBAR-*su-nu*	their silver (equivalent) is
		5)	1 MA.NA KUG.BABBAR LAL 5 GÍN	55 shekels of silver;
		6)	3 ERÍN ANŠE.BAR.AN	3 teams of mules;
		7)	NÍG.ŠÁM	at the price of
		8)	[1 ANŠE.B]AR.AN	[1 mu]le for
		9)	[⅓ ŠA KUG.BABBAR]	[20 shekels of silver],
		10)	[KUG.BABBAR-*su-nu*]	[their silver (equivalent) is]
		11)	[4 MA.NA KUG.BABBAR]	[240 shekels of silver];
		12)	[1 *ki-li-lum* KUG.BABBAR]	[1 silver wreath],
		13)	[KI.LAL.BI ⅓ ŠA KUG.BABBAR]	[its weight is 20 shekels of silver];

	14)	[ŠU.NIGÍN 13 MA.NA KUG. BABBAR]	[the total of 780 shekels of silver];
	15)	[NÍG.KI.GAR GÁN]	[(this is) the additional payment of the field];
	16)	[1 ERÍN ANŠE.BAR.AN]	[1 team of mules],
	17)	[1 GIŠ.GIGIR.NÍG.ŠU]	[1 NÍG.ŠU chariot],
	18)	[1 *ki-li-lum* KUG.BABBAR]	[(and) 1 silver wreath],
iii	1)	KI.LAL.BI ⅓ ŠA KUG. BABBAR	its weight is 20 shekels of silver,
	2)	1 URUDU ḪA.ZI UD.KA. BAR	1 bronze axe,
	3)	1 TÚG.ŠU.DU$_7$.A.BAL	(and) 1 TÚG.ŠU.DU$_7$.A.BAL cloth
	4)	*Zu-zu*	(for) Z.
	5)	DUMU *Ur-Már-da*	son of U.,
	6)	DUMU.DUMU *I-ki-lum*	descendant of I.,
	7)	PA.TE.SI	the governor of
	8)	*Ki-babbar*^{KI}	Ki-babbar;
	9)	[1] TÚG.ŠU.DU$_7$.A.BAL	[1] TÚG.ŠU.DU$_7$.A.BAL cloth
	10)	[*T*]*u-tu*	(for) T.
	11)	[DUMU . . .]-*gi*	[son of PN]
	12)	[DUMU.DUMU PN$_2$]	[descendant of PN$_2$];
	13)	[1 TÚG.ŠU.DU$_7$.A.BAL]	[1 TÚG.ŠU.DU$_7$.A.BAL cloth]
	14)	[PN]	[(for) PN]
	15)	[DUMU PN$_2$]	[son of PN$_2$],
	16)	[DUMU.DUMU PN$_3$]	[descendant of PN$_3$];
	17)	[1 TÚG.ŠU.DU$_7$.A.BAL]	[1 TÚG.ŠU.DU$_7$.A.BAL cloth]
	18)	[PN]	[(for) PN]
	19)	[DUMU PN$_2$]	[son of PN$_2$],
	20)	[DUMU.DUMU PN$_3$]	[descendant of PN$_3$];
iv	1)	1 TÚG.ŠU.DU$_7$.A.BAL	1 TÚG.ŠU.DU$_7$.A.BAL cloth
	2)	*I-bí*-ZU.AB	(for) I.
	3)	DUMU *Ur-mes-an-ni*	son of U.;
	4)	1 TÚG.ŠU.DU$_7$.A.BAL	1 TÚG.ŠU.DU$_7$.A.BAL cloth
	5)	*Ti-ru-um*	(for) T.
	6)	DUMU *A-da-na-aḫ*	son of A.,
	7)	DUMU.DUMU *I-ti-É-a*	descendant of I.;
	8)	1 TÚG.ŠU.SÈ.GA	1 TÚG.ŠU.SÈ.GA cloth
	9)	*Amar-rí-rí*	(for) A.;
	10)	1 TÚG.ŠU.SÈ.GA	1 TÚG.ŠU.SÈ.GA cloth
	11)	*Be-lí-sa-tu*	(for) B.;
	12)	2 DUMU *Zu-zu*	(these are) 2 sons of Z.,
	13)	[DU]MU.DUMU *Ur-*[*Má*]*r-da*	descendants of U.
	14)	[*ši I*]-*ki-lum*	[Of] ⌜I.⌝;
	15)	[1 TÚG.ŠU.SÈ.GA]	[1 TÚG.ŠU.SÈ.GA cloth]
	16)	[PN]	[(for) PN];
	17)	[1 TÚG.ŠU.SÈ.GA]	[1 TÚG.ŠU.SÈ.GA cloth]
	18)	[PN$_2$]	[(for) PN$_2$];
	19)	[2 DUMU PN$_3$]	[(these are) 2 sons of PN$_3$];
	20)	[1 TÚG.ŠU.SÈ.GA]	[1 TÚG.ŠU.SÈ.GA cloth]
	21)	[PN]	[(for) PN];
v	1)	1 TÚG.ŠU.SÈ.GA	TÚG.ŠU.SÈ.GA cloth
	2)	*Ì-lí-a-ḫi*	for I.;
	3)	2 DUMU *A-ḫu-mu-bí*	(these are) 2 sons of A.,
	4)	DUMU.DUMU *Iš-dup*-DINGIR	descendants of I.
	5)	*ši É-a-a*	Of E.;
	6)	1 TÚG.ŠU.SÈ.GA	1 TÚG.ŠU.SÈ.GA cloth
	7)	*Ra-bí*-DINGIR	(for) R.
	8)	DUMU PÙ.ŠA-*É-a*	son of P.;
	9)	1 TÚG.ŠU.SÈ.GA	1 TÚG.ŠU.SÈ.GA cloth

	10)	*Ga-at-núm*	(for) G.;
	11)	1 TÚG.ŠU.SÈ.GA	1 TÚG.ŠU.SÈ.GA cloth
	12)	Su_4*-ma*-SIPA	(for) S.;
	13)	1 TÚG.ŠU.SÈ.GA	1 TÚG.ŠU.SÈ.GA cloth
	14)	*Be-lí-ba-ni*	(for) B.;
	15)	3 DUMU *Ur*-ZU.AB	(these are) 3 sons of U.,
	16)	DUMU.DUMU DINGIR-*su-la-ba*	descendants of I.;
	17)	[1] TÚG.ŠU.SÈ.GA	[1] TÚG.ŠU.SÈ.GA cloth
	18)	[. . .]-NI	[(for) P]N
	19)	[DUMU . . . *-l*]*a-ba*	[son of P]N_2;
	20)	[1 TÚG.ŠU.SÈ.GA]	[1 TÚG.ŠU.SÈ.GA cloth]
	21)	[PN]	[(for) PN]
	22)	[DUMU PN_2]	[son of PN_2],
	23)	[DUMU.DUMU PN_3]	[descendant of PN_3];
	24)	[1 TÚG.ŠU.SÈ.GA]	[1 TÚG.ŠU.SÈ.GA cloth]
vi	1)	*I-ki-lum*	(for) I.;
	2)	1 TÚG.ŠU.SÈ.GA	1 TÚG.ŠU.SÈ.GA cloth
	3)	*A-ḫu-ḫu*	for A.;
	4)	2 DUMU *Iš-má*-DINGIR	(these are) 2 sons of I.;
	5)	1 TÚG.ŠU.SÈ.GA	1 TÚG.ŠU.SÈ.GA cloth
	6)	GAL.ZU	(for) G.
	7)	DUMU *Ur-sag*-UD.KIB.NUN^{KI}	son of U.;
	8)	1 TÚG.ŠU.SÈ.GA	1 TÚG.ŠU.SÈ.GA cloth
	9)	*Dup-si-ga*	(for) D.;
	10)	1 TÚG.ŠU.SÈ.GA	1 TÚG.ŠU.SÈ.GA cloth
	11)	*Šu-ì-li*	(for) Š.;
	12)	2 DUMU GAL.ZU	(these are) 2 sons of G.,
	13)	DUMU.DUMU *Ur-sag*-UD.KIB.NUN^{KI}	descendants of U.;
	14)	5 DUMU.DUMU	(these are) 5 descendants of
	15)	MES-*na-at*	M.;
	16)	1 TÚG.ŠU.SÈ.GA	1 TÚG.ŠU.SÈ.GA cloth
	17)	*Dup-si-ga*	(for) D.
	18)	DUMU *I-ki-lum*	son of I.,
	19)	DUMU.DUMU *Ur-nin*	descendant of U.;
	20)	1 TÚG.ŠU.SÈ.GA	1 TÚG.ŠU.SÈ.GA cloth
	21)	*Ma-la-ni-su*	(for) M.
	22)	[DU]MU *Dup-si-ga*	[so]n of D.,
	23)	[DU]MU.DUMU *I-*[*k*]*i-lum*	descendant of I.,
	24)	[. . .]*-a-a*	⌜the . . .⌝;
vii	1)	1 TÚG.ŠU.SÈ.GA	1 TÚG.ŠU.SÈ.GA cloth
	2)	ME-ŠEŠ.ŠEŠ	(for) M.
	3)	DUMU *Barag-gi-si*	son of B.,
	4)	DUMU.DUMU *Ur*-^{d}*En-líl*	descendant of U.;
		(blank)	
	5)	ŠU.NIGÍN 1 ERÍN ANŠE.BAR.AN	total of 1 team of mules,
	6)	ŠU.NIGÍN 1 GIŠ.GIGIR.NÍG.ŠU	total of 1 NÍG.ŠU chariot,
	7)	ŠU.NIGÍN 1 *ki-li-lum* KUG.BABBAR	total of 1 silver wreath,
	8)	ŠU.NIGÍN 1 URUDU ḪA.ZI UD.KA.BAR	total of 1 bronze axe,
	9)	ŠU.NIGÍN 6 TÚG.ŠU.DU_7.A.BAL	total of 6 TÚG.ŠU.DU_7.A.BAL cloths;
	10)	ŠU.NIGÍN 20 TÚG.ŠU.SÈ.GA	total of 20 TÚG.ŠU.SÈ.GA cloths;
	11)	NÍG.BA GÁN	(this is) the gift of the field;
	12)	ŠU.NIGÍN 26 GURUŠ	total of 26 men,

	13)	DUMU.DUMU *Pù-uš*-GAL	descendants of P.,
	14)	PA.TE.SI	the governor of
	15)	*Ki-babbar*^{KI}	Ki-babbar,
	16)	*be-lu* GÁN	the "lords of the field,"
	17)	KÚ KUG.BABBAR	the recipients of the silver.

C_2	18)	3(ŠÁR) 3(BÙR.GUNU) 3(BÙR) GÁN	3834 iku of land;
	19)	NÍG.ŠÁM-*su*	its price is
	20)	3 ŠE GUR_7 1980 GUR. SAG.GÁL	12780. gsg of barley;
	21)	NÍG.ŠÁM	at the price of
	22)	1 GÍN KUG.BABBAR	1 shekel of silver for
	23)	1 ŠE GUR.SAG.GÁL	1. gsg of barley,
	24)	KUG.BABBAR-*su*	its silver (equivalent) is
viii	1)	3 GÚ 33 MA.NA KUG. BABBAR	12780 shekels of silver;
	2)	NÍG.ŠÁM GÁN	(this is) the price of the field;
	3)	40 GÚ SÍG	2400 pounds of wool;
	4)	NÍG.ŠÁM	at the price of
	5)	1 GÍN KUG.BABBAR	1 shekel of silver for
	6)	4 MA.NA SÍG	4 pounds of wool,
	7)	KUG.BABBAR-*si-in*	its silver (equivalent) is
	8)	10 MA.NA KUG.BABBAR	600 shekels of silver;
	9)	3 *ki-li-lu* KUG.BABBAR	3 silver wreaths,
	10)	KI.LAL.BI 1 MA.NA KUG. BABBAR	their weight is 60 shekels of silver;
	11)	6 URUDU ḪA.ZI UD.KA. BAR	6 bronze axes,
	12)	4 URUDU *na-ap-la-aq-tum* UD.KA.BAR	4 bronze battle-axes,
	13)	3 URUDU *maš-sa-tum* UD. KA.BAR	(and) 3 bronze . . . ;
	14)	NÍG.ŠÁM 1 GIŠ.TUKUL	the price of 1 weapon is
	15)	5 GÍN KUG.BABBAR	5 shekels of silver;
	16)	KUG.BABBAR-*su-nu*	their silver (equivalent) is
	17)	1 MA.NA 5 GÍN KUG. BABBAR	65 shekels of silver;
	18)	3 ERÍN ANŠE.BAR.AN	3 teams of mules;
	19)	NÍG.ŠÁM	the price of
	20)	1 ANŠE.BAR.AN	1 mule is
	21)	⅓ ŠA KUG.BABBAR	20 shekels of silver;
	22)	KUG.BABBAR-*su-nu*	their silver (equivalent) is
	23)	4 MA.NA KUG.BABBAR	240 shekels of silver;
	24)	40 Ì DUG	40 jars of oil;
	25)	NÍG.ŠÁM	at the price of
	26)	1 GÍN KUG.BABBAR	1 shekel of silver for
ix	1)	10 Ì SILÀ	10 quarts of oil,
	2)	KUG.BABBAR-*su*	its silver (equivalent) is
	3)	2! MA.NA KUG.BABBAR	120 shekels of silver;
	4)	5 SAG.NITA	5 male slaves
	5)	4 SAG.SAL	(and) 4 female slaves;
	6)	NÍG.ŠÁM	the price of
	7)	1 SAG	1 slave is
	8)	⅓ ŠA KUG.BABBAR	20 shekels of silver;
	9)	KUG.BABBAR-*su-nu*	their silver (equivalent) is
	10)	3 MA.NA KUG.BABBAR	180 shekels of silver;
	11)	1 DUMU.SAL	1 girl,
	12)	NÍG.ŠÁM-*sa*	her price is

	13)	13 GÍN KUG.BABBAR (blank)	13 shekels of silver;
	14)	ŠU.NIGÍN 21⅔ ŠA MA.NA LAL 2 GÍN KUG.BABBAR	total of 1278 shekels of silver;
	15)	NÍG.KI.GAR GÁN	(this is) the additional payment of the field;
	16)	1 ERÍN ANŠE.BAR.AN	1 team of mules,
	17)	1 GIŠ.GIGIR.NÍG.ŠU	1 NÍG.ŠU chariot,
	18)	1 *ki-li-lum* KUG.BABBAR	1 silver wreath,
	19)	KI.LAL.BI ⅓ ŠA KUG. BABBAR	its weight is 20 shekels of silver,
	20)	1 URUDU *na-ap-la-aq-tum* UD.KA.BAR	1 bronze battle-axe,
	21)	1 TÚG.ŠU.DU$_7$.A.BAL	(and) 1 TÚG.ŠU.DU$_7$.A.BAL cloth
	22)	*I-ti-É-a*	(for) I.
	23)	DUMU *Ur-Már-da*	son of U.,
	24)	DUMU.DUMU *Ur-Kèš*^{KI}	descendant of U.
x	1)	*ši Dup-si-ga*	Of T.;
	2)	1 TÚG.ŠU.DU$_7$.A.BAL	1 TÚG.ŠU.DU$_7$.A.BAL cloth
	3)	*I-ti*-DINGIR	(for) I.
	4)	DUMU DINGIR-*su*-GÀR	son of I.;
	5)	1 TÚG.ŠU.DU$_7$.A.BAL	1 TÚG.ŠU.DU$_7$.A.BAL cloth
	6)	PÙ.ŠA-*Eš$_4$-dar*	(for) P.;
	7)	1 TÚG.ŠU.DU$_7$.A.BAL	1 TÚG.ŠU.DU$_7$.A.BAL cloth
	8)	*É-ku-ku*	(for) E.;
	9)	2 DUMU *Su-mu*-GI	(these are) 2 sons of S.,
	10)	DUMU.DUMU *Gal-pum*	descendants of K.;
	11)	1 TÚG.ŠU.SÈ.GA	1 TÚG.ŠU.SÈ.GA cloth
	12)	*Da-da*	(for) D.
	13)	DUMU *Ur-Már-da*	son of U.;
	14)	1 TÚG.ŠU.SÈ.GA	1 TÚG.ŠU.SÈ.GA cloth
	15)	KA-*Ma-ma*	(for) P.
	16)	DUMU DINGIR-GÀR	son of I.;
	17)	2 DUMU.DUMU *Ur-Kèš*^{KI}	(these are) 2 sons of U.
	18)	*ši Dup-si-ga*	Of D.;
	19)	1 TÚG.ŠU.SÈ.GA	1 TÚG.ŠU.SÈ.GA cloth
	20)	*Dam-ba-ba*	(for) D.
	21)	DUMU DINGIR-GÀR	son of I.;
	22)	1 TÚG.ŠU.SÈ.GA	1 TÚG.ŠU.SÈ.GA cloth
	23)	*Sá-lim-a-ḫu*	(for) S.
	24)	DUMU *Da-da*	son of D.;
	25)	2 DUMU.DUMU	(these are) 2 sons of
	26)	*Ra-bí*-DINGIR	R.;
xi	1)	1 TÚG.ŠU.SÈ.GA	1 TÚG.ŠU.SÈ.GA cloth
	2)	*Su-mu-É-a*	(for) S.;
	3)	1 TÚG.ŠU.SÈ.GA	1 TÚG.ŠU.SÈ.GA cloth
	4)	*É-da-da*	(for) E.;
	5)	2 DUMU PÙ.ŠA-*Eš$_4$-dar*	(these are) 2 sons of P.,
	6)	DUMU.DUMU *Gal-pum*	descendants of K.;
	7)	1 TÚG.ŠU.SÈ.GA	1 TÚG.ŠU.SÈ.GA cloth
	8)	DINGIR-*nu-id*	(for) I.
	9)	DUMU *I-ti-É-a*	son of I.,
	10)	DUMU.DUMU *Ur-Már-da*	descendant of U.
	11)	*ši Ur-Kèš*^{KI}	Of U.;
	12)	1 TÚG.ŠU.SÈ.GA	1 TÚG.ŠU.SÈ.GA cloth
	13)	*I-si-im*-DINGIR	(for) I.
	14)	DUMU *Im-tum*	son of I.,
	15)	DUMU.DUMU *Ur-Kèš*^{KI} (blank)	descendant of U.;
	16)	ŠU.NIGÍN 1 ERÍN ANŠE. BAR.AN	total of 1 team of mules,

	17)	ŠU.NIGÍN 1 GIŠ.GIGIR. NÍG.ŠU	total of 1 NÍG.ŠU chariot,
	18)	ŠU.NIGÍN 1 *ki-li-lum* KUG. BABBAR	total of 1 silver wreath,
	19)	ŠU.NIGÍN 1 URUDU *na-ap-la-aq-tum* UD.KA.BAR	total of 1 bronze battle-axe,
	20)	ŠU.NIGÍN 4 TÚG.ŠU.DU_7.A. BAL	total of 4 TÚG.ŠU.DU_7.A.BAL cloths,
	21)	ŠU.NIGÍN 8 TÚG.ŠU.SÈ.GA	total of 8 TÚG.ŠU.SÈ.GA cloths;
	22)	NÍG.BA GÁN	(this is) the gift of the field;
	23)	ŠU.NIGÍN 12 GURUŠ	total of 12 men,
	24)	DUMU.DUMU *Dup-si-ga*	descendants of T.
xii	1)	*ši* PÙ.ŠA-*ru-um*	Of P.,
	2)	NU.BANDA	the captain of
	3)	*Ša-at-bar-rí-im*^{KI}	Šat-bar(r)im,
	4)	*be-lu* GÁN	the "lords of the field,"
	5)	KÚ KUG.BABBAR	the recipients of the silver.

		(blank)	
C_3	6)	1(BÙR.GUNU) 7(BÙR) GÁN	306 iku of land;
	7)	NÍG.ŠÁM-*su*	its price is
	8)	1020 ŠE GUR.SAG.GÁL	1020. gsg of barley;
	9)	NÍG.ŠÁM	at the price of
	10)	1 GÍN KUG.BABBAR	1 shekel of silver for
	11)	1 ŠE GUR.SAG.GÁL	1. gsg of barley,
	12)	KUG.BABBAR-*su*	its silver (equivalent) is
	13)	17 MA.NA KUG.BABBAR	1020 shekels of silver;
	14)	NÍG.ŠÁM GÁN	(this is) the price of the field;
	15)	7 GÚ LAL 12 MA.NA SÍG	408 pounds of wool;
	16)	NÍG.ŠÁM	at the price of
	17)	1 GÍN KUG.BABBAR	1 shekel of silver for
	18)	4 MA.NA SÍG	4 pounds of wool,
	19)	KUG.BABBAR-*si-in*	its silver (equivalent) is
	20)	1⅔ ŠA MA.NA 2 GÍN KUG. BABBAR	102 shekels of silver;
	21)	NÍG.KI.GAR GÁN	(this is) the additional payment of the field;
	22)	1 TÚG.ŠU.SÈ.GA	1 TÚG.ŠU.SÈ.GA cloth
	23)	*Zu-zu*	(for) Z.;
	24)	1 TÚG.ŠU.SÈ.GA	1 TÚG.ŠU.SÈ.GA cloth
	25)	*Ìr-e-pum*	(for) I.;
	26)	2 DUMU *Iš-má*-DINGIR	(these are) 2 sons of I.
	27)	*ši* NIGIR	Of N.,
xiii	1)	DUMU.DUMU *Ur-ur*	descendants of U.
	2)	*ši* PA.ḪI	Of P.;
		(blank)	
	3)	ŠU.NIGÍN 2 TÚG.ŠU.SÈ.GA	total of 2 TÚG.ŠU.SÈ.GA cloths;
	4)	NÍG.BA GÁN	(this is) the gift of the field;
	5)	ŠU.NIGÍN 2 GURUŠ	total of 2 men,
	6)	DUMU.DUMU *Ur-ur*	descendants of U.
	7)	*ši* PA.ḪI	Of P.,
	8)	*be-lu* GÁN	the "lords of the field,"
	9)	KÚ KUG.BABBAR	the recipients of the silver.
		(blank)	
	10)	ŠU.NIGÍN 6(ŠÁR) GÁN	The total of 6480 iku of land;
	11)	GÁN.NINDÁ	the field's border
	12)	IM.MIR	to the north is
	13)	ÍD.ZI.KALAM.MA	the ZI.KALAM.MA canal;
	14)	GÁN.NINDÁ	the field's border
	15)	IM.U_5	to the south is

	16)	É.GIŠ.MA.NU^{KI}	É.GIŠ.MA.NU;
	17)	GÁN.NINDÁ	the field's border
	18)	IM.KUR	to the east is
	19)	ÍD *A-maš-ti-ak*	the Amaštiak canal;
	20)	GÁN.NINDÁ	the field's border
	21)	IM.MAR.TU	to the west is
	22)	^{d}*A-ba$_4$-iš-da-gal*	(the property of) A.
	23)	DUMU *Sar-ru-*GI	son of Š.;
	24)	SUG-^{d}*Nin-ḫur-sag*	(this is the field of) SUG-^{d}Nin-ḫur-sag.
	25)	1 TÚG.ŠU.SÈ.GA	1 TÚG.ŠU.SÈ.GA cloth
	26)	1 URUDU ḪA.ZI UD.KA.BAR	(and) 1 bronze axe
xiv	1)	*Ba-ša-aḫ*-DINGIR	(for) B.,
	2)	LÚ.ÉŠ.GÍD	the field-surveyor,
	3)	DUMU *Ur-ur*	son of U.;
	4)	1 TÚG.ŠU.SÈ.GA	1 TÚG.ŠU.SÈ.GA cloth,
	5)	1 URUDU ḪA.ZI UD.KA.BAR	(and) 1 bronze axe
	6)	*Ib*-LUL-DINGIR	(for) I.,
	7)	DUB.SAR	the scribe,
	8)	DUMU *Nu-gal*	son of N.;
	9)	1 TÚG.ŠU.SÈ.GA	1 TÚG.ŠU.SÈ.GA cloth
	10)	1 URUDU ḪA.ZI UD.KA.BAR	(and) 1 bronze axe
	11)	*Ur-*^{d}*Nin-kar*	(for) U.,
	12)	SAG.DU$_5$	the field recorder,
	13)	DUMU *Barag-ki-ba*	son of B.,
	14)	DUMU.DUMU *A-ku-ì-lum*	descendant of A.;
		(blank)	
	15)	ŠU.NIGÍN 3 TÚG.ŠU.SÈ.GA	total of 3 TÚG.ŠU.SÈ.GA cloth,
	16)	ŠU.NIGÍN 3 URUDU ḪA.ZI UD.KA.BAR	total of 3 bronze axes;
	17)	NÍG.BA	(this is) the gift of
	18)	LÚ.GÁN.GÍD.DA	the men who measured the field;
		(blank)	
	19)	1 PÙ.ŠA-*Lu-lu*	27 PNs;
	20)	DUMU DINGIR-*a-zu*	
	21)	DI.TAR	
	22)	1 GAL.ZU-DINGIR	
	23)	*šu* NIN	
	24)	SANGA	
	25)	^{d}*Lugal-Már-da*	
	26)	1 DINGIR-*ba-na*	
	27)	AB+ÁŠ.URU	
xv	1)	DUMU *Šà-gú-ba*	
	2)	1 *Be-lí-a-mi*	
	3)	DUMU *Ur-Ab-ra*	
	4)	*ši Su$_4$-a-tum-mu-da*	
	5)	1 *A-bu-bu*	
	6)	DUMU *I-mi*-DINGIR	
	7)	UGULA KA-*zu-ra-ak*^{KI}	
	8)	1 *Iš-dup*-DINGIR	
	9)	DUMU *Amar-rí-rí*	
	10)	DUMU.DUMU	
	11)	SANGA	
	12)	1 *Mi-su$_4$-a*	
	13)	DUMU *I-ki-lum*	
	14)	NU.BANDA *Eš$_4$-na-na-ak*^{KI}	
	15)	1 *Ti-ir-su*	
	16)	DUMU PÙ.ŠA-*Lu-lu*	

	17)	DUMU.DUMU SABRA	
	18)	1 *Ì-lí-a-ḫi*	
	19)	DUMU *Ne-sag*	
	20)	NU.BANDA	
	21)	1 *Ma-an-sa-ki-su*	
	22)	DUMU *A-bí-da*	
	23)	1 DINGIR-*ba-ni*	
	24)	NU.BANDA MÁ.GUR$_8$	
	25)	DUMU *Gal-pum*	
	26)	1 *Na-mu-ru-um*	
	27)	DUMU *I-da*-DINGIR	
	28)	1 DINGIR-GÚ	
	29)	DUMU *Su-mu*-^{d}EN.ZU	
xvi	1)	1 *Mi-it-lik*	
	2)	DUMU *Iš-dup*-DINGIR	
	3)	NU.BANDA	
	4)	1 DINGIR-*ba-ni*	
	5)	DUMU *Mi-su$_4$-a*	
	6)	1 SI.A-*um*	
	7)	DUMU *I-ti*-^{d}*Da-gan*	
	8)	1 *Tu-tu*	
	9)	DUMU *Ì-lí*	
	10)	1 *A-ku-É-a*	
	11)	DUMU PÙ.ŠA-*É-a*	
	12)	1 *Ur*-^{d}EN.ZU	
	13)	DUMU *Ur-ezen*	
	14)	NU.BANDA GIŠ.KIN.TI	
	15)	1 *Ur-En-gal*-DU.DU	
	16)	DUMU *Ur*-^{d}*Ezínu*(ŠE.TIR)	
	17)	NU.BANDA *É-mar-za*^{KI}	
	18)	1 *Tu-tu*	
	19)	DUMU *Ì-la-la*	
	20)	ŠEŠ *Ra-bí*-DINGIR	
	21)	1 DINGIR-GÀR	
	22)	DUMU *Ti-li-lum*	
	23)	1 *Ik-ru-ub*-DINGIR	
	24)	DUMU PÙ.ŠA-*su*	
	25)	1 DINGIR-*mu-da*	
	26)	DUMU *I-me-a*	
	27)	1 *Su$_4$-ma*-SIPA	
	28)	DUMU *I-nin-sa-tu*	
	29)	1 *Ur*-^{d}PA.BÌL.SAG	
xvii	1)	DUMU *É-ní-íl*	
	2)	ENGAR LUGAL	
	3)	1 *A-ḫu*-GIŠ.ERÍN	
	4)	DUMU *A-ḫa-ar-ši*	
	5)	DUMU.DUMU *Lugal-ezen*	
		(blank)	
	6)	ŠU.NIGÍN 3 DUB.SAR	total of 3 scribes;
	7)	ŠU.NIGÍN 30 LAL 3 AB+ÁŠ. AB+ÁŠ	total of 27 witnesses;
	8)	1 *Be-lí-sa-tu*	10 PNs,
	9)	DUMU *Ba-ša-aḫ*-DINGIR	
	10)	LÚ.ÉŠ.GÍD	
	11)	1 *Iš*-LUL-DINGIR	
	12)	DUMU *Iš-dup*-DINGIR	
	13)	1 *I-mi*-DINGIR	
	14)	DUMU *Pù-be-lí*	
	15)	1 DINGIR-GI	
	16)	DUMU GAL.ZU-DINGIR	
	17)	*šu* NIN	

	18)	SANGA	
	19)	^{d}*Lugal-Már-da*	
	20)	1 *Ti-ru-um*	
	21)	DUMU *Bur-zum*	
	22)	GAL.SUKKAL	
	23)	DUMU.DUMU *I-rí-iš-be-lí*	
	24)	1 *Iq-bí*-GI	
	25)	DUMU *Be-lí*-GÚ	
	26)	NU.BANDA LÚ.IGI	
	27)	1 *I-da*-DINGIR	
	28)	DUMU *Ib*-LUL-DINGIR	
	29)	DUMU.DUMU *Nu-gal*	
xviii	1)	1 DINGIR-*a-ḫa*	
	2)	DUMU *Be-lí*-GÚ	
	3)	NU.BANDA	
	4)	1 *Nu-ni-da*	
	5)	DUMU *Be-lí-a-mi*	
	6)	DUMU.DUMU *Ur-Ab-ra*	
	7)	*ši Su*$_4$*-a-tum-mu-da*	
	8)	1 *Li-sa-núm*	
	9)	DUMU *Ur*-AN.KI	
	10)	*šu* KUG.DÍM	
		(blank)	
	11)	ŠU.NIGÍN 10 DUMU.DUMU	total of 10 "sons" of
	12)	AB+ÁŠ.AB+ÁŠ	the witnesses;
	13)	1 *Be-lí*-GÚ	12 PNs,
	14)	DUMU *Ra-bí*-DINGIR	
	15)	1 *A-nu-zu*	
	16)	DUMU *Ik-ru-ub*-DINGIR	
	17)	1 *Iš-má*-DINGIR	
	18)	DUMU *Ik-ru-ub-É-a*	
	19)	1 *I-ti*-DINGIR	
	20)	DUMU *Ḫa-da-bi*	
	21)	1 PÙ.ŠA-*Eš*$_4$*-dar*	
	22)	DUMU KA-*Ma-ma*	
	23)	1 *Ur-Ab-ra*	
	24)	DUB.SAR	
	25)	DUMU *Su-mu-núm*	
	26)	1 SIG$_5$*-ì-lum*	
	27)	DUMU *Ra-bí*-DINGIR	
	28)	1 PÙ.ŠA-*Lu-lu*	
	29)	GAL.UKÙ	
	30)	*Ša-at-bar-rí-im*^{KI}	
xix	1)	1 *Ga-at-núm*	
	2)	DUMU *Ra-bí*-DINGIR	
	3)	*Ḫa-ar-ḫa-mu-na-ak*^{KI}	
	4)	1 *Ur-ur*	
	5)	DUMU *Su*-NI-*um*	
	6)	MAR.X^{KI}	
	7)	1 *Ra-bí*-DINGIR	
	8)	DUMU DINGIR-*su-a-ḫa*	
	9)	KA-*ul-lum*^{KI}	
	10)	1 *I-da*-DINGIR	
	11)	DUMU *I-ku-É-a*	
	12)	KA-*zu-ra-ak*^{KI}	
		(blank)	
	13)	ŠU.NIGÍN 12 NU.BANDA *ù* UGULA	total of 12 overseers and foremen;
	14)	ŠU.NIGÍN.ŠU.NIGÍN 52 GURUŠ	the grand total of 52 men of
	15)	*Már-da*^{KI}	Marda,

	16)	AB+ÁŠ.AB+ÁŠ	the witnesses of
	17)	GÁN	the field.
	18)	600 GURUŠ	600 men
	19)	*in Ga-za-lu*^{KI}	in Kazalu
	20)	NINDA Ì.KÚ	ate bread;
	21)	600 GURUŠ	600 men
	22)	*šu* 1 UD	for one day,
	23)	1200 GURUŠ	1200 men
	24)	*šu* 2 UD	for two days (= 600 men during two days),
	25)	*in maš-ga-ni Be-lí-ba-ni*	in the settlement of B.,
	26)	AGRIG ^{d}*A-ba*$_4$*-iš-da-gal*	the steward of A.,
	27)	NINDA Ì.KÚ	ate bread;
	28)	LÚ *Már-da*^{KI}	the citizens of Marda.
		(blank)	
		(xix 1 to xxiv 24 = A x 22 to xvi 17 = 49 citizens of Akkadē)	
		(blank)	
xxiv	25)	GÁN *Már-da*^{KI}	Field of Marda
	26)	*Ma-an-iš-tu-su*	M.
	27)	LUGAL	king of
	28)	KIŠ	the totality
	29)	Ì.ŠÁM	bought.

Side D (= old Side B)

		(first three columns missing, here marked a, b, and c)	
a	1)	[4(BÙR.GUNU) 4(BÙR) 2(IKU) GÁN]	[794 iku of land];
	2)	[NÍG.ŠÁM-*su*]	[its price is]
	3)	[2646(GUR) 2(PI) 4(BÁN) ŠE GUR.SAG.GÁL]	[2646.2.4 gsg of barley];
	4)	[NÍG.ŠÁM]	[at the price of]
	5)	[1 GÍN KUG.BABBAR]	[1 shekel of silver for]
	6)	[1 ŠE GUR.SAG.GÁL]	[1. gsg of barley],
b	1)	[KUG.BABBAR-*su*]	[its silver (equivalent) is]
	2)	[44 MA.NA 6 GÍN 2 MA.NA.TUR KUG.BABBAR]	[2646⅔ shekels of silver];
	3)	[NÍG.ŠÁM GÁN]	[(this is) the price of the field];
	4)	[17 GÚ 38⅔ MA.NA SÍG]	[1058⅔ pounds of wool];
	5)	[NÍG.ŠÁM]	[at the price of]
	6)	[1 GÍN KUG.BABBAR]	[1 shekel of silver for]
	7)	[4 MA.NA SÍG]	[4 pounds of wool],
c	1)	[KUG.BABBAR-*si-in*]	[its silver (equivalent) is]
	2)	[4⅓ ŠA MA.NA 4 GÍN 2 MA.NA.TUR KUG.BABBAR]	[264⅔ shekels of silver];
	3)	[NÍG.KI.GAR GÁN]	[(this is) the additional payment of the field];
	4)	[1 *ki-li-lum* KUG.BABBAR]	[1 silver wreath],
	5)	[KI.LAL.BI x GÍN KUG.BABBAR]	[its weight is x shekels of silver],
	6)	[1 TÚG.ŠU.DU$_7$.A.BAL]	[(and) 1 TÚG.ŠU.DU$_7$.A.BAL cloth]
	7)	[PN]	[(for) PN]
	8)	[DUMU DINGIR-GÀR]	[son of I.],
i	1)	[DUMU].DUMU [*Da*]-*tum*	[desce]ndant of D.;
	2)	[1 *ki*]-*li*-[*lu*]*m* KUG.BABBAR	[1] silver ⌜wreath⌝,
	3)	[KI].LAL.BI ⌜x⌝ GÍN KUG.BABBAR	its weight is ⌜x⌝ shekels of silver,
	4)	[1] TÚG.ŠU.DU$_7$.A.BAL	(and) [1] TÚG.ŠU.DU$_7$.A.BAL cloth
	5)	*Sag-gul-lum*	(for) S.;
	6)	⌜1⌝ TÚG.ŠU.SÈ.GA	[1] TÚG.ŠU.SÈ.GA cloth
	7)	[*A*]-*ḫu-mu-bí*	(for) A.;

	8)	[1] TÚG.ŠU.SÈ.GA	[1] TÚG.ŠU.SÈ.GA cloth
	9)	*Pù-pù*	(for) P.;
	10)	[3 DU]MU *É-a-ra-bí*	[(these are) 3 so]ns of E.;
	11)	[1] TÚG.ŠU.SÈ.GA	[1] TÚG.ŠU.SÈ.GA cloth
ii	1)	*Eš*$_4$*-dar-al-su*	(for) E.
	2)	DUMU *Iš-tu-tu*	son of I.;
	3)	4 DUMU.DUMU *ši A-pù-lum*	(these are) 4 descendants of A.;
	4)	1 TÚG.ŠU.SÈ.GA	1 TÚG.ŠU.SÈ.GA cloth
	5)	*Iš-má*-DINGIR	(for) I.;
	6)	1 TÚG.ŠU.SÈ.GA	1 TÚG.ŠU.SÈ.GA cloth
	7)	*I-ti*-DINGIR	(for) I.,
	8)	DUB.SAR	the scribe;
	9)	2 DUMU DINGIR-GÀR	(these are) 2 sons of I.;
	10)	1 TÚG.ŠU.SÈ.GA	1 TÚG.ŠU.SÈ.GA cloth
	11)	*É-a*-GÚ	(for) E.
	12)	DUMU *Iš-tu-tu*	son of I.;
iii	1)	1 TÚG.ŠU.SÈ.GA	1 TÚG.ŠU.SÈ.GA cloth
	2)	ARÁD-*zu-ni*	(for) A.
	3)	DUMU *La-mu-um*	son of L.;
	4)	4 DUMU.DUMU *Da-tum*	(these are) 4 descendants of D.;
	5)	1 TÚG.ŠU.SÈ.GA	1 TÚG.ŠU.SÈ.GA cloth
	6)	PÙ.ŠA-^{d}*Za-ba*$_4$*-ba*$_4$	(for) P.
	7)	DUMU *Mu-mu*	son of M.,
	8)	DUMU.DUMU *Ìr-am-*^{d}*Ma-lik*	descendant of I.;
	9)	1 TÚG.ŠU.SÈ.GA	1 TÚG.ŠU.SÈ.GA cloth
	10)	*Nu-ra*	(for) N.,
	11)	GEMÉ.DINGIR	the temple servant,
	12)	DUMU.SAL PÙ.ŠA-*Nu-ni*	daughter of P.,
	13)	DUMU.DUMU *Bu-im*	descendant of B.,
iv	1)	MÁ.LAḪ$_4$	the boatman;
		(blank)	
	2)	ŠU.NIGÍN 2 *ki-li-lum* KUG.BABBAR	total of 2 silver wreaths,
	3)	ŠU.NIGÍN 2 TÚG.ŠU.DU$_7$.A.BAL	total of 2 TÚG.ŠU.DU$_7$.A.BAL cloths,
	4)	ŠU.NIGÍN 10 LAL 1 TÚG.ŠU.SÈ.GA	total of 9 TÚG.ŠU.SÈ.GA cloths;
	5)	NÍG.BA GÁN	(this is) the gift of the field;
	6)	ŠU.NIGÍN 11 GURUŠ	total of 11 men,
	7)	*be-lu* GÁN	the "lords of the field,"
	8)	KÚ KUG.BABBAR	the recipients of the silver;
	9)	1 *Šu*-AD.MU	9 PNs,
	10)	DUMU *La-mu-um*	
	11)	1 *I-da-tum*	
	12)	1 *Su-ru-uš*-GI	
	13)	2 DUMU DINGIR-*su*-GÀR	
	14)	1 *Zi-ra*	
v	1)	DUMU DINGIR-*dan*	
	2)	1 *A-da-da*	
	3)	DUMU ^{d}KA-*Me-ir*	
	4)	5 DUMU.DUMU *Da-tum*	
	5)	1 *Šu-Eš*$_4$*-dar*	
	6)	DUMU ME-*Sá-lim*	
	7)	DUMU.DUMU KA-KA	
	8)	1 DINGIR-*a-zu*	
	9)	DUMU *I-zu*-GÍD	
	10)	1 PÙ.ŠA-*Il-la*	
	11)	DUMU *Ur-*^{d}*Nin-kar*	
	12)	2 DUMU.DUMU *A-pù-lum*	
	13)	1 DINGIR-*ga-lí*	

	14)	DUMU *Ì-lu-lu*	
	15)	DUMU.DUMU *Ìr-am-*^{d}*Ma-lik*	
vi		(blank)	
	1)	ŠU.NIGÍN 10 LAL 1 GURUŠ	total of 9 men,
	2)	ŠEŠ *be-lu* GÁN	the "brother-lords of the field";
		(blank)	
	3)	GÁN.NINDÁ	the field's border
	4)	IM.MIR	to the north is
	5)	DUMU.DUMU *Ku-ku*	(the property of) the descendants of K.;
	6)	GÁN.NINDÁ	the field's border
	7)	IM.U$_5$	to the south is
	8)	*ša-at Gu-lí-zi*	(the field?) of ox-drivers;
	9)	GÁN.NINDÁ	the field's border
	10)	IM.KUR	to the east is
	11)	ME-*Sá-lim*	(the property of) M.,
	12)	DUMU LUGAL	son of the king;
	13)	GÁN.NINDÁ	the field's border
	14)	IM.MAR.TU	to the west is
	15)	*Bar*^{KI}	Bar;
	16)	GÁN *Ba-ra-az*-EDIN^{KI}	(this is) the field of Baraz-EDIN,
vii	1)	*in Kiš*^{KI}	(located) in Kish.
		(blank)	
	2)	80 DUMU.DUMU	80 citizens of
	3)	*Kiš*^{KI}	Kish
	4)	*in Ga-za-lu*^{KI}	in Kazalu
	5)	NINDA Ì.KÚ	ate bread.
		(blank)	
		(vii 6 to xiv 16 = A x 22 to xvi 17 = 49 citizens of Akkadē)	
		(blank)	
xiv	17)	GÁN *Ba-ra-az*-EDIN^{KI}	Field of Baraz-EDIN,
	18)	*in Kiš*^{KI}	(located) in Kish,
	19)	*Ma-an-iš-tu-su*	M.
	20)	LUGAL	king of
	21)	KIŠ	the totality
	22)	Ì.ŠÁM	bought.

Notes

A xv 14.—The same PN is spelled *A-ḫu-ḫu* in B xxi 7.

A xvi 10.—For this toponym, see Steinkeller, *Vicino Oriente* 6 (1986) p. 36 line 209.

B xiv 12.—For the form of PÉŠ, see Krebernik, *Die Beschwörungen aus Fara und Ebla* (Hildesheim, 1984) p. 287f., examples C1, C2, and C3.

B xv 1.—Against *RGTC* 1 p. 151, which reads this GN as ŠID-bar^{KI}, the first sign is assuredly MES. Compare the form of ŠID in, e.g., B xv 5.

C xii 3 and xviii 30.—*Ša-at-bar-rí-im*^{KI} may be the same toponym as *Sa*/*Ša-at-ba-ri*^{KI} of lexical texts. See Steinkeller, *Vicino Oriente* 6 (1986) p. 34 n. 36.

C xv 14.—The toponym *Eš*$_4$*-na-na-ak*^{KI} may be identical with the city of Eshnuna (actually Eshnunak or Ashnunak), variously written Eš-nun(-na), Iš-nun(-na), and Aš-nun(-na) in third millennium texts (see *RGTC* 1 p. 80f.; 2 p. 18). For the evidence that Eshnuna's name ended in /k/, see Jacobsen, *AS* 6 pp. 11–16.

C xv 19.—The Sumerian word ne-sag, frequent as a PN in third millennium texts (see, e.g., examples listed in Hackman, *BIN* 8 p. 41f.) is equated with the Semitic *ba-ga-lu(-um)* /*bakrum* or *bukrum*/ "first-born" in Pettinato, *MEE* 4 p. 226 line 243 (cf. also DUMU.SAG = *bù-gú-lu*, *bù-ga-lu*/*ru*$_{12}$ *ibid.* p. 229 line 270). For the Ebla entries, see Krebernik, *ZA* 73 (1983) p. 13. Civil suggests to us (personal communication) that ne-sag is a syllabic spelling of nisag "first/early fruit," and brings our attention to the meaning "früh" of *bakrum* (said of dates), given in *AHWB* p. 97.

C xvi 14.—In the title NU.BANDA GIŠ.KIN.TI, GIŠ.KIN.TI is either "workshop" (Akk. *kiškattûm*) or, but less likely, the toponym Kishkattûm/GIŠ.KIN.TI, for which see *RGTC* 1 p. 94; 2 p. 106.

C xix 6.—The sign read here as X is probably É. Compare *RGTC* 1 p. 116.

C xix 9.—This toponym is probably to be interpreted as *Zú-ul-lum*^{KI}. Compare *RGTC* 1 p. 148.

No. 41 Sippar Stone

Photographs: Plates 73 and 74, Istanbul Archaeological Museum.

Copy: None; collated by Gelb in 1947 and 1963.

Synopsis: Plates 110 and 111.

Provenience: Probably Sippar (Abū Habba)—this provenience is supported by the mention of three geographical names in the text: *A-ga-dè*^{KI} (i 1′, rev. vii′ 17′), *U*$_4$*-bí-um*^{KI} (nisbe?) (viii 1′, 17′), and *I-lib*^{KI} (viii 7′, rev. vii′ 8′), all situated in northern Babylonia. In the same direction points the occurrence of ^{d}*A-ba*$_4$ (v 5′), the god of Akkadē. The eleven other geographical names occurring in the text are all *hapax legomena*.

Date: Sargonic.
Language: Akkadian.
Present location: Istanbul Museum, EŞEM 1022. The tablet entered the Museum by acquisition from a certain Camekian sometime between 1889 and 1891.
Publications: H. V. Hilprecht, *BE* 1 p. 53 and pls. VI–VIII (photographs from the cast); Scheil, *RT* 22 (1900) pp. 29–36 (transliteration); Gelb, "Old Akkadian Stone Tablet from Sippar," *RSO* 32 (1957) pp. 83–94 (photographs, transliteration, and translation). Compare also the references to discussions of the Sippar Stone noted in Gelb, *op. cit.* pp. 83f.; Diakonoff, *Obščestvenny i gosudarstvenny stroy Drevnego Dvurečya. Šumer* (Moscow, 1959) p. 79f.
Description: Large fragment of a limestone tablet measuring 15.6 × 25.3 cm. The thickness, varying from 5.1 cm on the outside to 7.4 cm on the inside, increases from left to right and from top to bottom. The preserved fragment constitutes about one-fourth of the original, most probably the top left quarter of the original. One side is flat, the other is rounded.
Text: Since one side is slightly rounded in comparison with the flat surface of the other side, we must assume that what was taken by Hilprecht and Scheil as the obverse must really be the reverse, and vice versa, in accordance with the general convention for the form of cuneiform tablets in early periods. This is also indicated by the position of the left edge, which normally begins at a point near the left bottom of the obverse on tablets of the Sargonic period. As a final reason for taking the present obverse as the reverse, we should note that the old column iii′ of the reverse, containing a list of gifts for the witnesses of Zuzu of Abu-ilum, should follow, rather than precede, the old column iv′ of the reverse, containing the main provisions concerning the transfers of the property of Zuzu and Abu-ilum. Similar conclusions can be derived on the basis of the old column v′ of the reverse. All that means that the old sequence of columns of the reverse should be reversed, so that the old reverse ix′ should become obverse i, and so on; and similarly, that the old obverse ix should become reverse i′, and so on.

The list of correspondences between the old and new sequences of columns is given here to make it easier to find the citations given in the old sequence in previous publications:

Old obv.	i	=	New rev.	ix′
	ii	=		viii′
	iii	=		vii′
	iv	=		vi′
	v	=		v′
	vi	=		iv′
	vii	=		iii′
	viii	=		ii′
	ix	=		i′
Old rev.	i′	=	New obv.	ix
	ii′	=		viii
	iii′	=		vii
	iv′	=		vi
	v′	=		v
	vi′	=		iv
	vii′	=		iii
	viii′	=		ii
	ix′	=		i

The text is preserved in nine columns of writing each on the obverse and reverse and in one column on the left edge. The right edge, now missing, could have contained the name of the buyer.

The preserved portions of the text deal with the acquisition of about twenty-seven parcels of land by an unknown person. Considering that the preserved portions constitute only about one-fourth of the original, and assuming that the destroyed portions listed a more or less corresponding number of parcels, we may be allowed to project the total of purchased parcels of land as over one hundred. This total is by far the highest among the texts in this collection.

Sample Interpretation

Obv. vi 10′–27′: PN (= seller) received 73⅓ of shekels of silver as the price of the field seeded with 3,300 quarts of barley, at 60 quarts per (1 iku), that is, 110 iku of land, and 7⅓ shekels of silver and 1 ŠU.ZA.GA cloth as the additional payment. Location of the field is given in E, W, N, and S directions.

Other transactions add information about x commodities offered to the witnesses of the sellers and to the surveyors.

Transliteration and Translation

Obv. i		(beg. destr.)	
	1′)	[*A*]-*ga-dè*^{KI}	
	2′)	[10] LAL 1 GUR GÁN 3(BÁN)	⌜2,700⌝ quarts (of seed barley), (at the rate of) 30 quarts per iku (= 90 iku of land);
	3′)	NÍG.ŠÁM-*su*	its price is
	4′)	2 KUG.BABBAR MA.NA	120 shekels of silver;
	5′)	NÍG.KI.GAR	the additional payment is
	6′)	12 GÍN KUG.BABBAR	12 shekels of silver
	7′)	4 TÚG.ŠU.ZA.GA	(and) 4 TÚG.ŠU.ZA.GA cloths;

	8′)	*in A-za-ra*	in Azara,
	9′)	1 *Iš-dup-Il*	3 PNs,
	10′)	DUMU *Ma-la-ni-su*	
	11′)	1 *Ib-bu-bu*	
	12′)	DUMU *A-mur-rúm*	
	13′)	1 *A-bí*-AN.NA	
	14′)	GEMÉ.DINGIR	
	15′)	SAL.DUMU *Na-ni*	
	16′)	DUMU.DUMU	descendants of
	17′)	*A-nu-nu*	A.,
	18′)	*ma-ḫi-ru*	are the recipients
	19′)	[KUG.B]ABBAR	of the silver.
		(rest destr.)	
ii		(beg. destr.)	
	1′)	1 SÍ[G MA.NA]	1 [pound of] wo[ol]
	2′)	1 *A-ḫu*-GIŠ.ERÍN	for A.
	3′)	*šu* SU.Ù.SAL	Of S.,
	4′)	DUB.SAR.GÁN	the scribe of the field.
	5′)	4 GUR GÁN 1(PI)	1,200 quarts (of seed barley), (at the rate of) 60 quarts per iku (= 40 iku of land);
	6′)	NÍG.ŠÁM-*su*	its price is
	7′)	1/3 ŠA 7 GÍN LAL 1 MA.NA. TUR KUG.BABBAR	26 2/3 shekels of silver;
	8′)	NÍG.KI.GAR	the additional payment is
	9′)	2 1/2 TAR GÍN KUG.BABBAR	2 1/4 shekels of silver;
	10′)	GÁN *šu Sa-ba-ra*?	field of S.;
	11′)	1 *Iš-má-ì-lum*	(the property of) I.
	12′)	*šu* LÚ.KAS$_4$	Of L.
	13′)	IM.KUR	to the east is
	14′)	GÁN.NINDÁ	the field's border;
	15′)	1 *I-bí*-ZU	(the property of) I.,
	16′)	DUMU LUGAL	the king's son,
	17′)	IM.MAR.TU	to the west is
	18′)	GÁN.NINDÁ	the field's border;
	19′)	1 *Ì-lum*-GIŠ.ERÍN	(the property of) I.
	20′)	[*šu Ku*]?-*ru*	[Of] ⌜K.⌝
		(rest destr.)	
iii		(beg. destr.)	
	1′)	IM.MIR	to the north is
	2′)	GÁN.NINDÁ	the field's border;
	3′)	*ša-at*	(the field) of
	4′)	*Sar-ra-tum*^{KI}	Šarratum
	5′)	IM.MAR.TU	to the west is
	6′)	GÁN.NINDÁ	the field's border;
	7′)	1 *Dam-ma*	(the property of) D.
	8′)	DUMU *A-pù*-BÀD	son of A.
	9′)	*šu Ba-lu-lu*	Of B.
	10′)	IM.KUR	to the east is
	11′)	GÁN.NINDÁ	the field's border;
	12′)	1 *A-mu-mu*	(the property of) A.
	13′)	*šu Ba-zi-gú*!	Of B.
	14′)	IM.U$_5$	to the south is
	15′)	GÁN.NINDÁ	the field's border;
	16′)	KUG.BABBAR	the silver of
	17′)	NÍG.ŠÁM	the price of
	18′)	3 GÁN	3 fields
	19′)	1 *A-ḫu*-DÙG	A.

	20′)	DUMU *Ì-lum-sar*	son of I.
	21′)	*šu* PA.TE.SI	Of the governor
	22′)	*im-ḫur*	received.

	23′)	[. . .]-ḪA	
		(rest destr.)	
iv		(beg. destr.)	
	1′)	KAS^{KI}	KAS
	2′)	IM.KUR	to the east is
	3′)	GÁN.NINDÁ	the field's border;
	4′)	1 *I-ti-sum*	(the property of) I.
	5′)	IM.U$_5$	to the south is
	6′)	GÁN.NINDÁ	the field's border;
	7′)	1 *A-bí-ra*	6 persons,
	8′)	*šu* ŠU.A	
	9′)	1 *Ì-lum*-GIŠ.ERÍN	
	10′)	*šu Ku?-ru*	
	11′)	1 *Šu-Ma-ma*	
	12′)	DUMU *Da-ba*$_4$*-la*	
	13′)	1 *Šu-Ba-ba*	
	14′)	*šu A-da* LÚ.GUNU+ÚŠ	
	15′)	1 *Su*$_4$-NI-*um*	
	16′)	*šu A-nu-nu*	
	17′)	1 *Šum-Ma-lik*	
	18′)	*šu Si-na*	
	19′)	AB+ÁŠ.AB+ÁŠ	the witnesses of
	20′)	GÁN *šu* KÁ.T[I]?	the field of KÁ.[T]I?;
	21′)	1 TÚG.ŠU.ZA.GA	1 TÚG.ŠU.ZA.GA cloth
	22′)	1 SÍG MA.NA	(and) 1 pound of wool
	23′)	1 *Na-ni*	for N.
	24′)	*šu Ḫu-bí-a*	Of Ḫ.,
	25′)	DUB.SAR.GÁN	the scribe of the field.
		(blank)	

v		(beg. destr.)	
	1′)	[1 . . .]	[(the property of) PN]
	2′)	*šu Bu-e-im*	Of B.
	3′)	IM.U$_5$	to the south is
	4′)	GÁN.NINDÁ	the field's border;
	5′)	^{d}*A-ba*$_4$	(the property of) A.
	6′)	IM.MAR.TU	to the west is
	7′)	GÁN.NINDÁ	the field's border;
	8′)	1 *A-ḫu*-DÙG	(the property of) A.
	9′)	*šu* PA.TE.SI	Of the governor
	10′)	IM.KUR	to the east is
	11′)	GÁN.NINDÁ	the field's border;
	12′)	1 *Ì-lí-a-ḫi*	I.
	13′)	*šu Bu-ḫu-lum*	Of B.,
	14′)	AB+ÁŠ.AB+ÁŠ	the witness(!) of
	15′)	GÁN *šu* Ù.SIG$_7$	the field of Ù.SIG$_7$.

	16′)	3 GUR GÁN 1(PI)	900 quarts (of seed barley), (at the rate of) 60 quarts per iku (= 30 iku of land);
	17′)	NÍG.ŠÁM-*su*	its price is
	18′)	⅓ ŠA KUG.BABBAR	20 shekels of silver;
	19′)	NÍG.KI.GAR	the additional payment is
	20′)	1½ TAR GÍN KUG.BABBAR	1¼ shekels of silver
	21′)	1 TÚG.ŠU.ZA.GA	(and) 1 TÚG.ŠU.ZA.GA cloth;

	22′)	*Da-bí-bí*	D.
	23′)	*šu Bí-za*	Of B.
	24′)	*dam-ḫur*	received (it);
	25′)	1 PA.TE.SI	(the property of) the governor
	26′)	IM.MIR	to the north is
	27′)	GÁN.NINDÁ	the field's border;
	28′)	1 PA.TE.SI	(the property of) the governor
	29′)	IM.KUR	to the east is
	30′)	[GÁN.NINDÁ]	[the field's border];
		(rest destr.)	
vi		(beg. destr.)	

	1′)	[x GUR GÁN 1(PI)?]	[x iku of land];
	2′)	NÍG.[ŠÁM-*su*]	[its pri]ce is
	3′)	1/3 ŠA 1/2 TAR GÍN KUG. BABBAR	20 1/4 shekels of silver;
	4′)	NÍG.KI.GAR	the additional payment is
	5′)	2 GÍN KUG.BABBAR	2 shekels of silver;
	6′)	1 *Zu-zu*	Z.
	7′)	ŠEŠ *Du-du*	brother of D. of
	8′)	BÀD-ḪU.GAN?^{KI}	BÀD-ḪU.GAN?
	9′)	*im-ḫur*《*-ra*》	received (it).

	10′)	11(wr. 12) GUR GÁN 1(PI)	3,300 quarts (of seed barley), (at the rate of) 60 quarts per iku (= 110 iku of land);
	11′)	NÍG.ŠÁM-*su*	its price is
	12′)	1 MA.NA KUG.BABBAR 13 GÍN 1 MA.NA.TUR	73 1/3 shekels of silver;
	13′)	NÍG.KI.GAR	the additional payment is
	14′)	7 GÍN KUG.BABBAR 1 MA. NA.TUR	7 1/3 shekels of silver
	15′)	1 TÚG.ŠU.ZA.GA	(and) 1 TÚG.ŠU.ZA.GA cloth;
	16′)	*A-pù-ì-lum*	A.
	17′)	*šu A-ki*	Of A. of
	18′)	URUDU?^{KI}	URUDU?
	19′)	*im-ḫur*	received (it);
	20′)	^{d}LUGAL-*bar-ga-ad*	(the property of) L.
	21′)	IM.KUR	to the east is
	22′)	GÁN.NINDÁ	the field's border;
	23′)	SI.A	(the property of) S.
	24′)	*šu ša-ti*	of the mountain(?) of
	25′)	*Ša-da-an*^{KI}	Šadan
	26′)	IM.MAR.TU	to the west is
	27′)	[GÁN.NINDÁ]	[the field's border];
		(rest destr.)	

---

vii		(beg. destr.)	
	1′)	⸢X X⸣ [. . .]	⸢. . .⸣
	2′)	*ù*	and
	3′)	*a-na* GÁN	for the field of
	4′)	*Zu-zu*	Z.
	5′)	ŠEŠ *Du-du*	brother of D.;
	6′)	1 MA.NA SÍG	1 pound of wool
	7′)	1 *I-kùn-núm*	for I.
	8′)	*šu* LÚ	Of L.;
	9′)	1 SÍG MA.NA	1 pound of wool
	10′)	1 PÙ.ŠA-*ru*	for P.,
	11′)	PAB.ŠEŠ	the PAB.ŠEŠ priest;
	12′)	1 *Šu-pù-la*	3 PNs,

13′)	1 *Ì-lum*-A.ZU	
14′)	1 *Iš-má-ì-lum*	
15′)	AB+ÁŠ.AB+ÁŠ	the elders
16′)	*šu* URU^{KI}.URU^{KI}	of the towns of (i.e., which are located on)
17′)	*ša* E	the Irḫan canal;
18′)	^{d}*Irḫan*$_{x}$(MUŠ)$^{ir\text{-}ḫa}$	
19′)	*a-na* GÁN	(they are the witnesses) for the field of
20′)	*A-pù-ì-lum*	A.

21′)	10(GUR) LAL 2(PI) GUR GÁN 1(PI)	2,880 quarts (of seed barley), (at the rate of) 60 quarts per iku (= 96 iku of land);
22′)	NÍG.ŠÁM-*su*	its price is
23′)	1 MA.NA 4 GÍN KUG. BABBAR	64 shekels of silver;
24′)	NÍG.KI.GAR	the additional payment is
25′)	6 GÍN [KUG.BABBAR 1? MA.NA TUR]	6+[⅓]? shekels [of silver];
	(rest destr.)	

viii	(beg. destr.)	
1′)	*U*$_4$*-bí-um*[^{KI}]	[x]+9 PNs,
2′)	1 *Ìr-da-pu*[*m*]	
3′)	1 *Pù-su*-DÙG	
4′)	1 IGI.SI$_4$	
5′)	ŠEG$_9$-*da*^{KI}	
6′)	1 *Zi-lu-lu*	
7′)	*I-lib*^{KI}	
8′)	1 *A-ḫu-ì-lum*	
9′)	1 *Šu-Eš*$_4$*-dar*	
10′)	*A-za-me-um*^{KI}	
11′)	1 *Su*$_4$-NI-*da*	
12′)	1 *Na-ni*	
13′)	*Šim*-SAR^{KI}	
14′)	AB+ÁŠ.AB+ÁŠ	the witnesses
15′)	*a-na* GÁN	for the field
16′)	*šu Be-la-su*(sic)*-nu*	of B. of
17′)	*U*$_4$*-bí-um*^{KI}	Upiʾum;
18′)	1 ŠE GUR	300 quarts of barley
19′)	1 TÚG.ŠU.ZA.GA	(and) 1 TÚG.ŠU.ZA.GA cloth
20′)	1 *Na-ni*	for N.
21′)	*šu Ḫu-bí-a*	Of Ḫ.,
22′)	DUB.SAR.GÁN	the scribe of the field.
	(rest destr.)	

ix	(beg. destr.)	
1′)	DUM[U . . .]	so[n of . . .]
2′)	[. . .]	[. . .]
3′)	LUGA[L. . .]	(the property of) ⸢L.⸣
4′)	I[M? . . .]	to [the . . . is]
5′)	GÁ[N.NINDÁ]	the fi[eld's border];
6′)	1 *Bu*-[. . .]	(the property of) ⸢B.⸣,
7′)	MU [. . .]	the ⸢. . .⸣
8′)	IM [. . .]	to [the . . . is]
9′)	GÁN.[NINDÁ]	the field's [border];
10′)	[. . .]	[(the property of) PN]
11′)	[. . .]	[. . .]
12′)	I[M . . .]	to [the . . . is]
13′)	GÁ[N.NINDÁ]	the fi[eld's border];
14′)	[. . .]	[(the property of) PN]

	15′)	I[M . . .]	to [the . . . is]
	16′)	[GÁN.NINDÁ]	[the field's border];
		(rest destr.)	

Rev. i′		(beg. destr.)	
	1′)	I[M? . . .]	
	2′)	*Ra-b*[*í-ì?-lum*?]	
	3′)	*šu Li-*[*gi?-im*?]	
	4′)	IM [. . .]	
		(rest destr.)	
ii′		(beg. destr.)	
	1′)	1 *Ḫu-*[. . .]	
	2′)	DUMU *Ba-*[. . .]	
	3′)	1 *Ú-*⌜*x*⌝-[. . .]	
	4′)	DUMU *Ḫa-la-*[X]	
	5′)	1 *Be-lí-lí*	
	6′)	DUMU *Bur-zi-*[*a*]?	
	7′)	1 *Ra-bí-ì-lum*	
	8′)	DUMU *Li-gi-i*[*m*]	
	9′)	1 *Ba-ša*	
	10′)	DUMU *Ku-ku* PAB.ŠEŠ	
	11′)	1 BALA-*ì-lum*	
	12′)	DUMU *Zi-at*	
	13′)	1 [. . .]	
	14′)	DUMU [. . .]	
	15′)	1 *Du-du*	
	16′)	DUMU *Tim-mu*	
	17′)	1 *Ku-ku*	
	18′)	DUMU *I-ti-*ÍD	
	19′)	1 *Ba-ša*	
	20′)	DUMU *Gi*$_4$-[. . .]	
	21′)	1 *U-ḫúb* [. . .]	
	22′)	DUMU *Zi-*[. . .]	
	23′)	1 *Sa-*[. . .]	
		(rest destr.)	

---

iii′		(beg. destr.)	
	1′)	3+[3 GÍN IGI].⌜4.GÁL⌝ [KUG. BABBAR]	⌜6¼⌝ [shekels of silver],
	2′)	1(GUR) 1(PI) ŠE GUR	360 quarts of barley,
	3′)	2 TÚG.A.SU	2 TÚG.A.SU cloths,
	4′)	12 BAPPIR	12 beer-breads,
	5′)	12 SILÀ Ì	(and) 12 quarts of oil
	6′)	*Šu-Eš*$_4$*-dar*	Š.
	7′)	*ù*	and
	8′)	1 SI.A-*um*	S.
	9′)	*šu Ḫa-a*[*r*?(-*x*)-*m*]*u*?	Of Ḫ.
	10′)	*im-ḫu*(*r*)*-ru*	received.

	11′)	1(GUR) 2(BÁN) GUR GÁN 2(BÁN)	320 quarts (of seed barley), (at the rate of) 20 quarts per iku (= 10⅔ iku of land);
	12′)	NÍG.ŠÁM-*su*	its price is
	13′)	⅓ ŠA 1 GÍN KUG.BABBAR 1 MA.N[A].T[UR]	21⅓ shekels of silver;
	14′)	NÍG.KI.GAR	the additional payment is
	15′)	1 GÍN KUG.BABBAR	1 shekel of silver,
	16′)	1(PI) ŠE	60 quarts of barley,
	17′)	2 BAPPIR	2 beer-breads,

	18′)	2 ⌜SILÀ Ì⌝	(and) 2 ⌜quarts of oil⌝;
		(rest destr.)	
iv′		(beg. destr.)	
	1′)	[. . .]	[. . .]
	2′)	*šu* X	Of X
	3′)	[I]M.MAR.TU	to the west is
	4′)	[GÁ]N.NINDÁ	the field's border;
	5′)	[LU]GAL?	(the property) of the [ki]ng(?)
	6′)	[I]M.KUR	to the east is
	7′)	GÁN.NINDÁ	the field's border;
	8′)	1 *Pù*-GI	(the property of) P.
	9′)	*šu Na-ba-li*	Of N.
	10′)	IM.MIR	to the north is
	11′)	GÁN.NINDÁ	the field's border;
	12′)	1 *A-bí-ra*	(the property of) A.
	13′)	*šu Iš-lam*-GI	Of I.
	14′)	IM.U_5	to the south is
	15′)	GÁN.NINDÁ	the field's border.

	16′)	3(GUR) LAL 2(PI) GUR GÁN 2(BÁN)	780 quarts (of seed barley), (at the rate of) 20 quarts per iku (= 26 iku of land);
	17′)	NÍG.ŠÁM-*su*	its price is
	18′)	1 MA.NA KU.BABBAR LAL 8 GÍN	52 shekels of silver;
	19′)	NÍG.KI.GAR	the additional payment is
	20′)	2½ TAR GÍN KUG	2¼ shekels of silver,
	21′)	2(PI) 3(BÁN) ŠE	150 quarts of barley,
	22′)	5 BAPP[IR]	5 beer-breads,
	23′)	5 SILÀ Ì	(and) 5 quarts of oil;
	24′)	1 ME-*Sá-lim*	M.
	25′)	*im-ḫur*	received (it).

	26′)	1 GUR [. . .]	300 quarts [of barley]
		(rest destr.)	
v′		(beg. destr.)	

	1′)	[3(GUR) 2(PI) GUR GÁN 2(BÁN)?]	[1,020 quarts (of seed barley), (at the rate of) 20(?) quarts per iku (= 34 iku of land)];
	2′)	NÍG.Š[ÁM-*su*]	[its] pr[ice is]
	3′)	1 MA.NA 8 GÍN [KUG. BABBAR]	68 shekels [of silver];
	4′)	NÍ[G.KI.GAR]	the addi[tional payment is]
	5′)	[3½ TAR GÍN KUG. BABBAR]	[3¼ shekels of silver],
	6′)	[3(PI) 3(BÁN) ŠE]	[210 quarts of barley],
	7′)	[7 BAPPI]R	[7 beer-bre]ads,
	8′)	7 SILÀ Ì	(and) 7 quarts of oil;
	9′)	1 *É-a-ra-bí*	E.
	10′)	*šu Ku-ru-*^{d}*Irra*$_{x}$(KIŠ)^{ra}	Of K.
	11′)	*im-ḫur*	received (it).
	12′)	A.SI	(The property of) A.,
	13′)	UM.LIBIR	the old . . . ,
	14′)	IM.MIR	to the north (is the field's border);
	15′)	1 *Šu-Ma-ma*	(the property of) Š.
	16′)	*šu A-ku-si-im*	Of A.
	17′)	IM.U_5	to the south
	18′)	*ù*	and
	19′)	IM.MAR.TU	to the west is
	20′)	GÁN.NINDÁ	the field's border;

	21′)	A.SI	(the property of) A.,
	22′)	UM.GIBIL	the new . . . ,
	23′)	IM.KUR	to the east is
	24′)	GÁN.NINDÁ	the field's border.

	25′)	2(GUR) ⸢2(PI)⸣ [GU]R [GÁN 2(BÁN)]	720 quarts (of seed barley), [(at the rate of) 20 quarts per iku (= 24 iku of land)];
		(rest destr.)	
vi′		(beg. destr.)	
	1′)	[IM.MAR.T]U	[to the wes]t is
	2′)	GÁN.NINDÁ	the field's border
	3′)	*ù*	and
	4′)	IM.U_5	to the south is
	5′)	GÁN.NINDÁ	the field's border;
	6′)	1 *A-ša-su*-GIŠ.ERÍN	(the property of) A.
	7′)	DUMU *I-mi-ì-lum*	son of I.
	8′)	IM.MIR	to the north is
	9′)	GÁN.NINDÁ	the field's border.

	10′)	2(PI) LAL 1(BÁN) GÁN 2(BÁN)	110 quarts (of seed barley), (at the rate of) 20 quarts per iku (= 3⅔ iku of land);
	11′)	NÍG.ŠÁM-*su*	its price is
	12′)	7½ GÍN KUG	7½ shekels of silver;
	13′)	NÍG.KI.GAR	the additional payment is
	14′)	1 MA.NA.TUR KUG	⅓ shekel of silver,
	15′)	2(BÁN) ŠE	20 quarts of barley,
	16′)	1 BAPPIR	1 beer-bread,
	17′)	1 SILÀ Ì	(and) 1 quart of oil;
	18′)	1 *E-mi*	E.
	19′)	*im-ḫur*	received (it).
	20′)	1 *Ì-lum*-GÀR	I.
	21′)	*šu La-ba*-Ù	Of L.,
		(rest destr.)	
vii′		(beg. destr.)	
	1′)	[*A*]?-*l*[*i*?-*l*]*i*?	⸢PN⸣
	2′)	*im*-[*ḫur*]	received.
	3′)	1 *A-mu*-[. . .]	(The property of) A.
	4′)	*šu La-ba*-Ù	Of L.
	5′)	IM.MIR	to the north is
	6′)	GÁN.NINDÁ	the field's border;
	7′)	1 *En-bu*-DINGIR	(the property of) E. of
	8′)	*I-lib*^{KI}	Ilib
	9′)	IM.KUR	to the east is
	10′)	GÁN.NINDÁ	the field's border;
	11′)	1 PÙ.ŠA-*A-a*	(the property of) P.
	12′)	*šu É-bí*-[*r*]*a*?	Of E.
	13′)	IM.U_5	to the south is
	14′)	GÁN.NINDÁ	the field's border;
	15′)	1 *Sa-tu-na*	(the property of) S.,
	16′)	SIMUG	the smith of
	17′)	*A-ga-dè*^{KI}	Akkadē,
	18′)	IM.MAR.TU	to the west is
	19′)	GÁN.NINDÁ	the field's border.

	20′)	4(BÁN) GÁN 1(BÁN) 5(SILÀ)	40 quarts (of seed barley), (at the rate of) 15 quarts per iku (= 1⅓ iku of land);
	21′)	NÍG.ŠÁM-*su*	its price is
	22′)	4 GÍN 1 MA.NA.TUR KUG. BABBAR	4⅓ shekels of silver;

	23′)	NÍG.KI.GAR	the additional payment is
	24′)	IGI.⌜4.GÁL⌝ KUG.BABBAR	¼ shekel of silver,
	25′)	[1(BÁN) 5(ŠILÀ) ŠE]	[15 quarts of barley],
	26′)	[1? BAPPIR]	[1(?) beer-bread],
	27′)	[1? SILÀ Ì]	[(and) 1(?) quart of oil].
		(rest destr.)	
viii′		(beg. destr.)	
	1′)	[2 GUR GÁN 3(BÁN)]	[600 quarts (of seed barley), (at the rate of) 30 quarts per iku (= 20 iku of land)];
	2′)	[NÍG.ŠÁM-*su*]	[its price is]
	3′)	[⅓ ŠA 7 GÍN LAL 1 MA.NA.TUR KUG.BABBAR]	[26⅔ shekels of silver];
	4′)	[NÍG.KI].GAR	[the additional pay]ment is
	5′)	[1] GÍN 1 MA.NA.TUR	[1] ⅓ shekels of silver,
	6′)	1(PI) 2(BÁN) ŠE	80 quarts of barley,
	7′)	3 BAPPIR	3 beer-breads,
	8′)	3 SILÀ Ì	(and) 3 quarts of oil;
	9′)	1 *Su-ru-uš*-GI	S.
	10′)	*šu* NA.GADA	Of N. of
	11′)	KI.SAR^{KI}	KI.SAR
	12′)	*im-ḫur*	received (it).
	13′)	1 *Ì-lum*-GÀR	(The property of) I.
	14′)	*šu La-ba*-Ù	Of L.
	15′)	IM.MAR.TU	to the west is
	16′)	GÁN.NINDÁ	the field's border;
	17′)	1 *Pù*-GI	(the property of) P.
	18′)	*šu Na-ba-li*	Of N.
	19′)	IM.U_5	to the south is
	20′)	GÁN.NINDÁ	the field's border;
	21′)	1 *A-li-li*	(the property of) A.
	22′)	*šu* GÁN	Of G.
	23′)	IM.KUR	to the east is
	24′)	GÁN.NINDÁ	the field's border;
	25′)	1 *Wa*-X-*rúm*	(the property of) W.
	26′)	*šu Mu-mu*	Of M.
	27′)	IM.MIR	to the north is
	28′)	GÁN.NINDÁ	the field's border.
		(rest destr.)	
ix′		(beg. destr.)	
	1′)	[11(GUR) 4(PI) G]UR GÁN 2(BÁN)	[3,540] quarts (of seed barley), (at the rate of) 20 quarts per iku (= 118 iku of land);
	2′)	NÍG.ŠÁM-*su*	its price is
	3′)	4 MA.NA KUG.BABBAR LAL 4 GÍN	236 shekels of silver;
	4′)	NÍG.KI.GAR	the additional payment is
	5′)	12 GÍN KUG.BABBAR	12 shekels of silver,
	6′)	2(GUR) 2(PI) ŠE GUR	720 quarts of barley,
	7′)	1 TÚG.ŠU.ZA.GA	1 TÚG.ŠU.ZA.GA cloth,
	8′)	24 BAPPIR	24 beer-breads,
	9′)	2(BÁN) 4(SILÀ) Ì	(and) 24 quarts of oil;
	10′)	1 *Iš-má-ì-lum*	
	11′)	KUG.GÁL	
	12′)	1 *Bí-bí*	
	13′)	DUMU *Šu-la-pi*	
	14′)	1 *Zi-ra*	
	15′)	DUMU *Ib-bu-ru*	
	16′)	1 *Ḫu-li-um*	
	17′)	DUMU *I-bí*-^{d}EN.ZU	
	18′)	[D]UMU.DUMU	

	19′)	[*Ì*]?-*lu-lu*	
	20′)	[. . .]-⸢X⸣	
		(rest destr.)	
L. E.		(beg. destr.)	
	1′)	[NÍG].⸢KI.GAR⸣	the additional payment is
	2′)	2½ TAR GÍN KUG.BABBAR	2¼ shekels of silver,
	3′)	2(PI) 3(BÁN) ŠE	150 quarts of barley,
	4′)	5 BAPPIR	5 beer-breads,
	5′)	5 SILÀ Ì	(and) 5 quarts of oil;
	6′)	*Ì-lum-dan*	I.
	7′)	*šu Ḫa*-X-*da*	Of Ḫ.,
	8′)	1 *I*-NI	I.
	9′)	*šu* KI.LAM	Of K.,
	10′)	1 *I-nin-sa-tu*	(and) I.
	11′)	*šu Su*$_4$*-mu-É-a*	Of S.
	12′)	*im-ḫu*(*r*)-*ru*	received (it).
	13′)	1 PÙ.ŠA-DÙG!(wr. UD)	(The property of) P.
	14′)	*šu* GÁN.DAR	Of G.
	15′)	IM.MIR	to the north is
	16′)	[GÁ]N.NINDÁ	the field's border;
	17′)	[1 *Šu*]-⸢*ì*⸣?-*lí-su*	(the property of) Š.
	18′)	[. . .] ⸢X⸣ [. . .]	
		(rest destr.)	

Notes

i 2′, ii 5′, v 16′, and *passim*.—The determination of land areas is based on the assumption that the seeding rate is the constant 30 quarts per iku. See in detail chapter 9 under *No. 41 Sippar Stone*.

i 9′.—The name interpreted here as *Iš-dup-Il* was read, with some misgivings, as *Iš-dup-ir-pum*? in *RSO* 32 p. 92 and *MAD* 3 pp. 61 and 291.

iv 14′—*A-da* LÚ.GUNU+ÚŠ is probably to be interpreted as $^{\text{a-da}}$*Adda*(LÚ.GUNU.ÚŠ). For the syllabic adda, see Adda-ga-nu^{KI}, alternating with ᵓÀ-da-ga-nu^{KI}, in the Abu Salabikh / Ebla Geographical List line 32 (Pettinato, *MEE* 3 p. 230).

v 22′–24′.—The masculine determinative pronoun *šu* in *Da-bí-bí šu Bí-za dam-ḫur* /*tamḫur*/ is used here in place of the expected feminine *šat*.

v 22′, vi 16′, rev. i′ 2′, iii′ 6′, and L. E. 6′.—Contrary to the general usage in this text and elsewhere, in these five occurrences the scribe failed to write a *Personenkeil* in front of the main entries.

vi 8′.—The interpretation of the GN BÀD-ḪU.GAN?^{KI} is unknown. The questionable sign looks very much like GAN in *RTC* 80:25.

vi 10′.—Both the price and the *iškinū* "additional payment" indicate that the number here should be 11 and not 12. In the photograph the final wedge of 12 appears to be crossed by a diagonal line as if the stonecutter had attempted to cross it out.

vi 16′–18′.—PN *šu A-ki* URUDU?^{KI} is structured like PN *šu ša-ti* GN^{KI} in the same column lines 23′–25′ (see below), suggesting that *A-ki* is a noun with an unknown meaning. The questionable sign looks like an incomplete URUDU. The interpretation A.KI. URUDU?^{KI} is theoretically also possible.

vi 20′.—^{d}LUGAL-*bar-ga-ad* stands here for a DN or a PN. If the name is a DN, then it can simply be interpreted as "King of (a GN) Bar-ga-ad." If the name is a PN, then *-bar-ga-ad* has to be interpreted as a stative, perhaps *parqad* (of *naparqudum*) structurally parallel to *palku*ᵓ (A. Heidel, *AS* 11 p. 79) and *parku*ᵓ (*ARM* 1, 37:27).

vi 23′–25′.—If PN *šu ša-ti Ša-da-an*^{KI} should be interpreted as "PN of the mountain of Šadan," then we would have here another example of *šadjum* "mountain" ("East") noted in *MAD* 3 pp. 264f.

vii 8′.—The sign LÚ in *šu* LÚ looks exactly like LÚ in *šu* LÚ.KAS$_4$ (obv. ii 12′), and not like the expected AŠGAB.

vii 17′–18′.—For the canal Irḫan$_{\text{x}}$ (also Urḫan$_{\text{x}}$), see the following: ÍD.AN.MUŠ.DIN.TIR.BALAG is glossed ir-ḫa-an and equated with Araḫtum and Purattum, and ^{ÍD}Ir-ḫa-an is equated with Purattum at Abu Salabikh and later (Biggs, *OIP* 99 p. 55); BALAG.DIN. AN.MUŠ^{KI} at Abu Salabikh (*OIP* 99, 331 v′ 7) corresponds to Ur$_4$-ḫa-an^{KI} at Ebla (Pettinato, *MEE* 3 p. 237 line 223); and $^{\text{ir-ḫa}}$MUŠ is equated with *Ir-ḫa-núm* (Pettinato, *MEE* 4 p. 357 line 0138). Living examples of this canal are rare, as in gú ^{ÍD}MUŠ "on the shore of the Irḫan canal" (Sollberger, *TCS* 1, 360:8, Ur III). The deified canal occurs in the form $^{\text{(d)}}$MUŠ$^{\text{ir-ḫa}}$.DIN.DÚB.NUN in the Early Dynastic (*UET* 2, 142 i 5, 190 i 3), and as ^{d}MUŠ$^{\text{ir-ḫa}}$DIN.DÚB.DU in the Ur III period (*UET* 3, 189:9, 191:16, 1110:1; 9, 37:9); see also PN Ur-^{d}MUŠ (no. 32 iii 10, no. 40 A xiii 7, and *passim* in Sargonic sources) and PN Gemé-^{d}MUŠ$^{\text{ir-ḫa}}$.DIN.DÚB.DU attested in the Ur III period (*UET* 3, 1040 ii 16). Compare G. J. P. McEwan, *Or.* n.s. 52 (1983) pp. 215–29; Krebernik, *Beschwörungen* pp. 298ff.

viii 4′.—This PN is also attested in no. 48 iv 16, *TSA* 18 iii 18, *HSS* 10, 13 i 10, and *MAD* 1, 232 i 17.

viii 5′.—The interpretation of the GN ŠEG$_9$-da^{KI} is unknown.

rev. ii′ 21′.—Note the unusual form of the reversed U sign in the name *U-ḫúb*.

iv′ 2′.—The sign read here as X has the same form as the third sign in *šu Ḫa*-X-*da* in L. E. 7′. It is possibly PÉŠ (= LAK-245, 246, and 247). For the paleography of PÉŠ and related signs, see Krebernik, *Beschwörungen* pp. 287–97.

iv′ 16′ and 18′.—Assuming a price of 1⅓ gín per 1 iku leads to the interpretation of line 18′ as 1 MA.NA LAL 8 GÍN (= 52 gín), and of line 16′ as 3(GUR) LAL 2(PI) GUR GÁN 2(BÁN).

v′ 10′.—For the reading ^{d}*Irra*$_{\text{x}}$(KIŠ)^{ra}, see Steinkeller, *ZA* 77 (1987) pp. 165ff.

v′ 13′ and 22′.—The meaning of UM, which is designated in these lines as LIBIR "old" and GIBIL "new," is unknown to us.

v′ 16′.—Scheil's reading *A-ku-si-im* is preferable to Gelb's *A-ra*?!-*im* (*RSO* 32 p. 88, *MAD* 3 p. 60). This PN is probably a nisbe of the GN Akusum (Steinkeller, *Vicino Oriente* 6 [1986] p. 34).

vii′ 12′.—Scheil's reading *-ra* in *É-bí-ra* is not confirmed by the photograph, although it may find support in the clearly written *A-bí-ra* in iv 7′ and rev. iv′ 12′.

viii′ 6′.—The unusual writing of 1(PI) 2(BÁN) as 1(PI) written over 2(BÁN) finds parallels in *PBS* 9, 39, 59, and 84 (*passim*).

viii′ 25′.—Even after renewed collations, the reading of the middle sign as *-at-* in *Wa-at?-rúm* of *MAD* 2^2 p. 75 and *RSO* 32 p. 87 offers great difficulties. The sign looks like GIŠ.ERÍN in ii 2′, iv 9′, and rev. vi′ 6′. [See now Wu-^{GIŠ}sur$_x$-rúm in *N.A.B.U.* 1990/1 p. 10.]

L. E. 7′.—For the reading of -X-, see note to rev. iv′ 2′.

No. 42 Eshnuna Stone Fragment

Photograph: Plate 75, Oriental Institute, The University of Chicago, negative N. 33718.
Copy: Plate 76, copied by Green.
Synopsis: Plate 112.
Provenience: Eshnuna (Tell Asmar), Field no. TA 1931, 130; found in Private House G 19:5, stratum IVa (Sargonic period)—see Delougaz *et al.*, *OIP* 88 pp. 225 and 310.
Date: Sargonic.
Language: Akkadian.
Present location: Oriental Institute, The University of Chicago, on loan from the Iraq Museum, Baghdad.
Publication: Gelb, *MAD* 1, 168.
Description: Fragment of a black diorite tablet measuring 8.1 × 13.7 × 6 cm. Since only one side is preserved, the original thickness is unknown. It has the ends of five columns, and a lower edge (uninscribed).
Text: If the preserved portion was part of the obverse, the order of the columns is left to right, giving a sequence of individual fields with price and additional payment, total of fields, and witnesses (with gifts). This is the expected order of the text.

Sample Interpretation

ii′ 2′–iii′ 3′: ⌈PN⌉ (= seller) received 8(?) shekels of silver and 12,000 quarts of barley as the price of [x] iku of land, and 420 quarts of barley and x commodities as the additional payment.

Transliteration and Translation

i′		(beg. destr.)	
	1′)	[ŠÁM]-⌈*su*⌉	its [price] is
	2′)	[x] GÍN [KU]G.BABBAR	[x] shekels of silver,
	3′)	[x] ŠE GUR	[x] quarts of barley;
ii′		(beg. destr.)	
	1′)	[*im-ḫu*]-*ru*	[rec]eived.

	2′)	[x(IKU)] GÁN	[x iku] of land;
	3′)	[ŠÁM]-*su*	its [price] is
	4′)	⌈8⌉? GÍN KUG.BABBAR	⌈8?⌉ shekels of silver
	5′)	40 ŠE GUR	(and) 12,000 quarts of barley;
	6′)	*iš-ki-nu-su*	its additional payment is
	7′)	1(GUR) 2(PI) ŠE GUR	420 quarts of barley;
iii′		(beg. destr.)	
	1′)	[DUMU] ⌈*Gi-x*⌉-*ra*	[son of] ⌈PN⌉
	2′)	*ši A-a*-BE	Of A.
	3′)	*im-ḫur*	received (it).
		(blank)	

	4′)	ŠU.NIGÍN 1(BURʾU) 3(BÙR) 1(IKU) GÁN	Total of 235 iku of land,
	5′)	*šu kir-ba-ti*	(the field located) in (lit.: of) the field district of
	6′)	*Ar-da-na-an*^{KI}	Ardanan,
	7′)	*in* E+PAB *At-li*	on the Atli-canal.
iv′		(beg. destr.)	
	1′)	1 [PN]	PN,
	2′)	NÀ[D? . . .]	the ⌈. . .⌉,
	3′)	*šu E*-[. . .]-*rí*-⌈*x*⌉-[(. . .)]	Of ⌈PN_2⌉;
	4′)	1 BA.AN ŠE.⌈TA⌉	1 BA.AN container of barley each,
	5′)	1 SÍG.GAN.⌈TA⌉	1 SÍG.GAN (measure of wool) each,
	6′)	1 *Pù-pù*	for P.
	7′)	*šu Bur-zi-a*	Of B.,
	8′)	1 *Na-bí-um*	N.,
v′		(beg. destr.)	
	1′)	*Ar*-[*da*]-*na-a*[*n*^{KI}]	

Notes

iii′ 7′.—The same canal is mentioned in no. 43 xii 2.
iv′ 4′–5′.—For the measures BA.AN (ŠE) and SÍG.GAN, see chapter 9 under Nos. 43 and 44.

No. 43 Eshnuna Clay Tablet

Photographs: Plates 75 and 77, Oriental Institute, The University of Chicago, negatives N. 42203, 42204. Fragment with obv. ii is slightly misaligned.
Copy: Plates 76 and 78, copied by Green, assisted by Whiting.
Synopsis: Plates 112 and 113.
Provenience: Eshnuna (Tell Asmar)—found in locus E 15, a robber hole that was cut into the walls of the building that was called "Northern Palace" by the excavators. See Gelb, *MAD* 1 pp. xiv–xvii, and Delougaz *et al.*, *OIP* 88 pp. 196 and 252. This tablet was found together with the twelve fragments published as no. 44.
Date: Sargonic.
Language: Akkadian.
Present location: Oriental Institute, The University of Chicago, TA 1931, 5A, 4.
Publication: The fragments which have been joined to form this tablet were published individually in *MAD* 1 under the following numbers: 45 (TA 1931, 5A, 4 + 6A, 5), 50 (TA 1931, 6A, 1), 51 (TA 1931, 6A, 2 + 6), 52 (TA 1931, 6A, 3), and 58 (TA 1931, 6A, 9).
Description: Five fragments as published in *MAD* 1 have been joined after baking and cleaning to form a tablet which measures 17.4 × 18.6 × 3.9 cm. One of the joins was made by Westenholz, the rest by Whiting. All the fragments join physically, except for the left edge piece (*MAD* 1, 50), which, though it does not involve any overlapping text, still fits snugly in its proper place. Both left and right edges of the tablet are preserved, showing the entire width of the original. The upper and lower edges are not preserved, but in places the text is preserved to within a line or two of these edges. Adding the necessary 1.5–2 cm, the original tablet must have been square. The obverse is flat, the reverse rounded. More of the reverse is missing than of the obverse.
Text: The tablet is inscribed in six columns on the obverse and six columns on the reverse. The text contained a record of at least seventeen individual purchases of land. The name of the buyer is not preserved. The individual transactions occupy columns i through x. In column xi is found a summary of the prices paid and commodities given for the land. Presumably this summary also gave the total amount of land purchased and the name of the buyer. Column xii has only a brief inscribed portion which records the general location of the land purchased. There is no space in the text for a lengthy list of witnesses that is usually part of the ancient kudurru. Either the list of witnesses was very brief and occupied the end of column x or else no list of witnesses was included in this inscription.

Sample Interpretation

i 1–14: PN, PN$_2$, and PN$_3$ (= sellers) received 24 shekels of silver and 48 gsg of barley as the price of 36 iku of land, and 2 shekels of silver and x commodities as the additional payment.

Transliteration and Translation

Obv. i	1)	[2(BÙR)] ⸢GÁN⸣	[36 iku] ⸢of land⸣;
	2)	[ŠÁ]M-*su*	its [pri]ce is
	3)	⸢⅓⸣ ŠA 4 GÍN KUG.BABBAR	⸢24⸣ shekels of silver
	4)	50 LÁ 2 ŠE GUR.SAG.GÁL	(and) 48. gsg of barley;
	5)	*iš-ki-nu-*[*su*]	[its] additional payment is
	6)	2 GÍN KUG.[BABBAR]	2 shekels of sil[ver],
	7)	[4 ŠE GUR.SAG.GÁL]	[4. gsg of barley],
	8)	1 *ḫa-zi-*[*núm*]?	1 ḫ. axe,
	9)	6 SÍG.GAN	6 SÍG.GAN measures of wool,
	10)	6 BA.AN	(and) 6 BA.AN containers;
	11)	*Bí-bí*	B.,
	12)	⸢*Pù*⸣?-*ì-li*	P.,
	13)	[*Ì-lí*]-TAB.BA	⸢(and) I.⸣
	14)	[*im-ḫu*]-⸢*ru*⸣?	[received(?) (it)].
	15)	[x(IKU) GÁN]	[x iku of land];
	16–23)	[. . .]	
ii	1–5)	[. . .]	
	6)	[*im-ḫu-ru*]	[received (it)].
	7)	[1(BÙR) 1(EŠE) GÁN]	[24 iku of land];
	8)	[ŠÁM-*su*]	[its price is]
	9)	12+[4 GÍN KUG.BABBAR]	12+[4 shekels of silver]
	10)	30+[2 ŠE GUR.SAG.GÁL]	(and) 30+[2. gsg of barley];

11)	*iš-ki-n*[*u-su*]	[its] additional payment is
12)	[1 GÍN 1 MA.NA⟨.TUR⟩ KUG.BABBAR]	[1⅓ shekel of silver],
13)	[2(GUR) 2(PI) 4(BÁN) ŠE GUR.SAG.GÁL]	[2.2.4 gsg of barley],
14)	[4 SÍG.GAN]	[4 SÍG.GAN measures of wool],
15)	[4 BA.AN]	[(and) 4 BA.AN containers];
16)	[PN]	[PN]
17)	[DUMU PN_2]	[son of PN_2]
18)	[*ši* PN_3]	[Of PN_3],
19)	[PN_4]	[(and) PN_4]
20)	[DUMU PN_5]	[son of PN_5]
21)	[*im-ḫu-ra*]	[received (it)].

---

22)	[x(IKU) GÁN]	[x iku of land];
23–24)	[. . .]	
iii 1–9)	[. . .]	
10)	[. . .]-⸢*x*⸣-*a-ḫ*[*u*]	⸢PN⸣
11)	[*Sá*]-*lim-a-ḫu*	⸢(and) S.⸣
12)	DUMU *ši Ga-ra-az-ni-iš*	son of G.
13)	*im-ḫu-ru*	received (it).

---

14)	1(EŠE) 2(IKU) GÁN	8 iku of land;
15)	*šu* DINGIR-GÀR	(the property) of I.
16)	[*ši*]? ⸢*Bu-la*⸣-*la*	[Of]? ⸢B.⸣;
17)	[ŠÁM]-*me-su*	its [pri]ce is
18)	[12]+4 ŠE GUR.SAG.GÁL	⸢16.⸣ gsg of barley;
19)	*iš-ki-nu-su*	its additional payment is
20)	1 MA.NA⟨.TUR⟩ KUG. BABBAR	⅓ shekel of silver,
21)	1 ŠE GUR.SAG.GÁL	1. gsg of barley,
22)	[x] ⸢SÍG.GAN⸣	[x] ⸢SÍG.GAN⸣ measures of wool,
23)	[x BA.AN]	(and) [x BA.AN containers];
iv 1)	[PN]	[PN]
2)	[*im-ḫur*]	[received (it)].

---

3)	[2(EŠE)] ⸢GÁN⸣	[12 iku] ⸢of land⸣;
4)	[ŠÁM]-*su*	its [price is]
5)	[8 GÍN] KUG.BABBAR	[8 shekels] of silver
6)	[16 ŠE] GUR.SAG.GÁL	[(and) 16.] gsg of barley;
7)	[*iš-ki*]-*nu-su*	its [additional payment] is
8)	[2 MA.N]A⟨.TUR⟩ KUG. BABBAR	[⅔] shekel of silver,
9)	[1(GUR)] 1(PI) 2(BÁN) ŠE GUR.SAG.GÁL	[1.]1.2 gsg of barley,
10)	2 SÍG.GAN	2 SÍG.GAN measures of wool,
11)	[2] BA.AN	(and) [2] BA.AN containers;
12)	⸢*I*⸣-*mi*-DINGIR	⸢I.⸣
13)	[DUMU] *Pù-*^{d}*Tišpak*	[son] of P.
14)	[*š*]*i*? *Ù-su*	[O]f? U.,
15)	[. . .]-⸢X⸣	[(and) PN]
16)	DUMU ⸢*I*⸣?-[*bi-b*]*í*?	son of ⸢I.⸣
17)	⸢*ši*⸣? [. . .]	⸢Of?⸣ [. . .]
18)	[*im-ḫu-ra*]	[(received it)].

---

19)	1(BÙR) [GÁN]	18 iku of land;
20)	ŠÁM-[*su*]	[its] price is
21)	12 GÍ[N KUG.BABBAR]	12 she[kels of silver]

	22)	24 ŠE GUR.SAG.GÁL	(and) 24. gsg of barley;
	23)	*iš-ki-nu-su*	its additional payment is
	24)	1 GÍN ⸢KUG.BABBAR⸣	1 shekel of ⸢silver⸣,
	25)	[2 ŠE GUR.SAG.GÁL]	[2. gsg of barley],
	26)	⸢3⸣ [SÍG.GAN]	⸢3⸣ [SÍG.GAN measures of wool],
	27)	[3 BA.AN]	[(and) 3 BA.AN containers];
v	1)	[PN]	[PN]
	2)	[PN_2]	[(and) PN_2]
	3)	*im-ḫ*[*u-ra*]	rece[ived (it)].

	4)	2(EŠE) [GÁN]	12 iku of [land];
	5)	ŠÁM-[*su*]	[its] price is
	6)	8 GÍN [KUG.BABBAR]	8 shekels of [silver]
	7)	16 ŠE GUR.⸢SAG.GÁL⸣	(and) 16. ⸢gsg⸣ of barley;
	8)	*iš-ki-nu-su*	its additional payment is
	9)	2 MA.NA⟨.TUR⟩ KUG. BABBAR	⅔ shekel of silver,
	10)	1(GUR) 1(PI) 2(BÁN) ŠE GUR.⸢SAG.GÁL⸣	1.1.2 ⸢gsg⸣ of barley,
	11)	2 SÍG.G[AN]	2 SÍG.G[AN] measures of wool,
	12)	2 B[A.AN]	(and) 2 B[A.AN] containers;
	13)	[PN]	[PN]
	14)	[DUMU PN_2]	[son of PN_2]
	15)	*ši* ⸢. . .⸣	Of ⸢. . .⸣
	16)	*im-ḫur*	received (it).

	17)	1(BÙR) 1(EŠE) GÁN	24 iku of land;
	18)	ŠÁM-*su*	its price is
	19)	12 GÍN KUG.BABBAR	12 shekels of silver
	20)	36 ŠE GUR.SAG.GÁL	(and) 36. gsg of barley;
	21)	*iš-ki-nu-su*	its additional payment is
	22)	[1 G]ÍN 1 MA.NA⟨.TUR⟩ K[UG.BABBAR]	⸢1⅓⸣ shekels of s[ilver],
	23)	⸢2(GUR) 2(PI) 4 (BÁN)⸣ ŠE GUR.⸢SAG.GÁL⸣	⸢2.2.4 gsg⸣ of barley
	24)	4 [SÍG.GAN]	4 [SÍG.GAN measures of wool],
	25)	[4 BA.AN]	[(and) 4 BA.AN containers];
	26)	[PN]	[PN]
vi	1)	[DUMU PN_2]	[son of PN_2]
	2)	[*im-ḫur*]	[received (it)].

	3)	[x(IKU) GÁN]	[x iku of land];
	4)	[ŠÁM-*su*]	[its price is]
	5)	[x KUG.BABBAR]	[x shekels of silver]
	6)	[x ŠE GUR.SAG.GÁL]	[(and) x gsg of barley];
	7)	[*iš-ki-nu-su*]	[its additional payment is]
	8)	[x KUG.BABBAR]	[x shekels of silver],
	9)	[x ŠE GUR.SAG.GÁ]L	[x] ⸢gsg⸣ [of barley],
	10)	[x SÍG.GA]N	[x SÍG.GA]N measures of wool,
	11)	[x BA].AN	[(and) x BA].AN containers;
	12)	[*Iš-má*]-DINGIR	⸢I.⸣
	13)	[*šu Za-a*]*b-tim*	[Of] ⸢Z.⸣,
	14)	[*Ìr*]-⸢*e*⸣-*um*	⸢(and) I.⸣
	15)	⸢DUMU⸣ [PN]	⸢son⸣ [of PN],
	16)	*im-ḫu-r*[*a*]	received (it).

	17)	2(EŠE) GÁN	12 iku of land;
	18)	ŠÁM-⸢*su*⸣	⸢its⸣ price is

19)	5 GÍN KU[G.BABBAR]	5 shekels of si[lver]
20)	14(GUR) 1(PI) 2(BÁN) [ŠE GUR.SAG.GÁL]	14.1.2 [gsg of barley],
21)	⌜2⌝+[x . . .]	⌜2⌝+[x . . .],
22–26)	[. . .]	
Rev. vii 1–4)	[. . .]	
5)	[*im-ḫu-ru*]	[received (it)].

---

6)	[2(EŠE) GÁN]	[12 iku of land],
7)	*šu* ⌜SAG⌝?-[. . .]	the property of ⌜S⌝.
8)	*ši Bar*?-DU$_8$-[. . .]	Of ⌜B.⌝;
9)	ŠÁM-*su*	its price is
10)	8 GÍN KUG.BABBAR	8 shekels of silver
11)	16 ŠE GUR.SAG.GÁL	(and) 16. gsg of barley;
12)	*iš-ki-nu-su*	its additional payment is
13)	2 MA.NA⟨.TUR⟩ KUG. BABBAR	⅔ shekel of silver,
14)	1(GUR) 1(PI) 2(BÁN) ŠE GUR.SAG.GÁL	1.1.2 gsg of barley,
15)	[2] ⌜SÍG⌝.GAN	[2] ⌜SÍG⌝.GAN measures of wool,
16)	⌜2⌝ BA.AN	(and) ⌜2⌝ BA.AN containers;
17)	*Ìr-e-um*	I.
18)	DUMU *Iš-má*-DINGIR	son of I.
19)	*ši Za-ab-tim*	Of Z.,
20)	DINGIR-*ra*-⌜*bí*⌝	(and) I.
21)	[DUMU PN]	⌜son⌝ [of PN]
22)	[*im-ḫu-ra*]	[received (it)].

---

23)	[x(IKU) GÁN]	[x iku of land];
24–25)	[. . .]	
viii 1–7)	[. . .]	
8)	[. . .]-⌜X⌝-[. . .]	[PN],
9)	[SAL].⌜BALAG.DI⌝	the singer of lamentations,
10)	[X].UD.DU-*na*	[(and?) P]N$_2$
11)	[*i*]*m-ḫu-ra*	received (it).

---

12)	1(EŠE) GÁN	6 iku of land;
13)	ŠÁM-*su*	its price is
14)	4 GÍN KUG.BABBAR	4 shekels of silver
15)	8 ŠE GUR.SAG.GÁL	(and) 8. gsg of barley;
16)	[*iš-ki-nu-su*]	[its additional payment is]
17)	[1 MA.NA⟨.TUR⟩ KUG. BABBAR]	[⅓ shekel of silver],
18)	[2(PI) 4(BÁN) ŠE GUR.SAG. GÁL]	[0.2.4 gsg of barley],
19)	[1 SÍG.GAN]	[1 SÍG.GAN measure of wool],
20)	[1 BA.AN]	[(and) 1 BA.AN container];
21)	[PN]	[PN]
22)	[DUMU PN$_2$]	[son of PN$_2$]
23)	[*im-ḫur*]	[received (it)].

---

24)	[1(BÙR) 1(EŠE) GÁN]	[24 iku of land];
25)	[ŠÁM-*su*]	[its price is]
26)	[16 GÍN KUG.BABBAR]	[16 shekels of silver]
27)	[32 ŠE GUR.SAG.GÁL]	[(and) 32. gsg of barley];
ix 1)	[*iš-ki-nu-su*]	[its additional payment is]
2)	[1 GÍN 1 MA.NA⟨.TUR⟩ KUG.BABBAR]	[1⅓ shekel of silver],

	3)	[2(GUR) 2(PI) 4(BÁN) ŠE GUR.SAG.GÁL]	[2.2.4 gsg of barley],
	4)	⌜4⌝ [SÍG GAN]	⌜4⌝ [SÍG.GAN measures of wool],
	5)	4 BA.[AN]	(and) 4 BA.[AN] containers;
	6)	*Tu-tu*	T.
	7)	*šu Ib-la*-NI-⌜*x*⌝	Of I.
	8)	*I-te*-[. . .]	(and) I.
	9)	DUMU [. . .]	son of [PN]
	10)	*i*[*m-ḫu-ra*]	re[ceived (it)].

	11)	[x(IKU) GÁN]	[x iku of land];
	12–22)	[. . .]	
	23)	[*im-ḫur*]	[received (it)].

	24)	[1(BÙR) 1(EŠE) GÁN]	[24 iku of land];
	25)	[ŠÁM-*su*]	[its price is]
	26)	[16 GÍN KUG.BABBAR]	[16 shekels of silver]
	27)	[32 ŠE GUR.SAG.GÁL]	[(and) 32. gsg of barley];
x	1)	[*iš-ki-nu-su*]	[its additional payment is]
	2)	[1 GÍN 1 MA.NA⟨.TUR⟩ KUG.BABBAR]	[1⅓ shekel of silver],
	3)	⌜2(GUR) 2(PI) 4(BÁN) ŠE GUR.SAG⌝.GÁL	⌜2.2.4 gsg of barley⌝,
	4)	4 SÍG.GAN	4 SÍG.GAN measures of wool,
	5)	4 BA.AN	(and) 4 BA.AN containers;
	6)	[*W*]*u-zum-tum*	⌜W.⌝,
	7)	SAL.BALAG.DI	the singer of lamentations,
	8)	KA$_5$.A	K.,
	9)	[*M*]*a-ga-ga*	⌜M.⌝
	10)	[PN]	(and) PN
	11)	[DUMU PN$_2$]	[son(s) of PN$_2$]
	12)	[*im-ḫu-ru*]	[received (it)].
		(rest destr., perhaps nothing missing)	

xi		(beg. destr.)	
	1′)	ŠÁM 1 GÍN 1 MA.NA⟨.TUR⟩ KUG.BABBAR	(its) price is 1⅓ shekel of silver;
	2′)	ŠU.NIGÍN 40 MA.NA SÍG	total of 40 pounds of wool—
	3′)	ŠÁM 6 GÍN 2 MA.NA⟨.TUR⟩ KUG.BABBAR	(its) price is 6⅔ shekels of silver;
	4′)	ŠU.NIGÍN 20 SILÀ Ì	total of 20 quarts of oil—
		(rest destr.)	
xii		(beg. destr., perhaps nothing missing)	
		(blank)	
	1)	GÁN *Bi-ìr-ti-in*	field of B.,
	2)	E+PAB *At-li*	(located on) the A. canal
	3)	*ù* E+PAB PA.TE.SI	(and on) the P. canal;
	4)	⌜*šu*⌝ *Ib-me-rí*^{KI} (= *Ib-rí-me*^{KI})	(field) ⌜of⌝ GN.
		(rest uninscribed)	

Notes

iii 20 etc.—Even after a renewed collation of the tablets, we could find no trace of TUR after MA.NA; we must assume therefore that MA.NA stands for MA.NA⟨.TUR⟩ in all the above cases. The sign TUR may have been omitted by the scribe because the context made the meaning of MA.NA as MA.NA.TUR explicit.

vi 12–13.—Reconstructed on the basis of vii 18–19.

ix 7.—Read perhaps *Ib-la-ì-i*[*m*], a nisbe of Ebla.

xii 2.—The same canal is mentioned in no. 42 iii′ 7′.

No. 44 Eshnuna Clay Fragments

Photographs: Plates 77–79, Oriental Institute, The University of Chicago, negative nos. 44a = N. 42201, 42202;

44b = N. 43969; 44c = N. 43966; 44d = N. 43945; 44e = N. 43968; 44f = N. 43948; 44g = N. 43963, 43964; 44h = N. 43946; 44i = N. 43947; 44j = N. 43967; 44k = N. 43965; 44l = N. 43962.

Copies: Plates 77–79, copied by Green, assisted by Whiting.

Synopsis: Plates 114 and 115.

Provenience: Eshnuna (Tell Asmar)—all texts were excavated "above the Northern Palace" at locus E 15, with the exception of *MAD* 1, 111, which comes from locus 16 (level unknown). The former pieces were found together with no. 43. Locus E 15 is a robber hole which cut into the walls of the building that was designated "Northern Palace" by the excavators. For a discussion of the find spots, see Gelb, *MAD* 1 pp. xiv–xvii, and Delougaz *et al.*, *OIP* 88 pp. 196 and 252. For the field numbers, see the listing below.

Date: Sargonic.

Language: Akkadian.

Present location: Oriental Institute, The University of Chicago.

Publication: All the texts included here have been published individually in *MAD* 1. A number of improvements have been made in the present edition, mostly due to the baking and cleaning of the texts. For a concordance of the *MAD* 1 numbers of the texts, see the list below.

Description: All texts are on clay and all deal with multiple field transactions. All have a content similar to no. 43, but none of them belongs to that tablet. Although no physical joins can be made among these fragments, it is possible that some of them may be part of the same tablet. On the other hand, differences in textual characteristics such as column width, size, and style of the writing, and especially the size of the holes made with the end of the stylus for numbers, indicate that more than one tablet must have been involved.

Frag.	*MAD* 1	Field No.	Mst. *(cm)*
a	25	TA 1931, 1A, 24	4.3 × 4.3 × 1.7 (rev. flaked off)
b	26	TA 1931, 1A, 25	3.4 × 3.7 × 1.4 (rev. flaked off)
c	36	TA 1931, 1A, 35	1.8 × 2.8 × 1.6 (rev. flaked off)
d	48	TA 1931, 5A, 7	7.4 × 6.4 × 3.2 (rev. flaked off)
e	67	TA 1931, 6A, 18	5.8 × 7.5 × 2.5 (rev. flaked off)
f	74	TA 1931, 6A, 25	4.1 × 3.8 × 2.1 (rev. flaked off)
g	111	TA 1931, 12	2.7 × 2.8 × 1.7
h	119	TA 1931, 12A, 8	5.7 × 5.8 × 2.6
i	120	TA 1931, 12A, 9	4.6 × 4 × 1.5 (rev. flaked off)
j	122	TA 1931, 12A, 11	3.5 × 3.2 × 1.2 (rev. flaked off)
k	128	TA 1931, 10A, 21 +12A, 17	6.3 × 7.4 × 2.2 (rev. flaked off)
l	161	TA 1931, 23	5.1 × 7.5 × 3

Sample Interpretation

44k ii′ 5′–12′: PN (= seller), son of PN_2, received 10 bushels (of barley), corresponding to 10 shekels of silver, and 26. gsg of barley, as the price of 18 iku of land.

Transliteration

No. 44a

Obv. i′ (beg. destr.)
1′) [x ŠE GUR].SAG.GÁL
2′) [*Ì-l*]*í-dan*
3′) [X]-*tu-um*
4′) [*A-ḫ*]*u-ḫu*
5′) [DUMU]? *Ga*-NI-*am-me-me*
6′) [x(IKU)] GÁN
7′) [x G]ÍN KUG.BABBAR
8′) [x] ⸢ŠE⸣ GUR.SAG.GÁ[L]
(rest destr.)
ii′ (traces of several lines)
Rev. (only small fragment of surface)

No. 44b

(beg. destr.)
1′) *A-bí-su*
2′) *šu Ú-húb*

3′) 2(EŠE) GÁN
4′) [ŠÁ]M-*su*
5′) ⸢8⸣?(GUR) 1(PI) 4(BÁN) ŠE GUR
6′) [ŠÁM 8? GÍN 1 MA.NA⟨.TUR⟩ KUG.BABBAR]
(rest destr.)

No. 44c

i′ (beg. destr.)
1′) [*im-ḫ*]*u-ra*

2′) [x(IKU) G]ÁN?
(rest destr.)
ii′ (beg. destr.)
1′) *Sa-lim-*⸢*a*⸣-[*ḫu*]
2′) DUMU *ši G*[*a*]?!-*ra-az-*[*ni-iš*]
(rest destr.)

No. 44d

i′ (beg. destr.)
1′) [. . . -*a*]*t*
2′) [. . . -*t*]*um*
3′) [. . .]-*lu*
4′) [. . .]-ZU
5′) [. . .]-DINGIR
(rest destr.)
ii′ (beg. destr.)
1′) *Be-lí-mu-*[*da*]
2′) *šu Iš-gu-*[*núm*]?

3′) 1(EŠE) GÁN 20 S[AR]
4′) ŠÁM-⸢*su*⸣
5′) 20 LÁL 2 ŠE GU[R].S[AG.GÁL]
6′) *Li-mu-*[*um*]?
(rest destr.)

No. 44e

i′ (beg. destr.)
1′) [*I*?-*b*]*í*?-*bí*
2′) [DUMU]? *Ù-ù*
(rest destr.)
ii′ (beg. destr.)
1′) [. . .]-⸢X⸣-SU_4
2′) *im-ḫu-ra*

3′) 1(BÙR) 2(EŠE) GÁN
4′) ŠÁM-*su*
5′) 10 GÍN KUG.BABBAR
6′) 15 ŠE GUR
7′) [ŠÁM 15] ⸢GÍN KUG.BABBAR⸣
8′) [32]+3 [ŠE GUR.SAG.GÁL]
(rest destr.)

---

iii′ (beg. destr.)
1′) ŠÁM 12 GÍ[N] KUG.[BABBAR]
2′) 40 LAL 2 ŠE GUR.SAG.GÁL
3′) *Ma-šum*
4′) *šu I-bi-*⸢*bí*⸣
5′) *im-*[*ḫur*]

6′) 2(EŠE) G[ÁN]
(rest destr.)

No. 44f

i′ (beg. destr.)
1′) 2(EŠE) GÁN
2′) ŠÁM-*su*
3′) 13 GÍN KUG.BABBAR
4′) [12]+5 ŠE GUR.SAG.GÁL
5′) [X]-*ba*-[X]
6′) [. . .]-ḪUR-[. . .]
(rest destr.)
ii′ (almost completely destr.)

No. 44g

Obv. (beg. destr.)
1′) [x(IKU)] GÁN
2′) [ŠÁM]-*su*
3′) [x]+2 GÍN KUG.BABBAR
4′) [20]+20 MA.NA SÍG
5′) [ŠÁM 4]+2 GÍN 2 ⸢MA.NA⟨.TUR⟩ KUG.BABBAR⸣
(rest destr.)
Rev. (beg. destr.)
1′) [1 SÍG].GAN
2′) [. . .-^{d}]*Tišpak*
3′) [. . .]-*sar*
(rest destr.)

No. 44h

i′ (beg. destr.)
1′) [*šu*] É
2′) 1(EŠE) GÁN
3′) [Š]ÁM-*su*
4′) [x]+1 ŠE GUR.SAG.GÁL
5′) [*Te-m*]*i-tum*
6′) [DUMU.SAL? *G*]*a-lí-tim*
7′) [. . .]-*bu*
8′) [. . .]-*si*?-*da*
(rest destr.)

---

ii′ (beg. destr.)
1′) [1 GÚ] SÍG
2′) ŠÁM 10 GÍN
3′) 14 ŠE GUR.SAG.GÁL
4′) ⸢*Ša*⸣-*a*
5′) ⸢SAL⸣.BALAG.DI
6′) *dam-ḫur*

7′) 1(EŠE) 4(IKU) GÁN
8′) *šu* É
9′) 5(IKU) GÁN
10′) ŠÁM-*su*
11′) [x ŠE GUR.SA]G.GÁL
(rest destr.)

No. 44i

(beg. destr.)
1′) [1 SÍG].GAN
2′) [*Ì*]*r-e-um*
3′) [*š*]*u*? *Ma-ga-ga*
4′) [*š*]*i* TE.LAL
5′) 1 BA.AN ŠE
6′) [1] SÍG.GAN
7′) DINGIR-IGI.D[U]
8′) SABRA.⸢É⸣
(rest destr.)

No. 44j

(beg. destr.)
1′) *im-ḫu-ru*
(blank)
2′) GÁN E-AKKIL-*tim*
(blank)
(rest destr.)

No. 44k

i′ (beg. destr.)
1′) [1]+2(BÙR) 1(EŠE) 1(IKU) GÁN
2′) [ŠÁ]M-*su* 2 GÍN KUG.BABBAR
3′) [10]+13 ŠE GUR

4′) [ŠÁM] ⅓ ŠA [3 G]ÍN KUG.BABBAR
(rest destr.)

ii′ (beg. destr.)
1′) ŠÁM 1+[x GÍN KUG.BABBAR]
2′) ⌜*We*⌝-*tum*
3′) DUMU *ši Ìr-e-um*
4′) *im-ḫur*

5′) 1(BÙR) GÁN
6′) ŠÁM-*su*
7′) 10 ŠE GUR
8′) ŠÁM 10 GÍN KUG.BABBAR
9′) 26 ŠE GUR.SAG.GÁL
10′) *É-a*
11′) [DUMU *G*]*a-li-l*⌜*i*⌝
12′) [*im-ḫu*]*r*

(rest destr.)

iii′ (beg. destr.)
(blank)
1′) *šu Ša-at-b*[*e*]-DINGIR
2′) 1(BÙR) GÁN
3′) ŠÁM-[*su*]
4′) 12 [ŠE GUR]
5′) ŠÁM 10+[2 GÍN KUG.BABBAR]
(rest destr.)

No. 44l

Obv. i′ (beg. destr.)
1′) [*In*?-*zi*?-*b*]*a-nim*
2′) *A*-ŠI-*a-lí*
3′) DUMU *Gi-šum*
4′) DUMU *Be-lí-sa-tu*
5′) PA.TE.SI
6′) *Tu-tu-ub*^KI^
(rest destr.)

ii′ (beg. destr.)
1′) 1 SÍG.GAN
2′) *I-da*-DINGIR
3′) DUMU *A-bu-lum*
4′) *ši*! *Lu-ga-tim*
5′) 1 BA.AN ŠE
6′) 1 SÍG.GA[N]
7′) *Iš-lam*-G[I]?
(rest destr.)

iii′ (beg. destr.)
1′) PAB+E [. . .]
2′) *A*-[. . .]
3′) *šu L*[*i*?- . . .]
4′) *M*[*u*- . . .]
5′) ⌜*šu*⌝ [. . .]
(rest destr.)

Rev. (rev. is ruled into 3 cols. but is blank)

Notes

44c ii′ 1′–2′.—The reconstruction of these two lines is based on no. 43 iii 11–12.

44e i′ 2′.—For the name *Ù-ù*, see *MAD* 5, 98 ii 5.

44h i′ 1′.—Reconstructed on the basis of ii′ 8′.

ii′ 4′.—For this PN, see clear *Ša-a* in IM 43381:1, Sargonic, unpublished.

44l i′ 1′.—The name is reconstructed on the basis of clear *In-zi-ba-nim* in *MAD* 1, 126:3, also from Tell Asmar.

No. 45 Assur Stone Fragment

Photograph: Plate 80—old photograph of the Staatliche Museen, Assur-Photo. S 5963.
Copy: None, collated by Westenholz.
Provenience: Assur—found in the area of the "Alter Palast" at the deepest level, corresponding to about levels H and G of the Ishtar temple, which are dated to the Sumerian-Sargonic periods. See W. Andrae, *Die archaischen Ischtar-Tempel in Assur* (Leipzig, 1922) p. 9; E. Forrer, *RLA* 1 p. 230.
Date: Sargonic.
Language: Akkadian, though note the sequence x URUDU MA.NA.
Present location: Berlin, Staatliche Museen zu Berlin, VA 5689 (formerly S 18208, on Assur-Photo. 5963).
Description: Described by E. Forrer, *RLA* 1, p. 230b, only as a "steinerne Kaufurkunde Assur 18208 auf Assur-Photo. 5963." From a photograph it has been possible to determine the size of the fragment as 6.1 × 6.3 cm. The reverse is completely broken away. Only part of one column with a left edge remains. Westenholz examined the stone and states in his letter that there may be "possibly traces of writing on the left edge." In addition, Forrer, *loc. cit.*, mentions a "Bruchstück (. . .) einer Stein?-Tafel [20876 on Assur-Photo. 6461] mit strichförmiger Keilinschrift von vier Zeichen."
Text: The eight preserved lines mention garments (TÚG.BAL) and 30 minas of copper which were presented as a gift (NÍG.BA) to the persons named in the following lines.

Transliteration

i′ (beg. destr.)
1′) [. . .] ⌜X⌝
2′) [x]+2 TÚG.BAL
3′) 30 URUDU MA.NA
4′) NÍG.BA
5′) 1 *Mu-m*[*u*?- . . .]
6′) 1 *Su-mu*-[. . .]
7′) 1 *Be-lí*-[. . .]
8′) 1 *Ig*-[. . .]
(rest destr.)

ii′ (destr.)

No. 46 TIM IX 97

Photograph: Plate 80, Iraq Museum, Baghdad, courtesy J. N. Postgate.
Copy: Plate 80, J. J. van Dijk, *TIM* 9, 97.
Provenience: Unknown.
Date: Pre-Sargonic(?).
Language: Akkadian.

Present location: Iraq Museum (Baghdad), IM 24684, located through the special efforts of Dr. Beijeh Khalil Ismail.

Publication: Van Dijk, *TIM* 9, 97.

Description: Fragment of a stone vessel measuring (with writing vertical) ca. 7.7 × 8.5 cm.

Text: The fragment contains portions of two columns. The sign ⸢X⸣ which follows Ì.IR "scented oil" in ii′ 3′ apparently denotes a capacity measure or a container, but none of the measures or containers (such as dug, šagan, and á-gam) usually used in connection with oils fits the traces (see the photograph). However, the sign in question could conceivably be read as umbin?, the container used for ì-udu "sheep oil" in nos. 14 and 15 (see note to no. 14 i 7).

Transliteration

i′ (beg. destr.)
1′) [. . .]-⸢X⸣-LI
2′) [. . .] ⸢TI⸣?
(rest destr.)
ii′ (beg. destr.)
1′) [x]+1 SÍG ⸢MA⸣.NA
2′) ⸢1⸣? ŠE GUR
3′) 1 Ì.IR ⸢X⸣
4′) NÍG.BA A.ŠÀ
5′) *Me-me* ⸢X⸣
(rest destr.)

No. 47 UM 32-40-436

Photograph: Plate 80, Oriental Institute, The University of Chicago, print nos. P64233 and P64234—the inscription on loan from the University Museum, University of Pennsylvania.

Copy: Plate 80, copied by Steinkeller.

Provenience: Ur—surface find at the site Diqdiqqah, 2 km northeast of the ziggurat at Ur, field no. U 17717. See L. Woolley, *UE* 4 p. 186. For Diqdiqqah, see Woolley and Mallowan, *UE* 7 pp. 81–87.

Date: Pre-Sargonic.

Language: Akkadian(?).

Present location: University Museum, University of Pennsylvania (Philadelphia), UM 32-40-436.

Description: Fragment of a light-gray limestone(?) tablet measuring 8.1 × 6.2 × 2.7 cm. The lower edge is preserved; the reverse is broken away. The surface slopes down gently toward the lower edge.

Text: The inscription consists only of ten signs preserved on the bottom portions of two columns. One noteworthy feature is the sequence KUG ½ MA.NA, paralleled only in no. 39 iii′ 3′, in Sumerian.

This text was kindly communicated to us by Westenholz.

Transliteration

i′ (beg. destr.)
1′) [. . .] ⸢X⸣
2′) [. . . D]U
ii′ (beg. destr.)
1′) [D]A? ÚR?
2′) NÍG.ŠÁM
3′) KUG ½ MA.N[A]
iii′ (destr.)

No. 48 BM 91068

Photographs: Plates 81 and 83. British Museum, London.

Copy: Plates 82 and 84, copy by T. G. Pinches, provided through the courtesy of E. Sollberger.

Provenience: Sippar (Abū Habba)—see C. B. F. Walker and D. Collon in L. de Meyer, ed., *Tell ed-Dēr* 3 (Leuven, 1980) p. 103 no. 66 and p. 111. On the reverse is a later, Neo-Babylonian, inscription stating that the document is the property of Shamash, chief god of Sippar.

Date: Sargonic.

Language: Akkadian.

Present location: British Museum (London), BM 91068 (= 82-7-14, 1045).

Publication: Described in *British Museum: A Guide to the Babylonian and Assyrian Antiquities* (London, 1922) p. 91 no. 91,068, as an "archaic Sumerian document containing a deed of sale with an Assyrian inscription of the Sargonic [meaning 'Neo-Assyrian'] period on the reverse."

Description: Thin, light-buff limestone slab measuring 23 × 24.5 × 2.7–3.7 cm. All four edges are preserved.

Text: There are nine columns of writing on the obverse, with about 21–24 lines each. There are only three inscribed columns on the right side of the reverse. Its surface is so badly worn that very little of the inscription can be read. The left side of the reverse contained only a later, Neo-Babylonian, addition. See below.

The beginning of column i is lost. What is visible in the rest of the column is the object of the transaction, [x] GÁN "x land," its price expressed in 10 ŠE GUR "10 bushels of barley" and possibly other commodities, and some unreadable names of the sellers(?). In column ii several sections deal with [x] TÚG.SU.A PN "[x] SU.A cloth (of/for) PN," that is, x SU.A clothes paid to PN as the additional payment. From column iii to ix 7 there is a list of originally about sixty-four witnesses, subsumed as AB+ÁŠ.AB+ÁŠ $^{d?}$UTU?-[X] "witnesses of P[N]." The name of each witness is preceded by a single wedge, and is identified by a profession or as LÚ PN "of (the household of) PN" or, occasionally, as DUMU PN "son of PN." A similar list of originally about twenty names from ix 8 to rev. ii 9 ends with AB+ÁŠ.AB+ÁŠ *Ab-za-*⸢*x*⸣^{KI} "witnesses of Ab-za-⸢x⸣." It is tempting to identify this geographical name with the one written *Ab-za-an*^{KI}, *Ab-sa-an*^{KI}, and *Ab-za-ab*^{KI} in the Old Babylonian geographical lists (see, for instance, McEwan, *WO* 11 [1980] p. 162, and *MSL* 11 p. 102 line 180 and p. 140 ii 1), or *Ab-sa-an*^{KI} and *Ab-šá-an*^{KI} in the late versions of the Cruciform Monument (see Sollberger, *JEOL* 20 [1968] p. 56). The latter sources place Apšan in the general area of later Opis, near Baghdad. The occurrence of this geographical name in our kudurru would help in circumscribing its area to northern Babylonia.

The readable names in these two lists of witnesses are *A-ḫu-ḫu* (iii 19′), *Ur-ur* (iv 4, vi 3, vii 13), *Du-du* (iv 11), *I-rí-sum* (iv 12), *Ur-ezen* (iv 14), IGI.SI_4 (iv 16), [*S*]*ar-ru-ru* (iv 19), ⸢*A-ḫa*⸣*-ì-lum* (v 6, 14), *Lú*-d⸢X⸣*-da* (v 17), *I-lu-lu* (v 18), *Lú*-[d]*En*-⸢*líl*⸣? (vi 8), *A*-SI.A LÚ.Ù? dUTU (vi 13–14), *I-ti-lum* (vi 15), *La-gi-um* (vii 9), and ŠEŠ ⸢*Pù-pù*⸣ (vii 14).

In the second half of rev. ii there are about five illegible lines, followed by: [1 X]-*bu*, [L]Ú [*Z*]*u-zu*, 1 *Pù-Il*, LÚ BÀD-*si*, AB+ÁŠ, *A*-⸢. . .⸣ "[X]-bu of (the household of) [Z]uzu; Pu-Il of (the household of) BÀD-si, the witness of A. (a GN?)."

Column iii lists personal names that are not preceded by a *Personenkeil* but are qualified by a profession and the genealogical relationship DUMU "son" or SAL. DUMU "daughter" or the designation LÚ PN "of (the household of) PN." This list of names is identified in lines 14–15 as GURUŠ.GURUŠ ⸢PN⸣ "men of ⸢PN⸣."

For a possible occurrence of the preposition *áš-ti* (rev. iii 8), see discussion of no. 26 under *Text*.

The interpretation of the last three lines of rev. iii is the most tantalizing. We can read ⸢ŠÀ/KI GÁN⸣ "in(?) the field," followed by NÍG.ŠÁM "price," followed by IN. ⸢GÀR?.MU?.MU?⸣. To judge from the parallel NÍG.ŠÁM PN at the end of no. 37, we expect that the signs in the last line should stand for the name of the buyer.

In the empty space of the reverse are two lines (written upside down of the text) in Neo-Babylonian script: NÍG.GA dUTU *šá* [TÙM(-*lu*)], MU-*šú liḫ-liq* "property of Šamaš; whosoever [removes it] may his name perish."

Transliteration

Rev. ii
1′) [1 X]-*bu*
2′) [L]Ú [*Z*]*u-zu*
3′) 1 *Pù-Il*
4′) LÚ BÀD-*si*
5′) AB+ÁŠ
6′) *A*-⸢. . .⸣

Rev. iii
1) ⸢DUMU⸣
2) *I-lu-lu*
3) ⸢GÌR?.BÀD⸣
4) DUMU
5) *Da-da*
6) *Ib-bu-bu*
7) LÚ *Kag-gú-tum*
8) *áš-ti*
9) LU GAR MA
10) SAL.DUMU
11) *Íl-li-l*[*i*]?
12) SANGA
13) *Ù-šu?-ti*
14) GURUŠ.GURUŠ
15) ⸢NIN?.DUB?⸣
16) ⸢ŠÀ/KI GÁN⸣
17) NÍG.ŠÁM
18) IN.⸢GÀR?.MU?.MU?⸣

No. 49 BM 90909

Photograph: Plate 85, British Museum (PS 097078).
Copy: Plate 86, copied by Steinkeller from a photograph and collations by K. Maekawa.
Provenience: Supposedly from Sippar—see Walker and Collon in L. de Meyer, ed., *Tell ed-Dēr* 3 (Leuven, 1980) p. 102 no. 58 and p. 111.
Date: Sargonic.
Language: Akkadian.
Present location: British Museum (London), BM 90909 (previously BM 12037).
Description: Fragment of a limestone slab measuring 8.4 × 10.5 × 5 cm. One side is inscribed, the other is defaced.
Text: In its present condition, the inscription is preserved in portions of four columns. It is impossible to tell whether it represents the obverse or the reverse.

This text was kindly communicated to us by C. B. F. Walker.

Transliteration

i′ (completely destr.)
ii′ (beg. destr.)
1′) [. . .]
2′) 1 DINGIR-*su-ra-bí*
3′) DUMU *Ìr-ra*-⸢*Il*⸣?
4′) [. . .]-⸢TU⸣?
(rest destr.)
iii′ (beg. destr.)
1′) [SÍ]G? 1 MA.NA K[UG?.BABBAR?]
2′) NÍG.KI.GAR GÁ[N]
3′) 1 ÁB
4′) *a-na* NÍG.ŠÁM
5′) 1 GIŠGIGIR
(rest destr.)
iv′ (beg. destr.)
1′) 2?+[x? . . .]
(rest destr.)

No. 50 BM 33429

Photographs: Plate 85, British Museum (PS 097079, 097080).
Copy: Plate 86, copied by Steinkeller from photographs and collations by K. Maekawa and Whiting.
Provenience: Registered as coming from Babylon.
Date: Sargonic.
Language: Akkadian.
Present location: British Museum (London), BM 33429 (= Rm III 106).
Description: Fragment of a dark-gray irregular stone slab measuring 6.8 × 13.5 × 6.8 cm. Preserved are the portions of two sides. The original shape of the piece cannot be determined.
Text: The inscription is preserved on two sides of the stone (classified here as Sides A and B), each side bearing three columns of writing. Since Side B lists the totals of commodities, it is certain that it recorded the

end of the inscription. However, the exact relationship of Side A to Side B cannot be determined.

This text was kindly communicated to us by C. B. F. Walker.

Transliteration

Side A	i′		(beg. destr.)
		1′)	[. . .] ⌜X⌝ UDU?
		2′)	[. . .] ⌜NÍG⌝?.BA
	ii′		(beg. destr.)
		1′)	[. . .-*u*]*m*?
		2′)	KA-*Me-ir*
		3′)	⌜*I-zu*-GÍD⌝
		4′)	[. . .]-⌜X⌝-LUM
	iii′		(beg. destr.)
		1′)	LÚ?.TÚG?
		2′)	*I-nin-me-šum*
		3′)	*Barag*?-*ga-mes*?
		4′)	*im-ḫu-ru*
		5′)	⌜DUMU⌝ [. . .]
Side B	i′		(3? lines destr.)
		1′)	[Š]U.NIGÍN ⌜3 GÍN? Ì.NUN?⌝
		2′)	[Š]U.NIGÍN 6 ⌜x⌝? MA.NA ⌜x⌝ URUDU
	ii′		(several lines destr., numbers only)
		1′)	ŠU.NIGÍN 40+[x? . . .]
	iii′	1)	⌜SAG⌝? [. . .]
			(rest destr.)

Notes

Side A iii′ 2′.—Note that the sign ŠUM is broken up into two parts.

No. 51 BM 45593

Photograph: Plate 85, British Museum (PS 097081).
Copy: Plate 86, copied by Steinkeller from a photograph and collations by Maekawa.
Provenience: Supposedly from Cuthah—the tablet was marked TI (= Tell Ibrahim = Cuthah).
Date: Sargonic.
Language: Akkadian.
Present location: British Museum (London), BM 45593 (= 81-7-1, 3354).
Description: Fragment of a light-gray alabaster(?) cylinder, originally about 9 or 10 cm in diameter. Measurements are 3.6 × 5.7 × 2.4 cm.
Text: Portions of two columns are preserved, one of which is inscribed and the other blank. Of the inscribed column, only one line remains: ŠU.NIGÍN 30+[10] plus a small circle. In the line below, now almost completely obliterated, two circles representing the number 20 are still visible.

The information concerning this fragment was kindly communicated to us by C. B. F. Walker.

No. 52 BM 139507

Photograph: Plate 85.
Copy: Plate 86, copied by Green.
Provenience: Unknown—in answer to our query, C. B. F. Walker writes:

> We have no information on the provenance of this particular item, but while registering it Julian [Reed] noticed that it had a small red number '91' painted on it. Such numbers are also found on items from George Smith's Daily Telegraph expedition, so it is possible that this stone was brought back on that occasion.

Date: Sargonic.
Language: Akkadian.
Present location: British Museum (London), BM 139507 (= 1983-1-1-50).
Description: Fragment of gray limestone, measuring 12 × 11 × 6 cm.

Transliteration

Rev.	i′		(beg. destr.)
		1′)	[. . .]-DINGIR
		2′)	[. . .-*z*]*um*
		3′)	[. . .-N]I
		4′)	[. . .]
			(rest destr.)
	ii′		(beg. destr.)
		1′)	1 *Ma-šum*
		2′)	DUMU PÙ.ŠA-^{d}*Za-ba*$_4$-*ba*$_4$
		3′)	1 *I-sa-ru-um*
		4′)	DUMU *Du-du*
		5′)	1 *Nu-nu*
		6′)	DUMU ⌜. . .⌝
		7′)	1 [. . .]
			(rest destr.)
	iii′		(beg. destr.)
		1′)	D[UMU]/A[RÁD] [. . .]
		2′)	1 È-[. . .] KISAL [. . .]
		3′)	ARÁD [. . .]
		4′)	1 DIN[GIR- . . .]
		5′)	AR[ÁD? . . .]
			(rest destr.)

CHAPTER 4

INDEXES TO ANCIENT KUDURRUS

These indexes list the personal, divine, geographical, and professional names found in the ancient kudurrus, with the exclusion of the archaic kudurrus nos. 1–9. Note that in these indexes primes are not indicated in the references and italics are not employed to distinguish Akkadian from Sumerian words in the transliterations.

4.1. *Personal Names*

A-a-BE: [PN DUMU] ⸢Gi-x⸣-ra ši A-a-BE, 42 iii 2
A-a-[. . .] UK[Ù.GAL], 16d A iii 4
A-ar-DINGIR DUMU Pù-ba-lum SIPA . . . DUMU. DUMU Ìr-ra-ra, 40 A iv 13
  ^{d}EN.ZU-al-su DUMU A-ar-DINGIR ši Pù-ba-lum . . . DUMU.DUMU Ìr-ra-ra, 40 A iv 17
A-ar-É-a: ^{d}EN.ZU-a-ar DUMU A-ar-É-a . . . DUMU. DUMU Ši-ù-ni, 40 A vii 14
  ^{d}EN.ZU-GIŠ.ERÍN Ì-la-la Šu-ì-lí-su 3 DUMU Zu-zu ši A-ar-É-a, 40 A x 9
  Zu-zu DUMU A-ar-É-a . . . DUMU.DUMU Ši-ù-ni, 40 A vii 3
^{d}A-ba$_4$-iš-da-gal DUMU Sar-ru-GI, 40 C xiii 22
  Be-lí-ba-ni AGRIG ^{d}A-ba$_4$-iš-da-gal, 40 C xix 26
A-bí-AN.NA GEMÉ.DINGIR SAL.DUMU Na-ni DUMU. DUMU A-nu-nu, 41 i 13
A-bí-bí, 32 iii 4
A-bí-da: Ma-an-sa-ki-su DUMU A-bí-da . . . DUMU. DUMU Lugal-ezen, 40 C xv 22
A-bí-ra šu Iš-lam-GI, 41 rev. iv 12
A-bí-ra šu ŠU.A, 41 iv 7
A-bí-su šu Ú-ḫúb, 44b i 1
A-bìl-dan BÀD-su-nu 2 DUMU Su-ru-uš-GI ši PAB. ŠEŠ PA.TE.SI GIŠ.ÙḪ^{KI}, 40 A xii 19
A-bu-bu, 15 iii 2, 12
  A-bu-bu DUMU I-mi-DINGIR UGULA KA-zu-ra-ak^{KI} . . . DUMU.DUMU SANGA, 40 C xv 5
A-bu-lum: I-da-DINGIR DUMU A-bu-lum ši! Lu-ga-tim, 44l ii 3
  A-pù-lum, 16a ii 3
  A-pù-lum: DUMU.DUMU A-pù-lum include families of Sag-gul-lum, [A]-ḫu-mu-bí, Pù-pù, Eš$_4$-dar-al-su, DINGIR-a-zu, and PÙ.ŠA-Il-la, 40 D ii 3, v 12
A-da: Šu-Ba-ba šu A-da LÚ.GUNU+ÚŠ, 41 iv 14
A-da-da DUMU ^{d}KA-Me-ir . . . 5 DUMU.DUMU Da-tum, 40 D v 2
A-da-na-aḫ: I-bí-ZU.AB DUMU Ur-mes-an-ni Ti-ru-um DUMU A-da-na-aḫ DUMU.DUMU I-ti-É-a, 40 C iv 6
A-DU-nàd gemé Bíl-làl-la, App. to no. 32 vii 5
A-geštin simug, 21 i 31
A-GÍR-gal, 12 Inscription on Side D
A-gu-tim: Ì-lu-lu DUMU Ik-ru-ub-DINGIR ši A-gu-tim, 40 A xiv 23
A-ḫa-ar-ši: A-ḫu-GIŠ.ERÍN DUMU A-ḫa-ar-ši DUMU. DUMU Lugal-ezen, 40 C xvii 4
  En-na-É-a DUMU A-ḫa-ar-ši NAGAR, 40 B xiii 3
⸢A-ḫa⸣-ì-lum, 48 v 6, 14
A-ḫu-ba-lik: DINGIR-ba-ni DUMU A-ḫu-ba-lik DUMU. DUMU Zi-im-tum, 40 B xi 12
A-ḫu-DÙG DUMU Ì-lum-sar šu PA.TE.SI, 41 iii 19
  A-ḫu-DÙG (var. A-ḫu-ḫu in B) DUMU Šu-Nu-nu ši Ḫa-lum, 40 A xv 14 (also in C and D)
  A-ḫu-DÙG šu PA.TE.SI, 41 v 8
A-ḫu-GIŠ.ERÍN DUMU A-ḫa-ar-ši DUMU.DUMU Lugal-ezen, 40 C xvii 3
  A-ḫu-GIŠ.ERÍN šu SU.Ù.SAL DUB.SAR.GÁN, 41 ii 2
A-ḫu-ḫu, 48 iii 19
  A-ḫu-ḫu (var. A-ḫu-DÙG in A, C, and D) DUMU Šu-Nu-nu ši Ḫa-lum, 40 B xxi 7
  I-ki-lum A-ḫu-ḫu 2 DUMU Iš-má-DINGIR . . . 5 DUMU.DUMU MES-na-at, 40 C vi 3
  [Ì-l]í-dan [X]-tu-um [A-ḫ]u-ḫu [DUMU]? Ga-NI-am-me-me, 44a i 4
  Bí-su-šè-ib-nim É-a-ra-bí 2 DUMU A-ḫu-ḫu ši Al-lu-lu, 40 A xi 23
  Im$_4$-da-lik DUMU I-su-DINGIR DUMU.DUMU A-ḫu-ḫu Da-mi-gi^{KI}, 40 A xv 23
A-ḫu-ì-lum, 41 viii 8
[A]-ḫu-mu-bí [DU]MU É-a-ra-bí . . . 4 DUMU.DUMU ši A-pù-lum, 40 D i 7
  [PN] Ì-lí-a-ḫi 2 DUMU A-ḫu-mu-bí DUMU.DUMU Iš-dup-DINGIR ši É-a-a, 40 C v 3
A-ki: A-pù-ì-lum šu A-ki URUDU?^{KI}, 41 vi 17
A-ki-gal, 15 vi 15, viii 25, x 18, xi 6
A-ku-É-a DUMU PÙ.ŠA-É-a . . . DUMU.DUMU Lugal-ezen, 40 C xvi 10

A-ku-ì-lum, 28 ii
A-ku-ì-lum DUMU PÉŠ-ì-lum ši Ur-^{d}AB, 40 B xiv 11
DUMU.DUMU A-ku-ì-lum include families of Ba-ša-aḫ-DINGIR, Ib-LUL-DINGIR, and Ur-^{d}Nin-kar, 40 C xiv 14
A-ku-si-im: Šu-Ma-ma šu A-ku-si-im, 41 rev. v 16
A-li-a-ḫu DUMU NI-ba-rí-im ŠEŠ LUGAL, 40 A x 22
[A]?-l[i?-l]i?, 41 rev. vii 1
A-li-li šu GÁN, 41 rev. viii 21
A-lum-DÙG: Ur-Ab-ra DUMU A-lum-DÙG DUMU.DUMU Ur-ma, 37 rev. i 13
A-ma-^{d}EN.ZU DUMU Ga-zu-a-lum ši Ì-lu-lu, 40 A v 3
A-mu-m[i], 15 v 6
A-mu-mu šu Ba-zi-gú!, 41 iii 12
A-mu-[. . .] šu La-ba-Ù, 41 rev. vii 3
A-mur-rúm: Ib-bu-bu DUMU A-mur-rúm . . . DUMU.DUMU A-nu-nu, 41 i 12
A-NI-NI, 37 rev. ii 19
A-NI-NI/GAR, 16d A i 3
⸢A⸣-nu-GÁN, 15 xiv 26
A-nu-nu: DUMU.DUMU A-nu-nu include families of Iš-dup-Il, Ib-bu-bu, and A-bí-AN.NA, 41 i 17
Su$_4$-NI-um šu A-nu-nu, 41 iv 16
A-nu-zu DUMU Ik-ru-ub-DINGIR, 40 C xviii 15
A-pù-BÀD: Dam-ma DUMU A-pù-BÀD šu Ba-lu-lu, 41 iii 8
A-pù-ì-lum, 41 vii 20
A-pù-ì-lum šu A-ki URUDU?^{KI}, 41 vi 16
A-pù-lum, see A-bu-lum
A-rúm, 35 ii 3
A.SI, 34 iii 8; 41 rev. v 12, 21
A-SI.A LÚ.Ù? ^{d}UTU, 48 vi 13
A-ša-su-GIŠ.ERÍN DUMU I-mi-ì-lum, 41 rev. vi 6
A-ŠI-a-lí DUMU Gi-šum DUMU Be-lí-sa-tu PA.TE.SI Tu-tu-ub^{KI}, 44l i 2
A-ŠI-gu-ru-ud: DINGIR-a-zu DUMU A-ŠI-gu-ru-ud attached to the lineage of Me-zi-zi, 40 A v 7
A-šu-El: DUG.RU-ma-da-ág Di-Utu A-šu-El dumu Ba-ni-me, 22 iii 52
A-tum: Ú-bí-bí šu Da-tum ⸢X⸣.GAL A-tum, 31 iv 5
A-za-šum, 28 ii
A-ZU.AB-si: Mes-sa dumu A-ZU.AB-si 22 [iii 10], 43
A-⸢. . .⸣: ⸢En-SAL⸣.UŠ.⸢DI-zi⸣ Inim-ma-ni-zi Nin-⸢kal-SI.A⸣ Lugal-⸢x⸣-ni-[x] Me-kisal-[si]? A-⸢. . .⸣ Lú-[. . .] dumu Amar-[tùr] sag-⸢du$_5$⸣, 22 [iv 14], 47
A-⸢. . .⸣ ⸢DUMU⸣ I-lu-lu, 48 rev. ii 4
A-[. . .] SAL.DI.UŠ É-sír-ág, 32 vi 4
Á-kal-li, 14 iii 15
Á!-ni-kur-ra, 33 rev. ii 2
Ib-mud dumu Á-ni-kur-ra ⸢É⸣-ib-zi-ka, App. to nos. 22–23 i 4
Ab-ba, 32 v 3
Ab-ba-ba, 33 rev. iii 3
Ab-ra-Il: DUMU.DUMU Ab-ra-Il include the families of Iq-bí-GI, Al-la, and Pù-su-GI, 40 B iv 4, v 3, 4
Ad-da, 15 ii 13, iii 29, iv 29, ix 16
[Ad]?-da, 31 iv 8
Ad-da ugula anše, 15 vi 16, vii 12, viii 28
Ad-da-tur: Ba-ni Ba-lum dumu Ad-da-tur [p]ab-⸢šeš⸣, 22 iii 4, [34], 38
Ag, 12 Inscription on Side B–C i 6
Ag gal-ukkin, 12 Adscription to Side B
Ag-a: ⸢Pù-pù⸣ DUMU Ag-a, 34 iii 4
Ag-^{d}En-líl INNIN.ÙḪ, 30b ii 3
AG.EN.NAM, 18 obv. 1, 5, 6, 7, 8, rev. iv 1
AGRIG: I-ti-DINGIR DUMU La-mu-sa ši AGRIG . . . DUMU.DUMU Su-mu-núm, 40 A ii 17
Su-ru-uš-GI DUMU I-ti-DINGIR šu La-mu-sa ši AGRIG . . . DUMU.DUMU Su-mu-núm, 40 A iii 16
SI.A-um DUMU La-mu-sa ši AGRIG . . . DUMU.DUMU SU-mu-núm, 40 A iv 12
Al-la: Iq-bí-GI Al-la 2 DUMU Ab-ra-Il DUMU.DUMU Iš-dup-BE . . . 3 DUMU.DUMU Ab-ra-Il, 40 B iv 3
Al-la-la: Pù-^{d}Da-gan DUMU Al-la-la attached to the lineage of Me-zi-zi, 40 A v 9
Al-lu-lu: Bí-su-šè-ib-nim É-a-ra-bí 2 DUMU A-ḫu-ḫu ši Al-lu-lu, 40 A xi 24
DINGIR-su-su DUMU Mu-mu ŠU.I ši Al-lu-lu, 40 A xii 18
ALAM.NE.PAB.KÍD?.GÍR.DU engar èš, 10:4
Ama-barag-si [dam Ur-^{d}Dumu-zi-da]? ⸢En-SAL⸣.UŠ.⸢DI-zi⸣ Inim-ma-ni-zi Nin-⸢kal-SI.A⸣ Lugal-[x]-ni-[x] Me-kisal-[si]? A-⸢. . .⸣ Lú-[. . .] dumu Amar-[tùr] sag-⸢du$_5$⸣, 22 [iv 7], 39
[. . .]-⸢ma⸣? [dumu X]-⸢barag-si⸣, 23 rev. iii 3, [33], obv. iv 7
Amar-aš?-è, 14 xii 16, xiii 15
[A]mar-Dilmun-na?^{KI}, 36 i 8, ii 12
Amar-^{d}EN.ZU, 15 iv 30
Amar-^{d}Ezínu(ŠE.TIR), 15 xii 10
Amar-GUL šu-i, 33 iii 5
Amar-rí-rí Be-lí-sa-tu 2 DUMU Zu-zu [DU]MU.DUMU Ur-[Má]r-da [ši I]-ki-lum, 40 C iv 9
Iš-dup-DINGIR DUMU Amar-rí-rí DUMU.DUMU SANGA, 40 C xv 9
Amar-^{d}Samàn(NUN.ŠE.ÉŠ.BU) dub-sar, 21 iii 33
Amar-tùr, 21 i 33, v 4
Ama-barag-si ⸢En-SAL⸣.UŠ.⸢DI-zi⸣ Inim-ma-ni-zi Nin-⸢kal-SI.A⸣ Lugal-⸢x⸣-ni-[x] Me-kisal-[si]? A-⸢. . .⸣ Lú-[. . .] dumu Amar-[tùr] sag-⸢du$_5$⸣, 22 [iv 16], 49
AN.DAM.ŠE.DU.A, 12 Inscription on Side A 1, E–D 5
AN.GÍR.JN-312.NUNUZ.SAG, 11:16
AN.MAŠ.LU.UŠ, 14 xv 4
An-na-bí-kúš dumu Ur-ur šeš Bíl-làl-la sanga Kèš, App. to no. 32 v 4
An-nu-me, 25 iii 5
AN.RU.KÈŠ.TA dumu-SAL [U]d-da, 33 rev. iv 6
AN-⸢x⸣-[. . .], 15 vii 9
A[N-. . .], 15 vii 8
Ar-rí-im: La-lí DUMU Iš-má-GÁR ši Ar-rí-im, 40 A xiv 20
ARÁD-zu-ni DUMU Gu-lí-zum ši SAL.ANŠE, 40 B xii 14
ARÁD-zu-ni DUMU Iš-dup-DINGIR . . . DUMU.DUMU Ši-ù-ni, 40 A vi 20
ARÁD-zu-ni DUMU Iš-dup-pum DUMU.DUMU Ši-na-na-tim, 40 B vii 8
ARÁD-zu-ni DUMU La-mu-um 4 DUMU.DUMU Da-tum, 40 D iii 2
ARÁD-zu-ni DUMU Me-zé-ì-lum attached to the lineage of Me-zi-zi, 40 A v 10

ARÁD-zu-ni DUMU Pù-pù LÚ.IGI, 40 B xiii 16
Da-kum DUMU ARÁD-zu-ni, 40 A xvi 4
La-gi-pum DUMU ARÁD-zu-ni, 40 B xiii 12
Su-NI-um DUMU ARÁD-zu-ni IŠ . . . DUMU.DUMU Ši-ù-ni, 40 A vi 17
Aš-dar-BALA?, 17 ii 2
^{d}ÁŠ?.TE?: Iš-[. . .] DUMU Ti-ti šu ^{d}ÁŠ?.TE?, 31 ii 4
ÁŠ?.UR?.[X]?, 13 rev. i 1

Ba-lu-lu: Dam-ma DUMU A-pù-BÀD šu Ba-lu-lu, 41 iii 9
Ba-lum: Ba-ni Ba-lum dumu Ad-da-tur [p]ab-⸢šeš⸣, 22 iii 3, 37
Ba-ni Ba-lum dumu [A]d-da-[tur] [p]ab-⸢šeš⸣, 22 iii 2, [33], 64
DUG.RU-ma-da-ág Di-Utu A-šu-El dumu Ba-ni-me, 22 iii 53
Ba-ša DUMU Gi$_{4}$-[. . .], 41 rev. ii 19
Ba-ša DUMU Ku-ku PAB.ŠEŠ, 41 rev. ii 9
Ba-ša-aḫ-DINGIR LÚ.ÉŠ.GÍD DUMU Ur-ur . . . DUMU.DUMU A-ku-ì-lum, 40 C xiv 1
Be-lí-sa-tu DUMU Ba-ša-aḫ-DINGIR LÚ.ÉŠ.GÍD . . . DUMU.DUMU I-rí-iš-be-li, 40 C xvii 9
Ba-zi-gú!: A-mu-mu šu Ba-zi-gú!, 41 iii 13
Ba-[. . .]: Ḫu-[. . .] DUMU Ba-[. . .], 41 rev. ii 2
BÀD-Il: Su-mu-GI U-li-id-ì-lum 2 DUMU BÀD-Il DUMU.DUMU Ib-bu-bu, 40 B v 9
BÀD-si AB+ÁŠ A-⸢. . .⸣, 48 rev. ii 4
Bàd-si-du, 15 v 8
Šà-gú-ba dumu Bàd⟨-si⟩-du, 15 v 11
BÀD-su-nu: A-bìl-dan BÀD-su-nu 2 DUMU Su-ru-uš-GI ši PAB.ŠEŠ PA.TE.SI GIŠ.ÙḪ^{KI}, 40 A xii 20
BALA-É-a: U-bi-in-LUGAL-rí DUMU BALA-É-a ARÁD-da-ni^{KI}, 40 A xv 12
Bala-ga: UD-ti-ru Sar-ru-GI-ì-lí 2 DUMU Bala-ga ši NAR, 40 A xii 9
BALA-ì-lum DUMU Zi-at, 41 rev. ii 11
Barag?-ga-mes?, 50 Side A iii 3
Barag-ga-[ni]: Igi-zi-barag-gi Ur-^{d}Nin-PA Ur-^{d}GUR$_{8}$-⸢x⸣ Barag-ga-[ni] dumu In[im-ma]-ni-[zi-me], 22 iv 60
Barag-gan-ni engar, 15 i 25, ii 24, iii 22, iv 22, v 21, vi 27, vii 25, ix 26, x 25, xiii 12, xiv 8, L. E. 6
Barag-gi-si: ME-ŠEŠ.ŠEŠ DUMU Barag-gi-si DUMU.DUMU Ur-^{d}En-líl, 40 C vii 3
Barag-ki-ba: Ur-^{d}Nin-kar SAG.DU$_{5}$ DUMU Barag-ki-ba DUMU.DUMU A-ku-ì-lum, 40 C xiv 13
Barag?-me?-⸢x⸣-GAR, 14 xv 8
Barag-^{sá}sag$_{7}$(GAN)-nu-di, 32 iv 8
Barag-^{sá}sag$_{7}$-nu-di!, 15 xii 1
Pab-ki-gal dumu Barag-$^{sá!}$sag$_{7}$-nu-di!, 15 xii 9
Barag-ul-tu: Làl?-li-l[i]? Barag-ul-tu dumu Ur-^{d}Dumu-zi-da-me, 22 iv 53
Be-la-su(sic)-nu U$_{4}$-bí-um^{KI}, 41 viii 16
Be-lí-a-mi DUMU Ur-Ab-ra ši Su$_{4}$-a-tum-mu-da . . . DUMU.DUMU SANGA, 40 C xv 2
Nu-ni-da DUMU Be-lí-a-mi DUMU.DUMU Ur-Ab-ra ši Su$_{4}$-a-tum-mu-da, 40 C xviii 5
Be-lí-ba-ni: Ga-at-núm Su$_{4}$-ma-SIPA Be-lí-ba-ni 3 DUMU Ur-ZU.AB DUMU.DUMU DINGIR-su-la-ba, 40 C v 14
Be-lí-ba-ni AGRIG ^{d}A-ba$_{4}$-iš-da-gal, 40 C xix 25
Be-lí-BALA SIPA, 38 i 3
Be-lí-GI: PÙ.ŠA-ì-li DUMU Be-lí-GI GÌR.NITA LÚ.GIŠ.TI, 40 A xii 4
Be-lí-GÚ, 38 ii 11
Be-lí-GÚ DUMU Ra-bí-DINGIR, 40 C xviii 13
DINGIR-a-ḫa DUMU Be-lí-GÚ NU.BANDA . . . DUMU.DUMU Ur-Ab-ra ši Su$_{4}$-a-tum-mu-da, 40 C xviii 2
Iq-bí-GI DUMU Be-lí-GÚ NU.BANDA LÚ.IGI . . . DUMU.DUMU Nu-gal, 40 C xvii 25
Be-lí-iš-lí: É-dam-si dumu Be-lí-iš-lí, 32 rev. i 18
Be-lí-lí DUMU Bur-zi-[a]?, 41 rev. ii 5
Šu-^{d}Da-gan DUMU Be-lí-lí ši Na-zi-tim SABRA.É, 40 A xi 16
Be-lí-mu-da DUMU Su-mi-su . . . DUMU.DUMU Zi-im-tum, 40 B xi 7
Be-lí-mu-[da] šu Iš-gu-[núm]?, 44d ii 1
Be-lí-sa-tu DUMU Ba-ša-aḫ-DINGIR LÚ.ÉŠ.GÍD . . . DUMU.DUMU I-rí-iš-be-lí, 40 C xvii 8
A-ŠI-a-lí DUMU Gi-šum DUMU Be-lí-sa-tu PA.TE.SI Tu-tu-ub^{KI}, 44l i 4
Amar-rí-rí Be-lí-sa-tu 2 DUMU Zu-zu [DU]MU.DUMU Ur-[Má]r-da [ši I]-ki-lum, 40 C iv 11
Be-lí-[. . .], 45 i 7
Bi-e-tim: DINGIR-a-ḫa šu Bi-e-tim . . . DUMU.DUMU Zi-im-tum, 40 B x 14
Bi-im: Su-NI-um DUMU Bi-im ši Zi-zi, 40 B xiv 3
Bi-li-li, 15 xii 20, xiii 4
Bí-bí, 43 i 11
Bí-bí DUMU Šu-la-pi, 41 rev. ix 12
Bí-su-šè-ib-nim É-a-ra-bí 2 DUMU A-ḫu-ḫu ši Al-lu-lu, 40 A xi 21
Bí-za: Da-bí-bí šu Bí-za, 41 v 23
Bí-zi-zi RÉC-349.A.TU, App. to no. 32 v 8
Bíl-làl-la, App. to no. 32 i 6
É-da-da Bíl-làl-la Ur-^{d}En-líl [dumu] Munsub$_{x}$, 32 ii 6
Bíl-làl-la sanga Kèš, App. to no. 32 ii 11
Lugal-ezen dumu Bíl-làl-la, App. to no. 32 iv 5
Ur-^{d}En-líl X-ma-ni-dùg Ur-^{d}Šul-pa-è É-úr-bi-dùg Ú-ú-a É-me-me Ur-ur šeš Bíl-làl-la-me, App. to no. 32 iv 14
An-na-bí-kúš dumu Ur-ur šeš Bíl-làl-la sanga Kèš, App. to no. 32 v 6
Làl-la dam Bíl-làl-la sanga Kèš, App. to no. 32 vi 2
9 PNs arád-me 1 PN gemé arád-gemé Bíl-làl-la-me, App. to no. 32 vii 7
Bìl-zum, 38 ii 10
Bu-e-im: [. . .] šu Bu-e-im, 41 v 2; see also Bu-im
Bu-ḫu-lum: Ì-lí-a-ḫi šu Bu-ḫu-lum, 41 v 13
Bu-im: Nu-ra GEMÉ.DINGIR DUMU.SAL PÙ.ŠA-Nu-ni DUMU.DUMU Bu-im MÁ.LAḪ$_{4}$, 40 D iii 13; see also Bu-e-im
⸢Bu-la⸣-la: GÁN šu DINGIR-GÀR [ši]? ⸢Bu-la⸣-la, 43 iii 16
Bu-pum, 19a i 6
BU.TUŠ.ḪU, 15 vi 14, viii 24
BU.TUŠ.ḪU-da dam É-ZU.AB, 15 v 28
Bu-[x]-nu-[x], 32 vii 8
Bu-[. . .], 41 ix 6
Bur-si EN.LU, 12 Inscription on Side D

Bur-zi-a: Pù-pù šu Bur-zi-a, 42 iv 7
Be-lí-lí DUMU Bur-zi-[a]?, 41 rev. ii 6
Bur-zum: Ti-ru-um DUMU Bur-zum GAL.SUKKAL DUMU.DUMU I-rí-iš-be-lí, 40 C xvii 21

Da-ba$_4$-la: Šu-Ma-ma DUMU Da-ba$_4$-la, 41 iv 12
Da-bí-bí šu Bí-za, 41 v 22
Da-da, 15 xiv 13
É-geštin-sir Da-d[a] Gu-ni-du dumu UD.MÁ.NINA.ŠUM-pa-⸢è⸣-[me], 22 ii 4, [32]
Da-da DUMU Ur-Már-da KA-Ma-ma DUMU DINGIR-GÀR 2 DUMU.DUMU Ur-Kèš^{KI} ši Dup-si-ga, 40 C x 12
UD.MÁ.NINA.ŠUM-pa-è dumu Da-da, 22 ii 41
Dam-ba-ba DUMU DINGIR-GÀR Sá-lim-a-ḫu DUMU Da-da 2 DUMU.DUMU Ra-bì-DINGIR, 40 C x 24
⸢GÌR?.BÀD⸣ DUMU Da-da, 48 rev. iii 5
Da-da-LUM: Mu-sa-ìr-su-nu DUMU Da-da-LUM DUB.SAR, 40 A xvi 6
Da-da-rí-im: GÁN šu ba-la-ag Da-da-rí-im, 38 i 9
Da-kum DUMU ARÁD-zu-ni, 40 A xvi 3
Da-núm DUMU Iš-kùn-DINGIR GAL.UKÙ, 40 A xiv 11
D[a]?-ti?, 15 xiv 30
Da-tum: DUMU.DUMU Da-tum include families of [X], Iš-má-DINGIR, I-ti-DINGIR, É-a-GÚ, ARÁD-zu-ni, Šu-AD.MU, I-da-tum, Su-ru-uš-GI, Zi-ra, and A-da-da, 40 D [i 1], iii 4, v 4
Ú-bí-bí šu Da-tum ⸢X⸣.GAL A-tum, 31 iv 4
Da-⸢x⸣-[. . .], 39 iii 2
Dam-ba-ba DUMU DINGIR-GÀR Sá-lim-a-ḫu DUMU Da-da 2 DUMU.DUMU Ra-bí-DINGIR, 40 C x 20
I-nin-me-šum DUMU Dam-ba-ba . . . DUMU.DUMU Ši-ù-ni, 40 A vii 18
Dam-ma DUMU A-pù-BÀD šu Ba-lu-lu, 41 iii 7; cf. also UD-ma
Dan-ì-li DUMU Ìr-e-^{d}Ma-lik ši MAŠKIM.GI$_4$, 40 A xiv 4
Dar-a-a, 38 rev. 2
DÉ.DÉ: Ìr-e-pum DUMU DINGIR-a-ḫa ši DÉ.DÉ . . . DUMU.DUMU Zi-im-tum, 40 B xi 3
Di-Utu, 21 iii 2
DUG.RU-ma-da-ág Di-Utu A-šu-El dumu Ba-ni-me, 22 iii 51
Ur-⸢^{d}Aš$_7$⸣-[gi$_4$-. . .] dumu Di-Utu, 33 rev. ii 9
Dingir-⸢azu⸣?-šè, 15 xiii 29
Dingir-gá-ab-⸢e⸣ arád Bíl-làl-la, App. to no. 32 vi 14
Dingir-pa-è dub-sar, 21 iii 4
DINGIR-. . ., see after Ì-lum-
D[u]-⸢ba?-ba?⸣ DAM Šu-Eš$_4$-dar LÚ Su$_4$-be-lí, 36 iii 7
Du-du, 48 iv 11
Du-d[u] engar, App. to nos. 22–23 viii 4
Du-du DUMU Tim-mu, 41 rev. ii 15
I-sa-ru-um DUMU Du-du, 52 rev. ii 4
Zu-zu ŠEŠ Du-du BÀD-ḪU.GAN?^{KI}, 41 vi 7, vii 5
DU$_6$.A, 33 rev. i 8
DUG.RU-ma-da-ág Di-Utu A-šu-El dumu Ba-ni-me, 22 iii 50
Dug?-[. . .], 22 iv 62
Dug$_4$-ga-ni, 23 [rev. iii 2], [rev. iii 29], [obv. iv 5], obv. iv 21
Dug$_4$-ga-ni TE.GAL UŠ-gal, 21 i 37
DUN-tur, 21 iii 35
Dup-si-ga, 37 R. E. 15
Dup-si-ga Šu-ì-li 2 DUMU GAL.ZU . . . 5 DUMU.DUMU MES-na-at, 40 C vi 9
Dup-si-ga DUMU I-ki-lum DUMU.DUMU Ur-nin, 40 C vi 17
Ma-la-ni-su [DU]MU Dup-si-ga [DU]MU.DUMU I-[k]i-lum [. . .]-a-a, 40 C vi 22
DUMU.DUMU Dup-si-ga ši PÙ.ŠA-ru-um NU.BANDA: lineage includes descendants of Ur-Kèš^{KI}, Gal-pum, and Ra-bí-DINGIR, 40 C x 1, 18, xi 24

E-bi-ir-ì-lum DUMU Iš-dup-^{d}EN.ZU . . . DUMU.DUMU Ìr-ra-ra, 40 A iii 7
E-bi-ir-mu-bí: Lam-gi-um DUMU E-bi-ir-mu-bí . . . DUMU.DUMU Su-mu-núm, 40 A iii 5
E-da-da NU.SAR GIŠ.SAR PAB.PAB, 38 ii 14
E-mi, 41 rev. vi 18
⸢E⸣-mi-^{d}EN.ZU, 28 ii; see also I-mi-^{d}EN.ZU
E-[. . .]-rí-⸢x⸣-[(. . .)]: [. . .] šu E-[. . .]-rí-⸢x⸣-[(. . .)], 42 iv 3
É-a [DUMU G]a-li-l⸢i⸣, 44k ii 10
É-a-a: [PN] Ì-lí-a-ḫi 2 DUMU A-ḫu-mu-bí DUMU.DUMU Iš-dup-DINGIR ši É-a-a, 40 C v 5
É-a-GÚ DUMU Iš-tu-tu . . . 4 DUMU.DUMU Da-tum, 40 D ii 11
É-a-ra-bí: Bí-su-šè-ib-nim É-a-ra-bí 2 DUMU A-ḫu-ḫu ši Al-lu-lu, 40 A xi 22
Pù-pù [DU]MU É-a-ra-bí . . . 4 DUMU.DUMU ši A-pù-lum, 40 D i 10
É-a-ra-bí šu Ku-ru-^{d}Irra$_x$(KIŠ)^{ra}, 41 rev. v 9
É-amar-si, 19a ii 6
É-Anzud$_x$(AN.MI.MUŠEN) engar, 15 i 26, ii 25, iii 23, iv 23, v 22, vi 28, vii 26, [ix 27], x 26, xiii 13, xiv 9, L. E. 7
É-barag-šu-du$_7$ ⸢dam⸣ Amar-tùr s[ag-du$_5$], 22 iv 4, 38
É-bí-[r]a?: PÙ.ŠA-A-a šu É-bí-[r]a?, 41 rev. vii 12
É-da-da: É-da-da Bíl-làl-la Ur-^{d}En-líl [dumu] Munsub$_x$, 32 ii 3
Su-mu-É-a É-da-da 2 DUMU PÙ.ŠA-Eš$_4$-dar DUMU.DUMU Gal-pum, 40 C xi 4
É-dam-si dumu Be-lí-iš-li, 32 rev. i 16
É-du-du, 33 rev. i 7
É-ga-lum DUMU Sa-NI, 40 A xi 19
É-GÁN, 15 vi 9, vii 11, 17
É-geštin-sir (or: É-geštin-sug$_4$) Da-d[a] Gu-ni-du dumu UD.MÁ.NINA.ŠUM-pa-⸢è⸣-[me], 22 ii 3, rev. [31]
Sag?-šu-du$_7$ dumu É-geštin-sir, 22 ii 39
É-gissu(GIŠ.MI)-bi, 33 iv 5
É-ib-zi: Ib-mud dumu Á-ni-kur-ra ⸢É⸣-ib-zi-ka, App. to nos. 22–23 i 5
Lugal-šà-pàd-da Lugal-⸢ù⸣-ma [d]umu É-[i]b-zi-me, App. to nos. 22–23 iii 11
É-igi-nim-pa-è GAR-en$_5$-si Adab^{KI}, App. to no. 32 viii 1
⸢É?.KI?.SÁR?.X⸣, 12 Inscription on Side A 4
É-ki-tuš: Igi-gùn dumu É-ki-tuš, 15 xii 13
É-ku-ku: PÙ.ŠA-Eš$_4$-dar É-ku-ku 2 DUMU Su-mu-GI DUMU.DUMU Gal-pum, 40 C x 8
É-kur-rí, 14 xv 17
É-Ma-ma, 14 xv 11

É-me-me šeš Bíl-làl-la sanga Kèš, App. to no. 32 iv 12
É-me-nam-nun [dumu Luga]l?-[z]i?-dè, 22 [ii 1], [27], 54
[Lu]gal-šà-pàd [dumu] É-me-nam-nun-ka, 22 ii 37
É-muš-si?, 20 vii 5
É-nam-zu-še GAL.UKÙ ìr é-šà-ga, 23 obv. x 5; App. to nos. 22–23 v 10
É-NI, 21 i 21
É-ní-íl: Ur-^{d}PA.BÌL.SAG DUMU É-ní-íl ENGAR LUGAL DUMU.DUMU Lugal-ezen, 40 C xvii 1
É-ní-nu-DU, 21 i 36
É-pirig-sír (or: É-nè-sug$_4$), 32 rev. i 12
É-sír-ág, 32 [v 15], [vi 2], [14], [vii 18], rev. ii 13, 15
Gu-ni-du [dumu É-sír-ág], 32 [vi 10]
A-[. . .] SAL.DI.UŠ É-sír-ág, 32 obv. vi 6
É-ti, 21 i 19
É-ti-la-dùg, 33 rev. iii 9
É.TÙR?.ḪÚB?, 12 Inscription on Side A 2
É-U+É-X, 15 ii 4
[É]-úr-bi-dùg!, 15 xiv 27
É-úr-bi-dùg šeš Bíl-làl-la sanga Kèš, App. to no. 32 iv 10
É-zi, 32 rev. i 9
É-zi engar, 14 vi 8
É-zi dumu TAR.ḪU, 22 [iii 11], 44
É-ZU.AB, 15 v 7
BU.TUŠ.ḪU-da dam É-ZU.AB, 15 v 30
⸢É⸣?-[. . .], 15 viii 19
È-[. . .], 52 rev. iii 2
È-du, 15 iv 14
Edin-ni-si: Ur-sag-ki-gal-la dumu Edin-ni-si, 15 i 17
Edin-ri, 14 viii 11, ix 3
Inim-ma-zi dumu Edin-ri, 14 ix 10
Ur-sag-Utu dumu Edin-ri, 14 ix 7
En-an-na-túm: Lum-ma-tur dumu En-an-na-túm en$_5$-si Lagaš^{KI}, 22 i 7, ii 9, [iii 15], [iv 19]; 23 [obv. i 9], [obv. ii 7], [obv. iii 11], [rev. iii 8], [obv. iv 30], obv. v 16, [rev. v 36], [rev. vi 21], [rev. vii 28]; App. to nos. 22–23 i 7
En-bu-DINGIR I-lib^{KI}, 41 rev. vii 7
En-bu-DINGIR DUMU Im$_4$-da-lik ši GAL.SUKKAL-li, 40 A xiii 17
En-bu-DINGIR šu NIN, 40 A ix 22
En-gil-sa: Uru-KA-gi-na DUMU En-gil-sa PA.TE.SI ŠIR.BUR.LA^{KI}, 40 A xiv 8
En-ḫé-gal, 12 Inscription on Side F
En-hé-gál lugal, 20 iii 5
En-ḫé-gál lugal Lagaš, 20 [i 6], ii 9, iv 9
^{d}En-ki: Su-mi-su DUMU Lu-zu-zum ši ^{d}En-ki, 40 B xiv 10
^{d}En-líl-IGI.SI.A [ŠE]Š PA.TE.SI, 30b i 2
En-na-É-a DUMU A-ḫa-ar-ši NAGAR, 40 B xiii 2
I-zi-núm En-na-É-a 2 DUMU Ur-sa(g)-núm DUMU.DUMU Ti-ti, 40 B ix 14
I-nin-sa-tu DUMU En-na-É-a DAM.GÀR, 40 B xiv 6
Ku-ku DUMU En-na-É-a DUMU.DUMU Zi-zi, 40 B vii 1
En-na-Il, 14 xvii 10
En-na-Il LUGAL Kiš, 26 ii 1
Men-mu DUMU En-na-Il, 37 rev. ii 18
En-na-núm AB+ÁŠ.URU BÀD-^{d}EN.ZU^{KI} DUMU I-mi-^{d}EN.ZU . . . DUMU.DUMU Ši-ù-ni, 40 A vi 11
Ì-lí-dan I-mi-^{d}EN.ZU 2 DUMU En-na-núm AB+ÁŠ.URU BÀD-^{d}EN.ZU^{KI} . . . DUMU.DUMU Ši-ù-ni, 40 A vii 10
Im$_4$-da-lik DUMU Ì-la-la MU ši En-na-núm AB+ÁŠ.URU BÀD-^{d}EN.ZU^{KI}, 40 A x 13
En-ra-rúm, 15 ii 14
⸢En-SAL⸣.UŠ.⸢DI-zi⸣: ⸢En-SAL⸣.UŠ.⸢DI-zi⸣ Inim-ma-ni-zi Nin-⸢kal-SI.A⸣ Lugal-⸢x⸣-ni-[x] Me-kisal-[si]? A-⸢. . .⸣ Lú-[. . .] dumu Amar-[tùr] sag-⸢du$_5$⸣, 22 [iv 9], 42
^{d}EN.ZU-a-ar DUMU A-ar-É-a . . . DUMU.DUMU Ši-ù-ni, 40 A vii 13
En-ZU.AB engar, 14 vi 7, xiv 16
^{d}EN.ZU-al-su DUMU A-ar-DINGIR ši Pù-ba-lum . . . DUMU.DUMU Ìr-ra-ra, 40 A iv 16
^{d}EN.ZU-GIŠ.ERÍN Ì-la-la Šu-ì-lí-su 3 DUMU Zu-zu ši A-ar-É-a, 40 A x 5
Engur-làl, 14 ii 16, iii 5
Engur-ušum, 14 x 12
Eš$_4$-dar-al-su DUMU Iš-tu-tu 4 DUMU.DUMU ši A-pù-lum, 40 D ii 1
Eš$_4$-dar-ra!, 38 ii 18
^{d}Ezínu(ŠE.TIR)-ur-sag, 33 rev. i 9

Ga-at-núm DUMU Ra-bí-DINGIR Ḫa-ar-ḫa-mu-na-ak^{KI}, 40 C xix 1
Ga-at-núm Su$_4$-ma-SIPA Be-lí-ba-ni 3 DUMU Ur-ZU.AB DUMU.DUMU DINGIR-su-la-ba, 40 C v 10
Ga-la-ab-É-a DUMU I-ši-me SIPA . . . DUMU.DUMU Zi-im-tum, 40 B xi 4
[G]a-li-l⸢i⸣: É-a [DUMU G]a-li-l⸢i⸣, 44k ii 11
Ga-lí-ì-li DUMU La-mu-sa GÚ.DU$_8$.A^{KI}, 40 A xiv 24
Ga-lí-su(wr. ZU)-ma DUMU Ur-é, 34 rev. i 3
[G]a-lí-tim: [Te-m]i-tum [DUMU.SAL? G]a-lí-tim, 44h i 6
Ga-NI-am-me-me: [Ì-l]í-dan [X]-tu-um [A-ḫ]u-ḫu [DUMU]? Ga-NI-am-me-me, 44a i 5
Ga-ra-az-ni-iš: [Sá]-lim-a-ḫu DUMU ši Ga-ra-az-ni-iš, 43 iii 12
Sá-lim-⸢a⸣-[ḫu] DUMU ši G[a]?!-ra-az-[ni-iš], 44c ii 2
Ga-zu-a-lum: A-ma-^{d}EN.ZU DUMU Ga-zu-a-lum ši Ì-lu-lu, 40 A v 4
Gal-pum, 33 ii 7
DINGIR-ba-ni NU.BANDA MÁ.GUR$_8$ DUMU Gal-pum . . . DUMU.DUMU Lugal-ezen, 40 C xv 25
DUMU.DUMU Gal-pum, of the lineage of Dup-si-ga ši PÙ.ŠA-ru-um, include families of I-ti-DINGIR, 40 C x 10, xi 6
GAL.SUKKAL-li: En-bu-DINGIR DUMU Im$_4$-da-lik ši GAL.SUKKAL-li, 40 A xiii 19
U-bi-in-LUGAL-rí DUMU Ur-ur ši GAL.SUKKAL-li, 40 A xv 7
GAL.ZU DUMU Ur-sag-UD.KIB.NUN^{KI} . . . 5 DUMU.DUMU MES-na-at, 40 C vi 6
Dup-si-ga Šu-ì-li 2 DUMU GAL.ZU . . . 5 DUMU.DUMU MES-na-at, 40 C vi 12

GAL.ZU-DI.TAR DUMU I-ti-DINGIR.DINGIR UD.KIB.NUN^{KI}, 40 A xiii 20
  Iš-dup-^{d}EN.ZU I-bí-^{d}EN.ZU 2 DUMU GAL.ZU-DI.TAR DUMU.DUMU Su-mu-núm, 40 A iv 2
GAL.ZU-DINGIR šu NIN SANGA ^{d}Lugal-Már-da . . . DUMU.DUMU SANGA, 40 C xiv 22
  DINGIR-GI DUMU GAL.ZU-DINGIR šu NIN SANGA ^{d}Lugal-Már-da . . . DUMU.DUMU I-rí-iš-be-lí, 40 C xvii 16
Gala, 14 vi 9
GAM.GAM, 14 xii 6
GÁN: A-li-li šu GÁN, 41 rev. viii 22
GÁN.DAR: PÙ.ŠA-DÙG(wr. UD) šu GÁN.DAR, 41 L. E. 14
Gi-ni-šè ì-du$_8$, 33 rev. iii 7
Gi-šum: A-ŠI-a-lí DUMU Gi-šum DUMU Be-lí-sa-tu PA.TE.SI Tu-tu-ub^{KI}, 44l i 3
⌜Gi-x⌝-ra: [PN DUMU] ⌜Gi-x⌝-ra ši A-a-BE, 42 iii 1
Gi$_4$-[. . .]: Ba-ša DUMU Gi$_4$-[. . .], 41 rev. ii 20
⌜GÌR?.BÀD⌝ DUMU Da-da, 48 rev. iii 3
GIŠ.BU, 14 iv 5
GIŠ.TUKUL-ga-su-al-si-in DUMU UD-ma, 40 A xiii 5
GIŠGAL-ir-nun Lum-ma-ki-gal-la dumu Ú-ti-me, 22 iii 47
Gu-da-ì-lí!, 33 iv 7
Gu-lí-zum: ARÁD-zu-ni DUMU Gu-lí-zum ši SAL.ANŠE, 40 B xii 15
  SI.A-um DUMU Gu-lí-zum . . . DUMU.DUMU Zi-im-tum, 40 B xi 10
  see also Gu-lí-zi under GNs
Gu-ni-du, 33 iv 6
  Gu-ni-du [dumu É-sír-ág], 32 vi 8
  É-geštin-sir Da-d[a] Gu-ni-du dumu UD.MÁ.NINA.ŠUM-pa-⌜è⌝-[me], 22 ii 5, [33]
  Lugal-Anzud$_x$(AN.IM.MI.MUŠEN) dumu Gu-ni-du, 22 ii 43
Gú-KALAM?, 20 iv 8

Ḫa-a[r?(-x)-m]u?: Šu-Eš$_4$-dar ù SI.A-um šu Ḫa-a[r?(-x)-m]u?, 41 rev. iii 9
Ḫa-da-bi: I-ti-DINGIR DUMU Ḫa-da-bi, 40 C xviii 20
Ḫa-la-[X]: Ù-[. . .] DUMU Ḫa-la-[X], 41 rev. ii 4
Ḫa-lum: A-ḫu-DÙG (var. A-ḫu-ḫu in B) DUMU Šu-Nu-nu ši Ḫa-lum, 40 A xv 16
Ḫa-X-da: Ì-lum-dan šu Ḫa-X-da, 41 L. E. 7
Ḫar-tu engar, 14 xiv 12
  Ḫar-tu dumu Pab-geštin, 14 vii 6
ḪAŠḪUR.LÀL, 11:15
Ḫu-bí-a: Na-ni šu Ḫu-bí-a DUB.SAR.GÁN, 41 iv 24, viii 21
ḪU.É?.⌜X⌝, 13 rev. ii 3
Ḫu-li-um DUMU I-bí-^{d}EN.ZU [D]UMU.DUMU [Ì]?-lu-lu, 41 rev. ix 16
⌜Ḫu⌝-[. . .] DUMU Ba-[. . .], 41 rev. ii 1
Ḫul-KAL-igi: Ušùr-r[a-ni]? Mes-ZU.A[B] Ur-^{d}Nin-Gír-su Tur-tur Úr-kug Ḫul-KAL-igi SAL-tur dumu ⌜X⌝-[x-m]e, 22 i 44
Ḫur-rúm, see GN Ḫur-rúm
Ḫur-sag, 14 xii 5

I-b[í]?-bí, 16f ii 2
  ⌜I⌝?-[bí-b]í?, 43 iv 16
  [I?-b]í?-bí [DUMU]? Ù-Ù, 44e i 1
  Ma-ma-ḪU DUMU I-bí-bí NU.BANDA Ša-na-e, 40 A xv 9
  Ma-šum šu I-bí-⌜bí⌝, 44e iii 4
I-bí-DINGIR, 16d A ii 5
I-bí-^{d}EN.ZU: Iš-dup-^{d}EN.ZU I-bí-^{d}EN.ZU 2 DUMU GAL.ZU-DI.TAR DUMU.DUMU Su-mu-núm, 40 A iv 1
  Ḫu-li-um DUMU I-bí-^{d}EN.ZU [D]UMU.DUMU [Ì]?-lu-lu, 41 rev. ix 17
I-bí-ì-lum: Im$_4$-da-lik DUMU I-bí-ì-lum šu MES.BAR^{KI} 2 DUB.SAR, 40 B xiv 18
I-bí-^{d}UTU [DUM]U Na-ni, 35 i 8
I-bí-ZU DUMU LUGAL, 41 ii 15
I-bí-ZU.AB DUMU Ur-mes-an-ni Ti-ru-um DUMU A-da-na-aḫ DUMU.DUMU I-ti-É-a, 40 C iv 2
I-b[í-. . .], 16b B ii 4
I-da-DINGIR DUMU A-bu-lum ši! Lu-ga-tim, 44l ii 2
  I-da-DINGIR DUMU I-ku-É-a KA-zu-ra-ak, 40 C xix 10
  I-da-DINGIR DUMU Ib-LUL-DINGIR DUMU.DUMU Nu-gal, 40 C xvii 27
  ^{d}Ma-lik-zi-in-su DUMU I-da-DINGIR GAL.SUKKAL, 40 A xi 10
  Na-mu-ru-um DUMU I-da-DINGIR . . . DUMU.DUMU Lugal-ezen, 40 C xv 27
I-da-tum Su-ru-uš-GI 2 DUMU DINGIR-su-GÀR . . . 5 DUMU.DUMU Da-tum, 40 D iv 11
I-dur-ma-at: PÙ.ŠA-^{d}IM DUMU I-dur-ma-at, 40 B xii 7
I-gu-ì-lí, 15 vi 19
I-GU-KU-DINGIR DUMU U$_9$-zi-um, 35 i 6
  Il-sù-LAK-647 I-KU-GU-Il Ur-^{d}DUB-an DUMU.DUMU Ur-PA, 37 iii 4
I-KA-lum, see I-pù-lum
I-ki-lum A-ḫu-ḫu 2 DUMU Iš-má-DINGIR . . . 5 DUMU. DUMU MES-na-at, 40 C vi 1
  Dup-si-ga DUMU I-ki-lum DUMU.DUMU Ur-nin, 40 C vi 18
  Ma-la-ni-su [DU]MU Dup-si-ga [DU]MU.DUMU I-[k]i-lum [. . .]-a-a, 40 C vi 23
  Ik-ru-ub-É-a DUMU I-ki-lum a-bi URU Elam^{KI}, 40 B xii 3
  Mi-su$_4$-a DUMU I-ki-lum NU.BANDA Eš$_4$-na-na-ak^{KI} . . . DUMU.DUMU SABRA, 40 C xv 13
  Zu-zu DUMU Ur-Már-da DUMU.DUMU I-ki-lum PA.TE.SI Ki-babbar^{KI}, 40 C iii 6
  Amar-rí-rí Be-lí-sa-tu 2 DUMU Zu-zu [DU]MU.DUMU Ur-[Má]r-da [ši I]-ki-lum, 40 C iv 14
I-ku-É-a: I-da-DINGIR DUMU I-ku-É-a KA-zu-ra-ak^{KI}, 40 C xix 11
I-KU-GU-Il, see I-GU-KU-DINGIR
I-ku-La-im: Ì-lu-lu Ma-z[u?-z]u 2 DUMU I-ku-La-im, 37 i 7
I-ku-tum DUMU Ú-ḫúb, 36 iv 7
I-kùn-núm šu LÚ, 41 vii 7
I-lu-lu, 48 v 18
  I-lu-[lu]? DUMU Ì-lí-⌜x⌝-[x] PA.TE.[SI], 35 rev. ii 14

Ì-lu-lu Ma-z[u?-z]u 2 DUMU I-ku-La-im, 37 i 4
Ì-lu-lu DUMU Ik-ru-ub-DINGIR ši A-gu-tim, 40 A xiv 21
[Ì]?-⸢lu-lu⸣ DUMU Pù-pù Kiš^{KI}, 34 i 10
DINGIR-a-ḫa DUMU Ì-lu-lu GAL.UKÙ . . . DUMU.DUMU Ìr-ra-ra, 40 A iv 8
DINGIR-ga-lí DUMU Ì-lu-lu DUMU.DUMU Ìr-am-^{d}Ma-lik, 40 D v 14
A-ma-^{d}EN.ZU DUMU Ga-zu-a-lum ši Ì-lu-lu, 40 A v 5
DUMU.DUMU [Ì]?-lu-lu include Iš-má-ì-lum, Bí-bí, Zi-ra, and Ḫu-li-um, 41 rev. ix 19
A-[. . .] DUMU I-lu-lu, 48 rev. iii 2
I-me-a: DINGIR-mu-da DUMU I-me-a . . . DUMU.DUMU Lugal-ezen, 40 C xvi 26
I-mi-DINGIR DUMU Pù-be-lí . . . DUMU.DUMU I-rí-iš-be-lí, 40 C xvii 13
⸢I⸣-mi-DINGIR [DUMU] Pù-^{d}Tišpak [š]i? Ù-su, 43 iv 12
A-bu-bu DUMU I-mi-DINGIR UGULA KA-zu-ra-ak^{KI} . . . DUMU.DUMU SANGA, 40 C xv 6
I-mi-^{d}EN.ZU: Ì-lí-dan I-mi-^{d}EN.ZU 2 DUMU En-na-núm AB+ÁŠ.URU BÀD-^{d}EN.ZU^{KI} . . . DUMU.DUMU Ši-ù-ni, 40 A vii 9
En-na-núm AB+ÁŠ.URU BÀD-^{d}EN.ZU^{KI} DUMU I-mi-^{d}EN.ZU . . . DUMU.DUMU Ši-ù-ni, 40 A vi 14
see also ⸢E⸣-mi-^{d}EN.ZU
I-mi-ì-lum: A-ša-su-GIŠ.ERÍN DUMU I-mi-ì-lum, 41 rev. vi 7
I-mu-mu: KIL-da-DINGIR DUMU I-mu-mu, 16d B ii 2
I-mu-tum, 38 ii 13
I-NI šu KI.LAM, 41 L. E. 8
I-nin-me-šum, 50 Side A iii 2
I-nin-me-šum DUMU Dam-ba-ba . . . DUMU.DUMU Ši-ù-ni, 40 A vii 17
I-nin-núm, 35 ii 10
I-nin-sa-tu DUMU En-na-É-a DAM.GÀR, 40 B xiv 5
I-nin-sa-tu šu Su$_{4}$-mu-É-a, 41 L. E. 10
Su$_{4}$-ma-SIPA DUMU I-nin-sa-tu . . . DUMU.DUMU Lugal-ezen, 40 C xvi 28
Innin-sar engar, 20 vi 4
INNIN.TAB.AMAR, 12 Inscription on Side D
INNIN?.ZI?, 13 ii 7
I-pù-lum DUMU DINGIR-su-ra-bí PA.TE.SI Ba-si-me^{KI}, 40 A xiv 14
Ib-ni-DINGIR DUMU I-KA(= pu$_{x}$)-lum, 36 iv 10
I-rí-iš-be-lí: DUMU.DUMU I-rí-iš-be-lí include families of Be-lí-sa-tu, Iš-LUL-DINGIR, I-mi-DINGIR, DINGIR-GI, and Ti-ru-um, 40 C xvii 23
I-rí-sum, 48 iv 12
I-sa-ru-um DUMU Du-du, 52 rev. ii 3
I-si-im-DINGIR DUMU Im-tum DUMU.DUMU Ur-Kèš^{KI}, 40 C xi 13
I-su-DINGIR: Im$_{4}$-da-lik DUMU I-su-DINGIR DUMU.DUMU A-ḫu-ḫu Da-mi-gi^{KI}, 40 A xv 22
I-ši-me: Ga-la-ab-É-a DUMU I-ši-me SIPA . . . DUMU.DUMU Zi-im-tum, 40 B xi 5
Ik-su-zi-na-at DUMU I-ši-me NU.BANDA AB+ÁŠ.AB+ÁŠ, 40 A xv 3
I-te-[. . .], 43 ix 8
I-ti-^{d}Da-gan: SI.A-um DUMU I-ti-^{d}Da-gan . . . DUMU.DUMU Lugal-ezen, 40 C xvi 7
I-ti-DINGIR: Iš-má-DINGIR I-ti-DINGIR DUB.SAR 2 DUMU DINGIR-GÀR . . . 4 DUMU.DUMU Da-tum, 40 D ii 7
I-ti-DINGIR DUMU DINGIR-su-GÀR . . . DUMU.DUMU Gal-pum, 40 C x 3
I-ti-DINGIR DUMU Ḫa-da-bi, 40 C xviii 19
I-ti-DINGIR DUMU La-mu-sa ši AGRIG . . . DUMU.DUMU Su-mu-núm, 40 A ii 15
Su-ru-uš-GI DUMU I-ti-DINGIR šu La-mu-sa ši AGRIG . . . DUMU.DUMU Su-mu-núm, 40 A iii 14
I-ti-DINGIR.DINGIR: GAL.ZU-DI.TAR DUMU I-ti-DINGIR.DINGIR UD.KIB.NUN^{KI}, 40 A xiii 21
I-ti-É-a DUMU Ur-Már-da DUMU.DUMU Ur-Kèš^{KI} ši Dup-si-ga, 40 C ix 22
DINGIR-nu-id DUMU I-ti-É-a DUMU.DUMU Ur-Már-da ši Ur-Kèš^{KI}, 40 C xi 9
I-bí-ZU.AB DUMU Ur-mes-an-ni Ti-ru-um DUMU A-da-na-aḫ DUMU.DUMU I-ti-É-a, 40 C iv 7
I-ti-Eš$_{4}$-dar: DINGIR-a-ḫa DUMU I-ti-Eš$_{4}$-dar DUMU.DUMU LÚ.IGI, 40 B vii 5
I-ti-ÍD: Ku-ku DUMU I-ti-ÍD, 41 rev. ii 18
I-ti-lum, 48 vi 15
I-ti-sum, 41 iv 4
Ì-lí-sar-ru DUMU I-ti-sum GÌR.NITA LÚ.GIŠ.GÍD.DA, 40 A xii 12
I-ti-ti: Na-bí-um DUMU I-ti-ti Da-mi-gi^{KI} in Dan-ni-rí-iš-tim, 40 A xvi 9
I-zi-ir-gul-la-zi-in DUMU Šu-ì-li SILÀ.ŠU.DU$_{8}$, 40 A xii 25
I-zi!-núm Iš-dup-Il PÙ.ŠA-sù-DÙG DUMU Su$_{4}$-ma-Ma-lik, 37 ii 1
I-zi-núm En-na-É-a 2 DUMU Ur-sa(g)-núm DUMU.DUMU Ti-ti, 40 B ix 13
⸢I-zu-GÍD⸣, 50 Side A ii 3
DINGIR-a-zu DUMU I-zu-GÍD PÙ.ŠA-Il-la DUMU Ur-^{d}Nin-kar 2 DUMU.DUMU A-pù-lum, 40 D v 9
⸢I⸣-[x]-lum-[x] DUMU ⸢X-x⸣, 30a iii 1
⸢I⸣?-⸢x⸣-[. . .], 30a i 2
Ì-a-ki-na-ni DAM Ur-^{d}Gú-gú DUMU Ur-túl-sag Pù-sa-an^{KI}, 37 R. E. 9
Ì-la-la: ^{d}EN.ZU-GIŠ.ERÍN Ì-la-la Šu-ì-lí-su 3 DUMU Zu-zu ši A-ar-É-a, 40 A x 6
Im$_{4}$-da-lik DUMU Ì-la-la MU ši En-na-núm AB+ÁŠ.URU BÀD-^{d}EN.ZU, 40 A x 11
Tu-tu DUMU Ì-la-la ŠEŠ Ra-bí-DINGIR . . . DUMU.DUMU Lugal-ezen, 40 C xvi 19
Ma-ma-ḫir-su DUMU Ra-bí-DINGIR ši Ì-la-la, 40 A xiii 14
Ì-la-lum, see GN gán É-Ì-la-lum
Ì-lí: Tu-tu DUMU Ì-lí . . . DUMU.DUMU Lugal-ezen, 40 C xvi 9
Ì-lí-a-ḫi DUMU DINGIR-a-ḫa, 40 A xvi 1
[PN] Ì-lí-a-ḫi 2 DUMU A-ḫu-mu-bí DUMU.DUMU Iš-dup-DINGIR ši É-a-a, 40 C v 2
Ì-lí-a-ḫi DUMU Ne-sag NU.BANDA . . . DUMU.DUMU Lugal-ezen, 40 C xv 18

Zi-gur-mu-bí DUMU Ì-lí-a-ḫi ši TE.LAL.GAL, 40 A xiii 10
Ì-lí-a-ḫi šu Bu-ḫu-lum, 41 v 12
Ì-lí-dan I-mi-^{d}EN.ZU 2 DUMU En-na-núm AB+ÁŠ. URU BÀD-^{d}EN.ZU^{KI} . . . DUMU.DUMU Ši-ù-ni, 40 A vii 8
[Ì-l]í-dan [X]-tu-um [A-ḫ]u-ḫu [DUMU]? Ga-NI-am-me-me, 44a i 2
Ì-lí-lí: Tu-li-id-da-nam DUMU Ì-lí-lí ši Mu-na, 40 A xvi 13
Ì-lí-sa-lik DUMU Im$_4$-da-lik . . . DUMU.DUMU Ši-ù-ni, 40 A vii 15
Ì-lí-sa-lik DUMU Šu-da-ti, 40 A xiv 27
Ì-lí-sar-ru DUMU I-ti-sum GÌR.NITA LÚ.GIŠ.GÍD.DA, 40 A xii 11
[Ì-lí⸣-TAB.BA, 43 i 13
Ì-lí-⸢x⸣-[x]: I-lu-[lu]? DUMU Ì-lí-⸢x⸣-[x] PA.TE.[SI], 35 ii 15
Ì-lu-lu, see I-lu-lu
Ì-lum-A.ZU: Šu-pù-la Ì-lum-A.ZU Iš-má-ì-lum AB+ÁŠ. AB+ÁŠ šu URU^{KI}.URU^{KI}, 41 vii 13
Ì-lum-dan šu Ḫa-X-da, 41 L. E. 6
Ì-lum-GÀR 35 i 3
Ì-lum-GÀR šu La-ba-Ù, 41 rev. vi 20, viii 13
Ì-lum-GIŠ.ERÍN [šu K]u?-ru, 41 ii 19
Ì-lum-GIŠ.ERÍN šu Ku?-ru, 41 iv 9
Ì-lum-sar: A-ḫu-DÙG DUMU Ì-lum-sar šu PA.TE.SI, 41 iii 20
Ì-l[um]?-[. . .], 16f ii 1
DINGIR-a-ḫa DUMU Be-lí-GÚ NU.BANDA . . . DUMU. DUMU Ur-Ab-ra ši Su$_4$-a-tum-mu-da, 40 C xviii 1
DINGIR-a-ḫa DUMU I-ti-Eš$_4$-dar DUMU.DUMU LÚ.IGI, 40 B vii 4
DINGIR-a-ḫa DUMU Ì-lu-lu GAL.UKÙ . . . DUMU. DUMU Ìr-ra-ra, 40 A iv 7
DINGIR-a-ḫa DUMU Su$_4$-ma-ba-ni UGULA . . . DUMU.DUMU Zi-im-tum, 40 B x 3
DINGIR-a-ḫa šu Bi-e-tim . . . DUMU.DUMU Zi-im-tum, 40 B x 13
Ì-lí-a-ḫi DUMU DINGIR-a-ḫa, 40 A xvi 2
Ìr-e-pum DUMU DINGIR-a-ḫa ši DÉ.DÉ . . . DUMU. DUMU Zi-im-tum, 40 B xi 2
DINGIR-a-zu DUMU A-ŠI-gu-ru-ud attached to the lineage of Me-zi-zi, 40 A v 6
DINGIR-a-zu DUMU I-zu-GÍD PÙ.ŠA-Il-la DUMU Ur-^{d}Nin-kar 2 DUMU.DUMU A-pù-lum, 40 D v 8
PÙ.ŠA-Lu-lu DUMU DINGIR-a-zu DI.TAR . . . DUMU.DUMU SANGA, 40 C xiv 20
DINGIR-ba-na AB+ÁŠ.URU DUMU Šà-gú-ba . . . DUMU.DUMU SANGA, 40 C xiv 26
DINGIR-ba-ni DUMU A-ḫu-ba-lik DUMU.DUMU Zi-im-tum, 40 B xi 11
DINGIR-ba-ni NU.BANDA MÁ.GUR$_8$ DUMU Gal-pum . . . DUMU.DUMU Lugal-ezen, 40 C xv 23
DINGIR-ba-ni DUMU Mi-su$_4$-a . . . DUMU.DUMU Lugal-ezen, 40 C xvi 4
DINGIR-ba-ni DUMU Ra-bí-DINGIR ši La-mu-um SANGA ^{d}Za-ba$_4$-ba$_4$, 40 A viii 17
DINGIR-dan: Šu-Nu-nu DUMU DINGIR-dan SANGA ^{d}A-ba$_4$ I-bí-rí^{KI}, 40 A xv 18
Zi-ra DUMU DINGIR-dan . . . 5 DUMU.DUMU Da-tum, 40 D v 1
DINGIR-en-ni, 15 xii 23, xiii 2
DINGIR-ga-lí DUMU Ì-lu-lu DUMU.DUMU Ìr-am-^{d}Ma-lik, 40 D v 13
DINGIR-GÀR DUMU Ti-li-lum . . . DUMU.DUMU Lugal-ezen, 40 C xvi 21
Da-da DUMU Ur-Már-da KA-Ma-ma DUMU DINGIR-GÀR 2 DUMU.DUMU Ur-Kèš^{KI} ši Dup-si-ga, 40 C x 16
Dam-ba-ba DUMU DINGIR-GÀR Sá-lim-a-ḫu DUMU Da-da 2 DUMU.DUMU Ra-bí-DINGIR, 40 C x 21
Iš-má-DINGIR I-ti-DINGIR DUB.SAR 2 DUMU DINGIR-GÀR . . . 4 DUMU.DUMU Da-tum, 40 D ii 9
GÁN šu DINGIR-GÀR [ši]? ⸢Bu-la⸣-la, 43 iii 15
DINGIR-GI DUMU GAL.ZU-DINGIR šu NIN SANGA ^{d}Lugal-Már-da . . . DUMU.DUMU I-rí-iš-be-lí, 40 C xvii 15
DINGIR-GÚ DUMU Su-mu-^{d}EN.ZU . . . DUMU.DUMU Lugal-ezen, 40 C xv 28
DINGIR-IGI.D[U] SABRA.É, 44i 7
DINGIR-mu-da DUMU I-me-a . . . DUMU.DUMU Lugal-ezen, 40 C xvi 25
Ti-da-nu DUMU DINGIR-mu-da DUMU.DUMU Ur-^{d}SI.LU, 40 B vi 7
DINGIR-nu-id DUMU I-ti-É-a DUMU.DUMU Ur-Már-da ši Ur-Kèš^{KI}, 40 C xi 8
Dingir-nu-me-a: PÙ.ŠA-^{d}Nu-muš-da šu Dingir-nu-me-a . . . DUMU.DUMU Zi-im-tum, 40 B x 18
DINGIR-ra-⸢bí⸣, 43 vii 20
DINGIR-su-a-ḫa: Ra-bí-DINGIR DUMU DINGIR-su-a-ḫa KA-ul-lum^{KI}, 40 C xix 8
DINGIR-su-GÀR: I-da-tum Su-ru-uš-GI 2 DUMU DINGIR-su-GÀR . . . 5 DUMU.DUMU Da-tum, 40 D iv 13
I-ti-DINGIR DUMU DINGIR-su-GÀR . . . DUMU. DUMU Gal-pum, 40 C x 4
DINGIR-su-la-ba: DUMU.DUMU DINGIR-su-la-ba include the families of Ra-bí-DINGIR, Ga-at-núm, Su$_4$-ma-SIPA, and Be-lí-ba-ni, 40 C v 16
DINGIR-su-ra-bí DUMU Ìr-ra-⸢Il⸣?, 49 ii 2
I-pù-lum DUMU DINGIR-su-ra-bí PA.TE.SI Ba-si-me^{KI}, 40 A xiv 15
DINGIR-su-su DUMU Mu-mu ŠU.I ši Al-lu-lu, 40 A xii 15
DIN[GIR-. . .], 52 rev. iii 4
Ì-ši-ši: Ù-na-gàr DUMU Ì-ši-ši NU.BANDA Ša-na-e, 40 A xiv 2
Ib-bu-bu DUMU A-mur-rúm . . . DUMU.DUMU A-nu-nu, 41 i 11
Ib-bu-bu LÚ Kag-gú-tum, 48 rev. iii 6
Su-mu-GI U-li-id-ì-lum 2 DUMU BÀD-Il DUMU. DUMU Ib-bu-bu, 40 B vi 1
Ib-bu-ru: Zi-ra DUMU Ib-bu-ru, 41 rev. ix 15
Ib-la-NI-⸢x⸣: Tu-tu šu Ib-la-NI-⸢x⸣, 43 ix 7
[I]b?-lu-DINGIR, 35 i 15
Ib-LUL-DINGIR DUB.SAR DUMU Nu-gal . . . DUMU. DUMU A-ku-ì-lum, 40 C xiv 6

I-da-DINGIR DUMU Ib-LUL-DINGIR DUMU.DUMU Nu-gal, 40 C xvii 28
Ib-LUL-Ịl: Pù-šu-tum DUMU Ib-LUL-Il!, 31 iii 4
Ib-mud dumu Á-ni-kur-ra ⸢É⸣-ib-zi-ka, App. to nos. 22–23 i 3, iii 7, v 5
Ib-ni-DINGIR DUMU I-KA-lum, 36 iv 9
Ig-[. . .], 45 i 8
Igi-gùn, 15 ii 11, vi 10, viii 22, xiv 18
Igi-gùn dumu É-ki-tuš, 15 xii 11
IGI.RU?.NUN ÉŠ.A dumu Me-si pab-šeš É-nun, 12 Adscription to Side C
IGI.SI$_4$, 48 iv 16
IGI.SI$_4$ ŠEG$_9$-da^{KI}, 41 viii 4
IGI.UR, 15 vii 16
IGI.ZA, 14 xv 19
Igi-zi-barag-gi Ur-^{d}Nin-PA Ur-^{d}GUR$_8$-⸢x⸣ Barag-ga-[ni] dumu In[im-ma]-ni-[zi-me], 22 iv 57
Ik-ru-ub-DINGIR DUMU PÙ.ŠA-su . . . DUMU.DUMU Lugal-ezen, 40 C xvi 23
A-nu-zu DUMU Ik-ru-ub-DINGIR, 40 C xviii 16
Ì-lu-lu DUMU Ik-ru-ub-DINGIR ši A-gu-tim, 40 A xiv 22
Ik-ru-ub-É-a DUMU I-ki-lum a-bi URU Elam^{KI}, 40 B xii 2
Iš-má-DINGIR DUMU Ik-ru-ub-É-a, 40 C xviii 18
Ik-su-zi-na-at DUMU I-ši-me NU.BANDA AB+ÁŠ.AB+ÁŠ, 40 A xv 2
Il-GIŠ.ERÍN LÚ GÁN, 34 ii 9
Il-su(wr. zu)-ERÍN+X: Zu-zu Ra-bí-ì-lum DUMU.DUMU Il-su(wr. zu)-ERÍN+X PA.TE.SI, 34 iv 10
⸢Il⸣-su-ra-b[í], 30a vii 3
Il-sù-LAK-647 I-KU-GU-Il Ur-^{d}DUB-an DUMU.DUMU Ur-PA, 37 iii 3
Íl-li-l[i]? SANGA, 48 rev. iii 11
^{d}IM-[G]Ú?.GAL, 36 iv 15
Im-li[k?-X], 16b B ii 3
Im-ta-è-e, 14 vi 3
Im-ta-kas$_4$-e nagar arád Bíl-làl-la, App. to no. 32 vi 8
Im-tum: I-si-im-DINGIR DUMU Im-tum DUMU.DUMU Ur-Kèš^{KI}, 40 C xi 14
Im$_4$-da-lik DUMU I-bí-ì-lum šu MES.BAR^{KI} 2 DUB.SAR, 40 B xiv 17
Im$_4$-da-lik DUMU I-su-DINGIR DUMU.DUMU A-ḫu-ḫu Da-mi-gi^{KI}, 40 A xv 21
Im$_4$-da-lik DUMU Ì-la-la MU ši En-an-núm AB+ÁŠ.URU BÀD-^{d}EN.ZU^{KI}, 40 A x 10
Im$_4$-da-lik DUMU Ur-nin Kiš^{KI}, 40 A x 2
En-bu-DINGIR DUMU Im$_4$-da-lik ši GAL.SUKKAL-li, 40 A xiii 18
Ì-lí-sa-lik DUMU Im$_4$-da-lik . . . DUMU.DUMU Ši-ù-ni, 40 A vii 16
In-su-mi-su-da-nu DUMU Iš-a-lum ši TE.LAL.GAL, 40 A xi 25
[In?-zi?-b]a-nim, 44l i 1
Inim-ma-ni?-⸢zi⸣?, 26 i 12
[In]im-ma-⸢ni⸣-zi, 23 [obv. vii 33], [obv. viii 14], obv. ix 8
⸢En-SAL⸣.UŠ.⸢DI-zi⸣ Inim-ma-ni-zi Nin-⸢kal-SI.A⸣ Lugal-⸢x⸣-ni-[x] Me-kisal-[si]? A-⸢. . .⸣ Lú-[. . .] dumu Amar-[tùr] sag-⸢du$_5$⸣, 22 [iv 10], 43
Igi-zi-barag-gi Ur-^{d}Nin-PA Ur-^{d}GUR$_8$-⸢x⸣, Barag-ga-[ni] dumu In[im-ma]-ni-[zi-me], 22 iv 61
Nin-uru-ni-šè-ḫi-li dam Inim-ma-ni-zi, 22 iv 55
Inim-ma-zi dumu Edin-ri, 14 ix 8
Innin-. . . , see I-nin-
Iq-bí-GI Al-la 2 DUMU Ab-ra-Il DUMU.DUMU Iš-dup-BE . . . 3 DUMU.DUMU Ab-ra-Il, 40 B iii 6
Iq-bí-GI DUMU Be-lí-GÚ NU.BANDA LÚ.IGI . . . DUMU.DUMU Nu-gal, 40 C xvii 24
Ìr-a-mu: Pù-su-GI SAG.DU$_5$ DUMU Ìr-a-mu DUMU.DUMU Ab-ra-Il 3 DUMU.DUMU Ab-ra-Il . . . DUMU.DUMU Iš-dup-BE, 40 B v 2
Ìr-am-^{d}Ma-lik: DINGIR-ga-lí DUMU Ì-lu-lu DUMU.DUMU Ìr-am-^{d}Ma-lik, 40 D v 15
PÙ.ŠA-^{d}Za-ba$_4$-ba$_4$ DUMU Mu-mu DUMU.DUMU Ìr-am-^{d}Ma-lik, 40 D iii 8
Ìr-da-pu[m], 41 viii 2
Ìr-DU?-[. . .], 16c A ii 2
Ìr-e-^{d}Ma-lik: Dan-ì-li DUMU Ìr-e-^{d}Ma-lik ši MAŠKIM.GI$_4$, 40 A xiv 5
Ìr-e-pum DUMU DINGIR-a-ḫa ši DÉ.DÉ . . . DUMU.DUMU Zi-im-tum, 40 B xi 1
Zu-zu Ìr-e-pum 2 DUMU Iš-má-DINGIR ši NIGIR DUMU.DUMU Ur-ur ši PA.ḪI, 40 C xii 25
Ìr-ì-pum [šu] Pù-šu-tum, 31 iii 12
[Ìr]-⸢e⸣-um, 43 vi 14
Ìr-e-um DUMU Iš-má-DINGIR ši Za-ab-tim, 43 vii 17
⸢We⸣-tum DUMU ši Ìr-e-um, 44k ii 3
[Ì]r-e-um [š]u? Ma-ga-ga [š]i TE.LAL, 44i 2
Ìr-ì-pum, see Ìr-e-pum
Ìr-ra-⸢Il⸣?: DINGIR-su-ra-bí DUMU Ìr-ra-⸢Il⸣?, 49 ii 3
Ìr-ra-ra: DUMU.DUMU Ìr-ra-ra, of the lineage of Me-zi-zi, include families of ^{d}EN.ZU-al-su, UD.IŠ, Zu-zu, and E-bi-ir-ì-lum, 40 A v 2
Ìr-ru-zum: U-bìl-ga-zu DUMU Ìr-ru-zum LÚ.IGI, 40 A xiii 24
Isin$_x$(IN)^{KI}-dùg, 14 ii 15, xvii 9
Iš-a-lum: In-su-mi-su-da-nu DUMU Iš-a-lum ši TE.LAL.GAL, 40 A xii 1
Iš-dup-BE: DUMU.DUMU Iš-dup-BE include the families of Iq-bí-GI, Al-la, and Pù-su-GI, 40 B iv 5
Iš-dup-DINGIR DUMU Amar-rí-rí DUMU.DUMU SANGA, 40 C xv 8
[PN] Ì-lí-a-ḫi 2 DUMU A-ḫu-mu-bí DUMU.DUMU Iš-dup-DINGIR ši É-a-a, 40 C v 4
ARÁD-zu-ni DUMU Iš-dup-DINGIR . . . DUMU.DUMU Ši-ù-ni, 40 A vi 21
Iš-LUL-DINGIR DUMU Iš-dup-DINGIR . . . DUMU.DUMU I-rí-iš-be-lí, 40 C xvii 12
Mi-it-lik DUMU Iš-dup-DINGIR NU.BANDA . . . DUMU.DUMU Lugal-ezen, 40 C xvi 2
Iš-dup-DINGIR.DINGIR: Ra-bí-ì-lum DUMU Iš-dup-DINGIR.DINGIR, 37 iv 13
Iš-dup-^{d}EN.ZU I-bí-^{d}EN.ZU 2 DUMU GAL.ZU-DI.TAR DUMU.DUMU Su-mu-núm, 40 A iii 17
E-bi-ir-ì-lum DUMU Iš-dup-^{d}EN.ZU . . . DUMU.DUMU Ìr-ra-ra, 40 A iii 8
Lugal-ezen UGULA DUMU Iš-dup-^{d}EN.ZU . . . DUMU.DUMU Zi-im-tum, 40 B x 8

UD.IŠ Zu-zu 2 DUMU Iš-dup-^{d}EN.ZU DUMU.DUMU Ìr-ra-ra, 40 A v 1
Iš-dup-Il, 14 i 14
Iš-dup-Il DUMU Ma-la-ni-su . . . DUMU.DUMU A-nu-nu, 41 i 9
I-zi!-núm Iš-dup-Il PÙ.ŠA-sù-DÙG DUMU Su$_4$-ma-Ma-lik, 37 ii 2
Iš-dup-pum: ARÁD-zu-ni DUMU Iš-dup-pum DUMU. DUMU Ši-na-na-tim, 40 B vii 9
Iš-gu-[núm]?: Be-lí-mu-[da] šu Iš-gu-[núm]?, 44d ii 2
Iš-kùn-DINGIR: Da-núm DUMU Iš-kùn-DINGIR GAL. UKÙ, 40 A xiv 12
Iš-lam-G[I]?, 44l ii 7
A-bí-ra šu Iš-lam-GI, 41 rev. iv 13
Iš-LUL-DINGIR DUMU Iš-dup-DINGIR . . . DUMU. DUMU I-rí-iš-be-lí, 40 C xvii 11
Iš-má-DINGIR DUMU Ik-ru-ub-É-a, 40 C xviii 17
Iš-má-DINGIR I-ti-DINGIR DUB.SAR 2 DUMU DINGIR-GÀR . . . 4 DUMU.DUMU Da-tum, 40 D ii 5
I-ki-lum A-ḫu-ḫu 2 DUMU Iš-má-DINGIR . . . 5 DUMU.DUMU MES-na-at, 40 C vi 4
Ìr-e-um DUMU Iš-má-DINGIR ši Za-ab-tim, 43 vii 17
Zu-zu Ìr-e-pum 2 DUMU Iš-má-DINGIR ši NIGIR DUMU.DUMU Ur-ur ši PA.ḪI, 40 C xii 26
[Iš-má]-DINGIR [šu Za-a]b-tim, 43 vi 12
Iš-má-GÁR: La-lí DUMU Iš-má-GÁR ši Ar-rí-im, 40 A xiv 19
Iš-má-ì-lum KUG.GÁL, 41 rev. ix 10
Šu-pù-la Ì-lum-A.ZU Iš-má-ì-lum AB+ÁŠ.AB+ÁŠ šu URU^{KI}.URU^{KI}, 41 vii 14
Iš-má-ì-lum šu LÚ.KAS$_4$, 41 ii 11
Iš-me-ì-lum engar, 15 i 24, ii 23, iii 21, iv 21, v 20, vi 26, vii 24, ix 25, xiii 11, xiv 7, L. E. 5
Iš-tu-tu: É-a-GÚ DUMU Iš-tu-tu . . . 4 DUMU.DUMU Da-tum, 40 D ii 12
Eš$_4$-dar-al-su DUMU Iš-tu-tu 4 DUMU.DUMU ši A-pù-lum, 40 D ii 2
Iš-[. . .] DUMU Ti-ti šu ^{d}ÁŠ?.TE?, 31 ii 2

KA-ba-ni-maḫ um-mi-a, App. to no. 32 ix 1
KA-GÍR-gal, 11:6
KA+IM-t[i]?: Ú-ti KA+IM-t[i]? dumu Mu-ni-kalam-m[a-m]e, 22 iii 7, 40
KA-KA: Šu-Eš$_4$-dar DUMU ME-Sá-lim DUMU.DUMU KA-KA, 40 D v 7
KA-ki-bi-šè, 32 iv 4
KA-Ma-ma: Da-da DUMU Ur-Már-da KA-Ma-ma DUMU DINGIR-GÀR 2 DUMU.DUMU Ur-Kèš^{KI} ši Dup-si-ga, 40 C x 15
PÙ.ŠA-Eš$_4$-dar DUMU KA-Ma-ma, 40 C xviii 22
KA-Me-ir, 38 ii 8; 50 Side A ii 2
A-da-da DUMU ^{d}KA-Me-ir . . . 5 DUMU.DUMU Da-tum, 40 D v 3
KA$_5$.A: [W]u-zum-tum SAL.BALAG.DI KA$_5$.A, 43 x 8
Kag-gú-tum, 48 rev. iii 7
Kar-ki-rúm, 35 ii 7
Kèš-pa-è arád Bíl-làl-la, App. to no. 32 vi 13
KI.LAM: I-NI šu KI.LAM, 41 L. E. 9
Ki-lí-lí, 15 iii 13
KI.⌜NA⌝?.LUGAL.ŠIR.UR?, 13 rev. i 4
Ki-ti-ti: U-za-si-na-at DUMU Ki-ti-ti, 40 A xiii 4
KIL-da-DINGIR DUMU I-mu-mu, 16d B ii 1
Ku-ku DUMU En-na-É-a DUMU.DUMU Zi-zi, 40 B vi 10
Ku-ku DUMU I-ti-ÍD, 41 rev. ii 17
Ba-ša DUMU Ku-ku PAB.ŠEŠ, 41 rev. ii 10
DUMU.DUMU Ku-ku, 40 D vi 5
[K]u?-ru: Ì-lum-GIŠ.ERÍN [šu K]u?-ru, 41 ii 20
Ì-lum-GIŠ.ERÍN šu Ku?-ru, 41 iv 10
Ku-ru-^{d}Irra$_x$(KIŠ)^{ra}: É-a-ra-bí šu Ku-ru-^{d}Irra$_x$(KIŠ)^{ra}, 41 rev. v 10
KUG.DÍM: Li-sa-núm DUMU Ur-AN.KI šu KUG.DÍM, 40 C xviii 10
Kum-tuš-šè, 14 i 12; 15 xiii 3; 33 rev. iii 4
Kun?-LAGAB?: Nin-SAL-zi dumu Kun?-LAGAB?, 14 xi 6
Kun?-si, 15 L. E. 12
Kur-mu-gam, 33 rev. i 5
KURUŠDA: Zu-zu DUB.SAR šu KURUŠDA DUMU La-mu-um, 40 A xi 4

La-a-GUR DUMU Rí-pum ši Wa-gi-rí, 40 B xiii 5
La-ba-Ù: A-mu-[. . .] šu La-ba-Ù, 41 rev. vii 4
Ì-lum-GÀR šu La-ba-Ù, 41 rev. vi 21, viii 14
La-ga-tum sagi, 33 rev. iii 5
La-gi-pum DUMU ARÁD-zu-ni, 40 B xiii 11
La-gi-pum DUMU Pù-pù ši ŠU.I, 40 B xiii 13
La-gi-um, 48 vii 9
La-lí DUMU Iš-má-GÁR ši Ar-rí-im, 40 A xiv 18
La-lí arád Bíl-làl-la, App. to no 32 vi 7
La-mu-sa: Ga-lí-ì-li DUMU La-mu-sa GÚ.DU$_8$.A^{KI}, 40 A xiv 25
SI.A-um DUMU La-mu-sa ši AGRIG . . . DUMU. DUMU Su-mu-núm, 40 A iv 11
I-ti-DINGIR DUMU La-mu-sa ši AGRIG . . . DUMU. DUMU Su-mu-núm, 40 A ii 16
Su-ru-uš-GI DUMU I-ti-DINGIR šu La-mu-sa ši AGRIG . . . DUMU.DUMU Su-mu-núm, 40 A iii 15
La-mu-um, 40 A ix 15
ARÁD-zu-ni DUMU La-mu-um 4 DUMU.DUMU Da-tum, 40 D iii 3
Šu-AD.MU DUMU La-mu-um . . . 5 DUMU.DUMU Da-tum, 40 D iv 10
Zu-zu DUB.SAR šu KURUŠDA DUMU La-mu-um, 40 A xi 5
DINGIR-ba-ni DUMU Ra-bí-DINGIR ši La-mu-um SANGA ^{d}Za-ba$_4$-ba$_4$, 40 A viii 19
DUMU.DUMU La-mu-um SANGA ^{d}Za-ba$_4$-ba$_4$ include descendants of Ra-bí-DINGIR and Ur-^{d}Nin-kar, 40 A ix 7
Lagaš^{KI} nigir, 21 iii 6
LÁL.È, 21 i 32
Làl-ad-da-na, 15 i 9
Làl-la: Làl-la dam Bíl-làl-la, App. to no. 32 iii 11
Làl-la dam Bíl-làl-la sanga Kèš, App. to no. 32 vi 1
Làl?-li-l[i]? Barag-ul-tu dumu Ur-^{d}Dumu-zi-da-me, 22 iv 52
Lam-gi-um DUMU E-bi-ir-mu-bí . . . DUMU.DUMU Su-mu-núm, 40 A iii 4

Li-gi-i[m]?: Ra-bí-ì-lum DUMU Li-gi-i[m]?, 41 rev. ii 8
Ra-b[í-ì?-lum?] šu Li-[gi?-im?], 41 rev. i 3
Li-mu-[um]?, 44d ii 6
Li-sa-núm DUMU Ur-AN.KI šu KUG.DÍM, 40 C xviii 8
Lu-da-na-at: Su-mi-su DUMU Lu-da-na-at SIPA, 40 B xiii 9
Lu-ga-tim: I-da-DINGIR DUMU A-bu-lum ši! Lu-ga-tim, 44l ii 4
Lu-lu sanga, 19a rev. i 1
Lu-zu-zum: Su-mi-su DUMU Lu-zu-zum ši ^{d}En-ki, 40 B xiv 9
LÚ, 16d A iii 3
I-kùn-núm šu LÚ, 41 vii 8
Lú-barag-si, 14 iv 7, v 6, vi 2
Lú-dingir-mu, 14 vi 5
Šeš-GÍR-*gunû*-gal dumu Lú-dingir-mu, 14 vii 11
Lú-[^{d}]En-⸢líl⸣?, 48 vi 8
LÚ.IGI: DINGIR-a-ḫa DUMU I-ti-Eš$_4$-dar DUMU.DUMU LÚ.IGI, 40 B vii 6
LÚ.KAS$_4$: Iš-má-ì-lum šu LÚ.KAS$_4$, 41 ii 12
Lú-lum-ma, 32 v 9; 33 i 6
Lú-pàd sag-du$_5$ Umma^{KI}, 21 ii 3
Lú-pàd sag-du$_5$ Umma^{KI} dumu Na-dù sag-du$_5$, 21 i 1
Lú-^{d}⸢X⸣-da, 48 v 17
⸢Lú⸣?-⸢x⸣-nàd-a, 30a vi 8
Lú-[. . .]: ⸢En-SAL⸣.UŠ.⸢DI-zi⸣ Inim-ma-ni-zi Nin-⸢kal-SI.A⸣ Lugal-⸢x⸣-ni-[x] Me-kisal-[si]? A-⸢. . .⸣ Lú-[. . .] dumu Amar-[tùr] sag-⸢du$_5$⸣, 22 [iv 15], 48
Lugal-a-mu, 33 ii 8
Lugal-á-zi-da, 14 xv 5
Lugal-Anzud$_x$(AN.IM.MI.MUŠEN) dumu Gu-ni-du, 22 ii 42
Lugal-barag-ga-ni-dùg nu-banda é Lum-ma-tur-ka, App. to nos. 22–23 x 1
Lugal-bí-túm, 15 ii 12, 16, vi 18
Lugal-da-gur-ra, 14 xvii 4, xviii 1, 10, 16; 15 L. E. 24
Lugal-[é]?-mes-[lam]?, 21 vi 6
Lugal-^{d}En-líl lú-u$_5$ Akšak^{KI}, App. to nos. 22–23 vi 7
Lugal-ezen(sic), 14 xv 12
Lugal-ezen engar, 15 i 23, ii 22, iii 20, iv 20, v 19, vi 25, vii 23, ix 24, xiii 10, xiv 6, L. E. 4
Lugal-ezen dumu Bíl-làl-la, App. to no. 32 iv 4
Lugal-ezen UGULA DUMU Iš-dup-^{d}EN.ZU . . . DUMU.DUMU Zi-im-tum, 40 B x 6
Maš-lugal dumu Lugal-ezen, 14 iii 8
PÙ.ŠA-PAB.PAB DUMU Lugal-ezen . . . DUMU.DUMU Ur-^{d}SI.LU, 40 B vi 4
DUMU.DUMU Lugal-ezen include families of Ì-lí-a-ḫi, Ma-an-sa-ki-su, DINGIR-ba-ni, Na-mu-ru-um, DINGIR-GÚ, Mi-it-lik, SI.A-um, Tu-tu, A-ku-É-a, Ur-^{d}EN.ZU, Ur-En-gal-DU.DU, DINGIR-GÀR, Ik-ru-ub-DINGIR, DINGIR-mu-da-, Su$_4$-ma-SIPA, Ur-^{d}PA.BÌL.SAG, and A-ḫu-GIŠ.ERÍN, 40 C xvii 5
Lugal-gal-zu, 15 x 6, xi 7; 32 iv 6
Lugal-GÁR.KAG: Nam-maḫ dumu Lugal-GÁR.KAG, 14 xi 1
Lugal-geštúg-gíd, 14 ii 14
Lugal-Giríd$^{K[I]}$ [. . .], 21 iii 8
Lugal-ḫé-gál-sir dub-sar-maḫ, 23 obv. x 3; App. to nos. 22–23 v 8
Lugal-i-mu engar, 14 xiv 15
Lugal-kar-si, 14 xvi 13
Lugal-ki, 20 iv 5
Lugal-ki-gal-la išib ^{d}Nin-Gír-su, 20 rev. ii 1
Lugal-ki-ni, 14 xiv 6
Lugal-ku-li: Ur-^{d}MUŠ DUMU Lugal-ku-li, 40 A xiii 8
Lugal-kur-da-kúš, 32 rev. i 11
Lugal-maš-usu(Á.KAL), 14 xvi 12
Lugal-mu-da-kúš ugula-é, App. to no. 32 viii 5
Lugal-mu-dù, 15 iii 11
Lugal-mu-dùg, 33 rev. ii 4
Lugal-na-nam, 14 xv 6
Lugal-nam-mu-šub-bi dub-sar lú-gán-[gíd-da], 23 obv. xi 3
Lugal-níg-BE-dùg, 14 iii 4
Lugal-níg-lu-lu, 23 U. E. x 34
Lugal-nim-du sag-du$_5$, 20 iii 8, v 11
Lugal-nir-gál, 32 rev. i 8
[Lu]gal-šà-pàd [dumu] É-me-nam-nun-ka, 22 ii 36
Lugal-šà-pàd-da Lugal-⸢ù⸣-ma dumu É-[i]b-zi-me, App. to nos. 22–23 iii 9, [iv 4?]
Lugal-šà-sud(wr. BU), 15 iv 6
LUGAL-šag$_5$-ga, 32 iv 5
Lugal-šùd(SAG+ŠU)-dè, 20 Lo. E. 1
[L]ugal-[t]ir? ugula e-me-a [(x)], App. to nos. 22–23 viii 2
Lugal-ù-ma, 14 xv 14
Lugal-šà-pàd-da Lugal-⸢ù⸣-ma dumu É-[i]b-zi-me, App. to nos. 22–23 iii 10, ⸢iv 6?⸣
Lugal-uru-bar, App. to nos. 22–23 vi 6
[Lugal]?-[z]i?-dè: É-me-nam-nun dumu [Lugal]?-[z]i?-dè, 22 ii 2, 28
Lugal-⸢x⸣-ni-[x]: ⸢En-SAL⸣.UŠ.⸢DI-zi⸣ Inim-ma-ni-zi Nin-⸢kal-SI.A⸣ Lugal-⸢x⸣-ni-[x] Me-kisal-[si]? A-⸢. . .⸣ Lú-[. . .] dumu Amar-[tùr] sag-⸢du$_5$⸣, 22 [iv 12], 45
Lugal-x-nun, 34 iii 9
Lugal-⸢x-x⸣, 14 xv 7
Lum-ma, 14 xv 3
Lum-ma-en-TE.ME-na, App. to nos. 22–23 ix 3
Lum-ma-EZEN+⸢X⸣-gal, App. to nos. 22–23 ix 4
Lum-ma-ki-gal-la: GIŠGAL-ir-nun Lum-ma-ki-gal-la dumu Ú-ti-me, 22 iii 48
Lum-ma-tur dumu En-an-na-túm en$_5$-si Lagaš^{KI}-ka, 22 i 6, ii 8, [iii 14], [iv 18]; 23 [obv. i 8], [obv. ii 6], [obv. iii 10], [rev. iii 7], [obv. iv 29], obv. v 15, [rev. v 35], [rev. vi 20], [rev. vii 27]; App. to nos. 22–23 i 6
Šu-ni-al-dugud dumu Lum-ma-tur, App. to nos. 22–23 xi 3
Lugal-barag-ga-ì-dùg nu-banda é Lum-ma-tur-ka, App. to nos. 22–23 x 2
L[um-ma]-^{d}[X], App. to nos. 22–23 vii 8

Ma-an-iš-tu-su LUGAL KIŠ, 40 A i 5, xvi 20, B xxii 14, C xxiv 26, D xiv 19
Ma-an-sa-ki-su DUMU A-bí-da . . . DUMU.DUMU Lugal-ezen, 40 C xv 21
[M]a-ga-ga, 43 x 9
[Ì]r-e-um [š]u? Ma-ga-ga [š]i TE.LAL, 44i 3
Ma-la-ni-su [DU]MU Dup-si-ga [DU]MU.DUMU I-[k]i-lum [. . .]-a-a, 40 C vi 21

Iš-dup-Il DUMU Ma-la-ni-su . . . DUMU.DUMU A-nu-nu, 41 i 10
^{d}Ma-lik-zi-in-su DUMU I-da-DINGIR GAL.SUKKAL, 40 A xi 9
Ma-ma-ḫir-su DUMU Na-ni GÌR.NITA, 40 A xi 12
  Ma-ma-ḫir-su DUMU Ra-bí-DINGIR ši Ì-la-la, 40 A xiii 12
Ma-ma-ḪU DUMU I-bí-bí NU.BANDA Ša-na-e, 40 A xv 8
Ma-síg-be-lí arád Bíl-làl-la, App. to no. 32 vi 6
Ma-šum DUMU PÙ.ŠA-^{d}Za-ba$_4$-ba$_4$, 52 rev. ii 1
  Ma-šum šu I-bí-⸢bí⸣, 44e iii 3
  Ma-šum šu Ur-Ì-šum ḪI.MA.KI?, 31 iii 7
Ma-z[u?-z]u: Ì-lu-lu Ma-z[u?-z]u 2 DUMU I-ku-La-im, 37 i 5
^{d}Maḫ-URUDU-e, 33 iv 4
Maḫ?-[. . .], 15 vii 10
Maš engar, 20 vii 4, 7
  Maš GU.SUR.NUN, 20 iii 9, v 9, vi 5
  Maš dumu Šeš-a, 32 rev. i 13
Maš-lugal dumu Lugal-ezen, 14 iii 6
MAŠKIM.GI$_4$: Dan-ì-li DUMU Ìr-e-^{d}Ma-lik ši MAŠKIM. GI$_4$, 40 A xiv 6
Me-é-mug!-si, 15 viii 15, 21
ME.KA-zà-me, 18 rev. vi 2
Me-kar-si, 14 xv 18
Me-kisal-[si]?: ⸢En-SAL⸣.UŠ.⸢DI-zi⸣ Inim-ma-ni-zi Nin-⸢kal-SI.A⸣ Lugal-⸢x⸣-ni-[x] Me-kisal-[si]? A-⸢. . .⸣ Lú-[. . .] dumu Amar-[tùr] sag-⸢du$_5$], 22 [iv 13], 46
Me-me, 46 ii 5
ME-Sá-lim, 41 rev. iv 24
  ME-Sá-lim DUMU LUGAL, 40 D vi 11
  Šu-Eš$_4$-dar DUMU ME-Sá-lim DUMU.DUMU KA-KA, 40 D v 6
Me-si: IGI.RU?.NUN ÉŠ.A dumu Me-si pab-šeš É-nun, 12 Adscription to Side C
ME-ŠEŠ.ŠEŠ DUMU Barag-gi-si DUMU.DUMU Ur-^{d}En-líl, 40 C vii 2
Me-^{d}Tud, 14 vii 5
Me-zé-ì-lum: ARÁD-zu-ni DUMU Me-zé-ì-lum is attached to the lineage of Me-zi-zi, 40 A v 11
Me-zi-zi: DUMU.DUMU Me-zi-zi include descendants of Su-mu-núm, Ìr-ra-ra, Ì-la-la, and attached personnel of A-ŠI-gu-ru-ud, Al-la-la, and Me-zé-ì-lum, 40 A v 16
Men-mu DUMU En-na-Il, 37 rev. ii 16
Mes-barag-si, App. to nos. 22–23 ix 2
Mes-ki?-núm, App. to nos. 22–23 vi 10
MES-na-at: 5 DUMU.DUMU MES-na-at include families of I-ki-lum, A-ḫu-ḫu, Dup-si-ga, GAL.ZU, and Šu-ì-lí, 40 C vi 15
⸢MES⸣-nàd, 30a i 6
Mes-níg-bur-LUL, 15 iii 1, 10, 14
  dam Mes-níg-bur-LUL, 15 iii 9
Mes-sa dumu A-ZU.AB-si, 22 [iii 9], 42
Mes-U+É engar, 14 xiv 13
MES-zi UM.MI.A DUB.SAR, 40 A xi 6
Mes-ZU.A[B], 14 xii 3, xv 13
  Ušùr-r[a-ni]? Mes-ZU.A[B] Ur-^{d}Nin-Gír-su Tur-tur Úr-kug Ḫul-KAL-igi SAL-tur dumu ⸢X⸣-[x-m]e, 22 i 40
Mi-it-lik DUMU Iš-dup-DINGIR NU.BANDA . . . DUMU.DUMU Lugal-ezen, 40 C xvi 1
Mi-su$_4$-a DUMU I-ki-lum NU.BANDA Eš$_4$-na-na-ak^{KI} . . . DUMU.DUMU SABRA, 40 C xv 12
  DINGIR-ba-ni DUMU Mi-su$_4$-a . . . DUMU.DUMU Lugal-ezen, 40 C xvi 5
Mi-zu-a-NI-im, see GN GÁN Mi-zu-a-NI-im
Mir-ki-ág ì-DU.DU, 39 ii 3
MU-ì-lí, 15 ii 15
Mu-mu DUMU Ur-Már-da, 40 A xiii 15
  DINGIR-su-su DUMU Mu-mu ŠU.I ši Al-lu-lu, 40 A xii 16
  PÙ.ŠA-^{d}Za-ba$_4$-ba$_4$ DUMU Mu-mu DUMU.DUMU Ìr-am-^{d}Ma-lik, 40 D iii 7
  Wa-X-rúm šu Mu-mu, 41 rev. viii 26
  Mu-mu [šu]? ⸢Um⸣-ma-DÙG, 31 ii 8
Mu-m[u?-. . .], 45 i 5
Mu-na: Tu-li-id-da-nam DUMU Ì-lí-lí ši Mu-na, 40 A xvi 14
Mu-ni-gár, 15 iii 30, iv 7, 10
  see also GN gán Mu-ni-gár
Mu-ni-ḫur-sag, 15 vii 14
Mu-ni-kalam-ma: Ú-ti KA+IM-t[i]? dumu Mu-ni-kala[m-ma-m]e, 22 iii 8, 41
Mu-sa-ìr-su-nu DUMU Da-da-LUM DUB.SAR, 40 A xvi 5
Mug-si, App. to no. 32 i 2
MUL?.MUD um-me ^{d}TIR, 13 rev. iii 1
Munsub$_x$(PA.USAN): É-da-da Bíl-làl-la Ur-^{d}En-líl [dumu] Munsub$_x$, 32 i 4, iii 1, v 11, rev. ii 8

Na-ʾà-šum: Ur-ezen DUMU Na-ʾà-šum DAM.GÀR, 40 B xi 15
Na-ba-li: Pù-GI šu Na-ba-li, 41 rev. iv 9, viii 18
[Na]-ba-lu$_5$ [n]agar-gal, 24 rev. iv 4
Na-bí-um, 42 iv 8
  Na-bí-um DUMU I-ti-ti Da-mi-gi^{KI}, 40 A xvi 8
Na-dù: Lú-pàd sag-du$_5$ Umma^{KI} dumu Na-dù sag-du$_5$, 21 i 4
NA.GADA: Su-ru-uš-GI šu NA.GADA KI.SAR^{KI}, 41 rev. viii 10
Na-mu-ra-[zu]?, 35 ii 4
Na-mu-ru-um [DUM]U I-da-DINGIR . . . DUMU. DUMU Lugal-ezen, 40 C xv 26
Na-n[a], 15 viii 14
[Na-n]ar, 32 iii 12
  Na-nar lú-ašlág, 33 rev. i 1
Na-ni [DUMU]? ⸢X⸣-zu-zu, 34 i 4
  I-bí-^{d}UTU DUMU Na-ni, 35 i 9
  Ma-ma-ḫir-su DUMU Na-ni GÌR.NITA, 40 A xi 13
  A-bí-AN.NA GEMÉ.DINGIR SAL.DUMU Na-ni . . . DUMU.DUMU A-nu-nu, 41 i 15
  Na-ni šu Ḫu-bí-a DUB.SAR.GÁN, 41 iv 23, viii 20
  Na-ni Šim-SAR^{KI}, 41 viii 12
Na-zi-tim: Šu-^{d}Da-gan DUMU Be-lí-lí ši Na-zi-tim SABRA.É, 40 A xi 17
NÀ[D? . . .] šu E-[. . .]-rí-⸢x⸣-[(. . .)], 42 iv 2
Nagar?-[. . .], 21 vi 7
Nam-lugal-ni-dùg ⸢lú⸣ [. . .], App. to nos. 22–23 x 3

Nam-maḫ dumu Lugal-GÁR.KAG, 14 x 14
Nam?-maḫ dumu Sum-du-du, 15 i 4
Nanna, see ŠEŠ.KI/NA and ŠEŠ.KI-na
^{d}Nanše-nu-me-a, 21 iii 3
NAR: UD-ti-ru Sar-ru-GI-ì-lí 2 DUMU Bala-ga ši NAR, 40 A xii 10
Ne-sag: Ì-lí-a-ḫi DUMU Ne-sag NU.BANDA . . . DUMU.DUMU Lugal-ezen, 40 C xv 19
NE.USAN LÚ ⸢Su⸣(wr. ⸢ZU⸣)-ba-rí-um, 34 ii 7
NI-ba-rí-im: A-li-a-ḫu DUMU NI-ba-rí-im ŠEŠ LUGAL, 40 A x 23
Ni-su-NI, 14 iv 6
NI-X, 15 iv 9
Níg-šà arád Bíl-làl-la, App. to no. 32 vii 1
NIGIR: Zu-zu Ìr-e-pum 2 DUMU Iš-má-DINGIR ši NIGIR DUMU.DUMU Ur-ur ši PA.ḪI, 40 C xii 27
NIN: En-bu-DINGIR šu NIN, 40 A ix 23
GAL.ZU-DINGIR šu NIN SANGA ^{d}Lugal-Már-da . . . DUMU.DUMU SANGA, 40 C xiv 23
DINGIR-GI DUMU GAL.ZU-DINGIR šu NIN SANGA ^{d}Lugal-Már-da . . . DUMU.DUMU I-rí-iš-be-lí, 40 C xvii 17
Nin-dalla, 14 i 4
Nin-Gír-su-⸢zà-me⸣, 18 rev. vi 3
Nin-⸢kal-SI.A⸣: ⸢En-SAL⸣.UŠ.⸢DI-zi⸣ Inim-ma-ni-zi Nin-⸢kal-SI.A⸣ Lugal-⸢x⸣-ni-[x] Me-kisal-[si]? A-⸢. . .⸣ Lú-[. . .] dumu Amar-[tùr] sag-⸢du$_5$⸣, 22 [iv 11], 44
^{d}Nin-kar: Su$_4$-ma-mu-tum DUMU Ra-bí-DINGIR ši ^{d}Nin-kar, 40 B xii 13
Nin-⸢PA?.PI⸣, 15 xiii 27
Nin-SAL-zi dumu KUN?.LAGAB?, 14 xi 4
Nin-uru-ni-šè-ḫi-li dam Inim-ma-ni-zi, 22 iv 55
Nu-gal: Ib-LUL-DINGIR DUB.SAR DUMU Nu-gal . . . DUMU.DUMU A-ku-ì-lum, 40 C xiv 8
DUMU.DUMU Nu-gal include families of Iq-bí-GI and I-da-DINGIR, 40 C xvii 29
Nu-ni-da DUMU Be-lí-a-mi DUMU.DUMU Ur-Ab-ra ši Su$_4$-a-tum-mu-da, 40 C xviii 4
Nu-nu DUMU ⸢. . .⸣, 52 rev. ii 5
Nu-ra GEMÉ.DINGIR DUMU.SAL PÙ.ŠA-Nu-ni DUMU.DUMU Bu-im MÁ.LAḪ$_4$, 40 D iii 10

PA.ḪI: Zu-zu Ìr-e-pum 2 DUMU Iš-má-DINGIR ši NIGIR DUMU.DUMU Ur-ur ši PA.ḪI, 40 C xiii 2, 7
PA.TE.SI: A-ḫu-DÙG DUMU Ì-lum-sar šu PA.TE.SI, 41 iii 21
A-ḫu-DÙG šu PA.TE.SI, 41 v 9
PA.UR.NIGIR?.⸢X⸣, 13 U. E. i 2
Pab-da-maḫ, 14 ix 4
Pab-geštin: Ḫar-tu dumu Pab-geštin, 14 vii 8
Pab-kalam-dùg, 33 ii 6
Pab-ki-gal dumu Barag-^{sá}sag$_7$(GAN)-nu-di, 15 xii 7
Pab-rúm, see gán Pab-rúm
PAB.ŠEŠ: A-bìl-dan BÀD-su-nu 2 DUMU Su-ru-uš-GI ši PAB.ŠEŠ PA.TE.SI GIŠ.ÙḪ^{KI}, 40 A xii 22
Pab-ur-sag, 15 xiii 28
PÉŠ-ì-lum: A-ku-ì-lum DUMU PÉŠ-ì-lum ši Ur-^{d}AB, 40 B xiv 12
Pù-ba-lum: A-ar-DINGIR DUMU Pù-ba-lum SIPA . . . DUMU.DUMU Ìr-ra-ra, 40 A iv 14
^{d}EN.ZU-al-su DUMU A-ar-DINGIR ši Pù-ba-lum . . . DUMU.DUMU Ìr-ra-ra, 40 A iv 18
Pù-be-lí: I-mi-DINGIR DUMU Pù-be-lí . . . DUMU.DUMU I-rí-iš-be-lí, 40 C xvii 14
Pù-^{d}Da-gan DUMU Al-la-la attached to the lineage of Me-zi-zi, 40 A v 8
Pù-GI šu Na-ba-li, 41 rev. iv 8, viii 17
⸢Pù⸣?-ì-li, 43 i 12
Pù-Il LÚ BÀD-si AB+ÁŠ A-⸢. . .⸣, 48 rev. ii 3
Pù-la-lí nu-banda é-gal, 23 obv. x 1
⸢Pù-Ma⸣-[ma]?: ⸢X⸣-[. . .] ⸢Pù-Ma⸣-[ma]? DUMU.DUMU.ME, 30a iv 2 Pù-⸢Ma?-ma?⸣, 30a v 3
Pù-Nu-nu SIPA, 38 i 5
Pù-pù, 48 vii 14
⸢Pù-pù⸣ DUMU Ag-a, 34 iii 3
Pù-pù [DU]MU É-a-ra-bí . . . 4 DUMU.DUMU ši A-pù-lum, 40 D i 9
Pù-pù DUMU Šeš-ENGUR-na . . . DUMU.DUMU Ur-ma, 37 rev. i 8
ARÁD-zu-ni DUMU Pù-pù LÚ.IGI, 40 B xiii 17
[Ì]?-⸢lu-lu⸣ DUMU Pù-pù Kiš^{KI}, 34 ii 1
La-gi-pum DUMU Pù-pù ši ŠU.I, 40 B xiii 14
Pù-pù šu Bur-zi-a, 42 iv 6
Pù-su-DÙG, 41 viii 3
Pù-su-GI, 35 i 4
Pù-su-GI SAG.DU$_5$ DUMU Ìr-a-mu DUMU.DUMU Ab-ra-Il 3 DUMU.DUMU Ab-ra-Il . . . DUMU.DUMU Iš-dup-BE, 40 B iv 8
PÙ.ŠA-A-a šu É-bí-[r]a?, 41 rev. vii 11
⸢PÙ⸣.ŠA-⸢^{d}⸣[A]-ba$_4$, 28 i
PÙ.ŠA-be-lí DUMU Su-mu-^{d}A-a, 35 i 12
PÙ.ŠA-DÙG(wr. UD), 41 L. E. 13
PÙ.ŠA-É-a: A-ku-É-a DUMU PÙ.ŠA-É-a . . . DUMU.DUMU Lugal-ezen, 40 C xvi 11
Ra-bí-DINGIR DUMU PÙ.ŠA-É-a . . . DUMU.DUMU DINGIR-su-la-ba, 40 C v 8
PÙ.ŠA-Eš$_4$-dar DUMU KA-Ma-ma, 40 C xviii 21
PÙ.ŠA-Eš$_4$-dar É-ku-ku 2 DUMU Su-mu-GI DUMU.DUMU Gal-pum, 40 C x 6
Su-mu-É-a É-da-da 2 DUMU PÙ.ŠA-Eš$_4$-dar DUMU.DUMU Gal-pum, 40 C xi 5
PÙ.ŠA-ì-li DUMU Be-lí-GI GÌR.NITA LÚ.GIŠ.TI, 40 A xii 3
PÙ.ŠA-Il-la: DINGIR-a-zu DUMU I-zu-GÍD PÙ.ŠA-Il-la DUMU Ur-^{d}Nin-kar 2 DUMU.DUMU A-pù-lum, 40 D v 10
PÙ.ŠA-^{d}IM DUMU I-dur-ma-at, 40 B xii 6
PÙ.ŠA-Lu-lu GAL.UKÙ Ša-at-bar-rí-im^{KI}, 40 C xviii 28
PÙ.ŠA-Lu-lu DUMU DINGIR-a-zu DI.TAR . . . DUMU.DUMU SANGA, 40 C xiv 19
Ti-ir-su DUMU PÙ.ŠA-Lu-lu DUMU.DUMU SABRA, 40 C xv 16
PÙ.ŠA-Ma-ma DUMU Ur-^{d}Nin-kar . . . DUMU.DUMU La-mu-um, 40 A viii 22
Ù-ì-lí DUMU PÙ.ŠA-Ma-ma ši Tu-gul-tim, 40 B xii 9
PÙ.ŠA-^{d}Nu-muš-da šu Dingir-nu-me-a . . . DUMU.DUMU Zi-im-tum, 40 B x 11

PÙ.ŠA-Nu-ni: Nu-ra GEMÉ.DINGIR DUMU.SAL PÙ.ŠA-Nu-ni DUMU.DUMU Bu-im MÁ.LAḪ$_4$, 40 D iii 12
PÙ.ŠA-PAB.PAB DUMU Lugal-ezen . . . DUMU.DUMU Ur-^{d}SI.LU, 40 B vi 3
PÙ.ŠA-ra-ra DUMU Ur-Ma-ma, 36 v 10
PÙ.ŠA-ru PAB.ŠEŠ, 41 vii 10
DUMU.DUMU Dup-si-ga ši PÙ.ŠA-ru-um NU.BANDA, 40 C xii 1
PÙ.ŠA-su: Ik-ru-ub-DINGIR DUMU PÙ.ŠA-su . . . DUMU.DUMU Lugal-ezen, 40 C xvi 24
PÙ.ŠA-sù-DÙG: I-zi!-núm Iš-dup-Il PÙ.ŠA-sù-DÙG DUMU Su$_4$-ma-Ma-lik, 37 ii 3
PÙ.ŠA-^{d}Za-ba$_4$-ba$_4$ DUMU Mu-mu DUMU.DUMU Ìr-am-^{d}Ma-lik, 40 D iii 6
Ma-šum DUMU PÙ.ŠA-^{d}Za-ba$_4$-ba$_4$, 52 rev. ii 2
Pù-šu-tum DUMU Ib-LUL-Il!, 31 iii 3
Ìr-ì-pum [šu] Pù-šu-tum, 31 iii 13
Pù-^{d}Tišpak: ⌜I⌝-mi-DINGIR [DUMU] Pù-^{d}Tišpak [š]i? Ù-su, 43 iv 13
Pù-uš-GAL: DUMU.DUMU Pù-uš-GAL PA.TE.SI Kibabbar^{KI} include descendants of I-ki-lum, I-ti-É-a, É-a-a, DINGIR-su-la-ba, MES-na-at, Ur-nin, and Ur-^{d}En-líl, 40 C vii 13
Pù-za-um, 35 i 11

Ra-bí-DINGIR DUMU DINGIR-su-a-ḫa KA-ul-lum^{KI}, 40 C xix 7
Ra-bí-DINGIR DUMU PÙ.ŠA-É-a . . . DUMU.DUMU DINGIR-su-la-ba, 40 C v 7
Be-lí-GÚ DUMU Ra-bí-DINGIR, 40 C xviii 14
DINGIR-ba-ni DUMU Ra-bí-DINGIR ši La-mu-um SANGA ^{d}Za-ba$_4$-ba$_4$, 40 A viii 18
Ga-at-núm DUMU Ra-bí-DINGIR Ḫa-ar-ḫa-mu-na-ak, 40 C xix 2
Ma-ma-ḫir-su DUMU Ra-bí-DINGIR ši Ì-la-la, 40 A xiii 13
SIG$_5$-ì-lum DUMU Ra-bí-DINGIR, 40 C xviii 27
Su$_4$-ma-mu-tum DUMU Ra-bí-DINGIR ši ^{d}Nin-kar, 40 B xii 12
Dam-ba-ba DUMU DINGIR-GÀR Sá-lim-a-ḫu DUMU Da-da 2 DUMU.DUMU Ra-bí- DINGIR, 40 C x 26
Tu-tu DUMU Ì-la-la ŠEŠ Ra-bí-DINGIR . . . DUMU.DUMU Lugal-ezen, 40 C xvi 20
Ra-bí-ì-lum DUMU Iš-dup-DINGIR.DINGIR, 37 iv 11
Ra-bí-ì-lum DUMU Li-gi-i[m]?, 41 rev. ii 7
Ra-b[í-ì?-lum?] šu Li-[gi?-im?], 41 rev. i 2
Zu-zu Ra-bí-ì-lum DUMU.DUMU Il-su(wr. ZU)-ERÍN+X PA.TE.SI, 34 iv 8
Ra-bí-Il, 33 ii 5
Ri-ti, 14 xii 14, xiii 13; 32 v 4; 33 iii 1
Rí-iṣ-DINGIR, 38 ii 12
Rí-pum: La-a-GUR DUMU Rí-pum ši Wa-gi-rí, 40 B xiii 6

Sa-ba-ra?, see GN GÁN šu Sa-ba-ra?
Sa-NI: É-ga-lum DUMU Sa-NI, 40 A xi 20
Sa-tu-na SIMUG A-ga-dè^{KI}, 41 rev. vii 15
Sa-tu-ni: Su-mu-núm DUMU Sa-tu-ni . . . DUMU.DUMU Zi-im-tum, 40 B x 10
Sa-[. . .], 41 rev. ii 23
Sá-lim-a-ḫu DUMU ši Ga-ra-az-ni-iš, 43 iii 11; 44c ii 1
Dam-ba-ba DUMU DINGIR-GÀR Sá-lim-a-ḫu DUMU Da-da 2 DUMU.DUMU Ra-bí- DINGIR, 40 C x 23
⌜Sá⌝-lim-a-lum, 28 i
SABRA: DUMU.DUMU SABRA include families of Mi-su$_4$-a and Ti-ir-su, 40 C xv 17
Sag-an-tuku, 32 iv 3
Sag-^{d}Aš$_7$-gi$_4$-da sagi, 33 ii 1
Sag-^{d}Aš$_7$-gi$_4$-da sukkal, 33 iii 7
Sag-gul-lum [DU]MU É-a-ra-bí . . . 4 DUMU.DUMU ši A-pù-lum, 40 D i 5
Sag-kud, App. to no. 32 v 1
Sag?-šu-du$_7$ dumu É-geštin-sir, 22 ii 38
SAL.ANŠE: ARÁD-zu-ni DUMU Gu-lí-zum ši SAL.ANŠE, 40 B xiii 1
SAL-tur: Ušùr-r[a-ni]? Mes-ZU.A[B] Ur-^{d}Nin-Gír-su Turtur Úr-kug Ḫul-KAL-igi SAL-tur dumu ⌜X⌝-[x-m]e, 22 i 45
SANGA: DUMU.DUMU SANGA include families of PÙ.ŠA-Lu-lu, GAL.ZU-DINGIR, DINGIR-ba-na, Be-lí-a-mi, A-bu-bu, and Iš-dup-DINGIR, 40 C xv 11
SAR.KI, 13 rev. ii 6
Sar-ru-BÀD: Sar-ru-ì-lí DUMU Sar-ru-BÀD EN.ME.LI, 40 A xv 26
Sar-ru-GI: ^{d}A-ba$_4$-iš-da-gal DUMU Sar-ru-GI, 40 C xiii 23
Sar-ru-GI-ì-lí: UD-ti-ru Sar-ru-GI-ì-lí 2 DUMU Bala-ga ši NAR, 40 A xii 8
Sar-ru-ì-lí DUMU Sar-ru-BÀD EN.ME.LI, 40 A xv 25
[S]ar-ru-ru, 48 iv 19
SI.A-um DUMU Gu-lí-zum . . . DUMU.DUMU Zi-im-tum, 40 B xi 9
SI.A-um DUMU I-ti-^{d}Da-gan . . . DUMU.DUMU Lugal-ezen, 40 C xvi 6
SI.A-um DUMU La-mu-sa ši AGRIG . . . DUMU.DUMU Su-mu-núm, 40 A iv 10
Šu-Eš$_4$-dar ù SI.A-um šu Ḫa-a[r?(-x)-m]u?, 41 rev. iii 8
Si-dù, 20 ii 3, 10, ⌜v 12⌝?, vi 6, [10]?
Si-gar, 15 iv 11, vi 13, viii 27?
Si-im-tum, see GN GÁN Si-im-tum
Si-lu-ga-ru$_9$-ut, 40 A ix 12
Si-na: Šum-Ma-lik šu Si-na, 41 iv 18
SIG?.GÍN?.[X]?, 13 Lo. E. iii 3
SÍG.BU-šè, 15 viii 1, 16
SIG$_5$-ì-lum DUMU Ra-bí-DINGIR, 40 C xviii 26
SU.KUR.RU, 13 rev. i 7
Su-mi-su DUMU Lu-da-na-at SIPA, 40 B xiii 8
Su-mi-su DUMU Lu-zu-zum ši ^{d}En-ki, 40 B xiv 8
Be-lí-mu-da DUMU Su-mi-su . . . DUMU.DUMU Zi-im-tum, 40 B xi 8
Su-mu-^{d}A-a: PÙ.ŠA-be-lí DUMU Su-mu-^{d}A-a, 35 i 13
Su-mu-É-a É-da-da 2 DUMU PÙ.ŠA-Eš$_4$-dar DUMU.DUMU Gal-pum, 40 C xi 2
I-nin-sa-tu šu Su$_4$-mu-É-a, 41 L. E. 11
Su-mu-^{d}EN.ZU: DINGIR-GÚ DUMU Su-mu-^{d}EN.ZU . . . DUMU.DUMU Lugal-ezen, 40 C xv 29
Su-mu-GI U-li-id-ì-lum 2 DUMU BÀD-Il DUMU.DUMU Ib-bu-bu, 40 B v 6

PÙ.ŠA-Eš$_4$-dar É-ku-ku 2 DUMU Su-mu-GI DUMU. DUMU Gal-pum, 40 C x 9
Su-mu-núm DUMU Sa-tu-ni . . . DUMU.DUMU Zi-im-tum, 40 B x 9
Ur-Ab-ra DUB.SAR DUMU Su-mu-núm, 40 C xviii 25
DUMU.DUMU Su-mu-núm, of the lineage of Me-zi-zi, include families of Su-ru-uš-GI, SI.A-um, X, Lam-gi-um, E-bi-ir-ì-lum, Iš-dup-^{d}EN.ZU, and I-bí- ^{d}EN.ZU, 40 A iv 3
Su-mu-[. . .], 45 i 6
Su-NI-um DUMU ARÁD-zu-ni IŠ . . . DUMU.DUMU Ši-ù-ni, 40 A vi 16
Su-NI-um DUMU Bi-im ši Zi-zi, 40 B xiv 2
Ur-ur DUMU Su-NI-um MAR.X^{KI}, 40 C xix 5
Su$_4$-NI-um šu A-nu-nu, 41 iv 15
Su-ru-uš-GI: I-da-tum Su-ru-uš-GI 2 DUMU DINGIR-su-GÀR . . . 5 DUMU.DUMU Da-tum, 40 D iv 12
Su-ru-uš-GI DUMU I-ti-DINGIR šu La-mu-sa ši AGRIG . . . DUMU.DUMU Su-mu-núm, 40 A iii 13
Su-ru-uš-GI šu NA.GADA KI.SAR^{KI}, 41 rev. viii 9
A-bìl-dan BÀD-su-nu 2 DUMU Su-ru-uš-GI ši PAB. ŠEŠ PA.TE.SI GIŠ.ÙH̬^{KI}, 40 A xii 21
Su-tu-ì-lum, 33 iv 3
SU.Ù.SAL: A-h̬u-GIŠ.ERÍN šu SU.Ù.SAL DUB.SAR. GÁN, 41 ii 3
Su$_4$-a-tum-mu-da: Be-lí-a-mi DUMU Ur-Ab-ra ši Su$_4$-a-tum-mu-da . . . DUMU.DUMU SANGA, 40 C xv 4
DUMU.DUMU Ur-Ab-ra ši Su$_4$-a-tum-mu-da, 40 C xviii 7
Su$_4$-be-lí: D[u]-⸢ba?-ba?⸣ DAM Šu-Eš$_4$-dar LÚ Su$_4$-be-lí, 36 iii 10
Su$_4$-ma-ba-ni: DINGIR-a-h̬a DUMU Su$_4$-ma-ba-ni UGULA . . . DUMU.DUMU Zi-im-tum, 40 B x 4
Su$_4$-ma-Ma-lik: I-zi!-núm Iš-dup-Il PÙ.ŠA-sù-DÙG DUMU Su$_4$-ma-Ma-lik, 37 ii 5
Su$_4$-ma-mu-tum DUMU Ra-bí-DINGIR ši ^{d}Nin-kar, 40 B xii 11
Su$_4$-ma-SIPA DUMU I-nin-sa-tu . . . DUMU.DUMU Lugal-ezen, 40 C xvi 27
Ga-at-núm Su$_4$-ma-SIPA Be-lí-ba-ni 3 DUMU Ur-ZU.AB DUMU.DUMU DINGIR-su-la-ba, 40 C v 12
Su$_4$?-ma-⸢. . .⸣, 31 i 8
Su$_4$-mu-É-a, see Su-mu-É-a
Su$_4$-NI-da, 41 viii 11
Su$_4$-NI-um, see Su-NI-um
Sum-du-du: Nam?-mah̬ dumu Sum-du-du, 15 i 6
Sum-ti, 14 i 5

⸢Ša⸣-a ⸢SAL⸣.BALAG.DI, 44h ii 4
Ša-at-b[e]-DINGIR, 44k iii 1
Šà-da-nu-NE, 32 v 5
Šà-gú-ba, 32 iv 2
[Šà-gú]-ba, 33 i 3
Šà-gú-ba guruš-tab, 32 v 7
Šà-gú-ba [P]A.URU, 32 iv 9
Šà-gú-ba dumu Bàd⟨-si⟩-du, 15 v 9
DINGIR-ba-na AB+ÁŠ.URU DUMU Šà-gú-ba . . . DUMU.DUMU SANGA, 40 C xv 1
Šà-tar dub-sar lú-gán-[gíd-da], 23 obv. xi 2
Šag$_5$-šag$_5$ nar?, 15 v 12
^{d}Šará-igi-zi-ZU.AB dumu Ušum-gal ÉŠ.A, 12 Adscription to Side D
^{d}Šará-men arád Bíl-làl-la, App. to no. 32 vi 12
Šeš-a: Maš dumu Šeš-a, 32 rev. i 15
Šeš-ENGUR-na: Pù-pù DUMU Šeš-ENGUR-na . . . DUMU.DUMU Ur-ma, 37 rev. i 10
Šeš-GÍR-*gunû*-gal, 14 vi 4; 15 x 12, xi 9
dam Šeš-GÍR-*gunû*-gal, 14 viii 9
Šeš-GÍR-*gunû*-gal sanga, 14 viii 6
Šeš-GÍR-*gunû*-gal dumu Lú-dingir-mu, 14 vii 9
ŠEŠ+IB-geštin engar, 20 v 3, 10
ŠEŠ.KI/NA ugula-ukkin, 12 Adscription to Side B
ŠEŠ.KI-na Uru!-⟨SAG.⟩H̬ÚB.DU^{KI}, 33 rev. ii 5
⸢ŠEŠ.KI⸣-na dumu Ur-^{d}En-líl, 14 x 9
Ur-DUN dumu ŠEŠ.KI-na, 14 vi 17
Šeš-pàd-da sagi, 33 ii 3
Šeš-šeš, 32 iii 8
Ši-na-na-tim: ARÁD-zu-ni DUMU Iš-dup-pum DUMU. DUMU Ši-na-na-tim, 40 B vii 10
Ši-ù-ni: DUMU.DUMU Ši-ù-ni include descendants of I-me-^{d}EN.ZU, Iš-dup-DINGIR, A-ar-É-a, Im$_4$-da-lik, and Dam-ba-ba, 40 A viii 4
ŠU.A: A-bí-ra šu ŠU.A, 41 iv 8
Šu-AD.MU DUMU La-mu-um . . . 5 DUMU.DUMU Da-tum, 40 D iv 9
Šu-Ba-ba šu A-da LÚ.GUNU+ÚŠ, 41 iv 13
Šu-^{d}Da-gan DUMU Be-lí-lí ši Na-zi-tim SABRA.É, 40 A xi 15
Šu-da-ti: Ì-lí-sa-lik DUMU Šu-da-ti, 40 A xv 1
[Šu-Eš$_4$]-dar, 36 v 19
Šu-Eš$_4$-dar A-za-me-um^{KI}, 41 viii 9
Šu-Eš$_4$-dar DUMU ME-Sá-lim DUMU.DUMU KA-KA, 40 D v 5
Šu-Eš$_4$-dar ù SI.A-um šu H̬a-a[r?(-x)-m]u?, 41 rev. iii 6
D[u]-⸢ba?-ba?⸣ DAM Šu-Eš$_4$-dar LÚ Su$_4$-be-lí, 36 iii 9
ŠU.I: La-gi-pum DUMU Pù-pù ši ŠU.I, 40 B xiii 15
Šu-ì-lí AB+ÁŠ.URU^{KI}, 38 ii 4
Dup-si-ga Šu-ì-li 2 DUMU GAL.ZU . . . 5 DUMU. DUMU MES-na-at, 40 C vi 11
I-zi-ir-gul-la-zi-in DUMU Šu-ì-li SILÀ.ŠU.DU$_8$, 40 A xiii 1
[Šu]-⸢ì⸣?-lí-su, 41 L. E. 17
^{d}EN.ZU-GIŠ.ERÍN Ì-la-la Šu-ì-lí-su 3 DUMU Zu-zu ši A-ar-É-a, 40 A x 7
Šu-la-pi: Bí-bí DUMU Šu-la-pi, 41 rev. ix 13
Šu-Ma-ma DUMU Da-ba$_4$-la, 41 iv 11
Šu-Ma-ma šu A-ku-si-im, 41 rev. v 15
Šu-ni-al-dugud dumu Lum-ma-tur, App. to nos. 22–23 xi 1
Šu-Nu-nu DUMU DINGIR-dan SANGA ^{d}A-ba$_4$ I-bí-rí^{KI}, 40 A xv 17
A-h̬u-DÙG (var. A-h̬u-h̬u in B) DUMU Šu-Nu-nu ši H̬a-lum, 40 A xv 15
Šu-pù-la Ì-lum-A.ZU Iš-má-ì-lum AB+ÁŠ.AB+ÁŠ šu URU^{KI}.URU^{KI}, 41 vii 12
⸢Šu?-x⸣-[. . .], 16g ii 1
⸢Šubur⸣? ìr en$_5$-si-⸢GAR⸣, App. to nos. 22–23 vii 10
Šum-Ma-lik šu Si-na, 41 iv 17

TAR.ḪU: É-zi dumu TAR.ḪU, 22 [iii 12], 45
TE.LAL: [Ì]r-e-um [š]u? Ma-ga-ga [š]i TE.LAL, 44i 4
TE.LAL.GAL: In-su-mi-su-da-nu DUMU Iš-a-lum ši TE.LAL.GAL, 40 A xii 2
  Zi-gur-mu-bí DUMU Ì-lí-a-ḫi ši TE.LAL.GAL, 40 A xiii 11
[Te-m]i-tum [DUMU.SAL? G]a-lí-tim, 44h i 5
Ti-da-nu DUMU DINGIR-mu-da DUMU.DUMU Ur-^{d}SI.LU, 40 B vi 6
Ti-ir-su DUMU PÙ.ŠA-Lu-lu DUMU.DUMU SABRA, 40 C xv 15
Ti-li-lum: DINGIR-GÀR DUMU Ti-li-lum . . . DUMU.DUMU Lugal-ezen, 40 C xvi 22
Ti-ru-um DUMU Bur-zum GAL.SUKKAL DUMU.DUMU I-rí-iš-be-lí, 40 C xvii 20
  I-bí-ZU.AB DUMU Ur-mes-an-ni Ti-ru-um DUMU A-da-na-aḫ DUMU.DUMU I-ti- É-a, 40 C iv 5
[T]i-[t]i [A]?.ZU, 30a i 11
  Iš-[. . .] DUMU Ti-ti šu ^{d}ÁŠ?.TE?, 31 ii 3
  I-zi-núm En-na-É-a 2 DUMU Ur-sa(g)-núm DUMU.DUMU Ti-ti, 40 B x 2
Tim-mu: Du-du DUMU Tim-mu, 41 rev. ii 16
Tu-gul-tim: Ù-ì-lí DUMU PÙ.ŠA-Ma-ma ši Tu-gul-tim, 40 B xii 10
Tu-li-id-da-nam DUMU Ì-lí-lí ši Mu-na, 40 A xvi 12
Tu-tu DUMU Ì-la-la ŠEŠ Ra-bí-DINGIR . . . DUMU.DUMU Lugal-ezen, 40 C xvi 18
  Tu-tu DUMU Ì-lí . . . DUMU.DUMU Lugal-ezen, 40 C xvi 8
  [T]u-tu [DUMU . . .]-gi [DUMU.DUMU PN], 40 C iii 10
  Tu-tu šu Ib-la-NI-⌜x⌝, 43 ix 6
Túl-li-li kurušda, 33 rev. i 3
Túl-sag muḫaldim lú-banšur-íl, 33 iii 2
Túl-ta, 38 ii 9
Tur-tur: Ušùr-r[a-ni]? Mes-ZU.A[B] Ur-^{d}Nin-Gír-su Tur-tur Úr-kug Ḫul-KAL-igi SAL-tur dumu ⌜X⌝-[x-m]e, 22 i 42

U-bi-in-LUGAL-rí DUMU BALA-É-a ARÁD-da-ni^{KI}, 40 A xv 11
  U-bi-in-LUGAL-rí DUMU Ur-ur ši GAL.SUKKAL-li, 40 A xv 5
U-bìl-ga-zu DUMU Ìr-ru-zum LÚ.IGI, 40 A xiii 23
U+É-šum kug-gál, 15 xiv 15
U-ḫúb [. . .] DUMU Zi-[. . .], 41 rev. ii 21; see also Ú-ḫúb
U-li-id-ì-lum: Su-mu-GI U-li-id-ì-lum 2 DUMU BÀD-Il DUMU.DUMU Ib-bu-bu, 40 B v 8
U-za-si-na-at DUMU Ki-ti-ti, 40 A xiii 3
U-zé-^{d}Ma-lik [nu]-banda Mar-tu-[n]e, 24 rev. iii 7
Ú-bí-bí šu Da-tum ⌜X⌝.GAL A-tum, 31 iv 3
Ú-da-ur$_4$, 14 xv 20
Ú-ḫúb: I-ku-tum DUMU Ú-ḫúb, 36 iv 8
  A-bí-su šu Ú-ḫúb, 44b i 2
  see also U-ḫúb
Ú-ti KA+IM-t[i]? dumu M[u-ni]-kalam-m[a-m]e, 22 iii 6
  GIŠGAL-ir-nun Lum-ma-ki-gal-la dumu Ú-ti-me, 22 iii 49
Ú-tum-ma-ì-lum ašgab arád Bíl-làl-la, App. to no. 32 vi 10
Ú-ú-a šeš Bíl-làl-la sanga Kèš, App. to no. 32 iv 11
Ú-⌜x⌝-[. . .] DUMU Ḫa-la-[X], 41 rev. ii 3
Ú-[. . .], 15 viii 20
Ù-Aš-dar, 17 ii 1
Ù-ì-lí DUMU PÙ.ŠA-Ma-ma ši Tu-gul-tim, 40 B xii 8
Ù-mes, 16d i 4
Ù-mu-ì-lí, 33 rev. i 6
Ù-na-gàr DUMU Ì-ši-ši NU.BANDA Ša-na-e, 40 A xiv 1
Ù-su: ⌜I⌝-mi-DINGIR [DUMU] Pù-^{d}Tišpak [š]i? Ù-su, 43 iv 14
Ù-šu?-ti, 48 rev. iii 13
Ù-Ù: [I?-b]í?-bí [DUMU]? Ù-Ù, 44e i 2
⌜Ù⌝-⌜x⌝-[. . .], 30a vii 4
U$_9$(EZEN+AN)-zi-um, 35 i 5
  I-GU-KU-DINGIR DUMU U$_9$-zi-um, 35 i 7
UD.A, 15 iv 12
Ud-da simug, 33 rev. iv 3
  AN.RU.KÈŠ.TA dumu-SAL [U]d-da, 33 rev. iv 8
UD.IŠ Zu-zu 2 DUMU Iš-dup-^{d}EN.ZU DUMU.DUMU Ìr-ra-ra, 40 A iv 19
⌜UD⌝-la, 15 ix 18
UD-ma: GIŠ.TUKUL-ga-su-al-si-in DUMU UD-ma, 40 A xiii 6; cf. also Dam-ma
UD.MÁ.NINA.KI.ŠUM-dùg dumu Ur-^{d}Dumu-⌜zi-da⌝, 23 [rev. vi 16], obv. vii 7, [29]
UD.MÁ.NINA.ŠUM-pa-è dumu Da-da, 22 ii 40
  É-geštin-sir Da-d[a] Gu-ni-du dumu UD.MÁ.NINA.ŠUM-pa-⌜è⌝-[me], 22 ii 6, 34
UD.NUN.GUR?.NÁM, 13 Lo. E. iii 1
UD-ti-ru Sar-ru-GI-ì-lí 2 DUMU Bala-ga ši NAR, 40 A xii 7
⌜Um⌝-ma-DÙG: Mu-mu [šu]? ⌜Um⌝-ma-DÙG, 31 ii 9
Um-me-DÙG, 38 ii 19
Ur-^{d}AB: A-ku-ì-lum DUMU PÉŠ-ì-lum ši Ur-^{d}AB, 40 B xiv 13
Ur-Ab-ra, 14 i 13; 15 ix 9, 17
  Ur-Ab-ra DUMU A-lum-DÙG . . . DUMU.DUMU Ur-ma, 37 rev. i 11
  Ur-Ab-ra DUB.SAR DUMU Su-mu-núm, 40 C xviii 23
  Be-lí-a-mi DUMU Ur-Ab-ra ši Su$_4$-a-tum-mu-da . . . DUMU.DUMU SANGA, 40 C xv 3
  DUMU.DUMU Ur-Ab-ra ši Su$_4$-a-tum-mu-da include families of DINGIR-a-ḫa and Nu-ni-da, 40 C xviii 6
Ur-AN.KI: Li-sa-núm DUMU Ur-AN.KI šu KUG.DÍM, 40 C xviii 9
Ur-AN.U+É: Ur-PA dumu Ur-AN.U+É, 14 ix 13
Ur-AN.UR.GÁN?.GA.IGI?, 14 xiii 8
Ur-⌜^{d}Aš$_7$(SÁR+DIŠ)⌝-[gi$_4$- . . .] dumu Di-Utu, 33 rev. ii 7
Ur-dingir-ra, 14 xvi 1
Ur-^{d}DUB-an: Il-sù-LAK-647 I-KU-GU-Il Ur-^{d}Dub-an DUMU.DUMU Ur-PA, 37 iii 5
Ur-^{d}Dumu-zi-da, 33 rev. ii 1
  Làl?-li-l[i]? Barag-ul-tu dumu Ur-^{d}Dumu-zi-da-me, 22 iv 54
Ur-DUN, 33 iii 9
  Ur-DUN dumu ŠEŠ.KI-na, 14 vi 15
Ur-é: Ga-lí-su(wr. ZU)-ma DUMU Ur-é, 34 rev. i 4

Ur-é-maḫ, 32 rev. i 10
Ur-En-gal-DU.DU DUMU Ur-^{d}Ezínu NU.BANDA É-mar-za^{KI} . . . DUMU.DUMU Lugal-ezen, 40 C xvi 15
Ur-^{d}En-ki, 14 iv 4; 15 x 9, xi 10, xiii 1
  Ur-^{d}En-ki agrig, 15 L. E. 14
  Ur-^{d}En-ki sukkal, 33 iv 1
Ur-^{d}En-líl, 14 vi 1, xii 15, xiii 14; 15 xiii 19; 33 rev. iv 10
  É-da-da Bíl-làl-la Ur-^{d}En-líl dumu Munsub$_{x}$, 32 ii 9
  Ur-^{d}En-líl šeš Bíl-làl-la sanga Kèš, App. to no. 32 iv 7
  ME-ŠEŠ.ŠEŠ DUMU BARAG-gi-si DUMU.DUMU Ur-^{d}En-líl, 40 C vii 4
  ⸢ŠEŠ.KI⸣-na dumu Ur-^{d}En-líl, 14 x 11
  Zi-gàr-su DUMU Ur-^{d}En-líl DUB.SAR, 40 B xiv 15
Ur-^{d}EN.ZU DUMU Ur-ezen NU.BANDA GIŠ.KIN.TI . . . DUMU.DUMU Lugal-ezen, 40 C xvi 12
⸢Ur⸣-^{d}⸢EN⸣.[X], 33 rev. iii 10
Ur-ezen, 48 iv 14
  Ur-ezen DUMU Na-ʾà-šum DAM.GÀR, 40 B xi 14
  Ur-^{d}EN.ZU DUMU Ur-ezen NU.BANDA GIŠ.KIN. TI . . . DUMU.DUMU Lugal-ezen, 40 C xvi 13
Ur-^{d}Ezínu(ŠE.TIR): Ur-En-gal-DU.DU DUMU Ur-^{d}Ezínu NU.BANDA É-mar-za . . . DUMU.DUMU Lugal-ezen, 40 C xvi 16
Ur-^{d}Gu-nu-ra, 14 v 5, xiv 9, xv 10, xvii 13; 15 vi 12, viii 26
  Ur-^{d}Gu-nu-ra engar, 14 xiv 14
Ur-^{d}Gú-gú DUMU Ur-túl-sag Pù-sa-an^{KI} husband of Ì-a-ki-na-ni, 37 R. E. 10
Ur-^{d}GUR$_{8}$-⸢x⸣: Igi-zi-barag-gi Ur-^{d}Nin-PA Ur-^{d}GUR$_{8}$-⸢x⸣ Barag-ga-[ni] dumu In[im-ma]-ni-[zi-me], 22 iv 59
Ur-ḪAR, 15 vi 8
Ur-Ì-šum: Ma-šum šu Ur-Ì-šum ḪI.MA.KI?, 31 iii 8
Ur-igi-sag, 32 iv 7
Ur-Kèš^{KI}: I-ti-É-a DUMU Ur-Már-da DUMU.DUMU Ur-Kèš^{KI} ši Dup-si-ga, 40 C ix 24
  Da-da DUMU Ur-Már-da KA-Ma-ma DUMU DINGIR-GÀR 2 DUMU.DUMU Ur-Kèš^{KI} ši Dup-si-ga, 40 C x 17
  I-si-im-DINGIR DUMU Im-tum DUMU.DUMU Ur-Kèš^{KI}, 40 C xi 15
  DINGIR-nu-id DUMU I-ti-É-a DUMU.DUMU Ur-Már-da ši Ur-Kèš^{KI}, 40 C xi 11
Ur-ma: DUMU.DUMU Ur-ma include families of Pù-pù and Ur-Ab-ra, 37 rev. i 18
  GÁN Ur-ma in Lugal-kalam-ma, 37 rev. iii 15
Ur-Ma-ma: PÙ.ŠA-ra-ra DUMU Ur-Ma-ma, 36 v 11
Ur-Már-da: Mu-mu DUMU Ur-Már-da, 40 A xiii 16
  Da-da DUMU Ur-Már-da KA-Ma-ma DUMU DINGIR-GÀR 2 DUMU.DUMU Ur-Kèš^{KI} ši Dup-si-ga, 40 C x 13
  I-ti-É-a DUMU Ur-Már-da DUMU.DUMU Ur-Kèš^{KI} ši Dup-si-ga, 40 C ix 23
  DINGIR-nu-id DUMU I-ti-É-a DUMU.DUMU Ur-Már-da ši Ur-Kèš^{KI}, 40 C xi 10
  Zu-zu DUMU Ur-Már-da DUMU.DUMU I-ki-lum PA.TE.SI Ki-babbar^{KI}, 40 C iii 5
  Amar-rí-rí Be-lí-sa-tu 2 DUMU Zu-zu [DU]MU.DUMU Ur-[Má]r-da [ši I]-ki-lum, 40 C iv 13
Ur-mes, 16i ii 3
Ur-mes-an-ni: I-bí-ZU.AB DUMU Ur-mes-an-ni Ti-ru-um DUMU A-da-na-aḫ DUMU.DUMU I-ti-É-a, 40 C iv 3
Ur-^{d}MUŠ, 32 iii 10
  Ur-^{d}MUŠ DUMU Lugal-ku-li, 40 A xiii 7
Ur-NE-ra: Ur-PA dumu Ur-NE-ra, 14 xiv 4
Ur-nin, 15 xiv 19
  Im$_{4}$-da-lik DUMU Ur-nin Kiš^{KI}, 40 A x 3
  Dup-si-ga DUMU I-ki-lum DUMU.DUMU Ur-nin, 40 C vi 19
Ur-^{d}Nin-Gír-su: Ušùr-r[a-ni]? Mes-ZU.A[B] Ur-^{d}Nin-Gír-su Tur-tur Úr-kug Ḫul-KAL-igi SAL-tur dumu ⸢X⸣-[x-m]e, 22 i 41
Ur-^{d}Nin-kar SAG.DU$_{5}$ DUMU Barag-ki-ba DUMU. DUMU A-ku-ì-lum, 40 C xiv 11
  DINGIR-a-zu DUMU I-zu-GÍD PÙ.ŠA-Il-la DUMU Ur-^{d}Nin-kar 2 DUMU.DUMU A-pù-lum, 40 D v 11
  PÙ.ŠA-Ma-ma DUMU Ur-^{d}Nin-kar . . . DUMU. DUMU La-mu-um, 40 A ix 1
Ur-^{d}Nin-PA: Igi-zi-barag-gi Ur-^{d}Nin-PA Ur-^{d}GUR$_{8}$-⸢x⸣ Barag-ga-[ni] dumu In[im-ma]-ni-[zi-me], 22 iv 58
Ur-PA, 14 xv 15
  Ur-PA ašgab?, 21 i 35
  Ur-PA dumu Ur-NE-ra, 14 xiv 3
  Ur-PA dumu Ur-AN.U+É, 14 ix 11
  Il-sù-LAK-647 I-KU-GU-Il Ur-^{d}DUB-an DUMU. DUMU Ur-PA, 37 iii 7
Ur-^{d}PA.BÌL.SAG DUMU É-ní-íl ENGAR LUGAL . . . DUMU.DUMU Lugal-ezen, 40 C xvi 29
Ur-sag-a-me-nàd: gán Gúg dumu Ur-sag-a-me-nàd, 14 iii 13
Ur-sag-gur?-ra?!, 14 xviii 5
Ur-sag-Kèš, App. to no. 32 v 2
Ur-sag-ki-gal-la dumu Edin-ni-si, 15 i 15
Ur-sa(g)-núm: I-zi-núm En-na-É-a 2 DUMU Ur-sa(g)-núm DUMU.DUMU Ti-ti, 40 B x 1
Ur-sag-UD.KIB.NUN^{KI}: GAL.ZU DUMU Ur-sag-UD. KIB.NUN^{KI}, 40 C vi 7
  Dup-si-ga Šu-ì-li 2 DUMU GAL.ZU DUMU.DUMU Ur-sag-UD.KIB.NUN^{KI}, 40 C vi 13
Ur-sag-Utu dumu Edin-ri, 14 ix 5
Ur-^{d}SI.LU: DUMU.DUMU Ur-^{d}SI.LU include families of PÙ.ŠA-PAB.PAB and Ti-da-nu, 40 B vi 8
Ur-^{d}Sud-da, 15 vi 11, vii 15, viii 23
Ur-^{d}Šul-pa-è, 32 iii 6
  Ur-^{d}Šul-pa-è šeš Bíl-làl-la sanga Kèš, App. to no. 32 iv 9
Ur-^{d}Tud, 33 rev. ii 3
Ur-túl-sag: Ur-^{d}Gú-gú DUMU Ur-túl-sag Pù-sa-an^{KI}, 37 R. E. 11
Ur-ú, 20 ii 1
Ur-ur, 15 i 8; 48 iv 4, vi 3, vii 13
  Ur-ur šeš Bíl-làl-la sanga Kèš, App. to no. 32 iv 13
  An-na-bí-kúš dumu Ur-ur šeš Bíl-làl-la sanga Kèš, App. to no. 32 v 5
  Ur-ur DUMU Su-NI-um MAR.X^{KI}, 40 C xix 4
  Ba-ša-aḫ-DINGIR LÚ.ÉŠ.GÍD DUMU Ur-ur . . . DUMU.DUMU A-ku-ì-lum, 40 C xiv 3

U-bi-in-LUGAL-rí DUMU Ur-ur ši GAL.SUKKAL-li, 40 A xv 6
Zu-zu Ìr-e-pum 2 DUMU Iš-má-DINGIR ši NIGIR DUMU.DUMU Ur-ur ši PA.ḪI, 40 C xiii 1, 6
Ur-Utu, 16a ii 4
Ur-^{d}Za-b[a$_4$?-ba$_4$?], 28 ii
Ur-ZU.AB: Ga-at-núm Su$_4$-ma-SIPA Be-lí-ba-ni 3 DUMU Ur-ZU.AB DUMU.DUMU DINGIR-su-la-ba, 40 C v 15
Ur?-[. . .], 23 rev. v 11
U[r-. . .], 15 viii 18; 16a iii 1
Úr-kug: Ušùr-r[a-ni]? Mes-ZU.A[B] Ur-^{d}Nin-Gír-su Tur-tur Úr-kug Ḫul-KAL-igi SAL-tur dumu ⸢X⸣-[x-m]e, 22 i 43
Úr-ni, 14 xv 16
Uru-KA-gi-na DUMU En-gil-sa PA.TE.SI ŠIR.BUR.LA^{KI}, 40 A xiv 7
Uru-mu, 30a v 4
UŠ-ág-Kèš IB, App. to no. 32 vii 12
UŠ-gal, 21 i 34, 39
Ušum-gal, 12 Inscription on Side C
Ušum-gal pab-šeš ^{d}Šará?, 12 Adscription to Side A
^{d}Šará?-igi-zi-ZU.AB dumu Ušum-gal ÉŠ.A, 12 Adscription to Side D
Ušum-ma, 15 iv 13
Ušùr(LÁL+LAGAB)-r[a-ni]? MES-ZU.A[B] Ur-^{d}Nin-Gír-su Tur-tur Úr-kug Ḫul-KAL-igi SAL-tur dumu ⸢X⸣-[x-m]e, 22 i 39
Utu-mu-kúš, 32 v 6
Utu-šeš-mu, 33 rev. iii 2
Ùz-da-DU sipa arád Bíl-làl-la, App. to no. 32 vii 2

Wa-gi-rí: La-a-GUR DUMU Rí-pum ši Wa-gi-rí, 40 B xiii 7
Wa-X-rúm šu Mu-mu, 41 rev. viii 25
⸢We⸣-tum DUMU ši Ìr-e-um, 44k ii 2
[W]u-zum-tum SAL.BALAG.DI KA$_5$.A, 43 x 6

Za-ab-tim: Ìr-e-um DUMU Iš-má-DINGIR ši Za-ab-tim, 43 vii 19
[Iš-má]-DINGIR [Šu Za-a]b-tim, 43 vi 13
Za-la, 15 iv 8
⸢Za-NI-NI⸣, 33 rev. i 10
Zag-mu IB, App. to no. 32 vii 11
Zi-at: BALA-ì-lum DUMU Zi-at, 41 rev. ii 12
Zi-gàr-su DUMU Ur-^{d}En-líl DUB.SAR, 40 B xiv 14
Zi-gur-mu-bí DUMU Ì-lí-a-ḫi ši TE.LAL.GAL, 40 A xiii 9
Zi-im-tum: DUMU.DUMU Zi-im-tum include families of DINGIR-a-ḫa, Lugal-ezen, Su-mu-núm, PÙ.ŠA-^{d}Nu-muš-da, DINGIR-a-ḫa, Ìr-e-pum, Ga-la-ab-É-a, Be-lí-mu-da, SI.A-um, and DINGIR-ba-ni, 40 B xi 13
Zi-lu-lu I-lib^{KI}, 41 viii 6
Zi-lú-AŠ-da IB, App. to no. 32 vii 10
Zi-ma-na-ak, see under GNs
Zi-ra DUMU DINGIR-dan . . . 5 DUMU.DUMU Da-tum, 40 D iv 14
Zi-ra DUMU Ib-bu-ru, 41 rev. ix 14
Zi-rí-gúm IB, App. to no. 32 vii 9
Zi-zi: Ku-ku DUMU En-na-É-a DUMU.DUMU Zi-zi, 40 B vii 2
Su-NI-um DUMU Bi-im ši Zi-zi, 40 B xiv 4
Zi-[. . .]: U-ḫúb [. . .] DUMU Zi-[. . .], 41 rev. ii 22
Zu-zu DUMU A-ar-É-a . . . DUMU.DUMU Ši-ù-ni, 40 A vii 2
Zu-zu DUMU Ur-Már-da DUMU.DUMU I-ki-lum PA.TE.SI Ki-babbar^{KI}, 40 C iii 4
Zu-zu Ìr-e-pum 2 DUMU Iš-má-DINGIR ši NIGIR DUMU.DUMU Ur-ur ši PA.ḪI, 40 C xii 23
UD.IŠ Zu-zu 2 DUMU Iš-dup-^{d}EN.ZU DUMU.DUMU Ìr-ra-ra, 40 A iv 20
Zu-zu Ra-bí-ì-lum DUMU.DUMU Il-su(wr. ZU)-ERÍN+X PA.TE.SI, 34 iv 7
Amar-rí-rí Be-lí-sa-tu 2 DUMU Zu-zu [DU]MU.DUMU Ur-[Má]r-da [ši I]-ki-lum, 40 C iv 12
^{d}EN.ZU-GIŠ.ERÍN Ì-la-la Šu-ì-lí-su 3 DUMU Zu-zu ši A-ar-É-a, 40 A x 8
Zu-zu ŠEŠ Du-du BÀD-ḪU.GAN?^{KI}, 41 vi 6, vii 4
Zu-zu DUB.SAR šu KURUŠDA DUMU La-mu-um, 40 A xi 2
[X]-bu [L]Ú [Z]u-zu, 48 rev. ii 2
Zur-zur, 14 i 15; 15 xiv 29

[. . .]-⸢a⸣, 32 rev. i 7
[. . .]-a-a: Ma-la-ni-su [DU]MU Dup-si-ga [DU]MU.DUMU I-[k]i-lum [. . .]-a-a, 40 C vi 24
[. . .]-a-nà[d-. . .], 23 [obv. v 11], [rev. v 2], 10, [24]
[. . .]-⸢^{d}Aš$_7$(SÁR+DIŠ)⸣-[gi$_4$-. . .], 33 rev. ii 10
[X]-⸢barag-si⸣: [. . .]-⸢ma⸣? [dumu X]-⸢barag-si⸣, 23 [rev. iii 3, 33], obv. iv 7
⸢X⸣-bí-bí, 28 i
[X]-bu [L]Ú [Z]u-zu, 48 rev. ii 1
[. . .]-bu, 44h i 7
[. . .]-DINGIR, 52 rev. i 1
[. . .]-gi: [T]u-tu [DUMU . . .]-gi [DUMU.DUMU PN], 40 C iii 11
[. . .]-⸢GÍN?-zi?⸣, 21 ii 2
[. . .]-⸢ì-lí⸣, 32 rev. i 6
[. . .]-KA-[. . .]-zi, 33 i 8
X-kar, 14 xviii 14
X.KU.EN gal-nigir, 12 Adscription to Side B
[. . .-l]a-ba: [. . .]-ni [DUMU . . .-l]a-ba, 40 C v 19
[X]-la-m[u(-x)], 16e 2
[. . .]-⸢ma⸣? [dumu X]-⸢barag-si⸣, 23 obv. iv 6
X-ma-ni-dug$_4$ šeš Bíl-làl-la sanga Kèš, App. to no. 32 iv 8
[. . .-m]u: [PN DUMU . . .-m]u . . . DUMU.DUMU Su-mu-núm, 40 A iii 2
[. . .]-⸢mu⸣-[. . .]-zu, 23 [obv. iv 25], [rev. iv 19], obv. v 7
⸢X⸣-NI, 23 rev. x 35
[. . .]-NI [DUMU . . .-l]a-ba, 40 C v 18
[. . .-N]I, 52 rev. i 3
[X]-NI-bí-zi-⸢x-x⸣, 28 i
X-nigir, 15 xiv 28
⸢X⸣-pirig ⸢X⸣-[x dumu PN-me], 22 [i 2, 27, 38], 57
[. . .]-sar, 44g rev. i 3
[. . .]-si guruš-[tab], 33 i 4
[. . .]-si?-da, 44h i 8

X-si-ga, 14 xi 3
LAK-483-TAR, 14 i 16
[. . .-^{d}]Tišpak, 44g rev. i 2
[X]-tu-um: [Ì-l]í-dan [X]-tu-um [A-ḫ]u-ḫu [DUMU]? Ga-NI-am-me-me, 44a i 3
[X].UD.DU-na, 43 viii 10
⸢X⸣-zu-zu: Na-ni [DUMU]? ⸢X⸣-zu-zu, 34 i 5
[. . .-z]um, 52 rev. i 2
⸢X⸣-[x]: ⸢X⸣-pirig ⸢X⸣-[x dumu PN], 22 [i 3, 31] Ušùr-r[a-ni]? Mes-ZU.A[B] Ur-^{d}Nin-Gír-su Tur-tur, Úr-kug Ḫul-KAL-igi SAL-tur dumu ⸢X⸣-[x-m]e, 22 i 46
⸢X-x⸣: ⸢I⸣-[x]-lum-[x] DUMU ⸢X-x⸣, 30a iii 2
[X]-⸢x⸣-Eš$_{4}$-dar, 35 i 16
⸢X⸣-[. . .]: ⸢X⸣-[. . .] ⸢Pù-Ma⸣-[ma]? DUMU.DUMU.ME, 30a iv 1
[. . .]-⸢x⸣-a-ḫu, 43 iii 10
[. . .]-⸢x⸣-dùg, 33 rev. iii 1
[. . .]-⸢x⸣-[L]UM, 16d A iii 1
[. . .]-⸢X⸣-LUM, 50 Side A ii 4

4.2. *Divine Names*

^{d}A-a, see PNs PÙ.ŠA-A-a and Su-mu-^{d}A-a
^{d}A-ba$_{4}$, 40 A xv 19; 41 v 5
see PNs ⸢PÙ⸣.ŠA-⸢^{d}⸣[A]-ba$_{4}$ and ^{d}A-ba$_{4}$-iš-da-gal
^{d}AB, see PN Ur-^{d}AB
Ab-ra, see PNs Ab-ra-Il and Ur-Ab-ra
Anzud$_{x}$(AN(.IM).MI.MUŠEN), see PNs É-Anzud$_{x}$ and Lugal-Anzud$_{x}$
Aš-dar, see Eš$_{4}$-dar
^{d}ÁŠ?.TE?, see under PNs
^{d}Aš$_{7}$(SÁR+DIŠ)-gi$_{4}$, see PNs Sag-^{d}Aš$_{7}$-gi$_{4}$-da, Ur-⸢^{d}Aš$_{7}$⸣-[gi$_{4}$-. . .], and [. . .]-⸢^{d}Aš$_{7}$⸣-[gi$_{4}$-. . .]

Ba-ba, see PN Šu-Ba-ba

^{d}Da-gan, see PNs I-ti-^{d}Da-gan, Pù-^{d}Da-gan, and Šu-^{d}Da-gan
^{d}DUB-an, see PN Ur-^{d}DUB-an
^{d}Dumu-zi, see PN Ur-^{d}Dumu-zi-da

É-a, see PNs A-ku-É-a, BALA-É-a, É-a-GÚ, É-a-ra-bí, En-na-É-a, Ga-la-ab-É-a, I-ku-É-a, I-ti-É-a, Ik-ru-ub-É-a, PÙ.ŠA-É-a, and Su/Su$_{4}$-mu-É-a
En-gal-DU.DU, see PN Ur-En-gal-DU.DU
^{d}En-ki, see under PNs
see PN Ur-^{d}En-ki
^{d}En-líl, see PNs Lú-⸢^{d}⸣En-⸢líl⸣?, Lugal-^{d}En-líl, and Ur-^{d}En-líl
^{d}EN.ZU, see PNs A-ma-^{d}EN.ZU, Amar-^{d}EN.ZU, ^{d}EN.ZU-a-ar, ^{d}EN.ZU-al-su, ^{d}EN.ZU-GIŠ.ERÍN, I-bí-^{d}EN.ZU, I-mi-^{d}EN.ZU, Iš-dup-^{d}EN.ZU, Su-mu-^{d}EN.ZU, and Ur-^{d}EN.ZU
Eš$_{4}$-dar, see PNs Eš$_{4}$-dar-al-su, Eš$_{4}$-dar-ra!, PÙ.ŠA-Eš$_{4}$-dar, Šu-Eš$_{4}$-dar, and [X]-⸢x⸣-Eš$_{4}$-dar
see PNs Aš-dar-BALA? and Ù-Aš-dar

^{d}Ezínu(ŠE.TIR), see PNs Amar-^{d}Ezínu, ^{d}Ezínu-ur-sag, and Ur-^{d}Ezínu

^{d}Gá-tùm-dùg, 19a iii 7, v 7
^{d}Gu-nu-ra, see PN Ur-^{d}Gu-nu-ra
^{d}Gú-gú, see PN Ur-^{d}Gú-gú
^{d}GUR$_{8}$-⸢x⸣, see PN Ur-^{d}GUR$_{8}$-⸢x⸣

Ì-šum, see PN Ur-Ì-šum
ÍD, see PN I-ti-ÍD
Il, see PNs Ab-ra-Il, BÀD-Il, En-na-Il, Ib-LUL-Il, Il-GIŠ.ERÍN, Ìr-ra-⸢Il⸣?, Iš-dup-Il, Pù-Il, and Ra-bí-Il
Il-la, see PN PÙ.ŠA-Il-la
^{d}IM, see PNs ^{d}IM-[G]Ú?.GAL and PÙ.ŠA-^{d}IM
^{d}Innin, 16d B iii 2; 26 ii 7
see PNs I-nin-me-šum, I-nin-sa-tu, and Innin-sar
Ìr-ra, see PN Ìr-ra-⸢Il⸣?
^{d}Irra$_{x}$(KIŠ)^{ra}, see PN Ku-ru-^{d}Irra$_{x}$(KIŠ)^{ra}

La-im, see PN I-Ku-La-im
Lu-lu, see PN PÙ.ŠA-Lu-lu
^{d}Lugal-^{GIŠ}asal$_{x}$(RÉC-65.A), 36 ii 10
^{d}LUGAL-bar-ga-ad, 41 vi 20
^{d}Lugal-Már-da, 40 C xiv 25, xvii 19

^{d}Ma-lik, see PNs Ìr-am-^{d}Ma-lik, Ìr-e-^{d}Ma-lik, ^{d}Ma-lik-zi-in-su, Su$_{4}$-ma-Ma-lik, Šum-Ma-lik, and U-zé-^{d}Ma-lik
Ma-ma, see PNs É-Ma-ma, KA-Ma-ma, PÙ.ŠA-Ma-ma, Šu-Ma-ma, and Ur-Ma-ma
^{d}Maḫ, see PN ^{d}Maḫ-URUDU-e
Me-ir, see PN KA-$^{(d)}$Me-ir
^{d}MUŠ, see PN Ur-^{d}MUŠ
^{d}MUŠ$^{ir\text{-}ḫa}$, see GN E ^{d}MUŠ$^{ir\text{-}ḫa}$

^{d}Nanše, see PN ^{d}Nanše-nu-me-a
see GN gán ^{d}Nanše-gar-ra
^{d}Nin-gal, 38 i 10
NIN-GÍR.ḪA.RAD, 10:1
$^{(d)}$Nin-Gír-su, 18 rev. ii 1, 4, iii 2, 4; 20 rev. ii 2
see PNs Nin-Gír-su-⸢zà-me⸣ and Ur-^{d}Nin-Gír-su
^{d}Nin-ḫur-sag, see GN SUG-^{d}Nin-ḫur-sag
^{d}Nin-kar, see under PNs
see PN Ur-^{d}Nin-kar
^{d}Nin-mug, App. to no. 32 i 4
^{d}Nin-PA, see PN Ur-^{d}Nin-PA
^{d}Nu-muš-da, see PN PÙ.ŠA-^{d}Nu-muš-da
Nu-ni, see PN PÙ.ŠA-Nu-ni
Nu-nu, see PNs Pù-Nu-nu and Šu-Nu-nu

^{d}PA.BÌL.SAG, see PN Ur-^{d}PA.BÌL.SAG

^{d}Samàn(NUN.ŠE.ÉŠ.BU), see PN Amar-^{d}Samàn
^{d}SI.LU, see PN Ur-^{d}SI.LU
^{d}Sud-da, see PN Ur-^{d}Sud-da

^{d}Šará?, 12 Adscription on Side A
see PNs ^{d}Šará?-igi-zi-ZU.AB and ^{d}Šará-men
^{d}Šul-pa-è, see PN Ur-^{d}Šul-pa-è

^{d}TIR, 13 rev. iii 2
^{d}Tišpak, see PNs Pù-^{d}Tišpak and [. . .-^{d}]Tišpak
^{d}Tud, see PNs Me-^{d}Tud and Ur-^{d}Tud

^{d}UTU, 48 vi 14, rev. Neo-Babylonian adscription
see PNs I-bí-^{d}UTU and Ur-Utu

^{d}Za-ba$_4$-ba$_4$, see PNs PÙ.ŠA-^{d}Za-ba$_4$-ba$_4$ and Ur-^{d}Za-b[a$_4$?-ba$_4$?]

^{d}⸢X⸣-da, see PN Lú-^{d}⸢X⸣-da

4.3. *Geographical Names*

A-ga-dè^{KI}, 24 rev. iv 9; 40 A xvi 16; 41 i 1, rev. vii 17
A.Ḫ[A . . .], 20 vii 2
[a-šà?] E-ga-rin, 21 v 3
a-šà ḪU.TUŠ.BU-rúm, 21 iii 30, v 1, 5
A-za-me-um^{KI}, 41 viii 10
A-za-ra, 41 i 8
A-⸢x⸣-[. . .], 19 rev. ii 2
Ab-za-⸢x⸣^{KI}, 48 rev. ii 9
Adab^{KI}, App. to no. 32 viii 3
Akšak^{KI}, App. to nos. 22–23 vi 9
AN.GÁN, 19 rev. i 2
An-za-ma-tim, see GÁN An-za-ma-tim
Ar-da-na-an^{KI}, 42 iii 6, v 1
ARÁD-da-ni^{KI}, 40 A xv 13
Áš-na-ak^{KI}, 38 i 15
At-li, see E+PAB At-li

Ba-az^{KI}, see GÁN Ba-az^{KI}
ba-la-ag Da-da-rí-im, see GÁN šu ba-la-ag Da-da-rí-im
Ba-ra-az-EDIN^{KI}, see GÁN Ba-ra-az-EDIN^{KI}
Ba-si-me^{KI}, 40 A xiv 17
BÀD-^{d}EN.ZU^{KI}, 40 A vi 13, vii 12, x 15, 20, xvi 19
Bàd-giš-gi$_4$, 20 v 2
BÀD-ḪU.GAN?^{KI}, 41 vi 8
BÀD [. . .], 15 viii 12
Bar^{KI}, 40 D vi 15
Bar-sag?-šag$_5$, 20 iv 7
BE.SUG, 18 rev. i 6
Bi-ìr-ti-in, see GÁN Bi-ìr-ti-in

da im-ru, see gán Ur-^{d}Gu-nu-ra ENGUR! da im-ru
da lugal, 21 i 22
Da-mi-gi^{KI}, 40 A xv 24, xvi 10
Dan-ni-rí-iš-tim, 40 A xvi 11
Dilmun^{KI}, see PN Amar-Dilmun-na?^{KI}

E-AKKIL-tim, see GÁN E-AKKIL-tim
E ^{d}Irḫan$_x$(MUŠ)$^{\text{ir-ḫa}}$: AB+ÁŠ.AB+ÁŠ šu URU^{KI}.URU^{KI} ša E ^{d}Irḫan$_x$(MUŠ)$^{\text{ir-ḫa}}$, 41 vii 17–18
E+PAB At-li, see GÁN Bi-ìr-ti-in . . .
E+PAB.KAS^{KI}, 20 iii 6
E+PAB PA.TE.SI, see GÁN Bi-ìr-ti-in . . .
É-dúr-BAḪÁR . . . , see (gán) É-dúr-BAḪÁR . . .
[É-du]r$_5$-en$_5$-si, see gán [É-du]r$_5$-en$_5$-si
É-dur$_5$-Me-me, 37 iv 2
É-dur$_5$-sabra, see ⸢gán⸣ É-dur$_5$-sabra
É.GIŠ.MA.NU^{KI}, 40 C xiii 16

É-gud, 14 xviii 13; 15 xi 13
see also gán É-gud
É-ki-im, see GÁN ša-at É-ki-im ù Zi-ma-na-ak
É-mar-za^{KI}, 40 C xvi 17
é Mug-si, App. to no. 32 i 2
é ^{d}Nin-mug, App. to no. 32 i 4
É-nun, 12 Adscription to Side C
É-sag-ki-ti, 14 xvi 3
⸢É⸣.TU[M], 15 viii 11
Elam^{KI}, 40 B xii 5
Eš$_4$-na-na-ak^{KI}, 40 C xv 14

Ga-za-lu^{KI}, 40 C xix 19′, D vii 4
gán A.UŠ, 20 v 8; 21 v 14
gán A+X-a-X-è/sag?, 20 vi 3
GÁN An-za-ma-tim, 40 B ix 3
GÁN Ba-az^{KI}, 40 A x 1, xvi 18
GÁN Ba-ra-az-EDIN^{KI} in Kiš^{KI}, 40 D vi 16, xiv 17
GÁN Bi-ìr-ti-in E+PAB At-li ù E+PAB PA.TE.SI ⸢šu⸣ Ib-me-rí^{KI} (= Ib-rí-me^{KI}), 43 xii 1–4
gán Da-da, 15 xiv 13
GÁN.DAR, see under PNs
gán ⸢DU⸣?, 20 i 5
[gá]n DÙG?, 39 i 4
gán DUN, 14 i 2, ii 7, viii 3, xviii 4; 15 ii 2, 29, iii 27, vii 1, xiii 17, L. E. 22
GÁN E-AKKIL-tim, 44j 2
gán É-ad-KID, 14 iv 16, vi 13
(gán) É-dúr-BAḪÁR!.DU, 15 L. E. 11
gán É-dúr-BAḪÁR!.A.DU.GÍN, 15 vii 30
gán É-dúr-BAḪÁR!.ZA.NUN.DU, 15 x 3
gán É-dúr-BAḪÁR.ZA.NUN, 15 xii 17
gán [É-du]r$_5$-en$_5$-si, 39 i 2
⸢gán⸣ É-dur$_5$-sabra, 39 i 1
gán É-GAM.GAM-maḫ-zu-zu, 15 v 26
gán É-gud, 15 i 2, iv 27
see also É-gud
gán É-Ì-la-lum, 14 v 3
gán É-kas, 32 i 1, v 12?
gán É-udu-ninda-kú, 14 viii 5, x 4
gán ganun(GÁ+NUN)-dù, 20 ii 4
gán GI.LAGAB, 12 Inscription on Side D, twice
gán Gi-lugal-la-ka, App. to nos. 22–23 i 2, xi 4
gán Gír-gír-maḫ, 24 rev. iii 5
GÁN Gir$_{13}$-tab^{KI}, 40 B xxii 13
gán gud, 20 vi 8
gán Gúg, 14 iii 11
GÁN KI, 17 ii 3
gán ki, 20 ii 5
gán Kug-gál^{KI}, 14 xvii 2
gán ⸢Lagaš⸣, 20 vii 8
GÁN LUGAL, 40 A ix 16
GÁN.MAḪ, 30 i 2
GÁN Mi-zu-a-NI-im, 40 B ix 9
gán Mu-ni-gár, 14 xvi 7
gán ^{d}Nanše-gar-ra, 24 rev. ii 1
GÁN NI.SUM, 18 rev. i 1
gán Níg-è, 20 vi 7
GÁN ^{d}Nin-gal, 38 i 10
gán Pab-rúm, 14 xiii 11

gán SAG.A, 15 viii 4
gán sag-[du$_5$-ka], 22 iv 3
GÁN Si-im-tum, 40 B ix 12
gán SUG ⸢AB?.ZAG?⸣, 39 ii 1
gán sug Lagaš^{KI}, 24 rev. iii 4
GÁN ša-at É-ki-im ù Zi-ma-na-ak, 40 B viii 11–12
gán ŠÀ.GIBIL, 19 rev. i 1
[g]án [^{GIŠ}Š]E.DÙG, 24 rev. iv 1
GÁN šu ba-la-ag Da-da-rí-im, 38 i 9
GÁN šu É, 44h ii 7–8
GÁN šu KÁ.T[I]?, 41 iv 20
GÁN šu kir-ba-ti Ar-da-na-an^{KI} in E+PAB At-li, 42 iii 4–7
GÁN šu Sa-ba-ra?, 41 ii 10
GÁN šu Ù.SIG$_7$, 41 v 15
GÁN TAR.⸢X⸣, 31 ii 5
GÁN Tu-la(l)-tim, 38 i 11
gán Ú.PAD.ME, 20 ii 8
gán Ù-a-dùg-ga, 24 rev. ii 3
[g]án Ù-[dùg]-⸢KU$_4$⸣, 24 obv. 1
gán Ur-^{d}Gu-nu-ra ENGUR! da im-ru, 14 xvii 13–14
GÁN Ur-ma in Lugal-kalam-ma, 37 rev. iii 15
gán [. . .]-⸢x⸣-lú, 39 i 3
gán X.PAB.ÚŠ, 14 xii 9, xiii 3
GÌR.ŠÀ, 19 rev. i 4
Gir$_{13}$-tab^{KI}, 40 B xv 5, 8
see also GÁN Gir$_{13}$-tab^{KI}
GIŠ.ÙḪ^{KI}, see Umma^{KI}
Gu-lí-zi: GÁN.NINDÁ IM.U$_5$ ša-at Gu-lí-zi, 40 D vi 8
see PN Gu-lí-zum
GÚ.DU$_8$.A^{KI}, 40 A xiv 26
gú-⸢nu⸣-[. . .], 15 xi 20
Gúg-bar-rúm^{KI}, 14 iv 9

Ḫa-ar-ḫa-mu-na-ak^{KI}, 40 C xix 3
ḪI.MA.KI?, 31 iii 9
ḪU.TUŠ.BU-rúm, see a-šà ḪU.TUŠ.BU-rúm
Ḫur-rúm, 34 rev. i 2

I-bí-rí^{KI}, 40 A xv 20
I-lib^{KI}, 41 viii 7, rev. vii 8
Ib-me-rí^{KI} (= Ib-rí-me^{KI}), see GÁN Bi-ìr-ti-in . . .
Ib-rí-me^{KI}, see Ib-me-rí^{KI}
ÍD A-maš-ti-ak, 40 C xiii 19
ÍD.IDIGNA or ÍD.ZUBI, 40 A ix 19
ÍD.NUN.ME, 40 B ix 6
ÍD.ZI.KALAM.MA, 40 C xiii 13
ÍD.ZUBI, see ÍD.IDIGNA
Isin$_x$(IN)^{KI}, see PN Isin$_x$(IN)^{KI}-dùg

KA-ul-lum^{KI}, 40 C xix 9
KA-zu-ra-ak^{KI}, 40 C xv 7, xix 12
KAS^{KI}, 41 iv 1
KAS.E+PAB^{KI}, 20 iii 6
Kèš^{KI}, App. to no. 32 ii 12, v 7, vi 3
see PNs Kèš-pa-è, Ur-Kèš^{KI}, Ur-sag-Kèš, and UŠ-ág-Kèš
Ki-babbar^{KI}, 40 C iii 8, vii 15
KI.SAR^{KI}, 41 rev. viii 11
Kiš$^{(KI)}$, 26 ii 2; 34 ii 2; 40 A x 4, D vii 1, 3, xiv 18

Lagaš^{KI}, 20 i 6, ii 9, iv 10; 22 i 9, ii 11, [iii 17], [iv 21]; 23 [obv. i 11], [obv. ii 9], [obv. iii 13], [rev. iii 10], [obv. iv 32], obv. v 18, [rev. v 38], [rev. vi 23], [rev. vii 30]; App. to nos. 22–23 i 9; 40 A xiv 10
see also gán ⸢Lagaš⸣ and gán sug Lagaš^{KI}
see PN Lagaš^{KI}
LAL?.KI, 20 iii 7
Lugal-kalam-ma, 37 rev. iii 16

ma-ta Urua(URU+A)^{KI}, App. to no. 32 vi 4
Mar-tu, 24 rev. iii 8
MAR.X^{KI}, 40 C xix 6
Már-da^{KI}, 40 C xix 15, 28, xxiv 25
see PN Ur-Már-da
see DN ^{d}Lugal-Már-da
ME.NAM?.⸢X⸣, 18 rev. i 3
MES.BAR^{KI}, 40 B xv 1

NI.DU$_6$, 18 rev. i 5
NUN.UD.KIB^{KI}, see Sippar^{KI}

Pù-sa-an^{KI}, 37 R. E. 12

SAR.LAK-175, 18 rev. i 2, ii 5
Sar-ra-tum^{KI}, 41 iii 4
Sippar^{KI}, 35 i 2; 40 A xiii 22
see PN Ur-sag-UD.KIB.NUN^{KI}
⸢Su⸣-ba-rí-um: LÚ ⸢Su⸣(wr. ⸢Zu⸣)-ba-rí-um, 34 ii 8
SUG-^{d}Nin-ḫur-sag, 40 C xiii 24

Ša-at-bar-rí-im^{KI}, 40 C xii 3, xviii 30
Ša-da-an^{KI}, 41 vi 25
Ša-na-e: PN NU.BANDA Ša-na-e, 40 A xiv 3, xv 10
ŠEG$_9$-da^{KI}, 41 viii 5
Šim-SAR^{KI}, 41 viii 13
ŠIR.BUR.LA^{KI}, see Lagaš^{KI}

Tu-la(l)-tim, see GÁN Tu-la(l)-tim
Tu-tu-ub^{KI}, 44l i 6

Ú-sá-la-tim, 38 i 7
U$_4$-bí-um^{KI}, 41 viii 1, 17
UD.KIB.NUN^{KI}, see Sippar^{KI}
UD.MÁ.NINA(.KI).ŠUM, see PNs UD.MÁ.NINA.ŠUM-pa-è and UD.MÁ.NINA.KI.ŠUM-dùg
UD.NUN^{KI}, see Adab^{KI}
UD.ÙḪ^{KI}, see Akšak^{KI}
UM.GIBIL, 41 rev. v 22
UM.LIBIR, 41 rev. v 13
Umma^{KI}, 21 i 3, ii 5; 40 A xii 24
Ur-šag$_5$?^{KI}, 26 i 3
Uru!-⟨SAG.⟩ḪÚB.DU^{KI}, 33 rev. ii 6
Urua(URU+A)^{KI}, see ma-ta Urua^{KI}
URUDU?^{KI}, 41 vi 18

Zi-ma-na-ak, see GÁN ša-at É-ki-im ù Zi-ma-na-ak

X.EDIN^{KI}, 38 i 13
[X].ME.RU^{KI}, 31 i 5
⸢X⸣-na-ma-nu^{KI}, 16d A iii 2

4.4. *Professions and Titles*

[A]?.ZU (*asûm*) "physician," 30a i 11
AB+ÁŠ.URU^{KI} (*šîbu âlim*) "city elder," 38 ii 5
AB+ÁŠ.URU, 40 C xiv 27
AB+ÁŠ.URU GN, 40 A vi 12–13, vii 11–12, x 14–15
AB+ÁŠ.AB+ÁŠ, see NU.BANDA AB+ÁŠ.AB+ÁŠ
a-bi URU Elam^{KI} (gen.), 40 B xii 4–5
ad-KID (*atkuppum*) "reed-mat maker," see GN gán É-ad-KID
agrig (*abarakkum*) "steward," 15 L. E. 15
AGRIG ^{d}A-ba$_4$-iš-da-gal, 40 C xix 26
AGRIG, see under PNs
arád (*wardum*) "slave," App. to no. 32 vii 4
arád-gemé, App. to no. 32 vii 7
see also ìr
ašgab (*aškāpum*) "leather worker," 21 i 35; App. to no. 32 vi 11

BALAG.DI, see SAL.BALAG.DI

DAM.GÀR (*tamkārum*) "merchant," 40 B xii 1, xiv 7
DI.TAR (*dajjānum*) "judge," 40 C xiv 21
dub-sar (*tupšarrum*) "scribe," 21 iii 5, 34; 40 A xi 3, xvi 7, B xiv 16, xv 2, C xiv 7, xvii 6, xviii 24, D ii 8
DUB.SAR.GÁN, 41 ii 4, iv 25, viii 22
dub-sar-maḫ, 23 obv. x 4; App. to nos. 22–23 v 9
dub-sar-me lú-gá[n-gíd-da-me], 23 obv. xi 4–5
see UM.MI.A DUB.SAR
DUMU LUGAL (*marʾu šarrim*) "prince," 40 D vi 12; 41 ii 16

EN.ME.LI, see ensi
en$_5$-si (Akk. *iššiakkum*) "governor," 34 iv 11; 35 ii 16; 41 v 25, 28
PA.TE.SI Ba-si-me^{KI}, 40 A xiv 16–17
en$_5$-si-⸢GAR⸣, see ìr en$_5$-si-⸢GAR⸣
PA.TE.SI GIŠ.ÙḪ^{KI}, 40 A xii 23–24
PA.TE.SI Ki-babbar^{KI}, 40 C iii 7–8, vii 14–15
en$_5$-si Lagaš^{KI}, 22 i 8–9, ii 10–11, [iii 16–17], [iv 20–21]; 23 [obv. i 10–11], [obv. ii 8–9], [obv. iii 12–13], [rev. iii 9–10], [obv. iv 31–32], obv. v 17–18, [rev. v 37–38], [rev. vi 22–23], [rev. vii 29–30]; App. to nos. 22–23 i 8–9; 40 A xiv 9–10
[PA.TE].SI [NUN.U]D.KIB^{KI}, 35 i 1–2
PA.TE.SI Tu-tu-ub^{KI}, 44l i 5–6
see GAR-en$_5$-si and [ŠE]Š PA.TE.SI
see under PNs
see GNs E+PAB PA.TE.SI and gán [É-du]r$_5$-en$_5$-si
engar (*ikkarum*) "farmer," "agronomos," 20 v 4, 10, vi 4, vii 4, 7
engar èš, 10:5
engar ki-gu[b], App. to nos. 22–23 viii 5
ENGAR LUGAL, 40 C xvii 2
engar zag durun-durun, 14 vi 10–11 (three men), xiv 17–18 (ki durun-durun; five men); 15 i 27–28 (four men), ii 26–27 (four men), iii 24–25 (four men), iv 24–25 (four men), v 23–24 (four men), vi 29–30 (four men), vii 27–28 (four men), ix 28–x 1 (four men), x 27–28 (four men), xiii 14–15 (four men), xiv 10–11 (four men), L. E. 8–9 (four men)
ensi (*ensûm, šāʾilum*) "dream-interpreter," 40 A xv 27

gal-nigir "chief herald," 12 Adscription to Side B
see nigir
GAL.SUKKAL "senior messenger," 40 A xi 11, C xvii 22
see sukkal
see under PNs
gal-ukkin "chief of the assembly," 12 Adscription to Side B
gal-ukù "military commander," 16d A iii 5; 40 A iv 9, xiv 13
gal-ukù ìr é-šà-ga, 23 obv. x 6–7; App. to nos. 22–23 [vi 1–2]
GAL.UKÙ Ša-at-bar-rí-im^{KI}, 40 C xviii 29
galla, see TE.LAL
galla-gal, see TE.LAL.GAL
GAR-en$_5$-si "retired(?) governor"
GAR-en$_5$-si Adab^{KI}, App. to no. 32 viii 2–3
see en$_5$-si-⸢GAR⸣
gemé (*amtum*) "slave woman," App. to no. 32 vii 6
GEMÉ.DINGIR, 40 D iii 11; 41 i 14
see arád-gemé
GÌR.NITA (Sum. šagina, Akk. *šakkanakkum*) "governor-general," 40 A xi 14
GÌR.NITA LÚ.GIŠ.GÍD.DA, 40 A xii 13–14
GÌR.NITA LÚ.GIŠ.TI, 40 A xii 5–6
GIŠ.KIN.TI, see NU.BANDA GIŠ.KIN.TI
gu-lí-zum "ox driver," see under PNs
gu-lí-zi, see under GNs
GU.SUR.NUN "field assessor," 20 iii 9, v 9, vi 5
guruš-tab (*batūlum*) "bachelor," 32 v 8; 33 i 5

ì-DU.DU (*muraqqiʾum*) "perfumer," 39 ii 4
ì-du$_8$ (*atûm*) "gatekeeper," 33 rev. iii 8
IB (meaning unknown), App. to no. 32 vii 13
INNIN.ÙḪ, see ÙḪ.INNIN
ìr "servant"
ìr en$_5$-si-⸢GAR⸣, App. to nos. 22–23 viii 1
ìr é-šà-ga, see gal-ukù ìr é-šà-ga
see also arád
IŠ (Akk. *kizûm*) "equerry," 40 A vi 18
išib (*išippum*) "purification priest"
išib ^{d}Nin-gír-su, 20 rev. ii 2

KUG.DÍM (*kutimmum*) "silversmith," see under PNs
kug-gál (*gugallum*) "canal inspector," 15 xiv 16; 41 rev. ix 11
see GN gán Kug-gál^{KI}
kurušda (*mārûm*) "animal fattener," 33 rev. i 4
see under PNs

lú-ašlág(GIŠ.TÚG.KAR.DU) (*ašlākum*) "bleacher," "fuller," 33 rev. i 2
lú-banšur-íl, see muḫaldim lú-banšur-íl
LÚ.ÉŠ.GÍD (*šādid ašlim*) "surveyor," 40 C xiv 2, xvii 10
lú-gán-gíd-da (*šādid ašlim*) "field surveyor," 23 obv. xi 5; App. to nos. 22–23 ix 1
LÚ.GIŠ.GÍD.DA, see GÌR.NITA LÚ.GIŠ.GÍD.DA

LÚ.GIŠ.TI, see GÌR.NITA LÚ.GIŠ.TI
LÚ.IGI (meaning unknown), 40 A xiii 25, B xiv 1
see NU.BANDA LÚ.IGI
see under PNs
LÚ.KAS$_4$ (*lāsimum*) "courier," see under PNs
lú-še-íl "grain-carrier," App. to no 32 vii 8
LÚ?.TÚG? "tailor," 50 Side A iii 1
lú-u$_5$ (*rakkābum*?) "mounted messenger"
lú-u$_5$ Akšak^{KI}, App. to nos. 22–23 vi 8–9
⸢lú⸣-[. . .], App. to nos. 22–23 x 4
lugal (*šarrum*) "king," 21 i 22; 41 ix 3, rev. iv 5
LUGAL KIŠ, 40 A i 6–7, xvi 21–22, B xxii 15–16, C xxiv 27–28, D xiv 20–21
LUGAL Kiš, 26 ii 2
lugal Lagaš, 20 i 6, ii 9, iv 10
see ENGAR LUGAL, DUMU LUGAL, and ŠEŠ LUGAL
see GNs da lugal and GÁN LUGAL

MÁ.LAH̲$_4$ (*malāh̲um*) "boatsman," 40 D iv 1
MAŠKIM.GI$_4$, see under PNs
MU, see muh̲aldim
muh̲aldim (Akk. *nuh̲atimmum*) "cook," 40 A x 12
muh̲aldim lú-banšur-íl, 33 iii 3–4

NA.GADA (*nāqidum*) "shepherd," see under PNs
nagar (*naggārum*) "carpenter," App. to no. 32 vi 9; 40 B xiii 4
[n]agar-gal, 24 rev. iv 5
nar (*nârum*) "singer/musician," 15 v 13
see under PNs
nigir (*nāgirum*) "herald," 21 iii 7
nigir-gal, 19 rev. i 3
see gal-nigir
see under PNs
NIN (*bêlatum*) "Lady," "Queen," see under PNs
NU.BANDA (*laputtûm*) "overseer," 40 C xv 20, xvi 3, xviii 3
NU.BANDA AB+ÁŠ.AB+ÁŠ, 40 A xv 4
nu-banda é-gal, 23 obv. x 2
nu-banda é Lum-ma-tur-ka, App. to nos. 22–23 x 2
NU.BANDA É-mar-za^{KI}, 40 C xvi 17
NU.BANDA Eš$_4$-na-na-ak^{KI}, 40 C xv 14
NU.BANDA GIŠ.KIN.TI, 40 C xvi 14
NU.BANDA LÚ.IGI, 40 C xvii 26
NU.BANDA MÁ.GUR$_8$, 40 C xv 24
[nu]-banda Mar-tu-[n]e, 24 rev. iii 8
NU.BANDA Ša-at-bar-rí-im^{KI}, 40 C xii 2–3
NU.BANDA Ša-na-e, 40 A xiv 3, xv 10
NU.SAR (*nukaribbum*) "gardener"
NU.SAR GIŠ.SAR PAB.PAB, 38 ii 15–17

PA.TE.SI, see en$_5$-si
[P]A.URU "gang leader," 32 iv 10
pab-šeš (*pašīšum*) (a type of priest), 22 iii 5; 41 vii 11, rev. ii 10
pab-šeš É-nun, 12 Adscription to Side C
PAB.ŠEŠ ^{d}Innin, 16d B iii 1–2
pab-šeš ^{d}Šará?, 12 Adscription to Side A
see under PNs

RÉC-349.A.TU (meaning unknown), App. to no. 32 v 9

sabra (*šapīrum*) "majordomo," "temple steward"
SABRA.É, 40 A xi 18; 44i 8
see GN ⸢gán⸣ É-dur$_5$-sabra
see under PNs
sag-du$_5$ (*šassukkum*) "field recorder," 20 iii 8, v 11; 21 i 5; 22 iv 6, [16a], 50; 40 B v 1, C xiv 12
sag-du$_5$ Umma^{KI}, 21 i 2–3, ii 4–5
see GN gán sag-[du$_5$-ka]
sagi (*šāqijum*) "cupbearer," 33 ii 2, 4, rev. iii 6; 40 A xiii 2
SAL.BALAG.DI (*ṣārih̲tum*) "singer of lamentations," 43 viii 9, x 7; 44h ii 5
sanga (*šangûm*) "temple-administrator," 14 viii 7; 48 rev. iii 12
SANGA ^{d}A-ba$_4$ I-bí-rí^{KI}, 40 A xv 19–20
sanga Kèš, App. to no. 32 ii 12, v 7, vi 3
SANGA ^{d}Lugal-Már-da, 40 C xiv 24–25, xvii 18–19
SANGA ^{d}Za-ba$_4$-ba$_4$, 40 A viii 20, ix 8
[SAN]GA?.GAR, 30a i 8
sanga ⸢X⸣.GAR/KAG, 19a rev. i 1
see under PNs
SIG$_7$ (meaning unknown), 14 iv 8
SILÀ.ŠU.DU$_8$, see sagi
simug (*nappāh̲um*) "smith," 21 i 31; 33 rev. iv 4
SIMUG A-ga-dè^{KI}, 41 rev. vii 16–17
SIPA (*rēʾijum*) "shepherd," 38 i 3, 5; 40 A iv 15, B xi 6, xiii 10
sukkal (*šukkallum*) "messenger," "secretary," 33 iii 8, iv 2
see GAL.SUKKAL

šagina, see GÌR.NITA
ŠEŠ LUGAL (*ah̲u šarrim*) "brother of the king," 40 A xi 1
[ŠE]Š PA.TE.SI (*ah̲u iššiakkim*) "brother of the governor," 30b i 3
šu-i (*gallābum*) "barber," 33 iii 6; 40 A xii 17
see under PNs

TE.GAL (possibly tiru, Akk. *tīrum* "servant"), 21 i 38
TE.LAL (= galla) "policeman," see under PNs
TE.LAL.GAL (= galla-gal) "senior policeman," see under PNs

ugula (*waklum*) "foreman," 40 B x 5, 7
ugula anše, 15 vi 17, vii 13, ix 1
ugula e-me-a [(x)], App. to nos. 22–23 viii 3
ugula-é, App. to no. 32 viii 6
UGULA KA-zu-ra-ak^{KI}, 40 C xv 7
ugula-ukkin, 12 Adscription to Side B
ÙH̲.INNIN (written INNIN.ÙH̲) (*uruh̲h̲um*) "undertaker," 30b ii 4
UKÙ.GAL, see gal-ukù
um-me "master scribe(?)"
um-me ^{d}TIR, 13 rev. iii 2
um-mi-a (*ummiʾānum*) "master scribe," App. to no. 32 ix 2
UM.MI.A DUB.SAR, 40 A xi 7–8

⸢X⸣.GAL, 31 iv 5

CHAPTER 5

LISTING OF ANCIENT KUDURRUS AND SALE DOCUMENTS

The following three listings offer a bird's-eye view of the main features of all the ancient kudurrus and purchase/sale transactions on clay.

5.1. *Listing of Ancient Kudurrus*

	Sigla	*Date*	*Provenience*	*Language*	*Material and Form*	*Size in cm* *lg. x wd. x th.*			*Notes*
1	Hoffman Tablet	Uruk III	Unknown	Sumerian(?)	Black stone	9.1	8.9	1.0–2.6	
2	Walters Tablet	Uruk III	Unknown	Sumerian(?)	Reddish stone	6.5	6.5	0.8–2.3	
3	Philadelphia Tablet	Uruk III	Unknown	Sumerian(?)	Greenish-black stone	7.2	7.4	?–1.8	
4	Louvre Tablet	Uruk III	Unknown	Sumerian(?)	Light-green onyx spheroid	4.0	4.0	2.0–4.0	
5	Yale Tablet I	Uruk III	Unknown	Sumerian(?)	Black stone	7.7	7.7	1.0–2.2	
6	Yale Tablet II	Uruk III	Unknown	Sumerian(?)	Light-brown stone	8.8	8.8	0.5–2.0	
7	Leiden Tablet	Uruk III	Unknown	Sumerian(?)	Black stone	10.0	9.5	0.5–3.0	
8	Sheep(?) Figurine	Uruk III	Unknown	Sumerian(?)	Stone figurine in the shape of a recumbent sheep(?)	4.0	11.0	4.0	
9	Khafajah Bird	Uruk III	Tutub	Sumerian(?)	Schist(?) figurine of a lion-headed bird	25.0	9.5	3.5	Excavated
10	Blau Obelisk	Uruk III	Unknown	Sumerian(?)	Greenish serpentine or dark shale(?)	18.0	4.3	1.3	Human representations
11	Blau Plaque	Uruk III	Unknown	Sumerian(?)	Greenish serpentine(?) or dark shale(?)	15.9	7.2	1.5	Human representations
12	Ushumgal Stela	ED I–II	Umma(?)	Sumerian(?)	Light to dark brown gypsum	22.0	14.0	9.5	Human representations
13	*RA* VI p. 143	Fara or earlier	Shuruppak(?)	Sumerian(?)	Light-buff limestone	10.5	10.0	4.0	
14	Chicago Stone	Fara or early Pre-Sargonic	Unknown	Sumerian	Black basalt	25.0	32.0	2.5–5.5	
15	Baltimore Stone	Fara or early Pre-Sargonic	Unknown	Sumerian	Reddish-brown stone slab	25.0	26.0	4.4	
16	Kish Stone Fragments I	Fara	Kish	Akkadian	Fragments of a white limestone cube(?)	12.0	12.0	12.0 (estimated)	Excavated
17	Kish Stone Fragment II	Fara or earlier	Kish	Akkadian(?)	Fragment of a red stone slab	9.2	6.9	3.0	Excavated
18	Figure aux Plumes	ED I–II	Girshu	Sumerian	White limestone tablet	15.7	13.4	3.5	Excavated; human representations
19	Lagash Stela	ED I–II	Girshu	Sumerian(?)	Fragment of a gray limestone stela	?	21.0	?	Excavated; human representations
19a	*DC* II p. XXXV 3	Pre-Sargonic or earlier	Girshu	Sumerian(?)	Fragment of a black stone	7.8	11.5	2.0–5.3	Excavated
19b	Cros, *NFT* p. 222	Pre-Sargonic or earlier	Girshu	Sumerian(?)	Fragment of a black stone slab	8.0	9.3	2.3	Excavated
20	Enḫegal Tablet	Fara	Girshu(?)	Sumerian	Light-buff limestone	12.4	12.8	3.8	
21	Lupad Statue	Fara	Girshu	Sumerian(?)	Dark-gray diorite	42.0	30.0	20.0	Excavated
22	Lummatur Tablet I	Pre-Sargonic	Girshu	Sumerian	Black stone	32.5	23.0	3.0–8.6	Excavated; unfinished
23	Lummatur Tablet II	Pre-Sargonic	Girshu	Sumerian	Light-buff limestone	52.0	40.0	8.2 (reconstructed)	Excavated

5.1. *Listing of Ancient Kudurrus—continued*

Sigla	*Date*	*Provenience*	*Language*	*Material and Form*	*Size in cm lg. x wd. x th.*	*Notes*
App. to nos. 22–23 = no. 144 *Bibl. Mes.* III 10	Pre-Sargonic	Lagash	Sumerian	Clay tablet	13.3 13.3 4.5	Excavated
24 Stela of Victory	Sargonic	Girshu	Sumerian	Fragment of a limestone tablet	29.0 26.0 (inscribed piece only)	Excavated
25 Nippur Statue	Fara	Nippur	Akkadian	White gypsum	75.8	Excavated
26 Enna-Il Statue	Fara	Nippur	Akkadian	Limestone	10.2 10.7 8.8	Excavated
27 10 NT 1	Pre-Sargonic	Nippur	Sumerian(?)	Fragment of a red stone tablet	6.2 4.0 5.5	Excavated
28 *PBS* XV 3	Pre-Sargonic	Nippur	Akkadian	Fragments of a buff limestone tablet	15.0 11.5 2.8	Excavated
29 *PBS* XV 17	Pre-Sargonic	Nippur	Sumerian(?)	Fragment of a dark-gray shale or slate tablet	4.8 5.5 0.9	Excavated
30 *PBS* XV 20	Pre-Sargonic	Nippur	Sumerian(?)	Fragment of a buff "schist" tablet	4.5 4.5 1.3	Excavated
30a Nippur Disk	Pre-Sargonic	Nippur	Akkadian	limestone fragment, about ⅓ of the original of c. 62.5 cm diameter	39.6 34.6 ? (estimated)	Excavated
30b IM 57944	Fara	Nippur	Akkadian(?)	Fragment of a slate tablet	7.2 7.5 ?	Excavated
30c A 33678	Pre-Sargonic	Nippur	Unknown	Fragment of a black shale tablet	3.9 2.4 0.7	Excavated
31 Adab Stone Fragment	Pre-Sargonic	Adab	Akkadian	Fragment of an alabaster tablet	11.6 8.2 2.0–3.7	Excavated
32 Adab Clay Fragment I	Pre-Sargonic	Adab	Sumerian	Fragment of a clay tablet	19.0 13.5 4.8	Excavated
Appendix to no. 32 = *Mesopotamia* VIII pp. 68f.	Pre-Sargonic	Adab	Sumerian	Clay tablet	11.0 11.0 1.5	
33 Adab Clay Fragment II	Pre-Sargonic	Adab	Akkadian(?)	Fragment of a clay tablet	13.5 9.9 5.4	Excavated
34 *BIN* II 2	Pre-Sargonic	Kish(?)	Akkadian	Gray, soft limestone slab	15.0 12.0 3.5	Unfinished
35 *DP* 2	Pre-Sargonic	Sippar(?)	Akkadian	Fragment of a reddish "syénite" tablet	6.7 9.0 3.1	
36 *CT* V 3	Pre-Sargonic	Sippar(?)	Akkadian	Fragment of a limestone slab	18.5 25.0 3.5–5.7	Said to be from Sippar
37 *CT* XXXII 7f.	Pre-Sargonic	Dilbat(?)	Akkadian	Fragment of a light-buff limestone tablet	17.0 19.1 5.1	Said to be from Dilbat
38 Dar-a-a Tablet	Sargonic	Sippar(?)	Akkadian	Limestone, c. ½ preserved	16.0 8.2 5.1	Said to be from Sippar
39 YBC 2409	Sargonic	Girshu(?)	Sumerian	Fragment of a light-buff stone	20.0 21.0 12.0	
40 Manishtushu Obelisk (MO)	Sargonic	Sippar(?)	Akkadian	Black diorite	144.0 12.0 tops 39.0–52.0 bases	Excavated at Susa; originally from northern Babylonia
41 Sippar Stone	Sargonic	Sippar(?)	Akkadian	Fragment of a limestone slab, less than ¼ of original	15.6 25.3 5.1–7.4	Said to be from Sippar
42 Eshnuna Stone	Sargonic	Eshnuna	Akkadian	Fragment of a black diorite tablet	8.1 13.7 6.0	Excavated
43 Eshnuna Clay Tablet	Sargonic	Eshnuna	Akkadian	Clay	17.4 18.6 3.9	Excavated
44 Eshnuna Clay Fragments	Sargonic	Eshnuna	Akkadian	12 fragments		Excavated
45 Assur Stone Fragment	Sargonic	Assur	Akkadian	Fragment of a stone tablet	6.1 6.3 ?	Excavated
46 *TIM* IX 97	Pre-Sargonic	Unknown	Akkadian	Fragment of a stone vessel	7.7 8.5 ?	
47 UM 32-40-436	Pre-Sargonic	Ur	Akkadian(?)	Fragment of a light-gray limestone(?) tablet	8.1 6.2 2.7	Excavated
48 BM 91068	Sargonic	Sippar	Akkadian	Light-buff limestone slab	23.0 24.5 2.7–3.7	Excavated
49 BM 90909	Sargonic	Sippar(?)	Akkadian	Fragment of a limestone slab	8.4 10.5 5.0	Registered as from Sippar

5.1. *Listing of Ancient Kudurrus—continued*

	Sigla	Date	Provenience	Language	Material and Form	Size in cm lg. x wd. x th.			Notes
50	BM 33429	Sargonic	Babylon(?)	Akkadian	Fragment of a dark-gray stone slab	6.8	13.5	6.8	Registered as from Babylon
51	BM 45593	Sargonic	Cuthah(?)	Akkadian	Fragment of a gray alabaster(?) cylinder	3.6	5.7	2.4	Marked as from Cuthah
52	BM 139507	Sargonic	Unknown	Akkadian	Fragment of a gray limestone tablet	12.0	11.0	6.0	

5.2. *Listing of Sale Documents*

	Sigla	Date	Provenience	Language	Object of Sale	Notes
100	*Fara* III 30	Fara	Shuruppak	Sumerian	House	
101	*Fara* III 31	Fara	Shuruppak	Sumerian	House	
102	*TSŠ* 66	Fara	Shuruppak	Sumerian	House	
103	*TMH* V 71	Fara	Shuruppak	Sumerian	House	
104	*RTC* 13	Fara	Shuruppak	Sumerian	House	
105	*RA* XXXII p. 126	Fara	Shuruppak	Sumerian	House	
106	Lambert in *Unger AV* pp. 33–34	Fara	Shuruppak	Sumerian	House	
107	De Marcellis	Fara	Shuruppak	Sumerian	2 houses	
108	IM 14182	Fara	Shuruppak	Sumerian	House	
109	*TMH* V 75	Fara	Shuruppak	Sumerian	House	
110	*TMH* V 78	Fara	Shuruppak	Sumerian	House	
111	*PBS* IX 3	Fara	Shuruppak	Sumerian	House	
112	*L'Oeil* nos. 221–222 p. 78 (= no. 113c)	Fara	Shuruppak	Sumerian	House	
113	*SEL* III p. 11	Fara	Shuruppak	Sumerian	House	
113a	*MVNS* X 82	Fara	Shuruppak	Sumerian	House	
113b	*MVNS* X 83	Fara	Shuruppak	Sumerian	House	
113c	*MVNS* X 85 (= no. 112)	Fara	Shuruppak	Sumerian	House	
114	*Fara* III 32	Fara	Shuruppak	Sumerian	Field	
115	*Fara* III 33	Fara	Shuruppak	Sumerian	Field	
116	*Fara* III 34	Fara	Shuruppak	Sumerian	Field	
117	*Fara* III 36	Fara	Shuruppak	Sumerian	Field	
118	*Fara* III 37	Fara	Shuruppak	Sumerian	Field	
119	*TSŠ* pls. XXXIII–XXXIV	Fara	Shuruppak	Sumerian	Field	
120	*PBS* XIII 24	Fara	Shuruppak	Sumerian	Field	
121	*ZA* LXIII pp. 209–210 no. 4a	Fara	Shuruppak	Sumerian	Field	Excavated at Uruk
122	Lambert in *Unger AV* pp. 29–30	Fara	Shuruppak	Sumerian	Field	
123	Lambert in *Unger AV* pp. 37–38	Fara	Shuruppak	Sumerian	Field	
124	Lambert in *Unger AV* pp. 41–42	Fara	Shuruppak	Sumerian	Field	
125	*AOr* XXXIX p. 14	Fara	Shuruppak	Sumerian	Field	
126	*AOr* XXXIX p. 15	Fara	Shuruppak	Sumerian	Field	
127	*Or.* n.s. XLIV p. 436 no. 1	Fara	Shuruppak	Sumerian	Field	
127a	*MVNS* X 84	Fara	Shurrupak	Sumerian	Field	
127b	*MVNS* X 86	Fara	Shuruppak	Sumerian	Field	
128	*Fara* III 38	Fara	Shuruppak	Sumerian	Field	
129	*Fara* III 40	Fara	Shuruppak	Sumerian	Field	
130	*RTC* 14	Fara	Shuruppak	Sumerian	Field	
131	*RTC* 15	Fara	Shuruppak	Sumerian	Field	
132	Edzard, *SRU* p. 31	Fara	Shuruppak	Sumerian	Field	
133	A 33676	Fara	Shuruppak	Sumerian	Field	
134	*Fara* III 39	Fara	Shuruppak	Sumerian	Field	
135	YBC 12305	Fara	Shuruppak	Sumerian	Field	
136	*WO* VIII p. 180	Fara	Shuruppak	Sumerian	Field	
137	*BIN* VIII 352	Pre-Sargonic	Girshu	Sumerian	House	
138	De Genouillac, *FT* I pl. XLIII	Pre-Sargonic	Girshu	Sumerian	House	
139	*Dok.* I 317	Pre-Sargonic	Girshu	Sumerian	House	Written on a clay cone
140	*DP* 31	Pre-Sargonic	Girshu	Sumerian	House	Written on a clay cone
141	*DP* 32	Pre-Sargonic	Girshu	Sumerian	House	Written on a clay cone
142	Hallo in *Gelb AV* p. 236	Pre-Sargonic	Girshu	Sumerian	House	
143	*RTC* 18	Pre-Sargonic	Girshu	Sumerian	2 Houses	
144	*Bibl. Mes.* III 10	Pre-Sargonic	Lagash	Sumerian	Field	

5.2. *Listing of Sale Documents—continued*

	Sigla	*Date*	*Provenience*	*Language*	*Object of Sale*	*Notes*
145	*Bibl. Mes.* III 11	Pre-Sargonic	Lagash	Sumerian	Field	Written on a clay cone
146	Cros, *NFT* p. 220	Pre-Sargonic	Girshu	Sumerian	Orchard	Written on brick
147	*Dok.* I 318	Pre-Sargonic	Girshu	Sumerian	Unidentified real estate	Written on clay cone
148	*TIM* IX 94	Pre-Sargonic	Girshu	Sumerian	Unidentified real estate	Written on a clay cone
149	*Or.* IX p. 173	Pre-Sargonic	Girshu	Sumerian	Person	
150	*RTC* 16	Pre-Sargonic	Girshu	Sumerian	Person	
151	*RTC* 17	Pre-Sargonic	Girshu	Sumerian	Person	
152	*VAS* XIV 141	Pre-Sargonic	Girshu	Sumerian	Person	
153	*VAS* XIV 144	Pre-Sargonic	Girshu	Sumerian	Person	
154	*BIN* VIII 363	Pre-Sargonic	Girshu	Sumerian	Person	
155	*Dok.* I 17	Pre-Sargonic	Girshu	Sumerian	Person	
156	*Dok.* I 293	Pre-Sargonic	Girshu	Sumerian	3 persons	
156a	*BIN* VIII 11	Pre-Sargonic	Unknown	Akkadian	2 Fields	
157	*BIN* VIII 177	Sargonic	Adab	Sumerian	Person	
158	A 713	Sargonic	Adab	Sumerian	Person	
159	Ist. Mus. Adab 397	Sargonic	Adab	Sumerian	Person	
160	Ist. Mus. Adab 398	Sargonic	Adab	Sumerian	Person	
161	Ist. Mus. Adab 399	Sargonic	Adab	Sumerian	Person	
162	Ist. Mus. Adab 426	Sargonic	Adab	Sumerian	Person	
163	A 815	Sargonic	Adab	Sumerian	Person	
164	*BIN* VIII 38	Sargonic	Isin	Sumerian	House	
165	NBC 6844	Sargonic	Isin	Sumerian	2 houses and fields	
166	*BIN* VIII 17	Sargonic	Isin	Sumerian	3 houses	*Sammelurkunde*
167	NBC 6900	Sargonic	Isin	Sumerian	House	*Sammelurkunde*
168	NBC 10198	Sargonic	Isin	Sumerian	House (and other matter)	
169	*BIN* VIII 80	Sargonic	Isin	Sumerian	Field	
170	*BIN* VIII 158	Sargonic	Isin	Sumerian	Field	
171	*BIN* VIII 171	Sargonic	Isin	Sumerian	Field	
172	*BIN* VIII 172	Sargonic	Isin	Sumerian	Field	
173	*BIN* VIII 178	Sargonic	Isin	Sumerian	Field	
174	*BIN* VIII 179	Sargonic	Isin	Sumerian	Field	
175	*MAD* IV 151	Sargonic	Isin	Sumerian	Field	
176	*MAD* IV 152	Sargonic	Isin	Sumerian	Field	
177	*MAD* IV 153	Sargonic	Isin	Sumerian	Field	
178	*MAD* IV 155	Sargonic	Isin	Sumerian	Field	
179	*MAD* IV 169	Sargonic	Isin	Sumerian	2 fields	
180	*MVNS* III 25	Sargonic	Isin	Sumerian	Field	
181	*MVNS* III 13	Sargonic	Isin	Sumerian	4 orchards and 1 house	*Sammelurkunde*
182	*MVNS* III 53	Sargonic	Isin	Sumerian	Orchard	
182a	Lambert Tablet	Sargonic	Isin	Sumerian	20 fields and 12 orchards	*Sammelurkunde*
183	NBC 10204	Sargonic	Isin	Sumerian	Canal(?)	
184	*MAD* IV 77	Sargonic	Isin	Sumerian	Person	
185	*MAD* IV 78	Sargonic	Isin	Sumerian	Person	
186	*MAD* IV 81	Sargonic	Isin	Sumerian	Person	
187	*MAD* IV 150	Sargonic	Isin	Sumerian	Person	
188	*MAD* IV 158	Sargonic	Isin	Sumerian	Person	
189	*BIN* VIII 39	Sargonic	Isin	Sumerian	2 persons (and other matter)	*Sammelurkunde*
190	*BIN* VIII 66	Sargonic	Isin	Sumerian	Person (and other matter)	*Sammelurkunde*
191	*BIN* VIII 175	Sargonic	Isin	Sumerian	Person	*Sammelurkunde*
192	Böhl Coll. 929	Sargonic	Isin	Sumerian	Person	
193	*MAD* IV 80	Sargonic	Isin	Sumerian	Person	
194	NBC 10294	Sargonic	Isin	Sumerian	Person	
195	*ITT* I 1040	Sargonic	Girshu	Sumerian	2 persons (related)	
196	*ITT* I 1041	Sargonic	Girshu	Sumerian	Person	
197	*ITT* II 4518	Sargonic	Girshu	Sumerian	Person	
198	*ITT* II 4578	Sargonic	Girshu	Sumerian	Person	
199	*ITT* II 4588	Sargonic	Girshu	Sumerian	Person	
200	*RTC* 79	Sargonic	Girshu	Sumerian	Person	

5.2. *Listing of Sale Documents—continued*

	Sigla	*Date*	*Provenience*	*Language*	*Object of Sale*	*Notes*
201	*RTC* 80	Sargonic	Girshu	Sumerian	6 persons	
202	*RTC* 81	Sargonic	Girshu	Sumerian	Person	
203	*ZA* LIII p. 79 no. 19	Sargonic	Girshu	Sumerian	Person(?)	
204	*PBS* IX 9	Sargonic	Nippur	Sumerian	House	
205	*TMH* V 128	Sargonic	Nippur	Sumerian	House	
206	IM 58820	Sargonic	Nippur	Sumerian	House	
207	*PBS* IX 8	Sargonic	Nippur	Sumerian	Field	
208	*TMH* V 47	Sargonic	Nippur	Sumerian	Person	
209	*PBS* IX 78	Sargonic	Nippur	Sumerian	Person(?)	
210	*PBS* IX 7	Sargonic	Nippur	Sumerian	3 houses	*Sammelurkunde*
211	PBX IX 51+52	Sargonic	Nippur	Sumerian	2 fields	*Sammelurkunde*
212	*PBS* IX 86+107	Sargonic	Nippur	Sumerian	2 fields	*Sammelurkunde*
213	*PBS* IX 4	Sargonic	Nippur	Sumerian	2 persons	*Sammelurkunde*
214	*Dok.* II 68	Sargonic	Umma	Sumerian	Person	
215	*TIM* IX 99	Sargonic	Unknown	Sumerian	Person	
216	IM 43431	Sargonic	Unknown	Sumerian	Person	
217	NBC 10221	Sargonic	Unknown	Sumerian	Person	
218	*CT* L 77	Sargonic	Unknown	Sumerian	House	
219	IM 43451	Sargonic	Unknown	Sumerian	Person	
220	IM 43741	Sargonic	Unknown	Sumerian	Person	
221	MLC 1251	Sargonic	Unknown	Sumerian	2 persons (related?)	
222	*MVNS* III 100	Sargonic	Unknown	Sumerian	2 equids	
223	YBC 12312	Sargonic	Unknown	Sumerian	Equid	
224	*MAD* IV 15	Sargonic	Unknown	Sumerian	Dates	
225	*MAD* IV 51	Sargonic	Unknown	Sumerian	Equid	
226	Serota Coll. A 10	Sargonic	Unknown	Sumerian	Gold	
227	*Or.* n.s. LI pp. 355–56	Sargonic	Unknown	Akkadian	House	
228	*FM* 4	Sargonic	Eshnuna	Akkadian	House	
229	*MAD* V 48	Sargonic	Kish	Akkadian	Field	
230	*MAD* V 65	Sargonic	Kish	Akkadian	Field	
231	*HSS* X 99	Sargonic	Gasur	Akkadian	Person	
232	*MVNS* III 80	Sargonic	Unknown	Akkadian	2 persons (related?)	
233	*MVNS* III 102	Sargonic	Unknown	Akkadian	Person	
234	IM 43612	Sargonic	Unknown	Akkadian	Person	
235	*Or.* n.s. LI p. 363	Sargonic	Unknown	Akkadian	Equid	
236	*MAD* IV 4	Sargonic	Eshnuna	Akkadian	Gold	
237	*JCS* X p. 26	Sargonic	Unknown	Akkadian	House	
238	*MAD* V 82	Sargonic	Umm el-Jīr	Akkadian	House	
239	*UCP* IX p. 204 no. 83	Sargonic	Eshnuna	Akkadian	Field	
240	*CT* L 78	Sargonic	Sippar*	Akkadian	2 persons (related)	*See *CT* L p. 8
241	*HSS* X 211	Sargonic	Gasur	Akkadian	Person	
242	*FM* 1	Sargonic	Eshnuna	Akkadian	House	
243	*FM* 2	Sargonic	Eshnuna	Akkadian	House	
244	*MAD* I 336	Sargonic	Eshnuna	Akkadian	House	
245	IM 2886/D	Sargonic	Eshnuna	Akkadian	House	
246	YBC 12310	Sargonic	Eshnuna(?)	Akkadian	Field	
247	*MVNS* III 213	Ur III	Umma	Sumerian	House	
247a	A 22108	Ur III	Eshnuna	Sumerian	House	
248	*ZA* LIII p. 82 no. 21	Ur III	Nippur	Sumerian	House	
249	*UET* III 31	Ur III	Ur	Sumerian	House	
250	*NSATN* 782	Ur III	Nippur	Sumerian	House	
251	*UET* III 27	Ur III	Ur	Sumerian	House	
252	*NSATN* 911	Ur III	Nippur	Sumerian	House	
253	*NSATN* 966	Ur III	Nippur	Sumerian	House	
254	Yondorf Coll. B	Ur III	Unknown	Akkadian	House	
255	*YOS* IV 4	Ur III	Umma	Sumerian	House	
256	*YOS* XV 100	Ur III	Umma	Sumerian	House	
257	*NRVN* I 223 + 251	Ur III	Nippur	Sumerian	House	
258	TA 1930, 249	Ur III	Eshnuna	Sumerian	Empty lot	
259	*ITT* V 6837 + *NSGU* III pl. 8 no. 100	Ur III	Girshu	Sumerian	House	
260	*NRVN* I 222	Ur III	Nippur	Sumerian	House(?)	
261	*NSATN* 19	Ur III	Nippur	Sumerian	House	
262	*TIM* V 8	Ur III	Nippur	Sumerian	House	
263	Oppenheim, *Eames Coll.* pl. XIV Noor II	Ur III	Nippur	Sumerian	House	Written on clay cone

5.2. *Listing of Sale Documents—continued*

	Sigla	*Date*	*Provenience*	*Language*	*Object of Sale*	*Notes*
264	*BE* III/1 14	Ur III	Nippur	Sumerian	Orchard	
265	*NRVN* I 224	Ur III	Nippur	Sumerian	Orchard	
266	*NSATN* 762	Ur III	Nippur	Sumerian	Orchard	
267	*MVNS* III 263	Ur III	Nippur	Sumerian	Orchard	
268	*NSATN* 777	Ur III	Nippur	Sumerian	Orchard	
269	*NSATN* 497	Ur III	Nippur	Sumerian	2 orchards	
270	BM 15464	Ur III	Unknown	Sumerian	Orchard	
271	*NSATN* 607	Ur III	Nippur	Sumerian	Person	
272	AUAM 73.1110	Ur III	Nippur	Sumerian	Person	
273	*NSATN* 123	Ur III	Nippur	Sumerian	Person	
274	AUAM 73.3097	Ur III	Umma	Sumerian	Person	
274a	AUAM 73.1265	Ur III	Umma	Sumerian	Person	
275	NBC 11300	Ur III	Nippur	Sumerian	Person	
276	*RA* VIII pp. 185–186 no. 4	Ur III	Nippur	Sumerian	Person	
277	*BE* III/1 15 + *NSATN* 367 (seal)	Ur III	Nippur	Sumerian	Person	
278	*NSATN* 255	Ur III	Nippur	Sumerian	Person	
279	NBC 7174	Ur III	Nippur	Sumerian	2 persons (related)	
280	*RA* X p. 66 no. 105	Ur III	Unknown	Sumerian	Person	
281	*UET* III 26	Ur III	Ur	Sumerian	Person	
282	NBC 5652	Ur III	Nippur	Sumerian	Person	
283	*TIM* V 12	Ur III	Unknown	Sumerian	Person	
284	*UET* III 30	Ur III	Ur	Sumerian	Person	
285	*NSATN* 761	Ur III	Nippur	Sumerian	3 persons (related)	
286	AUAM 73.3096	Ur III	Unknown	Sumerian	Person	
287	*UET* III 29	Ur III	Ur	Sumerian	Person	
288	*NRVN* I 216	Ur III	Nippur	Sumerian	Person	
289	*MDP* XXVIII 410	Ur III	Susa	Sumerian	Person	
290	*NRVN* I 215	Ur III	Nippur	Sumerian	Person	
291	*ZA* XXV p. 206 no. 1	Ur III	Unknown	Sumerian	Person	
292	*NSATN* 713	Ur III	Nippur	Sumerian	Person	
293	*TMH* n.F. I/II 51	Ur III	Nippur	Sumerian	Person	
294	*ITT* III 6370	Ur III	Girshu	Sumerian	Person	
295	*BIN* V 346	Ur III	Umma(?)	Sumerian	3 persons (related)	
296	*MAOG* IV p. 191 MD 3	Ur III	Unknown	Sumerian	2 persons (related)	
297	*TIM* IX 103	Ur III	Unknown	Sumerian	Person	
298	*NSATN* 498	Ur III	Nippur	Sumerian	Person	
299	Forde, *NCT* 63	Ur III	Umma	Sumerian	Person	
300	*NSATN* 610	Ur III	Nippur	Sumerian	Person	
301	*NSATN* 265	Ur III	Nippur	Sumerian	Person	
302	Ist. Mus. Nippur 5446	Ur III	Nippur	Sumerian	Person	
303	YBC 9827	Ur III	Nippur	Sumerian	Person	
304	*NRVN* I 214	Ur III	Nippur	Sumerian	Person	
305	*AOr* VII pl. III no. 1	Ur III	Nippur	Sumerian	Person	
306	*NSATN* 903	Ur III	Nippur	Sumerian	Person	
307	*PBS* VIII/2 157 + *NSATN* 5 (seals)	Ur III	Nippur	Sumerian	Person	
308	*NRVN* I 213	Ur III	Nippur	Sumerian	Person	
309	*UET* III 39	Ur III	Ur	Sumerian	Person	Self-sale
309a	Limet, *TSDU* 16	Ur III	Unknown	Sumerian	Person	
310	*NRVN* I 212	Ur III	Nippur	Sumerian	Person	
311	*PBS* IX 41	Ur III	Nippur	Sumerian	Person	
312	*NSATN* 850	Ur III	Nippur	Sumerian	4 persons (related)	
313	*NSATN* 884	Ur III	Nippur	Sumerian	2 persons (related)	
314	AUAM 73.2128	Ur III	Nippur(?)	Sumerian	Person	
315	*UET* III 47	Ur III	Ur	Sumerian	Person	
316	*NSATN* 741	Ur III	Nippur	Sumerian	Bovid	
317	*NRVN* I 218	Ur III	Nippur	Sumerian	Bovid	
318	Chiera, *CBTC* Ex 695	Ur III	Umma	Sumerian	Equid	
319	*JMEOS* XV pp. 41–42 no. 2	Ur III	Nippur	Sumerian	Bovid	
320	*TMH* n.F. I/II 52	Ur III	Nippur	Sumerian	2 equids	
321	*NRVN* I 220	Ur III	Nippur	Sumerian	Bovid	
322	*NRVN* I 219	Ur III	Nippur	Sumerian	Bovid	
323	*NRVN* I 221	Ur III	Nippur	Sumerian	3 equids	
324	*UET* III 32	Ur III	Ur	Sumerian	Unknown	
325	*BE* III/1 21	Ur III	Nippur	Sumerian	Unknown	
326	*ITT* III 6582 + *NSGU* III pl. 1 no. 9	Ur III	Lagash	Sumerian	Unknown	

5.2. *Listing of Sale Documents—continued*

	Sigla	*Date*	*Provenience*	*Language*	*Object of Sale*	*Notes*
327	*MVNS* III 330	Ur III	Nippur	Sumerian	Unknown	
328	6 N-T 436	Ur III	Nippur	Sumerian	Unknown	
329	*NRVN* I 217	Ur III	Nippur	Sumerian	Unknown	
330	*NRVN* I 225	Ur III	Nippur	Sumerian	Unknown	
331	*MVNS* III 268	Ur III	Adab	Sumerian	House	
332	*UET* III 19	Ur III	Adab	Sumerian	Person	Found at Ur
333	AUAM 73.3098	Ur III	Umma(?)	Sumerian	Person	
334	*UET* III 14	Ur III	Adab	Sumerian	Person	Found at Ur
335	*UET* III 15	Ur III	Adab	Sumerian	Person	Found at Ur
336	*UET* III 46	Ur III	Adab	Sumerian	Person	Found at Ur
337	*UET* III 44	Ur III	Adab	Sumerian	Person	Found at Ur
338	*UET* III 18	Ur III	Adab	Sumerian	Person	Found at Ur
339	Szlechter, *TJA* I pl. LXVIII JES 134	Ur III	Garshana(?)	Sumerian	Person	
340	*UET* III 9	Ur III	Adab	Sumerian	Unknown	Found at Ur
341	*YOS* XV 101	Ur III	Unknown	Sumerian	Person	
342	*ITT* II 3512	Ur III	Lagash	Sumerian	Person	Self-sale
343	*NRVN* I 226	Ur III	Unknown	Akkadian	Person	Found at Nippur
344	*YOS* IV 2	Ur III	Umma	Sumerian	Person	
345	IM 61558	Ur III	Nippur	Sumerian	Person	
346	*ZA* LIII p. 79 no. 18	Ur III	Nippur(?)	Sumerian	Person	
347	*NSATN* 937	Ur III	Nippur	Sumerian	Person	
348	*ZA* LIII p. 80 no. 20	Ur III	Nippur	Sumerian	Bovid(?)	
349	IM 61706	Ur III	Nippur	Sumerian	Person	
350	A 31164	Ur III	Nippur	Sumerian	Person	
351	*NSATN* 145	Ur III	Nippur	Sumerian	Person	
352	*UET* III 33	Ur III	Ur	Sumerian	Person	
353	IM 61712	Ur III	Nippur	Sumerian	Unknown	
354	*ITT* II 2766	Ur III	Girshu	Sumerian	Person	
355	AUAM 73.1042	Ur III	Umma	Sumerian	House	
356	*ITT* II 3470 + Buccellati, *Amorites* pl. XIV no. 25	Ur III	Girshu	Sumerian	Several persons (man, wife, children)	
357	Pinches, *BTBC* 53	Ur III	Girshu	Sumerian	Person	
358	De Genouillac, *FT* II pl. L AO 13019	Ur III	Girshu	Sumerian	Person	
359	*MAOG* IV pp. 188–189, MD 2	Ur III	Unknown	Sumerian	Person	
360	*UET* III 36	Ur III	Ur	Sumerian	Orchard	
361	Oppenheim, *Eames Coll.* pl. II TT 4	Ur III	Unknown	Sumerian	Person	
362	Oppenheim, *Eames Coll.* pl. XI TT 1	Ur III	Unknown	Akkadian	Person	
363	Oppenheim, *Eames Coll.* pl. IX TT 2	Ur III	Unknown	Sumerian	Person	
364	*TMH* n.F. I/II 50	Ur III	Nippur	Sumerian	Person	
365	*UET* III 41	Ur III	Ur	Sumerian	Person	
366	*MDP* XVIII 199	Ur III	Susa	Sumerian	Person	
367	*TLB* III 170	Ur III	Girshu	Sumerian	2 persons (related)	
368	*JCS* XIX p. 27 no. 2	Ur III	Unknown	Akkadian	Equid	
369	*TMH* n.F. I/II 53	Ur III	Nippur	Sumerian	5 persons (man, wife, 3 children)	
370	Yondorf Coll. A	Ur III	Unknown	Akkadian	Person	

5.3. *Concordance of Ancient Kudurrus and Sale Documents*

This section contains all references to ancient kudurrus and sale documents that were cited in the previous sections, 5.1 and 5.2. The entries include the sigla used in these two sections and the publications in which the sources were published. Unpublished sources are cited by the name of the museum in which they are housed.

Text	*No.*
A, see Oriental Institute	
Adab, see Istanbul Archaeological Museum	
Adab Clay Fragment I	32
Adab Clay Fragment II	33
Adab Stone Fragment	31
Andrews University Archeological Museum, Berrien Springs, Michigan	
AUAM 73.1042	355
AUAM 73.1110	272
AUAM 73.1265	274a

5.3. *Concordance of Ancient Kudurrus and Sale Documents—continued*

Text	*No.*
AUAM 73.2128	314
AUAM 73.3096	286
AUAM 73.3097	274
AUAM 73.3098	333
AO, see Louvre	
AOr VII pl. III no. 1	305
AOr XXXIX p. 14	125
AOr XXXIX p. 15	126
App. to nos. 22–23, see *Bibl. Mes.* III 10	
App. to no. 32, see *Mesopotamia* VIII pp. 68f.	
Ashmolean Museum, Oxford	
Kish 1928, 423	17
Kish 1930, 153–156, 178a, b, 179a, b, 180	16
Kish 1931, 162	16
Assur Stone Fragment	45
AUAM, see Andrews University	
Baghdad, see Iraq Museum	
Baltimore, see Walters Art Gallery	
Baltimore Stone	15
BE III/1 14	264
BE III/1 15	277
BE III/1 21	325
Berlin, see Staatliche Museen	
Berrien Springs, see Andrews University	
Bibl. Mes. III 10 (= App. to nos. 22–23)	144
Bibl. Mes. III 11	145
BIN II 2	34
BIN V 346	295
BIN VIII 1	5
BIN VIII 2	6
BIN VIII 11	156a
BIN VIII 17	166
BIN VIII 38	164
BIN VIII 39	189
BIN VIII 66	190
BIN VIII 80	169
BIN VIII 158	170
BIN VIII 171	171
BIN VIII 172	172
BIN VIII 175	191
BIN VIII 177	157
BIN VIII 178	173
BIN VIII 179	174
BIN VIII 352	137
BIN VIII 363	154
Blau Obelisk	10
Blau Plaque	11
BM, see British Museum	
Böhl Coll., see Liagre Böhl Collection	
British Museum, London	
BM 15464	270
BM 33429	50
BM 45593	51
BM 0909	49
BM 91068	48
BM 139507	52
Buccellati, *Amorites* pl. XIV no. 25	356
Chicago, see Oriental Institute	
Chicago Stone	14
Chiera, *CBTC* Ex 695	318
Cros, *NFT* p. 220	146
Cros, *NFT* p. 222	19b
Cros, *NFT* pp. 262–66	23
CT V 3	36
CT XXXII 7f.	37
CT L 77	218
CT L 78	240
Dar-a-a Tablet	38
DC II p. XXXIV	18
DC II p. XXXV 2	19
DC II p. XXXV 3	19a
DC II p. XLIX	22
DC II p. LIVf.	21
DC II p. LVII	24
De Genouillac, *FT* I pl. XLIII	138
De Genouillac, *FT* II pl. L AO 13019	358
De Marcellis	107
Dok. I 17	155
Dok. I 293	156
Dok. I 317	139
Dok. I 318	147
Dok. II 68	214
DP 2	35
DP 31	140
DP 32	141
Edzard, *SRU* p. 31	132
Enḫegal Tablet	20
Enna-Il Statue	26
EŞEM, see Istanbul Archaeological Museum	
Eshnuna Clay Fragments	44
Eshnuna Clay Tablet	43
Eshnuna Stone Fragment	42
Fara III 30	100
Fara III 31	101
Fara III 32	114
Fara III 33	115
Fara III 34	116
Fara III 36	117
Fara III 37	118
Fara III 38	128
Fara III 39	134
Fara III 40	129
Figure aux Plumes	18
FM 1	242
FM 2	243
FM 4	228
Forde, *NCT* 63	299
Gelb *AV* p. 236	142
Hallo in *Gelb AV*, see *Gelb AV*	
Hoffman Tablet	1
HSS X 99	231
HSS X 211	241
IM, see Iraq Museum	
Iraq Museum, Baghdad	
IM 2886/D	245
IM 14182	108
IM 43431	216
IM 43451	219
IM 43612	234
IM 43741	220
IM 56506	25
IM 57944	30b
IM 58820	206
IM 61558	345
IM 61706	349

5.3. *Concordance of Ancient Kudurrus and Sale Documents—continued*

Text	No.
IM 61712	353
10 NT 1	27
Istanbul Archaeological Museum	
Adab 397	159
Adab 398	160
Adab 399	161
Adab 426	162
EŞEM 4808	23
Nippur 5446	302
ITT I 1040	195
ITT I 1041	196
ITT II 2766	354
ITT II 3470	356
ITT II 3512	342
ITT II 4518	197
ITT II 4578	198
ITT II 4588	199
ITT III 6370	294
ITT III 6582	326
ITT V 6837	259
JCS X p. 26	237
JCS XV pp. 107–08	26
JCS XIX p. 27 no. 2	368
JMEOS XV pp. 41–42 no. 2	319
Khafajah Bird	9
Kish, see Ashmolean Museum	
Kish Stone Fragments I	16
Kish Stone Fragment II	17
Lagash Stela	19
Lambert in *Unger AV*, see *Unger AV*	
Lambert Tablet (*RA* LXXIII pp. 10–19)	182a
LB, see Liagre Böhl Collection	
Leiden, see Liagre Böhl Collection	
Leiden Tablet	7
Liagre Böhl Collection, Nederlands Instituut voor het Nabije Oosten, Leiden	
LB 929	192
LB 1338	7
Ligabue, see *SEL* III p. 11	
Limet, *TSDU* 16	309a
L'Oeil nos. 221–22 p. 78 (= *MVNS* X 85)	112 = 113c
London, see British Museum	
Louvre, Paris	
AO 4464	23
Louvre Tablet	4
Lummatur Tablet I	22
Lummatur Tablet II	23
Lupad Statue	21
MAD I 25	44
MAD I 26	44
MAD I 36	44
MAD I 45	43
MAD I 48	44
MAD I 50	43
MAD I 51	43
MAD I 52	43
MAD I 58	43
MAD I 67	44
MAD I 74	44
MAD I 111	44
MAD I 119	44
MAD I 120	44

Text	No.
MAD I 122	44
MAD I 128	44
MAD I 161	44
MAD I 168	42
MAD I 336	244
MAD IV 4	236
MAD IV 15	224
MAD IV 51	225
MAD IV 77	184
MAD IV 78	185
MAD IV 80	193
MAD IV 81	186
MAD IV 150	187
MAD IV 151	175
MAD IV 152	176
MAD IV 153	177
MAD IV 155	178
MAD IV 158	188
MAD IV 169	179
MAD V 48	229
MAD V 65	230
MAD V 82	238
Manishtushu Obelisk	40
MAOG IV pp. 188–89 MD 2	359
MAOG IV p. 191 MD 3	296
MDP II pls. I–X	40
MDP XVIII 199	366
MDP XXVIII 410	289
Mesopotamia VIII pp. 68f.	App. to no. 32
Metropolitan Museum, New York 58.29	12
MLC, see Yale Babylonian Collection	
MO, see Manishtushu Obelisk	
MVNS III 13	181
MVNS III 25	180
MVNS III 53	182
MVNS III 80	232
MVNS III 100	222
MVNS III 102	233
MVNS III 213	247
MVNS III 263	267
MVNS III 268	331
MVNS III 330	327
MVNS X 82	113a
MVNS X 83	113b
MVNS X 84	127a
MVNS X 85 (= *L'Oeil* nos. 221–222 p. 78)	113c = 112
MVNS X 86	127b
MVNS X 87	38
NBC, see Yale Babylonian Collection	
Nederlands Instituut, see Liagre Böhl Coll.	
New Haven, see Yale Babylonian Collection	
Nippur, see Istanbul Archaeological Museum	
Nippur Disk	30a
Nippur Statue	25
NRVN I 212	310
NRVN I 213	308
NRVN I 214	304
NRVN I 215	290
NRVN I 216	288
NRVN I 217	329
NRVN I 218	317
NRVN I 219	322
NRVN I 220	321
NRVN I 221	323
NRVN I 222	260
NRVN I 223	257

5.3. *Concordance of Ancient Kudurrus and Sale Documents—continued*

Text	No.
NRVN I 224	265
NRVN I 225	330
NRVN I 226	343
NRVN I 251	257
NSATN 5	307
NSATN 19	261
NSATN 123	273
NSATN 145	351
NSATN 255	278
NSATN 265	301
NSATN 367	277
NSATN 497	269
NSATN 498	298
NSATN 607	271
NSATN 610	300
NSATN 713	292
NSATN 761	285
NSATN 762	266
NSATN 777	268
NSATN 741	316
NSATN 782	250
NSATN 850	312
NSATN 884	313
NSATN 903	306
NSATN 911	252
NSATN 937	347
NSATN 966	253
NSGU III pl. 1 no. 9	326
NSGU III pl. 8 no. 100	259
NT, see Iraq Museum; Oriental Institute	
OECT VII 149	17
OIP XIV 48	31
OIP XIV 49	32
OIP XIV 51	33
OIP LVIII p. 289	9
Oppenheim, *Eames Collection*	
Noor II	263
TT 1	362
TT 2	363
TT 4	361
Oriental Institute, Chicago	
A 713	158
A 815	163
A 3669	8
A 22108	247a
A 25412	14
A 31164	350
A 33676	133
A 33678	30c
6 NT 436	328
TA 1930, 249	258
Or. IX p. 173	149
Or. n.s. XLIV p. 436 no. 1	127
Or. n.s. LI pp. 355–56	227
Or. n.s. LI p. 363	235
Oxford, see Ashmolean Museum	
Paris, see Louvre	
PBS VIII/2 157	307
PBS IX 1	3
PBS IX 2	20
PBS IX 3	111
PBS IX 4	213
PBS IX 7	210
PBS IX 8	207
PBS IX 9	204

Text	No.
PBS IX 41	311
PBS IX 51	211
PBS IX 52	211
PBS IX 78	209
PBS IX 86	212
PBS IX 107	212
PBS XIII 24	120
PBS XV 3	28
PBS XV 17	29
PBS XV 20	30
Philadelphia, see University Museum	
Philadelphia Tablet	3
Pinches, *BTBC* 53	357
RA VI p. 143	13
RA VIII pp. 185–86 no. 4	276
RA X p. 66 no. 105	280
RA XXIV p. 23	4
RA XXXII p. 126	105
RA LXXIII pp. 10–19 (Lambert Tablet)	182a
RSO XXXII pp. 83ff.	41
RTC 13	104
RTC 14	130
RTC 15	131
RTC 16	150
RTC 17	151
RTC 18	143
RTC 79	200
RTC 80	201
RTC 81	202
SEL III p. 11	113
Serota Coll. A 10	226
Sheep(?) Figurine	8
Sippar Stone	41
Staatliche Museen, Berlin	
VA 5689	45
Stela of Victory	24
Szlechter, *TJA* I pl. LXVIII JES 134	339
TA, see Oriental Institute	
TIM V 8	262
TIM V 12	283
TIM IX 94	148
TIM IX 97	46
TIM IX 99	215
TIM IX 103	297
TLB III 170	367
TMH V 47	208
TMH V 71	103
TMH V 75	109
TMH V 78	110
TMH V 128	205
TMH n.F. I/II 50	364
TMH n.F. I/II 51	293
TMH n.F. I/II 52	320
TMH n.F. I/II 53	369
TSŠ pls. XXXIII–XXXIV	119
TSŠ 66	102
UCP IX p. 204 no. 83	239
UET III 9	340
UET III 14	334
UET III 15	335
UET III 18	338
UET III 19	332
UET III 26	281

5.3. *Concordance of Ancient Kudurrus and Sale Documents—continued*

Text	No.
UET III 27	251
UET III 29	287
UET III 30	284
UET III 31	249
UET III 32	324
UET III 33	352
UET III 36	360
UET III 39	309
UET III 41	365
UET III 44	337
UET III 46	336
UET III 47	315
UM, see University Museum	
Unger *AV* pp. 29–30	122
Unger *AV* pp. 33–34	106
Unger *AV* pp. 37–38	123
Unger *AV* pp. 41–42	124
University Museum, Philadelphia	
UM 32-40-436	47
Ushumgal Stela	12
VAS XIV 141	152
VAS XIV 144	153
Walters Art Gallery, Baltimore 41.107	15
Walters Tablet	2
WO VIII p. 180	136
Yale Babylonian Collection, New Haven	
MLC 1251	221
NBC 5652	282
NBC 6844	165
NBC 6900	167
NBC 7174	279
NBC 10198	168
NBC 10204	183
NBC 10221	217
NBC 10294	194
NBC 11300	275
YBC 2409	39
YBC 9827	303
YBC 12305	135
YBC 12310	246
YBC 12312	223
Yale Tablet I	5
Yale Tablet II	6
YBC, see Yale Babylonian Collection	
Yondorf Coll. A	370
Yondorf Coll. B	254
YOS IV 2	344
YOS IV 4	255
YOS XV 100	256
YOS XV 101	341
ZA XXV p. 206 no. 1	291
ZA LIII p. 79 no. 18	346
ZA LIII p. 79 no. 19	203
ZA LIII p. 80 no. 20	348
ZA LIII p. 82 no. 21	248
ZA LXIII pp. 209–10 no. 4a	121

CHAPTER 6

STRUCTURE AND TYPOLOGY OF ANCIENT KUDURRUS AND SALE DOCUMENTS

6.1. *Introductory Remarks*

This chapter studies the general composition of the ancient kudurrus and clay sale documents. Our main objective here will be to distinguish the patterns underlying the internal structure of these texts. As far as the kudurrus are concerned, each document is treated separately. Excluded from the discussion are only those kudurrus which are either unintelligible (nos. 1, 2, 3, 4, 5, 6, 7, 8, 9, 10, 11, 12, 13, 18, 19a, 19b, and 20) or are not preserved sufficiently to judge their entire structure (nos. 17, 19, 24, 25, 26, 27, 28, 29, 30, 30a, 30b, 30c, 31, 39, 45, 46, 47, 48, 49, 50, and 51). Regarding the sale documents, patterns representative for groups of several texts each are established. Whenever it deems significant, the deviations from the respective patterns are noted. Not taken into consideration are a number of texts which lack a clearly defined pattern (nos. 154, 155, 156, 163, 166, 167, 180, 182a, 189, 190, 191, 192, 193, 194, 210, 211, 212, 213, and 224).

6.2. *Structure and Typology of Kudurrus*

Nos. 14 Chicago Stone and 15 Baltimore Stone

The Chicago Stone and the Baltimore Stone record sixteen and seventeen transactions, respectively, pertaining to the purchase of fields from different sellers by presumably the same buyer. The two inscriptions were unquestionably written at the same time, at the same place, and for the same occasion. This is demonstrated by the use of the same sign-forms, the identical formulary, and the occurrence of the same field and personal names in both inscriptions. Since the name of the buyer is not stated in either text, it seems likely that they were originally accompanied by yet another inscription (or inscriptions) which recorded additional transactions and ended with the name of the buyer. The individual transactions use two basic structures (Structures 1 and 2), with each showing further variations, such as the use of different verbs, different order of the component parts, etc. The existence of these variations strongly suggests that the Chicago Stone and the Baltimore Stone are composite copies of the clay tablets, now lost, which recorded individual transactions and were written by different scribes.

Structure 1

14. i 1–ii 5, iii 10–iv 14, vi 12–viii 1, viii 2–x 2, xviii 12–18; 15. i 1–28, ii 1–27, ii 28–iii 25, iii 26–iv 25, iv 26–v 24, v 25–vi 30, vi 31–vii 28, vii 29–ix 6, ix 7–x 1, x 2–28, xii 16–xiii 15, xiii 16–xiv 11, xiv 12–L. E. 9, L. E. 10–20, L. E. 21–29.

(1) x iku of land, the field FN.
x(iku) gán gán FN

(2) x shekels of silver (to) the seller(s) was weighed out.
x gín kug PN/PNs an-na-lal[1]

(3) PNs left the (buyer's?) house.
x PNs é-ta íb-è[2]

(4) Commodities (received by) PNs, the witnesses.
Commodities x PNs lú-ki-inim-ma[3]

(5) The oil was spread on the side.
ì-bi zag (ab-)ag

(6) This transaction "left the house."
inim-bi é-ta ab-è

(7) PNs, the "farmers," sat on the side.
x PNs engar zag durun-durun

Structure 2

14. ii 6–iii 9, iv 15–vi 11, x 3–xi 11, xi 12–xii 7, xii 8–xiii 1, xiii 2–9, xiii 10–xvi 1, xvi 2–14, xvii 1–11, xvii 12–xviii 2, xviii 3–11; 15. xi 1–11, xi 12–xii 15.

(1) x iku of land, the field FN.
x(iku) gán gán FN

(2) x shekels of silver (and) Commodities (to) the seller(s) were given.
x gín kug Commodities PN/PNs an-na-sum[4]

1. 14. viii 2–x 2 reads an-na-túm, "(it) was brought," in place of an-na-lal. 14. xviii 12–18 reads an-gi$_4$, "(it) was . . . ," in place of an-na-lal. 15. x 2–28, xii 16–xiii 15, and xiv 12–L. E. 9 have an-kú, "(the seller(s)) received (lit.: ate) (it)," in place of an-na-lal.

2. Attested only in 15. i 1–28.

3. 14. viii 2–x 2 adds after lú-ki-inim-ma: ki ⸢gán? šám?⸣ ì-durun-durun, "they sat in the place where the ⸢field? was bought?⸣."

4. 14. xvii 1–11 reads x kug (ma-na) PN an-na⟨-lal⟩, Commodities PN$_2$ PN$_3$ an-na-sum. 14. xi 12–xii 7, xii 8–xiii 1, and xiii 2–9 read é-ta íb-è, "(the sellers) took (it) from the (buyer's?) house," in place of

(3) PN took (it) from the (buyer's?) house.
PN é-ta íb-è[5]

(4) PNs are the witnesses.
x PNs lú-ki-inim-ma

(5) The oil was spread on the side.
ì-bi zag (ab-)ag

(6) This transaction "left the house."
inim-bi é-ta ab-è

(7) PNs, the "farmers," sat on the side.
x PNs engar zag durun-durun[6]

Comments on Structures 1 and 2

According to the interpretation adopted here, in the transactions using Structure 1 the price, paid in silver, was received by the sellers, while the commodities were received by the witnesses. In contrast, in the transactions with Structure 2, both the silver and the commodities were given to the sellers, while the witnesses received nothing. Since this interpretation looks suspiciously artificial, it is possible that the commodities listed in Structure 1 after the names of sellers and the verb were in fact received by the sellers, and not by the witnesses.

Also, it should be pointed out that in several transactions the numbers of witnesses may actually be lower than the numbers one obtains through the simple addition of personal names. This is suggested by the instances in which the same person is listed among both the sellers and the witnesses. One is tempted to speculate that in those cases the second mention of the seller is simply a description of the preceding witness: "(man of) PN." See the following examples:

Sellers: PN, PN_2, PN_3; first two witnesses: PN_4 (of?) PN_3 (14. ii 6–iii 9);
Sellers: PN, PN_2; first two witnesses: PN_3 (of?) PN_2 (14. vi 15–vi 11);
Sellers: PN, PN_2; first five witnesses: dam PN, PN_3 (of?) PN_2, PN_4, (of?) PN (15. ii 28–iii 25);
Sellers: PN, PN_2; first five witnesses: PN_3 (of?) PN_2, PN_4, PN_5 (of?) PN (15. iii 26–iv 25);
Sellers: PN, PN_2; witnesses: PN_3 (of?) PN_2, PN_4 (of?) PN (15. xii 16–xiii 15).

No. 16 Kish Stone Fragments I

The ten stone fragments classified as Kish Stone Fragments I could very well belong to the same tablet, in spite of the fact that none of them join physically. This possibility is suggested by the similarity in their coloring, writing, and contents. In their present state of preservation, the fragments deal with at least twenty-eight transactions, all of which appear to follow the same pattern.

(1) x iku of land;
x(IKU) GÁN

(2) (its) price is x shekels of silver;
ŠÁM x GÍN KUG.BABBAR

(3) the additional payment is x shekels of silver;
NÍG.KI.GAR x GÍN KUG.BABBAR

(4) the sellers received (lit.: ate) (it).
KÚ

Nos. 21 Lupad Statue, 22 Lummatur Tablet I, and 23 Lummatur Tablet II

For the structure of these three inscriptions, see below under nos. 137–153.

Nos. 32 Adab Clay Fragment I and 33 Adab Clay Fragment II

The Adab Clay Fragment I records two transactions concerning the purchase of two fields belonging to two different families by the same buyer (i 1–v 11 and v 12–Rev. ii 2). Following the second transaction, the inscription contains a summary of the commodities presented as gifts to the sellers: [šu-nigín] Commodities níg-ba dumu PN Commodities níg-ba dam PN_2 dumu PN_2 (Rev. ii 3–15). The very end of the inscription, now lost, probably recorded the name of the buyer. The Adab Clay Fragment II, consisting of a long list of witnesses, appears to have been part of a sale document whose structure paralleled that of Fragment I.

(1) x iku of land, (located in) GN.
x(iku) gán GN

(2) Its price (is) x pounds of silver.
šám-bi x ma-na kug

(3) The field of (the family of) PN.
gán PN

(4) Commodities (received by) PNs sons/children of PN, the sellers.
Commodities x PNs[7] dumu PN lú-šám-kú

(5) Commodities (received by) PNs, the secondary sellers (= primary witnesses).
Commodities x PNs[8] lú-ki-inim-ma[9]

(6) PNs, the (secondary) witnesses of (the family of) PN.
x D PNs lú-ki-inim-ma PN

No. 34 BIN II 2

This text contains the record of eight transactions, six of which follow the same pattern (i 1–7, i 8–ii 4, ii 5–9, ii 10–iii 5, iii 6–12, and iv 5–11). The remaining two

an-na-sum. 14. xii 10–xvi 1 reads x gín kug PN PN_2 PN_3 é-ta íb-è, Commodities PN_4 é-ta íb-è. 14. xvi 2–14 reads an?-ne-túm?, "(it) was brought," instead of an-na-sum. 14. xii 10–xvi 1 inserts after (2) the following clause: PN iš-gán nu-ag PN_2 ì-ag, "PN (i.e., the Buyer?) did not make the additional payment; PN_2 made it."

5. Attested only in 14. x 3–xi 11.

6. 14. xiii 10–xvi 1 reads ki durun-durun "sat in (this) place" and adds a list of twelve PNs, not described by any term. 15. xi 12–xii 15 reads šeš gán ki-ba ì-durun-durun, "the 'brothers of the field' sat in this place," instead(?) of engar zag durun-durun.

7. Written: Commodities PN, Commodities PN_2, etc.

8. Written: Commodities PN, Commodities PN_2, etc.

9. The second transaction does not seem to list primary witnesses.

transactions (iv 1–4 and rev. i 1–4) are not finished. The name of the buyer does not appear anywhere in the inscription.

(1) x pounds / x shekels of silver
x MA-NA / x GÍN KUG.BABBAR
(2) (is the price of) x iku of land.
X(IKU) GÁN
(3) The seller(s) received (lit.: ate) the price of the field.
PN/PNs ŠÁM GÁN KÚ[10]

No. 35 DP 2

As far as can be judged from the preserved part, *DP* 2 recorded a single transaction. Due to the fragmentary state of the inscription, its structure can be reconstructed only tentatively.

(1) [Size of the property?].
[. . .]
(2) [Its price?].
[. . .]
(3) [The sellers received it?].
[. . .]
(4) The sellers(?) spread the oil.
[x]+5 PNs
Ì *iš-du-du*
2 D PNs
[Ì] *iš-du-du*
[2 D P]Ns
[Ì *iš-du-d*]*u*!
(5) Description of the property.
⌜*è-da*⌝-[*su*]
⌜IM⌝.Ù PN PN_2
è-da-s[*u*]
IM.MAR.T[U]
PN
è-da-su
IM *sa-ti-um*
LÚ PN
(6) [20 PNs], the total of 20 witnesses, in the house of PN (i.e., the buyer), son of P[N_2], the governor, ate bread/food (and) drank beer.
[20 PNs] ŠU.NIGÍN 20 AB+ÁŠ *in* É PN DUMU P[N_2] PA.TE.[SI] NINDA KÚ(KA+⌜GAR⌝) KAŠ Ì.NA[G](K[A+A])

No. 36 CT V 3

In its present state of preservation, *CT* V 3 lists seven(?) transactions, pertaining to the sale of fields by different persons (i 1–ii 20, iii 1–11, iii 12–22, iv 1–11, iv 12–v 2, v 3–12, and v 13–22). The name of the buyer was conceivably recorded at the very end of the inscription, which is now broken away. The pattern of the transactions is as follows:

(1) x iku of land;
x(IKU) GÁN
(2) its price is x shekels of silver;
ŠÁM-*sù* x GÍN KUG.BABBAR
(3) the additional payment is Commodities;
NÍG.KI.GAR Commodities
(4) the seller(s) received (it).
PN/PNs ŠU.BA.TI

No. 37 CT XXXII 7f.

The preserved portions of *CT* XXXII 7f. contain a sequence of ten transactions which deal with the purchase of fields from different sellers by the same buyer (i′ 1–7, i′ 8–ii′ 5, ii′ 6–iii′ 7, iii′ 8–17, iv′ 1–13, iv′ 14–Rev. i 4, i 5–ii 8, ii 9–iii 12, iii 13–iv 14, and iv 15–17). The transactions closely follow the same pattern (see below). The inscription ends with the following statement: (a) the rates of barley, oil, and wool given as the additional payment (NÍG.DÚR.GAR); (b) the amount of barley received by one person, whose role in the transaction is unclear (24 ŠE.NI.KID.NI GUR PN DAM PN_x DUMU PN_y GN ŠU.BA.TI "PN, wife of PN_x, son of PN_y of GN, received 24 gur of . . ."); and (3) the identification of the purchased fields as NÍG.ŠÁM PN, "purchased (fields) of PN (i.e., the buyer)."

(1) x iku of land, (located in) GN;
x(IKU) GÁN[11] *in* GN[12]
(2) the price of the field is x gsg of barley;
ŠÁM GÁN[13] x(GUR) ŠE GUR.SAG.GÁL
(3) the additional payment is Commodities;
NÍG.DÚR.GAR Commodities[14]
(4) the gift is Commodities;
NÍG.BA Commodities[15]
(5) the seller(s) (received it).
PN/PNs

No. 38 Dar-a-a Tablet

The structure of this text finds no parallel among the extant kudurrus. The preserved part of the inscription, which appears to record a single transaction, has the following pattern:

(1) a number of animals and the names of two persons (possibly the price and the sellers);
(2) a list of six fields (= the object of sale?);

10. Transactions in ii 5–9 and iv 5–11 omit ŠÁM GÁN KÚ.

11. Transactions Rev. iii 13–iv 14 and iv 15–17 add ÉŠ.GÍD SI.SÁ after GÁN.

12. The location of the field is stated only in iv′ 1–13 and Rev. iii 13–iv 14.

13. Rev. iii 13–iv 14 has ŠÁM-*sù* instead of ŠÁM GÁN.

14. Rev. i 5–ii 8 reads NÍG.DÚR.GAR Commodities DUMU.DUMU PN NÍG.DÚ[R.GAR] K[Ú], "the additional payment, Commodities; the descendants of PN received (lit.: ate) the additional payment."

15. Attested only in ii′ 6–iii′ 7 and iv′ 1–13.

(3) a list of commodities and the names of two persons (possibly the additional payment and the secondary sellers);

(4) names of eight persons (the secondary sellers or witnesses).

The missing part of the text may have recorded other transactions. The text concludes with the statement: ŠU.NIGÍN 25 AB+ÁŠ PN, "total of 25 witnesses of PN," where PN may be the buyer.

No. 40 Manishtushu Obelisk

The Manishtushu Obelisk records four transactions (A, B, C, and D), pertaining to the purchase of eight parcels of land by one buyer (Manishtushu) from different sellers. The beginning of the inscription (preceding A) gives the grand totals of the purchased land and prices, and the name of the buyer. The transactions show the following pattern:

(1) x iku of land;
  x(IKU) GÁN

(2) its price is x gsg of barley.
  NÍG.ŠÁM-*su* x(GUR) ŠE GUR.SAG.GÁL
 Rate.
  1 GÍN KUG.BABBAR = 1 ŠE GUR.SAG.GÁL
 Its (of the barley) silver (equivalent) (is)
  KUG.BABBAR-*su*
 x pounds / x shekels of silver.
  x MA.NA / x GÍN KUG.BABBAR
 (This is) the price of the field.
  NÍG.ŠÁM GÁN

(3) x gsg of barley is the additional payment of the field.
  x(GUR) ŠE GUR.SAG.GÁL NÍG.KI.GAR GÁN

(4a) Commodities (received by) PNs.
  Commodities x PNs[16]

(4b) Total of Commodities, the gift of the field.
  ŠU.NIGÍN Commodities NÍG.BA GÁN

(4c) PNs (not receiving Commodities)
  x D PNs[17]

(4d) Total of PNs, the "lords of the field," the recipients of silver.
  ŠU.NIGÍN x GURUŠ *be-lu* GÁN KÚ KUG.BABBAR

(5) PNs, total of PNs, the "brother-lords of the field."
  x D PNs ŠU.NIGÍN x GURUŠ ŠEŠ *be-lu* GÁN[18]

(6) (Grand-total of PNs), descendants of (the clan of) PN.
  (ŠU.NIGÍN.ŠU.NIGÍN x GURUŠ) DUMU.DUMU PN[19]

(7) Description of the field.
  GÁN.NINDÁ IM.MIR
  PN/GN
  GÁN.NINDÁ IM.MAR.TU
  PN/GN
  GÁN.NINDÁ IM.KUR
  PN/GN
  GÁN.NINDÁ IM.U_5
  PN/GN
  GÁN FN (*in* GN)[20]

(8) PNs, total of PNs, the witnesses of the field (= witnesses of the sellers).
  x D PNs ŠU.NIGÍN x GURUŠ AB+ÁŠ.AB+ÁŠ GÁN[21]

(9) x men, citizens of GN, (in Kazalu) ate bread.
  x GURUŠ DUMU.DUMU GN (*in Ga-za-lu*^{KI}) NINDA Ì.KÚ[22]

(10) PNs, total of the citizens of Akkadē, the witnesses of the field (= witnesses of the buyer)
  x D PNs ŠU.NIGÍN x DUMU.DUMU *A-ga-dè*^{KI} AB+ÁŠ.AB+ÁŠ GÁN

(11) Manishtushu, king of the totality, bought the field FN (in GN).
  GÁN FN (*in* GN) *Ma-ni-iš-tu-su* LUGAL KIŠ Ì.ŠÁM

The distribution of the component parts in A, B, C, and D is as follows:

A:	1–6 (A_1)	B:	1
	1–4d, 6 (A_2)		2
	1–4b, 4d, 6 (A_3)		3
	7		4a
	8		4b
	9		4d
	10		7
	11		8
			9
			10
			11

16. Written: Commodities PN, Commodities PN_2, etc.
17. Only in A_1 and A_2.
18. Only in A_1 and D.
19. Missing in B and D.

20. In A and C, this part begins with the total of the fields listed in A_1, A_2, A_3 and in C_1, C_2, C_3, respectively.

21. In C, this section shows the following subdivisions:

(8a)	Commodities (received by) 3 PNs, the surveyors.	Commodities 3 D PNs (LÚ.ÉŠ.GÍD, DUB.SAR, and SAG.DU_5)
	Total of Commodities, the gift for the surveyors.	ŠU.NIGÍN Commodities NÍG.BA LÚ.GÁN.GÍD.DA
(8b)	27 PNs (not receiving Commodities)	27 D PNs
(8c)	Total of the scribes (i.e., the surveyors)	ŠU.NIGÍN 3 DUB.SAR
	Total of the witnesses.	ŠU.NIGÍN 27 AB+ÁŠ.AB+ÁŠ
(8d)	10 PNs, total of the sons of the witnesses.	10 D PNs ŠU.NIGÍN 10 DUMU.DUMU AB+ÁŠ.AB+ÁŠ
(8e)	12 PNs, total of the overseers and foremen.	12 D PNs ŠU.NIGÍN 12 NU.BANDA ù UGULA
(8f)	Grand-total of the citizens of GN, the witnesses of the field.	ŠU.NIGÍN.ŠU.NIGÍN 52 GURUŠ GN AB+ÁŠ.AB+ÁŠ GÁN

22. In C, this section is formulated as follows: 600 GURUŠ *in Ga-za-lu*^{KI} NINDA Ì.KÚ 600 GURUŠ *šu* 1 UD 1200 GURUŠ *šu* 2 UD

C:	1–4b, 4d, 6 (C_1)	D:	1
	1–4b, 4d, 6 (C_2)		2
	1–4b, 4d, 6 (C_3)		3
	7		4a
	8		4b
	9		4d
	10		5
	11		7
			9
			10
			11

No. 41 Sippar Stone

The preserved portions of the Sippar Stone list at least twenty-seven transactions pertaining to the sale of fields by different sellers to an unknown buyer. As far as the fragmentary state of the inscription allows us to ascertain, the individual transactions follow basically the same pattern. The name of the buyer was probably recorded at the very end of the inscription, which is now broken away.

(1) x iku of land (measured in grain-seed);
 x GUR GÁN 1(PI)

(2) its price is x pounds / x shekels of silver;
 NÍG.ŠÁM-*su* x MA.NA / x GÍN KUG.BABBAR

(3) the additional payment is Commodities;
 NÍG.KI.GAR Commodities

(4) the seller(s) received (it).
 D PN / x D PNs *im-ḫur* / *dam-ḫur* / *im-ḫu-ru*[23]

(5) Description of the property.
 D PN IM.MIR
 GÁN.NINDÁ
 D PN IM.MAR.TU
 GÁN.NINDÁ
 D PN IM.KUR
 GÁN.NINDÁ
 D PN IM.U_5
 GÁN.NINDÁ

(6) PNs, the witnesses of the field of the seller(s).
 x D PNs AB+ÁŠ.AB+ÁŠ (*a-na*) GÁN *šu* PN[24]

(7) Commodities (received by) PN, the scribe of the field.
 Commodities D PN DUB.SAR GÁN

Nos. 42 Eshnuna Stone Fragment, 43 Eshnuna Clay Tablet, and 44 Eshnuna Clay Fragments

Each of these three texts contains a sequence of individual transactions, following basically the same pattern. Due to the fragmentary state of the texts, it is difficult to describe their entire structure. It appears that in no. 42 the transactions were followed by a summary of the purchased fields, and then, by a list of witnesses, each of whom received commodities. In no. 43 the transactions were followed by a summary of the prices and the commodities given for the fields. That section probably continued with a total of the purchased fields and the name of the buyer. This list of witnesses was either very short, and followed immediately after the transactions, or was not included at all in the inscription.

(1) x iku of land;
 x(IKU) GÁN

(2) its price is x shekels of silver (and) x gur/gsg of barley;
 ŠÁM-*su* x GÍN KUG.BABBAR x(GUR) ŠE GUR(.SAG.GÁL)

(3) its additional payment is Commodities;
 iš-ki-nu-su Commodities[25]

(4) the seller(s) received (it).
 PN/PNs *im-ḫur* / *dam-ḫur* /*im-ḫu-ra* / *im-ḫu-ru*

6.3. *Structure and Typology of Sale Documents*

Nos. 100–136 Fara Sale Documents

The Fara sale documents are characterized by a highly standardized and regular structure, which shows only small variations from one text to another. Only three texts (nos. 128, 129, and 134) diverge from that pattern. With the exception of no. 107, the Fara sale documents pertain to single purchases of real property (houses or fields). No. 107 is atypical in that it records two purchases of houses belonging to two different sellers by the same buyer. The structure of the Fara sale documents nos. 100–127, 130–133, and 135–136 is as follows:

(1) The amount x (is) the price of the house/field.
 x ma-na urudu / x gín kug(-luḫ-ḫa) šám é/gán[26]

(2) Its (i.e., of the real estate) size is y.
 x sar é-bi / x(iku) gán-bi[27]

(3) Additional payments.
 (a) The amount z (is) the . . .
  x ma-na urudu MUNSUB.AN.TAR[28]
 (b) The amount z_2 (is) the additional payment.
  x ma-na urudu / x gín kug(-luḫ-ḫa) níg-dirig[29]
 (c) The amount z_3 (is) the gift.
  x ma-na urudu, x NI-ga/x(bán) še níg-ba[30]

(4) Commodities (received by) PN/PNs, the seller(s).
 Commodities PN/PNs lú-šám-kú[31]

in maš-ga-ni Be-li-ba-ni IGI.DUB ^{d}*A-ba*$_4$*-iš-da-gal* NINDA Ì.KÚ LÚ *Mar-da*^{KI}, "600 men in Kazalu ate bread; 600 men for one day, 1200 men for two days ate bread in the settlement of Bêlī-bāni, the steward of Abaish-takal; the citizens of (the district of) Marda."

23. Obv. i reads *ma-ḫi-ru* [KUG.B]ABBAR, "receivers of the silver."

24. In Obv. vii, two of the witnesses received commodities.

25. No. 44 does not list the additional payment.

26. No. 125 reads: 4(iku) gán-TUŠ.SAR.ḪAR 10 urudu-EN.DA 4 gín kug šám-kam. No. 136 reads: 1(bùr) gán 9 gín kug šám-bi.

27. Omitted in nos. 100, 101, 104, 107, and 108.

28. Attested only in nos. 115 and 117.

29. Omitted in no. 101. Nos. 103, 104, 105, 108, 109, and 110 add é-dù after níg-dirig.

30. Omitted in nos. 100, 101, 102, 104, 107, 108, 115, 117, 121, and 136.

31. No. 125 reads lú-níg-šám-kú-me instead of lú-šám-kú.

(5) Commodities (received by) PNs (= primary witnesses).
Commodities PNs[32]

(6) PNs, the (secondary) witnesses.
D PNs lú-ki-inim[33]

(7) In house-sales:
Commodities (received by) PN, the master-surveyor.
Commodities PN um-mi-a lú-é-éš-gar[34]
In field-sales:
Commodities (received by) PN, the surveyor (lit.: scribe of the field).
Commodities PN dub-sar-gán[35]

(8) In house-sales:
Commodities (received by) PN, the herald.
Commodities PN nigir-sila[36]
In field-sales:
Commodities (received by) PN, the . . .
Commodities PN ENGAR.UŠ[37]

(9) PN, (is) the buyer.
PN lú-é/gán-šám[38]

(10) "Office" of PN.
bala PN[39]

(11) Location of the sold property.
Varies[40]

The divergent sale documents nos. 128, 129, and 134 use a different formulation each:

No. 128

(1) The amount x (is) the price of the field.
5(gur) 2(bán) še-ḪAR NI-ga šám gán

(2) Its size is y.
1(eše) gán-bi

(3) (To) PN (= the seller) it (i.e., the price) was given.
PN an-na-sum

(4) PN (is) the witness.
PN lú-ki-inim

(5) PN (is) the buyer.
PN lú-šám-ag

No. 129

(1) The amount x (is) the price of the field.
8 gín kug šám gán

(2) PN (and) PN (are) the sellers.
PN PN lú-[šá]m-kú

(3) PN (is) the witness.
PN lú-ki-inim

(4) Commodities (received by) PN (= a primary witness).
Commodities PN

(5) Commodities (received by) PN (= a primary witness).
Commodities PN

(6) Commodities (received by) PN (= a primary witness).
Commodities PN

(7) Commodities (received by) PN (= $seller_1$).
Commodities PN

(8) Commodities (received by) PN (= $seller_2$).
Commodities PN

(9) It (i.e., the price) was given by PN (= the buyer) to him (= $seller_1$).
an-na-sum PN

(10) Rate.
ud-ba 2(bán) š[e] (1) ma-na (urudu)

No. 134

(1) The amount x [(is) the price of the field].
20 NI-ga še, 10 TÚG.A.SU [x si]là [ì šám gán]

(2) [Its size is y].
[x(iku) gán-bi]

(3) PN (is) the seller.
PN lú-šám-kú

(4) PNs (are) the witnesses.
3+[x] D PNs lú-ki-inim

(5) Commodities (received by) PN (= the seller).
Commodities PN

(6) Commodities (received by) PN (= a primary witness).
Commodities PN

(7) Location of the field.
gán-UD.KA.BAR

(8) PN (is) the buyer.
PN lú-šám-ag

32. Written Commodities, PN, Commodities, PN_2, etc. Omitted in nos. 100, 101, 103, 105, 109, 110, 111, 113, 115, 125, and 127b.

33. In no. 122 the witnesses are subdivided into two groups: 18 D PNs lú-ki-inim and 5 D PNs lú-ki-inim. No. 125 has lú-ki-inim-ma-me in place of lú-ki-inim. No. 114 omits lú-ki-inim; the witnesses are subdivided into two groups: 4 D PNs and 4 D PNs.

34. Omitted in nos. 101 and 113.

35. Omitted in nos. 124 and 127b. Nos. 119, 126, 127a, 130, and 136 read dub-sar instead of dub-sar-gán. No. 117 has dub-sar lú-inim-til instead of dub-sar-gán. No. 125 has PN dub-sar-bi Commodities níg-ba-ni.

36. Omitted in nos. 101, 104, 107, 113, 113a, and 113b. Nos. 100 and 108 read gal-nigir in place of nigir-sila.

37. Omitted in nos. 115, 116, 117, 118, 123, 127, and 127b. No. 119 omits ENGAR.UŠ. No. 122 adds lú-ki-inim after ENGAR.UŠ. No. 125 reads engar-bi instead of ENGAR.UŠ. No. 133 lists instead a sag-du_5 and a [GU.SUR].NUN, while no. 136 has a GU.SUR.NUN.

38. No. 125 reads lú-gán-šám-me in place of lú-é/gán-šám. No. 113a adds ½ sar é é rig_9(DU.TUKU) PN an-na-sum. No. 113b adds ½ sar PN ad-da-ni ama-ni ì-na-ba é rig_9(DU.TUKU) inim-ba šu nu-bala.

39. Omitted in nos. 100, 101, and 107. No. 111 reads bala PN PN_2 en_5-si-bi. No. 125 has en_5-si-bi PN.

40. Omitted in nos. 100, 101, 104, 106, 107, 111, and 125 (gives the name of the field in section (1)).

Nos. 137–153 Pre-Sargonic Sale Documents from Lagash, 21 Lupad Statue, 22 Lummatur Tablet I, and 23 Lummatur Tablet II

The Pre-Sargonic sale documents from Lagash follow basically three patterns, classified below as Structures 1, 2, and 3. One Lagash text (no. 149) uses a different formulation, which, however, can be linked to Structure 2. With the exception of no. 143, which records two house-sales involving two different sellers and the same buyer, all of the Lagash sale documents pertain to single transactions. The form of the individual transactions recorded in the Lummatur Tablets I and II, both of which also originated at Lagash, is closely related to Structure 1. As far as one can judge from its single preserved transaction, the Lupad Statue has the same pattern, too.

Structure 1

Nos. 137, 138, 139, 140, 141, 142, 144, 147, 148, and 150.

(1) The object x from the seller the buyer bought.
  Object PN(-šè) PN$_2$(-e) e-šè-šám[41]

(2) Its price, the amount y, the seller received.
  níg-šám-bi Amount PN(-e) šu-ba-ti[42]

(3) Its gift, the amount z, he received.
  níg-ba-bi Amount šu-ba-ti[43]

(4) Commodities PNs (= primary witnesses) received.
  Commodities x PNs šu-ba-ti[44]

(5) PNs are the (secondary) witnesses.
  x D PNs lú-ki-inim-ma-bi-me[45]

(6) Commodities PN, the herald, received.
  Commodities PN nigir šu-ba-ti[46]

(7) (PN, the herald) drove this nail into the wall.
  (PN nigir) kag-bi é-gar$_8$-ra bi/bí-dù[47]

(8) He (i.e., the herald?) spread the oil on the side.
  ì-bi zag-gi bi/bí-ag[48]

(9) (If) someone (else) holds it (i.e., the object of sale) in possession, this nail will be driven through his mouth.
  lú am$_6$-ma-dù-da kag-bi ka-ka(-na) e-gaz[49]

(10) Various clauses.[50]

(11) Date.[51]

The pattern of the transactions recorded in the Lummatur Tablets I and II, which is closely related to Structure 1, is as follows:

(1) x iku of land, (measured?) with purchase rope(?),
  x(iku) gán éš šám-ma-ta
 from the sellers,
  x PNs
 the owners of the field,
  lugal gán(-šè)
 the buyer bought.
  PN(-e) e-ne-šè-šám

(2) For 1 iku of land (the price is) x gsg of barley / x pounds of wool; its (i.e., of the field) barley (equivalent) is x gsg / its wool (equivalent) is x pounds.
  iku 1-a še x gur-sag-gál / síg x ma-na-ta še-bi x gur-sag-gál / síg-bi x ma-na
 The price of the field they received.
  níg-šám gán-kam šu-ba-ti

(3) Commodities the (main) seller as the gift received.
  Commodities PN níg-ba-šè šu-ba-ti

(4) The sellers$_{2\text{-}x}$, the owners of the field, (and) PNs, the "sons of the field" (= the secondary sellers), per 1 person Commodities as the gift received.
  x PNs lugal gán-me x PNs dumu gán-me lú 1-šè Commodities níg-ba-šè šu-ba-ti

(5) The (main) seller drove this nail into the wall.
  PN kag-bi é-gar$_8$-ra bi-dù

(6) He (i.e., the main seller) spread the oil on the side.
  ì-bi zag-gi bi-ag

Structure 2

Nos. 143, 146, 151, 152, and 153.

(1) The object x from the seller the buyer bought.
  Object PN(-šè) PN$_2$(-e) e-šè-šám[52]

41. Nos. 137, 138, and 142 place the buyer before the seller. In no. 139, there are three sellers, described as lugal [é], "owners of the [house]." In no. 139 the verb is e-ne-šè-šám.

42. Nos. 138 and 141 add níg-šám é-kam, "price of the house," after níg-šám-bi Amount. No. 144 reads Amount níg-šám gán-kam, "price of the field," in place of níg-šám-bi Amount. No. 150 reads níg-šám-ma-ni instead of níg-šám-bi. No. 137 omits níg-šám-bi.

43. No. 141 reads: Amount Seller níg-ba-šè šu-ba-ti. No. 144 reads: ⸢Amount⸣ [níg-ba-šè] Seller šu-ba-ti. Nos. 137, 138, and 150 list no gift. In no. 139 the verb is šu-ba-ti-éš.

44. No. 142 has no primary witnesses. No. 144 reads: [x]+1 PNs dumu gán⟨⟨-kam⟩⟩-me, "'sons' of the field," Commodities lú 1-šè [níg-ba-šè šu-ba-ti]. In nos. 137, 141, and 147 the primary witnesses are described as lú-ki-inim-ma-bi-me.

45. Nos. 137 and 141 have no secondary witnesses. In no. 140 the secondary witnesses receive gifts: 23 D PNs Rate lú-ki-inim-ma-bi-me lú 1-šè Amount šu-ba-ti. No. 139 has lú-ki-inim-ma-me in place of lú-ki-inim-ma-bi-me.

46. Nos. 138, 142, 144, and 150 do not contain this part. In no. 137 the herald is listed among the witnesses. No. 141 reads nigir-uru, "town-herald," in place of nigir.

47. In nos. 137, 138, and 150 this clause is omitted. In nos. 139 and 142 the subject of the clause is identified as PN nigir. No. 144 probably lists the seller in the place of the herald.

48. Omitted in nos. 137, 138, and 150.

49. Attested only in nos. 140 and 148.

50. No. 138: PN dub-[sar] im-bi ⸢e⸣?-sar, "PN, the scribe, wrote this tablet." No. 144: ud PN dumu-ni Buyer-ra gán FN e-na-šám-a ki-^{GIŠ}sur$_x$(ERÍN)-ra-bi ba-ba, "when PN, his (i.e., of the buyer) son, bought the field FN for the buyer, its border was divided." No. 150: ud an-dù inim an-gál ud ka-ka-na níg-NE.RU ba-gá-gá ^{GIŠ}kag ka-ka-na ešé-gaz, "if he (i.e., the seller) detains (the sold woman) or raises claims (to her), then he puts deceit in his mouth, (and) thus a wooden nail should be driven through his mouth."

51. Omitted in nos. 138, 139, 140, 141, and 147.

52. No. 146 reads Buyer Seller Object e-šè-šám. No. 151 reads Buyer-e Seller-šè e-šè-šám.

(2) Its price, the amount y, the buyer to the seller weighed out.
níg-šám-bi Amount PN_2(-ra) PN(-e) e-na-lal[53]

(3) The gift, Commodities.
níg-ba Commodities[54]

(4) PNs are the (secondary) witnesses.
x D PNs lú-ki-inim-ma-bi-me[55]

(5) PN, the town-herald, drove this nail into the wall.
PN nigir-uru kag-bi é-gar_8-ra bi-dù[56]

(6) He (i.e., the herald) spread the oil on the side.
ì-bi zag-[g]i bí-[a]g[57]

(7) Date.[58]

Text no. 149 is formulated as a payment of price, and, as such, shows some affinity with Structure 2:

(1) Amount x, the price of the object y, the buyer to the seller gave.
Amount níg-šám PN gala-kam PN_2 dam PN_x en_5-si $Lagaš^{KI}$-ke_4 PN_3 ab-ba-ni é-gal-ta e-na-sum

(2) Date
6

Structure 3

No. 145

(1) The object x.
⌜1(bùr)⌝ gán FN

(2) Its price, the amount y, the sellers, the [owners] ⌜of the field⌝, [received].
níg-šám-bi Amount 4 PNs [lugal] ⌜gán⌝-[me šu-ba-ti]

(3) Commodities, as the gift, the sel[lers] received.
Commodities níg-ba-šè 1+[3] PNs šu-ba-ti

(4) [The buyer gave? (it)].
[PN e-ne-sum?]

(5) [PNs are the witnesses].
[x D PNs lú-ki-inim-ma-bi-me]

(6) ⌜He (i.e., the herald?) drove the nail into the wall⌝.
[kag]-bi [é-g]ar_8-ra [b]i-dù

(7) [He (i.e., the herald) spread the oil] ⌜on the side⌝.
[ì-bi zag-g]i [bi-ag]

No. 156a Pre-Sargonic Sale Document of Unknown Provenience

Apart from the Lagash texts discussed above, the only other sale document that can be dated confidently to Pre-Sargonic times is no 156a. This text, which is written in Akkadian, contains two transactions recording the purchase of two separate fields from the same seller by different buyers. Both transactions show the identical pattern:

x iku of land;	x(IKU) GÁN
(from) the buyer(s)	PN/PNs
the amount x (as its price)	x GÍN / MA.NA KUG
the seller	PN
received.	KÚ

Following the two transactions, no. 156a lists two secondary sellers, described as LÚ.ŠEŠ.EN "'brother-lords' (of the field)," and twenty witnesses, not identified by any term.

Nos. 157–246 Sargonic Sale Documents

Regarding their form, Sargonic sale documents are much more irregular and diversified than their Fara and Pre-Sargonic counterparts. The fact that the individual documents differ greatly among themselves in respect to the clauses employed and their sequence in a text, makes it very difficult to establish standard patterns that would be fully representative of particular groups of texts. For this reason, Sargonic sale documents can be organized only according to the type of their "operative section," that is, the main part of the document listing the object of sale, the price, the names of the parties to the transaction, and the verb. The criterion which we adopted in differentiating among the types of operative section was the verb or verbs occurring in it. Though in most cases we are able to distinguish only three basic parts of the document: (a) operative section, (b) various clauses, and (c) list of witnesses, an attempt was made to establish, whenever possible, more subdivisions.

Operative Section of Type A

The operative section of Type A, which is characterized by the use of the verb šu . . . si, "to fill (someone's) hands," has two variants, classified here as Sub-types A_1 and A_2. The first sub-type is attested exclusively in the texts from Adab, whereas the second is employed in the documents of various provenience. As far as one can tell, the operative section of Type A appears only in the sale documents written in Sumerian.

Sub-type A_1

Nos. 157, 158, 159, 161, and 162.

(1) (With) the amount x, the price of the sold person, the hands of the sellers (by) the buyer were filled.
x gín kug-babbar níg-šám D PN x PNs PN šu-ne-ne-a ab-si

(2) They (i.e., the sellers) made (the sold person) cross over the stick.
giš-a íb-ta-bala-éš

(3) PNs are the witnesses.
x D PNs lú-ki-inim-ma-bi-me

53. Nos. 152 and 153 read níg-šám-ma-ni instead of níg-šám-bi. No. 152 and 153 read Seller-ra Buyer e-na-lal. No. 146 has Amount e-šè-lal. No. 143 reads níg-šám-bi Amount níg-ba-bi Amount Seller Buyer e-na-ba. No. 151 reads níg-šám-ma-ni-šè Amount e-na-sum.

54. The gift is listed only in nos. 143 and 146.

55. Nos. 146 and 152 have no witnesses.

56. Attested only in no. 151.

57. Attested only in no. 151.

58. Attested only in no. 153.

Sub-type A_2

Nos. 214, 215, 216, and 217.

(1) (With) the amount x, the price of the sold person, the hands of the seller(s) were filled (with this silver).
x gín kug-babbar[59] níg-šám[60] D PN[61] PN/PNs (kug-bi) šu-na / šu-ne-ne ab-si[62]

(2) He/they (i.e., the seller(s)) made (the sold person) cross over the pestle.
giš-gan-na . . . bala Clause[63]

(3) The buyer is the man who bought the slave.
PN lú-sag-šám-àm[64]

(4) Various clauses.[65]

(5) PNs are the witnesses.
x D PNs lú-ki-inim-ma-bi-me[66]

Operative Section of Type B

The operative section of this type is attested in the sale documents of various origin and written in Sumerian or Akkadian. It is formulated as a payment of price. The verbs used in it are sum, *nadānum*, "to give," lal, *šaqālum*, "to weigh out," and ág, "to measure out."

Nos. 170, 204, 205, 206, 208, 219, 220, 228, and 229.

(1) The amount x, the price of the object y, the buyer to the seller gave / weighed out / measured out.
Amount níg-šám[67] Object-kam/šè PN(-e) PN$_2$(-ra) sum / *nadānum* / lal / *šaqālum* / ág[68]

(2) Various clauses.[69]

(3) PNs are the witnesses.
x D PNs lú-ki-inim-ma-bi-me[70]

Operative Section of Type C

The operative section of Type C occurs in the sale documents of various origin, written in Akkadian or Sumerian. It is formulated as a receipt of price. The verbs used in it are *maḫārum* and šu . . . ti, both meaning "to receive."

Nos. 160, 164, 165, 168, 169, 171, 172, 174, 175, 176, 177, 183, 207, 209, 223, 227, 231, 233, 235, and 236.

(1) The amount x (as) the price of the object y, the seller from the buyer received.
Amount *a-na* (NÍG.)ŠÁM/ níg-šám(-bi)
Object(-kam) PN *iš-dè* PN$_2$ *maḫārum* / šu . . . ti[71]

(2) Various clauses.[72]

59. No. 214 reads kug instead of kug-babbar.

60. No. 214 reads šám instead of níg-šám.

61. Nos. 216 and 217 omit D before the name of the sold person.

62. No. 214 reads bi-si instead of ab-si.

63. Attested only in nos. 215 and 217. No. 215: giš-gan-na íb-ta-bala-e-éš; no. 217: [sa]g? giš-gan-na bala-a[m$_6$]?.

64. Omitted in no. 216. No. 214 reads: sag šám-a Buyer, "the purchased slave of the buyer." No. 217 omits -àm.

65. No. 214 has a date. No. 215: PN dam-gàr lú-giš-rín-dab$_5$-ba-àm, "PN, the merchant, was the man who held the scales"; dam sanga-ke$_4$ mu-gi$_4$, níg-na-me nu-da-tuku [ini]m-mu-ta ḫé-[š]ám-šám bí-dug$_4$, "the wife of the temple administrator answered(?): 'There are no claims on him (i.e., the sold person); he (i.e., the buyer) may buy him with my consent.'" No. 217: Seller-e zag in-šuš, "the seller branded (the sold woman)"; PN dam-gàr sag-ka[m]?, "PN is the 'merchant' of the slave."

66. No. 214 lists no witnesses.

67. Nos. 170, 204, and 206 read níg-šám-bi instead of níg-šám. Nos. 228 and 229 have *a-na* ŠÁM instead of níg-šám.

68. No. 170: ì-n[a?-sum?]. No. 204: ì-ne-sum. No. 208: an-na-sum. No. 220: e-na-sum. No. 228: *i-ti-in*. No. 204: ì-na-lal, ì-ne-lal. No. 206: an-ne-lal. No. 219: in-lal. No. 229: *da-áš-ku-ul*. No. 205: an-na-ág.

69. No. 170: inim-bi igi-ne-n[e]-t[a] a[l-til], "before them this transaction was [completed]"; mu ^{d}Nin-IN-na-šè PN dumu PN$_x$ PN$_2$ dumu PN$_y$-ka lú-lú nu-ba-gi$_4$-gi$_4$ inim-bi al-til, "by the name of Nin-Isina, PN son of PN$_x$, (and) PN$_2$, son of PN$_y$, completed this transaction that they will not contest one against the other." No. 204: LUL.GU PN ba-túm, "PN took the . . ." No. 205: še É.SUKAL.ḪU^{KI} [. . .] ki P[N? . . .], ". . . ." No. 206: 1 gín kug ⸢x x⸣ ŠA [. . .], ". . . ," [igi-ne-ne]-šè a-bi ab-ta-dé, "before [them] this transaction was completed (lit.: this water was poured out)." No. 219: PN ⸢ù⸣ PN$_2$ (i.e., the sellers) [x]-⸢x⸣-sag-gá-me, "are the [. . .] of the slave." No. 220: KUG.KUG è TUR.TUR è-àm, ". . ."

70. Nos. 204, 205, and 208 list no witnesses. No. 228: 4 PNs AB+ÁŠ ⸢*gu*⸣*-su-ra-im*, "witnesses of the transaction." No. 229: ⸢6⸣ D PNs [ŠU.NIGÍN] 6 AB+ÁŠ *in Kiš*$^{[KI]}$, "[total] of 6 witnesses, in Kish."

71. No. 227: *ma-ḫi-ir-da* KUG.BABBAR, "recipients of the silver." Nos. 231, 235, and 236: *im-ḫur*. No. 233: [*i*]*m-ḫu-ra*. Nos. 160, 164 (twice), 165 (twice), 168 (twice), 169 (twice), 171, 174, 175, 176, 177, 183, 207, 209, 223: šu-ba-ti. No. 172: šu-ba-ti-éš.

72. No. 160: [gi]š-a íb-ta-ba[la], "he (i.e., the seller) made (the sold person) cross over the stick"; [x] gín kug-babbar ⸢x x x x x⸣ [. . .], ". . ." No. 164: níg-š[ám? al-til?], "the pri[ce is completed?]." No. 165: Commodities ⸢iš-gán⸣-bi, "its ⸢additional payment⸣." No. 169: PN dumu P[N$_x$] gán-bi ì-g[íd], "PN, son of P[N$_x$] (i.e., the seller, measured this field." No. 171: Commodities šu-ba-ti iš-gán-bi; inim-pi a⸢l-til⸣ "this transaction is [completed]"; Buyer lú-šám-ag; Seller lú-šám-k[ú]. No. 172: inim-til-[à]m, "completed transaction"; lú gán-⸢ba⸣ am$_6$-ma-dù-da kug-da kug ⟨gur-⟩ru-dam inim-ma [a]n-gál, "he (i.e., the seller) made it stand in the agreement to ⟨return⟩ with the silver (of the price) the (equal amount of) silver, if somebody else holds the field in possession." No. 174: [Buyer? lú-šám-ag?]. No. 175: ud gán-ga lú ù-ma-a-dù-a 2(iku) gán-bi-šè 4(iku) gán ab-ši-gá-gá inim-ma an-gál, "he (i.e., the seller) made it stand in the agreement that, if somebody else holds the field in possession, he will replace the field of two iku with (another) field of four iku"; Buyer simug lú-šám-ag-àm; Seller nin PN lú-šám-kú-àm. No. 176: Bu[yer? lú-šám-ag?]; gán-⸢pi⸣ ⸢PN⸣ ⸢x⸣ [. . .] mu-[gíd], "this field ⸢PN⸣ [measured out]." No. 177: 2 gín kug PN dumu PN$_x$-ke$_4$ ba-túm šám ⸢x⸣-am$_6$, "PN, son of PN$_x$, took 2 shekels of silver; the price of . . ."; Buyer simug lú-šám-ag-am$_6$; ud lú am$_6$-ma-dù-da-a PN árad PN$_x$-ke$_4$ dam dumu-ni igi ba-a-DU-a inim-ma ì-gar, "he (i.e., the seller) made it stand in the agreement that, if somebody else holds the field in possession, PN, the slave of PN$_2$ (i.e., the seller's father), his wife (and) children will serve (him) (i.e., the buyer)." No. 183: inim PN šeš-na-ta, "with the order/permission of PN, his brother." No. 207: x gín kug iš-gán gán-gá-kam; Buyer dam-gàr lú-níg-šám-ag. No. 209: ⸢mu ^{d}Nin⸣-urta-šè mu lugal-šè a-bi ab-ta-dé, "⸢by the name of Nin⸣-urta, by the name of the king, its 'water was poured out'"; [lú l]ú la-ba-da-[g]i$_4$-gi$_4$ [inim]-⸢ma⸣ an-gál, "they made it stand in the transaction that they will not contest ⸢one against the other⸣." No. 227: Commodities PN *ù* PN$_2$ (i.e., the sellers) *a-ki-ìl-d*[*a*] *iš-ki-n*[*e*], "the 'eaters' of the additional payment"; Commodities PN DUB.SAR. No. 233: 2 D PNs *u-gi-ip*, "guaranteed."

(3) PNs are the witnesses.
x D PNs lú-ki-inim-ma-bi-me[73]

Operative Section of Type D

The operative section of Type D is attested in five documents from Isin. It is closely related to Type A, as it also uses the verb šu . . . si, "to fill (someone's) hands." In contrast to Type A, however, where the name of the buyer is included in the clause of šu . . . si, in Type D the buyer is placed in a separate clause, stating the payment of the price. The latter clause uses the verb lal, "to weigh out."

Nos. 184, 185, 186, 187, and 188.

(1) (With) the amount x, the price of the sold person, the hands of the sellers were filled.
x gín kug-babbar níg-ŠÁM+A/ŠÁM+ÀM PN-kam/šè x PNs[74] šu-ne-ne ab-si
The buyer weighed (it) out.
PN ì-ne-lal[75]

(2) They (i.e., the sellers) made (the sold person) cross over the pestle.
giš-gan-na ab-ta-bala[76]

(3) . . .
ì sag(-gá) zíd? sag(-gá)-bi a ba-sum[77]

(4) The buyer is the man who gave the price.
PN lú-níg-ŠÁM+A/ ŠÁM+ÀM-ag-àm[78]

(5) The (main) seller is the person who received the price.
PN lú-níg-ŠÁM+A/ ŠÁM+ÀM-kú-àm[79]

(6) By the name of the king, by the name of Nammaḫ, this transaction was completed; [he will not contest?].
mu lugal-šè mu Nam-maḫ-[šè] in[im-bi a]l-til [la-ba-gi$_4$-gi$_4$?]-da[80]

(7) PNs are the witnesses.
x D PNs lú-ki-inim-ma-bi-me

Operative Section of Type E

Like Type D, the operative section of Type E is composed of two parts. Its first part records the payment of the price by the buyer (sum, *nadānum*, "to give," lal, "to weigh out," or ág, "to measure out"), the second part states the receipt of the price by the seller (šu . . . ti, *maḫārum*, "to receive"). Type E has two sub-types (E$_1$ and E$_2$). The first of them occurs in the Sumerian documents from Lagash; the second sub-type is found in the texts of various provenience, written in Sumerian or Akkadian.

Sub-type E$_1$

Nos. 195, 196, 197, 198, 199, 200, 202, and 203.

(1) The amount x, the price of the sold person, the buyer weighed out.
x gín kug-babbar níg-šám D PN-kam[81] PN$_2$ ì-ši-lal[82]
The seller received (it).
PN$_3$[83] šu-ba-ti[84]

(2) He (i.e., the seller) made (the sold person) cross over the stick.
giš-a íb-ta-bala[85]

(3) PNs are the witnesses.
x D PNs lú-ki-inim-ma-bi-me

Sub-type E$_2$

Nos. 173, 178, 179, 181, 182, 218?, 222, 230, 232, and 234.

(1) The object x; (as) its price, the amount y, the seller received.
Object níg-šám-bi(-šè)[86] Amount PN(-e) šu . . . ti / *maḫārum*[87]
The buyer gave (it) / weighed (it) out / measured (it) out.
PN$_2$(-e) sum / *nadānum* / lal / ág[88]

(2) Various clauses.[89]

(3) PNs are the witnesses.
x D PNs lú-ki-inim-ma-bi-me[90]

Operative Section of Type F

The operative section of Type F is styled as a sale of the object of sale by the seller to the buyer. It is attested in

73. There are no witnesses listed in nos. 164, 168, 171, 183, and 231. No. 172: 1 D PN lú-inim-ma inim-til-a-kam, "witness of the completed transaction." No. 227: 5 D PNs SAL.A[B+ÁŠ Buyer?]. No. 233: 6 D PNs ŠU.NIGÍN 6 AB+ÁŠ-*bu-ut* Buyer. No. 235: 3+[x] D PNs SAL.AB+ÁŠ.SAL.AB+Á[Š]. No. 236: 4 D PNs AB+ÁŠ. AB+ÁŠ *gu-su$_4$-ra-im*.

74. In nos. 184, 186, and 187 (possibly also in no. 188) the sellers include the sold person.

75. Nos. 186 and 187 omit Buyer ì-ne-lal.

76. Attested only in nos. 184 and 187.

77. Attested only in nos. 184 and 187.

78. Omitted in no. 185.

79. Omitted in no. 185. No. 188 lists here also the other seller.

80. Attested only in no. 188.

81. In no. 195, there were sold two persons.

82. In no. 195 the verb is ì-ne-ši-[lal].

83. Nos. 196 and 200 have D before the name of the seller.

84. No. 199 reads: Seller kug-bi šu-[ba-ti].

85. No. 199 reads: PN (i.e., a third party) giš-a íb-[ta-bala].

86. Nos. 230 and 232 read *a-na* (NÍG.)ŠÁM instead of níg-šám-bi(-šè). No. 234 has *a-na* ŠÁM-*me*.

87. Nos. 173, 178, 179, 181 (five times), 182, 218, and 222: šu-ba-ti. No. 179: šu-ba-ti-[é]š. Nos. 230 and 232: *im-ḫur*. No. 234: *im-ḫu-ru*.

88. Nos. 173 and 181: ì-na-sum. Nos. 230 and 232: *i-ti-in*. Nos. 178 and 179: ì-na-lal. No. 218: íb-ši-lal. No. 222: ⸢ì⸣-lal. No. 234: Ì.LAL. No. 182: še-pi-ta ⸢ì⸣-na-⸢ág⸣?, "he measured out(?) (the price) with this barley."

89. No. 178: Seller lú-níg-ŠÁM+A-kú⟨-àm⟩; Buyer lú-níg-ŠÁM+A-ag-àm. No. 179: Sellers lú-níg-ŠÁM+A-kú-a-me; Buyer lú-níg-Š[ÁM+A-ag-à]m. No. 182: Commodities níg-ba; šám al-til, "the price was completed." No. 232: ŠE LIBIR *šu* GUR$_7$ [*š*]*i-bu-tim*, "the old barley of the silo of the [wi]tnesses."

90. There are no witnesses in no. 173. No. 230: *in* É-*ti* PN DUMU.SAL PN$_x$ *in A-ga-dè*^{KI} ⸢10⸣ D PNs ŠU.NIGÍN ⸢10⸣ AB+ÁŠ Buyer *in* [*A*]-*ga-dè*$^{[KI]}$ KUG.BABBAR *iš$_{11}$-ku-*⸢*lu*⸣, "in the house of PN, daughter of PN$_2$, in Akkadē, ⸢10⸣ PNs, the total of ⸢10⸣ witnesses (to the fact) that the buyer weighed out the silver in Akkadē." No. 234: 7 D PNs ŠU.NIGÍN 7 AB+ÁŠ.

two Akkadian texts, stemming from Eshnuna and Nuzi, respectively.

Nos. 239 and 241.

(1) The object x, for the price, the amount y, the seller to the buyer gave (i.e., sold).
Object *a-na* ŠÁM Amount PN *a-na* PN_2 *i-ti-in*

(2) Various clauses.[91]

(3) PNs are the witnesses.
x D PNs AB+ÁŠ(.AB+ÁŠ)[92]

Operative Section of Type G

The operative section of Type G is styled as a purchase of the object of sale from the seller by the buyer. It is found in the texts of various origin, written in Akkadian or Sumerian.

Nos. 201, 226, 237, 238, and 240.

(1) The object x, (for) its price, the amount y, from the seller the buyer took/bought.
Object ŠÁM[93] Amount *iš-dè* PN PN_2 *aḫāzum* / *laqāʾum* / šám[94]

(2) Various clauses.[95]

(3) PNs are the witnesses.[96]

Operative Section of Type H

The operative section of Type H is composed of two parts, recording the purchase of the object of sale from the seller by the buyer and the payment of the price by the buyer, respectively. The only sale document that uses it is no. 225; its origin is unknown.

(1) The object x from the seller the buyer bought.
1 ANŠE.BAR.AN-nita PN-šè PN_2-e ì-šè-šám
The amount y (as its price) he (i.e., the buyer) weighed out.
11 gín kug ì-na-lal

(2) PNs are the witnesses.
4? D PNs lú-ki-inim-ma-me

Operative Section of Type I

Under this type we have included a group of five Akkadian documents which deal with the transfer of real property (houses, field) and show a similar structure (nos. 242, 243, 244, 245, and 246). All five of them appear to have originated at Eshnuna. In nos. 242, 243, and 244, the key verb is *šadādum*, "to measure," and in no. 245, *nadānum*, "to give." No. 246 does not contain a verb, but the mention of *šiddatum*, "measuring," in the body of the text links it closely with the other documents. The structure of these texts can be summarized as follows:

(1) Dimensions of the four sides of the property, according to the four cardinal points.[97]

(2) Total area and the identification of the property.[98]

(3) The statement that the seller measured it off (*šadādum*) / gave (*nadānum*) to the buyer.[99]

(4) Witnesses.

It is not clear whether the *šadādum* texts are to be analyzed as outright sale documents or as the records of the preliminary procedure of measuring and evaluating the property that preceded the actual sale transaction. The use of the terminology distinctly different from that of the regular sale documents seems to support the latter view (compare Gelb, *FM* pp. 188ff.). Still another possibility is suggested by the fact that in nos. 243, 244, and 245 the seller is in all probability the same person in each case (called *Da-ba-lum* in nos. 244 and 245, and *I-da-bí-ì-li* / *Da-bi-lum* in no. 243). If this is correct, then the occurrence of the same person in three different documents would mean that they came from his archive. This, in turn, would indicate that the *šadādum* text was prepared for the seller, and that it functioned as a counterpart of the regular sale document. Whereas the sale document was intended to protect the rights of the buyer, by recording such information as the fact that the buyer paid the full price and that the seller was satisfied with it, it is possible that the *šadādum* text, stating the size of the sold property and the fact that the seller measured it off to the buyer, protected the rights of the seller against any future claims that the property proved smaller than it had been described by him.

91. No. 239: PN SABRA É, "PN, (was) the majordomo"; UD.BA PN SAL.SILÀ.ŠU.DU_8 *ì-nu-mi* PN_2 EN_5.SI-*ki Iš-nun*^{KI}, "on that day PN (was) the female cupbearer; on that day PN_2 (was) the governor of Eshnuna"; PN NAR [*i*]-*gu-un*, "PN, the singer (i.e., the buyer?), . . ."; PN [D]UB.SAR [*š*]*a-ti-ir* DUB, "PN, the scribe, wrote (this) tablet"; GIŠ.KAG ⌜*a*⌝-*na* ⟪KI/NA⟫ TI.LA Na-ra-am-^{d}EN.ZU [*m*]*a-aḫ*(wr. ḪI)-*za-at*, "the peg was driven in by the 'life of Naram-Sin'"; *mu-ba-al-ki-tum* [KUG.BAB]BAR 1 MA.NA ⌜*i*⌝-*sa-gal*, "the transgressor will weigh out 1 mina of silver." No. 241: PN EN_5.SI [DI].E Ì.KUD, "PN, the governor, decided (this) case"; [P]N MAŠKIM, "PN (was) the bailiff."

92. No. 239: 8 D PNs AB+ÁŠ GÁN *ši Maš-gán*^{KI}, "witnesses of the field of Mashkan."

93. There is no price in no. 201. No 226: níg-šám. Nos. 237 and 240: ŠÁM-*su-nu*. No. 238: ŠÁM.

94. Nos. 237 and 240?: *i-ḫu-uz*. No. 238: *il-ga*. No. 201: ì-ne-ši-šám. No. 226: e-šè-šám.

95. No. 201: D PN dumu PN_x [š]eš Seller-ke_4 [A-g]a-dè^{KI}-ta [m]u-lah_4-ḫi-éš giš-a íb-ta-bala-éš, "PN, son of PN_x, [bro]ther of the seller, brought them (i.e., the sold persons) from Akkadē and made them cross over the stick." No. 237: *a-na* NÍG.KI.GAR É Commodities Commodities *a-na* Ì.ZAG Buyer *i-ti-in*, "as the additional payment for the house the commodities (the buyer gave), as the . . . the commodities the buyer gave."

96. No. 201: 10 D PNs. There are no witnesses in nos. 226 and 238. No. 237: 18 D PNs 1 MA.NA KUG.BABBAR PN [DU]MU PN_x [19 A]B+ÁŠ.AB+ÁŠ *in* É Buyer NINDA K[Ú], "18 PNs; 1 mina of silver (for) PN; [19 wit]nesses in the house of the buyer at[e] bread." No. 240: ⌜11⌝ D PNs ŠU.NIGÍN 11 AB+ÁŠ.A[B+ÁŠ] Commodities [PN DUB.SAR?], "11 PNs; the total of 11 witnesses; the commodities (for) [PN, the scribe?]."

97. Nos. 242 and 243 do not record the dimensions.

98. No. 242 does not give the area.

99. No. 242: Seller House *a-na* Buyer *iš-du-da*. No. 243: House Seller *a-na* Buyer *iš-du-ud*. No. 244: ⟨*a-na*⟩ Buyer House *šu-ut* Sellers *iš-du-tu*. No. 245: House Seller *a-na*? Buyer *i-di*[n_x]?(DÍ[M]?). No. 246 omits the name of the buyer and the verb.

Nos. 247–370 Ur III Sale Documents

While the Ur III sale documents use fewer types of the operative section than their Sargonic counterparts, they display a much greater diversity as regards the choice and sequence of other component parts. For this reason, it is not possible to present a single pattern which could serve as a model for all the extant texts and would at the same time comprise all the attested clauses. In view of these difficulties, only a general outline of the structure of the Ur III sale document can be drawn:

(1) Operative Section
(2) Completion-of-price clauses
  (a) The construction kug-bi šu . . . si
  (b) The construction kug-bi-ta . . . è
  (c) The construction kug-bi-ta . . . til
  (d) The construction níg-šám . . . til
(3) Completion-of-transaction clause
  (a) The construction inim-bi . . . til
  (b) The construction inim-bi . . . dug_4
(4) giš-gana . . . bala clause
(5) Delivery clause
(6) No-contest clause
  (a) The verb gi_4
  (b) The verb inim . . . gar
  (c) The verb inim . . . kúr
  (d) The verb inim . . . gar
(7) Eviction clause
  (a) The verb dù
  (b) The verb inim . . . gar
  (c) The verb inim . . . gi-(n)
  (d) The construction *arugimānē rašājum*
  (e) Seller's confirmation of his title to the sold object
(8) Delinquency clause
(9) Oath
(10) Guarantor
(11) Weigher of silver
(12) Authorizing official
(13) Scribe
(14) Witnesses
(15) Location of sale transaction
(16) Date formula
(17) Seal impressions

In the following discussion, we shall limit ourselves to describing the Ur III operative sections. Five types of such sections can be distinguished, classified here as Types a, b, c, d, and e. Cf. Steinkeller, *Sale Documents* pp. 8–29.

Operative Section of Type a

This is by far the most common type of operative section in the Ur III period. It occurs in 100 out of the total of 127 texts. There are attested two variants of this operative section, Sub-type a_1 and Sub-type a_2. Sub-type a_1 is employed in the documents from Eshnuna, Lagash, Nippur, Susa, Umma, and Ur, as well as in the texts of unknown provenience, while Sub-type a_2 is found in the texts from Adab and Umma. Nos. 309 and 342 are self-sale documents. Two of the texts using this operative section are written in Akkadian (nos. 254 and 343). The overwhelming majority of the documents use the verb šám; no. 254 uses *šaʾāmum*, while no. 343 has *aḫāzum* (doubtful). The Ur III Type a corresponds to the Sargonic operative section of Type G.

Sub-type a_1

Nos. 247–330, 341, 342, and 343.

The object x,	Object of Sale
for its price,	Term for Price
the amount y,	Amount(-šè)
from the seller	PN(-šè/ra/a) / ki PN-ta
the buyer	PN_2(-e)
bought / took in possession.	šám / *šaʾāmum* / *aḫāzum*

Sub-type a_2

Nos. 331, 332, 333, 334, 335, 336, 337, 338, 339, and 340.

The object x,	Object of Sale
the property of the seller,	Property PN(-kam)
for the amount y	Amount(-šè)
the buyer	PN_2(-e)
bought.	šám

Operative Section of Type b

The operative section of Type b is attested in four texts from Nippur (nos. 345, 346, 347, and 348), in one text from Umma (no. 344), and in one self-sale document of unknown origin, which is written in Akkadian (no. 370). The corresponding Sargonic operative section is Type F.

Nos. 344, 345, 346, 347, 348, and 370.

The object x,	Object of Sale
for its price,	Term for Price
the amount y,	Amount(-šè)
the seller	PN(-e)
to buyer	PN_2(-ra)
gave (i.e., sold).	sum / *nadānum*

Operative Section of Type c

Four sale documents from Nippur (nos. 349, 350, 351, and 353), one from Lagash (no. 354), and one from Ur (no. 352) use the operative section of Type c. The corresponding type of the Sargonic operative section is Type B.

Nos. 349, 350, 351, 352, 353, and 354.

The object x;	Object of Sale
its price,	Term for Price
the amount y,	Amount

to the seller	PN(-ra)
the buyer	PN_2(-e)
weighed out / gave.	lal / sum

Operative Section of Type d

The operative section of Type d occurs in three documents of Lagash origin (nos. 356, 357, and 358), in one text from Umma (no. 355), and in one text of unknown origin (no. 359). Type d corresponds to the Sargonic operative section of Type C.

Nos. 355, 356, 357, 358, and 359.

The amount x,	Amount
as the price	Term for Price
of the object y,	Object of Sale(-šè)
from the buyer	ki PN-ta
the seller	PN_2(-e)
received.	šu . . . ti

Operative section of Type e

The operative section of this type is employed in ten documents. Two of them come from Nippur (nos. 364 and 369), two from Ur (nos. 360 and 365), one from Lagash (no. 367), and one from Susa (no. 366); the provenience of the remaining four texts (nos. 361, 362, 363, and 368) is unknown. The corresponding operative section in Sargonic sale documents is Type H.

Nos. 360, 361, 362, 263, 364, 365, 366, 367, 368, and 369.

The object x	Object of Sale
from the seller	PN(-šè/ra) / ki PN
the buyer	PN_2(-e)
bought.	šám
The amount y,	Amount
as its price,	Term for Price(-šè)
the buyer	PN_2(-e)
to the seller	PN(-ra)
weighed out.	lal

CHAPTER 7

TERMS AND CLAUSES

7.1. *Introductory Remarks*

This chapter presents the terms and clauses occurring in the kudurrus and sale documents. The order of the discussion follows that in which these component parts generally appear in the texts, i.e., beginning with the description of the object of sale and ending with the date formula and sealings. The references to the texts are given in chronological order, with the references to the kudurrus preceding those to the sale documents.

For the formulary of the third millennium sale documents, see Edzard, *SRU*; Krecher, *ZA* 63 (1974) pp. 145–271; *idem*, *RLA* 5 pp. 490–98 ("Kauf. A.I. Nach sumerischen Quellen vor der Zeit der III. Dynastie von Ur"); Wilcke, *RLA* 5 pp. 498–512 ("Kauf. A.II. Nach Kaufurkunden der Zeit der III. Dynastie von Ur"); Steinkeller, *Sale Documents* pp. 30–117.

7.2. *Objects of Sale and Their Description*

As noted earlier, ancient kudurrus record exclusively multiple purchases of fields. In contrast, sale documents deal with 1) fields, 2) orchards, 3) canals(?), 4) houses, 5) humans, 6) animals, and 7) commodities. The temporal distribution of the types of objects sold in sale documents is as follows:

Fara period: fields and houses
Pre-Sargonic period: fields, orchards, houses, and humans
Sargonic period: fields, orchards, canals(?), houses, humans, animals, and commodities
Ur III period: orchards, houses, humans, and animals

7.2.1. Fields

In addition to the ancient kudurrus (nos. 1–52), fields are purchased in the following sale documents:
Fara: nos. 114–136
Pre-Sargonic: nos. 144–145 and 156a
Sargonic: nos. 169–180, 182a, 207, 210–212, 229–230, 239, and 246

The most common description of a sold field contains its size, the term gán "field," and the name of the field. In some instances, the text gives the field's location, usually the town or *Flur* in which the field was situated:

gán Kug-gál^{KI} "field (located in) Kug-gál" (no. 14 xvii)
gán E+PAB.KAS^{KI} LAL?.KI "field (located on) the E+PAB.KAS canal (in) LAL?" (no. 20 iii)
gán sug Lagaš^{KI} "field (located in) the marshes of Lagash" (no. 24 rev. iii)
GÁN É? ḪA? GUD? X? *in Ur-šag*$_5$^{KI} "field (called) . . . (located) in Ur-šag$_5$" (no. 26 i)
GÁN [. . .].⸢X⸣.KI [X].ME.RU^{KI} "field ⸢. . .⸣ (located? in) [X].ME.RU" (no. 31 i)
GÁN *Ur-ma in Lugal-kalam-ma* "field (of) Ur-ma (located) in Lugal-kalam-ma" (no. 37 rev. iii)
GÁN *in É-dur*$_5$*-Me-me* "field (located) in É-dur$_5$-Me-me" (no. 37 U. E. iv′)
GÁN *in Ú-sá-la-tim* "field (located) in Ú-sá-la-tim" (no. 38 i)
GÁN *šu ba-la-ag Da-da-rí-im* "field (located) on (lit.: of) the canal of Da-da-rí-im" (no. 38 i)
GÁN ⟨*in*⟩? *Tu-la(l)-tim* "field (located?) in(?) Tu-la(l)-tim" (no. 38 i)
GÁN *in* X.EDIN^{KI} "field (located) in X.EDIN" (no. 38 i)
GÁN *in Áš-na-ak*^{KI} "field (located) in Ashnak" (no. 38 i)
⸢gán⸣ É-dur$_5$-sabra "⸢field⸣ (located in) É-dur$_5$-sabra" (no. 39 i)
gán [É-du]r$_5$-en$_5$-si "field (located in) [É-du]r$_5$-en$_5$-si" (no. 39 i)
gán SUG ⸢AB?.ZAG?⸣ "field (located in) the ⸢AB?.ZAG?⸣ marshes" (no. 39 ii)
GÁN *Ba-az*^{KI} "field (of) Baz" (no. 40 A x, xvi)
SUG-^{d}*Nin-ḫur-sag* "(field located in) the Nin-ḫur-sag marshes" (no. 40 C xiii)
GÁN *Ba-ra-az*-EDIN^{KI} *in Kiš*^{KI} "field (of) Ba-ra-az-EDIN (located) in Kish" (no. 40 D vi, xiv)
GÁN *šu kir-ba-ti Ar-da-na-an*^{KI} *in* E+PAB *At-li* "field (located) in (lit.: of) the Ar-da-na-an *Flur*, on the At-li canal" (no. 42 iii)

It should also be noted that the majority of the Fara sale documents state the name of the field/*Flur* or household in which the sold estate was located. This information is contained at the end of the text. The following locations are attested:

É-nar (no. 114)
Gán-é-nar (no. 130)
Du$_6$-e-lum (no. 115)
É-^{d}Dumu-zi (no. 116)
Sa-a (no. 117)
Gán-kug (no. 118)
Mar-ŠIR.BUR.MUŠEN (nos. 119, 122, and 136)
Gán-si-LAK-50 (no. 120)
É-MUNSUB$_x$(PA.USAN) (no. 123)
É-DUN (no. 124)
Gán-A.GAR.TUR (no. 126)
Gán-NA (no. 127)
Gán-sar-ul$_x$(LAK-384) (no. 127a)
⸢X⸣.TUR (no. 127b)
Gán-e-maḫ-X (no. 131)
Gán-mar-DU (no. 132)
Gán-é-ḪU.UN.SAR (no. 133)
Gán-UD.KA.BAR (no. 134)

Three of the kudurrus (nos. 35, 40, and 41), all of which are written in Akkadian, define the location of the sold field by naming the estates which border it on four sides:

1) No. 35, once:

[*è-da-su* IM.MIR PN]
[*è-d*]*a*-[*su*] ⸢IM⸣.Ù PN$_2$ PN$_3$
è-da-s[*u*] IM.MAR.TU PN$_4$
è-da-su IM *sa-ti-um* PN$_5$

"[its side: north—PN (i.e., the owner of the neighboring field)]"
"south—PN$_2$ (and) PN$_3$"
"west—PN$_4$"
"east—PN$_5$"

2) No. 40, *passim*—the order of the cardinal points varies:

GÁN.NINDÁ IM.MIR PN
GÁN.NINDÁ IM.MAR.TU PN$_2$
GÁN.NINDÁ IM.KUR PN$_3$
GÁN.NINDÁ IM.U$_5$ PN$_4$

"field's side(?): north—PN (i.e., the owner of the neighboring field)"
"west—PN$_2$"
"east—PN$_3$"
"south—PN$_4$"

3) No. 41, *passim*—the order of the cardinal points varies:

D PN IM.MIR GÁN.NINDÁ
D PN$_2$ IM.MAR.TU GÁN.NINDÁ
D PN$_3$ IM.KUR GÁN.NINDÁ
D PN$_4$ IM.U$_5$ GÁN.NINDÁ

"PN (i.e., the owner of the neighboring field)—field's side(?) (to) the north"
"PN$_2$—west"
"PN$_3$—east"
"PN$_4$—south"

A different method of describing fields is employed in three of the so-called *išdud* texts (nos. 244, 245, and 246), dating to the Sargonic period, which give the length of the four sides of the property, oriented according to the four points of the compass.

In some instances, the description of a field contains the name of the adjacent property or the name of its owner, or the name of the canal on which the field is located:

gán Ur-^{d}Gu-nu-ra ENGUR! da im-ru "the Ur-^{d}Gu-nu-ra field (located) at (the holdings?) of the ENGUR clan(?)" (no. 14 xvii)
(gán) zag PN "side of (the property of) PN" (nos. 21, *passim*; 34 rev. i)
[gán É-gud]-ka [pa$_5$-d]a-na-ke$_4$ [a]b-uš "[É-gud field], bordering on the [D]a-na canal" (no. 169)
[gán] ÉŠ.SA[L? . . .] an-[gál] "[field] ⸢located⸣ at/in the ⸢. . .⸣" (no. 173)
gán da pa$_5$-dub-sar-ka an-gál "field located on the Dub-sar canal" (no. 175)
gán pa$_5$-dub-sar-ka "field (located) on the Dub-sar canal" (no. 176)
gán da é Tu-tu-ka-kam "field bordering on the household of Tu-tu" (no. 178)
gán da Ki-ša-nu-dar-ra-ni "field bordering on the Ki-ša-nu-dar-ra-ni(-field?)" (no. 179, twice)
gán É-gud pa$_5$-dub-sar gán ab-uš "the É-gud field, the field bordering on the Dub-sar canal" (no. 182a A)
gán pa$_5$-ib-ka al-gál ki Ur-DUN sag-du$_5$-ke$_4$ ab-uš "field located on the Ib canal, bordering on the territory of Ur-DUN, the field registrar" (no. 182a C)
gán É-gud ⟨pa$_5$-⟩da-na-ka "the É-gud field, (located) on the Da-na (canal)" (no. 182a D)
gán É-gud ki Ma-ḫir ab-uš "the É-gud field, bordering on the territory of Ma-ḫir" (no. 182a E)
gán É-gud pa$_5$-da-na-ke$_4$ ab-uš "the É-gud field, bordering on the Da-na canal" (no. 182a F)
gán pa$_5$-da-na-ka "field (located) on the Da-na canal" (no. 182a G)
gán pa$_5$-da-na-ka gán dam? MI.MI ab-uš "field (located) on the Da-na canal, bordering on the field of the wife(?) of MI.MI" (no. 182a H)
gán gú DÍM+SU É-X [g]án sag-SAL.KAB.DU Barag-me-zi-da dam Ur-ki "field (located) on the bank of . . . of É-X, the field of the oblate(?) of Barag-me-zi-da, wife of Ur-ki" (no. 182a I)
gán pa$_5$-di?-⸢x⸣-kam "field (located) on the . . . canal" (no. 182a J)
gán pa$_5$-^{d}Innin gán Ur-DUN Inim-ma-ni-zi ab-uš du$_6$ giš-zag-ga-an-ke$_4$ ab-uš "field (located on) the Innin canal, bordering on the field of Ur-DUN, (the man) of Inim-ma-ni-zi, (and) bordering on the Giš-zag-ga-an hill" (no. 182a K)
gán DU$_6$?-DU?-an-ni "field (located) on the DU?-an-ni hill(?)" (no. 182a O)
gán pa$_5$-^{d}Innin gán É-erín a-gál "field located on the Innin canal, in the É-erín *Flur*" (no. 182a P, Q, and R)
gán gú DÍM+SU "field (located) on the bank of . . ." (no. 182a U and V)

gán ⸢X⸣-da pa$_5$-Da-da "⸢X⸣-da field, (located) on the Da-da canal" (no. 182a DD)
gán Ma-šeg$_9$^{KI} pa$_5$-Da-da, "field (located) in Ma-šeg$_9$, on the Da-da canal" (no. 182a EE)
gán Áb-za-an-na an-gál "field located in Áb-za-an-na" (no. 207)
GÁN IGI *na-ra-tim* "field (located) opposite the canals" (no. 230)

A different type of description is found in kudurrus nos. 30a ii and 37 rev. iii, iv, where the purchased fields are classified as ÉŠ.GÍD SI.SÁ "(measured? with) the standard measuring-rope." Perhaps related to this description is the phrase gán éš šám-ma-ta "field (measured?) with the purchase(?)-rope," which is attested in nos. 22, 23, and App. to nos. 22–23. The latter expression was translated by Krecher, *RLA* 5 p. 497, as "Areal, für das ein Kaufpreis gezahlt werden könnte" = "verkäufliches Areal."

7.2.2. Orchards

The following sale documents deal with the purchase of orchards:

Pre-Sargonic: no. 146
Sargonic: nos. 181, 182, and 182a
Ur III: nos. 264–270 and 360

The description of an orchard usually contains the size and the term for orchard. The term used is either the standard ^{GIŠ}kiri$_6$ (*passim*) or $^{\text{ki GIŠ}}$kiri$_6$, the latter found in three of the Ur III sale documents from Nippur (nos. 264, 265, and 269). In four Ur III texts (nos. 266, 267, 268, and 360), the orchard is described not in terms of its size but the number of date palms growing in it. In two instances (nos. 267 and 269), the orchard is qualified as giš-gub-ba "planted with trees (i.e., date palms)," and once (no. 264), as gišimmar "(planted with) date palms."

The following documents specify the orchard's location:

^{GIŠ}kiri$_6$ gú pa$_5$-kur$_6$ al-gál "orchard located on the bank of the Kur$_6$ canal" (no. 181)
^{GIŠ}kiri$_6$ gú pa$_5$-kur$_6$ "orchard (located) on the bank of the Kur$_6$ canal" (no. 181, three times)
^{GIŠ}kiri$_6$ pa$_5$-kur$_6$ GADA+GAR PN lú-u$_5$-ke$_4$ ab-uš "orchard (located) on the Kur$_6$ canal, bordering on the . . . of PN, the currier" (no. 182)
^{GIŠ}kiri$_6$ gú túl ^{GIŠ}kiri$_6$ Ur-é-nu-na ab-uš ^{GIŠ}kiri$_6$ É-muš ab-uš "orchard (located) on the bank of a well, bordering on the orchard of Ur-é-nu-na (and) the orchard of É-muš" (no. 182a B)
^{GIŠ}kiri$_6$ Da-da IŠ ab-uš "orchard bordering on the orchard of Da-da, the equerry" (no. 182a L)
^{GIŠ}kiri$_6$ Du-du Ur-tur X-a-gud al-gál "orchard of Du-du of (the household of) Ur-tur, (located) in . . ." (no. 182a M)
^{GIŠ}kiri$_6$ gú pa$_5$-kur$_6$ ^{GIŠ}kiri$_6$ Me-zu-an-da "orchard (located) on the bank of the Kur$_6$-canal, the orchard of Me-zu-an-da" (no. 182a N)
^{GIŠ}kiri$_6$ pa$_5$-a-zu pa$_5$-mu-tuku Ḫur-sag-ke$_4$ ab-uš "orchard bordering on the A-zu canal (and) Mu-tuku canal of Ḫur-sag" (no. 182a S)
⟨^{GIŠ}kiri$_6$⟩ túl-mun ki-ba Ur-gu dumu Nigìn-kam "⟨orchard⟩ (located) at the 'Salinated Well,' in its middle (there is a property?) of Ur-gu, son of Nigìn" (no. 182a W)
^{GIŠ}kiri$_6$ túl-mun "orchard (located) at the 'Salinated Well'" (no. 182a X, Y, Z, AA, and BB)
^{GIŠ}kiri$_6$ gú GADA+GAR ^{GIŠ}kiri$_6$ Ti-ti ab-uš "orchard (located) on the bank of . . . , bordering on the orchard of Ti-ti" (no. 182a CC)
35 ^{GIŠ}gišimmar gú kar-anše "35 date palms (growing) on the bank of the 'Quay of Donkeys'" (no. 266)
$^{\text{ki GIŠ}}$kiri$_6$ giš-gub-ba . . . KI.UD a-šà du$_6$-an-na-gu-la "orchard planted with trees (i.e., date palms) (and) empty lot, (both located) in the Du$_6$-an-na-gu-la field" (no. 269)

In one instance, the object of sale consisted of an empty lot located in an orchard: KI.UD šà *gunû*-LÚ-*šeššig* (= rin$_x$)-na-ra ^{GIŠ}kiri$_6$ "empty lot (located) in the . . . of an orchard" (no. 270). An empty lot (KI.UD) was sold, together with an orchard, also in no. 269 (see above).

7.2.3. Canals(?)

A single (and uncertain) instance of the sale of a canal is recorded in the Sargonic document no. 183. The text gives only the name of the canal: níg-šám pa$_5$-A-b[a(-kam)] "price of the A-b[a] canal."

7.2.4. Houses

Houses are sold in the following sale documents:

Fara: nos. 100–113c
Pre-Sargonic: nos. 137–143
Sargonic: nos. 164–168, 204–206, 210, 218, 227–228, 237–238, and 242–245
Ur III: nos. 247–263, 331, and 355

The description of a house usually contains the size and term for house. The most commonly used term is é "house, house lot" (*passim*). The other attested terms are:

é-dù-a "built-up house lot" (nos. 247a, 250, and 257)
é-dù "built-up house lot" (nos. 103, 104, 106, 108, 109, and 110, all occurring only in the phrase níg-dirig é-dù "additional payment for the built-up house lot")
é al-dù-dù "built-up house lot" (no. 165)
é-dù-a ù KI.UD "built-up house lot and empty lot" (nos. 248, 263, and 331)
é-KI.UD "empty house lot" (nos. 165 and 256)
é-ki "empty(?) house lot" (no 252)
ki-⸢é?-šub?⸣ "ruined(?) house lot(?)" (no. 251)
ki-gál "empty ground" (no. 258)

The location of the sold house is noted in the following instances:

[é] é P[N] ab-uš "[house] bordering on the house of P[N]" (no. 167)
é uru-bar abulla$_x$(KÁ.GAL)-tur-ra-ka an-gál "house located outside of the small city-gate" (no. 204)
é-dù-a É-DUN^{KI}-ka "built-up house lot (located) in É-DUN" (no. 250)
é-dù-a é-šu-sì-ga "built-up house lot (located at?) the é-šu-sì-ga (a type of building—meaning uncertain)" (no. 257)

Several of the sale documents from Fara give the name of the place (most probably a city quarter) where the sold house was situated. The following locations are attested:

KI-KA.Ú (nos. 103, 105, and 108)
Dag-^{d}En-líl (no. 109)
Ki-lam-maḫ (read probably Ganba-maḫ) (no. 110)
É-me-DILMUN-la (no. 113)
^{GIŠ}má-ka (nos. 113a and 113b)
URU+UD^{ki} (no. 113c = 112)

7.2.5. Humans

The documents dealing with the sale of humans (men, women, and children) are as follows:

Pre-Sargonic: nos. 149–156
Sargonic: nos. 157–163, 184–203, 208, 213–217, 219–221, 231–234, and 240–241
Ur III: nos. 271–315, 332–339, 341–347, 349–352, 354, 356–359, 361–367, and 369

In the Pre-Sargonic and Sargonic sale documents, sold persons most often are identified simply by their personal names, usually preceded by a *Personenkeil.* Occasionally, they are described by specific terms, such as sag-nita "male 'head'" or "slave," gemé "female 'head'" or "slave woman," and igi-nu-du$_8$ "blind(?)." In contrast, in the Ur III texts sold persons are usually described by the terms sag-nita "male 'head'" or "slave" and sag-SAL "female 'head'" or "slave woman," in most instances combined with the phrase PN mu-ni-im "his/her name being PN." However, the method of describing sold persons by giving their names only is used sporadically also in Ur III times.
The following terms are attested:

sag-nita (PN mu-ni-im) "'male head,' (his name is PN)" (no. 156, *passim* in the Ur III sale documents)
sag-SAL (PN mu-ni-im) "'female head,' (her name is PN)" (no. 150, *passim* in the Ur III sale documents)
gemé "slave woman" (nos. 163, 194, and 240)
DUMU.SAL "daughter, girl" (no. 240)
igi-nu-du$_8$ "blind(?)" (nos. 152, 153, and 156)

In addition, the following qualifications are attested, which follow after either the above terms or the name of the sold person:

SAL "female" (no. 295)
nita "male" (no. 295)
guruš-am$_6$ "grown man" (no. 155)
[ARÁ]D *Lu-lu-bi-im* "Lulubean [sla]ve" (no. 231)
túl-ta-pàd-da-am$_6$ "foundling" (no. 150)
ama-tu-am$_6$ "house-born slave" (no. 192)
gemé Seller(-kam) "slave woman of the seller" (nos. 332, 333, 335, and 338)
arád Seller(-kam) "slave of the seller" (nos. 334, 336, and 339)
dumu-sag-ri[g$_x$](PA.SAL.KA[B.DU]) Seller dam [PN-kam] "young oblate of the seller, wife [of PN]" (no. 337)
gala "cantor" (nos. 149, 151, and 154)
nu-kiri$_6$ É-^{d}Nisaba^{KI}-kam "gardener of É-^{d}Nisaba" (no. 208)
su$_4$?-NE-a ". . ." (no. 301)
SIG$_7$ ". . ." (no. 336)
1½ kùš-ni-ta (envelope: 1 kùš-ni-ta) "1½ (envelope: 1) cubit tall" (no. 281, describing a boy)
dumu-SAL gaba-na b[í-tab]-bi "daughter is pressed to her breast" (no. 279, following 1 sag-SAL-àm PN m[u]-ni-i[m] "one female 'head,' her name is PN")
dumu gaba-na-a ab-tab "child is pressed to her breast" (no. 285, following 1 sag-SAL PN mu-ni-im "one female 'head,' her name is PN")

7.2.6. Animals

Animals are sold in the following sale documents:

Sargonic: nos. 222, 223, 225, and 235
Ur III: nos. 316–323, 348(?), and 368

The types of animals dealt with in the above texts are equids and bovids. The terms and qualifications attested for each group are as follows:

Equids

anše "donkey" (no. 223)
emè(ANŠE.SAL) "she-ass, jenny" (nos. 323 and 368)
emè(ANŠE.SAL)-máḫ "mature she-ass" (no. 318)
amar-ga anše "suckling ass" (no. 323)
ANŠE.BAR.AN(= kungá)-nita "male mule" (no. 225)
[ANŠE].BAR.AN 1 "one-year-old [mu]le" (no. 235)
ANŠE.LIBIR(= dusú) "dusú-equid" (no. 222)
ANŠE.LIBIR-nita 3 "three-year-old male dusú-equid" (no. 222)
ANŠE.NITA.LIBIR "male dusú-equid" (no. 320)

Bovids

[g]ud mu 2 [x] IM DA GÍR SI ZU KI [Ḫ]AR?-a ḪAR?-a íb-su?-éš? "two-year-old bull, . . ." (no. 322)
gud-giš "yoke-ox" (nos. 319, 321, and 348?)
gud-niga(ŠE) "barley-fed bull" (no. 317)
GIR mu 2 "two-year-old heifer" (no. 316)

7.2.7. Commodities

Only three sale documents, all of which come from the Sargonic period, deal with the sale of commodities. The commodities are:

zú-lum "dates" (no. 224)
kug-GI "gold" (nos. 226 and 236)

No special descriptions or qualifications are used for either commodity.

7.3. *Terms for Price*

7.3.1. Introductory Remarks

Throughout the Fara–Ur III periods the standard Sumerian term for "price" is šám or níg-šám. The form šám is the older one; it is used mainly in the Fara sale documents, but it occasionally occurs also in the later periods, especially in the texts written in Akkadian. Apart from the regular spelling with the sign ŠÁM (= NINDÁ+ŠE), the word is also written with the signs ŠÁM+ÀM (frequent—e.g., in no. 184) and ŠÁM+A (rare—in nos. 178, 179, 185, 186, 187, 188, 269, and 272). The terms šám and níg-sám were recently discussed by Krecher, *ZA* 63 pp. 151f., *idem*, *RLA* 5 pp. 495ff., and by Steinkeller, *Sale Documents* pp. 153ff., 161f.

During the same periods, the corresponding Akkadian term for "price" is usually written logographically as ŠÁM or NÍG.ŠÁM, or with syllabic indicators which show that the Akkadian word was a plural tantum *šiʾmū* or *šîmū*. See the spelling *a-na* ŠÁM-*me* (no. 234), which stands for *ana šiʾmē* "for the price"; for other examples, see Gelb, *MAD* 3 p. 259. The unique syllabic spelling *si-im-sù* /*šiʾm-šu*/, which is found in the Ur III sale document no. 368, indicates that, at least in the Ur III period, a singular form *šiʾmum* was also used.

In the Pre-Sargonic and later texts, the word šám / níg-šám is commonly followed by a pronominal possessive suffix, which refers to the object of sale. In the documents dealing with the sale of objects belonging to the class of things, such as real property (fields, orchards, and houses), animals, and commodities, the suffix used is -bi "its." In contrast, the texts involving the sale of single humans employ the suffix -ani (written -(m)a-ni, -a-ni, or -ni) "his/her." This distinction is not observed in several Ur III sale documents, where the expected suffix -ani is replaced by -bi, even though the object of sale is a single person in each case (nos. 274, 276, 286, 297, 302, 304, and 366). Interestingly enough, however, in the same texts the corresponding possessive suffix in the phrase PN mu-ni-im "his/her name is PN," which describes the sold person, is without exception -ani and not -bi. The use of -ani, in place of expected -bi, in no. 360, which deals with an orchard, is evidently a mistake.

In the documents involving the sale of two or more humans, the respective suffix is the plural possessive pronoun -anene "their" (written -ne-ne or -(k)a-ne-ne—attested only in nos. 279 and 295) or the singular pronoun -bi "its" (attested only in nos. 285 and 312), where -bi has a collective force, referring to the persons in question as a group: "its (of the group)," i.e., "their." In one instance (no. 367), -ani is used for a plural object of sale.

The pronominal suffixes used in the Akkadian texts are written -*sù* or -*su* "his/her/its" in singular, both referring to the class of things and the class of persons, and -*su-nu* "their" in plural. A unique usage of the suffix -*su-nu* is attested in the Sargonic sale document no. 237, where -*su-nu* refers not to the object of sale but to the sellers: Object of Sale ŠÁM-*su-nu* Amount "OS, their (of the sellers) price (is) A."

In the Ur III texts written in Sumerian, šám / níg-šám can be combined with the verbal adjective til-la, Akk. *gamrum*, "complete, completed," as in, e.g., níg-šám-til-la "completed price" (no. 354).

Another expression for "price," attested only in sale documents from the Ur III period, is kug or kug-babbar, "silver." Naturally, this usage is documented only in those transactions in which the price was paid in silver. Some of the Ur III sale documents use a special construction which combines kug or kug-babbar with šám or níg-šám. See, e.g., [ku]g-babbar šám-ma-ni "silver of his price" (no. 291) and kug-babbar níg-šám-bi "silver of its price" (no. 258).

The following is a complete list of the occurrences of the terms for "price" in the kudurrus and sale documents.

7.3.2. šám

1) Without a Pronominal Suffix

Amount šám Object of Sale "A, the price of OS": nos. 20 and 100–134
Amount ŠÁM Object of Sale: no. 238
Object of Sale ŠÁM "OS, (its) price": no. 26
Amount Object of Sale Seller ŠÁM GÁN KÚ "A (for) OS; the seller consumed the price of the field": no. 34
Object of Sale šám Amount "OS, (its) price (is) A": nos. 166 and 247a
Object of Sale ŠÁM Amount: no. 36
Object of Sale ŠÁM GÁN Amount: no. 37
Amount šám Object of Sale-kam "A is the price of OS": no. 182a (twice)
Amount šám Object of Sale-am$_6$: no. 214
Amount šám (of Object of Sale) ba-gar "A, the price (of OS), was set": no. 192
Amount *a-na* ŠÁM Object of Sale "A, as the price of OS": nos. 228, 229, 231, 232, and 233
Object of Sale *a-na* ŠÁM Amount "OS for the price, A": nos. 239(?) and 241
Amount *a-na* ŠÁM-*me* Object of Sale: no. 234
Amount šám-til-⌜la⌝ Object of Sale "A, the complete price of OS": no. 341
Amount šám-til-a Object of Sale-šè "A, as the complete price of OS": no. 357

2) With -bi

Object of Sale šám-bi Amount "OS, its price (is) A": nos. 32, 166, and 366
Object of Sale Amount šám-bi "OS, A (is) its price": no. 136
ŠÁM.BI (envelope: *si-im-su*) (of Object of Sale) Amount "its price (of OS) (is) A": no. 368
Object of Sale šám-bi Amount-šè "OS, for its price, A": no. 263

Object of Sale Amount šám-til-la-bi-šè "OS, for A, its complete price": no. 312
Object of Sale kug šám-bi Amount "OS, the silver of her price (is) A": no. 286
Object of Sale kug-babbar šám-bi Amount "OS, the silver of its price (is) A": no. 317
Object of Sale šám-bi kug Amount "OS, her price (is) the silver, A": no. 289

3) With -(m)a-ni

Object of Sale šám-ma-ni Amount "OS, her price (is) A": no. 311
šám-ma-ni (of Object of Sale) Amount "their(!) price (of OS) (is) A": no. 367
Object of Sale Amount ŠÁM+ÀM-til-la-ni-šè "OS, for A, his complete price": nos. 287 and 352
ŠÁM+ÀM-til-la-ni-šè (of Object of Sale) Amount "as its(!) (of OS) full price, A": no. 360
Amount ŠÁM+ÀM-til-la-ni-šè (of OS) "A, as his (of OS) full price": no. 365.
Object of Sale [ku]g-babbar šám-ma-ni Amount "OS, the silver of her price (is) A": no. 291
Object of Sale KUG.BABBAR ŠÁM.MA.NI Amount: no. 370

4) With *-sù* or *-su*

Object of Sale ŠÁM-*sù* Amount "OS, its price (is) A": nos. 36 and 37
Object of Sale ŠÁM-*su* Amount: nos. 42, 43, and 44
Object of Sale [ŠÁM]-*me-su*: no. 43 iii 17
Amount ŠÁM-*su* (of Object of Sale) "A, its price (of OS)": no. 362

5) With *-su-nu*

Object of Sale ŠÁM-*su-nu* Amount "OS, their (of the sellers) price (is) A": no. 237
Object of Sale ŠÁM-*su-nu* Amount "OS, their (of the sold persons) price (is) A": no. 240

7.3.3. níg-šám

1) Without a pronominal suffix

Amount níg-šám Object of Sale "A, the price of OS": nos. App. to no. 32, 157, 158, 159, 160, 161, 162, 193, 195, 196, 197, 198, 199, 200, 202, 204, 205, 208, 210, 217, 219, 221, and 226
Amount NÍG.ŠÁM Object of Sale: no. 40
Amount níg-šám Object of Sale-kam: nos. 22, 23, 138, 141, 144, 149, 164, 169 (twice), 171, 172, 183, 189 (twice), 191, 215, and 216
(Amount) níg-šám Object of Sale-kam: no. 190
Amount níg-ŠÁM+ÀM Object of Sale-kam: no. 184
Amount níg-ŠÁM+A Object of Sale-kam: nos. 186, 187, and 188
Amount níg-šám Object of Sale-šè "A, as the price of OS": nos. 154 and 220
Amount níg-ŠÁM+ÀM Object of Sale-šè: nos. 355 and 359
Amount níg-ŠÁM+A Object of Sale-šè: no. 185
(Amount) níg-šám Object of Sale-šè: nos. 168 and 180
Object of Sale níg-šám Amount "OS, (its) price (is) A": nos. 30, 282, and 314
Object of Sale [(NÍG)].ŠÁM Amount: no. 227
Object of Sale níg-šám Amount-šè "OS, for the price, A": nos. 347 and 356
Object of Sale níg-ŠÁM(wr. ÁG)+ÀM-e Amount, "OS, (its) price (is) A": no. 301
Amount *a-na* NÍG.ŠÁM Object of Sale "A, as the price of OS": nos. 49, 230, 235, and 236
Amount níg-ŠÁM+ÀM-til-la Object of Sale "A, the complete price of OS": no. 342
Amount níg-šám-til-la Object of Sale-kam?: no. 354
Amount níg-ŠÁM+ÀM-til-la Object of Sale-ka: no. 358
Amount níg-šám PN "A, the price of (i.e., due to) PN (i.e., the seller)": Appendix to no. 32
NÍG.ŠÁM PN "the purchased (fields) of PN (i.e., the buyer)": no. 37
KUG.BABBAR NÍG.ŠÁM 3 GÁN "the silver, the price of 3 fields": no. 41
NÍG.ŠÁM IN ⌜GÀR? MU? MU?⌝ "the price . . .": no. 48
Object of Sale ŠÁM.GAR (for NÍG.ŠÁM?) Amount "OS, (its) price? (is) A": no. 254
[. . .] NÍG.ŠÁM Amount: nos. 27 and 47
[NÍG].ŠÁM [. . .]: no. 30b

2) With -bi

Object of Sale níg-šám-bi Amount "OS, its price (is) A": nos. 165, 167, 170, 173, 175, 177, 204, 206, 207, 209, 211, 212, 218, 297, 304, 320, and 322
Object of Sale níg-ŠÁM+ÀM-bi Amount: nos. 250, 252, 267, 276, 316, and 319
Object of Sale níg-ŠÁM+A-bi Amount: nos. 178, 179, and 269
Object of Sale níg-šám-pi Amount: nos. 169, 176, 181, 182, 182a, and 210
Object of Sale níg-šám-bi Amount-šè "OS, for its price, A": nos. 248, 253, 257, 262, 265(?), 285(?), and 325
Object of Sale níg-ŠÁM+ÀM-bi Amount-šè "OS, for its price, A": nos. 266 and 321
Object of Sale Amount níg-šám-bi-šè "OS, for its price, A": no. 222
Object of Sale níg-ŠÁM+ÀM-til-la-bi Amount-šè "OS, for its full price, A" no. 259
Object of Sale kug-babbar níg-šám-bi Amount "OS, the silver of its price (is) A": no. 258
níg-šám-bi (of Object of Sale) Amount "its price (of OS), A": nos. 21, 139, 140, 142, 143, and 145
níg-šám-bi Amount níg-šám Object of Sale-kam "its price, A, the price of OS": nos. 138 and 141

3) With -(m)a-ni

Object of Sale níg-šám-ni Amount "OS, her price (is) A": nos. 194(?), 290, and 308
Object of Sale níg-šám-ma-ni Amount: nos. 273, 283, 298, 307, 310, 349, 350, and 351
Object of Sale níg-šám-a-ni Amount: no. 305

Object of Sale níg-ŠÁM+ÀM-ma-ni Amount: nos. 271 and 306
Object of Sale níg-ŠÁM+A-ma-ni Amount: no. 272
Object of Sale [ní]g-šám-ga-ni /nig-šam-ak-ani/ Amount "OS, her A of the price (is x)": no. 300
Object of Sale níg-šám-ma-ni Amount-šè "OS, for his/her price, A": nos. 275, 278, 292, and 345
Object of Sale níg-ŠÁM+ÀM-ma(wr. BA)-ni Amount-⸢šè⸣: no. 293
níg-šám-ma-ni (of Object of Sale) Amount "his price (of OS) (is) A": nos. 152 and 153
Amount níg-šám-ma-ni (of Object of Sale) "A (is) her price (OS)": no. 150
níg-šám-ma-ni-šè (of Object of Sale) Amount "for his price (of OS), A": no. 151
Object of Sale Amount níg-šám-ma⟨-ni⟩-šè "OS, for A, his price": no. 155
Object of Sale Amount níg-šám(wr. GAZ)-ma-ka-n[i-šè] /nig-šam-ak-ani-še/ "OS, for her A of the price": no. 346
Object of Sale níg-ŠÁM+ÀM-ma-ni-šè Amount "OS, for his price, A": no. 364
Amount níg-šám-ma-ni-šè (of Object of Sale) "A, as her price (of OS)": no. 361
Object of Sale kug níg-šám(wr. ÁG)-ma-ni Amount "OS, the silver of her price (is) A": no. 303
Object of Sale kug-babbar níg-šám-ma-ga-ni /nig-šam-ak-ani/ Amount "OS, her silver of the price (is) A": no. 288
Object of Sale Amount níg-ŠÁM+ÀM-til-a-ni-šè "OS, for A, her complete price": no. 294

4) With -ne-ne

Object of Sale níg-šám-ne-ne Amount-šè "OS, for their price, A": no. 295
Object of Sale níg-šám-ma-ka-ne-ne /nig-šam-ak-anene/ Amount-àm "OS, their A of the price is (x)": no. 279

5) With *-su*

Object of Sale NÍG.ŠÁM-*su* Amount "OS, his price (is) A": nos. 40 and 41

7.3.4. *šiʾmum*

si-im-sù (tablet: ŠÁM.BI) (of Object of Sale) A "its price (of OS) (is) A": no. 368

7.3.5. kug / kug-babbar

Object of Sale kug-bi Amount "OS, its silver (is) A": nos. 247, 249, 255, 261, 268, and 274
Object of Sale kug-babbar-bi Amount "OS, her silver (is) A": no. 302
Object of Sale kug Amount-šè "OS, for the silver, A": nos. 270 and 296

7.4. *Statement of Rate*

Ancient kudurrus and sale documents occasionally note the rates of commodities included in prices and additional payments. The statement of rate can take the following forms:

1) Introduced by ud(-ba) "on (that) day, then"

a) With the copula -àm "to be"

ud-ba 3(bán) še (1) ma-na (urudu) "on that day, 30 quarts of barley (were the equivalent of) (1) mina (of copper)" (nos. 101 and 119)
ud-ba 2(bán) š[e] (1) ma-na (urudu) "on that day, 20 quarts of barley (were the equivalent of) (1) mina (of copper)" (no. 129)
ud-ba (1 gur) š[e] kug gín 1-àm "on that day, (1 bushel of) barley was (the equivalent of) 1 shekel of silver" (no. 140)
ud-ba kug-luḫ-ḫa 1 gín še-bi 1(ul) 2(bán)-am_6 "on that day, 1 shekel of purified silver was (the equivalent of) 80 quarts of barley" (no. 142)

b) With the verb ág "to measure out"

ud še kug-ga 2(pi) gur al-ág(wr. NINDÁ+ŠE)-gá "on (that) day, for (1 shekel of) silver 120 quarts of barley were measured out" (no. 175)
ud še kug-ga 2(pi) še gur al-ág-a (no. 180)
ud-ba 1(gur) še gur al-ág "on that day, (for 1 shekel of silver) 1 bushel of barley was measured out" (no. 189)
ud-ba še 1 gín kug-babbar 3(bán) ì-ág "one that day, for 1 shekel of silver 30 quarts of barley were measured out" (no. 222)
ud zú-lum 1 kug gín-a 3(pi) 2(bán) al-ág-gá "on (that) day, for 1 shekel of silver 200 quarts of dates were measured out" (no. 224)
kug-GI-bi 6 gub-ba-ta ì-á[g]? "(on that day), gold was exchanged (for silver) at the rate of 6 (to 1)" (no. 226)
ud-ba še 1 g[ín-ta] 1(bán)-àm ì-ág "on that day, for 1 shekel (of silver) 10 quarts of barley were measured out" (no. 226)

c) With the verb dé "to pour out"

ud-ba 6 silà ì al-dé "on that day, (for 1 shekel of silver) 6 quarts of oil were poured out" (no. 189)

2) Not introduced by ud(-ba)

a) Amount x Commodity A (níg-)šám Amount y Commodity B "the amount x of the commodity A (is) the price/equivalent of the amount y of the commodity B" (nos. 37 R. E., 40 [*passim*], 44 [*passim*], 181, and 232 [two examples])

b) Amount x Commodity A Amount y Commodity B(-kam) "the amount x of the commodity A (corresponds to) the amount y of the commodity B" (nos. 137, 142, 143, 164, 168, 172, 174, 177, 183, 189 [four examples], 191 [four examples], 341, and 359)

For a complete list of rates, see chapter 10.

7.5. *Terms for Additional Payments*

7.5.1. Introductory Remarks

One of the characteristic features of the pre-Ur III kudurrus and sale documents are the so-called "additional payments" (henceforth abbreviated as AP or APs), i.e., payments in excess of the purchase price, which can be given to the sellers, secondary sellers, primary witnesses, and officials. It should be noted that not a single example of APs is found in sale documents from the Ur III period. [But see now the occurrence of níg-ba in an Ur III sale document from Umma, which was published by Steinkeller, *Sale Documents* pp. 275–78 no. 88*.] APs are attested almost exclusively in the texts dealing with the sale of immovables, i.e., fields, houses, and orchards. The only exceptions here are nos. 150 (Pre-Sargonic) and 240 (Sargonic), both involving the sale of persons. In the first document, the recipient of APs is the seller's daughter, in the second, an unknown individual, most probably the scribe who wrote the tablet. The commodities given as APs are usually designated by specific terms, such as níg-ba "gift," etc., but they can also be listed without any description. The terms used for APs in the Fara-Sargonic texts are NÍG.KI.GAR, NÍG.DÚR.GAR, *iškinū*, iš-gán, níg-dirig, níg-ba, MUNSUB(.AN).TAR, and Ì.ZAG. In the following discussion, we will study each of these terms, and will attempt to establish the function of APs in the sale transaction.

For the relationships between the value of APs and that of prices, see chapter 9.

7.5.2. NÍG.KI.GAR, NÍG.DÚR.GAR, *iškinū*, and *iš-gán*

These four terms will be discussed together, since they are apparently etymologically related and denote the same type of AP.

The AP NÍG.KI.GAR is listed in five kudurrus (nos. 16, 36, 40, 41, and 49) and in one Sargonic sale document dealing with the sale of a house (no. 237). All of these texts are written in Akkadian. In each case where the names of the parties to the transaction are preserved, the recipients of NÍG.KI.GAR are the sellers. In no. 16, NÍG.KI.GAR is the only AP listed, and it is paid in silver (NÍG.KI.GAR x GÍN KUG.BABBAR). Due to the fragmentary state of the inscription, the ratio of the NÍG.KI.GAR to the price cannot be established. In the transactions recorded in no. 36, NÍG.KI.GAR most often consists of silver and oil (NÍG.KI.GAR x GÍN KUG.BABBAR, x SILÀ Ì), but can also include barley and TÚG.A.SU cloths. It is the only AP listed in this text, and is constant at 10 percent of the price. In no. 40, NÍG.KI.GAR is given together with NÍG.BA. It consists of silver (x GÍN KUG.BABBAR, NÍG.KI.GAR GÁN—A$_1$, A$_2$, A$_3$), wool (C$_3$, D), barley (B), wool, silver, copper, and bronze objects, mules, and slaves (C$_1$, C$_2$), and constitutes 15 percent of the price in A$_1$, A$_2$, and A$_3$, and 10 percent in all other transactions. NÍG.KI.GAR is the only AP given in no. 41. It is fairly constant at around 10 percent of the price. In the transactions listed on the obverse, NÍG.KI.GAR includes silver and TÚG.ŠU.ZA.GA cloths (NÍG.KI.GAR x GÍN KUG.BABBAR, x TÚG.ŠU.ZA.GA), while in the transactions found on the reverse, it consists of silver, barley, BAPPIR, and oil. The commodities included in the NÍG.KI.GAR listed in no. 49 are preserved only partially: [. . . SÍ]G? 1 MA.NA K[UG?.BABBAR?] NÍG.KI.GAR GÁ[N]. In the sale document no. 237, NÍG.KI.GAR is given to the sellers together with another AP, designated as Ì.ZAG: *a-na* NÍG.KI.GAR É 5(GUR) ŠE GUR, 6 SILÀ Ì, 10 MA.NA SÍG, 1 TÚG.A.SU, 1 *ḫa-la-um*^{TÚG}; 2(PI) ŠE, 1 SILÀ Ì, 1 MA.NA SÍG, 1 GIŠ.DU.DA^{URUDU} *a-na* Ì.ZAG Buyer *i-ti-in* "Buyer gave 5 bushels of barley, 6 quarts of oil, 10 pounds of wool, 1 TÚG.A.SU cloth, (and) 1 *ḫala*ʾ*um* cloth as the NÍG.KI.GAR of the house; 120 quarts of barley, 1 quart of oil, 1 pound of wool, (and) 1 copper GIŠ.DU.DA, as the Ì.ZAG."

The only example of NÍG.DÚR.GAR (or NÍG.TUŠ.GAR) comes from the kudurru no. 37. It is given to the sellers together with NÍG.BA, and it consists of barley, wool, and oil (NÍG.DÚR.GAR x GUR.SAG.GÁL ŠE, x MA.NA SÍG, x SILÀ Ì). The NÍG.DÚR.GAR is constant at 10 percent of the price. In the transaction recorded on rev. i–ii, the receivers of the NÍG.DÚR.GAR are persons other than the primary sellers (most probably secondary sellers): NÍG.DÚR.GAR Com. DUMU.DUMU PN NÍG.DÚ[R.GAR] K[Ú] "the NÍG.DÚR.GAR (is) Com.; the descendents of PN received (lit.: ate) the NÍG.DÚR.GAR."

Two kudurrus (nos. 42 and 43) and one Sargonic sale document (no. 227) mention the AP called *iškinū*. The *iškinū* is the only AP occurring in these texts, and it is given to the sellers. In nos. 42 and 43, *iškinū* consists of silver, barley, wool, and BA.AN containers (*iš-ki-nu-su* x GÍN KUG.BABBAR, x GUR.SAG.GÁL ŠE, x SÍG.GAN, x BA.AN); in one instance (no. 43 i), it also includes a *ḫaṣṣinnum* "axe." The *iškinū* received by the sellers in no. 227 has a similar content: 1(GUR) ŠE GUR, 2 [MA.NA SÍG], 5 BA.[AN], 1 G[ÍN] KUG.BABBAR P[N] *ù* P[N$_2$] *a-ki-ìl-d*[*a*] *iš-ki-n*[*e*] "PN and PN$_2$ (i.e., the sellers—two women) are the receivers (lit.: consumers) of the additional payment (which consists of) 1 bushel of barley, 2 [pounds of wool], 5 BA.AN containers, (and) 1 shekel of silver." The term *iškinū* is also attested in the Sargonic administrative text *MAD* 5, 3:1–3, which lists among the expenditures an amount of barley paid as *iškinū*: 3(GUR) 2(PI) 3(BÁN) ŠE GUR *A-ga-dè*^{KI} *a-na iš-gi-ni* GÁN *be-lu* GÁN *im-ḫur-ru* "the owners of the field received 3 bushels and 150 quarts of barley, by the bushel of Akkadē, as the additional payment of the field."

The AP iš-gán is given to the sellers in twelve Sargonic sale transactions (nos. 165, 166, 169, 171, 172, 182a F, 182a J, 182a X, 182a Y, 182a Z, 182a CC, and 207). It is the only AP listed in these texts, with the exception of nos. 169, 182a F, and 182a J, where iš-gán is given together with níg-ba. The content of iš-gán is as follows:

- 1 A.SU^{TÚG}, 1 ÍB.BA.DÙ^{TÚG}, 1(gur) 1(pi) 2(bán) še gur, 1 igi-3-gál si[là] ⌜ì⌝-šáḫ, 1 ma-na síg, ⌜iš-gán⌝-bi (no. 165)
- 1(gur) še iš-gán (no. 166)
- 2(pi) 4(bán) še gur, iš-gán še-kam; 2(pi) 4(bán) še gur, iš-gán síg-kam (nos. 169 and 182a F)
- 1 bar-síg^{TÚG}, 1(gur) še gur, 1 silà ì-šáḫ šu-ba-ti, iš-gán-pi (no. 171)
- 2(pi) 2(bán) zu-lúm gur, iš-[gán-bi] (no. 172)
- 4(gur) še gur, iš-gán še-kam; 3 umbin? ì-udu, iš-gán síg-kam (no. 182a J)

10(gur) še iš-gán (no. 182a X)
[x še iš-gán] (no. 182a Y)
2(pi) še iš-gán (no. 182a Z)
2(pi) še iš-gán; 2(pi) še iš-gán; 2(pi) še iš-gán (no. 182a CC)
1 gín lal igi-6 kug, iš-gán gán-ga-kam (no. 207)

The term iš-gán is also mentioned in the following passages: PN iš-gán nu-ag PN_2 ì-ag "PN (i.e., the buyer?) did not give (lit.: make) the iš-gán; PN_2 gave (it)" (no. 14 xiv 6–10); iš-gán ì-kú "(the seller) received the iš-gán" (no. 212). And finally, note the occurrences of iš-gán in connection with commodities in nos. 14 and 15, discussed in note to no. 14 i 9, where the meaning of iš-gán is unclear.

The following interpretations of the terms NÍG.KI.GAR, NÍG.DÚR.GAR, *iškinū*, and iš-gán are found in previous literature:

1) V. Scheil, *MDP* 2 p. 7, interpreted NÍG.KI.GAR as "additionnellement au prix du champ."
2) F. Hrozný, *WZKM* 21 (1907) p. 16, agreed with Scheil's interpretation of NÍG.KI.GAR, and suggested a connection with the NB *atru*.
3) F. Thureau-Dangin, *RA* 6 (1907) p. 154, translated NÍG.KI.GAR as "tout ce qui a été bâti" or "(supplément au prix pour) les constructions de toute sorte," on account of the expression níg-dirig é-dù in *RTC* 13 (our no. 104).
4) H. de Genouillac, *TSA* p. XXXVf., agreed with the opinion of Thureau-Dangin cited above, and noted that "(. . .) les mots *nig-diri(g)-é-dū*, 'prix supplémentaire pour la maison bâtie,' (*RTC* 13) correspondent assez bien au complexe sumérien *nig-ki-gar* dont les deux derniers éléments *ki-gar* sont expliqués par l'assyrien *šikittu ša biti*, 'construction, [se dit] d'une maison.'"
5) According to L. Matouš, *AOr* 22 (1954) p. 435, the term *iškinū* "durch seine Ableitung von der Wurzel *škn* 'legen' entschpricht (. . .) dem (. . .) Ideogram *nì-ki-gar* im Sinne von 'was auf die Erde gelegt ist.' Man kann also in dem Ausdruck *iškinū* das altakkadische, in Nordbabylonien gebrauchte Äquivalent des *nì-ki-gar* = Zugabe (zum Kaufpreis) sehen." At the same time, Matouš read the term NÍG.DÚR.GAR as NÍG.KU.GAR, and interpreted it as a phonetic spelling of NÍG.KI.GAR. Matouš rejected the interpretation of NÍG.KI.GAR as the payment for the buildings erected on the sold property, on the grounds that in the Manishtushu Obelisk (no. 40) NÍG.KI.GAR stands in a set relation to the price and also, that in the kudurrus from the Diyala area (nos. 43 and 44) *iškinū* can be as low as one shekel of silver.
6) Gelb, *MAD* 3 p. 268, translated *iškinū* as "amount of money paid in addition to the price of a field or house," and analyzed NÍG.KI.GAR and NÍG.DÚR.GAR (transliterated NÍG.KU.GAR) as its logographic spellings. According to Gelb, *iškinū* evidently corresponds to the Fara níg-dirig and to SI.BI of the OB sale documents.
7) Edzard, *ZA* 56 (1964) p. 276, was the first scholar to study the term iš-gán. According to him: "iš-gána, Lehnwort von akkadisch *iškinū*, einer der Ausdrücke für "Zugabe" in Kaufverträgen; (. . .) lautliche Entwicklung wohl *iškin + a > iškana, geschrieben iš-gána (regressive Vokalangleichung)." Edzard translated iš-gán as "Zugabe" also in *SRU* p. 44, where he equated it with NÍG.KI.GAR.
8) The terms in question were discussed most recently by Krecher, *ZA* 63 (1974) pp. 154–58; *Acta Antiqua* 22 (1974) pp. 31f., who believed that iš-gán is a loanword from the Akkadian *iškinū*, also expressed by the pseudo-Sumerograms NÍG.KI.GAR and NÍG.TUŠ.GAR (our NÍG.DÚR.GAR). Krecher interpreted *iškinū* as "Äquivalent für Objekte bzw. Zustände, die durch *šakānu* ('anlegen' bzw. 'eine Sache (Akk.) (gleichsam) mit einer Ausstattung (Akk.) versehen') beschafft bzw. herbeigeführt sind," that is, "Entgelt für vorhandene Anlagen" (*ZA* 63 p. 156). Krecher deduced the same meaning from the etymologies of NÍG.KI.GAR and NÍG.TUŠ.GAR: since the elements ki-gar and tuš-gar mean "Gründung" and "Wohnsitz," respectively, both NÍG.KI.GAR and NÍG.TUŠ.GAR denote "Äquivalent für die Anlage eines Wohnhauses" (*Acta Antiqua* 22 p. 31). According to Krecher, *iškinū* and related terms represent the compensation for a house both in the sales of houses and in the sales of fields.

As the above interpretations show, there is a general consensus that the terms NÍG.KI.GAR, NÍG.DÚR.GAR, *iškinū*, and iš-gán are all etymologically related, and that they denote the same type of payment. This payment was analyzed by some scholars as the noncommital "additional payment," and by others, as the compensation for the buildings or other structures erected on the sold property. The latter interpretation, most fully expounded by Krecher, is primarily based on the etymologies of *iškinū*, NÍG.KI.GAR, and NÍG.DÚR.GAR. In our opinion, the proposed etymologies are far from conclusive. Thus the term *iškinū*, an *ipris* formation from *šakānum*, can equally well be analyzed as "things which were established/placed down" (result of an action created by *šakānum*), parallel to *išpikū* "produce, storage bin" (lit.: "grain accumulations") (result of an action created by *šapākum* "to pile up"). Similarly, NÍG.KI.GAR, which is a derivative of the verb ki . . . gar "to found (a house, temple, city, etc.)" (see Gudea Cyl. A iii 2, ix 11; *ZA* 50 [1952] p. 70 l. 80; *JCS* 21 [1967] p. 31 v 6, 23), "to place (an object) on the ground" (see W. W. Hallo and J. J. A. van Dijk, *YNER* 3 p. 81), "to establish (as a regular offering)" (see *BE* 1, 12 iii′ 3′–9′), can be simply translated "things (níg) which were founded (ki-gar)," that is, "foundation, establishment," or the like. For NÍG.KI.GAR, see now also Pettinato, *MEE* 4 p. 211 line 125: NÍG.KI.GAR = *maš-ga-nu* "threshing floor, settlement"; for NÍG.DÚR.GAR, see *ibid.*, p. 209 line 117b, p. 367 line 0276: NÍG.DÚR.GAR = *si-ti-a-núm*, where the meaning of the Semitic gloss is, unfortunately, unclear. Finally, the word NÍG.DÚR.GAR, which derives from dúr . . . gar, "to sit, to dwell, to make someone sit" (see Falkenstein, *Götterlieder* p. 191), is to be translated "things (níg) which were set up (dúr-gar)" (cf. also the chair called ^{GIŠ}dúr-gar [see, e.g., *BIN* 8, 20 i 8], corresponding to the Akkadian *durgarûm* [wr. *du-ur-ga-ru-ù* in *CT* 18, 3 rev. iii 1; cf. *CAD* D p. 191]). Krecher's proposal that NÍG.KU.GAR is to be read NÍG. TUŠ.GAR (or NÍG.DÚR.GAR) is confirmed by the examination of the photographs of no. 37, which show that the sign in question is square, and that the horizontal wedge in the middle of the sign does not cross it completely. In contrast, the sign KU in the same text is tall and narrow with the horizontal wedge crossing it completely in the middle (see, e.g., the personal names *I-ku-La-im* [i′ 7] and *I*-KU-GU-*Il* [iii′ 4]). For the formal distinction between DÚR and KU in the early periods, see Biggs, *JCS* 20 (1966) p. 77 n. 37.

Beside the insufficient etymological grounds, Krecher's interpretation of NÍG.KI.GAR and the related terms appears unacceptable also for the following reasons:

1) NÍG.KI.GAR, NÍG.DÚR.GAR, *iškinū*, and iš-gán stand in the same relationship to the object of sale as (níg-)šám. This is demonstrated by the existence of such constructions as NÍG.KI.GAR GÁN/É, parallel to (níg-)šám gán/é "(commodities given as) the price of the field/house." Accordingly, NÍG.KI.GAR GÁN/É must mean "(commodities given *as*) the 'foundation' of the field/house," and not "(commodities given *for*) the 'foundation' of the field/house."
2) In no. 165, the object of sale is described as 1 sar ⸢x⸣ ša-na [x] gín é-KI.UD, ⅓ ša-na é al-dù-dù "1 (and) ⸢x⸣ sar (and) [x] gín of an empty house lot, (and) ⅓ sar of a built-up house lot." The text then states the price and iš-gán paid for this property: níg-šám-bi, Com., PN [šu-ba-t]i; [Com.], PN_2 šeš-ni šu-ba-ti; Com., ⸢iš-gán⸣-bi, "its price, Com., PN received; [Com.], PN_2, his brother, received; Com., (it is) its 'additional payment.'" This example clearly shows that both the price and the iš-gán refer to the *whole* property, and not to any particular parts of it.
3) As already pointed out by Matouš, the payments designated as NÍG.KI.GAR, NÍG.DÚR.GAR, and *iškinū* stand in a set relationship to the price. Such a situation would be impossible if the "additional payment" represented a compensation for the buildings erected on the sold property, since the value of buildings would necessarily have differed from one case to another.
4) Another argument against Krecher's interpretation is provided by one of the transactions recorded in no. 37 (rev. i–ii). Following the price and the names of the sellers, the text lists the NÍG.DÚR.GAR and its recipients: NÍG.DÚR.GAR Amount DUMU.DUMU *Ur-ma* NÍG.DÚ[R.GAR] K[Ú] "the descendants of Ur-ma received (lit.: consumed) the NÍG.DÚR.GAR." This example demonstrates that the price and the NÍG.DÚR.GAR were payments that were distributed among the sellers depending on their relationship to the real estate, rather than payments for the two different parts of this real estate.

In light of the above, we assume that NÍG.KI.GAR and related terms designate the payments made in excess of the purchase price, representing the value of the whole property. It is possible that these payments, even though received by the sellers, actually served to compensate their relatives.

As far as the precise meanings of NÍG.KI.GAR, NÍG. DÚR.GAR, *iškinū*, and iš-gán are concerned, we believe that no adequate solution of this question can be offered at this time. One of the possibilities is that *šakānum* is used in *iškinū* in the sense "to impose" (for this meaning of *šakānum*, see Gelb, *MAD* 3 p. 267). Accordingly, *iškinū* could denote "payments which were imposed," i.e., placed on top of the price or in addition to it. This interpretation may find support in the fact that the verb which is used to express the payment of the OB "additional payment" called SI is also *šakānum* (in contrast to the payment of price, which is expressed by *šaqālum*/lal "to weigh out").

7.5.3. níg-dirig

The AP níg-dirig is found exclusively in the Fara sale documents. It is regularly given to the sellers, together with MUNSUB(.AN).TAR, níg-ba, and the commodities which are not designated by any term. It is lacking only in four texts (nos. 101, 128, 129, and 134). With two exceptions, níg-dirig consists of the same commodity as the price (copper or silver); in no. 121, níg-dirig is paid in silver, whereas the price consists of copper; and in no. 125, it consists of barley, in contrast to the price, which is paid in copper and silver. It is significant that in most instances (14) níg-dirig is larger than the price (nos. 103, 105, 106, 108, 109, 113, 115, 118, 119, 121, 122?, 124, 125?, and 127b). It is lower than the price in ten cases (nos. 100 107 [first transaction], 107 [second transaction], 116, 117, 120, 127a, 130, 132, and 136), and equal with the price, in eight (nos. 104, 112 = 113c, 113a, 113b, 114, 123, 127, and 133); the ratio cannot be established in five texts (nos. 102, 110, 111, 126, and 131). In six of the house-sales which list níg-dirig (nos. 103, 104, 106, 108, 109, and 110), níg-dirig is followed by the description é-dù "built-up house lot"; this description is missing in the other house-sales (nos. 100, 102, 105, 107 [first transaction], 107 [second transaction], 111, 112 = 113c, 113, 113a, and 113b).

The term was discussed by the following scholars:

1) Thureau-Dangin, *RA* 6 (1907) p. 154; "Au lieu de *nig-diri*(*g*) (= *atru* 'supplément' dans les contracts néo-babyloniens), l'Obélisque de Maništusu [our no. 40], la Pierre de Sippar [our no. 41] et le fragment B. M. 22506 [our no. 36] ont *nig-ki-gar*. Il est à noter que *RTC* no. 13 spécifie que le *nig-diri*(*g*), ici particulièrement élevé, représente la valeur d'une maison construite sur le terrain vendu. Ceci pourrait donner la clé de *nig-ki-gar*. En effet, cette expression signifie mot à mot 'tout ce qui a été bâti.' On est dons amené à traduire, en paraphrasant: '(Supplément au prix pour) les constructions de toute sorte.'"
2) De Genouillac, *TSA* pp. XXXVf.: "(. . .) le prix supplémentaire, *nig-diri*(*g*) ou *nig-ki-gar*: ces deux expressions, probablement de sens identique, désig-

neraient selon la remarque de M. Thureau-Dangin le prix des constructions, distingué dans l'acte de vente de celui du terrain; l'une et l'autre en effet ne sont employées que pour des surfaces de terre, et les mots *nig-diri(g)-é-dū*, 'prix supplémentaire pour la maison bâtie,' (*RTC* 13) correspondent assez bien au complexe sumérien *nig-ki-gar* dont les deux elements *ki-gar* sont expliqués par l'assyrien *šikittu ša biti*, 'construction, [se dit] d'une maison.'"

3) Deimel, *Fara* 3 p. 11*: "(. . .) eine Zuschlagsumme (*níg-diri(g)*), die sich bei Häusern vielleicht auf das mitgekaufte Mobiliar, bei Feldern auf mitgekaufte Gebäulichkeiten und Feldgeräte bezieht."
4) Koschaker, *OLZ* 40 (1937) col. 425: "Zusatzgeld (*níg-dirig = watrum*)."
5) M. Lambert, *Sumer* 9 (1953) p. 208: "(. . .) le second prix est appelé *níg-dirig* 'chose de supplément,' c'est-à-dire, s'il s'agit d'un champ, suppléments pour les constructions, canaux ou emblavures qui s'y trouvent, et, s'il s'agit d'une maison, suppléments pour le jardin ou le mobilier."
6) Matouš, *AOr* 22 (1954) p. 435: "Zugabe."
7) Krecher, *ZA* 63 (1974) p. 157, assumed that níg-dirig must have a similar meaning as the terms NÍG.KI.GAR, NÍG.DÚR.GAR, *iškinū*, and iš-gán, which he translated "Anlagen" or "Ausstattung," and, since níg-SI.A (our níg-dirig) does not have this meaning, he proposed that SI.A was the "Fara-Orthographie für späteres si(-g), sè(-g) 'setzen,' 'anbringen' (= *mullû, nadû, uḫḫuzu, šakānu*) und dieses Wort deckte das gleiche Bedeutungsfeld wie altakkadisches *škn* in *iškinū*." Compare also *Acta Antiqua* 22 (1974) p. 32. Krecher, *ZA* 63 pp. 155f., agreed with Thureau-Dangin (see above) that, in the examples of níg-dirig é-dù, níg-dirig denotes the payment for the buildings erected on the house lot, but he extended this interpretation also to the house-sales in which níg-dirig is not followed by the description é-dù. According to him, níg-dirig, like the expressions NÍG.KI.GAR, NÍG.DÚR.GAR, *iškinū*, and iš-gán, signifies "(. . .) die Erstattung des Wertes der 'Ausstattung' des Grundstücks (. . .), die u.a. beim Feld vielleicht Geräte und (zu erwartende?) Ernte, beim Hausgründstuck das Gebaüde samt Einrichtung einschliessen könnte." In his later discussion of níg-dirig (*Acta Antiqua* 22 p. 31), Krecher proposed a slightly different interpretation, concluding, with some reservations, that níg-dirig, as well as NÍG.KI.GAR and related terms, denote the payment for the buildings not only in the house-sales, but also in the transactions involving the sale of fields.

As we can see from the above interpretations of níg-dirig, the prevailing opinion is that the element SI.A of this term is to be read dirig, and that it corresponds to the Akkadian root WTR. The only scholar dissenting from this opinion is Krecher, who analyzes SI.A as a Fara spelling of the verbs si(-g) and sè(-g). As far as we know, there is no evidence supporting this suggestion. Note that the Fara texts consistently express the verb si(-g) with the sign SI, as demonstrated by such personal names as Lugal-é-si (e.g., *Fara* 3, 33 viii 1) and Lú-barag-si (*TSŠ* 881 obv. x 5′), which correspond to the later personal names of the Lugal-zag-ge-si type (cf. Limet, *Anthroponymie* pp. 291f.); note also the personal name(?) Ki-si-ga, occurring in *TSŠ* 369 iii 7. Furthermore, the Fara texts maintain a clear distinction between dirig and si(-g); this is best exemplified by the text *TSŠ* 881, where both verbs appear side by side: níg-dirig (obv. viii 2′) and X NE na si-ga (obv. x 4′). The reading of SI.A as dirig also seems certain in *TSŠ* 292 (= *NTSŠ* 292) rev. i 1–2, where SI.A is likewise contrasted with si: gú-an-šè 8 lú-si, kur_6 dirig gud giš Ag. The interpretation of níg-SI.A as níg-dirig finds additional support in the existence of an OB additional payment called SI (abbreviated spelling of DIRIG) and the NB *atru* (see below). For all these reasons, we retain the traditional reading níg-dirig and translate this term "excess, addition," as describing the commodities given in excess of the equivalent (šám) of the object of sale.

The next and more difficult problem to be considered now is the function of níg-dirig. The examination of the Fara sale documents shows that the amount given as the "price" (šám) represents the actual value of the sold property. This is particularly clear in the field-sales in which the price is paid in copper. In these texts the value of one iku of land usually is two pounds of copper. In contrast to the fairly constant relationship between the amount of the price and the size of the property, the amount of níg-dirig varies widely from one text to another. This indicates that níg-dirig constitutes an "addition" to the actual equivalent of the property. The question thus arises: an addition for what? As we have seen, the most commonly accepted interpretation of níg-dirig, first proposed by Thureau-Dangin and most recently entertained by Krecher, has it that níg-dirig is a payment for the buildings or other structures erected on the sold land. It must be stressed here that this theory is based solely on the examples of the phrase níg-dirig é-dù, which occurs in some of the Fara house-sales (but note that níg-dirig occurs more often without é-dù). This phrase was translated by Thureau-Dangin and his followers as the "additional payment for the house," who distinguished é-dù from the term é "house (lot)," which describes the sold property elsewhere in the text. The main argument against this interpretation is that the term é-dù does not occur in the sales of fields, as one would expect if níg-dirig represented the payment for a house. Furthermore, the phrase níg-dirig é-dù closely parallels such expressions as NÍG.KI.GAR GÁN, iš-gán gán, and, especially, NÍG.KI.GAR É, in which the whole object of sale, and not a part of it or an addition to it, is meant. Accordingly, we assume that é-dù is simply a more specific description of the sold property: "built-up house lot." If we accept, as generally agreed, that there is a functional identity between níg-dirig and the Sargonic NÍG.KI.GAR, NÍG.DÚR.GAR, *iškinū*, and iš-gán, the arguments given earlier against interpreting these payments as a compensation for the buildings erected on the sold property would apply also to níg-dirig. We conclude, therefore, that níg-dirig is not a payment for some material "additions" to the land in question, but a payment in addition to the total value of the sold property, which most probably was intended to compensate the relatives of the seller(s).

In this connection, we should mention two APs known from the later periods, which may be related to níg-dirig, as regards both their names and function. The first of them, called SI, is attested in the OB sale documents from northern Babylonia (cf. Wilcke, *WO* 8 [1976] pp. 263–67), in a sale document from Uruk (*RA* 14 [1917] p. 153f.), and in an OB text from Khana (*Syria* 5 [1924] p. 272). This AP is named in a standard clause, which is placed immediately after the statement that the buyer paid the price: *ù* x GÍN KUG.BABBAR SI.BI *iškun* "(Buyer paid x shekels of silver as its full price) and *placed* x shekels of silver as its additional payment." The sale documents which record this clause deal indiscriminately with immovables and movables, with SI always constituting only a small fraction of the price. The sign SI in this context is undoubtedly an abbreviated writing of DIRIG; this is demonstrated by the fact that the OB clause ḫé-dirig ḫé-ba-lal "be it more or less" (e.g., *TCL* 10, 36:12), corresponding to the Akkadian *lītir limṭi* (e.g., Waterman, *Bus. Doc.* 26:2, 40:3, 69:6), is alternatively spelled ḫé-si ḫé-ba-lal (e.g., Jean, *Tell Sifr* 47:1) or ḫé-si ba-lal (e.g., Jean, *Tell Sifr* 60a:1; *BIN* 7, 63:1). Against Wilcke's reservation to accept the value DIRIG for SI in the texts from northern Babylonia (*WO* 8 p. 265), see the text Birot, *Tablettes* 70, almost certainly coming from northern Babylonia (cf. Birot, *Tablettes* p. 108), which is a roster of conscripted men, each entry stating: 1) name of the conscripted man; 2) name of his replacement (DAḪ), usually his brother; and 3) name of his supernumerary (SI), usually his father. As noted already by B. Landsberger (in Lautner, *Personenmiete* p. 225), SI in this context stands for DIRIG (Akk. *attarum*).

The other AP, called *atru*, is regularly listed in the Neo-Babylonian sales of real property (cf. E. Sonnenschein, *Rocznik Orjentalistyczny* 3 [1925] pp. 205–07; M. San Nicolò, *Or.* n.s. 16 [1947] pp. 273–302). This payment constitutes only a small fraction of the price, and it is given to the seller together with a garment (*lubāru* or TÚG.ḪI.A), which is usually intended for the seller's wife. It is important for our interpretation of níg-dirig that *atru*, exactly like the OB SI, is given in excess of the total value of the sold property. This point is made clear by the texts themselves, which state that the buyer named the price, bought the property in question for that price, and paid the full price, plus the *atru* and a garment; see, e.g., *VAS* 5, 96:13–17: Buyer KI.LAM *tam-bi-e-ma* 2 MA.NA 8 GÍN KUG.BABBAR BABBAR-*ú ta-ši-im ši-mi-šú gam-ru-tú ù* 4½ GÍN KUG.BABBAR *a-ta-ar ù* TÚG.ḪI.A *ta-ad-di-in-šú* "Buyer named the price, bought (the property for) 128 shekels of white silver, (and) paid its full price and 4½ shekels of silver (in lieu of) the additional payment and a garment."

7.5.4. níg-ba

An AP called níg-ba is regularly given to the sellers in the Fara sale documents, in addition to níg-dirig and the commodities which are not described by any term. It does not occur in thirteen instances (nos. 100, 101, 102, 104, 107, 108, 115, 117, 121, 128, 129, 134, and 136); in three texts this section is not preserved (nos. 118, 120, and 135). The níg-ba consists of barley (nos. 105, 109, 110, 111, 112 = 113c, 113, 113a, 113b, 126, 127a, 130, 131, and 132) or an amount of the same metal (urudu or kug-luḫ-ḫa) in which the price is paid (nos. 116, 119, 122, 127, and 129). In a few instances, níg-ba consists both of barley and metal (nos. 103, 106, 114, 123, 124, and 133?). In no. 125, which is rather atypical regarding its formulary, and which is probably slightly younger than the other Fara sale documents, níg-ba is the only AP given to the sellers, and it consists of wool, three different garments, oil, and bread (4 ma-na síg, 1 TÚG.A.SU, 1 TÚG. ÍB.DÙ, 2 silà ì, 1 níg-sag-kéš, 2 ninda). The same text describes the commodities given to a dub-sar gán likewise as níg-ba: ŠÁM+2 kug, 1 silà ì, níg-ba-ni "2/3 shekel of silver (and) 1 quart of oil, (is) his gift."

In the Pre-Sargonic kudurrus and sale documents from Lagash, níg-ba is the only term used for APs. In nos. 22, 23, and 144, it refers to the commodities given to the principal seller, as well as to the commodities given to the other sellers (lugal-gán-me) and secondary sellers (dumu-gán-me). In one of the transactions recorded in no. 23 (rev. ix–obv. x), the commodities described as níg-ba are presented to still another group of people, not designated by any term. The commodities which are given in these texts as níg-ba include wool, oil, fish, soup, various types of onions, various types of breads, and sheep (see pls. 100, 134, and 135).

In the other Pre-Sargonic sale documents from Lagash, the term níg-ba is used only in reference to the commodities received by the sellers (nos. 139, 140, 141, 142, 143, 145, and 146). These include silver, barley, wheat, wool, oil, soup, beer, various types of bread, and various garments (see pls. 134 and 135).

In the kudurru no. 32, which comes from Adab and dates to the Pre-Sargonic period, the term níg-ba is applied in the first of the two transactions to the commodities received by the sellers and secondary sellers (13 SU.A.TÚG, 70 ma-na síg, níg-ba dumu PN), and in the other transaction, to the commodities received by the sellers only (3 SU.A.TÚG, 10 ma-na síg, níg-ba dam PN_2, dumu PN_2). It is the only term for APs used in this text.

The term níg-ba appears in Sargonic times considerably less often than in the earlier periods. Only four Sargonic kudurrus use it as a description of APs. In no. 37, níg-ba is given to the sellers in addition to NÍG.DÚR.GAR; it consists of a single cloth (NÍG.BA 1 TÚG.SU.A). The Manishtushu Obelisk (no. 40) applies this term to the commodities received, in addition to NÍG.KI.GAR, by the sellers, as well as to the commodities given to the officials who surveyed the sold field (only in C_3). The commodities given as níg-ba in this document include various types of silver, bronze, and copper objects, various types of garments, and teams of equids (see pl. 107). The other two kudurrus which mention níg-ba are no. 45 ([. . .], [x]+2 TÚG.BAL, 30 URUDU MA.NA, NÍG.BA) and no. 46 ([. . .], [x]+1 SÍG ⌜MA⌝.NA, ⌜1⌝? ŠE GUR, 1 Ì.IR ⌜X⌝, NÍG.BA A.ŠÀ).

The AP níg-ba is also attested in the Sargonic sale transactions nos. 169, 182, 182a F, and 182a J. In nos. 169 and 182a F, níg-ba is presented to the sellers in addition to iš-gán še-kam and iš-gán síg-kam: [1(pi) 2(bán) še, ní]g-ba-pi (no. 169); 1(pi) 2(bán) ⟨še⟩, níg-ba (no. 182a F). In no. 182a J, níg-ba, given to the seller together with iš-gán še-kam and iš-gán síg-kam, is composed of two cloths and a measure of sheep-oil (1 A.SU.TÚG, 1 NI. TÚG, 1 umbin? ì-udu-dùg?, níg-[b]a). In no. 182, níg-ba is the only AP presented to the sellers in this text, and it consists of a single cloth (1 A.SU.TÚG, níg-ba).

To summarize these data, in most instances the term níg-ba describes an AP given to the sellers; less frequently, it denotes an AP given to the secondary sellers or the officials. It may be used as the only term for APs (Pre-Sargonic kudurrus and sale documents from Lagash, and nos. 32, 46, 47?, and 182), or it may appear in addition to another AP, such as níg-dirig (Fara sale documents), NÍG.KI.GAR (no. 40), NÍG.DÚR.GAR (no. 37), or iš-gán (no. 169). The commodities which are given as níg-ba usually include various foodstuffs, wool, and garments. Particularly characteristic is the inclusion in níg-ba of various types of garments. Note here especially nos. 37 and 182, in which níg-ba consists of a single TÚG.A.SU cloth. With the exception of the Fara sale documents, silver, copper, and barley, i.e., the standard media in which price is paid, are included in níg-ba only occasionally.

The traditionally accepted translation of níg-ba, Akk. *qīštum*, in the context of sale documents and other legal documents is "gift"; see, e.g., Falkenstein, *NSGU* 3 p. 148; Edzard, *SRU* p. 233. This interpretation has recently been questioned by Krecher, *ZA* 63 (1974) pp. 158ff.; *idem*, *Acta Orientalia* 22 (1974) p. 32, who proposed instead the meaning "allotment" ("Zuweisung"), pointing out that the original meaning of the verb ba is "to divide" ("abteilen"), Akk. *zuāzum*, *našārum*, and interpreting the original meaning of *qiāšum* likewise as "to divide." Another argument supplied by Krecher is that the meaning "to give as a gift" is expressed in Sumerian not by ba but by sag . . . rig_7. The interpretation of níg-ba as "allotment" led Krecher to the assumption that níg-ba was the only part of the purchase-payments which was actually distributed among the sellers. According to Krecher, the other two parts, (níg-)šám, i.e., the payment for the land, and NÍG. KI.GAR / NÍG.DÚR.GAR / *iškinū* / iš-gán, i.e., the payment for the buildings, were added in bulk to the family property and remained there undivided, until they were distributed through inheritance.

Although Krecher is unquestionably right that the original and basic meaning of níg-ba is "allotment," the derived sense "gift," "present," or the like is well documented from the earliest periods on. Because of this, we see no reason why the traditional interpretation of níg-ba as "gift" in the context of sale transactions should not be retained. The function of níg-ba in these documents, we believe, is to be considered in a broader perspective of the symbolic significance that underlines the act of gift-making. The presentation of a gift creates a bond between the donor and the receiver, and imposes on the receiver an obligation to reciprocate, which may materialize in a return gift, in the granting of favor or status, or simply in a favorable and friendly attitude towards the donor. The same principles appear to have been operating in the case of níg-ba; we may speculate that níg-ba was intended to make the sellers and their relatives favorably inclined towards the buyer, to establish a community between both parties to the transaction, and thus to create a propitious climate in which the property in question could be alienated.

7.5.5. MUNSUB(.AN).TAR

The only attestations of this AP come from the Fara sale documents nos. 115 and 117, both pertaining to the sale of fields. The MUNSUB(.AN).TAR is given in these two texts to the sellers, in addition to the níg-dirig and the commodities which are not labeled by any term; it is listed after the price and before the níg-dirig. There is no níg-ba mentioned in either text. The MUNSUB(.AN).TAR consists in both instances of copper, as do the price and níg-dirig.

Deimel, *Fara* 3 p. 11*, noting the absence of níg-ba in both texts, suggested that the meaning of MUNSUB(.AN). TAR may be similar to that of níg-ba. This view was rejected by Matouš, *AOr* 22 (1954) pp. 435f., on the grounds that, first, MUNSUB(.AN).TAR is listed after the price and before níg-dirig, whereas níg-ba always occurs after níg-dirig and, second, that MUNSUB(.AN). TAR consists of metal, in contrast to níg-ba, which is usually paid in barley. Matouš then suggested the meaning "abgeschnittenes Getreide oder Futter für Vieh, das dann in übertragenem Sinne bestimmte Zugabe zum Kaufpreis bedeuten würde," basing it on the misinterpreted occurrences of MUNSUB in *Fara* 2, 81 and Gudea Cyl. B xvi 5.

The meaning of MUNSUB(.AN).TAR was subsequently studied by Edzard, *SRU* p. 24, who proposed that the element (AN.)TAR is a verbal form ("er hat abgetrennt"), and speculated that this term may denote a "price-reduction" ("Kaufpreisminderung"). Most recently, MUNSUB(.AN). TAR was discussed by Krecher, *ZA* 63 (1974) p. 154, who was inclined to agree with the "price-reduction" interpretation of Edzard.

The meaning of MUNSUB(.AN).TAR is unclear. If the meaning of MUNSUB in this context is "hair," Akk. *šārtum* (see *AHWB* p. 1191; Pettinato, *MEE* 4 p. 307 l. 970: MUNSUB = *sa-rí-a-du*), and the form (AN.)TAR, as suggested by Edzard, is a verbal form, then the whole compound could be translated "the hair was cut off." Assuming the correctness of this interpretation, MUNSUB(.AN). TAR could denote an AP given in connection with some ritual action accompanying the sale transaction. As a possible parallel, we may cite here the AP called Ì.ZAG (see section 7.5.6), which is almost certainly connected with the practice of spreading or pouring the oil during the sale transaction. The "cutting off the hair" could perhaps be compared with the ritual of "cutting off the hem" (*sissiktam batāqum*) of the OB and MB legal documents, which symbolized the act of quittance (for this symbolic action, see most recently J. J. Finkelstein, *WO* 8 [1976] pp. 236–40). We may also recall here the practice of sending a lock of hair and a hem of garment from the person who transmitted a prophetic message, mentioned in the OB texts from Mari (see H. B. Huffmon, *The Biblical Archaeologist* 31/4 [Dec. 1968] pp. 121–24). As suggested by Huffmon, *op. cit.* p. 121, "(. . .) hair and hem must have been some kind of a guarantee from the person, a symbolic subjection to royal authority"; "(. . .) hair and hem might have been used to represent the person in some ritual that examined, in a more proper way, his or her reliability."

7.5.6. Ì.ZAG

An AP called Ì.ZAG is attested only in one sale document (no. 237). It is given to the sellers together with NÍG.KI.GAR: *a-na* NÍG.KI.GAR É 5(GUR) ŠE GUR, 6 SILÀ Ì, 10 MA.NA SÍG, 1 TÚG.A.SU, 1 *ḫa-la-um*^{TÚG}; 2(PI) ŠE, 1 SILÀ Ì, 1 MA.NA SÍG, 1 GIŠ.DU.DA^{URUDU} *a-na* Ì.ZAG Buyer *i-ti-in* "Buyer gave 5 bushels of barley, 6 quarts of oil, 10 pounds of wool, 1 TÚG.A.SU cloth, (and) 1 *ḫalaʾum* cloth as the NÍG.KI.GAR of the house; 120 quarts of barley, 1 quart of oil, 1 pound of wool, (and) 1 copper GIŠ.DU.DA, as the Ì.ZAG."

As proposed already by Sollberger, *JCS* 10 (1956) p. 15, the term Ì.ZAG seems to be connected with the ì . . . ag ritual, known from nos. 14 and 15 and the Pre-Sargonic kudurrus and sale documents from Lagash (see section 7.12.5.2). This ritual involved the spreading or pouring of oil at the conclusion of sale transaction, and was performed either by the herald or the seller. Accordingly, Ì.ZAG appears to signify the payments given to the sellers in connection with the above ritual, most probably, as their reward for performing this ritual.

7.5.7. Additional Payments without Description

In addition to the APs designated by the terms that were discussed above, kudurrus and sale documents also list commodities which are not labeled by any term. Such commodities are regularly attested in the Fara sale documents; they are given to the sellers, secondary sellers, and officials, among whom we find um-mi(-a) lú-é-éš-gar, nigir-sila, gal-nigir, dub-sar(-gán), ENGAR.UŠ, sag-du$_5$, and GU.SUR.NUN. The commodities given to the sellers are not attested only in three texts (nos. 101, 125, and 128); they are not preserved in three instances (nos. 118, 120, and 135). The secondary sellers receive commodities in twenty-five texts (nos. 102, 104, 106, 107, 108, 112 [= 113c], 113a, 113b, 114, 116, 117, 119, 121, 122, 123, 124, 125, 127, 127a, 129, 130, 131, 132, 134, and 135), and the officials, in thirty-three texts (nos. 100, 102, 103, 104, 105, 106, 107, 108, 109, 110, 111, 112 [= 113c], 113a, 113b, 114, 115, 116, 117, 118, 119, 122, 123, 124, 125, 126, 127, 127a, 130, 131, 132, 133, 135, and 136). For the amounts and types of the commodities given in the Fara sale documents, see pls. 123–128.

In the Pre-Sargonic texts from Lagash, the commodities are given to the secondary sellers, witnesses, and officials (nos. 137, 140, and 141), to the secondary sellers and official (no. 139), or to the secondary sellers only (nos. 138, 143, 147, 148, and 150). For the amounts and types of the commodities, see pls. 134–135.

The commodities are also listed in several Sargonic texts. They are given to the secondary sellers (nos. 41 obv. vii 6′–11′; 164, 165, 177, and 227) and officials (nos. 227, 237, and 240). For the amounts and types of the commodities, see the respective plates.

7.5.8. Concluding Remarks

In summary of the preceding discussion, the following facts stand out clear. APs are a regular component of the pre-Ur III sales of houses, fields, and orchards; with the exception of a few isolated instances, they are not attested in the sales of persons. The commodities given as APs are usually designated by specific terms, but can also be listed without any description. Among the terms for APs, níg-dirig, iš-gán and MUNSUB(.AN).TAR are found exclusively in the texts written in Sumerian, whereas NÍG.KI.GAR, NÍG.DÚR.GAR, and *iškinū* are attested only in Akkadian texts. The term níg-ba is used both in Sumerian and Akkadian texts. As far as the temporal distribution of these terms is concerned, níg-dirig and MUNSUB(.AN).TAR appear only in the Fara period, iš-gán, in the Fara and Sargonic periods, níg-ba and NÍG.KI.GAR, throughout the Fara-Sargonic periods, NÍG.DÚR.GAR, only in the Pre-Sargonic period, and *iškinū* and Ì.ZAG only in the Sargonic period. With the exception of níg-ba, none of these terms continues to be used beyond the end of the Sargonic period. According to the evidence provided by the texts, the recipients of APs can be sellers, secondary sellers, witnesses, and officials.

7.6. *Sellers*

7.6.1. Introductory Remarks

This section is primarily concerned with the terms for sellers. As already noted under 1.8, in the periods earlier than Ur III, two types of sellers can be distinguished: 1) primary sellers, who receive both the price and gifts (= additional payments), and 2) secondary sellers, who receive gifts only. Primary and secondary sellers are (usually) related to each other in a larger kinship grouping.

Throughout the Fara and Pre-Sargonic periods, both the kudurrus and sale documents differentiate between the two types of sellers fairly consistently. Secondary sellers become rare in the Sargonic period and disappear completely in Ur III times.

The terms used to identify primary sellers are the same as those for sellers in general. In contrast, secondary sellers are described by several special terms. It must be noted, though, that in most cases secondary sellers do not bear any designation.

There are also instances where secondary sellers are listed together with witnesses and described as lú-ki-inim-ma(-me) "witnesses." In those cases, secondary sellers may also be designated as "Primary Witnesses" (see section 7.9.4).

For the number and social status of sellers, see section 1.8.

7.6.2. Primary Sellers

The only texts which consistently employ special terms for sellers are the Fara sale documents. The usage of such designations in the Pre-Sargonic and Sargonic texts is much less frequent, while the sale documents of Ur III date do not know them at all.

The standard Sumerian term for "seller" is lú-šám-kú or lú-níg-šám-kú "man who received (lit.: 'ate') the price." The form lú-šám-kú is primarily used in the Fara sale documents. The other spelling, lú-níg-šám-kú, which is first attested in the Fara text no. 125, replaces lú-šám-kú in the Pre-Sargonic and Sargonic periods. In the Fara texts (with the exception on no. 125), the form lú-šám-kú stands both for singular and plural subjects. In the later documents, the plural is expressed by the suffix -me. The forms of lú(-níg)-šám-kú attested in our corpus are as follows:

lú-šám-kú: nos. 32, 100, 101, 102, 103, 104, 105, 106, 107, 108, 109, 110, 111, 112 (= 113c), 113, 113a, 113b, 114, 115, 116, 117, 119, 121, 122, 123, 124, 126, 127, 127a, 127b, 130, 131, 132, 133, 134, 136, and 171
lú-šám-kú-àm: no. 175
lú-níg-šám-kú: App. to no. 32
lú-níg-šám-kú-me: no. 125
lú-níg-ŠÁM+A-kú-àm: nos. 178, 186, and 187
lú-níg-[ŠÁM+ÀM-k]ú-àm: no. 184
lú-níg-ŠÁM+A-kú-a-me: no. 179
lú-níg-ŠÁM+A-kú《-àm》-me: no. 188

In the Sargonic texts written in Akkadian, the sellers are described by the use of the active participles of *maḫārum* "to receive" and *akalūm*, also meaning "to receive" (lit.: "to eat, to consume"):

ma-ḫi-ru KUG.BABBAR "recipients of the silver (i.e., the price)": no. 41
ma-ḫi-ir-da KUG.BABBAR "recipients (fem. dual) of the silver": no. 227
KÚ KUG.BABBAR "recipients of the silver": no. 40
a-ki-il-d[*a*] *iš-ki-n*[*e*] "recipients (fem. dual) of the additional payment": no. 227

In addition, the Pre-Sargonic texts dealing with the sale of fields designate the seller as lugal gán(-kam) "lord (= owner) of the field" (nos. 22 and 23), or, in plural, as lugal-gán-me (nos. 22, 23, and 145). In one of the Pre-Sargonic sales of houses from Lagash (no. 139), the respective term is lugal [é] "lord of the [house]." The Akkadian equivalent of lugal gán(-kam) is *be-lu* GÁN "lord of the field," which appears in no. 40. The seller is designated as lugal "owner" also in the Ur III sale documents nos. 276 and 277.

Another form for "owner of the field" is probably LÚ GÁN, attested in nos. 25 iii 10 and 34 ii 9.

Finally, we should mention here the obscure [x]-⌜x⌝ sag-gá-me "they are the [. . .] of the 'head,'" which describes the sellers in the Sargonic sale document no. 219, involving the sale of a person.

7.6.3. Secondary Sellers

The ancient kudurrus and sale documents use several terms for secondary sellers (henceforth abbreviated as SSs). In most instances, however, SSs are not designated by any specific terms. The terms attested are:

šeš-gán "'brothers' of the field": no. 15 xii, Fara
LÚ.ŠEŠ.EN "'brother-lords' (of the field)": no. 156a, Pre-Sargonic
dumu-gán-me "'sons' of the field": nos. 22, 23, and 144, Pre-Sargonic
ŠEŠ *be-lu* GÁN "'brother-lords' of the field": no. 40

In the following two sections, we shall discuss all the occurrences of SSs in the kudurrus and sale documents, including those in which SSs do not bear any description.

7.6.3.1. Fara Period

SSs are listed in eight Fara house sales (nos. 102, 104, 106, 107, 108, 112 [= 113c], 113a, and 113b) and in seventeen texts dealing with the sale of fields (nos. 114, 116, 117, 119, 121, 122, 123, 124, 126, 127, 127a, 129, 130, 131, 132, 134, and 135). No description is applied to SSs in any of these texts. The gifts presented to SSs do not have any label; they consist of commodities, usually the quantities of ninda "bread," gug "cake," tu_7 "soup," and NIGÍN+ḪA.A (meaning unknown). They occasionally also include še "barley" (nos. 106, 113a, 113b, 114, 122, 123, 124, 125, 127a, 130, 131, and 132), síg "wool" (nos. 121, 122, and 127), TÚG.ME(.A).GÁL cloth (nos. 117 and 118), and ì "oil" (no. 112). In three cases (nos. 123 [first SS], 129, and 134), gifts consist exclusively of barley.

One of the transactions recorded in the Baltimore Stone (no. 15 xii 7–15) lists three persons, among them the seller's son, who are described as šeš-gán ki-ba ì-durun-durun "'brothers' of the field who sat at this place (i.e., the place where the transaction took place)." Even though these individuals do not receive any gifts, they can assuredly be interpreted as SSs. In the Chicago and Baltimore Stones (nos. 14 and 15), SSs could also be sought among the persons designated as lú-ki-inim-ma "witnesses," depending on whether the gifts listed in these two kudurrus were meant for the sellers or the lú-ki-inim-ma (see the discussion of the operative sections of nos. 14 and 15 in section 6.2). Assuming that the latter was the case, the lú-ki-inim-ma would have to be interpreted as SSs (or Primary Witnesses).

7.6.3.2. Pre-Sargonic Period

The Pre-Sargonic document no. 156a, which deals with the sale of two fields and is written in Akkadian, contains a list of twenty-two personal names, each preceded by a personal wedge. The first two persons are described as LÚ.ŠEŠ.EN "'brother-lords' (of the field)," whereas the following twenty individuals lack any designation. In spite of the fact that the two LÚ.ŠEŠ.EN do not receive gifts, they can be identified as SSs, and the remaining persons, as witnesses.

Two Pre-Sargonic kudurrus (nos. 22 and 23) and one sale document from Lagash (no. 144) list several SSs, who are identified as dumu-gán-me "'sons' of the field" and receive additional payments, labeled as níg-ba "gift." In one of the transactions recorded in no. 23 (rev. ix–obv. xi), the dumu-gán-me are followed by another group of people, who likewise receive additional payments, but are not described by any term. The additional payments (níg-ba) given to the SSs in these documents include ninda-še "barley-bread," ninda-kalag (a type of bread), ku_6-dar-ra "dried fish," tu_7 "soup," udu "sheep," še-sa "roasted barley," and ga-raš^{SAR} "leek."

SSs appear, without any designation, in nine other sale documents from Lagash (nos. 137, 138, 139, 140, 141, 143, 147, 148, and 150). In nos. 137 and 141, the SSs are included in the same group as the witnesses, both of whom receive additional payments and are called lú-ki-inim-ma-bi-me "witnesses." In two instances, SSs are relatives of the seller: in no. 140, six out of the nine SSs are the seller's children, and in no. 150, the only SS listed there is the seller's daughter. The number of SSs appearing in the above texts and the commodities they receive are as follows:

- no. 137: two SSs, receiving 2(gur) še gur-2-UL, 2 ma-na síg, 20 ninda-KU-KU-na, 3 ninda-silà, ½ dug kas, and 2 m[a-na s]íg, 20 ninda, 3(silà) tu_7, ½ dug kas, respectively
- no. 138: one SS, receiving [. . .], 1 ^{TÚG}níg-lám-gíd-da
- no. 139: three(?) SSs, each receiving 5 ninda, 1 silà tu_7
- no. 140: nine SSs, receiving varying quantities of še, ninda, ninda-silà, and síg
- no. 141: six SSs, receiving varying quantities of síg, bar-si, ninda, tu_7, and ku_6-dar-ra; the first SS also receives one níg-sag-lal-SAL
- no. 143: two SSs, each receiving 10 ninda, 1 silà tu_7, 1 silà ì(-šáḫ)
- no. 147: [x] + three SSs, receiving varying quantities of ninda
- no. 148: seventeen + [x] SSs, receiving varying quantities of ninda and tu_7
- no. 150: one SS, receiving 3 SUR, 2 ninda-silà

The first of the two transactions recorded in the Adab kudurru no. 32, which also dates to the Pre-Sargonic period, contains a list of nine persons, called lú-ki-inim-ma "witnesses," four of whom receive one SU.A.TÚG cloth each, and the remaining five, one pound of wool each. They are followed by twenty-two(?) individuals, not receiving gifts, who are likewise designated as lú-ki-inim-ma. The gifts given to the first group of lú-ki-inim-ma, plus the gifts received by the primary sellers, are labeled in the total as níg-ba dumu PN "gift of the 'sons' of PN." The two groups of persons can be interpreted as the SSs (or Primary Witnesses) and witnesses, respectively.

7.6.3.3. Sargonic Period

There are only few occurrences of SSs in the Sargonic kudurrus and sale documents. The transactions A_1 and D of the Manishtushu Obelisk (no. 40) list several SSs, who are called ŠEŠ *be-lu* GÁN "'brother-lords' of the field." These persons do not receive any gifts. SSs are also attested, without any designation, in the following texts:

- no. 41 obv. vii 6′–11′: two SSs (listed at the beginning of the list of witnesses), each receiving 1 MA.NA SÍG
- no. 164: one SS, receiving 1 gín kug
- no. 165: one SS (brother of the seller), receiving [. . .]
- no. 177: one SS, receiving 2 gín kug
- no. 227: one SS, receiving 1 BA.A[N], 1 MA.N[A] SÍG

7.7. *Buyers*

This section discusses the terms for buyers, attested in ancient kudurrus and sale documents. The questions pertaining to the number and social status of buyers are discussed in section 1.8.

As in the case of the terms for sellers (7.6), the only group of texts which consistently use special designations for buyers are the Fara sale documents. Buyers are occasionally identified by the use of such terms also in the Pre-Sargonic and Sargonic texts, but not in the Ur III material.

The terms employed are 1) lú-šám-ag or lú-níg-šám-ag "man who 'made' the price" and 2) lú-Object of Sale-šám(-a) "man who bought the Object of Sale." Both terms are attested throughout the Fara-Sargonic periods. With the exception of the Fara text no. 127a, which uses lú-šám-kú for two buyers, the plurality of the subject is regularly expressed by the suffix -me. The following forms of these two terms are attested:

1) lú(-níg)-šám-ag "man who 'made' the price"

   - lú-šám-ag: nos. 128, 134, 171, 174, and 176
   - lú-šám-ag-àm "(PN) is the man who 'made' the price": nos. 175 and 177
   - lú-níg-šám-ag: App. to no. 32 and no. 207
   - lú-níg-ŠÁM+A-ag-àm: nos. 178, 179, 186, 187, and 188
   - lú-[níg-ŠÁM+ÀM-ag-àm]: no. 184

2) lú-Object of Sale-šám(-a) "man who bought the Object of Sale"

   - lú-é-šám "man who bought the house": nos. 100, 101, 103, 104, 105, 106, 107, 108, 109, 110, 111, 112 (= 113c), 113, 113a, and 113b
   - lú-gán-šám "man who bought the field": nos. 114, 115, 116, 117, 118, 119, 120, 122, 123, 124, 126, 127, 127a, 127b, 130, 131, 132, 133, and 136
   - lú-gán-šám-me "men who bought the field": no. 125
   - sag-šám-a "(the one) who bought the 'head'": no. 214

lú-sag-šám-àm "(PN) is the man who bought the 'head'": no. 215
[lú-sag]-šám: no. 217

7.8. *Terms for Buying and Selling*

7.8.1. Introductory Remarks

In this section, we list all the verbal forms found in the kudurrus and sale documents which express either 1) the payment/receipt of the price and/or the additional payment(s) or 2) the purchase/sale of the object of sale. The verbs are cited together with the phrases in which they occur. The following abbreviations are used:

A = Amount
AP = Additional Payment
B = Buyer
OS = Object of Sale
P = Price
S = Seller
Ss = Sellers

For the use of verbs in the operative sections, see section 6.2.

7.8.2. Verbs Expressing the Payment/Receipt of the Price and/or the Additional Payment(s)

7.8.2.1. lal, *šaqālum* "to weigh out"

OS A S(s) an-na-lal: nos. 14 and 15
OS A S an-šè-lal: no. 14 iii 16
A (B to S) e-šè-lal: no. 146
níg-šám-ma-ni A S-ra B e-na-lal: nos. 152 and 153
B ì-na-lal (P): nos. 178 and 179
kug-pi B an-ši-lal: no. 182a H
B ì-ne-lal (P to Ss): nos. 184, 185, and 188
A níg-šám OS B ì-ši-lal: nos. 196, 197, 198, 199, 200, 202, and 203
A níg-šám OS-kam B-e S-[ra] ì-na-lal: no. 204
A B níg-šám OS Ss ì-ne-lal: no. 204
OS [níg-š]á[m-bi] A B Ss an-ne-lal: no. 206
OS níg-šám-pi A S-ra B in-na-lal: no. 210
A níg-šám OS S B-e in-na-lal: no. 210
B íb-ši-lal (P): no. 218
B in-lal (P): no. 219
B ⌜ì-lal⌝ (P): no. 222
A (B) ì-na-lal: no. 225
B_1 *ù* B_2 Ì.LAL (P): no. 234
OS níg-šám-ma-ni A S B in-na-lal: nos. 349, 350, 352, and 353
OS níg-šám-ma-ni B S ì-[n]a-[lal]: no. 351
ŠÁM+ÀM-til-la-ni-šè A B-e S-ra in-na-lal: no. 360
A níg-šám-ma-ni-šè B-e S in-na-lal: no. 361
A ŠÁM-*su* B Ì.LAL *a-na* S: no. 362
A B ì-na-lal: no. 363
OS níg-ŠÁM+ÀM-ma-ni-šè A (B to S) ba-ši-lal: no. 364
A ŠÁM+ÀM-til-la-ni-šè (B to Ss) in-ne-lal: no. 365
OS šám-bi A (B to S) in-na-lal: no. 366
šám-ma-ni A (B to S) in-n[a?-lal?]: no. 367
[B P to Ss in-ne-lal?]: no. 369
[A *a*]-*na* ŠÁM OS of S B *da-áš-ku-ul*: no. 229

7.8.2.2. sum, *nadānum* "to give"

OS A S(s) an-na-sum: nos. 14 and 15
A (P) an-na-sum: no. 128
(P) an-na-sum B: no. 129
[B P to Ss e-ne-sum?]: no. 145
A níg-sám OS-kam B-e S e-na-sum: no. 149
níg-šám-ma-ni-šè A (B to S) e-na-sum: no. 151
OS níg-⌜šám-bi⌝ A B ì-n[a?-sum?]: no. 170
B [ì-na]-sum (P): no. 173
A níg-šám OS-šè B-e S-ra ì-na-sum: no. 180
[B P ì-na-sum?]: no. 181
OS [níg-šám]-pi A S-kam B ma-ši-sum?: no. 182a E
OS níg-šám-pi A B ì-na-su[m]: no. 182a U
níg-šám OS-kam B-e ì-ši-sum: no. 189
OS níg-šám-b[i] A B Ss ì-ne-sum: no. 204
A níg-šám OS-kam B S-ra an-na-sum: no. 208
[A níg-šám OS]-kam S B in-na-sum: no. 210
A B níg-šám OS-šè S e-na-sum: no. 220
A níg-šám-til-la OS-kam? B S-ra in-na-sum: no. 354
A *a-na* ŠÁM OS B *a-na* S *i-ti-in*: no. 228
B *i-ti-in* (P): no. 230
[B P *i-ti-in*?]: no. 232

7.8.2.3. šu . . . si "to fill hands (with price/silver)"

A níg-šám OS Ss B šu-ne-ne-a ab-si: nos. 157, 158, 159, 161, and 162
A níg-ŠÁM+A/ÀM OS-kam/šè Ss šu-ne-ne ab-si: nos. 184, 185, 186, 187, and 188
(A) S šu-na ab-si: no. 212
A šám OS S šu-na bi-si: no. 214
A [(níg-)šám] OS-kam Ss kug-bi šu-ne-ne ab-si: no. 215
A níg-šám OS-kam Ss B kug-bi šu-ne-ne ab-si: no. 216
A [(níg-)šá]m OS S šu-na ab-si: no. 217

7.8.2.4. ba "to give, to allot"

níg-šám-bi A níg-ba-bi A S B e-na-ba: no. 143

7.8.2.5. ág "to measure out (barley)"

še-pi-ta B ⌜ì⌝-na-⌜ág⌝?: no. 182
še-pi B an-na-ág: no. 182a D
A B S-ra an-na-ág níg-šám OS-kam: no. 205
A níg-šám OS-kam S B in-na-ág: no. 210

7.8.2.6. gar "to place"

4 PNs (= Buyers?) šám-ni ì-gar: no. 192

7.8.2.7. šu . . . ti, *maḫārum* "to receive"

A níg-šám OS-kam (S) šu-ba-ti: nos. 22 and 23
AP (S) níg-ba-šè šu-ba-ti: nos. 22 and 23
Ss lú-l-šè AP šu-ba-ti: nos. 22 and 23

OS ŠÁM A NÍG.KI.GAR A Ss ŠU.BA.TI: no. 36
A ŠE.NI.KID.NI S? ŠU.BA.TI: no. 37 R. E.
A S ti-la-ni šu-ba-ti: no. 137
[n]íg-[šám-bi] A níg-šám OS-kam S š[u-ba-ti]: no. 138
níg-šám-bi A (S) šu-ba-ti níg-ba-bi A Ss šu-ba-ti-éš: no. 139
níg-šám-bi A níg-ba-bi A S šu-ba-ti: no. 140
níg-šám-bi A níg-šám OS-kam A S níg-ba-šè šu-ba-ti: no. 141
níg-šám-bi A níg-ba-bi A S-e šu-ba-ti: no. 142
A níg-šám OS-kam (S) šu-ba-ti A [níg-ba-še] S šu-ba-ti: no. 144
níg-šam-bi A Ss [šu-ba-ti] A níg-ba-šè Ss šu-ba-ti: no. 145
A níg-šám-ma-ni S šu-ba-ti: no. 150
A [níg-šám] OS S B [šu]-ba-t[i]: no. 160
A níg-šám OS-kam S šu-ba-ti: no. 164
OS níg-šám-bi A S [šu-ba-t]i: no. 165
A S šu-ba-ti níg-šám OS-⸢šè⸣ [šu-b]a-ti: no. 168
OS [n]íg-šám-pi A A iš-gán še-kam A iš-gán síg-kam [A] [ní]g-ba-pi A níg-šám DU$_6$-kam S šu-ba-t[i]: no. 169
A níg-šám OS-kam S šu-ba-ti: nos. 171 and 172
OS níg-šám-bi A S [šu-b]a-ti: no. 173
A níg-šám OS-šè S šu-ba-t[i]: no. 174
OS níg-šám-bi A S šu-ba-ti: no. 175
OS níg-šám-pi A Ss šu-ba-ti: no. 176
OS níg-šám-bi A S šu-ba-ti: no. 177
OS níg-ŠÁM+A-bi A S šu-ba-ti: nos. 178 and 179
OS níg-ŠÁM+A-bi A Ss šu-ba-ti-[é]š: no. 179
OS níg-šám-pi A S šu-ba-ti: nos. 181 and 182a *passim*
A níg-šám OS[(-kam)] S ⸢šu⸣-ba-ti: no. 183
A Ss [š]u-ba-ti: no. 190
A S šu-ba-ti: no. 191
S [š]u-ba-ti (P): no. 195
S šu-ba-ti (P): no. 196
S [šu-ba-t]i (P): no. 197
S šu-ba-[ti] (P): no. 198
S kug-bi šu-[ba-ti]: no. 199
S šu-ba-t[i] (P): no. 200
S šu-ba-ti (P): nos. 202, 203, and 207
S (from) B (P) šu-b[a]-ti: no. 209
S [P šu-ba-ti?]: no. 218
OS A níg-šám-bi-šè S šu-ba-ti: no. 222
A (P) OS-kam Ss šu-ba-ti: no. 223
A [(níg-)ŠÁM]+ÀM OS-šè ki B-ta S šu-ba-ti: no. 355
A níg-šám OS-šè ki B-ta S šu-ba-ti: no. 356
A šám-til-a OS-šè ki B-ta S šu-ba-ti: no. 357
A níg-ŠÁM+ÀM-til-la OS-ka ki B-ta S [šu]-⸢ba⸣-an-ti: no. 358
A níg-ŠÁM+ÀM OS-šè ki B-ta S šu-ba-an-ti: no. 359
OS NÍG.ŠÁM-*su* A NÍG.KI.GAR A Ss *ma-ḫi-ru* [KUG.B]ABBAR: no. 41 obv. i
KUG.BABBAR NÍG.ŠÁM OS S *im-ḫur*: no. 41 obv. iii
OS NÍG.[ŠÁM-*su*] A NÍG.KI.GAR A S *im-ḫur*⟨⟨*-ra*⟩⟩: no. 41 obv. vi
OS NÍG.ŠÁM-*su* A NÍG.KI.GAR A S *im-ḫur*: no. 41 obv. vi, rev. iv, vi
[OS NÍG.ŠÁM-*su* A NÍG.KI.GAR] A Ss *im-ḫu*(*r*)-*ru*: no. 41 rev. iii
[OS] NÍG.Š[ÁM-*su*] A NÍ[G.KI.GAR] A S *im-ḫur*: no. 41 rev. v
[OS NÍG.ŠÁM-*su* A NÍG.KI].GAR A S *im-ḫur*: no. 4 rev. viii
[OS NÍG.ŠÁM A NÍG].⸢KI.GAR⸣ A Ss *im-ḫu*(*r*)-*ru*: no. 41 L.E.
[OS ŠÁM-*su* A *iš-ki-nu-su* A] S *im-ḫur*: no. 42
[OS ŠÁM-*su* A *iš-ki-nu-su* A Ss *im-ḫu*]-*ru*: no. 42
⸢OS⸣ [ŠÁ]M-*su* A *iš-ki-nu-*[*su*] A Ss [*im-ḫu-ru*]?: no. 43 i
[OS ŠÁM-*su*] A *iš-ki-n*[*u-su* A 2 Ss *im-ḫu-ra*]: no. 43 i–ii
[. . .] ⸢Ss⸣ *im-ḫu-ru*: no. 43 ii–iii
OS *šu* PN (P) A *iš-ki-nu-su* A [S *im-ḫur*]: no. 43 iii–iv
⸢OS⸣ [ŠÁM]-*su* A [*iš-ki*⸣-*nu-su* ⸢A 2 Ss⸣ [*im-ḫu-ra*]: no. 43 iv
⸢OS⸣ ŠÁM-[*su*] A *iš-ki-nu-su* A [2 Ss] *im-ḫ*[*u-ra*]: no. 43 iv–v
⸢OS⸣ ŠÁM-[*su*] A *iš-ki-nu-su* A [S] *im-ḫur*: no. 43 v
OS ŠÁM-*su* A *iš-ki-nu-su* A [S *im-ḫur*]: no. 43 v–vi
[OS ŠÁM-*su* A *iš-ki-nu-su*] A ⸢2 Ss⸣ *im-ḫu-r*[*a*]: no. 43 vi
OS ŠÁM-⸢*su*⸣ A [. . . *im-ḫu-ru*]: no. 43 vi–vii
[OS] *šu* PN ŠÁM-*su* A *iš-ki-nu-su* A ⸢2 Ss⸣ [*im-ḫu-ra*]: no. 43 vii
[OS . . .] ⸢2 Ss⸣ [*i*]*m-ḫu-ra*: no. 43 vii–viii
OS ŠÁM-*su* A [*iš-ki-nu-su* A S *im-ḫur*]: no. 43 viii
[OS ŠÁM-*su* A *iš-ki-nu-su*] A 2 Ss *i*[*m-ḫu-ra*]: no. 43 viii–ix
[OS . . . *im-ḫur*]: no 43 ix
[OS ŠÁM-*su* A *iš-ki-nu-su*] A ⸢Ss⸣ [*im-ḫu-ru*]: no. 43 ix–x
[. . . *im-ḫ*]*u-ra*: no. 44c
[. . .] ⸢x⸣ *im-ḫu-ra*: no. 44e
[. . .] A S *im-*[*ḫur*]: no. 44e
[. . .] A S *dam-ḫur*: no. 44h
[. . .] A S *im-ḫur*: no. 44k
OS ŠÁM-*su* A S [*im-ḫu*]*r*: no. 44k
[. . .] ⸢Ss⸣ *im-ḫu-ru*: no. 50
A *a-na* NÍG.ŠÁM OS S *im-ḫur*: no. 230
A [*a-n*]*a* ŠÁM OS S [*i*]*š-dè* B [*im*]-*ḫur*: no. 231
A *a-na* ŠÁM OS S *im-ḫur*: no. 232
A *a-na* ŠÁM OS 2 Ss [*i*]*m-ḫu-ra*: no. 233
A *a-na* ŠÁM-*me* OS Ss *im-ḫu-ru*: no. 234
A *a-na* NÍG.ŠÁM OS S *iš-dè* B *im-ḫur*: no. 236

7.8.2.8. kú, *akālum* "to consume, to receive"

OS A S an-kú: no. 15 *passim*
OS ŠÁM A S KA.GAR: no. 16
A OS S ŠÁM GÁN KÚ: no. 34
A S KÚ: no. 156a

7.8.2.9. túm "to carry away, to bring"

OS A Ss an-na-túm: no. 14 viii
OS A Ss an?-ne-túm?: no. 14 xvi
A níg-šám OS-šè S ba-túm: no. 154
OS A níg-šám-ma⟨-ni⟩-šè A S$_1$ ba-túm A S$_2$ ba-túm A S$_3$ ba-túm: no. 155

A S ba-túm šám-˹x˺-am$_6$: no. 177
OS níg-šám-pi A S ba-ší-túm: no. 182a N
OS níg-šám-pi A B ì-na-túm: no. 182a I
OS A B ì-na-túm: no. 182 J
A S$_1$? ba-túm A S$_2$? ba-túm A S$_3$? ba-túm: no. 189
A níg-šám OS S ba-túm: no. 193
A S$_1$? ba-túm A S$_2$? ba-túm A S$_3$? ba-túm: no. 194
OS níg-šá[m]-pi A S? ba-túm: no. 210

7.8.2.10. laḫ$_4$ "to carry away"

A (= 5 sheep) S? ba-laḫ$_4$: no. 190

7.8.2.11. è "to remove, to take away"

OS A AP Ss é-ta íb-è: no. 14 *passim*

7.8.2.12. gi$_4$ "to . . ."

OS A Ss an-gi$_4$: no. 14 xviii

7.8.3. Verbs Expressing the Purchase/Sale of the Object of Sale

7.8.3.1. šám, *šaʾāmum* "to buy"

OS B e-šè-šám: no. 21
OS Ss lugal gán-šè B e-ne-šè-šám: nos. 22 and 23
[OS S lugal gán-šè B-e e-šè]-sám: no. 23 obv. iii
OS B Ì.ŠÁM: no. 40
OS B-e [S-šè] e-šè-šám: no. 137
OB B ˹S˺-šè e-šè-šám: no. 138
OS ˹Ss˺ lugal [é-šè] B e-ne-šè-šám: no. 139
OS S-šè B-e e-šè-šám: nos. 140, 143, 144, and 150
OS [S-šè B]-e e-šè-šám: no. 141
OS B S-šè e-šè-šám: no. 142
OS B S e-šè-šám: no. 146
B-e S-šè OS e-šè-šám: no. 151
OS S-šè B e-šè-šám: nos. 152 and 153
B (OS) al-šám: no. 182a B
níg-šám OS-kam B an-šám: no. 190
OS B-e S-šè ì-ne-ši-šám: no. 201
OS S-šè B ì-ši-šám: no. 213
OS S-šè B-e ì-šè-šám: no. 225
A níg-šám OS S-šè B-e e-šè-šám: no. 226
OS kug-bi A S-šè B [i]n-ši-šám: no. 247
OS ˹šám˺ A ki S[(-ta)] B in-ša$_6$: no. 247a
OS níg-šám-bi A-šè B-e Ss [i]n-ne-ši-šám: no. 248
OS kug-bi A B-e S-˹šè˺ in-ši-šám(wr. GAZ): no. 249
OS [níg]-ŠÁM+ÀM-bi A Ss-ra B-e [i]n-ne-ši-ŠÁM+A: no. 250
OS A-šè Ss B in-ne-ši-in-šám: no. 251
OS níg-ŠÁM+ÀM-bi A B Ss-˹šè˺? in-ne-ši-ŠÁM+˹A˺: no. 252
OS níg-šám-bi A[(-šè)] B-e Ss in-˹ne˺-ši-šám: no. 253
OS kug-bi A S-eš B-e in-ši-šám: no. 255
OS A-šè S-šè B-e in-ši-šám: no. 256
OS níg-šám-bi A-šè S[(-šè)] B [in-ši-šám?]: no. 257
OS kug-babbar níg-šám-bi A ki S B in-šám: no. 258
OS níg-ŠÁM+ÀM-til-la-bi A-šè B-e S in-ši-š[ám]: no. 259
OS A-šè S-šè Bs in-ši-šám-áš: no. 260
OS kug-bi A B S-a ì-šám: no. 261
OS [níg-šám-b]i? A-šè S-ra in-ne-ši-šám: no. 262
OS sám-bi A-šè B Ss in-ši-šám: no. 263
OS A-šè S-šè B-e in-ši-šám: no. 264
OS níg-šám-bi A B-e Ss in-ne-ši-šá[m]: no. 265
OS níg-ŠÁM+ÀM-bi A-šè S-r[a] B in-ši-šám: no. 266
OS níg-ŠÁM+ÀM-bi A S-ra B in-ši-šám: no 267
OS kug-bi A ki S-ta B in-ši-šám: no. 268
OS níg-ŠÁM+A-bi A Ss B-e in-ne-ši-sà: no. 269
OS kug A-˹šè˺ B S-šè in-ši-ŠÁM+A: no. 270
OS níg-ŠÁM+À[M-ma-ni] A S B [in-š]i-šám!: no. 271
OS níg-ŠÁM+A-ma-ni A S-ra B-e in-ši-ŠÁM+A: no. 272
OS níg-šá[m-ma-ni] A [S] B in-[si-šám]: no. 273
OS kug-bi A S-ka B-e ì-ši-šám: no. 274
[OS níg-šám-ma-n]i A-šè B S-ra [i]n-ši-šám: no. 275
OS níg-ŠÁM+ÀM-bi A S lugal-a-ni-ir B-e in-ši-šám: no. 276
OS A-šè S lugal-a-ni-šè B in-ši-šám: no. 277
OS níg-šám-ma-ni A-šè B-e S-ka in-ši-šám: no. 278
OS níg-šám-ma-ka-ne-ne A-àm S B in-ši-šám: no. 279
OS A-šè B S-ra [i]n-ši-in-šám: no. 280
OS A-šè B Ss-šè ba-an-ši-šám: no. 281
OS níg-šám A B S in-ši-šám: no. 282
OS níg-šám-ma-ni A ki S-ta B in-ši-šám: no. 283
OS A-šè B-e S-ka in-ši-šám: no. 284
OS ˹níg˺-šám-bi A [S B in-ši-šám]: no. 285
OS kug šám-bi A ki S-ta B in-ši-šám: no. 286
OS A ŠÁM+ÀM-t[il-la-ni(-šè)] S B in-ši-[šám]: no. 287
OS kug-babbar níg-šám-ma-ga-ni A ki S-ta B in-ši-šám: no. 288
OS šám-bi kug A ki S$_1$-ta ù S$_2$ B in-ši-šám: no. 289
OS níg-šám-ni A[(-šè)] S-r[a] B in-ši-šám: no. 290
OS [ku]g-babbar šám-ma-ni A ki S-ta B in-ši-šám: no. 291
OS [níg-šám-ma]-ni A-šè B [S] in-ši-šám: no. 292
OS níg-ŠÁM+ÀM-ma-ni A-˹šè˺ [S B in-ši-šám]: no. 293
OS A níg-ŠÁM+ÀM-til-a-ni-šè B S-ra in-ši-šám: no. 294
OS níg-šám-ma-ne-ne A-šè S-ra B-e in-ši-šám: no. 295
OS kug A-šè S-šè B in-ši-šám: no. 296
OS [ní]g-šám-bi A [k]i S-ta B in-ši-šám: no. 297
OS níg-šám-ma-ni A B S-ra in-ši-šám: no. 298
OS A-šè S-šè B-e in-ši-šám: no. 299
OS [ní]g-šám-ma-ga-ni A ki S-ta B-e in-ši-šám: no. 300
OS níg-ŠÁM(wr. ÁG)+ÀM-e A B Ss in-ši-šám (wr. ÁG): no. 301
OS kug-babbar-bi A ki S-ta B-e in-ši-in-sà: no. 302
OS kug-níg-šám(wr. ÁG)-ma-ni A Ss B in-ne-ši-sà: no. 303
OS níg-šám-bi A ki Ss-ta B [i]n-šám: no. 304
OS níg-šám-a-ni A B-e S-ra in-ši-šám: no. 305
OS níg-ŠAM+ÀM-ma-ni A S ama-ni-ir B-e in-ši-šám: no. 306
OS níg-šám-ma-ni A S-ra B in-ši-šám: no. 307
OS níg-šám-ni [A] S[(-ra)] B in-ši-[šám]: no. 308
OS [na]m-gemé-[šè] B [i]n-šám: no. 309

OS [níg-šám]-ma-ni A S[(-ra)] B-⸢e⸣ [in-ši-šám]: no. 310
OS šám-ma-ni A S B-e in-ši-šám: no. 311
OS A šám-til-la-bi-šè S B in-ši-in-sà: no. 312
OS níg-šám A S-ra B in-ši-šám: no. 314
OS A-šè S B-e in-ši-šám: no. 315
OS níg-ŠÁM+ÀM-bi A S-ra B-e in-ši-šám: no. 316
OS kug-babbar šám-bi A ki S-ta B in-ši-šám: no. 317
OS A-šè B-e S-šè in-ši-šám: no. 318
OS níg-ŠÁM+ÀM-bi A B-e Ss in-ne-[ši-šám]: no. 319
OS níg-šám-bi A [S B in-ši-šám]: no. 320
OS [níg-ŠÁM+À]M-bi A-šè B-e S-ka [in-ši]-šám: no. 321
OS níg-šám-bi A S-ra B-e in-[ši]-šám: no. 322
OS A-šè S B [i]n-si-sà: no. 323
[. . .] in-ši-ša$_6$: no. 324
[OS níg-š]ám-bi A-šè Ss B-e [in]-ne-ši-šám(wr. GAZ): no. 325
[. . . B] S-ra in-ši-šám: no. 326
[. . .] A S B-e in-ši-šám: no. 327
[. . .] A B-e S-ra in-ši-šám: no. 329
[. . .] S-ra B in-ši-šám: no. 330
OS é S-kam A-šè B in-ši-šám: no. 331
OS [gemé S]-kam A-šè [B in]-ši-šám: no. 332
OS gemé S A-šè B in-ši-šám: no. 333
OS arád S-kam A-šè B-e in-ši-šám: no. 334
OS gemé S-kam A-šè B in-ši-šám: no. 335
OS [ar]ád S-kam A-šè B in-ši-šám: no. 336
OS dumu-sag-ri[g$_x$] S-[kam] A-šè B in-ši-š[ám]: no. 337
OS gemé S-kam A-šè B in-ši-šám: no. 338
OS arád S A-šè B [i]n-šám: no. 339
[. . . S-kam A-šè B in-ši-šám]: no. 340
A šám-til-la OS S-ra B-e in-ši-⸢šám⸣: no. 341
A níg-ŠÁM+ÀM-til-la OS dumu S B-e in-ši-šám: no. 342
OS S-ra B-e in-ši-šám: no. 360
OS S B in-ši-šám: no. 361
OS KI S B IN.ŠÁM: no. 362
OS ki S ad-da-ni B in-ši-šám: no. 363
(OS) S-[šè B in-ši-šám]: no. 364
OS Ss B in-ne-ši-ŠÁM+⸢A⸣: no. 365
(OS) ki S B [i]n-ši-šám: no. 366
OS S-šè B in-ši-šám: no. 367
OS ŠÁM.GAR (for NÍG.ŠÁM?) A *i-ti* S B *i-ša-am*: no. 254
OS *i-ti* S B *i-ša-am*: no. 368

7.8.3.2. sum, *nadānum* "to give (away for price), to sell"

OS S B-ra A-šè ì-na-sum: no. 224
OS A-šè Ss B-ra in-na-sum: no. 344
OS [níg]-šám-ma-ni A-šè S B-ra in-na-sum: no. 345
OS A níg-šám(wr. GAZ)-ma-ka-n[i-šè] B-ra S [i]n-na-sum: no. 346
OS níg-šám A-šè Ss B-a in-na-sum-mu-da (env.: in-ne-ši-šám): no. 347
⸢OS⸣ [A]-šè S B [in-n]a-an-sum: no. 348
[OS *a-na* ŠÁM A] ⸢S⸣ [*a-n*]*a* B *i-ti-in*: no. 239
OS *a-na* ŠÁM A *a-na* B ⸢*i*⸣-*ti-in*: no. 241
OS S *a-na*? B *i-di*[*n*$_x$]?(DÍ[M]?): no. 245
OS (= slave woman) KUG.BABBAR ŠÁM.MA.NI A *a-na* B *ga-ga-za* ⸢*a*⸣-*na* ŠÁM *i-ti-in*: no. 370

7.8.3.3. *aḫāzum* "to seize, to take into possession"

OS ŠÁM-*su-nu* A *iš-dè* Ss B *i-ḫu-uz*: no. 237
OS ŠÁM-*su-nu* A [*iš-dè* Ss B *i-ḫu-uz*?]: no. 240
OS A KI S B *ì-ḫu-uz*?: no. 343

7.8.3.4. *laqāʾum* "to take, to acquire"

A ŠÁM OS (of) S B *il-ga*: no. 238

7.8.3.5. *šadādum* "to measure out (real property in sale)"

(witnesses to the fact that) S OS *a-na* B *iš-du-da*: no. 242
OS S *a-na* B *iš-du-ud*: no. 243
OS ⟨*a-na*⟩ B OS *šu-ut* Ss *iš-du-tu*: no. 244

7.9. *Witnesses*

7.9.1. Introductory Remarks

The list of witnesses is a standard component of both the kudurrus and sale documents from the Fara period on. Due to the fact that most of the kudurrus are preserved incompletely, the presence of the list of witnesses is certain only in nos. 14, 15, 23, 28, 32, 33, 35, 38, 40, 41, and 48. The only kudurru which definitely does not have a list of witnesses is no. 20. Among the sale documents, the list of witnesses is wanting in nos. 146, 149, 152, 154, 156, 164, 166, 168, 171, 173, 180, 189, 190, 194, 204, 208, 212, 214, 226, 231, 263, 339, 346, 349, and 365.

In the kudurrus, which record multiple transactions, the list of witnesses is placed either 1) at the end of each transaction (nos. 32 and 40) or 2) following one or more transactions (nos. 14, 15, and 41) or 3) following all the transactions (nos. 23, 35, and 38)—apparently depending on whether the individual transactions that are recorded in one document were attended by the same or different witnesses. Note, however, that no. 40 does not follow this rule, as it has a list of witnesses following each of the four transactions, even though the same individuals were involved in each case. In nos. 28, 33, and 48, the relationship of the list of witnesses to the rest of the document is uncertain, due to the fragmentary state of their preservation. In the sale documents, which deal with single transactions, the list of witnesses is regularly placed at the end of the text, following the operative section and final clauses.

Throughout the Fara-Sargonic periods, the names of witnesses are regularly preceded by the cipher "1" (a semicircle), which functions as the so-called *Personenkeil*, for which see Krecher, *ZA* 63 pp. 161–65. In one Sargonic sale document (no. 217), the *Personenkeil* has the form of a vertical wedge, while in another (no. 224), a combination of igi "before" and the *Personenkeil* is used, both features being very rare before Ur III times. In the Fara, Pre-Sargonic, and Sargonic texts, the *Personenkeil* is wanting in only eleven instances (nos. 14, 15, 28, 38, 125, 129, 177, 216, 223, 243, and 244).

Although the *Personenkeil*, now shaped as a vertical wedge, is found in a considerable number of the Ur III sale documents, the more common method of marking witnesses in these texts is by the use of the construction igi . . . (-šè) "before." Some of the Ur III sale documents combine these two ways of identifying witnesses by construing the first name (or the first few names) appearing in the list with igi . . . -šè (or igi or -šè), while marking the following names with a *Personenkeil*. There are also instances where the first name is construed with igi . . . -šè or -šè alone, with the following names being unmarked. A unique way of identifying witnesses is found in no. 255, where the name of each witness is preceded by a *Personenkeil* and followed by -šè. In twelve of the Ur III sale documents (nos. 252, 259, 261, 262?, 271, 277?, 279, 282, 284, 333, 341, and 367), the names of witnesses lack any markings.

The following is a list of the ways used to mark the names of witnesses in the Ur III sale documents:

1) ᴵPN: nos. 250, 251, 256, 257, 260, 264, 265, 269, 273, 274, 276, 280(?), 288, 292, 295, 298, 305, 306, 308, 309a, 311, 317, 319, 321(?), 322, 323(?), 325, 326(?), 328, 330(?), 331, 332, 335, 336, 342, 344, 345, 350, 351, 354, and 355
2) igi PN-šè: nos. 247, 249(?), 258(?), 270, 281, 286, 291, 293, 294, 296, 299, 302, 303, 307, 309, 312, 315(?), 318, 324, 329, 347, 356, 357, 358, 359, 360, and 361
3) igi PN: nos. 247a, 254, 258(?), 267, 268, 283, 287, 289, 297, 301, 304, 343, 352, 362, 363, 366(?), 368, and 370
4) ᴵPN-šè: no. 255
5) first witness igi PN-šè, following ᴵPN: nos. 300, 316, and 327
6) first two witnesses igi PN-šè, following ᴵPN: no. 348
7) first witness igi PN-šè, following PN: no. 278
8) first witness igi PN, following ᴵPN: no. 338
9) first four witnesses igi PN, following ᴵPN: no. 334
10) first witness igi PN, following PN: no. 272
11) first witness PN-šè, following ᴵPN: no. 266

In the overwhelming majority of the kudurrus and sale documents, the list of witnesses is followed by a term identifying the preceding persons as "witnesses." While this description is wanting in quite a number of the Ur III sale documents (nos. 247, 247a, 254, 267, 270, 281, 286, 291, 293, 294, 296, 297, 299, 301, 302, 303, 308, 309, 312, 327, 347, 358, 359, 360, 368, and 370), the only earlier texts that do not have it are nos. 114, 156a, and 224.

7.9.2. Terms for Witnesses

Three terms for "witness" are attested in the kudurrus and sale documents: 1) lú-ki-inim-ma; 2) lú-inim-ma; 3) AB+ÁŠ, *šībum*.

In the texts dating to the Fara, Pre-Sargonic, and Sargonic periods, the terms lú-ki-inim-ma and AB+ÁŠ, apart from being used to identify witnesses, are occasionally applied also to secondary sellers and other participants of the transaction. See the following examples:

1) lú-ki-inim describing a secondary seller (no. 129)
2) lú-ki-inim-ma describing secondary sellers (no. 32)
3) lú-ki-inim-ma-bi-me describing secondary sellers (nos. 137 and 141)
4) lú-ki-inim describing an ENGAR.UŠ official (no. 122)
5) lú-ki-inim-ma-bi describing a nigir "herald" (no. 137)
6) AB+ÁŠ.AB+ÁŠ describing LÚ.GÁN.GÍD.DA "surveyors" (no. 40)
7) AB+ÁŠ describing a secondary seller (no. 237)

Apparently, while the narrow usage of lú-ki-inim-ma and AB+ÁŠ was limited to the witnesses proper, in a broader sense they could denote any participant of the transaction other than the buyer and the seller.

7.9.2.1. lú-ki-inim-ma

The term lú-ki-inim-ma is the standard word for "witness" from the Fara down to the Sargonic period in the texts written in Sumerian. It continues to be occasionally used as late as Ur III times, even though the usual term for "witness" in that period is lú-inim-ma (see under 7.9.2.2.).

Although the meaning "witness" of lú-ki-inim-ma is assured by the context of its occurrences, the analysis of this term is somewhat unclear. The two most likely choices are either to analyze it as a double genitive: lú ki inim-ak-ak "person of the place of the legal case / transaction," or to assume, with Krecher, *ZA* 63 pp. 160f., that it represents an abbreviation of *lú ki-inim-ma-ka gub-ba / tuš-ša, "person who stood / sat at the place of the legal case / transaction."

The earliest attested form of this term is lú-ki-inim. This spelling is found only in the Fara sale documents (nos. 100–113c, 115–124, and 126–136), where it is used both for the singular and the plural: "(this/these is/are) the witness(es)."

The form lú-ki-inim-ma makes its appearance in the Fara sale document no. 125, which, in view of its various textual peculiarities, may be actually younger than the other Fara sale documents, and in kudurrus nos. 14 and 15, whose date also seems to be slightly later than that of the Fara texts. While no. 125 adds the copula -me to mark the plural: "(these) are the witnesses," nos. 14 and 15 use the form lú-ki-inim-ma regardless of the number. The latter usage of lú-ki-inim-ma is also attested in Pre-Sargonic kudurrus nos. 32 and 33, both coming from Adab.

In the Pre-Sargonic kudurrus and sale documents from Lagash (nos. 23, 137, 138, 139, 140, 141, 142, 143, 144, 147, 148, 150, 151, 153, and 155), one finds for the first time the spelling lú-ki-inim-ma-bi, "(this) is the witness of this legal case / transaction," and the plural is regularly expressed by -me. The same spelling, with -pi occasionally replacing -bi, is the standard description of witnesses in the Sargonic texts (*passim*). It is also found in Ur III texts nos. 287, 292 (adds -éš), 344, and 355 (adds -éš).

The term lú-ki-inim-ma usually appears without any qualifications. The only exception is no. 32, in which the witnesses are described as lú-ki-inim-ma PN, "witnesses of (the family of) PN," i.e., witnesses of the sellers.

The following are the forms of lú-ki-inim-ma found in the texts belonging to the present corpus:

1) lú-ki-inim: nos. 100, 101, 102, 103, 104, 105, 106, 107, 108, 109, 110, 111, 112 (= 113c), 113, 113a, 113b, 115, 116, 117, 118, 119, 121, 122, 123, 124, 126, 127, 127a, 127b, 128, 129, 130, 131, 132, 133, 134, 135, and 136
2) lú-ki-inim-ma: nos. 14, 15, 32, and 33
3) lú-ki-inim-ma-me: nos. App. to no. 32, 125, 169, 192, 225, 274, and 318
4) lú-ki-inim-ma-bi: nos. 182 and 193 (5 persons)
5) lú-ki-inim-ma-bi-me: nos. 23, 137, 138, 139, 140, 141, 142, 143, 144, 147, 148, 150, 151, 153, 155, 157, 158, 159, 160, 161, 162, 163, 165, 176, 177, 178, 179, 184, 185, 186, 187, 188, 191, 195, 196, 197, 199, 200, 202, 203, 206, 207, 209, 211, 215, 216, 217, 218, 219, 220, 221, 222, 223, 287, and 344
6) lú-ki-inim-ma-pi-me: nos. 210 and 213
7) lú-ki-inim-ma-bi-me-éš: nos. 292 and 355

7.9.2.2. lú-inim-ma

The term lú-inim-ma, "person of the legal case / transaction," is the standard word for "witness" in Ur III times. Its origin, however, can be traced back to the Sargonic period, as in Sargonic sale documents nos. 170, 172, and 175. With the exception of the Ur III text no. 361, which is written in Akkadian, the use of lú-inim-ma is limited to the Sumerian documents.

In view of the fact that lú-inim-ma appears later than lú-ki-inim-ma, and that it replaces the latter completely by OB times, one may speculate that lú-inim-ma is a simplified form of lú-ki-inim-ma, introduced by the Sargonic scribes for reasons of economy (cf. Krecher, *ZA* 63 p. 160).

The only example of lú-inim-ma being qualified by another description comes from no. 172, which has lú-inim-ma inim til-a-kam "(this) is the witness of the completed transaction."

The term lú-inim-ma is attested in the following forms:

1) lú-inim-ma-bi: no. 175
2) lú-inim-ma inim til-a-kam: no. 172
3) lú-inim-ma-bi-me: nos. 170, 250, 252, 253, 255, 257, 258, 260, 261, 264, 265, 266, 268, 269, 271, 272, 273, 276, 277, 278, 279, 283, 284, 288, 289, 290, 298, 300, 305, 306, 307, 309a, 311, 314, 316, 319, 321, 322, 323, 324, 325, 331, 332, 333, 334, 335, 338, 341, 342, 348, 351, 352, 354, 356, 357, 361, 362, 363, and 369
4) lú-inim-ma-bi-me-éš: nos. 251, 256, 282, and 295

7.9.2.3. AB+ÁŠ, *šîbum*

The logogram AB+ÁŠ, which belongs to the variety of cuneiform that was dubbed by Gelb as the "Kish Tradition" (see *Syro-Mesopotamian Studies* 1/1 p. 13), stands for the Akkadian *šîbum* "elder, witness." A detailed discussion of AB+ÁŠ and *šîbum* has recently been offered by Gelb, *JNES* 43 (1984) pp. 263–76.

The earliest occurrences of AB+ÁŠ come from Akkadian kudurrus nos. 28 and 35, both of which date to the Pre-Sargonic period. This term is the standard description of witnesses in the Sargonic kudurrus and sale documents written in Akkadian. Although AB+ÁŠ is occasionally used in Akkadian texts as late as Ur III times (e.g., *TIM* 3, 150:15), it is found in none of the Ur III sale documents belonging to this corpus. However, one of the texts (no. 343) contains a unique example of *šîbum* written in Akkadian.

In nos. 227 and 235, where the witnesses were exclusively women, there is used the logogram SAL.AB+ÁŠ, standing for *šîbtum* "female witness." The plural is expressed by either the reduplication of the logogram (nos. 28, 40, 41, 45, 48, 235, 236, 237, 240, and 241) or the addition of *-bu-ut* (for *šîbūt*) to the unreduplicated form (nos. 233, 242, and 244). In several cases, however, the unreduplicated form is used for the plural (nos. 35, 38, 228, 229, 230, 234, 239, 243, and 246). In one instance (no. 41 obv. v), AB+ÁŠ.AB+ÁŠ describes a single witness.

While in most instances the term AB+ÁŠ (and its variants) is placed immediately after the list of witnesses, in agreement with the practice found in the Sumerian texts using the terms lú-ki-inim-ma and lú-inim-ma, some texts insert between the names of witnesses and AB+ÁŠ the phrase ŠU.NIGÍN NUMBER, which tallies the preceding persons (nos. 35, 38, 229, 230, 233, 234, 237, 240, 242, and 343). Also, in contrast to the terms lú-ki-inim-ma and lú-inim-ma, which usually appear without any qualifications, AB+ÁŠ tends to be combined with various descriptions. Thus we find: 1) "(witnesses) of the buyer" (nos. 38, 227?, and 233); 2) "(witnesses) of the seller" (no. 243); 3) "(witnesses) of the field (of GN/PN)" (nos. 40, 41, 43, and 239); 4) "(witnesses) of the compensation (*kušur-rā'um*)" (nos. 228, 236, and 343); 5) "(witnesses) of the measuring (*šiddatum*) of the field" (no. 246); 6) "(witnesses) who inspected the measuring (of the house)" (no. 244); 7) "(witnesses) that the seller measured out the house to the buyer" (no. 242); 8) "(witnesses) who ate bread (and drank beer) in the house of the buyer" (nos. 35 and 237); 9) "(witnesses) of/in GN" (nos. 48 and 229).

A completely unique pattern of the list of witnesses is found in no. 230: "in the house of PN, daughter of PN_x, in Akkadē, 10 PNs, the total of 10 witnesses (to the fact) that the buyer weighed out the silver in Akkadē."

The following list contains the extant examples of AB+ÁŠ, cited with the full contexts of their occurrences:

1) [x]+2 PNs AB+ÁŠ.AB+ÁŠ: no. 28
2) [20 PNs] ŠU.NIGÍN 20 AB+ÁŠ *in* É! Buyer NINDA KÚ(KA+⌜GAR⌝) KAŠ Ì.NA[G](K[A+A]): no. 35
3) 9+[16] PNs ŠU.NIGÍN 25 AB+ÁŠ Buyer: no. 38

4) 49 D PNs ŠU.NIGÍN 49 DUMU.DUMU *A-ga-dè*^{KI} AB+ÁŠ.AB+ÁŠ GÁN: no. 40 A, B, C, D
5) 5 D PNs ŠU.NIGÍN 5 GURUŠ AB+ÁŠ.AB+ÁŠ GÁN: no. 40 A
6) 30 D PNs ŠU.NIGÍN 30 GURUŠ AB+ÁŠ.AB+ÁŠ GÁN *Gir*$_{13}$-*tab*^{KI}: no. 40 B
7) 3 PNs (LÚ.ÉŠ.GÍD, DUB.SAR, and SAG.DU$_5$) receiving additional payments + 27 D PNs = ŠU.NIGÍN 3 DUB.SAR ŠU.NIGÍN 27 AB+ÁŠ.AB+ÁŠ; 10 D PNs ŠU.NIGÍN 10 DUMU.DUMU AB+ÁŠ.AB+ÁŠ; 12 D PNs ŠU.NIGÍN 12 NU.BANDA *ù* UGULA; ŠU.NIGÍN.ŠU.NIGÍN 52 GURUŠ *Már-da*^{KI} AB+ÁŠ.AB+ÁŠ GÁN: no. 40 C
8) 6 D PNs AB+ÁŠ.AB+ÁŠ GÁN *šu* KÁ.T[I]?: no. 41 obv. iv
9) 1 D PN AB+ÁŠ.AB+ÁŠ GÁN *šu* Ù.SIG$_7$: no. 41 obv. v
10) 3 D PNs AB+ÁŠ.AB+ÁŠ *šu* URU^{KI}.URI^{KI} *ša* E ^{d}*Irḫan*$_x$(MUŠ)$^{ir\text{-}ḫa}$ GÁN *A-pù-ì-lum*: no. 41 obv. vii
11) [x]+9 D PNs AB+ÁŠ.AB+ÁŠ *a-na* GÁN *šu* *Be-la-su-nu U*$_4$-*bí-um*^{KI}: no. 41 obv. viii
12) [x]+64 PNs AB+ÁŠ.AB+ÁŠ $^{d?}$UTU?-[X]: no. 48 iii–ix
13) [x]+20 PNs AB+ÁŠ.AB+ÁŠ *Ab-za-*⸢*x*⸣^{KI}: no. 48 ix–rev. ii
14) 5 D PNs SAL.A[B+ÁŠ Buyer?]: no. 227
15) 4 D PNs AB+ÁŠ ⸢*gu*⸣-*su-ra-im*: no. 228
16) 6 D PNs [ŠU.NIGÍN] 6 AB+ÁŠ *in Kiš*$^{[KI]}$: no. 229
17) *in* É PN DUMU.SAL PN$_x$ *in A-ga-dè*^{KI} 10 D PNs ŠU.NIGÍN ⸢10⸣ AB+ÁŠ Buyer *in* [*A*]-*ga-dè*$^{[KI]}$ KUG.BABBAR *iš*$_{11}$-*ku-*⸢*lu*⸣: no. 230
18) 6 D PNs ŠU.NIGÍN 6 AB+ÁŠ-*bu-ut* Buyer: no. 233
19) 7 D PNs ŠU.NIGÍN 7 AB+ÁŠ: no. 234
20) [x]+3 D PN SAL.AB+ÁŠ.SAL.AB+Á[Š]: no. 235
21) 4 D PNs AB+ÁŠ.AB+ÁŠ *gu-su*$_4$-*ra-im*: no. 236
22) 18 D PNs + 1 PN (receiving additional payments) [19 A]B+ÁŠ in É Buyer NINDA K[Ú]: no. 237
23) 8 D PNs AB+ÁŠ GÁN *ši Maš-gán*^{KI}: no. 239
24) 11 D PNs ŠU.NIGÍN 11 AB+ÁŠ.A[B+ÁŠ]: no. 240
25) 7 D PNs AB+ÁŠ.AB+ÁŠ: no. 241
26) 8 D PNs ŠU.NIGÍN 8 AB+ÁŠ-*bu-ut*: no. 242
27) 6 PNs AB+ÁŠ Seller: no. 243
28) 6 PNs *šu*⟨-*ut*⟩ AB+ÁŠ-*bu-ut si-da-t*[*im*] *i-mu-ru*: no. 244
29) 4 D PNs AB+ÁŠ *si-da-ti* GÁN: no. 246
30) 10 PNs (each preceded by IGI) ŠU.NIGÍN 10 GURUŠ *si-bu-tum gú-šu-ra-im*: no. 343

7.9.3. Distinctions among Witnesses

In the overwhelming majority of the texts, witnesses are listed as a single homogeneous group, within which no internal distinctions are detectable. In a few texts, however, witnesses are divided into two separate units. This is the pattern in Fara sale documents nos. 114 and 122, Sargonic kudurru no. 40, and Ur III sale documents nos. 327 and 332.

Given the fact that in nos. 114 and 122 the members of the second unit are in each case the sons of the buyer, they undoubtedly represented the witnesses of the buyer. Accordingly, the members of the first unit can be identified as the witnesses of the seller.

The same explanation applies to nos. 40 and 327. In no. 40, transactions A, B, and C contain in each case two lists of witnesses, described as AB+ÁŠ.AB+ÁŠ GÁN (GN), "witnesses of the field (of GN)," and DUMU.DUMU *A-ga-dè*^{KI} AB+ÁŠ.AB+ÁŠ GÁN, "citizens of Akkadē, witnesses of the field," respectively. Since the members of the second list are the same individuals in each of the three transactions, and further, since they are associated with Akkadē (i.e., the royal capital), they clearly represented the witnesses of the buyer (i.e., the king Manishtushu). The first group must therefore represent the witnesses of the sellers; this interpretation finds confirmation in the fact that, in transaction A, the first group of witnesses included four relatives of the sellers. In no. 327, the witnesses are divided into ušùr-da-gi$_4$-a-me "neighbors," and [d]am-gàr-me "merchants." Given that one of the "merchants" is the buyer's brother, the "merchants" can be identified as the witnesses of the buyer, and, accordingly, the "neighbors," as the witnesses of the seller.

Text no. 332 also divides witnesses into two groups: [ki]? ⸢x⸣ šám-a tuš-ša-me "persons who sat in the [place(?)] ⸢(where) the slave woman(?)⸣ was bought," and lú-inim-ma-bi-me "witnesses," respectively, but the reason for this distinction seems to be different from that of the earlier texts. One can speculate that the persons identified as lú-inim-ma-bi-me were the actual witnesses, who were brought by the parties involved for the purpose of witnessing the sale, whereas the members of the other group, probably to be translated as "bystanders," were persons who simply happened to be present during the transaction in question. A possible case of such a "bystander" occurs perhaps in the Sargonic sale document no. 206, where the name of one of the witnesses, described as lú-ki-inim-ma-b[i-me], is followed by the note ki-ba ì-tuš-a[m$_6$]? "he sat at this place." In this connection, note also the Sargonic legal case *AnOr* 7, 372 (collated by Westenholz), in which the first eight witnesses are identified as *mu-za-zu* "ones who stood (there)."

7.9.4. Witnesses and Secondary Sellers

Finally, we should comment on the question of the relationship between witnesses and secondary sellers in certain Fara and Pre-Sargonic documents.

In general, witnesses and secondary sellers are clearly distinguished from each other in the Fara and Pre-Sargonic kudurrus and sale documents: the first are marked with a *Personenkeil* and do not receive additional payments, whereas the latter lack a *Personenkeil* before their names and do receive additional payments. Another difference between the two groups lies in the sphere of terminology: witnesses are identified by the term lú-ki-inim-ma or AB+ÁŠ, whereas the secondary sellers (if identified at all) bear such descriptions as dumu-gán-me, šeš-gán, ŠEŠ *be-lu* GÁN, etc. (see under 7.6.3).

However, as already noted (see under 7.9.2), there are instances where the terms lú-ki-inim-ma and AB+ÁŠ are applied to secondary sellers as well. Furthermore, we have examples of witnesses receiving additional payments. A clear case in point is found in the Pre-Sargonic text no. 140, which contains, in addition to the secondary sellers (who receive additional payments and do not have a *Personenkeil* before their names), a list of twenty-three witnesses (lú-ki-inim-ma-bi-me), who are given additional payments (in the amount of four breads per person) and whose names are marked with a *Personenkeil.*

Although this interpretation is not as immediately obvious as in no. 140, it can be demonstrated that witnesses receive additional payments also in nos. 137 and 141, likewise dating to the Pre-Sargonic period. Each of the latter texts contains a list of persons, labeled as lú-ki-inim-ma-bi-me, all of whom receive additional payments and lack a *Personenkeil* before their names. Given that there is no other list of witnesses in either text, it necessarily follows that the list comprises both the secondary sellers and the witnesses. This interpretation is supported by the fact that, by comparing the types and quantities of commodities included in the additional payments, it is possible in each case to divide the list into two units, comprising secondary sellers and witnesses, respectively. Thus, in no. 137, the first two persons, receiving barley, wool, beer, soup, and several types of bread, can be identified as the secondary sellers, while the following twenty-three persons, receiving, in considerably smaller quantities, only soup and one type of bread, can be identified as the witnesses. Similarly, in no. 141, the first six persons, who receive several types of garments as well as wool, bread, soup, and fish, appear to have been the secondary sellers; the following nineteen individuals, each of whom receives two breads and one quart of soup (with the exception of one person, who has ten breads and five quarts of soup), may be interpreted as the witnesses.

A unique situation is found in the Sargonic text no. 192. This text contains a single list of witnesses, called lú-ki-inim-ma-me, who receive ten breads each (10 ninda-ta) and whose names are marked with a *Personenkeil.*

Other instances of witnesses (lú-ki-inim-ma) who receive additional payments are possibly attested in Fara kudurrus nos. 14 and 15. This, however, is not entirely certain, since these texts can alternatively mean that the additional payments in question were actually given to the sellers (see the discussion of the operative sections of nos. 14 and 15 in section 6.2).

The above facts obviously raise the following question: since, at least as far as the Fara and Pre-Sargonic periods are concerned, witnesses could receive additional payments, while secondary sellers could be described by the terms lú-ki-inim-ma and AB+ÁŠ, both meaning "witness," was there any qualitative difference between the two? If, as the facts seem to indicate, secondary sellers and witnesses were virtually indistinguishable from the legal point of view, it would perhaps be more appropriate to include both in one broad category of "witnesses," differentiating them specifically between "primary witnesses" (i.e., secondary sellers) and "secondary witnesses" (i.e., witnesses).

7.10. *Guarantors*

The only occurrence of a guarantor in sale documents before the Ur III period comes from the Sargonic text no. 233: D PN D PN_2 *u-gi-ip* "PN (and) PN_2 guaranteed (*uqīp*, D-stem from *qiāpum*; instead of the expected dual *uqippā*)." This passage may also be interpreted as "PN guaranteed (to) PN_2 (i.e., the buyer)" in accordance with Steinkeller, *RA* 74 (1980) p. 179. [For the verb, see now *JCS* 35 (1983) p. 168 no. 1:9–10: [P]N *šu* GUD [*u*]-*gi-ip-su*$_4$ "[P]N, man in charge of oxen, guaranteed for him (i.e., the seller)."] In contrast, the Ur III sale documents mention guarantors fairly frequently. There are attested four different terms for "guarantor" in those texts: 1) gáb-gi, 2) lú-gi-na-ab-túm, 3) lú-inim-gi-na, and 4) *muqippum.* In addition, in some texts the guarantor is identified not by one of the above terms, but by the verb gi-(n), Akk. *kuānum*, *kunnum* "to be firm," "to make firm, to guarantee."

1) gáb-gi (lit.: "may I guarantee for it": a frozen cohortative of the verb gi-(n))

PN gáb-gi-bi-im "PN is the guarantor": nos. 306, 308, and 319
PN gáb-gi-bi: no. 271
PN ga-ab-gi-bi: no. 303
PN gáb-gi-in sag-kam "PN is the guarantor of the 'head' ": no. 292

2) lú-gi-na-ab-túm

PN lú-gi-[na]-ab-túm-bi-im "PN is the guarantor": no. 304
PN lú-gi-na-ab-tum: no. 339
PN lú-ki-[na]-ab-túm-[bi-im]: no. 315
PN lú-ki-na-ab-tum-bi-im: no. 296
PN lú-ki-na-ab-dam-bi-im: no. 300
PN lú-ki-na-ab-dam-a-si-TUM-ma?-bi-im "PN is the guarantor of . . .": no. 299
PN nam-[l]ú-gi⟨-na⟩-ab-tum-bi-šè mu lugal-bi in-pàd "PN swore by the name of the king for the guarantorship": no. 294.

3) lú-inim-gi-na

PN lú-inim-[gi-na] "PN is the guarantor": no. 288
PN lú-inim-gi-[na]: no. 329
[P]N [l]ú-inim-gi-na: no. 332 (among witnesses)

4) *muqippum*

PN *ù* PN_2 DUMU.NI *mu-gi-bu* "PN and PN_2, her son, (are) the guarantors": no. 370

5) gi-(n)

PN íb-gi-ni /i-b-gin-e/ "PN guarantees": no. 298
PN íb-gi-ne: no. 352

For a detailed discussion of these terms and the legal importance of guarantors in the Ur III period, see Steinkeller, *Sale Documents* pp. 80–92.

7.11. *Other Participants of the Transaction*

Under this category, we have included the persons acting as neutral parties to the sale transaction, whose duties entailed the surveying and registration of sold real estate, the official authorization of transactions, the weighing of purchase price, the publicity of sales, and the preparation of sale documents.

7.11.1. Fara Period

The Fara sale documents were attended basically by four types of officials, um-mi-a lú-é-èš-gar "master house surveyor" and nigir-sila "street herald" (or gal-nigir "chief herald"), who appear in the house sales, and dub-sar(-gán) "(field) scribe" and ENGAR.UŠ ". . ." (in no. 125 called engar), who are attested in the transactions involving the sale of fields. In two of the field sales (nos. 133 and 136), we also find a sag-du$_5$ "field recorder" and GU.SUR.NUN "field assessor." The officials are not attested in six instances (nos. 101, 113, 127b, 128, 129, and 134); they are not preserved in two texts (nos. 120 and 121). All of these officials are given gifts, with the exception of no. 125, listing a dub-sar and an engar, of whom only the former receives a gift.

In the house sales, the um-mi-a lú-é-èš-gar is followed by nigir-sila (nos. 102?, 103, 105, 106, 109, 110, 111, and 112 = 113c) or preceded by gal-nigir (nos. 100 and 108). In two instances (nos. 104 and 107), um-mi-a lú-é-èš-gar appears alone. In the transactions in which the "master house surveyor" is listed together with the "street herald," the former official receives more gifts than the latter. The payments given to the "master house surveyor" include one pound of copper (disregarding whether the price is paid in copper or silver) and quantities of ninda, gúg, tu$_7$, and NIGÍN+ḪA.A, whereas the "street herald" usually receives quantities of barley, ninda, gúg, tu$_7$, and NIGÍN+ḪA.A. In contrast, the "master house surveyor" is given fewer gifts than the "chief herald"; he receives ½ pound of copper, plus quantities of ninda, gúg, tu$_7$, and NIGÍN+ḪA.A, whereas the "chief herald" gets one pound of copper.

In the texts involving the sale of fields, the official dub-sar(-gán) is followed by ENGAR.UŠ (engar in no. 125) in eleven instances (nos. 114, 119, 122, 124, 125, 126, 127a, 130, 131, 132, and 135?), by sag-du$_5$ and GU.SUR.NUN, in one (no. 133), and by GU.SUR.NUN alone, also in one (no. 136). The dub-sar(-gán) appears alone in six documents (nos. 115, 116, 117, 118, 123, and 127), whereas in one case (no. 124), the only official mentioned is ENGAR.UŠ. As a rule, dub-sar(-gán) receives more payments than ENGAR.UŠ and the two other officials (with the possible exception of no. 136, where the dub-sar is probably given the same amount as the GU.SUR.NUN). His payments usually include between 1 and 1½ pounds of copper, alternating with between ⅓ and 1½ shekels of silver, plus quantities of ninda, gúg, tu$_7$, and NIGÍN+ḪA.A. In some instances, dub-sar(-gán) receives also barley, wool, and oil. The official ENGAR.UŠ receives quantities of barley, ninda, gúg, tu$_7$, and NIGÍN+ḪA.A, with the exception of no. 124, the only text in which he appears alone, where he is given two shekels of silver. In no. 125, which differs considerably from the other Fara texts, both officials (called dub-sar and engar) are recorded, but only the former receives a gift: ŠÁM+2 (i.e., 2/3 shekel) kug, 1 silà ì, níg-ba-ni. The sag-du$_5$ and GU.SUR.NUN who follow dub-sar-gán in no. 133 each receive the same amounts of wool, ninda, gúg, tu$_7$, and NIGÍN+ḪA.A. In no. 136, the GU.SUR.NUN receives one shekel of silver; the same amount of silver is most probably received by the two scribes (dub-sar) listed in this document.

Since the "master house surveyor" and the "street herald" (or the "chief herald") are attested only in house sales, and the "(field) scribe" and ENGAR.UŠ, only in field sales, it is reasonable to assume that these officials performed complementary functions, depending on the type of real estate (houses or fields). This point seems to be assured in the case of the "master house surveyor" and the "(field) scribe," both of whom were clearly responsible for the surveying, and probably also for the registration, of real estate. The same is less certain in the case of the other two officials, for only the function of the "street herald" (or the "chief herald") is known. The nigir served as a town crier and thus was an instrument of publicity. We can assume, therefore, that, in the context of sales, the "street herald," and similarly the "chief herald," was responsible for the publicity of concluded transactions, more specifically, those transactions which involved estates located within the city limits, i.e., houses. The meaning and function of ENGAR.UŠ is not known, but, if his duties paralleled those of nigir-sila and gal-nigir, it would follow, then, that he was responsible for the publicity of field sales. It is significant that in no. 125, whose formulary diverges somewhat from that of the other Fara sale documents, this official is called engar. This may indicate that the function of ENGAR.UŠ was similar to that of engar, who in the early periods appears to have been a high administrative official in charge of agricultural activities (*agronomos* or the like). The engar was probably also involved in the surveying and registration of fields; this is suggested by the Pre-Sargonic texts from Lagash, where the same person, named Lugal-kur, is earlier documented as an engar (*VAS* 14, 173 iv 13–14—Lugalanda 4; *DP* 132 v 5–6—Lugalanda 5), and later, as a lú-èš-gíd "surveyor" (*DP* 133 viii 8–9—Urukagina 1). The ENGAR.UŠ, however, cannot be identical with the engar, since these two officials appear side by side in the Pre-Sargonic text *DP* 590.

The officials sag-du$_5$ and GU.SUR.NUN who replace the ENGAR.UŠ in nos. 133 and 136, are well documented as "field recorder" and "field assessor" respectively (for GU.SUR.NUN, see commentary to no. 20 iii 9). In the context of field sales, however, they may have been specifically responsible, like the ENGAR.UŠ, for the publicity of transactions.

In the Chicago and Baltimore Stones (nos. 14 and 15), dated to the Fara period, most of the transactions contain a list of persons, usually the same four men, who are described as engar zag/ki durun-durun "'farmers' who sat on a side / at (this) place." These persons do not receive any payments. The fact that the same individuals appear in this position in different transactions suggests that they are to be interpreted as the counterparts of the ENGAR. UŠ. This assumption may find support in the example of ENGAR.UŠ being replaced by engar in one of the Fara sale documents (no. 125). The identification of the engar officials of the Chicago and Baltimore Stones with the ENGAR.UŠ official, who appears exclusively in transactions involving the sale of fields, is further indicated by the fact that all of the transactions recorded in these two kudurrus are field sales.

The persons designated as sag-du$_5$, GU.SUR.NUN, and engar appear also in the Enḫegal Tablet (no. 21), likewise dated to the Fara period. However, the interpretation of these persons as the officials who attended the respective transactions is not certain on account of the difficulties involved in the interpretation of this document.

7.11.2. Pre-Sargonic Period

In five Pre-Sargonic texts from Lagash dealing with the sale of houses (nos. 137, 139, 140, 141, and 142), and in one slave sale (no. 151), there is listed a nigir "herald," in two instances called nigir-uru "town herald." This official performs the kag . . . dù and ì . . . ag rites, symbolizing the transfer of property and assuring the publicity of transaction, and receives gifts (with the exception of nos. 142 and 151). The payments given to the "herald" are different in each case: 1 dug kas (no. 137); 5 silà tu$_7$ (no. 139); 2(UL) še gur-2-UL, 1 dug kas, 30 ninda-KU-KU-na, 3 ninda-silà (no. 140); 1(gur) še gur-2-UL, 1 dug kas-gi$_6$, 10 ku$_6$-dar-ra (no. 141). Quite characteristically, the "herald" does not appear in the Lagash field sales (note that in these transactions the rites in question were performed by the seller!). Two of the latter texts (nos. 23 and 144) name in his place "scribes" (dub-sar), further described as lú-gán-gíd-da-me "field surveyors," who do not receive payments. No. 147, in which the object of sale is not preserved, lists a dub-sar with a gift: 1 [. . .], 1 dug-KIL.KIL kas, 10 ninda.

This particular distribution of officials seems to suggest that, in the Pre-Sargonic Lagash, the sales of houses and the sales of fields were attended and officially authorized by two different officials, nigir and dub-sar lú-gán-gíd-da, respectively. If so, we would find here continuation of the practice first documented in the Fara period (see section 7.11.1).

Scribes are also mentioned in two other Pre-Sargonic sale documents, where they are identified as the persons who wrote the tablets in question: PN um-mi-a dub mu-sar "PN, the master scribe, wrote (this) tablet" (App. to no. 32); PN dub-[sar] im-bi ⌜e⌝?-sar "PN, the scr[ibe], wrote this tablet" (no. 138).

In App. to no. 32, we find the earliest reference to the weigher of silver in a sale transaction. This person was responsible, usually on account of his professional familiarity with the scales, for the exact weight of the purchased silver (see, in detail, Steinkeller, *Sale Documents* pp. 92–97). In this particular instance, the weigher of silver also acted as a measurer of the purchased barley: PN ugula-é lú-kug-lal-a lú-še-ág "PN, the majordomo, (was) the weigher of silver (and) the measurer of barley."

7.11.3. Sargonic Period

Texts of Sargonic date do not yield any clear-cut evidence for the attendance of sale transactions by different officials, depending on the object of sale. Several of the Sargonic kudurrus and sale documents mention field-surveyors. In the transaction C_3 of the Manishtushu Obelisk (no. 40), three officials are listed, LÚ.ÉŠ.GÍD "surveyor," DUB.SAR "scribe," and SAG.DU$_5$ "field registrar," who in the total are identified as "scribes" (DUB.SAR). These officials receive payments, one TÚG. ŠU.SÈ.GA and one ^{URUDU}ḪA.ZI$^{\text{UD.KA.BAR}}$ in each case, which are labeled as NÍG.BA LÚ.GÁN.GÍD.DA "gift of the surveyors of the field." In no. 41, three transactions list a DUB.SAR GÁN "field scribe," who is given payments, consisting of either one pound of wool and one TÚG.ŠU.ZA.GA cloth (obv. ii 1′–4′, iv 21′–25′) or one bushel of barley and one TÚG.ŠU.ZA.GA cloth (obv. viii 18′–22′).

Finally, four of the transactions recorded in no. 182a name the persons who surveyed the sold fields, without, however, stating their official titles: D PN dumu PN$_x$ ì-gíd "PN, son of PN$_x$, measured (the field)" (C); (še-pi PN dam-gàr an-na-ág) gán-pi ì-gíd "(PN, the merchant, measured out this barley, i.e., the price, and) surveyed this field" (D, in this transaction PN is either the buyer or a third party); D PN PN$_x$ gán-pi ì-gíd "PN (of) PN$_x$ measured this field" (F = no. 169); D PN PN$_x$ D PN$_2$ PN$_y$ lú ^{GIŠ}kiri$_6$ gíd-da-me "PN (of) PN$_x$ (and) PN$_2$ (of) PN$_y$ are the men who measured the orchard" (L).

A "scribe" (DUB.SAR), who most probably prepared the sale document, receives a gift in no. 227: 1 BA.AN, 1 ŠÀ.GA.DÙ^{TÚG}. If our reconstruction is correct, another example of a scribe with a gift is found in no. 240: 1 TÚG.TUM-*gunû* [PN DUB.SAR?]. Note also no. 237, where the receiver of a gift, who, though not described by any term, may conceivably be a scribe: 1 MA.NA.TUR KUG.BABBAR PN [DU]MU PN$_2$. The scribe who wrote the tablet in question, but did not receive any payment, is listed in two other Sargonic sale documents: PN dub-sar-pi "PN (is) the scribe" (no. 224); PN [D]UB.SAR [*š*]*a-ti-ir* DUB "PN, the scribe, wrote the tablet" (no. 239).

The only occurrence of the weigher of silver in the Sargonic period is attested in no. 215: PN dam-gàr lú-giš-rín-dab$_5$-ba-àm "PN, the merchant, was the man who held the scales." See also 182a D, cited above, which may involve a similar case of the merchant who measured out the purchase barley.

Finally, we have among the Sargonic material two possible instances of the official authorization of sale transactions. Thus the transaction recorded in no. 215 appears to have been authorized by the wife of a temple administrator: dam sanga-ke$_4$ mu-gi$_4$ níg-na-me nu-da-tuku [ini]m-mu-ta ḫé-[š]ám-šám "the wife of the temple administrator replied(?): 'There are no claims on him (i.e., the sold person); he may buy him with my consent.'" The other example comes from no. 239, where the authorization was probably granted by a SABRA É "majordomo."

7.11.4. Ur III Period

Sale documents of the Ur III period name three types of officials: 1) the person who authorized the transaction, 2) the weigher of silver, and 3) the scribe who wrote the tablet in question.

The authorizing official either is listed separately or is included among the witnesses. He can be an en_5-si "governor" (nos. 331, 335, 338, and 340), a ḫa-za-núm "mayor" (nos. 258, 283, 291, 343, and 370), a di-kud "judge" (nos. 264 and 365), a nu-banda Adab^{KI} "military commander of Adab" (no. 334), and an egir en_5-si "'retainer' of the governor" (no. 332). In some instances, the authorizing official seals the tablet (nos. 264, 283, 332, 334, and 365).

The scribe is listed in eight texts (nos. 247a, 258, 324, 331, 334, 335, 338?, and 370). He usually appears as the last witness (nos. 324, 331, 334, 335, 338?, and 370); in nos. 247a and 258, both stemming from Eshnuna, he is listed apart from the witnesses. In one instance (no. 247a), he seals the tablet.

There are fourteen occurrences of the weigher of silver in the Ur III sale documents (nos. 247a, 258, 271, 296, 299, 300, 306, 308, 311, 314, and 332 [among witnesses], 334 [among witnesses], 350, and 362). He is either a simug "smith" (nos. 247a, 258, 271?, 300, 314, 332, 334, and 360) or a kug-dím "goldsmith" (nos. 296 and 299) or a dam-gàr "merchant" (nos. 306, 308, and 350); in one instance (no. 311), his profession is not stated. The weigher of silver is usually identified by the phrase (lú-)kug-lal-bi(-im) "the man who weighed out the silver." In nos. 314 and 332, he is simply called simug-bi "the smith (of the transaction)," whereas in no. 362 we find the statement PN SIMUG KUG.BI Ì.LAL "PN, the smith, weighed out the silver."

For a detailed discussion of the official authorization of sale transactions in Ur III times, see Steinkeller, *Sale Documents* pp. 97–103.

7.12. *Final Clauses*

7.12.1. Introductory Remarks

Following the operative section, which states the basic facts of the transaction (see section 6), both the kudurrus and the sale documents contain a variety of additional clauses and statements, dealing with such points as the completion of the payment of the price, completion of the transaction, transfer of the sold property to the buyer, ritual actions accompanying the transaction, legal obligations of the parties involved, etc. Their varied content notwithstanding, all these clauses and statements can be included under one broad category of "final clauses," in agreement with the classification introduced by M. San Nicolò, *Schlussklauseln* p. 20.

7.12.2. Completion-of-Price Clauses

The documents belonging to the present corpus use four different clauses to express the completion of the price by the buyer.

7.12.2.1. (níg-)šám . . . til Clause

Attested in two Sargonic and one Ur III sale documents.

níg-[šám? al-til] "the [price? was completed]": no. 164
šám al-til "the price was completed": no. 182
níg-šám-bi in-til "he (i.e., the buyer) completed the price": no. 356

For til, Akk. *gamārum* "to complete, to be completed," see Falkenstein, *NSGU* 3 p. 166.

7.12.2.2. kug(-bi)-ta . . . til Clause

Attested in four Ur III sale documents.

kug-ta ì-til "he (i.e., the buyer) completed (the price) with (this) silver": nos. 247 and 299
⸢kug⸣-bi-ta ì-til "he (i.e., the buyer) completed (the price) with this silver": no. 255
kug-ta in-til: no. 256

7.12.2.3. kug-bi-ta . . . è Clause

The only example of this clause comes from the Ur III sale document no. 294: kug-bi-ta íb⟨-ta⟩-ni-è "he (i.e., the buyer) issued this silver," lit.: "he went ⟨out⟩ of this silver." For kug-ta . . . è "to issue silver," see Falkenstein, *NSGU* 3 p. 105 under è(-d) 5.

7.12.2.4. kug-bi šu . . . si Clause

Attested in eight Ur III sale documents.

kug-bi šu-ne-ne(-a) ab-si "this silver filled their (i.e., of the sellers) hands": nos. 248, 252, 253, 262, and 328
⸢kug⸣-bi šu-na [ab-si] "this silver [filled] his (i.e., of the seller) hands": no. 310
kug-bi šu-na-a ab-si: no. 327
kug-bi šu-na ba-a-si: no. 330

For šu(-a) . . . si "to fill (someone's) hands," see Falkenstein, *NSGU* 3 pp. 155f. Note that the same clause is used in certain Sargonic sale documents as the main verb of the operative sections of types A and D (see section 6.3).

7.12.3. Completion-of-Transaction Clauses

There are extant three separate clauses which record the fact that the transaction has been completed, i.e., that the buyer has paid the price in full and has taken possession of the sold property.

7.12.3.1. inim-bi . . . til Clause

Attested in nine Sargonic and three Ur III sale documents.

inim-bi igi-ne-n[e]-t[a] a[l-til] "this transaction [was completed] before them (i.e., the witnesses)": no. 170
inim-pi al-til "this transaction was completed": nos. 171 and 190
mu lugal-šè mu Nam-maḫ-[šè] in[im-bi a]l-til "by the name of the king, by the name of Nam-maḫ, [this] transaction was completed": no. 188
inim-bi al-til: nos. 191 and 224
inim-ma-ni ì-til: "he (i.e., the buyer) completed his transaction": no. 191
ig[i]-ne-ne inim-pi al-til: no. 192
inim-bi ì-til "he (i.e., the buyer) completed this transaction": nos. 203, 318, 344, and 365
mu lugal inim-bi a[l-til] "by the name of the king, this transaction was [completed]": no. 211

See also the examples of inim-bi . . . til in conjunction with the nu-gi$_4$-gi$_4$ clause, cited under 7.12.6.1.2.

7.12.3.2. inim-bi é-ta . . . è Clause

This clause, which is found only in the Fara kudurrus nos. 14 and 15, reads: inim-bi é-ta ab-è "this transaction 'left the house'" or "this transaction 'was taken out from the house.'" The idiomatic sense of this statement appears to be that the sellers departed from the buyer's house having been satisfied with the price, i.e., that the transaction has been completed. For the house of the buyer as the usual location of sale transactions, see section 7.12.5.7. Alternatively, the clause could simply be translated: "this transaction 'has departed'"; this interpretation is suggested by the usage of é-ta . . . è in Sargonic economic texts (e.g., *BIN* 8, 124, 206, and 271), where this expression means "to take out, to issue," without referring to any specific house.

A possible parallel to this clause is found in the OB deeds of division of property from Susa. One of the clauses used in the latter texts reads: *zīzū mesû duppurū*, "they divided, they are 'cleared,' they removed themselves" (see Y. Muffs, *Studies in the Aramaic Legal Papyri from Elephantine* [Leiden, 1969] pp. 117–20). The verb *duppurum* denotes here the act of quittance (lit.: the act of departure) after the receipt of inheritance shares, and thus may convey a similar idea as é-ta . . . è in nos. 14 and 15.

7.12.3.3. inim-bi . . . dug$_4$ Clause

This clause is uniquely attested in the Ur III sale document no. 359. It reads: É-duru$_5$-nigìn-gar-ki-dùg gú ^{ÍD}Dur-ùl-ka inim-bi ba-ab-dug$_4$ "this transaction was negotiated in the hamlet Nigìn-gar-ki-dùg, (located) on the bank of the Dur-ùl." The sense "to negotiate" or "to come to an agreement" of inim . . . dug$_4$ is suggested by the context. In this meaning, inim . . . dug$_4$ probably corresponds to the Akkadian *dabābum*; compare KA-dug$_4$ = MIN (= *da-ba-bu*) in Nabnitu IV–IVa 98 (*MSL* 16 p. 80), and KA-dug$_4$ = *da-ba-[bu]* in Igituḫ I 197.

7.12.4. Transfer-of-Object-of-Sale Clause

This clause is attested only in the Ur III sale documents from Adab and Nippur. It states that the object of sale was purchased (šám) or transferred (sum) in the presence of witnesses or authorizing official(s).

igi-bi-šè é ba-šám "before them (i.e., the witnesses) the house was purchased": no. 331
igi-bi-šè sag ba-šám "before them (i.e., the witnesses) the 'head' was purchased": nos. 335 and 338
igi PN di-kud lugal-⌜ka⌝-šè ⌜in-na?-an?-sum⌝ "before PN, the royal judge, he (i.e., the seller) ⌜transferred⌝ it (i.e., the orchard)": no. 264
igi PN muḫaldim é-dub ù PN$_2$ IŠ-šè i[n]-⌜na⌝?-[an-s]um "before PN, the cook of the storehouse, and PN$_2$, the equerry, he (i.e., the seller) transferred him (i.e., the sold man)": no. 277
in-na-an-sum-ma "(before the witnesses) he (i.e., the seller) transferred them (i.e., the sold persons)": no. 312
[igi-bi-šè an]še ba-sum "[before them (i.e., the witnesses) the as]ses were transferred": no. 323
[igi P]N nu-banda-ni [ù] PN$_2$ engar-a-ni ⌜in⌝-na-⌜an⌝-sum-éš "before PN, his overseer, [and] PN$_2$, his farmer, they (i.e., the sellers) transferred it (the object of sale is not preserved)": no. 325
igi-bi sag ba-sum "before them (i.e., the witnesses) the 'head' was transferred": no. 334
[igi] PN ad-da en$_5$-si-ka-šè PN$_2$ egir en$_5$-si sag ba-sum "[before] PN, father of the governor, PN$_2$, the retainer of the governor, transferred the 'head'": no. 332

7.12.5. Symbolic Actions Accompanying the Sale Transaction

This category comprises the clauses recording various ritual actions that formed part of the sale transaction. Six such ritual actions can be distinguished: 1) kag . . . dù "driving of the nail into a wall"; 2) ì . . . ag "spreading of oil"; 3) a . . . dé "pouring of water"; 4) a . . . sì "putting (of oil and flour?) into the water"; 5) giš-gan(-na) . . . bala "crossing over the pestle"; 6) zag . . . šuš "branding."

7.12.5.1. kag . . . dù Clause

The kag . . . dù clause occurs in twelve Pre-Sargonic texts from Lagash (nos. 21?, 22, 23, 139, 140, 141, 142, 144, 145, 147, 148, and 151) and in one Sargonic document from Eshnuna (no. 239). Of those, nos. 21, 22, and 23 are stone kudurrus, nos. 139, 140, 141, 145, 147, and 148 are clay cones, and nos. 142, 144, 151, and 239 are clay tablets. Regarding their content, nos. 22, 23, 144, 145, and 239 deal with the sale of fields, nos. 139, 140, 141, and 142, with the sale of houses, and no. 151, with the sale of a person. In nos. 147 and 148 the object of sale is not preserved, but it almost certainly was real estate in each case.

In the Lagash texts, the clause reads: (PN-e) kag-bi é-gar$_8$(-ra) bí/bi-dù "(PN) drove this nail into the wall." In all of the extant examples, this statement is followed by the ì . . . ag clause (see section 7.12.5.2), with which it forms one syntactic unit: "(PN) drove this nail into the wall (and) spread its (i.e., of the transaction) oil on the side."

In no. 239, the form of the clause is as follows: GIŠ. KAG ⌜*a*⌝-*na* (erasure) TI.LA *Na-ra-am-*ᵈEN.ZU [*m*]*a-aḫ*(wr. ḪI)-*za-at* "the nail was driven in (by the seller?) by the life of Narâm-Sin."

In nos. 22 and 23, both of which deal with the sale of fields, the actor of the kag . . . dù rite is the seller. In contrast, in nos. 139, 140, 141, and 142, concerning the sale of houses, and in the slave-sale no. 151, this rite was performed by a nigir "herald" (nos. 139, 140, and 142), or a nigir-uru "town-herald" (nos. 141 and 151). In nos. 144, 145, 147, and 148, the actor is not preserved.

The "nail" (Sum. kag, Akk. *sikkatum*) referred to in the clause can be identified with the clay cones on which nos. 139, 140, 141, 145, 147, and 148 are recorded. Another example of such a cone is the Ur III house sale no. 263, whose text, however, makes no mention of the kag . . . dù rite.

These objects, whose shape is vaguely reminiscent of that of the votive nails, are inscribed in a characteristic manner, from the small end to the large end, contrary to the orientation found on the latter documents. Each of these cones has a hole along its axis, which originally accommodated a wooden peg, running through the cone and protruding at both ends. The cone was fastened to the peg with strings or leather thongs, the impressions of which can still be seen on the extant specimens. It appears that, after the cone had been attached to the peg, the protruding pointed end of the peg was driven into the wall, until the cone rested upon the wall's face. Cf. Steinkeller, *Sale Documents* pp. 238–41.

The point as to which "wall" these cones were hammered in is not entirely clear. Assuming that the clause means the wall of the sold property, in the sales of houses this would be the wall of the house in question, while in the case of transactions involving the sales of fields one thinks of the low mud-walls (Sum. im-dù-a, Akk. *pitiqtum*) that are known to have surrounded fields. However, this interpretation does not work for the slave-sales, which, as demonstrated by no. 151, were also accompanied by the kag . . . dù rite. As an alternative solution, one could speculate that all such cones, irrespectively of the nature of the object of sale, were exposed on the wall of a house, which was either the house of the buyer or some public building, such as a temple or city-gate, especially designated for this purpose. For a possible representation of such a cone *in situ*, see no. 12 under *Iconography and Text*.

In spite of this uncertainty, the meaning of the kag . . . dù rite is clear: it symbolized and, at the same time, made public the transfer of the sold property to the buyer. As far as one can tell from the extant data, this rite was performed either by the seller or the herald, the first acting in the sales of fields, the latter acting in the sale of houses and persons.

The fact that the kag . . . dù clause is included in nos. 142, 144, and 151, all three of which are written on clay tablets, suggests that in Pre-Sargonic Lagash each sale transaction was recorded on two types of documents: a clay cone, which was displayed publicly (either on the buyer's house or in a public place), and a clay tablet, which was kept by the buyer in his archive. On the other hand, the presence of this clause in the transactions recorded in the stone kudurrus nos. 22 and 23 demonstrates that the latter documents are collections of individual transactions, which were copied from either cones or clay tablets.

7.12.5.2. ì . . . ag Clause

This clause is attested in two Fara kudurrus (nos. 14 and 15) and in several Pre-Sargonic kudurrus and sale documents from Lagash (nos. 22, 23, 139, 140, 141, 142, 144, 145, 147, 148, and 151). With the exception of no. 151, which records the sale of a person, all of these texts deal with the transfer of immovables (fields and houses).

The clause reads: ì-bi zag (ab-)ag "the oil was spread (by him/them) on the side" (nos. 14 and 15); ì-bi zag-gi bí/bi-ag "he spread the oil on the side" (nos. 22, 23, 139, 140, 141, 142, 144, 145, 147, 148, and 151). In nos. 14 and 15, the clause appears following the inim-bi é-ta . . . è clause (see section 7.12.3.2); the only exception here is the transaction recorded in no. 14 xiii 10–xvi 1, where the two clauses occur separately from each other. In the Pre-Sargonic texts from Lagash, the ì . . . ag clause regularly follows after the kag . . . dù clause, with which it forms one syntactic unit: "he drove this nail into the wall (and) spread its (i.e., of the transaction) oil on the side."

In the Lagash texts, the person performing the ì . . . ag rite can be identified, by analogy with the kag . . . dù clause (see under 7.12.5.1), as either the seller or the herald, the first acting in the sales of fields, the latter acting in the sales of houses and persons. By extending this analogy to nos. 14 and 15, both of which record the sales of fields, we can assume that in the latter texts this rite was performed by the sellers too.

Although the Lagash examples could be taken as evidence that the kag . . . dù and the ì . . . ag clauses were parts of the same rite, the fact that in nos. 14 and 15 the ì . . . ag clause occurs by itself makes it clear that they must be interpreted as two independent ritual actions.

The construction ì Object-e . . . ag "to apply oil to an object," which is translated in lexical texts by *arāmum* "to stretch, to spread something over an object" (see ì ag-a = *a-ra-mu* in Erimhuš V 122 [*MSL* 17 p. 72]), is also attested in economic texts, where it serves as a technical term for treating various materials and objects with oil. See, e.g., ì túg-gi . . . ag "to apply oil to the cloth (in fulling)" (for the examples, see Waetzoldt, *UNT* p. 170); 1½ silà UD.KA.BAR ab-ag "1½ quart (of oil) was applied to the bronze (objects)" (*OIP* 14, 118:4); ì-šáḫ kuš-e ag-dè "the lard to be applied to the hides" (*OIP* 14, 126:1–2).

Although it is certain that, in the context of the present clause, the "applying of oil" denotes a ritual action, solemnizing the transfer of the sold property to the buyer, the question as to what this rite actually entailed is somewhat unclear. The answer to this question hinges on the meaning of zag, which can be interpreted either as an adverb, "here, on the side" (with Edzard, *SRU* p. 70) or as "border (of the sold property)." Of the two interpretations, the first one appears to be more likely, since, as proved by no. 151, this rite could be performed at the sales of people as well.

The same rite is probably also mentioned in the Pre-Sargonic kudurru no. 35 i, where three groups of persons, (probably the sellers) are said to have spread the oil: [x]+5 PNs Ì *iš-du-du* D PN D PN_2 DUMU PN_x [Ì] *iš-du-du* [D P]N_3 [D P]N_4 [Ì *iš-du-d*]*u!* "[x]+5 PNs spread the oil; PN (and) PN_2, son of PN_x, spread [the oil]; [P]N_3 (and) [P]N_4 [spre]ad [the oil]." The verb *šadādum*, whose usual meanings are "to pull, to drag, to measure (with a rope)," in this context probably means "to spread." This translation is suggested by the evidence from the OB oil-omen texts, where *šadādum* is used to describe the movement of oil on the surface of water (see Pettinato, *Die Ölwahrsagung bei den Babyloniern* 1 [Rome, 1966] pp. 166f.).

Yet another reference to this rite may be found in the Sargonic house-sale no. 237, which mentions, apart from the NÍG.KI.GAR, another payment called Ì.ZAG (see section 7.5.6). Since the term Ì.ZAG "oil of the 'side'" cannot but be connected with the rite in question, we can speculate that this payment represented a remuneration or gift that the buyer gave to the seller for the performance of the oil-ceremony.

The symbolic use of oil in connection with various legal transactions, such as sales, marriages, manumissions, etc., and in oath taking, is amply documented both in ancient Mesopotamia and in the ancient Near East in general. For a discussion of oil-symbolism in ancient Near Eastern law, see E. Kutsch, *Salbung als Rechtsakt im Alten Testament und im Alten Orient*, *ZAW* Beiheft 87 (1963); K. R. Veenhof, *BiOr* 23 (1966) pp. 308–13; S. Greengus, *JCS* 20 (1966) p. 72 and nn. 115–17; A. Drafkorn-Kilmer, *JAOS* 94 (1974) p. 182 n. 22. Compare also section 7.12.5.3 and the "oath by oil" (NAM.KUD Ì IR) in no. 36 ii, discussed in section 7.12.6.3.

7.12.5.3. a . . . dé Clause

The only examples of this clause come from two Sargonic sale documents from Nippur, involving the sale of houses: [igi-ne-ne]-šè [a-bi a]b-ta-dé "[before them (i.e., the witnesses) its (i.e., of the transaction) 'water] was poured out'" (no. 206); ⌜mu ^{d}Nin⌝-urta-šè mu lugal-šè a-bi ab-ta-dé "by the name of Ninurta, by the name of the king, its 'water was poured out'" (no. 209). The same clause also occurs in difficult contexts in two Sargonic legal documents: PN dumu PN_x PN_2 dumu PN_y igi-ne-ne a-pi ab-ta-dé "PN, son of PN_x, (and) PN_2, son of PN_y, before them, its 'water was poured out'" (*MVNS* 3, 52 ii 4′–9′); ki di-kud-ka a-bi šu-na ì-mi-dé "at the place of the judge/judgment its 'water he poured/was poured into his hands'" (*MVNS* 3, 77:18–19).

The basic meanings of a . . . dé are "to pour water, to sprinkle with water, to irrigate" (see Falkenstein, *NSGU* 3 p. 89; *AHWB* p. 1181), also "to perform a libation" (see Falkenstein, *NSGU* 1 p. 111 n. 5). In the present clause, the "pouring of water" can be understood either literally, namely, that the water was actually poured or libated, or figuratively, meaning that the transaction was irrevocably completed. In favor of the literal interpretation is the fact that in the above-cited text *MVNS* 3, 77, it is specifically said that the water was poured "into his hands." Further, the use of water as part of the symbolic actions accompanying various legal transactions is well documented in the ancient Near East. The washing of hands with water as a gesture of quittance, recorded in the Ugaritic text *MRS* 6, 55:11–14, and the Neo-Assyrian oath by "water and oil" (see K.-H. Deller, *Biblica* 46 [1965] pp. 349–52; Veenhof, *BiOr* 23 [1966] pp. 312f.; *CAD* A/1 p. 132 *adû* Ac) are two such examples.

Accordingly, if the present clause does in fact refer to the physical act of pouring water, we would be dealing here with either a form of libation, solemnizing the transfer of the sold property and reminiscent of the oil-ceremony, or a gesture of quittance, signifying that the parties involved have no outstanding claims.

7.12.5.4. a . . . sì Clause

Only two examples of this clause are extant, both coming from the Sargonic slave-sales. The clause reads: ì sag zíd? sag-bi a ba-SUM (no. 184); ì sag-gá zíd? sag-gá-[b]i a ba-SUM (no. 187). Its interpretation presents serious difficulties. Krecher, *ZA* 63 (1974) p. 233, translated it "das beste Fett und beste Mehl dabei sind *dazu gegeben*," on the assumption that, firstly, sag is used here as an adjective, meaning "first-quality," and secondly, that the element a represents an assimilated prospective prefix ù- (*ù-ba-SUM > a-ba-sum). This explanation, however, is highly questionable. Given the fact that in Sumerian the noun and its attributive cannot form a genitival construct, the possibility that sag could be an adjective here is unlikely. Furthermore, since the use of the prospective is limited to dependent clauses, the absence of the main clause in either text speaks strongly against interpreting a as a prospective prefix. As an alternative solution, one might consider the translation "the oil of the 'head' and the flour(?) of the 'head' were placed in the water." This interpretation would assume that sag denotes here the sold person, and that SUM stands for sì "to place," corresponding to the Akkadian *šakānum* (see Sollberger, *TCS* 1 p. 166).

If this interpretation is correct, we would find here yet another type of a symbolic action, which involved the placing of oil and flour(?) in water, perhaps as part of the oath-taking (cf. the Neo-Assyrian oath by "water and oil," cited under 7.12.5.3).

7.12.5.5. giš-gan(-na) . . . bala Clause

The giš-gan(-na) clause is attested in nineteen Sargonic and nine Ur III sale documents. With the exception of the Ur III text no. 368, which concerns the sale of a she-ass, they all deal with the sale of persons. The usual form of the clause is giš-gan(-na) íb-ta-bala "he (i.e., the seller) made him/her (i.e., the sold person) cross over the pestle (for the buyer)." In most of the Sargonic examples, the word giš-gan "pestle" is replaced by giš "wooden stick." The attestations of the clause are as follows:

giš-a íb-ta-bala(-éš) "he/they made him/her cross over the stick": nos. 157, 158, 159, 160, 161, 162, 195, 196, 200, 201, and 202

PN mu PN_2-šè giš-a ì-na-ta-bala "PN, in place of PN_2 (i.e., the seller?), made her cross over the stick for him (i.e., the buyer)": no. 163
giš-a ab-ta-bala "she made him cross over the stick": no. 191
PN giš-a íb-[ta-bala] "PN (i.e., the guarantor?) made him [cross] over the stick": no. 199
giš-a ab-t[a]-bala-e-é[š] "he made them cross over the stick": no. 213
giš-a ì-ta-bala-e-éš "he made them cross over the stick": no. 213
giš-gan-na ab-ta-bala "she made him cross over the pestle": nos. 184 and 187
giš-gan-na íb-ta-bala-e-éš "they made him cross over the pestle": no. 215
[sa]g? giš-gan-na bala-a[m_6]? "the ⌜'head'(?)⌝ (i.e., the sold woman?) crossed over the pestle": no. 217
[giš-gan]-na ib-ta-bala "he made her cross over the ⌜pestle⌝": no. 283
sag-bi ⌜giš⌝-g[an]-na [íb]-t[a]?-[ba]la "he made this 'head' (i.e., the sold woman) ⌜cross over the pestle⌝": no. 286
giš-gan íb-ta-ab-la "they made her cross over the pestle": no. 289
giš-gan(wr. TAG) in-bala "he made her cross over the pestle": no. 291
giš-gin_x(GIM)-na ba-ra-a-bala-eš "he made them cross over the pestle": no. 296
[sag? giš-g]i-na [íb-ta-ba]la "⌜he made⌝ [the 'head'? (i.e., the sold man)] ⌜cross over the pestle⌝": no. 297
giš-gin_x(GIM) ì-na-ra-bala "he made her cross over the pestle for him (i.e., the buyer)": no. 298
sa[g giš-ga]n?-na íb-[ta?]-[ba]la-e "he made the 'head' (i.e., the sold man) ⌜cross over the pestle⌝": no. 366
GIŠ.GUM ÍB.LA "he made it (i.e., the she-ass) cross over the pestle(?) (or: mortar)": no. 368

The rite of "crossing over the pestle/stick" can be interpreted as a symbolic action signifying the transfer of the sold person (and possibly also of the sold animal) from the authority of the seller to that of the buyer. Typologically, this symbolic action belongs to the so-called "rites of passage," i.e., rites which in traditional societies accompany the passage of a person from one situation or state to another; such rites are common at births, initiations, betrothals, marriages, and funerals. For a detailed discussion of this clause, see Edzard, *ZA* 60 (1969) pp. 8–53; Steinkeller, *Sale Documents* pp. 34–42.

7.12.5.6. zag . . . šuš Clause

This clause is uniquely attested in the Sargonic sale document no. 217, which records the sale of a woman. The clause reads: PN zag in-šuš "PN (i.e., the seller) branded (the sold woman with the branding-mark of the buyer)." For zag . . . šuš "to brand," see zag-šuš = *ši-im-tum* "branding-mark," Nabnitu IV-IVa 354 (*MSL* 16 p. 91); [z]ag-šuš = *ši-mat* [*bu-lim*] "branding-mark of cattle," Antagal F 281 (*MSL* 17 p. 220); udu-zag-šuš = MIN (= UDU) [*šim-ti*] "branded sheep," Hh. XIII 181 (*MSL* 8/1 p. 26). While the practice of branding farm animals is well documented in third millennium texts, references to the branding of humans are comparatively rare. The only such references come from Sargonic sources, where persons are occasionally classified as zag-šuš "branded" (e.g., *ITT* 2, 4543:2; *HSS* 10, 197:5; *MVNS* 3, 64 iv 7′), and zag-nu-šuš "not branded" (e.g., *ITT* 1, 1231; Gordon, *Smith College* 2 i 11, 16, 20, ii 4).

Although the act of branding is charged with symbolic significance, it cannot, however, be considered a symbolic action in the proper sense of the term. Nevertheless, it seems certain that, when performed during a sale transaction, its importance was largely symbolic. This interpretation finds support in the fact that, as demonstrated by no. 217, such branding was done by the seller, which parallels the situation found in the giš-gan(-na) . . . bala rite.

7.12.5.7. The Ceremonial Feast Concluding the Transaction

The kudurrus nos. 35 and 40, dating to the Pre-Sargonic and Sargonic periods respectively, and the Sargonic house-sale no. 237 offer evidence that the sales of real property were concluded with a ceremonial feast which was held by the buyer for the participants of the transaction. This feast is recorded in a special clause, whose extant examples read as follows:

ŠU.NIGÍN 20 AB+ÁŠ *in* É! P[N] DUMU P[N_x] PA.TE.[SI] NINDA KÚ(KA+⌜GAR⌝) KAŠ Ì.NA[G](K[A+A]) "total of twenty witnesses; they ate bread/food (and) drank beer in the house of P[N], son of P[N_x], the governor (i.e., the buyer)": no. 35
ŠU.NIGÍN 5 GURUŠ AB+ÁŠ.AB+ÁŠ GÁN 190 GURUŠ DUMU.DUMU BÀD-^{d}EN.ZU^{KI} NINDA Ì.KÚ "total of 5 men, the witnesses of the field; 190 men, citizens of Dûr-Sin, ate bread/food": no. 40 Side A
ŠU.NIGÍN 30 GURUŠ AB+ÁŠ.AB+ÁŠ GÁN *Gir*$_{13}$-*tab*^{KI} 94 GURUŠ DUMU.DUMU *Gir*$_{13}$-*tab*^{KI} NINDA Ì.KÚ "total of 30 men, the witnesses of the field of Girtab; 94 men, citizens of Girtab, ate bread/food": no. 40 Side B
ŠU.NIGÍN.ŠU.NIGÍN 52 GURUŠ *Már-da*^{KI} AB+ÁŠ.AB+ÁŠ GÁN 600 GURUŠ *in Ga-za-lu*^{KI} NINDA Ì.KÚ 600 GURUŠ *šu* 1 UD 1200 GURUŠ *šu* 2 UD *in maš-ga-ni Be-lí-ba-ni* AGRIG ^{d}*A-ba*$_4$-*iš-da-gal* NINDA Ì.KÚ LÚ *Már-da*^{KI} "grand-total of 52 men of Marda, the witnesses of the field; 600 men ate bread/food in Kazalu; 600 men for one day, 1200 men for two days (i.e., 600 men for two days), ate bread/food in the settlement of Bêlī-bāni, the steward of Abaiš-takal; the citizens of Marda": no. 40 Side C
80 DUMU.DUMU *Kiš*^{KI} *in Ga-za-lu*^{KI} NINDA Ì.KÚ "80 citizens of Kish ate bread/food in Kazalu": no. 40 Side D
[19 A]B+ÁŠ.AB+ÁŠ *in* É PN NINDA K[Ú] "[19] witnesses; they ate bread/food in the house of PN (i.e., the buyer)": no. 237

In nos. 35 and 237, the clause is placed immediately after the list of witnesses. In contrast, in no. 40, which divides witnesses into two groups: witnesses of the sellers and those of the buyer (with the exception of the transaction recorded on Side D, which has only witnesses of the buyer), it is inserted between the two lists. If one were to assume that the subject of the clause is, in each case, the persons immediately preceding it, the resulting conclusion would be that in nos. 35 and 237 the persons participating in the feast were the witnesses, while in no. 40 they were the unnamed citizens of Dûr-Sin, Girtab, Marda, and Kish. It is possible, however, that this clause functions as a semi-independent unit, whose subject is all of the persons listed before it. This would mean that, in nos. 35 and 237, the participants of the feast were the sellers, secondary sellers, and the witnesses; in the case of no. 40, they would include the sellers, secondary sellers, and witnesses of the sellers. The latter interpretation may find support in the fact that in the Mari sale documents *M.A.R.I.* 1 p. 80, and *ARMT* 8, 13, which use a similar clause, the subject of the clause appears to be all of the parties to the transaction (see below).

In no. 237, and probably also in no. 35, the feast was held in the buyer's house. In the case of no. 40, it appears that all four transactions recorded refer to one and the same feast, which took place in Kazalu, in the settlement (or on the threshing floor) of Bêlī-bāni, the steward of Abaiš-takal. The fact that Abaiš-takal is known to have been one of Maništushu's brothers (he is identified as a son of Sargon in C xiii 22–23 of the same text), provides the evidence linking Bêlī-bāni to Manishtushu, i.e., the buyer. Accordingly, we can assume that Bêlī-bāni, who seems to have owned a landed property in or near Kazalu, acted as Manishtushu's host for the occasion of the four sale transactions; in other words, the feast was held in the temporary quarters of Manishtushu. These facts combined point to the buyer's house as the usual location of this type of a ceremony.

As demonstrated by the Mari texts, *M.A.R.I.* 1 p. 80 (field-sale, *šakkanakku* period), and *ARMT* 8, 13 (house-sale, Old Babylonian), which contain a clause that is strikingly reminiscent of the examples discussed earlier, the custom of holding such ceremonial feasts was also known in the outlying regions of Mesopotamia. This clause, which is recorded after the list of witnesses, reads as follows:

> 6 PNs ÉŠ.GÍD *šu zi-ga-tim*$_x$(DIN) *tim-ḫa-zu* NINDA *ti-ku-lu* KAŠ *ti-iš-da-u ú* Ì *ti-il-tap-tu in* É PN *a-lu-zi-nim* "6 PNs, the measurers who drove the pegs in; they ate bread/food, drank beer, and anointed one another with oil in the house of PN, the jester (possibly a relative of the buyer)" (*M.A.R.I.* 1 p. 80 lines 14–26)
>
> [x]+10 PNs *ka-ra-am i-ku-lu ka-sa-am iš-tu-ú ù ša-am-na-am ip-ta-šu* "[x]+10 PNs; they ate 'bread' (or: from the platter), drank 'beer' (or: from the goblet), and anointed one another with oil" (*ARMT* 8, 13 rev. 1′–14′)

The only significant difference between the Mesopotamian and the Mari examples is that in the latter the parties to the transaction, in addition to having eaten and drank, also anointed one another with oil. Although none of the extant kudurrus and sale documents makes mention of that particular use of oil (but note that oil was used in the ritual actions discussed under 7.12.5.2 and 7.12.5.4), there are reasons to believe that this custom, too, was practiced as part of the Mesopotamian sale transaction. This is indicated by an early Old Babylonian field-sale from Khafajah (*JCS* 9 [1955] p. 107 no. 59:10), which records, after the giš-gan(-na) . . . bala clause and before the list of witnesses, the following statement: *ša-am-na qá-qá-sú-nu pa-ši-iš* "their (i.e., of the seller and the buyer, and possibly also of the witnesses) heads were(!) anointed with oil."

7.12.6. No-Contest Clause

The clause of no-contest records the sworn promise of either the seller alone or both the seller and the buyer that he/they will not contest the completed transaction in the future. The clause is usually composed of two parts: 1) the no-contest statement and 2) the oath. Six no-contest clauses can be distinguished, depending on the verb of the no-contest statement.

7.12.6.1. nu-gi$_4$-gi$_4$ Clause

This is by far the most common no-contest clause in the texts belonging to this corpus. Its time-range is the Sargonic and Ur III periods. The verb gi$_4$, Akk. *tuārum*, whose usual meaning is "to return," in this clause has the specialized sense of "to return (with claims), to go back (on an agreement)." In the legal context, lexical texts translate gi$_4$ by *enûm*, "to change, to revoke," see Ai. IV iv 49, VI i 53 (*MSL* 1 pp. 67, 78). The clause can be used in either one-sided (referring only to the seller) or reciprocal sense (referring both to the seller and the buyer). When used in the first sense, the no-contest statement contains only the verb. See, e.g., nu-gi$_4$-gi$_4$-da "(he swore by the name of the king) that he will not contest" (no. 356). The reciprocity is expressed either by lú lú(-ra), Akk. *awīlum awīlam* "one against the other," before the verb, or by the inclusion in the oath of the adverbial expression téš-bi/ba, Akk. *mitḫāriš*, *ištēniš* "together," "jointly." See, e.g., lú lú-ra nu-gi$_4$-gi$_4$-dè "(they swore by the name of the king) not to contest one against the other" (no. 298); [nu]-gi$_4$-gi$_4$-dè ⌜téš⌝-bi mu lugal íb-da-pàd "they swore together by the name of the king [not] to contest (one against the other)" (no. 325). For a detailed discussion of this clause and the oath in general, see Falkenstein, *NSGU* 1 pp. 63–72, 79f.; Edzard, *AS* 20 pp. 63–98; Steinkeller, *Sale Documents* pp. 44–50, 71–80. The following listing contains all the examples of the nu-gi$_4$-gi$_4$ clause grouped according to whether the clause is employed in one-sided or reciprocal sense.

7.12.6.1.1. One-Sided

é-a nu-ub-gi$_4$-gi$_4$-dè mu lugal-bi [in-pàd(-dè-éš)] "[they (i.e., the sellers) swore] by the name of the king that they will not raise claims to the house": no. 251

nu-ub-gi_4-gi_4-da-⌜gi⌝?! mu lugal-bi in-pàd "he (i.e., the seller) swore by the name of the king that he will not contest": no. 256

[nu-gi_4-gi_4-da] ⌜mu lu⌝[gal-bi in-pàd] "[he swore] by the name of the ki[ng not to contest]": no. 257

é-a nu-ù-[gi_4-gi_4-da Seller] m[u] lu[gal-bi in-pàd] "[the seller swore] ⌜by the name of the king⌝ not to [raise claims] to the house": no. 259

n[u-a]b-gi_4-g[i_4-da] mu lugal-bi [in-pàd] "[he (i.e., the seller) swore] by the name of the king ⌜not to contest⌝": no. 264

nu-gi_4-g[i_4-da] mu lugal-b[i in-pàd] "[he (i.e., the seller) swore] by the name of the king not to contest": no. 290

nu-ù-gi_4-g[i_4-da] mu lugal-bi in-[pàd] "[he (i.e., the seller) swore] by the name of the king that he will not contest": no. 294

nu-ub-gi_4-gi_4-[da] mu lugal-bi [in-pàd] "[he (i.e., the seller) swore] by the name of the king that he will not contest": no. 299

Seller Buyer-ra téš-bi nu-ub-gi_4-gi_4-da mu lugal-bi in-pàd "the seller swore for the buyer by the name of the king that he will not contest together (sic)": no. 300

nu-gi_4-gi_4-da mu lugal[al]-bi ì-pàd "he (i.e., the seller) swore by the name of the king not to contest": no. 305

[nu-gi_4-gi_4-da] mu lugal-bi in-[pàd] "[he (i.e., the seller) swore] by the name of the king [not to contest]": no. 317

nu-gi_4-gi_4-d[a] mu lugal-bi [in-pàd(-dè-éš)] "[they (i.e., the sellers) swore] by the name of the king not to contest": no. 319

nu-gi_4-gi_4-dè mu lugal-bi ì-pàd "he (i.e., the seller) swore by the name of the king not to contest": no. 324

nu-ù-gi_4-gi_4-da Seller-e mu lugal-bi in-pàd "the seller swore by the name of the king that he will not contest": no. 326

[nu-g]i_4-gi_4-da [mu lu]gal-bi ì-pàd "he (i.e., the seller) swore by the [name of the ki]ng [not] to contest": no. 346

nu-ub-gi_4-gi_4-da mu lugal-bi pàd "the oath was sworn that he (i.e., the seller) will not contest": no. 352

nu-gi_4-gi_4 mu nu-gi_4-g[i_4-šè] mu lugal-[bi] pàd-da "not to contest, on account of no contesting the oath by the name of the king was sworn": no. 354

nu-gi_4-gi_4-da mu lugal-bi in-pàd "he (i.e., the seller) swore by the name of the king not to contest": no. 356

ud-kúr lú lú nu-un-gi_4-gi_4-da Seller-ke_4 mu lugal-bi in-pàd "the seller swore by the name of the king that they (sic) will not contest one against the other in the future": no. 360

MU LUGAL IN.PÀD NU.UB.GI_4.GI_4.DA "he (i.e., the seller) swore by the name of the king that he will not contest": no. 370

7.12.6.1.2. Reciprocal

mu dNin-$Isin_x$(IN)-na-šè PN dumu PN_x PN_2 dumu PN_y lú lú nu-ba-gi_4-gi_4 inim-bi in-til "by the name of Nin-Isin, PN son of PN_x, (and) PN_2, son of PN_y, completed this transaction that they will not contest one against the other": no. 170

mu dNin-$Isin_x$(IN)-šè mu lugal-šè inim-pi ì-til lú ⟨lú⟩ nu-ba-gi_4-gi_4-da "by the name of Nin-Isin, by the name of the king, they completed this transaction that they will not contest one against the other": no. 192

[lú l]ú la-ba-da-[g]i_4-gi_4 [inim]-⌜ma⌝ an-gál "it is in the ⌜agreement⌝ that they will not contest ⌜one against the other⌝": no. 209

mu lugal lú lú nu-ba-gi_4-gi_4-da-a inim-bi al-til! "by the name of the king, this transaction was completed that they will not contest one against the other": no. 213

[lú lú]-⌜ù⌝ [la-b]a-an-gi_4-gi_4-[da] m[u dNin-urta mu lugal-bi in-pàd(-dè-éš)] "[they swore by] the na[me] of Ninurta (and) by the name of the king] that they will [not] contest ⌜one against the other⌝": no. 248

[l]ú [l]ú-ù la-gi_4-gi_4-da [m]u dNin-urta mu lugal-bi in-pàd-éš "they swore by the name of Ninurta (and) by the name of the king that they will not contest ⌜one against the other⌝": no. 250

lú lú-ù la-ba-an-gi_4-gi_4-da mu dNin-urta [m]u lugal-bi al-[p]àd "the oath was sworn by the name of Ninurta (and) by the name of the king that they will not contest one against the other": no. 252

[lú lú-ù l]a-ba-an-gi_4-gi_4-da [mu dNin-ur]ta [mu lugal-bi in-pàd(-dè-éš)] "[they swore by the name of Ninur]ta (and) [by the name of the king] that they will not contest [one against the other]": no. 253

[lú lú-ra] la?-[ba(-an)-gi_4-g]i_4-da mu [lu]gal-bi in-pàd "they swore by the name of the king that they will not ⌜contest⌝ [one against the other]": no. 255

lú lú-ù la-ba-an-gi_4-gi_4-da-a mu dNin-urta mu lugal-bi al-pàd "the oath was sworn by the name of Ninurta (and) by the name of the king that they will not contest one against the other": no. 262

téš-ba nu-gi_4-gi_4-dè mu lugal-bi ì-pàd "they swore together by the name of the king not to contest (one against the other)": no. 266

[l]ú lú [nu-g]i_4-g[i_4-da mu lugal-bi in-pàd(-dè-éš)] "[they swore by the name of the king not] to ⌜contest one against the other⌝": no. 275

ud-kúr nu-u[b-gi_4-gi_4-da] téš-bi mu [lugal-bi íb]-da-p[a] "they swore together by the name of the [king] that they will not [contest] (one against the other) in the future": no. 287

lú lú nu-gi_4⟨-gi_4⟩-dam mu lugal-bi in-pàd "they swore by the name of the king not to contest one against the other": no. 288

mu lugal-bi in-pàd lú lú nu-gi_4-gi_4-da "they swore by the name of the king not to contest one against the other": no. 291

lú l[ú n]u?-u[n]-gi_4-g[i_4-da] mu lug[al-bi in-pàd]-dè-[éš] "[they swore] by the name of the ki[ng] ⌜not to contest one against the other⌝": no. 292

lú lú nu-ù-gi_4-gi_4-da mu lugal-bi in-pàd "they swore by the name of the king that they will not contest one against the other": no. 295

lú lú-ra nu-gi_4-gi_4-dè mu lugal[al]-bi ì-pàd "they swore by the name of the king not to contest one against the other": no. 298

lú lú nu-ki-ki-dè mu lugal-bi in-pàd "they swore by the name of the king not to contest one against the other": no. 303

lú lú nu-gi$_4$-gi$_4$-da mu lugal-bi in-pàd "they swore by the name of the king not to contest one against the other": no. 306

lú lú nu-gi$_4$-gi$_4$-dè mu lugal-bi ì-pàd-éš "they swore by the name of the king not to contest one against the other": no. 307

[lú lú la-ba-g]i$_4$-gi$_4$-da-a [mu lugal-b]i in-p[àd-d]è-e[š] "⌜they swore⌝ [by the name of the king not] ⌜to contest⌝ [one against the other]": no. 310

[nu]-gi$_4$-gi$_4$-dè ⌜téš⌝-bi mu lugal íb-da-pàd "they swore ⌜together⌝ by the name of the king [not] to contest (one against the other)": no. 325

lú lú la-ba-an-gi$_4$-gi$_4$-da mu lugal-bi al-pàd "the oath was sworn by the name of the king that they will not contest one against the other": no. 327

lú lú-ù la-ba-an-[gi$_4$-gi$_4$-da] mu ^{d}Nin-urta mu lugal-bi al-[pàd] "the oath was [sworn] by the name of Ninurta (and) by the name of the king that they will not [contest] one against the other": no. 328

lú lú-ù la-ba-an-gi$_4$-gi$_4$-da mu lugal-bi ì-pàd-d[è-éš] "they swore by the name of the king that they will not contest one against the other": no. 330

lú lú nu-gi$_4$-gi$_4$-dè téš-bi mu lugal ì-pàd "they swore together by the name of the king not to contest one against the other": no. 363

lú lú nu-un-gi$_4$-gi$_4$-da mu lugal-bi in-pàd-dè-[éš] "they swore by the name of the king that they will not contest one against the other": no. 365

lú [(lú) nu-g]i$_4$-gi$_4$-⌜dè⌝? mu [lugal-bi in-p]àd "⌜they swore⌝ by the name of the [king not] to ⌜contest one against the other⌝": no. 366

7.12.6.2. nu-bala Clause

The only certain occurrence of this clause comes from the Ur III sale document no. 297. The clause reads: [nu]-bala-e-dè Seller [m]u lugal-bi in-pàd "the seller swore by the name of the king [not] to change/violate (the terms of the agreement)." When used in legal documents, the verb bala corresponds to the Akkadian *nakārum* "to change, to violate"; see lú lú-ra nu-bala-e-dè = LÚ *a-mi-lam la-a na-ka-ri* Ai. VI i 60–61 (*MSL* 1 p. 78); bala = *na-ka-rum šá a-ma-ti* Nabnitu XXI 217 (*MSL* 16 p. 198). Compare also bala = *nabalkutum*, with the same meanings (*AHWB* pp. 694f.). The same clause is commonly used in the OB sale documents from southern Babylonia, especially those from Kutalla (see San Nicolò, *Schlussklauseln* pp. 52f.; Matouš, *AOr* 18/4 [1950] p. 43).

Another example of the nu-bala clause is possibly found in the Ur III sale document no. 357: nu-GIBIL-da mu lugal-bi ì-pàd "he (i.e., the seller) swore by the name of the king not to . . . ," where GIBIL should perhaps be read bíl and interpreted as a phonetic spelling for bala. However, one cannot rule out the possibility that the verb is in fact to be read gibil and equated with the Akkadian *edēšum* "to be new, to renew." The latter interpretation would yield the translation "he swore by the name of the king not to 'renew' (this transaction)." It should be stressed, however, that neither gibil nor *edēšum* is documented in this meaning in other legal documents.

An early variant of the nu-bala clause is found in the Fara sale documents nos. 113a and 113b, which concern the sale of two adjoining(?) houses by the same sellers to the same buyer. Following the statement that the buyer had donated a section of each of the two houses to his parents, the clause stipulates (only in no. 113b) that the sellers shall not violate the status of those quarters: ½ sar é é rig$_9$(DU.TUKU) PN an-na-sum "½ sar of (that) house, a donated house, was presented to PN (by the buyer)" (no. 113a); ½ sar é PN ad-da-ni ama-ni ì-na-ba é rig$_9$(DU.TUKU) inim-ba šu nu-bala "½ sar of (that) house he (i.e., the buyer) presented to PN, his father, (and) to his mother; this is a donated house; (with respect to) this transaction, they (i.e., the sellers) shall not violate (its status)" (no. 113b). For the meaning "to violate, to transgress" of šu . . . bala, see H. Behrens and H. Steible, *FAOS* 6 p. 318.

7.12.6.3. inim nu-kúr Clause

This clause is attested only in the Ur III sale document no. 281. It reads: ud-ta ud-gur-ra inim nu-ši-gur-da mu lugal-bi in-pàd-dè-éš "they (i.e., the sellers) swore by the name of the king that from this day on, in the future, they will not change the agreement" (note the phonetic spelling gur for kúr). If our reconstruction is correct, another example of this clause is found in the Ur III sale document no. 304: inim [nu-ši-kúr-da?] mu [lugal-bi in]-pàd "⌜he (i.e., the seller) swore⌝ by the name [of the king that he will not change] the agreement." For inim . . . kúr "to change an agreement," corresponding to the Akkadian *awatam nukkurum*, see Falkenstein, *NSGU* 3 p. 123.

A possible precursor of the inim nu-kúr clause may be the clause found in the Pre-Sargonic kudurru no. 36 ii 4–11: NAM.KUD Ì IR LÚ.NA.ME *i-na-kir ap-lu* GÍR ^{d}*Lugal*-^{GIŠ}*asal*$_x$(RÉC-65.A) ḪI.ÚŠ "the oath by oil nobody should change/violate; (if somebody does change it), then the heirs(?) (of the sellers?) with the dagger of Lugal-asal will kill him," or "(the preceding persons) swore by oil that nobody should change/violate (the conditions of the transaction); (if somebody does change them), then etc." For a detailed discussion of this clause, see note to no. 36 ii 1–20.

7.12.6.4. inim nu-gá-gá Clause

The only example of this clause is preserved in the Ur III sale document no. 278. In this particular instance, the provisions of the clause apply not to the seller or the buyer, as it is the case in the other no-contest clauses, but to the seller's brothers, who promise under oath not to raise claims to the sold property. The clause reads: PN ù PN$_2$ šeš-a-ni-me inim nu-gá-gá-dè mu lugal-bi in-pàd-dè-éš "PN and PN$_2$, his (i.e., of the seller) brothers, swore by the name of the king not to raise claims." For inim . . . gar / gá-gá "to raise claims, to sue at law," corresponding to the Akkadian *ragāmum*, *paqārum*, see Falkenstein, *NSGU* 3 p. 124.

7.12.6.5. dù and inim . . . gál Clause

This clause is singularly attested in the Pre-Sargonic sale document no. 150. It reads: ud an-dù inim an-gál ud-da ka-ka-na níg-NE.RU ba-gá-gá ^{GIŠ}kag ka-ka-na ešé-gaz "if he (i.e., the seller) detains (the sold woman) or raises claims (to her), then he puts deceit in his mouth, (and thus) a wooden nail should be driven through his mouth." For a discussion of this clause, see Steinkeller, *Sale Documents* pp. 58–60.

7.12.6.6. *mubbalkitum* Clause

This clause is attested in the Sargonic sale document no. 239, which is written in Akkadian. The clause provides that whoever of the parties to the transaction violates/changes the agreement, he will pay one pound of silver as a penalty: *mu-ba-al-ki-tum* [KUG.BAB]BAR 1 MA.NA ⌜*i*⌝-*sa-gal* "the transgressor will weigh out one pound of [silv]er." For *nabalkutum*, "to cross over, to transgress, to violate (an agreement)," see *AHWB* pp. 694f. Closely related clauses are used in the OB sale documents from Susa and in the fictitious adoption texts from Nuzi. See the following examples: *šà ib-ba-[la-ka-tu]* 1 MA.NA KUG.[BABBAR] Ì.LA[L.E] "the one who transgresses (the agreement) will weigh out one pound of silver" (*MDP* 18, 216:28–30); *šà ib-ba-la-ak-ka-tu ri-it-ta-šu ù li-šà-an-šu i-na-ak-ki-sú* 10 MA.NA KUG.BABBAR Ì.LAL.E "the one who transgresses (the agreement), they will cut off his hand and tongue (or) he will weigh out ten pounds of silver" (*MDP* 18, 203:47–50); *ma-an-nu-um-me-e i-na be-ri-šu-nu ša* KI.BALA-*ak-ka*$_4$-*tu*$_4$ 1 MA.NA KUG.BABBAR 1 MA.NA KUG.GI *ú-ma-al-la* "whoever among them transgresses (the agreement), he will pay one pound of silver (and) one pound of gold" (*HSS* 14, 604:28–30); *šum-ma* ^{I}PN KI.BALA-*at* 5 MA.NA KUG.BABBAR 5 MA.NA KUG.GI *a-na* ^{I}PN$_2$ *ú-ma-al-la* "if PN (i.e., the adoptee) transgresses (the agreement), he will weigh out to PN$_2$ (i.e., the adopter) five pounds of silver (and) five pounds of gold" (*JEN* 1, 16:14–17).

7.12.7. Eviction Clauses

The eviction clause stipulates that, if the seller was not the rightful owner of the sold property and, as a result of it, the buyer was evicted from this property, the seller will meet a corporal punishment or will have to pay a compensation. Four separate eviction clauses can be distinguished, depending on the verb employed in the protasis of the clause.

7.12.7.1. dù Clause

This clause is attested in the sale documents dating to the Pre-Sargonic, Sargonic, and Ur III periods. The extant examples are as follows:

lú [am$_6$]-ma-d[ù-da] kag-bi ka-ka-n[a]! e-g[az] "if somebody else ⌜holds⌝ it (i.e., the house) in possession, this nail (i.e., the clay nail on which the transaction is recorded, see section 7.12.5.1), will be dr[iven] through his (i.e., of the seller) mouth": no. 140

lú am$_6$-ma-dù-da kag-bi ka-ka⟨-na⟩ e-gaz "if somebody else holds it (i.e., the real estate) in possession, this nail will be driven through (his) mouth": no. 148

lú gán-⌜ba⌝ am$_6$-ma-dù-da kug-da kug ⟨gur-⟩ru-dam inim-ma [a]n-gál "it is in the agreement to return with the silver (of the price) the (equal amount of) silver, if somebody else holds the field in possession": no. 172

ud gán-ga(= ašag-ga) lú ù-ma-a-dù-a 2(iku) gán-bi-šè 4(iku) gán ab-ši-gá-gá inim-ma an-gál "it is in the agreement that, if somebody else holds the field in possession, he will replace the field of two iku with (another) field of four iku": no. 175

ud lú am$_6$-ma-dù-da-a PN arád PN$_2$-ke$_4$ dam dumu-ni igi ba-a-DU-a inim-ma ì-gar "he (i.e., the seller) made it stand in the agreement that, if somebody else holds the field in possession, PN, the slave of PN$_2$ (i.e., the seller's father), his wife (and) children will serve (him) (i.e., the buyer)": no. 177

tukumbi(ŠU.GAR.BI.LAL) lú ba-a-dù ^{ki} ^{GIŠ}kiri$_6$ ki-ba! gá-gá-dam mu lugal^{al}-bi in-pàd-éš "they (i.e., the sellers) swore by the name of the king to replace it (i.e., the orchard) with (another) orchard, if somebody else holds it in possession": no. 269

As noted by Sollberger, *TCS* 1 p. 109, in the legal context the verb dù corresponds to the Akkadian *kullum* "to detain, to hold." In view of the fact that all of the examples of the dù clause involve immovables, it appears that, when used in that clause, dù is to be equated with *kullum* in its specialized sense of "to have possession of or to hold real estate" (see *CAD* K pp. 514f.). Accordingly, we can assume that the protasis of the clause is concerned with a situation in which the sold property is owned by somebody else other than the seller. The apodosis then spells out the form of punishment that the seller is to meet. This punishment can entail either facial mutilation (nos. 140 and 148), or the payment of a simple compensation (nos. 177? and 269) or the double amount of the price (nos. 172 and 175). For a detailed discussion of this clause, see Steinkeller, *Sale Documents* pp. 52–58.

7.12.7.2. inim . . . gar Clause

The only example of this clause comes from the Ur III sale document no. 267. The clause reads: tukumbi lú inim ba-an-gar 6 ^{GIŠ}gišimmar sum-mu-dam mu lugal-bi ì-pàd "he (i.e., the seller) swore by the name of the king to give (an orchard with) six date-palms (in place of the original orchard with three palms), if someone else (i.e., the real owner) raises claims to it."

7.12.7.3. inim . . . gi-in Clause

This clause is preserved in the Ur III sale document no. 270. The clause reads: tukumbi inim nu-⌜ba⌝?-gi-in ^{GIŠ}gišimmar-mu inim-ba ga-ra-ab-sum bí-dug$_4$ "he (i.e., the seller) declared: 'If it is not confirmed (i.e., the sold property to the buyer), I will give you (i.e., the buyer) my own date-palms (in place of the property in question) in this transaction.'" Assuming that the verb inim . . . gi-in has the same meaning as gi-in "to verify, adjudge, to confirm (something to someone)" (see Falkenstein, *NSGU* 3 pp. 114f.), the protasis of the clause appears to refer to a situation in which the sold property is claimed by a third party and the seller fails to defend the buyer's title to this property, i.e., to confirm this property to the buyer.

7.12.7.4. *ar(r)ugimānē rašājum* Clause

The only example of this clause comes from the Ur III text no. 370, which records the self-sale of a woman. For obvious reasons, the party guaranteeing against the eviction in this text is not the seller herself but the guarantors. The clause reads: PN *ù* PN_2 DUMU.NI *mu-gi-bu* PN *ni-iš* LUGAL *it-ma šu-ma* GEMÉ *a-ru-gi-ma-ni ir-da-ši-ì a-na-ku-ù lu* GEMÉ "PN and PN_2, her son, are the guarantors; PN swore by the name of the king: 'If the slave woman (i.e., the woman selling herself into slavery) has claims, I will become a slave woman (in her place).'" For the term *arugimānum* "claim," see [i]nim-gál = *a-ru-gi₄-ma-n*[*u-um*] Kagal D Section 11:7 (*MSL* 13 p. 249 misprinted as *a-ru-ru-gi₄-ma-n*[*u-um*]).

7.12.8. Seller's Guaranty for the Title

The Ur III sale document no. 302 contains a unique clause, in which the seller declares under oath that he is the rightful owner of the sold property: mu lugal gemé-gá ḫi-a bí-in-du(= bí-in-dug₄) "he declared: 'By the name of the king, she (i.e., the sold woman) is truly my slave woman.'" The legal significance of this clause appears to be that, by making such a declaration, the seller assumes the responsibility to defend the buyer's title in the case of a claim raised by a third party, or, if he fails to defend the title and the eviction is carried out, to give a compensation to the buyer.

7.12.9. Delinquency Clause

The only example of this clause is found in the Ur III sale document no. 303. The clause reads: tukumbi gá-la in-dag ne-me arád(wr. NITA) ḫa-me "if she (i.e., the sold woman) refuses to work, they (i.e., the sellers) will become slaves (in her place)." For the verb gá-la . . . dag, in the later periods spelled also gà(-la) . . . dag or gál-la . . . dag, "to desist from work, to retreat," which corresponds to the Akkadian *naparkûm* and *egûm*, see G. R. Castellino, *Two Šulgi Hymns (BC)* (Rome, 1972) p. 119. We assume that ne-me arád(wr. NITA) ḫa-me stands for /nemeš arad ḫemeš/, where /nemeš/, usually spelled ne-meš, is 3rd person plural demonstrative pronoun "these," corresponding to the Akkadian *annūtum.*

7.12.10. Oath without Any Clause

Several of the Ur III sale documents record an oath not accompanied by any clause or statement. It appears that all these examples are to be interpreted as abbreviations of the no-contest clause.

mu lugal-bi in-pàd "he (i.e., the seller) swore by the name of the king (not to contest): nos. 258, 286, 322, 331, 340, and 348
mu lugal-bi al-pa "the oath was sworn by the name of the king (that the seller will not contest)": no. 260
mu lugal-bi ì-p[àd(-dè-éš)] "[they (i.e., the sellers)] sw[ore] by the name of the king (not to contest)": no. 265
mu lugal in-pàd "he (i.e., the seller) swore by the name of the king (not to contest)": nos. 270, 289, and 341
[igi-ne-n]e Seller [mu lugal-bi i]n-pàd "[before th]em (i.e., the witnesses) the seller swore [by the name of the king] (not to contest)": no. 283
igi-bi-šè mu lugal-bi in-na-an-pàd "before them (i.e., the witnesses) he (i.e., the seller) swore for him (i.e., the buyer) by the name of the king (not to contest)": no. 312
mu lugal-bi ba-pàd "the oath was sworn by the name of the king (that the seller will not contest)": nos. 323 and 334
mu lugal ba-pàd "the oath was sworn by the name of the king (that the seller will not contest)": nos. 335 and 338
zi lugal ì-p[àd] "he (i.e., the seller) swore by the life of the king (not to contest)": no. 342
téš-bi mu lugal ib-da-pàd "they (i.e., the sellers and the buyer) swore together by the name of the king (not to contest one against the other)": no. 347
šu-ut ma-ḫa-ar-šu-nu ni-iš LUGAL-*im it-ma-ù* "these are (the witnesses) in whose presence he (i.e., the seller) swore by the life of the king (not to contest)": no. 362
MU LUGAL PÀD *a-na ba ki tu me* (unclear): no. 343
Compare also the occurences of NAM.KUD in no. 12 Side D.

7.12.11. Miscellaneous Clauses

In this category we include two clauses which cannot be satisfactorily explained at the present time.

ud Šu-ni-al-dugud-dè dumu-ni Lum-ma-tur-ra gán Gi-lugal-la-ka e-na-šám-a ki-^{GIŠ}ERÍN-ra-bi ba-ba "when Šu-ni-al-dugud, his (i.e., of Lum-ma-tur) son, bought the field Gi-lugal-la for Lum-ma-tur, its . . . was distributed" (no. 144, Pre-Sargonic, Lagash).

The enigmatic term ki-^{GIŠ}ERÍN-ra also appears in the place-name e-ki-ERÍN-ra (a canal?), for which see Bauer, *AWL* p. 103. Assuming that the verbal form ba-ba is to be translated "he divided" or "it was divided," the ki-^{GIŠ}ERÍN-ra could denote a type of payment or offering that was distributed in connection with the sale transaction. [See now Steinkeller, *N.A.B.U.* 1990/1 p. 9f., who proposes the reading ki-^{GIŠ}sur$_x$-ra-bi ba-ba "its border was divided."]

KUG.KUG è TUR.TUR è-àm (no. 220, Sargonic).

We are unable to offer any plausible interpretation of this clause. The expression KUG.KUG è is also attested in two Ur III texts, where, unfortunately, its meaning is equally obscure: 59 gín [kug-babbar] KUG.KUG è PN ba-a-DU ki PN$_2$-ta PN$_3$ ù PN$_4$ šu-ba-ti "59 shekels [of silver], the . . . PN . . . ; PN$_3$ and PN$_4$ received (the silver?) from PN$_2$" (*ITT* 4, 7116:1–8); 2 gín kug-babbar PN KUG.KUG è BIR? IM ki PN$_2$-ta PN$_3$ šu-ba-ti "2 shekels of silver, PN . . . , PN$_3$ received from PN$_2$" (*YOS* 4, 13:1–6).

7.13. *Place of the Transaction*

The location of the sale transaction is noted in the kudurrus and sale documents very rarely. The only kudurru which offers such information is no. 40: 600 GURUŠ *in Ga-za-lu*^{KI} NINDA Ì.KÚ 600 GURUŠ *šu* 1 UD 1200 GURUŠ *šu* 2 UD *in maš-ga-ni Be-lí-ba-ni* AGRIG ^{d}*A-ba*$_4$*-iš-da-gal* NINDA Ì.KÚ LÚ *Már-da*^{KI} "600 men ate bread/food in Kazalu; 600 men for one day, 1200 men for two days ate bread/food in the settlement of Bêlī-bāni, the steward of Abaiš-takal; the citizens of Marda" (Side C); 80 DUMU.DUMU *Kiš*^{KI} *in Ga-za-lu*^{KI} NINDA Ì.KÚ "80 citizens of Kish ate bread/food in Kazalu" (Side D).

In addition, the record of the sale's location is also given in three Sargonic and two Ur III sale documents:

in Kiš$^{[KI]}$ "in Kish" (following the list of witnesses): no. 229

in É-*ti* PN DUMU.SAL PN$_x$ *in A-ga-dè*^{KI} 10 PNs ŠU.NIGÍN ⌜10⌝ AB+ÁŠ Buyer *in* [*A*]*-ga-dè*$^{[KI]}$ KUG. BABBAR *iš*$_{11}$*-ku-*⌜*lu*⌝ "in the house of PN, daughter of PN$_x$, in Akkadē, 10 PNs, total of 10 witnesses (to the fact) that the buyer weighed out the silver in Akkadē": no. 230

šà [Du$_6$-sa-bar]-ra "in [Du$_6$-sa-bar]-ra": no. 304

É-duru$_5$-nigìn-gar-ki-dùg gú ^{ÍD}Dur-ùl-ka inim-bi ba-ab-dug$_4$ "this transaction was negotiated in the hamlet Nigìn-gar-ki-dùg, on the bank of the Dùr-ul": no. 359

7.14. *Date Notations*

The earliest example of a date notation in sale documents can be considered the formula bala PN "the office-term(?) of PN," which is attested in the Fara sale documents (nos. 103, 104, 105, 106, 108, 109, 110, 111, 112 = 113c, 113, 113a, 113b, 114, 115, 116, 117, 118, 119, 120, 122, 123, 124, 126, 127, 127a, 127b, 130, 131, 132, 133, and 136). The Fara sale document no. 125 uses a different dating formula, which reads: en$_5$-si-bi PN "PN (was) the governor (at that time)." The same formula may be found in no. 111, which adds, following bala PN, PN$_2$? en$_5$-si-bi.

Among the Pre-Sargonic sources, only the texts from Lagash are dated. In these documents, the date consists of either a number, corresponding to the consecutive year of the governor's term (nos. 144, 149, 153, 154, 155, and 156), or a more elaborate formula, which names the governor and/or another high official who served at that time (the so-called ud-ba date). The examples of the latter are:

En-[è]n-tar-zi sanga 17 "(at that time) En-[è]n-tar-zi (was) the temple-administrator (of Ningirshu); (his) (i.e., of En-èn-tar-zi) seventeenth (year)": no. 137

Du-du sanga "(at that time) Du-du (was) the chief temple-administrator (of Ningirshu)": no. 142

[u]d-ba [Ur]u-KA-⌜gi⌝-na lugal Lagaš^{KI} La-la nigir Gír-su^{KI} [it]i Ezen-[x] "at that time [Ur]u-KA-⌜gi⌝-na (was) the king of Lagash (and) La-la (was) the herald of Girshu; month of Ezen-[x]": no. 148

ud-ba En-te-me-na en$_5$-si Lagaš^{KI}-kam En-èn-tar-zi sanga ^{d}Nin-gír-su-ka-kam 19 "at that time En-te-me-na was the governor of Lagash (and) En-èn-tar-zi was the temple-administrator of Ningirshu; (his) (i.e., of En-te-me-na) nineteenth (year)": no. 150

Only two of the Sargonic sale documents contain a date formula. One of them (no. 214), which comes from Umma, uses the so-called mu iti date: 3 mu iti 3. The other text (no. 239), which is of Eshnuna origin, contains a formula of the ud-ba type: UD.BA PN SAL.SILÀ.ŠU.DU$_8$ *ì-nu-mi* PN$_2$ EN$_5$.SI-*ki Iš-nun*^{KI} "at that time PN (was) the female cupbearer; at that time (or: while) PN$_2$ (was) the governor of Eshnuna."

The date formula is a regular component of the Ur III sale documents. It is wanting in eight instances only (nos. 261, 263, 270, 274a, 312, 327, 343, and 368). In agreement with the practice found in administrative and legal documents from that period, the date consists of either 1) the year only (mu x, *passim*), or 2) the year and the month (mu x, iti y, *passim*), or 3) the year, the month, and the day (mu x, iti y, ud z(-kam), *passim*). Of special interest are the Umma sale documents nos. 247 and 274, which employ the identical ud-ba date: ud-ba Ur-^{d}Li$_9$-si$_4$(-na) en$_5$-si Umma^{KI} "on that day Ur-Lisi (was) the governor of Umma"; this form of dating is exceedingly rare in the Ur III period.

7.15. *Sealed Sale Documents*

The only example of a sealed sale document before the Ur III period is no. 141, which dates to the Pre-Sargonic period and comes from Lagash. This document, which is written on a clay nail (kag, Akk. *sikkatum*), bears the impression of an uninscribed seal.

Even though less than half of the extant Ur III sale documents (63 out of 127) are presently sealed, it appears that the original number of the sealed examples might have been much higher. This is suggested by the fact that very few of the Ur III sale documents came down to us with their envelopes preserved, on which sealings are more likely to be found than on the tablets.

The distribution of the ownership of the seals impressed on the Ur III sale documents is as follows:

1) texts sealed by the seller or sellers only: nos. 250 (three seals), 251(?), 256, 258, 269, 270, 276, 277, 280, 281 (two seals), 282, 284, 286, 288, 290, 292, 293(?), 296, 297, 299, 301, 302, 305, 306, 310, 312, 317, 318, 319, 320(?), 322, 324(?), 331, 335, 336, 338, 340, 343, 356, 359, 360, and 364

2) texts sealed both by the seller and the guarantor: nos. 298, 300, 304, and 308
3) text sealed both by the seller and the authorizing official (nu-banda Adab^{KI}): no. 334
4) text sealed both by the seller and the sold person: no. 307
5) text sealed both by the seller and his brother, who is not mentioned in the body of the text: no. 347
6) texts sealed by the authorizing official only: nos. 264 (di-kud lugal "royal judge"), 283 (ḫa-za-núm "mayor"), 332 (egir en$_5$-si "governor's 'retainer'"), and 365 (di-kud "judge"; in the seal's inscription, the same person is called ga-eš$_8$-a-ab-ba-ka "seafaring merchant")
7) text sealed by the guarantor only: no. 329
8) text sealed by the sold person only: no. 285
9) texts sealed by the buyer only: nos. 309 and 369(?) (both self-sales)
10) text sealed by the scribe only: no. 247a
11) text sealed with a seal of (the household of) the god Ninurta: no. 263
12) texts sealed with the seals whose inscriptions are illegible: nos. 267, 325, 330, and 368

As can be seen from the above listing, it is primarily the seller who seals the sale document. The seals of sellers are impressed on at least 45 tablets (49 with uncertain cases). In twelve instances, the seal of the seller is accompanied or replaced by either that of the guarantor or the authorizing official or the scribe. Two(?) texts, both of which are self-sale documents, bear an impression of the buyer's seal. Of special interest are the two examples of the sold person sealing the tablet.

The actual act of sealing the sale document is recorded in three texts: mu [PN-šè] kišib P[N$_2$ (ad-da-na)] íb-[ra], "in place [of the seal of PN (i.e., the man who sells himself into slavery)], the seal of P[N$_2$, (his father)], was [rolled]" (no. 342—the seal must have been impressed on the envelope, which is now wanting); mu PN-šè kišib PN$_2$ dumu-na íb-ra "in place of (the seal of) PN (i.e., the principal seller), the seal of PN$_2$ (i.e., the other seller), his son, was rolled" (no. 356—the envelope is sealed with PN$_2$'s seal); kišib PN di-kud íb-ra "the seal of PN, the judge, was rolled" (no. 365—the tablet bears an impression of PN's seal).

For the sealing of the Ur III sale documents, see also Steinkeller, *Sale Documents* pp. 112–16.

CHAPTER 8

CHARTS OF PRICES, RATES, AND ADDITIONAL PAYMENTS

8.1. *Introductory Remarks*

What follows below is the complete listing of the prices and additional payments attested in the kudurrus and sale documents, which is presented in the form of synoptic charts. The charts are organized according to the nature of the object of sale, starting with fields, and continuing with houses, orchards, humans, animals, and commodities.

In the charts dealing with real estate (fields, houses, and orchards), the following information is given: the description of the real estate, its size (in iku or sar), its total price, the price per one iku or sar as calculated from the context plus the rate given in the text, and the additional payment(s). The charts listing the prices of humans, animals, and commodities contain only the description of the object of sale and its price.

As it has been the practice throughout the commentary, the references to kudurrus always precede those to sale documents in the charts.

Note the following abbreviations: gur-sag-gál = gsg; kug-babbar = k.b.

8.2. *Kudurrus: Fields*

Text	Object of Sale + Description and Location	Size in iku	Price	Price of One iku + Rate	Additional Payments	Miscellaneous
1 Hoffman Tablet						
ii 1	gán	270	—	—	—	Total: 990 iku (i)
ii 2	(gán)	270	—	—	—	—
iii 1	(gán)	180	—	—	—	—
iii 2	(gán)	270	—	—	—	—
2 Walters Tablet						
	gán	180	—	—	—	—
3 Philadelphia Tablet						
ii 1	(gán)	54	—	—	—	Total: 180 iku (i)
ii 2	(gán)	36	—	—	—	Subtotal:
iii 2	gán	36	—	—	—	90 iku (ii 3)
iii 6	gán	54	—	—	—	—
4 Louvre Tablet						
ii 1	gán	1080	—	—	—	Total: 1890 iku (i)
ii 2	(gán)	810	—	—	—	—
5 Yale Tablet I						
ii 1	(gán)	360	—	—	—	Total: 450 iku (i)
ii 2	(gán)	90	—	—	—	—
6 Yale Tablet II						
	gán	180	—	—	—	—
7 Leiden Tablet						
i	gán	54	—	—	—	—
8 Sheep(?) Figurine						
ii 1		162	—	—	—	Total: 1224 iku (i)
ii 3		90	—	—	—	—
ii 4		72	—	—	—	—
iii 1		90	—	—	—	—
iii 2		36	—	—	—	—

8.2. *Kudurrus: Fields—continued*

Text	*Object of Sale + Description and Location*	*Size in iku*	*Price*	*Price of One iku + Rate*	*Additional Payments*	*Miscellaneous*
8 Sheep(?) Figurine						
iv 1		450	—	—	—	—
iv 3		288	—	—	—	—
v 1		36	—	—	—	—
9 Khafajah Bird						
		90	—	—	—	—
10 Blau Obelisk						
	gán	90	—	—	—	—
12 Ushumgal Stela						
		450	—	—	—	—
13 RA 6 p. 143						
i 1	gán	900(?)	—	—	—	—
i 3	[gán]	360(?)	—	—	—	—
i 6	[gán]	720(?)	—	—	—	—
iii 1	[gán]	180(?)	—	—	—	—
14 Chicago Stone						
i 1	gán gán DUN	6	10 gín kug	1.66 gín kug	1 umbin? ì-udu 2 ma-na síg 1 NI-ga iš-gán 10 ninda-bappir 3 ninda-banšur	—
ii 6	gán gán DUN	7	12 gín kug	1.71 gín kug	1 umbin? ì-udu 2 ma-na síg 1 NI-ga iš-gán 10 ninda-bappir 3 ninda-banšur!	—
iii 10	gán gán Gúg dumu PN	15	30 gín kug	2 gín kug	3 umbin? ì-udu 6 ma-na síg 2(NI-ga) 2(UL) NI-ga iš-gán 30 ninda-bappir 4 ninda-ban⟨šur⟩	—
iv 15	gán gán É-ad-KID	26	43.33 gín kug	1.66 gín kug	18 ma-na síg	—
	gán gán É-Ì-la-lum	30	50 gín kug	1.66 gín kug	9 NI-ga iš-gán 9 umbin? ì-udu 90 ninda-bappir	—
vi 12	gán gán É!-ad-KID	22	36 gín kug	1.64 gín kug	4 umbin? ì-udu 8 ma-na síg 4 NI-ga še iš-gán	—
viii 2	gán gán DUN	108	275 gín kug	2.08 gín kug	21 NI-ga še iš-gán	—
	gán gán É-udu-ninda-kú	24			42 ma-na síg 21 umbin? ì-udu	—
x 3	gán gán É-udu-ninda-⌜kú⌝	21	35 gín kug	1.66 gín kug	7 ma-na síg 4 umbin? ì-udu 3(NI-ga) 2(UL) NI-ga še iš-gán	—
xi 12	gán	39	65 gín kug	1.66 gín kug	13 ma-na síg 6(NI-ga) 2(UL) NI-ga iš-gán 7 umbin? ì-udu	—
xii 8	gán gán X.PAB.ÚŠ	39	65 gín kug	1.66 gín kug	13 ma-na síg 6(NI-ga) 2(UL) NI-ga iš-gán 7 umbin? ì-udu	—
xiii 2	gán gán X.PAB!.ÚŠ	39	65 gín kug	1.66 gín kug	13 ma-na síg 6(NI-ga) 2(UL) NI-ga iš-gán 7 umbin? ì-udu	—
xiii 10	gán gán Pab-rúm	54	90 gín kug	1.66 gín kug	9 NI-ga iš-gán 9 umbin? ì-udu 18 ma-na síg	—
xvi 2	gán É-sag-ki-ti	20	113 gín kug	1.69 gín kug	11 NI-ga še iš-gán	—
	gán gán DUN	25			22 ma-na síg	—
	gán gán Mu-ni-gár	22			11 umbin? ì-udu	—

8.2. *Kudurrus: Fields—continued*

Text	*Object of Sale + Description and Location*	*Size in iku*	*Price*	*Price of One iku + Rate*	*Additional Payments*	*Miscellaneous*
xvii 1	gán gán Kug-gál^{KI}	12	20 gín kug	1.66 gín kug	2 NI-ga iš-gán 2 umbin? ì-udu 4 ma-na síg	—
xvii 12	gán gán Ur-^{d}Gu-nu-ra ENGUR! da im-ru	12	20 gín kug	1.66 gín kug	2 NI-ga iš-gán 2 umbin? ì-udu 4 ma-na síg	—
xviii 3	gán gán DUN Ur-sag-gur?-ra?!	9	15 gín kug	1.66 gín kug	1(NI-ga) 2(UL) ⟨NI-⟩ga iš-gán 3 ma-na síg 3 silà ì	—
xviii 12	gán É-gud X-kar	15	25 gín kug	1.66 gín kug	5 silà ì	—
15 Baltimore Stone						
i 1	gán gán É-gud	18	30 gín kug	1.66 gín kug	2 NI-ga še iš-gán 6 ma-na síg 3 umbin? ì-udu 30 ninda-bappir	—
ii 1	gán gán DUN	12	20 gín kug	1.66 gín kug	2 NI-ga še iš-gán 4 ma-na síg 4 silà ì 20 ninda-bappir 4 ninda-banšur	—
ii 28	gán gán DUN	12	20 gín kug	1.66 gín kug	⌜2⌝ NI-ga [še] iš-gán 4 ma-na síg 4 silà ì 20 ninda-bappir 4 ninda-banšur	—
iii 26	gán gán DUN	6	10 gín kug	1.66 gín kug	1 NI-ga [še] iš-gán 2 ma-na síg 2 silà ì 10 ninda-bappir 5 ninda-banšur	—
iv 26	gán gán É-gud	15	25 gín kug	1.66 gín kug	[2(NI-ga)] ⌜2(UL)⌝ [NI-ga še iš]-⌜gán⌝ [5 ma-na síg] [5 silà ì] [23]+2 ninda-bappir [2]+4 ninda-banšur	—
v 25	gán gán É-GAM. GAM-maḫ-zu-zu	7	[. . .]		[. . .]	—
	gán PN dam PN$_x$	23				—
vi 31	gán gán D[UN]	30	⌜50⌝ gín kug	1.66 gín kug	—	—
vii 29	gán gán É-dúr-BAḪÁR!.A.DU. GÍN	6(?)	10 gín kug	1.66 gín kug	—	—
viii 3	gán SAG.A	6	10 gín kug	1.66 gín kug	—	—
viii 8	[gá]n [gán X]	[6]	10 gín kug	[1.66] gín kug	—	—
ix 7	gán	6	10 gín kug	1.66 gín kug	1 [NI-ga še iš-gán] ⌜2⌝ [ma]-n[a] síg 2 silà ì [10 ninda-bappir] [x ninda-banšur]	—
x 2	gán gán É-dúr-BAḪÁR!.ZA. NUN.DU	9	15 gín kug	1.66 gín kug	2(NI-ga) 2(UL) [NI]-g[a še i]š-gán 3 ma-na síg 3 ⌜silà⌝ ì ⌜15⌝ ninda-bappir 3 ninda-banšur	—
xi 1	gán	3	5 gín kug	1.66 gín kug	2(UL) NI-ga še iš-gán 1 ma-na síg 1 silà ì	—
xi 12	gán É-gud	⌜15⌝	28 gín kug	1.86 gín kug	2(NI-ga) 2(UL) NI-ga [še] iš-gán 5 ma-na síg 5 silà ì 25 ninda-bappir	—
xi 19	gán gú-⌜nu⌝-[. . .]	15	25 gín kug	1.66 gín kug	[. . .]	—
xii 16	gán gán! É-dúr-BAḪÁR.ZA.NUN	2.5	4 gín kug	1.6 gín kug	1 NI-g[a še] iš-[gán] 2 ma-na síg 2 [silà] ⌜ì⌝ 10 ninda-bap[pir]	—

8.2. *Kudurrus: Fields—continued*

Text	*Object of Sale + Description and Location*	*Size in iku*	*Price*	*Price of One iku + Rate*	*Additional Payments*	*Miscellaneous*
xiii 16	gán gán DUN	7	12 gín kug	1.71 gín kug	1(NI-ga) 2(UL) NI-ga iš-gán 3 ma-na síg 3 silà ì ⌜15⌝ [nin]da-bappir [x nin]da-banšur	—
xiv 12	gán gán Da-da gán U+É-šum kug-gál	10 5	28 gín kug	1.86 gín kug	3 NI-ga iš-gán 6 ma-na síg 3 umbin? ì-udu 30 ninda-bappir 4 ninda-banšur	—
L.E. 10	gán É-dúr-BAḪÁR!. DU	6	10 gín kug	1.66 gín kug	—	—
L.E. 21	gán gán DUN	6	10 gín kug	1.66 gín kug	—	—
16 Kish Stone Fragments I						
a) i	[. . .]	[x]	[. . .]	—	NÍG.KI.GAR: [x]+1 GÍN K.B.	—
ii 1′	[. . .]	[x]	[. . .]	—	NÍG.KI.GAR: 8 GÍN K.B.	—
ii 6′	GÁN	8	20(?) GÍN K.B.	2.5(?) GÍN K.B.	[. . .]	—
b) A i	GÁN	3	15 GÍN K.B.	5 GÍN K.B.	NÍG.KI.GAR: 1 GÍN K.B.	—
ii	⌜GÁN?⌝	12	34+[x] GÍN K.B.	3(?) GÍN K.B.	[. . .]	—
B ii	[. . .]	[x]	60+[x] GÍN K.B.	—	NÍG.KI.GAR: 3 GÍN K.B.	—
C i	GÁN	13	20 GÍN K.B.	1.54 GÍN K.B.	[. . .]	—
d) A i	[. . .]	[x]	[. . .]	—	NÍG.KI.GAR: ⌜1⌝+[x] GÍN K.B.	—
ii	GÁN	[x]+2	7 GÍN K.B.	—	—	—
B i	GÁN	8	[x]+4 GÍN K.B.	—	[. . .]	—
iii	GÁN	1+⌜x⌝	[. . .]	—	[. . .]	—
g) ii	[GÁN]	13+[x]	20 GÍN K.B.	—	[. . .]	—
h)	[. . .]	[x]	[x]?+60 GÍN K.B.	—	[. . .]	—
i) ii	[. . .]	[x]	[. . .]	—	NÍG.KI.GAR: 20+[x GÍN K.B.]	—
17 Kish Stone Fragment II						
i	[. . .]	[x]	[x]+47 MA.NA URUDU	—	[. . .]	—
ii	GÁN KI	7.5	[. . .]	—	[. . .]	—
18 Figure aux Plumes						
Rev. i 1	gán NI.SUM	72	—	—	—	—
2	SAR.LAK-175	180	—	—	—	—
3	ME.NAM?.⌜X⌝	90	—	—	—	—
4	X.A	54	—	—	—	—
5	NI.DU$_6$	54	—	—	—	—
6	BE.SUG	⌜18?⌝	—	—	—	—
19 Lagash Stela						
Obv.	gán DIN.SILÀ [PN]?	1,296,018	—	—	—	—
Rev. i 1	gán ŠÀ.GIBIL	720(?)	—	—	—	—
2	AN.GÁN	360(?)	—	—	—	—
3	ŠÀ nigir-gal	540(?)	—	—	—	—
4	GÍR.ŠÀ	360(?)	—	—	—	—
5	A.[?]	720(?)	—	—	—	—
ii 1	[. . .]	360(?)	—	—	—	—
2	A-⌜x⌝-[. . .]	180(?)	—	—	—	—
3	[. . .]	216(?)	—	—	—	—
4	[. . .]	360(?)	—	—	—	—
5	[. . .]	360(?)	—	—	—	—
20 Enḫegal Tablet						
i	gán ⌜DU⌝?	414	720 ma-na urudu 2. še 1. zíz	1.74 ma-na urudu +	—	—
i–ii	gán ganun-dù	126	⌜180⌝ ma-na urudu 2. še	1.43 ma-na urudu +	—	—

8.2. *Kudurrus: Fields—continued*

Text	*Object of Sale + Description and Location*	*Size in iku*	*Price*	*Price of One iku + Rate*	*Additional Payments*	*Miscellaneous*
ii	gán ki gán Ú.PAD.ME	198	300 ma-na urudu 2.2. še	1.51 ma-na urudu +	—	—
iii	gán E+PAB. KAS^{KI} LAL?.KI	144	1.2. še 20 BAL+U 11 šáḫ-niga	—	—	—
iii–iv	gán	504	720(!) ma-na urudu 4. še	1.43 ma-na urudu +	—	—
	gán Bar-sag?-šag$_5$ Gú-KALAM?	342	420 ma-na urudu 1.2. še	1.23 ma-na urudu +	—	—
iv–v	gán Bàd-giš-gi$_4$	252	720 ma-na urudu 2. še	2.86 ma-na urudu +	—	—
	gán A.UŠ	180	200 ma-na urudu 2. še	1.11 ma-na urudu +	—	—
vi	gán A+X-a- X-è?/sag?	144	3. še	—	—	—
vi–vii	gán níg-è gán gud	54	80 ma-na urudu	1.48 ma-na urudu	—	—
	gá[n] A.Ḫ[A . . .]	[162]+180	360 ma-na urudu 120 ma-na urudu	1.40 ma-na urudu	—	—
Rev. i		2700	3820 ma-na urudu 21.2. še zíz 20 BAL+U	1.41 ma-na urudu +	—	—

21 Lupad Statue

i 18	zag É-ti	[x]	15. gsg še	—	—	—
20	zag É-NI	21+[(x)]	9 ma-na síg	—	—	—
22	da lu[gal]	21	6(?) ma-na níg-	—	—	—
26	zag [. . .]	6	urudu-babbar	—	—	—
28	zag [. . .]	6	—	—	—	—
30	zag [. . .]-gal-[. . .] A-geštin simug	6	—	—	—	—
32	LÁL.È zag Amar-tùr	54	—	—	—	—
34	Uš-gal zag Ur-pa ašgab? É-ní-nu-DU zag Dug$_4$-ga-ni TE.GAL UŠ-gal	22	—	—	—	—
ii 19	zag [. . .] AN [. . .]	2+[x]	20 ma-na síg 10. gsg še(?)	—	Gift of [x]+4 PNs, each: 5 ma-na síg	—
21	[. . .]	72	3 TÚG.SU.A 1 níg-lal-sag 1 túg [. . .] [. . .]	—	—	—
iii	[a-šà ḪU.TUŠ. BU]-rú[m]	[x]	[. . .]	—	Gift of 2+[x] PNs, each: 5 ma-na síg	—
v	[. . .]	72	[. . .]	—	—	—
vi	[. . .]	[x]	[. . .]	—	Gift of 3+[x] PNs, each: 5 ma-na síg	—

22 Lummatur Tablet I

Obv. i– Rev. i	[gán éš šám-ma-ta]	[9.25]	18.2. gsg še	Rate: 1 iku = 2. gsg še	níg-ba of First Seller: 5 síg-bar-udu-bar 1 šakan [i] 1 ⌜ninda⌝-sag 1 ŠU.KEŠDA 40 ninda-še 10 ninda-kalag 40 ku$_6$-dar-ra 10 silà tu$_7$ [1] sa [ga-raš]^{SAR} [1 s]a [lu]^{SAR} [1 sa sum-si]kil! níg-ba of 12 Other Sellers, each: 5 ninda-še 1 ninda-kalag 3 silà tu$_7$ 3 ku$_6$-dar-ra 1 sa ga-raš^{SAR} 1 silà še-sa	—

8.2. *Kudurrus: Fields—continued*

Text	*Object of Sale + Description and Location*	*Size in iku*	*Price*	*Price of One iku + Rate*	*Additional Payments*	*Miscellaneous*
Rev. i– Rev. ii	gán [éš] šám-m[a- ta]	⸢9.25⸣	⸢18.2.⸣ gsg še	Rate: 1 iku = 2. gsg še	níg-ba of First Seller: 2.5(?) [síg-bar-udu-bar] 1(!) [šakan ì] 1 [ŠU.KEŠDA] 20 ninda-[še] 5 ni[nda]-kalag 20 ku$_6$-dar-ra 5 silà tu$_7$ 1 sa lu^{SAR} 1 sa ga-raš$^{[SAR]}$ níg-ba of 7 Other Sellers, each: 5 ninda-še 1 ninda-kalag 3 silà tu$_7$ 3 ku$_6$-dar-ra 1 ga-raš^{SAR} 1 silà še-sa	—
Obv. iii– Rev. iii	⸢gán⸣ éš šám-ma-ta	⸢9.25⸣	18.2. gsg še	Rate: 1 iku = 2. gsg še	níg-ba of First Seller: 3+[x] síg-bar-udu-[bar] [1] šakan ì [1] ⸢ŠU.KEŠDA⸣ [x] ninda-še [x ninda-kalag] [x ku$_6$-dar-ra] [x si]là tu$_7$ [1 sa lu^{SAR}] [1 sa ga-raš^{SAR}] níg-ba of 10 Other Sellers, each: 5 ninda-še 1 ninda-kalag 3 silà tu$_7$ 3 ku$_6$-dar-ra 1 sa ga-raš^{SAR} 1 silà še-sa	—
Rev. iii– Rev. iv	gán [gán . . .] gán g[án] sag-[du$_5$-ka]	⸢8.25⸣ 21	58.2. gsg še	Rate: 1 iku = 2. gsg še	níg-ba of First Seller: [x síg-bar-udu-bar] [1] ša[kan] ⸢ì⸣ 1 ŠU.[KEŠDA] [x ninda-še] [x ninda-kalag] [x ku$_6$-dar-ra] [x silà tu$_7$] + 3 unidentified Com. níg-ba of 15 Other Sellers, each: [5 ninda-še] 1 n[inda-kalag] [3 silà tu$_7$] [3 ku$_6$-dar-ra]	—
23 Lummatur Tablet II						
Obv. i– Rev. i	[gán éš šám-ma-ta]	[x]	[x] [x gur-2-ul še x ma-na síg]	Rate: 1 iku = 2. gur-2-ul še; 1 iku = 3 ma-na síg- ŠÀ.ŠÈ	níg-ba of First Seller: [x síg-bar-udu] [1 šakan ì] [1 ŠU.KEŠDA] [x ninda-še] [x ninda-kalag] [x ku$_6$-dar-ra] [x silà tu$_7$] [x silà še-sa] [x sa ga-raš^{SAR}] níg-ba of 7 Other Sellers, each: [x ninda-še] [1 ninda-kalag] [x ku$_6$-dar-ra]	—

8.2. *Kudurrus: Fields—continued*

Text	*Object of Sale + Description and Location*	*Size in iku*	*Price*	*Price of One iku + Rate*	*Additional Payments*	*Miscellaneous*
					[x silà tu$_7$] [1 udu] [1 silà še-sa] [1 sa ga-raš^{SAR}]	
Rev. i–Obv. iii	[gán éš šám-ma-ta]	[x]	[x gur-2-ul še] [x]+15 ma-na síg	Rate: 1 iku = 2. gur-2-ul še; 1 iku = 3 ma-na síg-ŠÀ.ŠÈ	níg-ba of First Seller: 43+⸢2?⸣ síg-b[ar-udu] [+ the same Com. as in Obv. i–Rev. i] níg-ba of 16 Other Sellers, each: [the same Com. as in Obv. i–Rev. i]	—
Obv. iii	[gán éš šám-ma-ta]	[22.33]	67 ma-na síg	Rate: 1 iku = 3 ma-na síg-ŠÀ.ŠÈ	níg-ba of First Seller: 33 síg-bar-udu [+ the same Com. as in Obv. i–Rev. i]	—
Rev. iii–Obv. iv	[gán éš šám-ma-ta]	[x]	[x gur-2-ul še x ma-na síg]	Rate: 1 iku = 2. gur-2-ul še; 1 iku = 3 ma-na síg-ŠÀ.ŠÈ	níg-ba of First Seller: [the same Com. as in Obv. i–Rev. i] níg-ba of 5 Other Sellers, each: [x udu] 5 ninda-še 1 ninda-kalag 3 silà tu$_7$ 3 ku$_6$-dar-ra 1 sa ga-raš^{SAR} 1 silà še-⸢sa⸣	—
Obv. iv–Rev. iv	[gán éš šám-ma-ta]	[x]	[x gur-2-ul še x ma-na síg]	Rate: 1 iku = 2 gur-2-ul še; 1 iku = 3 ma-na síg-ŠÀ.ŠÈ	níg-ba of First Seller: [x síg-bar-udu] [1 šakan ì] [1 ŠU.KEŠDA] [x ninda]-še 1 ninda-kalag 1 tu$_7$ silà 20 ku$_6$-dar-ra 1 ninda-ì 3 silà [x] 1 silà še-[sa] 1 silà [x] 1 sum-⸢gu⸣ 1 ⸢sa ga⸣-[raš^{SAR}] níg-ba of 3 Other Sellers, each: [the same Com. as in Obv. i–Rev. i]	—
Obv. v–Rev. v	[gán éš šám-ma-ta]	[x]	[x gur-2-ul še x ma-na síg]	Rate: 1 iku = 2. gur-2-ul še; 1 iku = 3 ma-na síg-ŠÀ.ŠÈ	níg-ba of First Seller: [the same Com. as in Obv. i–Rev. i] níg-ba of 3 Other Sellers, each: 13+[x] ⸢ninda⸣-[še] [+ the same Com. as in Obv. i–Rev. i]	—
Rev. v–Rev. vi	[gán éš šám-ma-ta]	[14.5 or 14.33]	29. gur-2-ul še 43 ma-na síg	Rate: 1 iku = 2. gur-2-ul še; 1 iku = 3 ma-na síg-ŠÀ.ŠÈ	níg-ba of First Seller: [x síg-bar-udu] [1 šakan ì] [1 ŠU.KEŠDA] [x ninda-še] 1 [ninda-kalag] 20 ku$_6$-[dar-ra] 1 [silà tu$_7$] 2+[x silà še-sa] 1 [sa ga-raš^{SAR}] níg-ba of 7 Other Sellers, each: [the same Com. as in Obv. i–Rev. i]	—

8.2. *Kudurrus: Fields—continued*

Text	*Object of Sale + Description and Location*	*Size in iku*	*Price*	*Price of One iku + Rate*	*Additional Payments*	*Miscellaneous*
Rev. vi– Obv. vii	[gán éš šám-ma-ta]	36+[x]	[x gur-2-ul še x ma-na síg]	Rate: 1 iku = 2. gur-2-ul še; 1 iku = 3 ma- na síg-ŠÀ.ŠÈ	níg-ba of First Seller: [x síg-bar-udu] [1 šakan ì] [1 ŠU.KEŠDA] [1 ninda-še] [x ninda]-kalag [x] ⸢ku$_6$⸣-dar-ra 2 silà tu$_7$ 1 ⸢udu⸣ 1 silà še-sa 1 sa ga-raš^{SAR} níg-ba of 3 Other Sellers, each: [the same Com. as in Obv. i–Rev. i]	—
Obv. vii– Obv. ix	[gán éš šám-ma-ta]	[14.5 or 14.33]	29. gur-2-ul še 43 ma-na síg	Rate: 1 iku = 2. gur-2-ul še; 1 iku = 3 ma- na síg-ŠÀ-ŠÈ	níg-ba of First Seller: 20 síg-⸢bar⸣-udu 1 šak[an] ì 1 ŠU.KEŠDA [x] ⸢ninda-še⸣ [x ninda-kalag] [x ku$_6$-dar-ra] [x silà tu$_7$] [x silà še-sa] [x sa ga-raš^{SAR}] níg-ba of [x] Other Sellers, each: 7 ninda-še ⸢1⸣ ninda-kalag 5 ku$_6$-dar-ra 1 silà tu$_7$ 1 udu 1 silà še-sa 1 sa ga-raš^{SAR}	—
24 Stela of Victory						
Obv. 1′	[g]án Ù-[dùg]-⸢KU$_4$⸣	[x]	—	—	—	—
Rev. ii′ 2′	gán ^{d}Nanše-gar-ra	[360]+ 360	—	—	—	—
3′	gán Ù-a-dùg-ga	360	—	—	—	—
iii′ 4′	gán sug Lagaš^{KI}	[54]+36	—	—	—	—
5′	gán Gír-gír-maḫ	90	—	—	—	—
iv′ 1′	[g]án $^{[GIŠ]}$ŠE.DÙG	[x]	—	—	—	—
25 Nippur Statue						
i 4	[GÁN]	6	10 [MA.NA URUDU]	1.66 MA.NA URUDU	—	—
i 7	[GÁN]	12	20 [MA.NA URUDU]	1.66 MA.NA URUDU	—	—
i 10	[GÁN]	6	10 [MA.NA URUDU]	1.66 MA.NA URUDU	—	—
ii 10	GÁN	3	5 MA.NA [URUDU]	1.66 MA.NA URUDU	—	—
iii 3	GÁN	5	9 MA.NA URUDU	1.8 MA.NA URUDU	—	—
iii 7	GÁN	18	40 MA.NA URUDU	2.2 MA.NA URUDU	—	—
26 Enna-Il Statue						
i 1′	GÁN É? ḪA? GUD? X? *in Ur-šag$_5$?^{KI}*	[x]+72	—	—	—	—
4′	GÁN ⸢X X X⸣ GÁN [. . .]	108	—	—	—	—
9′	GÁN GÁN ŠÁM	36	—	—	—	—
27 10 NT 1						
ii′	[. . .]	[x]	40 gín kug	—	—	—
Rev. ii′	[. . .]	[x]	⸢40⸣ gín kug	—	—	—

8.2. *Kudurrus: Fields—continued*

Text	*Object of Sale + Description and Location*	*Size in iku*	*Price*	*Price of One iku + Rate*	*Additional Payments*	*Miscellaneous*
30 PBS XV 20						
ii	gán-maḫ	21	10 gín kug	0.48 gín kug	—	—
30a Nippur Disk						
i	gán	36	180 gín k.b.	5 gín k.b.	—	—
ii	gán	25	125 gín k.b.	5 gín k.b.	—	—
iii	gá[n]	6.5(?)	32.5(?) gín k.b.	5(?) gín k.b.	—	—
iv	gán	7.5	37.5 gín k.b.	5 gín k.b.	—	—
v	gán	2	10 gín k.b.	5 gín k.b.	—	—
vi	⸢gán⸣	2.5(?)	12.5(?) gín k.b.	5(?) gín k.b.	—	—
31 Adab Stone Fragment						
i′ 3	GÁN [. . .]-⸢X⸣.KI [X].ME.RU^{KI}	[x]	[x] MA.NA URUDU	—	—	—
i′ 6	GÁN	[18?]+3	46 MA.NA URUDU	2.19 MA.NA URUDU	—	—
i′ 9	GÁN	18(?)+6	⸢62?⸣ MA.NA URUDU	2.58(?) MA.NA URUDU		
ii′ 6	GÁN	10	32 MA.NA URUDU	3.2 MA.NA URUDU	—	—
ii′ 10	GÁN	8	[x] MA.NA URUDU	—	—	—
iii′ 5′	GÁN ḪI.MA.KI?	9	45 MA.NA URUDU	5 MA.NA URUDU	—	—
iii′ 10′	GÁN	24	50 MA.NA URUDU	2.08 MA.NA URUDU	—	—
iv′ 1′	GÁN ⸢X⸣.GAL *A-tum*	[x]+9	[x]+4 MA.NA URUDU	—	—	—
iv′ 6′	GÁN	[6?]+9	⸢40⸣ MA.NA URUDU	2.66(?) MA.NA URUDU	—	—
32 Adab Clay Fragment I						
i–v	gán É-kas	122	80.66 gín k.b.	0.66 gín k.b.	níg-ba of ⸢9⸣ Sellers, each: 1 SU.A.TÚG 5 ma-na síg níg-ba of 4 Witnesses, each: 1 SU.A.TÚG níg-ba of ⸢5⸣ Witnesses, each: 5 ma-na síg	Total of Gifts: 13 SU. A.TÚG 70 ma-na síg
v–vii	gán É-[kas]?	84	[x] gín k.b.	—	níg-ba of Second Seller: [1 SU.A.TÚG] [5 ma-na síg] níg-ba of Third Seller: 1 SU.[A.TÚG] níg-ba of Fourth Seller: 5 ma-na síg níg-ba of Fifth Seller: [1 SU.A.TÚG]	Total of Gifts: 3 SU. A.TÚG 10 ma-na síg
34 BIN II 2						
i	GÁN	[15]	100 GÍN K.B.	6.66 GÍN K.B.	—	—
i–ii	GÁN	⸢6⸣	40 GÍN K.B.	6.66 GÍN K.B.	—	—
ii	GÁN	7	45 GÍN K.B.	6.43 GÍN K.B.	—	—
ii–iii	GÁN	13.5	[x]+5 GÍN K.B.	—	—	—
iii	GÁN	6	40 GÍN K.B.	6.66 GÍN K.B.	—	—
iv 5	[GÁN]	0.32	4 GÍN K.B.	12.5 GÍN K.B.		
Rev. i	GÁN ZAG *Ḫur-rúm*	0.47	—	—	—	—
36 CT V 3						
i	GÁN	96	320 GÍN K.B.	3.33 GÍN K.B.	NÍG.KI.GAR: 5 TÚG.	Ratio of NÍG.

8.2. *Kudurrus: Fields—continued*

Text	*Object of Sale + Description and Location*	*Size in iku*	*Price*	*Price of One iku + Rate*	*Additional Payments*	*Miscellaneous*
i—*continued*					A.SU 26 SILÀ Ì.ŠÁḪ 15.2. ŠE	KI.GAR (TÚG. A.SU + ŠE) to Price: 1:10(?)
iii 1	GÁN	[18]	[60 GÍN K.B.]	[3.33] GÍN K.B.	NÍG.KI.GAR: 6 GÍN K.B. 6 SILÀ Ì	Ratio of NÍG. KI.GAR (K.B. only) to Price: [1:10]
iii 12	GÁN	18	⸢60⸣ GÍN K.B.	3.33 GÍN K.B.	NÍG.KI.GAR: [6 GÍN K.B. 6 SILÀ Ì]	Ratio of NÍG. KI.GAR (K.B. only) to Price: [1:10]
iv	[GÁN]	[45]	[150 GÍN K.B.]	[3.33] GÍN K.B.	NÍG.KI.GAR: [15 GÍN K.B.] 15 SILÀ [Ì]	Ratio of NÍG. KI.GAR (K.B. only) to Price: [1:10]
iv–v	GÁN	4	13.33 GÍN K.B.	3.33 GÍN K.B.	—	—
v 3	[GÁN]	[12]	[40 GÍN K.B.]	[3.33] GÍN K.B.	NÍG.KI.GAR: ⸢2.⸣ [ŠE] 2 [GÍN K.B.] 4 SILÀ Ì	Ratio of NÍG. KI.GAR (ŠE + K.B.) to Price: [1:10]
v 13	GÁN	24	80 GÍN K.B.	3.33 GÍN K.B.	NÍG.KI.GAR: 4. ŠE 4 GÍN K.B. ⸢8⸣ SILÀ Ì	Ratio of NÍG. KI.GAR (ŠE + K.B.) to Price: 1:10
37 CT XXXII 7f.						
i′	[. . .]	[x]	[. . .]	[. . .]	NÍG.DÚR.GAR: 1. GSG ŠE 2 MA.NA SÍG 2 SILÀ Ì	—
i′–ii′	GÁN	[6]	[15. GSG ŠE]	[2.5] GÍN K.B.	NÍG.DÚR.GAR: [1. GSG ŠE 2 MA.NA SÍG 2 SILÀ Ì]	Ratio of NÍG. DÚR.GAR to Price: [1:10]
ii′–iii′	GÁN	6	15. GSG ŠE	2.5 GÍN K.B.	NÍG.DÚR.GAR: [1. GSG ŠE 2 MA.NA SÍG 2 SILÀ Ì] NÍG. BA: 1 TÚG.SU.A	Ratio of NÍG. DÚR.GAR to Price: [1:10]
iii′	GÁN	6	15. GSG ŠE	2.5 GÍN K.B.	NÍG.DÚR.GAR: [1. GS]G [ŠE 2 MA.N]A [SÍG 2 SILÀ Ì]	Ratio of NÍG. DÚR.GAR to Price: [1:10]
iv′ 1	GÁN *in É-dur*$_5$*-Me-me*	48	90. GSG ŠE	1.88 GÍN K.B.	NÍG.DÚR.GAR: 8. GSG ŠE 16 MA.NA SÍG 16 SILÀ Ì NÍG. BA: 1 TÚG.SU.A	Ratio of NÍG. DÚR.GAR to Price: 1:5.6
iv′ 14	GÁN	⸢6⸣	[15. GSG ŠE]	[2.5] GÍN K.B.	NÍG.DÚR.GAR: [1. GSG ŠE 2 MA.NA SÍG 2 SILÀ Ì]	Ratio of NÍG. DÚR.GAR to Price: [1:10]
Rev. i–ii	[GÁN]	[6]	[15.] GSG [ŠE]	[2.5] GÍN K.B.	NÍG.DÚR.GAR: 1. GSG ŠE 2 MA.NA SÍG 2 SILÀ Ì	Ratio of NÍG. DÚR.GAR to Price: [1:10]
ii–iii	[GÁN]	[6]	[15.] GSG [Š]E	[2.5] GÍN K.B.	NÍG.DÚR.GAR: 1. GSG ŠE 2 MA.NA SÍG 2 SILÀ Ì	Ratio of NÍG. DÚR.GAR to Price: [1:10]
iii–iv	[GÁN É]Š.GÍD SI.SÁ GÁN *Ur-ma in Lugal-kalam-ma*	[12]	30. GSG ŠE	[2.5] GÍN K.B.	NÍG.DÚR.GAR: [2. GSG ŠE 4 MA.NA SÍG 4 SILÀ Ì]	Ratio of NÍG. DÚR.GAR to Price: [1:10]
38 Dar-a-a Tablet						
i 6	GÁN *in Ú-sá-la-tim*	180	—	—	—	—
8	GÁN *šu ba-la-ag Da-da-rí-im*	18	—	—	—	—

8.2. *Kudurrus: Fields—continued*

Text	*Object of Sale + Description and Location*	*Size in iku*	*Price*	*Price of One iku + Rate*	*Additional Payments*	*Miscellaneous*
10	GÁN ^{d}*Nin-gal*	6	—	—	—	—
11	GÁN ⟨*in*⟩? *Tu-la(l)-tim*	6	—	—	—	—
12	GÁN *in* X.EDIN^{KI}	54	—	—	—	—
14	GÁN *in Áš-na-ak*^{KI}	18	—	—	—	—
39 YBC 2409						
i′ 1′	⌜gán⌝ É-dur$_5$-sabra	[x]+38.5(?)	—	—	—	—
2′	gán [É-du]r$_5$-en$_5$-si	[x]+52.5(?)	—	—	—	—
3′	gán [. . .]-⌜x⌝-lú	[x]+2.5	—	—	—	—
4′	[gá]n DÙG?	[x]	—	—	—	—
ii′ 1′	gán SUG ⌜AB?.ZAG?⌝	72	—	—	—	—
40 Manishtushu Obelisk						
A$_1$	GÁN *Ba-az*^{KI}	[439]	[1463.1.2] GSG ŠE = 1463.33 GÍN K.B.	3.33 GÍN K.B. Rate: 1 GÍN K. B. = 1. GSG ŠE	NÍG.KI.GAR GÁN: 219.5 GÍN K.B. NÍG.BA GÁN: 1 *su-ga-nu* K.B. *maš-ga-na-at* = 15 GÍN K.B. 1 TÚG.ŠU.DU$_7$.A.BAL 3 TÚG.ŠU.SÈ.GA	Ratio of NÍG. KI.GAR to Price: 1:6.66
A$_2$	(GÁN *Ba-az*^{KI})	821	2736.2.4 GSG ŠE = 2736.66 GÍN K.B.	3.33 GÍN K.B. Rate: 1 GÍN K.B. = 1 GSG ŠE	NÍG.KI.GAR GÁN: 410.5 GÍN K.B. NÍG.BA GÁN: 1 *su-ga-nu* K.B. *maš-ga-na-at* = 15 GÍN K.B. 1 TÚG.ŠU.DU$_7$.A.BAL 3 TÚG.ŠU.SÈ.GA	Ratio of NÍG. KI.GAR to Price: 1:6.66
A$_3$	(GÁN *Ba-az*^{KI})	73	243.1.2 GSG ŠE = 243.33 GÍN K.B.	3.33 GÍN K.B. Rate: 1 GÍN K.B. = 1. GSG ŠE	NÍG.KI.GAR GÁN: 36.5 GÍN K.B. NÍG.BA GÁN: 2 TÚG.ŠU.SÈ.GA	Ratio of NÍG. KI.GAR to Price: 1:6.66
B	GÁN *ša-at É-ki-im ù Zi-ma-na-ak*	⌜1116⌝	⌜3720.⌝ GSG ŠE = 3720 GÍN K.B.	3.33 GÍN K.B. Rate: 1 GÍN K.B. = 1. GSG ŠE	NÍG.KI.GAR GÁN: 372. GSG ŠE = 372 GÍN K.B. NÍG.BA GÁN: 1 ERÍN ANŠE.BAR.AN 1 GIŠ.GIGIR.NÍG.ŠU 2 *ki-li-lum* K.B. = 30 GÍN K.B. 1 URUDU *maš-sa-tum* K.B. 2 TÚG.ŠU.DU$_7$.A.BAL 8 TÚG.ŠU.SÈ.GA	Ratio of NÍG. KI.GAR to Price: 1:10
C$_1$	SUG-^{d}*Nin-ḫur-sag*	⌜2340⌝	⌜7800.⌝ GSG ŠE = 7800 GÍN K.B.	3.33 GÍN K.B. Rates: 1 GÍN K.B. = 1. GSG ŠE; 1 GÍN K.B. = 4 MA.NA SÍG	NÍG.KI.GAR GÁN: [1860 MA.NA SÍG = 465 GÍN K.B.] [5? URUDU ḪA.ZI? UD.KA.BAR] [5? URUDU *na-ap-la-aq-tum* UD.KA.BAR] 1 URUDU *ba-da-ru-um* UD.KA.BAR = 55 GÍN K.B. 3 ERÍN ANŠE.BAR.AN = [240 GÍN K.B.] [1 *ki-li-lum* K.B. = 20 GÍN K.B.] [Total Value: 780 GÍN K.B.] NÍG.BA GÁN: 1 ERÍN ANŠE.BAR.AN 1 GIŠ.GIGIR.NÍG.ŠU 1 *ki-li-lum* K.B. = 20 GÍN K.B.	Ratio of NÍG. KI.GAR to Price: 1:10

8.2. *Kudurrus: Fields—continued*

Text	*Object of Sale + Description and Location*	*Size in iku*	*Price*	*Price of One iku + Rate*	*Additional Payments*	*Miscellaneous*
C_1—*continued*					1 URUDU ḪA.ZI UD.KA.BAR 6 TÚG.ŠU.DU$_7$.A.BAL 20 TÚG.ŠU.SÈ.GA	
C_2	(SUG-^{d}*Nin-ḫur-sag*)	3834	12780. GSG ŠE = 12780 GÍN K.B.	3.33 GÍN K.B. Rates: 1 GÍN K.B. = 1. GSG ŠE; 1 GÍN K.B. = 4 MA.NA SÍG	NÍG.KI.GAR GÁN: 2400 MA.NA SÍG = 600 GÍN K.B. 3 *ki-li-lu* K.B. = 60 GÍN K.B. 6 URUDU ḪA.ZI UD.KA.BAR = 30 GÍN K.B. 4 URUDU *na-ap-la-aq-tum* UD.KA.BAR = 20 GÍN K.B. 3 URUDU *maš-sa-tum* UD. KA.BAR = 15 GÍN K.B. 3 ERÍN ANŠE.BAR.AN = 240 GÍN K.B. 1200 SILÀ Ì = 120 GÍN K.B. 5 SAG.NITA = 100 GÍN K.B. 4 SAG.SAL = 80 GÍN K.B. 1 DUMU.SAL = 13 GÍN K.B. Total Value: 1278 GÍN K.B. NÍG.BA GÁN: 1 ERÍN ANŠE.BAR.AN 1 GIŠ.GIGIR.NÍG.ŠU 1 *ki-li-lum* K.B. = 20 GÍN K.B. 1 URUDU *na-ap-la-aq-tum* UD.KA.BAR 4 TÚG.ŠU.DU$_7$.A.BAL 8 TÚG.ŠU.SÈ.GA	Ratio of NÍG. KI.GAR to Price: 1:10
C_3	(SUG-^{d}*Nin-ḫur-sag*)	306	1020. GSG ŠE = 1020 GÍN K.B.	3.33 GÍN K.B. Rates: 1 GÍN K.B. = 1. GSG ŠE; 1 GÍN K.B. = 4 MA.NA SÍG	NÍG.KI.GAR GÁN: 408 MA.NA SÍG = 102 GÍN K.B. NÍG.BA GÁN: 2 TÚG.ŠU.SÈ.GA NÍG.BA LÚ.GÁN. GÍD.DA (C_1, C_2, and C_3): 3 TÚG.ŠU.SÈ.GA 3 URUDU ḪA.ZI UD.KA.BAR	Ratio of NÍG. KI.GAR to Price: 1:10
D	GÁN *Ba-ra-az-* EDIN^{KI} *in* *Kiš*^{KI}	[794]	[2646.2.4] GSG ŠE = [2646.66] GÍN K.B.	[3.33 GÍN K.B.] Rates: 1 GÍN K.B. = 1. GSG ŠE; 1 GÍN K.B. = 4 MA.NA SÍG	NÍG.KI.GAR GÁN: [1058.66 MA.NA SÍG = 264.66 K.B.] GÍN NÍG.BA GÁN: 2 *ki-li-[lu]m* K.B. 2 TÚG.ŠU.DU$_7$.A.BAL 9 TÚG.ŠU.SÈ.GA	Ratio of NÍG. KI.GAR to Price: 1:10
41 Sippar Stone						
i	GÁN	90	120 GÍN K.B.	1.33 GÍN K.B.	NÍG.KI.GAR: 12 GÍN K.B. 4 TÚG.ŠU.ZA.GA	Ratio of NÍG. KI.GAR (K.B. only) to Price: 1:10
ii	GÁN GÁN *šu Sa-ba-ra*?	40	26.66 GÍN K.B.	0.66 GÍN K.B.	NÍG.KI.GAR: 2.25 GÍN K.B.	Ratio of NÍG. KI.GAR to Price: 1:11.85
v	GÁN GÁN.NINDÁ etc.	30	20 GÍN K.B.	0.66 GÍN K.B.	NÍG.KI.GAR: 1.25 GÍN K.B. 1 TÚG.ŠU.ZA.GA	Ratio of NÍG. KI.GAR (K.B. only) to Price: 1:16
vi 1′	[GÁN]	[x]	20.25 GÍN K.B.	—	NÍG.KI.GAR: 2 GÍN K.B.	Ratio of NÍG. KI.GAR to Price: 1:10.12
vi 10′	GÁN GÁN.NINDÁ etc.	110	73.33 GÍN K.B.	0.66 GÍN K.B.	NÍG.KI.GAR: 7.33 GÍN K.B. 1 TÚG.ŠU.ZA.GA	Ratio of NÍG. KI.GAR (K.B. only) to Price: 1:10
vii	GÁN	96	64 GÍN K.B.	0.66 GÍN K.B.	NÍG.KI.GAR: 6.[33? GÍN K.B.]	Ratio of NÍG. KI.GAR to Price: 1:10.11(?)

8.2. *Kudurrus: Fields—continued*

Text	*Object of Sale + Description and Location*	*Size in iku*	*Price*	*Price of One iku + Rate*	*Additional Payments*	*Miscellaneous*
Rev.iii′ 1′	[GÁN]	[x]	122.5 GÍN K.B.	—	NÍG.KI.GAR: 6.[25 GÍN K.B.] 1.1. ŠE 2 TÚG.A.SU 12 BAPPIR 12 SILÀ Ì	Ratio of NÍG. KI.GAR (without TÚG.A.SU) to Price: 1:9.8
iii′ 11′	GÁN	10.66	21.33 GÍN K.B.	2 GÍN K.B.	NÍG.KI.GAR: 1 GÍN K.B. .1. ŠE 2 BAPPIR 2 ˹SILÀ Ì˺	Ratio of NÍG. KI.GAR to Price: 1:10.66
iv′	GÁN	26	52(?) GÍN K.B.	2(?) GÍN K.B.	NÍG.KI.GAR: 2.25 GÍN K.B. .2.3 ŠE 5 BAPP[IR] 5 SILÀ Ì	Ratio of NÍG. KI.GAR to Price: 1:11.55(?)
v′	[GÁN] GÁN.NINDÁ etc.	[34]	68 GÍN K.B.	[2] GÍN K.B.	NÍG.KI.GAR: [3.25 GÍN K.B.] [.3.3 ŠE] [7 BAPPI]R 7 SILÀ Ì	Ratio of NÍG. KI.GAR to Price: [1: 10.46]
vi′	GÁN GÁN.NINDÁ etc.	3.66	7.5 GÍN K.B.	2.05 GÍN K.B.	NÍG.KI.GAR 0.33 GÍN KUG .2 ŠE 1 BAPPIR 1 SILÀ Ì	Ratio of NÍG. KI.GAR to Price: 1:11.36
vii′	GÁN	1.33	4.33 GÍN K.B.	3.25 GÍN K.B.	NÍG.KI.GAR: 0.25 GÍN K.B. [.1.5 SILÀ ŠE] [1? BAPPIR] [1? SILÀ Ì]	Ratio of NÍG. KI.GAR to Price: 1:8.6
viii′	[GÁN] GÁN.NINDÁ etc.	[20]	[26.66?] GÍN K.B.	[1.33?] GÍN K.B.	NÍG.KI.GAR: [1].33 GÍN K.B. .1.2 ŠE 3 BAPPIR 3 SILÀ Ì	Ratio of NÍG. KI.GAR to Price: [1:10.02]
ix′	GÁN	˹118˺	236 GÍN K.B.	2 GÍN K.B.	NÍG.KI.GAR: 12 GÍN K.B. 2.2 ŠE 1 TÚG.ŠU.ZA.GA 24 BAPPIR .2.4 SILÀ Ì	Ratio of NÍG. KI.GAR (without TÚG.ŠU.ZA. GA) to Price: 1:9.83
L. E.	[GÁN] GÁN.NINDÁ etc.	[25?]	[50?] GÍN K.B.	[2?] GÍN K.B.	NÍG.KI.GAR: 2.25 GÍN K.B. .2.3 ŠE 5 BAPPIR 5 SILÀ Ì	Ratio of NÍG. KI.GAR to Price: [1:11.11?]
42 Eshnuna Stone Fragment						
ii′	GÁN	[x]	˹8?˺ GÍN K.B. 40. ŠE	—	*iš-ki-nu-su*: 1.2. ŠE	Ratio of *iš-ki-nu* to Price: 1:34.28(?)
iii′	GÁN *šu kir-ba-ti Ar-da-na-an*^{KI} *in* E+PAB *At-li*	235	—	—	—	—
43 Eshnuna Clay Tablet						
i	˹GÁN˺	[36]	˹24˺ GÍN K.B. 48. GSG ŠE	[2] GÍN K.B. +	*iš-ki-nu-su*: 2 GÍN K.B. [4. GSG ŠE] 1 *ḫa-zi-[núm]*? 6 SÍG.GAN 6 BA.AN	Ratio of *iš-ki-nu* (K.B. + ŠE) to Price: 1:12
ii	[GÁN]	[24]	12+[4 GÍN K.B.] 30+[2. GSG ŠE]	[2] GÍN K.B.	*iš-ki-nu-su*: [1.33 GÍN K.B.]	Ratio of *iš-ki-nu*

8.2. *Kudurrus: Fields—continued*

Text	Object of Sale + Description and Location	Size in iku	Price	Price of One iku + Rate	Additional Payments	Miscellaneous
					⌜2.2.4 GSG ŠE⌝ 4 SÍG.GAN 4 BA.AN	(K.B. + ŠE) to Price: [1:12]
iii–iv	GÁN *šu* DINGIR-GÀR	8	⌜16.⌝ GSG ŠE	2 GÍN K.B.	*iš-ki-nu-su*: 0.33 GÍN K.B. 1. GSG ŠE [x] ⌜SÍG.GAN⌝ [x BA.AN]	Ratio of *iš-ki-nu* (K.B. + ŠE) to Price: 1:12
iv	⌜GÁN⌝	[12]	[8] GÍN K.B. [16.] GSG [ŠE]	[2] GÍN K.B.	*iš-ki-nu-su*: [0.66] GÍN K.B. [1.]1.2 GSG ŠE 2 SÍG.GAN [2] BA.AN	Ratio of *iš-ki-nu* (K.B. + ŠE) to Price: [1:12]
iv–v	[GÁN]	18	12 GÍ[N K.B.] 24. GSG ŠE	2 GÍN K.B.	*iš-ki-nu-su*: 1 GÍN ⌜K.B.⌝ [2. GSG ŠE] ⌜3⌝ [SÍG.GAN] [3 BA.AN]	Ratio of *iš-ki-nu* (K.B. + ŠE) to Price: [1:12]
v	[GÁN]	12	8 GÍN [K.B.] 16. GSG ŠE	2 GÍN K.B.	*iš-ki-nu-su*: 0.66 GÍN K.B. 1.1.2 ⌜GSG⌝ ŠE 2 SÍG.G[AN] 2 B[A.AN]	Ratio of *iš-ki-nu* (K.B. + ŠE) to Price: 1:12
v–vi	GÁN	24	12 GÍN K.B. 36. GSG ŠE	2 GÍN K.B.	*iš-ki-nu-su*: [1.]33 GÍN ⌜K.B.⌝ ⌜2.2.4⌝ GSG ŠE 4 [SÍG.GAN] [4 BA.AN]	Ratio of *iš-ki-nu* (K.B. + ŠE) to Price: [1:12]
vi–vii	GÁN	12	5 GÍN ⌜K.B.⌝ 14.1.2 [GSG ŠE] ⌜2⌝+[x . . .]	—	[. . .]	—
vii	[GÁN] *šu* ⌜SAG⌝?-[. . .]	[12]	8 GÍN K.B. 16. GSG ŠE	[2] GÍN K.B.	*iš-ki-nu-su*: 0.66 GÍN K.B. 1.1.2 GSG ŠE [2] ⌜SÍG⌝.GAN ⌜2⌝ BA.AN	Ratio of *iš-ki-nu* (K.B. + ŠE) to Price: 1:12
viii	GÁN	6	4 GÍN K.B. 8. GSG ŠE	2 GÍN K.B.	*iš-ki-nu-su*: [0.33 GÍN K.B.] [.2.4 GSG ŠE] [1 SÍG.GAN] [1 BA.AN]	Ratio of *iš-ki-nu* (K.B. + ŠE) to Price: [1:12]
viii–ix	[GÁN]	[24]	[16 GÍN K.B.] [32. GSG ŠE]	[2] GÍN K.B.	*iš-ki-nu-su*: [1.33 GÍN K.B.] [2.2.4 GSG ŠE] ⌜4⌝ [SÍG.GAN] 4 BA.[AN]	Ratio of *iš-ki-nu* (K.B. + ŠE) to Price: [1:12]
ix–x	[GÁN]	[24]	[16 GÍN K.B.] [32. GSG ŠE]	[2] GÍN K.B.	*iš-ki-nu-su*: [1.33 GÍN K.B.] ⌜2.2.4 GSG ŠE⌝ 4 SÍG.GAN 4 BA.AN	Ratio of *iš-ki-nu* (K.B. + ŠE) to Price: [1:12]
44 Eshnuna Clay Fragments						
b)	GÁN	12	⌜8.?⌝1.4 ŠE = [8.33?] GÍN K.B.	0.69(?) GÍN K.B.	—	—
d) ii′	GÁN	6.2	18. GSG ŠE	2.9 GÍN K.B.	—	—
e) ii′	GÁN	30	10 GÍN K.B. 15. ŠE = ⌜15⌝ GÍN K.B.	0.83 GÍN K.B.	—	—
iii′ 1′	[. . .]	[x]	12 GÍN K.B. 38. GSG ŠE	—	—	—
iii′ 6′	G[ÁN]	12	[. . .]	—	—	—
f) i′	GÁN	12	13 GÍN K.B. ⌜17.?⌝ GSG ŠE	2.5(?) GÍN K.B.	—	—
g)	GÁN	[x]	[x]+2 GÍN K.B. ⌜40⌝ MA.NA SÍG = ⌜6.⌝66 GÍN K.B. [. . .]	—	—	—

8.2. *Kudurrus: Fields—continued*

Text	*Object of Sale + Description and Location*	*Size in iku*	*Price*	*Price of One iku + Rate*	*Additional Payments*	*Miscellaneous*
h) i′	GÁN [*šu*] É 6 (IKU)	[x]	[x]+1. GSG ŠE	—	—	—
ii′ 1′	[. . .]	[x]	[60] MA.NA SÍG = 10 GÍN K.B. 14. GSG ŠE	—	—	—
ii′ 7′	GÁN *šu* É 5(IKU)	10	[x] GSG ŠE	—	—	—
k) i′	GÁN	⌜61⌝	2 GÍN K.B. ⌜23.⌝ ŠE = 23 GÍN K.B. [. . .]	—	—	—
ii′	GÁN	18	10. ŠE = 10 GÍN K.B. 26. GSG ŠE	—	—	—
iii′	GÁN	18	12. ŠE = ⌜12⌝ GÍN K.B. [. . .]	—	—	—

8.3. *Sale Documents*

8.3.1. Fields

Text	Sale + *Description and Location* (*Object of*)	*Size in iku*	*Price*	*Price of One iku + Rate*	*Additional Payments*	*Miscellaneous*
114 *Fara* III 32	gán	3	6 ma-na urudu	2 ma-na urudu	níg-dirig: 6 ma-na urudu níg-ba: 18 ma-na urudu 1 NI-ga še	—
115 *Fara* III 33	gán	2	4 ma-na urudu	2 ma-na urudu	níg-dirig: 18 ma-na urudu MUNSUB.AN.TAR: 2 ma-na urudu	—
116 *Fara* III 34	gán	3	12 ma-na urudu	4 ma-na urudu	níg-dirig: 10 ma-na urudu níg-ba: 8 ma-na urudu	—
117 *Fara* III 36	gán	6	12 ma-na urudu	2 ma-na urudu	níg-dirig: 4(?) ma-na urudu MUNSUB.TAR: 7 ma-na urudu	—
118 *Fara* III 37	gán	2	6 ma-na urudu	3 ma-na urudu	níg-dirig: 20 ma-na urudu níg-ba: [. . .]	—
119 *TSŠ* pls. XXXIII–XXXIV	gán	6	12 ma-na urudu	2 ma-na urudu Rate: 1 ma-na urudu = .3 še	níg-dirig: 14 ma-na urudu níg-ba: 13 ma-na urudu	—
120 PBS XIII 24	gán	37	60 ma-na urudu	1.62 ma-na urudu	níg-dirig: 39 ma-na urudu níg-ba: [. . .]	—
121 *ZA* LXIII pp. 209–10 no. 4a	gán	5	10 ma-na urudu	2 ma-na urudu	níg-dirig: 30.66 gín kug	—
122 Lambert in *Unger AV* pp. 29–30	gán	8	13+[x] ma-na urudu	2(?) ma-na urudu	níg-dirig: 32 ma-na urudu níg-ba: 46 ma-na urudu	—

8.3.1. Fields—*continued*

Text	Object of Sale + Description and Location	Size in iku	Price	Price of One iku + Rate	Additional Payments	Miscellaneous
123 Lambert in *Unger AV* pp. 37–38						
	gán	2	4 ma-na urudu	2 ma-na urudu	níg-dirig: 4 ma-na urudu níg-ba: 52 ma-na urudu .2. še	—
124 Lambert in *Unger AV* pp. 41–42						
	gán	12	24 ma-na urudu	2 ma-na urudu	níg-dirig: 60 ma-na urudu níg-ba: 92 ma-na urudu .2. še	—
125 *AOr* XXXIX p. 14						
	gán TUŠ.SAR.ḪAR	4	10 ma-na urudu-EN.DA 4 gín kug	—	níg-dirig: 6. še níg-ba: 1 TÚG.ÍB.DÙ 2 silà ì 1 níg-sag-kéš 2 ninda níg-ba of dub-sar: 0.66 gín kug 1 silà ì	—
126 *AOr* XXXIX p. 15						
	gán	4	[x] ma-na urudu	—	níg-dirig: 4 ma-na urudu níg-ba: 2 NI-ga še	—
127 *Or*. n.s. XLIV p. 436 no. 1						
	gán	3	6 ma-na urudu	2 ma-na urudu	níg-dirig: 6 ma-na urudu níg-ba: 18 ma-na urudu	—
127a *MVNS* X 84						
	gán	8	22 ma-na urudu	2.75 ma-na urudu	níg-dirig: 16 ma-na urudu níg-ba: 2 NI-ga še	—
127b *MVNS* X 86						
	gán	0.6	1 ma-na urudu	1.66 ma-na urudu	níg-dirig: 2 ma-na urudu níg-ba: 6 ma-na urudu	—
128 *Fara* III 38						
	gán	6	5 NI-ga .2. še-ḪAR 11 gín kug	—	—	—
129 *Fara* III 40						
	gán	—	8 gín kug	Rate: 1 ma-na urudu = .2 še	—	—
130 *RTC* 14						
	gán	8	20 gín kug-luḫ-ḫa	2.5 gín kug-luḫ-ḫa	níg-dirig: 10 gín kug níg-ba: 4 NI-ga še	—
131 *RTC* 15						
	gán	2	[x] gín [kug-l]uḫ-ḫa	—	níg-dirig: 5 gín kug-luḫ-ḫa níg-ba: 1 NI-ga še	—
132 Edzard, *SRU* p. 31						
	gán	2	2 gín kug-luḫ-ḫa	1 gín kug-luḫ-ḫa	níg-dirig: 1.5 gín kug níg-ba: .2. še	—
133 A 33676						
	gán	23	10 gín kug-luḫ-ḫa	0.43 gín kug-luḫ-ḫa	níg-dirig: 10 gín kug-luḫ-ḫa níg-ba: 25 gín kug-luḫ-ḫa [x NI-ga še]	—
134 *Fara* III 39						
	[gán]	[x]	20 NI-ga še 10 TÚG.A.SU [x si]là [ì]	—	—	—

8.3.1. Fields—*continued*

Text	*Object of Sale + Description and Location*	*Size in iku*	*Price*	*Price of One iku + Rate*	*Additional Payments*	*Miscellaneous*
136 *WO* VIII p. 180						
	gán	18	9 gín kug	0.5 gín kug	níg-dirig: 1 gín kug Gift of GU.SUR.NUN: 1 gín kug Gift of two dub-sar's: [1?] gín kug	—
144 *Bibl. Mes.* III 10						
	gán éš šám-ma-ta gán gi lugal-la	16.5	20.3 gsg še	1.1. 1+ silà gsg še	níg-ba: Com.	—
145 *Bibl. Mes.* III 11						
	gán du$_6$-[sír]-ra ⌜. . .⌝	⌜18⌝	61.2. gsg še	3.1.4 gsg še	níg-ba: Com.	—
156a *BIN* VIII 11						
	GÁN GÁN	15 13.5	30 GÍN KUG 27 GÍN KUG	2 GÍN KUG 2 GÍN KUG	— —	— —
166 *BIN* VIII 17						
	gán [. . .]	5	4 udu-bar-gál 3 ^{SAL}áš-gà[r]	—	—	—
	gán Ki-[. . .]	8	8 g[ín] kug 1 máš-bar-du$_8$	—	—	—
169 *BIN* VIII 80 = 182a F						
	[gán É-gud]-ka [pa$_5$-da]-na-ke$_4$ [a]b-uš	4.15	1 gín kug 1. še 1. še Total: 3(?) gín kug	0.24 gín kug	iš-gán še-kam: .2.4 še iš-gán síg-kam: .2.4 še níg-ba: [.1.2 še]	—
170 *BIN* VIII 158						
	gá[n . . .]⌜GAR⌝? [. . .]-KA	18+[x?]	0.5 ⌜x⌝ [. . .] 60. še	—	—	—
171 *BIN* VIII 171						
	Ki-numun-zi	—	15 gín bar-ra kug 15.2. še	—	iš-gán: 1 bar-síg^{TÚG} 1. še 1 silà ì-šáḫ níg-ba: [. . .]	—
172 *BIN* VIII 172						
	gán	—	3 gín kug 2 SU.A.TÚG = 2 gín kug	—	iš-gán: .2.2 zú-lum	—
	gán	—	4 gí[n] kug	—	—	—
173 *BIN* VIII 178						
	[gán] ÉŠ.SA[L? . . .] an-[gál]	3	4 gín kug 2 udu-nita bar- gál-la 1. še	—	—	—
174 *BIN* VIII 179						
	gán Ki-eme$_x$(SAL+ ḪÚB)	—	15. zú-lum = 30 gín kug	—	—	—
175 *MAD* IV 151						
	gán da pa$_5$-dub- sar-ka an-gál	2	4 gín kug 3. še .2 zíd-ba 0.5 silà ì	Rate: 1 gín kug = .2. še	—	—
176 *MAD* IV 152						
	gán pa$_5$-dub- sar-ka	8	32 gín kug 2. še 1 bar-dul$_5$ .2. še-ba	—	—	—

8.3.1. Fields—*continued*

Text	*Object of Sale + Description and Location*	*Size in iku*	*Price*	*Price of One iku + Rate*	*Additional Payments*	*Miscellaneous*
177 *MAD* IV 153						
	gán É-ad?	6	9 gín kug 7. še 1 bar-dul$_5$ = 2. še	3 gín kug = 3. še	Gift of 1 Sec. Seller: 2 gín kug	—
178 *MAD* IV 155						
	gán gán da é Tu- tu-ka-kam	1.5	2.5 gín kug	1.66 gín kug	—	—
179 *MAD* IV 169						
	gán da Ki-ša-nu- dar-ra-ni	6	10 gín kug	1.66 gín kug	—	—
	gán da Ki-ša-nu- dar-ra-ni	6	10 gín kug	1.66 gín kug	—	—
180 *MVNS* III 25						
	gán	—	7. še 3+⌜x?⌝ gín kug	—	—	—
182a Lambert Tablet						
A	gán É-gud pa$_5$-dub-sar gán ab-uš	24	20 gín kug [20] gín kug 6 udu-nita 1 túg ki-sì-ga = 10 gín kug 3 ma-na urudu Total: 64(?) gín kug	2.66(?) gín kug Rate: 1 udu-nita = [2?] gín kug Rate: 1 ma-na urudu = 0.66 gín kug	—	—
C	gán pa$_5$-ib-ka al-gál ki Ur-DUN sag-du$_5$-ke$_4$ ab-uš	7.75	37.2. še	—	—	—
D	gán É-gud da-na-ka	40.2	40. še	—	—	—
E	gán É-gud ki Ma-ḫir ab-uš	8	40. še	—	—	—
F	gán É-gud pa$_5$-da- na-ke$_4$ ab-uš	4.15	1 gín kug 1. še 1. še Total: 3 gín kug	0.72 gín kug	iš-gán še-kam: .2.4 še iš-gán síg-kam: .2.4 še níg-ba: 1.2 še	—
G	gán pa$_5$-da-na-ke$_4$	21	16.2. še 16. še 4.1.1 še Total: 36.3.1	1.3.4 še	—	—
H	gán pa$_5$-da-na-ke$_4$ gán dam? MI.MI ab-uš	7.5	[x]+3 gín kug	—	—	—
I	gán gú DIM+SU é-X [g]án sag-SAL.KAB.DU Barag-me-zi-da dam Uš-ki	24	30 gín kug 1. še 2.2. še 6 umbin? ì-udu	1.4(?) gín kug Rate: 1 umbin? ì-udu = 1 gín kug	—	—
J	gán pa$_5$-di?-⌜x⌝-kam	20+[x]	43.5 gín kug	—	iš-gán še-kam: 4. še iš-gán síg-kam: 3 umbin? ì-udu níg-[b]a: 1 A.SU.TÚG, 1 NI.TÚG, 1 umbin? ì-udu-dùg?	—
K	gán pa$_5$-^{d}Innin gán Ur-DUN Inim-ma-ni-zi ab-uš du$_6$ giš zag-ga-an-ke$_4$ ab-uš	180	59.(?) še	.1.4(?) še	—	—
O	gán DU$_6$?-DU?-an-ni	10	40. še	4. še	—	—

8.3.1. Fields—*continued*

Text	*Object of Sale + Description and Location*	*Size in iku*	*Price*	*Price of One iku + Rate*	*Additional Payments*	*Miscellaneous*
P	gán pa$_5$-^{d}Innin gán É-erín a-gál	3	10. še	3.1.4 še	—	—
Q	gán pa$_5$-^{d}Innin gán É-erín a-gál	3	[x] gín kug 2 silà ì-sáḫ	—	—	—
R	gán pa$_5$-^{d}Innin gán É-erín a-gál	3	[x] gín kug	—	—	—
T	gán É-X	6(?)	12. še	2.(?) še	—	—
U	gán gú DÍM+SU	12	10. še	.4.1 še	—	—
V	gán gú DÍM+SU	12	20. še 6.3. še	2.1 še	—	—
DD	gín ⌜X⌝-da pa$_5$-Da-da	6	20. še	3.1.4 še	—	—
EE	gán Ma-šeg$_9$^{KI} pa$_5$-Da-da	6	15. še	2.2.3 še	—	—
FF	gán gán A-[m]ud?-kam	2	10 gín kug	5 gín kug		
207 PBS IX 8						
	gán gán Áb-za-an-na	2	6.66 gín kug	3.33 gín kug	iš-gán gán-ga-kam: 0.8 gín kug	Ratio of iš-gán to Price: 1:8.32
210 PBS IX 7						
	gán	6	18 gín kug	3 gín kug	—	—
	gán	6	18(?) gín kug	3(?) gín kug	—	—
211 PBS IX 51+52						
	gán Á-[ti-ka]m? gán Bar-[. . .]	6 6	40 gín kug	3.33 gín kug	—	—
230 *MAD* V 65						
	GÁN IGI *na-ra-tim*	—	2 GÍN K.B.	—	—	—

8.3.2. Houses

Text	*Object of Sale + Description and Location*	*Size in sar*	*Price*	*Price of One sar + Rate*	*Additional Payments*
100 *Fara* III 30					
	é	—	13 ma-na urudu	—	níg-dirig: 2 ma-na urudu
101 *Fara* III 31					
	é	—	⌜3?⌝ ma-na urudu .3. še	Rate: 1 ma-na urudu = .3 še	—
102 *TSŠ* 66					
	é	[x]+0.5	[x] ma-na urudu	—	níg-dirig: 4 ma-na urudu
103 *TMH* V 71					
	é	1.5	15 ma-na urudu	10 ma-na urudu	níg-dirig: 30 ma-na urudu níg-ba: 25 ma-na urudu 1 NI-ga še

8.3.2. Houses—*continued*

Text	Object of Sale + Description and Location	Size in sar	Price	Price of One sar + Rate	Additional Payments
104	*RTC* 13				
	é	—	31.5 ma-na urudu	—	níg-dirig: 31.5 ma-na urudu
105	*RA* XXXII p. 126				
	é	1.16	10 ma-na urudu	8.62 ma-na urudu	níg-dirig: 20 ma-na urudu níg-ba: 1 NI-ga še
106	Lambert in *Unger AV* pp. 33–34				
	é	1.25	17.5 ma-na urudu	14 ma-na urudu	níg-dirig: 20 ma-na urudu níg-ba: 25.5 ma-na urudu 1 NI-ga še
107	De Marcellis				
	é	—	8 ma-na urudu	—	níg-dirig: 5.5 ma-na urudu
	é	—	8 ma-na urudu	—	níg-dirig: 5.5 ma-na urudu
108	IM 14182				
	é	—	13 ma-na urudu	—	níg-dirig: 41 ma-na urudu
109	*TMH* V 75				
	é	1.66	1+[x] gín ⸢kug-luḫ]-ḫa	—	níg-dirig: 10 gín kug-luḫ-ḫa níg-ba: [x NI-ga] ⸢še⸣
110	*TMH* V 78				
	é	1.16	[x]+5 gín kug-luḫ-ḫa	—	níg-dirig: 6 gín kug-luḫ-ḫa níg-ba: 2 NI-ga še
111	PBS IX 3				
	é	1.66	[x] gín kug-[luḫ]-ḫa	—	níg-dirig: 2 gín kug níg-ba: 1 NI-ga še
112	*L'Oeil* nos. 221–22 p. 78 (= no. 113c)				
	é	1.33	1.5 gín kug-luḫ-ḫa	1.13 gín kug-luḫ-ḫa	níg-dirig: 1.5 gín kug-luḫ-ḫa níg-ba: .2. še
113	Ligabue (= *SEL* III p. 11)				
	é	2	4 gín kug	2 gín kug	níg-dirig: 10 gín kug níg-ba: .2. še ninda 1 NI-ga še
113a	*MVNS* X 82				
	é	1.9	2 gín kug-luḫ-ḫa	1+ gín kug-luḫ-ḫa	níg-dirig: 2 gín kug-luḫ-ḫa níg-ba: .3. še
113b	*MVNS* X 83				
	é	1.9	2 gín kug-luḫ-ḫa	1+ gín kug-luḫ-ḫa	níg-dirig: 2 gín kug níg-ba: 1.2. še
137	*BIN* VIII 352				
	é	1.74	36. gur-2-ul še = 18 gín kug-luḫ-ḫa 10 gín kug	—	Com.
138	De Genouillac, *FT* Pl. XLIII				
	é	0.5	8.5 gín kug 4 ma-na síg 6. gur-2-ul zíd = [2?]+1 gín kug 1 ^{TÚG}níg-lám gíd-da = 1.5 gín kug	—	Com.
139	*Dok.* I 317				
	é	[x]	5 gín kug-luḫ-ḫa	—	níg-ba: Com.

8.3.2. Houses—*continued*

Text	Object of Sale + Description and Location	Size in sar	Price	Price of One sar + Rate	Additional Payments
140 *DP* 31					
	é	0.66	15. gsg še	22.5 gsg še Rate: 1 gín kug = 1. še	níg-ba: Com.
141 *DP* 32					
	é	[x]	20 gín kug-luḫ-ḫa	—	níg-ba: Com.
142 Hallo in *Gelb AV* p. 236					
	é	0.66	10 gín kug-luḫ-ḫa = ⸢6⸣.1.2 gur-2-ul še	16.66 gín kug-luḫ-ḫa = 11. gur-2-ul še Rate: 1 gín kug-luḫ-ḫa = .1.2 še	níg-ba: Com.
143 *RTC* 18					
	⟨é⟩	0.71	[10 gín kug?] = 20. gur-2-ul še	[14.08 gín kug?] = 28.17 gur-2-ul še	níg-ba: Com.
	é	1.25	15 gín kug	12 gín kug	níg-ba: Com.
164 *BIN* VIII 38					
	é	1	15. še 1 gín kug = 1. še	16 gín kug	—
165 NBC 6844					
	é-KI.UD é al-dù-dù	1.⸢x⸣ 0.33	119.1.2 še 6 gín kug [. . .]	— —	iš-gán: 1 A.SU.TÚG 1 ÍB.BA.DÙ^{TÚG} 1.1.2 še 1.33 si[là ì]-šáḫ 1 ma-na síg
166 *BIN* VIII 17					
	é [é]	[1].33 3	[x]+5. še 1 gín kug 1 bar-dul$_5$ ⸢x x⸣	— —	iš-gán: [x ba]r-dul$_5$ [x g]ín [kug] 1. še
167 NBC 6900					
	[é] é P[N$_x$] ab-uš é PN-ka[m]	1	2 gín kug —	2 gín kug —	— —
168 NBC 10198					
	é	—	2. z[ú]-lum 3.5 [sìla ì]-šáḫ 1 ^{TÚG}šu-ni-ra = 1 gín kug	—	—
181 *MVNS* III 13					
	é PN$_x$ sagi NI.KU-kurušda	1	10 gín kug = níg-šám uri^{URUDU}-kam	10 gín kug	—
204 PBS IX 9					
	é uru-bar abulla$_x$-tur-ra-ka an-gál	1	10 NI-g[a] še	10 NI-ga še	—
	é	—	5 gí[n] kug	—	—
	é	—	5 gí[n] kug	—	—
205 *TMH* V 128					
	é	—	15 NI-ga še	—	—
206 IM 58820					
	⸢é⸣	1.8	21 gín kug	11.66 gín kug	—

8.3.2. Houses—*continued*

Text	*Object of Sale + Description and Location*	*Size in sar*	*Price*	*Price of One sar + Rate*	*Additional Payments*
210 PBS IX 7					
	é	1.⌜x⌝	18.66 gín kug	—	—
	é	—	[5] gín [k]ug	—	—
	é	—	10 NI-ga še	—	—
218 *CT* L 77					
	é	0.66	5.5 gín k.b.	8.33 gín k.b.	—
227 *Or.* n.s. LI pp. 355–56					
	É	0.33 + 1 GÍN = (21 GÍN)	[20]+1 GÍN [KUG.BAB]BAR	60 GÍN K.B.	*iš-ki-ne*: 1. ŠE 2 [MA.NA SÍG] 5 BA.[AN] 1 G[ÍN] K.B. Gift of 1 Sec. Seller: 1 BA.A[N] 1 MA.N[A] SÍG Gift of Scribe: 1 BA.AN 1 ŠÀ.GA.DÙ^{TÚG}
228 *FM* 4					
	⌜É⌝	1 GIŠ.IŠ.DÈ 1 GÍN	11 GÍN K.B.	1 GIŠ.IŠ.DÈ = ca. 11 GÍN K.B.	—
237 *JCS* X p. 26					
	É	[x SA]R [x]+2 GÍN	42.66 GÍN K.B.	—	NÍG.KI.GAR É: 5. ŠE 6 SILÀ Ì 10 MA.NA SÍG 1 TÚG.A.SU 1 *ḫa-la-um*^{TÚG} Ì.ZAG: .2. ŠE 1 SILÀ Ì 1 MA.NA SÍG 1 GIŠ.DU.DA^{URUDU} Gift of 1 Person (Scribe?): 0.33 GÍN K.B.
238 *MAD* V 82					
	É	—	4. GSG ŠE 2.5 GÍN K.B.	—	—
247 *MVNS* III 213					
	é	1	1 gín k.b.	1 gín k.b.	—
247a A 22108					
	[é-dù-a]	[x g]u-za	⌜9⌝.5 gín k.b.	—	—
248 *ZA* LIII p. 82 no. 21					
	é-dù-a ù KI.UD	4.86	25 gín k.b.	5.14 gín k.b.	—
249 *UET* III 31					
	[é?]	1.5(?)	[x gín k.b.]	—	—
250 *NSATN* 782					
	é-dù-a É-DUN^{KI}-ka	[x]	6 gín k.b.	—	—
251 *UET* III 27					
	ki-⌜é?-šub?⌝	2.66	4(?) gín k.b.	1.5(?) gín k.b.	—
252 *NSATN* 911					
	é-ki	6	36 gín ⟨k.b.⟩	6 gín k.b.	—
253 *NSATN* 966					
	[é?]	3	12(?) gín [k.b.]	4(?) gín k.b.	—
254 Yondorf Coll. B					
	É	3.66	5 GÍN K.B.	1.36 GÍN K.B.	—

8.3.2. Houses—*continued*

Text	*Object of Sale + Description and Location*	*Size in sar*	*Price*	*Price of One sar + Rate*	*Additional Payments*
255	*YOS* IV 4				
	é	1.16	2.8 gín k.b.	2.41 gín k.b.	—
256	*YOS* XVI 100				
	é-KI.UD	1.16	2.66 gín k.b.	2.29 gín k.b.	—
257	*NRVN* I 223+251				
	é-dù-a é-šu-sì-ga	2	40 gín k.b.	20 gín k.b.	—
258	TA 1930, 249				
	ki-gál	23.33	40.5 gín k.b.	1.73 gín k.b.	—
259	*ITT* V 6837+*NSGU* III pl. 8 no. 100				
	[é?]	1.33	5.5 gín k.b.	4.13 gín k.b.	—
260	*NRVN* I 222				
	é [. . .]	[x]	[x] gín k.b.	—	—
261	*NSATN* 19				
	〈é〉	1.16	9 gín k.b.	7.76 gín k.b.	—
262	*TIM* V 8				
	[é?]	[x].14?	[x] gín k.b.	—	—
263	Oppenheim, *Eames Coll.* Pl. XIV Noor II				
	é-dù-a ⸢ù⸣ [KI.UD]	[x]+1.72	18.16 gín k.b.	—	—
331	*MVNS* III 268				
	é-dù-a ù KI.UD	1.42	4.33 gín k.b.	3.05 gín k.b.	—
355	AUAM 73.1042				
	é	3	[x] gín k.b.	—	—

8.3.3. Orchards

Text	*Object of Sale + Description and Location*	*Size in sar*	*Price*	*Price of One sar + Rate*	*Additional Payments*
146	Cross, *NFT* p. 220				
	gán [S]AR	2000(?)	180+[120?] gín kug	0.15(?) gín kug	níg-ba: 1 dug kas
181	*MVNS* III 13				
	^{GIŠ}kiri$_6$ gú pa$_5$-kur$_6$ al-gál	120	10 gín kug 7.2. še	0.14 gín kug	—
	^{GIŠ}kiri$_6$ gú pa$_5$-kur$_6$	300	20 gín kug 6. še	0.87 gín kug	—
	[^{GIŠ}kiri$_6$ gú pa$_5$-kur$_6$]	[x]	20 gín kug	—	—
	^{GIŠ}kiri$_6$ gú pa$_5$-kur$_6$	100	1 ANŠE.SAL [. . .]	—	—
182	*MVNS* III 53				
	^{GIŠ}kiri$_6$ kur$_6$ GADA+GAR PN lú-u$_5$-ke$_4$ ab-uš	300	30. še	.3 še = 0.1 gín kug	níg-ba: 1 A.SU.TÚG
182a	Lambert Tablet				
B	^{GIŠ}kiri$_6$ gú túl ^{GIŠ}kiri$_6$ Ur-é-nu-na ab-uš ^{GIŠ}kiri$_6$ É-muš ab-uš	300	27(?) gín kug 3. še	0.1(?) gín kug	—

8.3.3. Orchards—*continued*

Text	*Object of Sale + Description and Location*	*Size in sar*	*Price*	*Price of One sar + Rate*	*Additional Payments*
L	^{GIŠ}kiri$_6$ Da-da IŠ ab-uš	320	55. še 18. še	.1.1 še	—
M	^{GIŠ}kiri$_6$ Du-du Ur-tur X-a-gud al-gál	300	20.25 gín kug 1 gín kug .2. še 1 gín kug .2. še	0.08 gín kug	—
N	^{GIŠ}kiri$_6$ gú pa$_5$-kur$_6$ ^{GIŠ}kiri$_6$ Me-zu-an-da	300	6(iku) 20 sar ^{GIŠ}kiri$_6$ 1 sar é 10 gín kug	—	—
S	^{GIŠ}kiri$_6$ pa$_5$-a-zu pa$_5$-mu-tuku Ḫur-sag-ke$_4$ ab-uš	620	10. še 5 gín kug	0.02 gín kug	—
W	⟨^{GIŠ}kiri$_6$⟩ túl-mun ki-ba Ur-gu dumu Nigìn-kam	115	12. še	.3 še	—
X	^{GIŠ}kiri$_6$ túl-mun	115	7. še	.2 še	iš-gán: 10. še
Y	^{GIŠ}kiri$_6$ túl-mun	115	7. še	.2 še	iš-gán: [x še]
Z	^{GIŠ}kiri$_6$ túl-mun	115	7. še	.2 še	iš-gán: .2. še
AA	^{GIŠ}kiri$_6$ túl-mun	45	4. lal .2. še 2. še	.4 še	—
BB	[^{GIŠ}kiri$_6$ túl-mun]	⌜115?⌝	7. še	.2(?) še	—
CC	^{GIŠ}kiri$_6$ gú GADA+GAR ^{GIŠ}kiri$_6$ Ti-ti ab-uš	280	6 gín kug 6 gín kug 4. še 1 bar-dul$_5$ = 2 gín kug	0.06 gín kug	iš-gán: .2. še iš-gán: .2. še iš-gán: .2. še
211 PBS IX 51+52					
	⌜^{GIŠ}⌝kiri$_6$	1.33	18.66 gín kug	14.03 gín kug	—
264 *BE* III/1 14					
	$^{\text{ki GIŠ}}$kiri$_6$ gišimmar	40	38.5 gín k.b	0.96 gín k.b.	—
265 *NRVN* I 224					
	gán $^{\text{ki GIŠ}}$kiri$_6$	100	4. gín k.b.	0.04 gín k.b.	—
266 *NSATN* 762					
	^{GIŠ}gišimmar gú kar-anše	35 (Palms)	10 gín k.b.	1 Palm = 0.28 gín k.b.	—
267 *MVNS* III 263					
	^{GIŠ}gišimmar giš gub-ba	3 (Palms)	1 gín k.b.	1 Palm = 0.33 gín k.b.	—
268 *NSATN* 777					
	^{GIŠ}gišimmar	35 (Palms)	10 gín k.b.	1 Palm = 0.28 gín k.b.	—
269 *NSATN* 497					
	$^{\text{ki GIŠ}}$kiri$_6$ giš-gub-ba gán KI.UD a-šà du$_6$-an-na-gu-la	400 (or 500) 100	80 gín k.b.	0.16 (or 0.13) gín k.b.	—
270 BM 15464					
	KI.UD šà *gunû*-LÚ- *šeššig*(= rin$_x$)-na-⌜ra⌝ ^{GIŠ}kiri$_6$	8	0.66 gín k.b.	0.08 gín k.b.	—
360 *UET* III 36					
	^{GIŠ}gišimmar	18 (Palms)	4 gín k.b.	1 Palm = 0.22 gín k.b.	—

8.3.4. Persons

Text	*Object of Sale + Description*	*Price*
149	*Or.* IX p. 173	
	PN gala "cantor" (Boy)	10 gín kug-luḫ-ḫa
		1 iku gán še-mú-a
		1 [. . .]
		1 silà ì-nun
		1 ḫubur ku_6-KU?
		1 sá-dug_4 kas
		10 SUR
		5 ninda-silà
150	*RTC* 16	
	1 sag-SAL túl-ta-pàd-da-am_6 "foundling" (Woman/Girl)	10 gín kug-luḫ-ḫa
		.2. še
		Gift of 1 Sec. Seller:
		3 SUR
		2 ninda-silà
151	*RTC* 17	
	PN gala "cantor" (Boy)	20 gín kug
		1. gsg še
		1 dug kas
		20 SUR
		20 ninda-silà
152	*VAS* XIV 141	
	1 igi-nu-du_8 "blind" (Man)	15 gín kug
153	*VAS* XIV 144	
	1 igi-nu-du_8 "blind" (Man)	15 gín kug
154	*BIN* VIII 363	
	PN gala "cantor" (Boy)	30. gsg še
155	*Dok.* I 17	
	PN gala guruš-am_6 "grown cantor" (Man)	18 gín kug
156	*Dok.* I 293	
	1 igi-nu-du_8 "blind" (Man)	14 gín kug
	1 sag-nita (Man)	20 gín kug
	1 igi-nu-du_8 "blind" (Man)	14 gín kug
157	*BIN* VIII 177	
	D PN (Man)	[x] gín k.b.
158	A 713	
	D PN (Woman)	[x] gín k.b.
159	Ist. Mus. Adab 397	
	D PN (Girl?)	10 gín k.b.
160	Ist. Mus. Adab 398	
	D PN (Woman?)	⌜12?⌝ gín k.b.
161	Ist. Mus. Adab 399	
	[D P]N	[x] gín k.b.
162	Ist. Mus. Adab 426	
	[D PN]	[x] gín k.b.
163	A 815	
	1 gemé "slave woman"	15 gín k.b.
184	*MAD* IV 77	
	PN (Girl?)	9 gín kug

Text	*Object of Sale + Description*	*Price*
185	*MAD* IV 78	
	PN (Man?)	6 gín kug
186	*MAD* IV 81	
	PN (Boy)	6 gín kug
187	*MAD* IV 150	
	PN (Boy)	8 gín kug
188	*MAD* IV 158	
	[PN] (Child)	[x] gín kug
189	*BIN* VIII 39	
	dumu PN (Child)	2.4. še
		1 u_8 = 0.5 gín kug
		20 gín níg-kug
	PN (Woman)	6 gín kug
		5. še
		40 silà ì
190	*BIN* VIII 66	
	PN dumu PN_x (Woman)	[x].2. še
		5 udu
191	*BIN* VIII 175	
	PN (Child)	10.93 gín kug
192	Böhl Coll. 929	
	PN ama-tu-am_6 "house-born slave" (Woman)	10. še
193	*MAD* IV 80	
	PN (Man?)	5 gín kug
194	NBC 10294	
	1 gemé "slave woman"	22 gín kug
		36. še
195	*ITT* I 1040	
	[D PN ù D PN_2] dumu P[N_x(-me)]	[x] gín k.b.
196	*ITT* I 1041	
	[D PN]	[x] gín k.b.
197	*ITT* II 4518	
	D PN (Man)	15 gín k.b.
198	*ITT* II 4578	
	PN dumu PN_x (Man)	[x] gín k.b.
199	*ITT* II 4588	
	D PN (Man)	6.⌜33⌝ gín k.b.
200	*RTC* 79	
	D PN (Man)	15 gín k.b.
201	*RTC* 80	
	D PN (Man)	—
	D PN_2 (Woman)	—
	2 dumu-SA[L]-n[i] (Girls)	—
	dam dumu-ni-me	
	D PN_3 (Man)	—
	D PN_4 (Man)	—
	šeš-a-ni-me	—

8.3.4. Persons—*continued*

Text	*Object of Sale + Description*	*Price*
202	*RTC* 81	
	D PN dumu PN_x (Man)	⌜20⌝ gín k.b.
208	*TMH* V 47	
	PN nu-$kiri_6$ "gardener" É-^{d}Nisaba^{KI}-kam (Man)	10 gín k.b.
213	PBS IX 4	
	D PN (Woman?)	—
	D PN_2 (Woman?)	—
214	*Dok.* II 68	
	D PN (Man)	4 gín kug
215	*TIM* IX 99	
	D PN (Boy)	[x] gín k.b.
216	IM 43431	
	PN (Man?)	⌜5?⌝.16 gín k.b.
217	NBC 10221	
	PN (Woman)	[x] gín k.b.
219	IM 43451	
	PN (Woman?)	[x] gín k.b.
220	IM 43741	
	PN (Man?)	10 + [x] gín k.b.
221	MLC 1251	
	D PN (Man)	15 gín k.b.
	[D PN_2]	5 gín k.b.
231	*HSS* X 99	
	[ARÁ]D Lu-lu-bi-im "Lulubean [sla]ve"	[x]. ŠE
232	*MVNS* III 80	
	D PN (Boy)	3.2. ŠE = 6 GÍN K.B.
	[D PN_2]	4.4. ŠE = [8 GÍN K.B.?]
233	*MVNS* III 102	
	1 PN (Child)	10.33 GÍN K.B.
234	IM 43612	
	PN (Woman)	6.5 GÍN K.B.
240	*CT* L 78	
	1 GEMÉ "slave woman"	27 GÍN K.B.
	1 DUMU.SAL (Girl)	10 GÍN K.B.
241	*HSS* X 211	
	PN (Woman)	5 GÍN K.B.
271	*NSATN* 607	
	1 sag-[X]	[x].3 gín k.b.
272	AUAM 73.1110	
	1 sag-nita (Man)	2.66 gín k.b.
273	*NSATN* 123	
	1 sag-[X]	[x] gín k.b.
274	AUAM 73.3097	
	1 sag-nita sag-ba PN mu-ni (Man)	3 gín k.b.

Text	*Object of Sale + Description*	*Price*
275	NBC 11300	
	[1 sag-X]	[x]. še
276	*RA* VIII pp. 185–186 no. 4	
	1 sag-SAL PN mu-ni-im (Woman)	6.66 gín k.b.
277	*BE* III/1 15+*NSATN* 367	
	1 sag-nita [P]N mu-ni-im (Man)	11 gín k.b.
278	*NSATN* 255	
	1 sag-nita PN mu-ni-im (Man)	10 gín k.b.
279	NBC 7174	
	1 sag-SAL-àm PN m[u]-ni-i[m] dumu-SAL gaba-na-a b[í-tab]-bi (Woman and Female Infant)	8.2.3 še
280	*RA* X p. 66 no. 105	
	1 sag-nita PN mu-ni-im (Man)	3.1.4 še
281	*UET* III 26	
	1 sag-nita PN mu-ni 1½ kùš-ni-ta (env.: 1 kùš-ni-ta) (Boy)	2 gín k.b.
282	NBC 5652	
	1 sag-nita-àm PN mu-ni-im (Man)	7.33 gín k.b.
283	*TIM* V 12	
	1 sag-SAL PN mu-ni-im (Woman)	1.5 gín k.b.
284	*UET* III 30	
	1 sag-SAL PN mu-ni gemé Seller-kam (Woman)	8.5 gín k.b.
285	*NSATN* 761	
	1 sag-nita PN mu-ni-im (Man)	16 gín k.b.
	1 sag-SAL PN_2 mu-ni-im dumu gaba-na-a ab-tab (Woman and Infant)	
286	AUAM 73.3096	
	1 sag-⌜SAL⌝ PN mu-ni-im (Woman)	2.5 gín kug
287	*UET* III 29	
	1 sag-nita P[N] mu-[ni-im] (Man)	5 gín k.b.
288	*NRVN* I 216	
	1 sag-SAL PN mu-ni-im (Woman)	4.33 gín k.b.
289	*MDP* XXVIII 410	
	[1] sag-SAL P[N] mu-ni-i[m] (Woman)	7 gín kug
290	*NRVN* I 215	
	1 sag-SAL PN mu-n[i-im] (Woman)	12+[x?] gín k.b.
291	*ZA* XXV p. 206 no. 1	
	[1] sag-SAL PN mu-ni-im (Woman)	4 gín k.b.
292	*NSATN* 713	
	[1 sag]-SAL [P]N [mu-ni-i]m (Woman)	[x] gín k.b.

8.3.4. Persons—*continued*

Text	*Object of Sale + Description*	*Price*
293 *TMH* n.F. I/II 51		
	1 sag-nita PN mu-ni-im (Man)	⌜4?⌝ gín k.b.
294 *ITT* III 6370		
	1 dumu-SAL PN PN$_2$ mu-ni-im (Girl)	4.25 gín k.b.
295 *BIN* V 346		
	^{I}PN SAL (Woman) ^{I}PN$_2$ dumu-ni (Boy) ^{I}PN$_3$ nita (Man)	20 gín k.b.
296 *MAOG* IV p. 191 MD 3		
	1 sag-SAL PN mu-ni-im (Woman) 1 sag-nita dumu-nita-ni PN$_2$ mu-ni-im (Boy)	12 gín kug
297 *TIM* IX 103		
	1 sag-nita [P]N mu-ni-im (Man)	7 gín k.b.
298 *NSATN* 498		
	1 sag-SAL PN mu-ni (Woman)	2 gín k.b.
299 Forde, *NCT* 63		
	1 sag-SAL PN mu-ni (Woman)	6 gín k.b.
300 *NSATN* 610		
	1 sag-SAL PN mu-ni-im (Girl)	[x]+4.5 gín k.b.
301 *NSATN* 265		
	1 sag-SAL su$_4$?-NE-a PN mu-ne-im (Woman)	3.5 gín k.b.
302 Ist. Mus. Ni. 5446		
	1 sag-SAL PN mu-ni (Woman)	2 gín k.b.
303 YBC 9827		
	1 sag-SAL PN mu-ne ba-sa(for sa$_4$?) (Woman)	5 gín k.b.
304 *NRVN* I 214		
	1 sag-[nita] PN mu-ni-im (Girl)	3 gín k.b.
305 *AOr* VII pl. III no. 1		
	1 sag-SAL PN mu-ni-im (Woman)	5. še
306 *NSATN* 903		
	1 sag-SAL PN mu-ni-im (Girl)	4 gín k.b.
307 PBS VIII/2 157+*NSATN* 5		
	1 sag-[nita] PN mu-ni-im (Man)	10 gín k.b.
308 *NRVN* I 213		
	1 s[ag-SAL] PN m[u-ni-im] (Woman)	[x gín k.b.]
309 *UET* III 39		
	[^{I}PN dumu-[SAL PN$_x$] (Woman)	—
309a Limet, *TSDU* 16		
	1 sag-nita ⌜x⌝ PN mu-ni-im (Man)	10 gín k.b.
310 *NRVN* I 212		
	⌜1⌝ sa[g-ni]ta P[N m]u-ni-im (Man)	15 gín k.b.
311 PBS IX 41		
	1 sag-SAL (Woman)	9.16 gín k.b.
312 *NSATN* 850		
	^{I}PN ^{I}PN$_2$ ^{I}PN$_3$ ^{I}PN$_4$ dumu PN$_x$-me (Men)	41 gín kug
313 *NSATN* 884		
	[1] sag-nita PN mu-ni-im (Man) 1 sag-SAL PN$_2$ mu-ni-im (Woman)	[. . .]
314 AUAM 73.2128		
	1 sag-SAL (Woman)	5.5 gín k.b.
315 *UET* III 47		
	1 sag-nita PN mu-ni-im (Man)	17 gín k.b.
332 *UET* III 19		
	[1] sag-SAL [P]N [mu]-ni-im [gemé Sel]ler-kam (Woman)	[x gín] k.b.
333 AUAM 73.3098		
	[P]N gemé Seller (Woman)	4 gín k.b.
334 *UET* III 14		
	1 sag-nita PN mu-ni-im arád(wr. NITA) Seller-kam (Man)	10 gín k.b.
335 *UET* III 15		
	1 sag-SAL PN mu-ni-im gemé Seller-kam (Woman)	6.1.4 še
336 *UET* III 46		
	1 sag-nita SIG$_7$ PN mu-ni-im (Man) [ar]ád(wr. NITA) Seller-kam	[x]+2 gín k.b.
337 *UET* III 44		
	1 sag-nita PN mu-ni-[im] dumu-sag-ri[g$_x$] (PA.SAL.KA[B.DU]) Seller dam [PN$_x$-kam] (Boy?)	8 gín k.b.
338 *UET* III 18		
	1 sag-SAL PN mu-ni-im gemé Seller-kam (Woman)	8 gín k.b.
339 Szlechter, *TJA* I p. LXVIII JES 134		
	PN arád Seller (Man)	⌜x⌝ gín k.b.
341 *YOS* XV 101		
	PN (Man?)	[x] gín k.b.
342 *ITT* II 3512		
	^{I}PN dumu PN$_x$ (Man)	4.25 gín k.b.
343 *NRVN* I 226		
	1 SAG.SAL PN MU.NI (Woman)	0.66 GÍN K.B.
344 *YOS* IV 2		
	^{I}PN (Boy?)	9 gín kug-UD.UD

8.3.4. Persons—*continued*

Text	*Object of Sale + Description*	*Price*
345	IM 61558	
	[1 sag-X]	12 gín k.b.
346	*ZA* LIII p. 79 no. 18	
	1 sag-SAL P[N] mu-ni-im (Woman)	4 gín k.b.
347	*NSATN* 937	
	1 sag-nita PN mu-ni-im (Man)	5 gín k.b.
349	IM 61706	
	1 sa[g-nita?] P[N] mu-[ni-im] (Man?)	6 gín k.b.
350	A 31164	
	[1 s]ag-[X]	15 gín k.b.
351	*NSATN* 145	
	1 sag-SAL P[N] (Woman)	3 gín ⟨k.b.⟩
352	*UET* III 26	
	1 sag-nita PN mu-ni-im (Man)	3 gín k.b.
354	*ITT* II 2766	
	PN (Man)	14.5 gín k.b.
356	*ITT* II 3470	
	PN dam ù dumu (Man, Woman, and Children)	8 gín k.b.
357	Pinches, *BTBC* 53	
	PN (Woman)	6.66 gín k.b.
358	De Genouillac, *FT* II pl. L AO 13019	
	PN (Woman)	1 gín k.b.
359	*MAOG* IV pp. 188–189 MD 2	
	PN (Man)	15. še = 15 gín k.b.
361	Oppenheim, *Eames Coll.* pl. II TT 4	
	⟨1⟩ sag-SAL PN mu-ni (Woman)	0.5 gín k.b.
362	Oppenheim, *Eames Coll.* pl. XI TT 1	
	1 SAG.NITA PN MU.NI.IM (Man)	⸢8?⸣.33 GÍN K.B. 1 U$_8$.BAR.GÁL.LA
363	Oppenheim, *Eames Coll.* pl. IX TT 2	
	1 sag-SAL PN mu-ni-im (Girl)	3.33 gín k.b.
364	*TMH* n.F. I/II 50	
	1 sag-nita-àm PN mu-ni (Man)	5.5 gín k.b.
365	*UET* III 41	
	1 sag-nita PN mu-ni-im (Man)	55 gín k.b.
366	*MDP* XVIII 199	
	1 sag-nita PN mu-ni-im (Man)	2 gín k.b.
367	*TLB* III 170	
	[PN ù] PN$_2$ dumu PN$_x$-me (Two Boys?)	15 gín k.b.
369	*TMH* n.F. I/II 53	
	[^{I}P]N ^{I}PN$_2$ dam-ni ^{I}PN$_3$ ^{I}PN$_4$ ^{I}PN$_5$ dumu-ni-me (Man, Woman, and three Children)	43 gín k.b.

Text	*Object of Sale + Description*	*Price*
370	Yondorf Coll. A	
	1 SAG.SAL PN MU.NI.IM (Woman)	2.33 GÍN K.B.

8.3.5. Animals

Text	*Object of Sale + Description*	*Price*
222	*MVNS* III 100	
	1 ANŠE.LIBIR "dusú-equid" 1 ANŠE.LIBIR-nita 3 "three-year-old male dusú-equid"	13.66 gín k.b.
223	YBC 12312	
	anše "donkey"	5 gín kug
225	*MAD* IV 51	
	1 ANŠE.BAR.AN-nita "male mule"	11 gín kug
235	*Or.* n.s. LI p. 363	
	[1 ANŠE].BAR.AN 1 "one-year-old mule"	25 GÍN K.B. 10. ŠE 1 GÚ SÍG.UDU
316	*NSATN* 741	
	1 GIR mu-2 "two-year-old heifer"	6 gín k.b.
317	*NRVN* I 218	
	1 gud-niga "barley-fed bull"	10.5 gín k.b.
318	Chiera, *CBTC* Ex 695	
	1 emè(ANŠE.SAL)-máḫ "mature she-ass"	7.1. še
319	*JMEOS* XV pp. 41–42 no. 2	
	1 gud-giš "yoke-ox"	8.33 gín k.b.
320	*TMH* n.F. I/II 52	
	2 dusú-nita(wr. ANŠE.NITA. LIBIR) "male dusú-equid"	8.5 gín kug-UD.UD
321	*NRVN* I 220	
	[1 g]ud-giš "yoke-ox"	[x] gín k.b.
322	*NRVN* I 219	
	[1 g]ud mu-2 [x] IM DA GÍR SI ZU KI [Ḫ]AR?-a ḪAR?-a íb-su?-éš? "two-year-old bull . . ."	4.5 gín k.b.
323	*NRVN* I 221	
	2 emè(ANŠE.SAL) "she-ass" 1 amar-ga anše "suckling ass"	13 gín k.b.
348	*ZA* LIII p. 80 no. 20	
	[1 gud?-gi]š? "[yo]ke(?)-[ox?]"	[x gín k.b.]
368	*JCS* XIX p. 27 no. 2	
	⟨1⟩ EMÈ(ANŠE.SAL) "she-ass"	6. ŠE

8.3.6. Commodities

Text	*Object of Sale + Description*	*Price*	*Price per Unit*
224 *MAD* IV 15			
	10. zú-lum "dates"	10 gín kug	1. zú-lum = 1 gín kug
226 Serota Coll. A 10			
	10 gín kug-GI "gold"	2.2. gsg še	1 gín kug-GI = .1. gsg še Rates: 1 gín k.b. = .1 gsg še 1 gín kug-GI = 6 gín k.b.
236 *MAD* IV 4			
	2 GÍN KUG.GI "gold"	15 GÍN K.B.	1 GÍN KUG.GI = 7.5 GÍN K.B.

CHAPTER 9

RELATIONSHIPS AMONG ADDITIONAL PAYMENTS AND BETWEEN PRICES AND ADDITIONAL PAYMENTS

In several of the kudurrus and in some of the clay sale documents (Fara) the value of the commodities included in the additional payment stands in a definite relationship to the value of the price. Furthermore, in many instances proportional relationships among the amounts of the commodities in the additional payment can be discerned. In the following pages, all the attestations of these relationships, with the exception of a few uncertain cases, are discussed.

No. 14 *Chicago Stone and* No. 15 *Baltimore Stone*

The prices of fields in these two inscriptions are paid in silver, at the constant rate of 1.66 shekels of silver per one iku of land. In five of the transactions recorded on no. 14, the prices diverge slightly from that rate: 1.71 shekels per iku in ii 6; 2 shekels per iku in iii 10; 1.64 shekels per iku in vi 12; 2.08 shekels per iku in viii 2; and 1.69 per iku in xvi 2.

The commodities included in the additional payment are oil (or sheep oil), wool, an item called (še) iš-gán (see note to no. 14 i 9), beer-bread, and table(?)-bread.

The comparison of the amounts of the commodities given as the additional payment with those of the price (illustrated in fig. 13, p. 285) displays the existence of fairly constant proportional relationships between them. The ideal set of relationships is: 10 shekels of silver of the price to the additional payment composed of two quarts of oil (or 1 umbin? of sheep oil), two pounds of wool, 1 NI-ga (= gur) of (še) iš-gán, and ten units of beer-bread. The table(?)-bread, which is sometimes included in the additional payment, shows no numerical relationship to the other commodities.

The fact that two quarts of oil regularly interchange with one umbin? of sheep oil in the additional payment suggests that umbin? was a container of the capacity of two quarts. See note to no. 14 i 7.

There occur numerous deviations from the above set of proportions in both inscriptions. It is clear that the amounts of the commodities were calculated in relation to the price: if the price consists of one or more units of ten, then the proportions of the commodities are generally exact; however, if the price is not a multiple of ten, then the amounts of the commodities are only approximate. See, e.g., no. 14 xii–xiii, where the 65 shekels of silver of the price correspond to the additional payment composed of 7 umbin? of sheep oil, 13 pounds of wool, and 6.2.0 of (še) iš-gán.

The value of the additional payment in relation to the price can be estimated only approximately. Assuming that the rates of oil, wool, and barley are standard in both inscriptions, we can calculate the values shown in figure 14, p. 286.

This leaves us with 10 beer-breads, the value of which is not known, but probably not exceeding 0.3 shekel of silver. Accordingly, we can estimate that the value of the additional payment amounted to ca. 2 shekels of silver, that is, ca. 20 percent of the price composed of 10 shekels of silver.

No. 16 *Kish Stone Fragments I*

Both the prices and the additional payment (NÍG.KI.GAR) appearing in no. 16 are paid in silver. Only two transactions are preserved sufficiently to determine the relationship of the additional payment to the price. In the first transaction (16b A), the NÍG.KI.GAR represents $\frac{1}{15}$ of the price (1 GÍN KUG.BABBAR to 15 GÍN KUG.BABBAR), while in the other (16b B), ca. $\frac{1}{20}$ of the price (3 GÍN KUG.BABBAR to 60+[x] GÍN KUG. BABBAR).

No. 22 *Lummatur Tablet I and* No. 23 *Lummatur Tablet II*

In these two kudurrus, prices are paid in barley (no. 22) and in barley and wool (no. 23). The commodities included in the gifts (níg-ba), which were presented to the first (or primary) seller and other sellers, are: a type of wool called síg-bar-udu, oil, ŠU.KEŠDA (meaning unknown), barley-bread, kalag-bread, ku_6-dar-ra (dried fish), soup, roasted barley, leeks, turnips, and sheep.

As far as the fragmentary state of both inscriptions allows us to ascertain, the commodities given to the first seller appear to stand in set proportions. This is demonstrated by the transactions no. 22 Obv. i–Rev. i and no. 22 Rev. i–Rev. ii, where the relationships between five of the commodities are as follows: one unit of síg-bar-udu to eight units of barley-bread to two units of kalag-bread to eight units of ku_6-dar-ra to two quarts of soup. The remaining six commodities are always given in the amount of one unit (ŠU.KEŠDA and sheep) or one quart (roasted barley) or one šakan container (oil) or one bundle (leeks and turnips).

The gift presented to other sellers is always given in the same amounts. The proportions are: five units of barley-bread to one unit of kalag-bread to three units of ku_6-dar-ra to three quarts of soup to one quart of roasted barley to one bundle of leeks (illustrated in fig. 15, p. 286).

It appears that the value of the commodities included in the additional payment has no relationship to the value of the price (and thus to the size of the sold field) in these kudurrus; this is suggested by no. 22 Obv. i–Rev. i and no. 22 Rev. i–Rev. ii, where the amounts of the commodities differ, even though the prices and the sizes of the fields remain unchanged.

No. 36 *CT V 3*

In this document, prices are paid exclusively in silver, at the rate of 3⅓ shekels of silver per 1 iku of land. The commodities included in the additional payment (NÍG.KI.GAR) are silver, barley, (pig) oil, and TÚG.A.SU cloths.

In two of the transactions recorded in this kudurru (iii 1–11 and iv), the additional payment consists of silver and oil, which stand in the proportions of one shekel of silver to one quart of oil. In two other transactions (v 3–12 and v 13–22), the additional payment includes barley, silver, and oil, in the proportions: ½ gur of barley to ½ shekel of silver to one quart of oil. In the remaining transaction (i), the commodities of the additional payment are pig oil, barley, and TÚG.A.SU cloth. No clear correspondences between the amounts of these commodities can be detected.

With the exception of the transaction recorded in i, the proportional relationship between the price and the additional payment is: 10 shekels of silver of the price to the additional payment composed of 1 shekel of silver (or ½ gur of barley plus ½ shekel of silver) and one quart of oil (see fig. 16, p. 286).

The ratio of the additional payment to the price in this document can be analyzed in two different ways. One can either assume that the values of both silver (or barley plus silver) and oil were included in the additional payment, or that only silver (or barley plus silver) was counted. In the first case, the additional payment would amount to 1$^1/_{10}$ shekel of silver, i.e., 1 shekel of silver plus $^1/_{10}$ shekel of silver, the equivalent of one quart of oil (at the rate of $^1/_{10}$ shekel of silver per 1 quart of oil). Accordingly, the additional payment would represent ca. 9 percent of the price. Following the other alternative, the value of the additional payment would be exactly 1 shekel of silver, i.e., 10 percent of the price. The rule of simplicity suggests that the second interpretation is the correct one.

The value of the additional payment given in the transaction recorded in i is difficult to calculate, since the rate of TÚG.A.SU cloth is not specified in the text. However, if one assumes that the additional payment, as in other transactions, represents 10 percent of the price, then the value of the additional payment could be put at 32 shekels of silver (the price is 320 shekels in this transaction). By analogy with other transactions, one could then take it that the pig oil was not counted in the additional payment, thereby arriving at the equation: 15⅖ shekels of silver (= the equivalent of 15.2.0 gur of barley) plus 5 TÚG.A.SU cloth = 32 shekels of silver. Based on this equation, one would be able to establish that 5 TÚG.A.SU cloth cost 16 ⅗ shekels of silver, i.e., that the value of 1 TÚG.A.SU cloth was ca. 5⅓ shekels of silver.

No. 37 *CT XXXII 7f.*

In this inscription, the prices of fields are paid in barley, while the commodities included in the additional payment (NÍG.DÚR.GAR) are barley, wool, and oil.

The reconstruction of the prices and the amounts of the commodities included in the additional payment assumes that, throughout this document, the price of 1 iku of land is 2.5 GSG of barley (as recorded in Obv. ii′–iii′ and iii′), and that the proportions between the commodities of the additional payment are constant at 1 GSG of barley to two pounds of wool to two quarts of oil (as it is recorded in Obv. iv′, Rev. i–ii, and ii–iii). By combining these two sets of data, we can establish that the price, consisting of 15 GSG of barley, corresponds to the additional payment composed of 1 GSG of barley, two pounds of wool, and two quarts of oil (see fig. 17, p. 286).

The numerical relationships reconstructed above do not fit in Obv. iv′, where the price of 1 iku of land is 1.88 GSG of barley. One may observe, however, that the relationship between the size of the field and the amounts of the commodities of the additional payment is as expected in this transaction (48 iku of land to the additional payment composed of 8 GSG of barley, sixteen pounds of wool, and sixteen quarts of oil), and that it is only the amount of the price that does not fit the picture. All the relationships would be correct in this transaction if the price were not 90 but 120 GSG of barley. Therefore, one might suggest that the figure of 90 GSG is a scribal error.

The ratio of the additional payment to the price can be calculated in two different ways, depending on whether one includes only barley or barley plus wool and oil in the value of the additional payment. In the first case, the value of the additional payment would represent $^1/_{15}$ (6.66 percent) of the price. In the second case, the value of the additional payment would amount to $^1/_{10}$ (or 10 percent) of the price. The latter calculation is based on the rates of wool and oil given in the R. E. of the inscription, which are 0.25 shekel of silver per one pound of wool and 0.25 shekel of silver per one quart of oil (SÍG.GI_6 1 GÚ ŠÁM 15 KUG.BABBAR GÍN, [Ì . . . 1 (PI)] ŠÁM 14+[1 KUG.BABBAR] G[ÍN]). Assuming that SÍG has the same value as SÍG.GI_6 "black wool," and that 1 shekel of silver corresponds to 1 GSG of barley, the value of the additional payment composed of 1 GSG of barley, two pounds of wool, and two quarts of oil would be 1.5 GSG of barley, i.e., 10 percent of the price consisting of 15

GSG of barley. The fact that the usual ratio of the additional payment to the price is 1:10 shows that the second calculation is the correct one.

No. 40 *Manishtushu Obelisk*

In the Manishtushu Obelisk the prices of fields are paid exclusively in barley. The commodities included in the additional payment (NÍG.KI.GAR) are paid in:

1) silver (A_1, A_2, A_3)
2) barley (B)
3) wool (C_3 and D)
4) wool, teams of mules, and various metal objects (C_1)
5) oil, teams of mules, various metal objects, and human beings (C_2)

In the three instances where the additional payment consists of silver, its ratio to the price is 1:6.66 (i.e., 15 percent of the price). In all other transactions, the additional payment represents 1/10 (or 10 percent) of the price. The reason for this difference may be sought in the fact that silver was generally considered less desirable than barley, as evidenced in the Mesopotamian loan practices, according to which the interest on silver was lower than that on barley (20 percent against 33 percent).

No. 41 *Sippar Stone*

In this document the prices of fields are paid in silver. The additional payment (NÍG.KI.GAR) includes silver, barley, beer-bread (BAPPIR), oil, and TÚG.ŠU.ZA.GA cloths.

The determination of the size of the fields listed in the text and the price per iku of the fields is dependent on two assumptions. The first is that the price per iku of a field should be related to its seeding rate. That is, more productive land (with a lower seeding rate) should be more expensive (per iku) than less productive land (with a higher seeding rate). The second is that the amount of seed indicating the area of the field is determined by a standard seeding rate which is thirty quarts per iku. The second assumption is a necessary corollary of the first: otherwise, if the area of field were determined by dividing the amount of seed given by the seeding rate assigned to each field, calculation shows that the price per iku would be constant at ca. 1⅓ shekels of silver per iku. This would be contrary to our first assumption that the seeding rate affects the price per iku of land. Therefore, the amount of seed must be calculated at a standard rate and the figure of thirty quarts per iku was chosen on the basis of later sources. The area of field is thus determined by the relationship:

$$\text{number of iku} = \frac{\text{amount of seed in quarts}}{\text{standard rate of seeding (30 quarts per iku)}}$$

Since the price is given, it is a simple matter to calculate the price per iku using the formula:

$$\text{price per iku} = \frac{\text{price}}{\text{number of iku}}$$

These calculations yield the results given in figure 18, p. 286.

If we assume that the standard price per iku is based on the price of a field seeded at the standard rate of 30 quarts per iku, then the rate of seeding is related to the price per iku in the following manner:

$$\text{price per iku} = \text{standard price per iku} \times \frac{\text{standard rate of seeding (30 quarts)}}{\text{(1⅓ shekel per iku) seeding rate of field}}$$

In other words, a field that requires twice as much seed costs half as much.

An exception to the formula is found in the case of a small plot of exceptionally productive land. In Rev. vii′ we find 4(BÁN) of land with a seeding rate of fifteen quarts. The amount of land is 1⅓ iku and the price is 4⅓ shekels of silver, which indicates a price per iku of 3¼ shekels, while the relationship of the seeding rates indicates that the price should be 2⅔ shekels per iku. This distortion of the linear increase in price with increasing productivity is not surprising. The labor saved in working a small field with a high yield would compensate for a premium in price over the expected rate.

While the price of the land per iku varies according to its productivity, the additional payment is fairly constant at around 10 percent of the total price of the field. Disregarding one value of 7.5 percent (Obv. v), the values for the additional payment range from 9.37 percent to 10.67 percent with several at exactly 10 percent. The variations stem from the fact that small amounts are generally disregarded in the additional payment if they cannot be expressed as exact fractions and reflect the difficulties of trying to arrive at 10 percent of a number using a sexagesimal system.

As already mentioned, the price of the fields is given in silver only. On the obverse, the additional payment is also given in silver only, and the two figures establish the value of the additional payment as ca. 10 percent of the price. On the reverse, the additional payment consists of silver, barley, beer-bread, and oil. If we assume that the additional payment still constitutes ca. 10 percent of the price, it is immediately apparent that the value of the additional payment is divided as equally as possible between silver and barley plus beer-bread and oil, since the amount of silver is ca. 5 percent of the price. This fact taken together with the relationship between the other commodities allows us to postulate the values of the commodities. The easiest assumption is that 1 gur of barley (300 quarts) = 1 shekel of silver, and if this is so, then the value of barley in the additional payment is always ⅕ of the amount of silver, and the value of beer-bread plus oil must be $\frac{4}{5}$ of the value of silver. Thus silver is $\frac{1}{2}$ of the additional payment, barley is $\frac{1}{10}$, and beer-bread plus oil is $\frac{2}{5}$ ($\frac{5}{10} + \frac{1}{10} + \frac{4}{10} = 1$). Since the number of beer-breads is always the same as the number of the quarts of oil (both expressed in counted units, not measures), no further division of the value of these two commodities is possible, especially because of the wide range of values attested for oil during this period. Although it is obvious from the calculations that five beer-breads + five quarts of oil = 2 shekels of silver, there is no further evidence to show what portion of the value each makes up.

On both obverse and reverse, TÚG.ŠU.ZA.GA cloths are sometimes listed along with the additional payment, but their value cannot be included in the additional payment without severely distorting the calculations of the value of the additional payment. In the first place, the proportions of the other commodities which make up the additional payment and the relation of the additional payment (not counting the cloths) to the price are the same whether the cloths are included or not. Secondly, the amounts of the other commodities have a relationship to the price of the field, while the number of cloths (if any) does not. For these two reasons, it is obvious that the value of the cloths was not included in the additional payment.

No. 43 *Eshnuna Clay Tablet and* No. 44 *Eshnuna Clay Fragments*

Due to the close relationship between inscriptions nos. 43 and 44, they are considered together. In both kudurrus, the prices are paid in silver and barley, while the commodities given in the additional payment (*iškinū*) include silver, barley, wool (SÍG.GAN), and BA.AN-containers.

Examination of the prices and tariffs found in nos. 43 and 44 leads to contradictory conclusions. In no. 43, all prices except one (iii–iv) are given as a combination of silver in shekels and barley in GSG. In all instances except three, the amount of GSG is twice that of shekels, that is, one-third of the price is given in shekels (of silver) and two-thirds in GSG (of barley). If we assume, as in the Manishtushu Obelisk, that 1 shekel of silver equals 1 GSG of barley, then the totals of silver and barley yield a price of 2 shekels of silver per 1 iku of land. Further strengthening the assumption that 1 shekel of silver equals 1 GSG of barley is the fact that in those instances where the proportions of silver and barley given as the price are different from the normal one-third : two-thirds (iii–iv, v–vi), the totals of silver and barley still yield a price of 2 shekels of silver per 1 iku if 1 GSG of barley is figured at a rate of 1 shekel of silver. In addition, the totals of the additional payment, also given in silver and barley, add up to a rate of one-sixth shekel of silver per 1 iku if it is assumed that 1 shekel of silver = 1 GSG of barley. The figures for the additional payment show clearly that the GSG contains 240 quarts, since the normal one-third : two-thirds proportions of silver to barley is found in all cases except one (iii–iv). Thus one-third of a shekel (1 MA.NA.TUR) of silver is half of two-thirds of GSG (0.2.4 = 160 quarts [viii]) totaling 1 shekel of silver as the additional payment for 6 iku of land and so forth.

In no. 44, the prices and proportions are much more difficult to assess because of the fragmentary nature of the texts. Nevertheless, no. 44k shows a price similar to those of no. 43 in that the price of 18 iku of land is given as 10 shekels of silver plus 26 GSG of barley, totaling 36 shekels of silver (if 1 shekel of silver = 1 GSG of barley) or 2 shekels of silver per 1 iku. However, the 10 shekels of silver of the price are said to be the equivalent of 10 gur of barley which were given in place of silver. This statement indicates a rate of 1 shekel of silver to 1 gur of barley, leading to the paradox that both 1 GSG and 1 gur equal 1 shekel of silver. Since the gur and GSG contain different amounts (300 quarts for 1 gur, 240 quarts for 1 GSG), we should not expect them to have the same value in the same text. The first explanation which comes to mind is that gur is written as an abbreviation for GSG. However, this supposition is contradicted by several facts. First, in no. 44b we find a quantity of grain written as ⸢8⸣?.1.4 ŠE GUR. Although the equivalent and the rest of the price are lost, it must be taken into consideration that 0.1.4 (= 100 quarts) is one-third of a normal gur (= 300 quarts), while 0.1.2 is one-third of a GSG (= 240 quarts). Since the only fractions used in these two texts are $\frac{1}{3}$ and $\frac{2}{3}$, it is reasonable to assume that the writing ⸢8⸣?.1.4 ŠE GUR stands for $8\frac{1}{3}$ gur and not $8\frac{5}{12}$ GSG. Second, in several instances (43 iii–iv, 44d, and 44h) the price is given in barley alone instead of silver (or some equivalent) and barley. Therefore, it does not seem likely that the price in no. 44k would have been broken down into gur and GSG when it could have been given in GSG. We must conclude that gur is not an abbreviation for GSG and that the gur in these texts had 300 quarts while the GSG had 240. The reason for both 1 GSG and 1 gur being equal to 1 shekel of silver must be left to speculation.

The term *iškinū* is found in each preserved transaction in no. 43 but is not in no. 44. The *iškinū* is regularly one-twelfth of the price (i.e., $\frac{1}{6}$ shekel of silver per 1 iku of land, assuming that 1 shekel of silver = 1 GSG of barley), not including the value of the SÍG.GAN and BA.AN also given in each transaction in no. 43. In that text, the number of SÍG.GAN and the number of BA.AN (both are counted in units, not measures) are always equal to the amount of silver given in the additional payment. Thus for 12 iku of land the price (in silver and barley) would be 24 shekels (2 shekels per 1 iku), the additional payment (in silver and barley) would be 2 shekels ($\frac{1}{12}$ of the price) and 2 SÍG.GAN and 2 BA.AN.

The latter two items appear as SÍG.GAN and BA.AN ŠE in nos. 42 and 44, where they are given singly (one of each) to various individuals, who probably were witnesses or officials.

The SÍG.GAN is unknown elsewhere, but the evidence here suggests that it is a fixed quantity of wool and not a special kind of wool. The BA.AN is well attested in third millennium Mesopotamia as a vessel or container. See section 11.7.

In no. 43, the totals in column xi give 40 MA.NA SÍG and 20 SILÀ Ì (sic, not 2 [BÁN]). Since oil is not mentioned elsewhere in the preserved portions of the inscription, we can assume that the forty pounds is the total of the SÍG.GAN in the text, and that the twenty quarts of oil is the total of the BA.AN.

The striking thing about the totals of forty pounds of wool and twenty quarts of oil is the reappearance of the 2:1 relationship between barley and silver in the price and in the additional payment sections. In order to preserve the validity of this relationship, it must be assumed that one pound of wool has the same value as one quart of oil. The text gives 6⅔ shekels of silver as the equivalent of 40 pounds of wool and therefore 1 shekel of silver equals 6 pounds of wool. If our other assumptions are correct, 1 shekel of silver should also equal 6 quarts of oil. The actual size of the SÍG.GAN and the BA.AN depends on the total number of these, which is not preserved. The total preserved in the inscription is 35 SÍG.GAN and 35 BA.AN. In addition, there are five transactions where the numbers are not preserved or cannot be reconstructed. It is also possible that the end of column x contained a brief summary of the witnesses and the number of SÍG.BAN and BA.AN each received (as in no. 42). The repeated use of the fractions ⅓ and ⅔ in the inscription suggests that the total of SÍG.GAN and BA.AN should be reconstructed as 60 of each. Then the numbers 40 and 20 would indicate that the SÍG.GAN was ⅔ pound and the BA.AN was ⅓ quart. Regardless of the totals, the 2:1 relationship between the SÍG.GAN and the BA.AN holds true because the number of SÍG.GAN is always equal to the number of BA.AN. Reconstructing the totals as 60 allows the SÍG. GAN and the BA.AN to have values of simple fraction in keeping with the general tendency of the text. A reconstruction of the totals as 40 SÍG.GAN and BA.AN is barely possible (thirty-five preserved or reconstructed plus one each in the five broken sections), in which case the SÍG.GAN would be 1 pound and BA.AN ½ of a quart. The first reconstruction seems more plausible.

The value of wool is preserved in the text and is 6 pounds for 1 shekel of silver. If the SÍG.GAN is ⅔ pound, its value is ⅑ shekel of silver. If we follow the assumption that 1 pound of wool is the equivalent of one quart of oil, then the value of the BA.AN at ⅓ quart is 1/18 shekel of silver and the value of 1 SÍG.GAN plus 1 BA.AN is ⅙ shekel of silver.

Based on these reconstructions and calculations, the SÍG.GAN plus the BA.AN has a value of ⅙ of the value of the silver plus barley of the additional payment and 1/72 of the price.

The question remains as to whether the SÍG.GAN and the BA.AN are to be considered as part of the additional payment or to be considered separately. Without the SÍG.GAN and the BA.AN the value of the additional payment is 1/12 of the price. If the value of the SÍG.GAN and the BA.AN is added, the additional payment becomes 7/72 of the price. The rule of simplicity suggests that the first figure is correct. In addition, the first transaction in no. 43 includes a *haṣṣinnum* "axe" before the SÍG.GAN and the BA.AN. If the latter are to be included in the additional payment, then the axe must also be included and this would throw the calculation off. It seems then that the additional payment consists of silver and barley only, as does the price, and that the SÍG.GAN and BA.AN (and the axe) are additional gifts presented to the primary sellers, perhaps for distribution to others.

Nos. 100–136 *Fara Sale Documents*

In the Fara sale documents, the prices of houses and fields are paid either in copper or silver. The commodities which appear in the additional payments include more than twelve different items, among them metals, foodstuffs, and cloths. See plates 123–128 (not included there are the commodities of nos. 113a, 113b, 113c [= no. 112], 127a, and 127b). Among these commodities, only barley-bread (ninda-še) and cakes (gúg), both measured in units, and soup (tu_7) and NIGÍN+ḪA.A (a type of liquid), both measured in kúr, stand in definite numerical relationships. In most instances, the number of barley-breads corresponds to the number of cakes, while the amount of soup corresponds to the amount of NIGÍN.ḪA.A. The amounts of the first pair of the commodities are always higher than those of the latter, but, beyond that, no clear proportions can be established between them.

Figure 13. The Relationship between the Price and Additional Payment in Kudurrus nos. 14 and 15.

Price in Shekels (of Silver)	Additional Payment				
	Oil in Quarts (or sheep oil in umbin?)	Wool in pounds	(še) iš-gán in NI-ga (= gur)	Beer-Bread in Units	Table(?)-Bread in Units
10	2 (1)	2	1	10	varies

Figure 14. The Values of the Additional Payment in Kudurrus nos. 14 and 15.

2 quarts of oil	= 0.2 shekel of silver (at the rate of 0.1 shekel of silver per one quart of oil)
2 pounds of wool	= 0.5 shekel of silver (at the rate of 0.25 shekel of silver per one pound of wool)
1 NI-ga (= 1 gur) (še) iš-gán	= 1 shekel of silver (at the rate of 1 shekel of silver per 1 gur of barley)
Total:	1.7 shekels of silver

Figure 15. The Proportions between Commodities in Kudurrus nos. 22 and 23.

Seller	síg-bar-udu in Units	ì in šakan	ŠU. KEŠDA in Units	Barley-Bread in Units	kalag-Bread in Units	ku_6-dar-ra in Units	Soup in Quarts	Roasted Barley in Quarts	Leeks in Bundles	Turnips in Bundles	Sheep in Units
First	1	1	1	8	2	8	2	1	1	1	1
Other				5	1	3	3	1	1		

Figure 16. The Relationship between the Price and Additional Payment in Kudurru no. 36.

	Additional Payment		
Price in Shekels of Silver	Silver in Shekels	Barley in gur	Oil in Quarts
10	1 (0.5)	(0.5)	1

Figure 17. The Relationship between the Price and Additional Payment in Kudurru no. 37.

		Additional Payment		
Field in IKU	Price in GSG of Barley	Barley in GSG	Wool in Pounds	Oil in Quarts
6	15	1	2	2

Figure 18. The Price of the Field in Relation to Its Seeding Rate in Kudurru no. 41.

Price per iku in Shekels of Silver	Seeding Rate per iku in Quarts of Barley
2⅔	15
ca. 2	20
ca. 1⅓	30
1	45
⅔	60

CHAPTER 10

RATES OF COMMODITIES

The rates of commodities stated in prices and additional payments as attested in the kudurrus and clay sale documents are illustrated in figures 19–27. The following equations and abbreviations should be noted with reference to the figures below:

1 GUR	= 300 silà
1 GSG = gur-sag-gál	= 240 silà (Sargonic)
	= 144 silà (Pre-Sargonic Lagash)
1 gur-2-ul	= 72 silà (Pre-Sargonic Lagash)
1 MNT = ma-na-tur	= ⅓ gín = 60 še
K.B. = kug-babbar	

Figure 19. Rates of Barley

Text	*Barley*	*Its Silver/Copper Equivalent*	*Price of 1* gur *of Barley*
37 *CT* XXXII 7f.			
	[1.0.0 GSG]	[1 GÍN K.B.]	1 GÍN K.B.
40 Manishtushu Obelisk			
A_1	1.0.0 GUR	1 GÍN K.B.	1 GÍN K.B.
A_2	1.0.0 GUR	1 GÍN K.B.	1 GÍN K.B.
A_3	1.0.0 GUR	1 GÍN K.B.	1 GÍN K.B.
B	1.0.0 GUR	1 GÍN K.B.	1 GÍN K.B.
C_1	1.0.0 GUR	1 GÍN K.B.	1 GÍN K.B.
C_2	1.0.0 GUR	1 GÍN K.B.	1 GÍN K.B.
C_3	1.0.0 GUR	1 GÍN K.B.	1 GÍN K.B.
D	1.0.0 GUR	1 GÍN K.B.	1 GÍN K.B.
44 Eshnuna Clay Fragments			
b)	⸢8⸣?.1.4 GUR	[8? GÍN 1 MNT K.B.]	1 GÍN K.B.
e)	15.0.0 GUR	⸢15⸣ [GÍN K.B.]	1 GÍN K.B.
k) i	⸢23.0.0⸣ GUR	⸢23 GÍN K.B.⸣	1 GÍN K.B.
k) ii	10.0.0 GUR	10 GÍN K.B.	1 GÍN K.B.
k) iii	12.0.0 GUR	10+[2] GÍN K.B.	1 GÍN K.B.
101 *Fara* III 31			
	0.0.3 gur	(1) ma-na (urudu)	10 ma-na urudu
119 *TSŠ* Pls. XXXIII–XXXIV			
	0.0.3 gur	(1) ma-na (urudu)	10 ma-na urudu
129 *Fara* III 40			
	0.0.2 gur	(1) ma-na (urudu)	15 ma-na urudu
137 *BIN* VIII 352			
	36.0.0 gur-2-ul	18 gín kug-luḫ-ḫa	0.5 gín kug-luḫ-ḫa (for 1 gur-2-ul)

Figure 19. Rates of Barley

Text	*Barley*	*Its Silver/Copper Equivalent*	*Price of 1* gur *of Barley*
140	*DP* 31		
	1.0.0 (gur-2-ul)	1 gín kug	1 gín kug (for 1 gur-2-ul)
142	*Gelb AV* p. 236		
	⸢6⸣.1.2 gur-2-ul	10 gín kug-luḫ-ḫa	1.5 gín kug-luḫ-ḫa (for 1 gur-2-ul)
	0.1.2 gur-2-ul	1 gín kug-luḫ-ḫa	1.5 gín kug-luḫ-ḫa (for 1 gur-2-ul)
143	*RTC* 18		
	20.0.0 gur-2-ul	[10? gín kug]	0.5? gín kug (for 1 gur-2-ul)
164	*BIN* VIII 38		
	1.0.0 gur	1 gín kug	1 gín kug
175	*MAD* IV 151		
	0.2.0 gur	(1 gín) kug	2.5 gín kug
180	*MVNS* III 25		
	0.2.0 gur	(1 gín) kug	2.5 gín kug
183	NBC 10204		
	8.1.2 gur	8⅙ gín kug	ca. 1 gín kug
189	*BIN* VIII 39		
	1.0.0 gur	(1 gín kug)	1 gín kug
191	*BIN* VIII 175		
	6.0.0 gur	2 gín kug	⅓ gín kug (mu ḫé-gál-la "good year")
	0.2.0 gur	⅔ gín kug	1⅔ gín kug
222	*MVNS* III 100		
	0.0.3 gur	1 gín k.b.	10 gín k.b.
226	Serota Coll. A 10		
	0.0.1 gur	1 gín (kug)	30 gín kug
232	*MVNS* III 80		
	3.2.0 gur	6 GÍN K.B.	1.76+ GÍN K.B.
359	*MAOG* IV pp. 188–89 MD 2		
	15.0.0 gur	15 gín kug	1 gín kug

Figure 20. Rates of Dates

Text	*Dates*	*Its Silver Equivalent*	*Price of 1* gur *of Dates*
174	*BIN* VIII 179		
	15.0.0 gur	30 gín kug	2 gín kug
191	*BIN* VIII 175		
	(1.0.0 gur)	1 gín kug	1 gín kug (mu nu-gál-la "bad year")
224	*MAD* IV 15		
	0.3.2 gur	1 gín kug	1.5 gín kug

Figure 21. Rates of Oil

Text	*Oil*	*Its Silver Equivalent*	*Price of 1* silà/ umbin? *of Oil*
40 Manishtushu Obelisk			
C_2	10 SILÀ	1 GÍN K.B.	1/10 GÍN K.B.
182a Lambert Tablet I			
	6 umbin? ì-udu	1 gín kug	1/6 gín kug
189 *BIN* VIII 39			
	6 silà	(1 gín kug)	1/6 gín kug

Figure 22. Rates of Copper

Text	*Copper*	*Its Silver Equivalent*	*Price of 1* ma-na *of Copper*
182a Lambert Tablet A			
	3 ma-na	2 gín kug	2/3 gín kug

Figure 23. Rates of Wool

Text	*Wool*	*Its Silver Equivalent*	*Price of 1* ma-na *of Wool*
37 *CT* XXXII 7f.			
	1 GÚ SÍG.GI_6	15 GÍN K.B.	0.25 GÍN K.B.
40 Manishtushu Obelisk			
C_1	4 MA.NA SÍG	1 GÍN K.B.	0.25 GÍN K.B.
C_2	4 MA.NA SÍG	1 GÍN K.B.	0.25 GÍN K.B.
C_3	4 MA.NA SÍG	1 GÍN K.B.	0.25 GÍN K.B.
D	4 MA.NA SÍG	1 GÍN K.B.	0.25 GÍN K.B.
189 *BIN* VIII 39			
	4 [m]a-na síg	1 gín kug	0.25 gín kug

Figure 24. Rates of Cloths

1 ^{TÚG}šu-ni-ra (a type of cloth) = 1 gín kug (168 NBC 10198)
2 SU.A.TÚG (a type of cloth) = 2 gín kug (172 *BIN* VIII 172)
1 bar-dul_5 (a type of elaborate cloth) = 2. še (177 *MAD* IV 153)
1 bar-dul_5 = 2 gín kug (182a Lambert Tablet CC)
⟨1⟩ túg ki-sì-ga bala "funerary(?) cloth" = 10 gín kug (182a Lambert Tablet A)

Figure 25. Rates of Metal Objects

1 ^{URUDU}Ḫ̮A.ZI UD.KA.BAR "axe" = 5 GÍN K.B. (40 Manishtushu Obelisk C_1, C_2)
1 ḫa-zi^{URUDU} = 1 gín kug (189 *BIN* VIII 39)
1 ^{URUDU}*na-ap-la-aq-tum* UD.KA.BAR "battle-axe" = 5 GÍN K.B. (40 Manishtushu Obelisk C_1, C_2)
1 ^{URUDU}*ba-da-ru-um* UD.KA.BAR (a type of weapon) = 5 GÍN K.B. (40 Manishtushu Obelisk C_1, C_2)
(1) uri^{URUDU} (a container) = 10 gín kug (181 *MVNS* III 13)

Figure 26. Rates of Animals

1 u_8 "ewe" = 0.5 gín kug (189 *BIN* VIII 39)
1 udu-nita "ram" = 0.25 (gín) kug (191 *BIN* VIII 175)
6 udu-nita = [10?]+2 gín kug (182a Lambert Tablet A)
1 šáḫ-ú " 'grass'-fed pig" = 1 gín kug (189 *BIN* VIII 39)
1 ANŠE.BAR.AN "mule" = 20 GÍN KUG.BABBAR (40 Manishtushu Obelisk C_1, C_2)
1 ÁB "cow" = 1 ^{GIŠ}GIGIR "chariot" (49 BM 90909)

Figure 27. Rates of Human Beings

1 SAG.NITA "male head (= slave)" = 20 GÍN K.B. (40 Manishtushu Obelisk C_2)
1 SAG.SAL "female head (= slave-woman)" = 20 GÍN K.B. (40 Manishtushu Obelisk C_2)
1 DUMU.SAL "girl" = 13 GÍN K.B. (40 Manishtushu Obelisk C_2)

CHAPTER 11

COMMODITIES

11.1. *Introductory Remarks*

This chapter contains listings of all the commodities that are included in prices and additional payments. The examples are culled both from the kudurrus and sale documents (with the exclusion of the earliest kudurrus, nos. 1–12). The commodities are organized into the following typological categories: 1) grains and grain products, 2) fruits and vegetables, 3) liquids, 4) wool and cloths (garments), 5) metals, 6) metal, stone, and wooden objects, 7) animals, 8) human beings, and 9) miscellaneous. Within each category, the commodities are listed in alphabetic order of Sumerian/Akkadian. Whenever possible, English translations are given, and, if the word is Sumerian, also its Akkadian equivalent. Unless the item appears *passim*, all of the occurrences are listed. The order of references is chronological, with the references to kudurrus always preceding those to sale documents. If the commodity is attested only in price, the occurrence is marked as "Price"; if the commodity is attested both in price and additional payment, the occurrence is marked as "Price and AP." The occurrences of the commodity in additional payment alone are left unmarked. Where deemed necessary, short notes discussing the meaning of the commodity and offering lexical references are appended.

11.2. *Grains and Grain Products*

BAPPIR(ŠIM+GAR), Akk. *bappirum* "beer bread," in units (of loaves).
See *CAD* B pp. 95ff; *AHWB* pp. 103f.
Sargonic no. 41
Compare ninda-bappir below.

gúg, Akk. *kukkum* (a type of bread or cake), in units. See *CAD* K p. 498; *AHWB* p. 500; A. J. Ferrara, *Nanna-Suen's Journey to Nippur* (Rome, 1973) pp. 148f.; Civil, *OA* 21 (1982) pp. 12ff.
Fara (*passim* in nos. 100–136)

ninda, Akk. *akalum* "bread," in units (of loaves). See *CAD* A/1 pp. 238–45; *AHWB* p. 26.
Fara (*passim* in nos. 100–136)
Pre-Sargonic no. 19b
Pre-Sargonic (*passim* in nos. 137–156)

ninda 1(ul) (a type of bread), in units (of loaves).
Pre-Sargonic no. 140: 10 ninda
The interpretation of this bread as "bread (in the amount of) 1 ul" is of course impossible because of the enormous size (thirty-six quarts) involved. Compare ninda 2(ul) below.

ninda 2(ul) (a type of bread), in units (of loaves).
Pre-Sargonic no. 140: 10 ninda
This bread cannot be interpreted as the "bread (in the amount of) 2 ul" because of the enormous size (seventy-two quarts) involved. Compare ninda 1(ul) above.

ninda-banšur "table bread," in units (of loaves). See H. A. Hoffner, *Alimenta* pp. 193f.
Fara nos. 14 and 15
This type of bread, written ninda-banšur$_x$(ASARI), is frequently mentioned in the Sargonic beer-and-bread texts from Umma; for examples, see Foster, *Umma in the Sargonic Period* (Hamden, Conn., 1982) pp. 14f., 111. For the reading banšur$_x$ of ASARI/ASAL, see Steinkeller, *RA* 74 (1980) p. 6 n. 7.

ninda-bappir(BI+GAR) Akk. *bappirum* "beer bread," in units of loaves.
See *CAD* B pp. 95ff.; *AHWB* pp. 103f.
Fara nos. 14 and 15
Compare BAPPIR above.

ninda-ì "bread (mixed with) oil," in units (of loaves).
Pre-Sargonic no. 23
According to M. Sigrist, *Les sattukku dans l'Ešumeša durant la période d'Isin et Larsa* (Malibu, Cal., 1984) p. 14, ninda-ì is an abbreviation for ninda-ì-dé-a (Akk. *mirsum*). Note, however, that Hoffner, *Alimenta* p. 196, treats ninda-ì and ninda-ì-dé-a as two different types of bread.

ninda-kalag (a type of bread), in units (of loaves).
Pre-Sargonic nos. 22, 23, and 144
The meaning of the qualification kalag is not clear; the same description probably also occurs in ninda-gu-KALAG, zíd-KALAG(= sig$_{15}$), and kas-KALAG. See Bauer, *AWL* p. 172.

ninda-KU.KU-na (a type of bread), in units (of loaves).
Pre-Sargonic nos. 137, 140, and 145
Civil, *OA* 21 (1982) p. 10 n. 9, suggests the reading ninda-durun$_x$(TUŠ.TUŠ)-na "oven(-baked) bread." See also note to no. 14 vi 11.

ninda-sag (a type of bread), in units (of loaves).
Fara 30b
Pre-Sargonic nos. 22 and 23
Probably to be connected with SAG.NINDA (to be read ninda-sag?), attested in the Sargonic texts *ITT* 5, 9263 i 1, 2, 4, 5; *RTC* 123:2′, 126 i 1′ and *passim*; MAH 16670 (unpubl.).

ninda-silà (a type of bread), in units (of loaves).
Pre-Sargonic (*passim* in nos. 137–156)
Pre-Sargonic nos. 149 and 151 (both Price)
This commodity is possibly to be read ninda-sal$_4$, and to be connected with ninda-sal-la "thin bread," cited by B. A. Levine and W. W. Hallo, *HUCA* 38 (1967) p. 57. For the interchange of sal$_4$ with sal, see Gelb, *AJSL* 55 (1938) p. 71.

ninda-še "barley bread," in measures of dry capacity or in units (of loaves). See Hoffner, *Alimenta* p. 203.
Fara nos. 106, 110, 114, and 130 (in silà)
Fara no. 109 (in silà and in units)
Pre-Sargonic nos. 22, 23, and 144 (in units)

SUR (bread in size of one-half of a standard loaf), in units. See F. Hrozný, *Getreide* p. 116; Deimel, *Or.* 9–13 p. 173; *idem*, *AnOr* 2 p. 38; Civil, *OA* 21 (1982) pp. 9f.
Pre-Sargonic nos. 141 and 150
Pre-Sargonic nos. 149 and 151 (both Price)

še, Akk. *šeʾum* "barley," in measures of dry capacity.
Fara no. 20
Fara (*passim* in nos. 100–36)
Fara nos. 101 and 134 (both Price)
Fara no. 129: 2(ul) še šám kaš (wr. še kaš šám) "barley as the price of beer(?)." Attested also in *TSŠ* 881 vii 8, 14.
Pre-Sargonic (*passim* in nos. 137–156)
Pre-Sargonic no. 19b (measured in dug)
Pre-Sargonic nos. 21, 22, 23, 137, 140, 144, 145, 150, and 151 (all Price)
Pre-Sargonic no. 29 (Price?)
Pre-Sargonic nos. 36 and 46
Pre-Sargonic no. 37 (Price and AP)
Sargonic nos. 38, 41, 227, and 237
Sargonic nos. 44, 164, 165, 166, 170, 171, 173, 175, 176, 177, 180, 181, 182, 189, 190, 192, 194, 204, 205, 210, 226, 231, 232, 235, and 238 (all Price)
Sargonic no. 45 (Price?)
Sargonic nos. 40, 42, 43, 165, 166, 169, 171, and 182a (all Price and AP)
Ur III nos. 275, 279, 280, 305, 318, 335, 359, and 368 (all Price)

še-ba "barley allotment(?)," in measures of dry capacity.
Sargonic no. 176: 2(pi) še-ba (Price)
The meaning of še-ba in this context is uncertain. Krecher, *ZA* 63 (1974) p. 218, proposed the translation "Gerste, zugeteilt," i.e., "'Gerste' als 'Zuweisung' neben dem Gerste-Anteil des Kaufpreises im engeren Sinne." Compare also zíd-ba below.

še-ḪAR (meaning uncertain), in measures of dry capacity.
Fara no. 128 (Price)
Compare A. Deimel, *ŠL* 367.199, who interprets ŠE.ḪAR as "geröstete Gerste," and further note še-ḪAR-ra gul-la for sheep and cattle (*TCL* 2, 5538:1–2; *PDT* 1, 374:2; *SET* 134:4). Compare also *CAD* M/2 pp. 201f. under *mundu* (= Sum. NÍG.ḪAR.RA) "groats."

ŠE.NI.KID.NI (meaning unknown), in measures of dry capacity.
Pre-Sargonic no. 37: 24 ŠE.NI.KID.NI GUR
Is it a mistake for ŠE Ì.GIŠ.Ì "sesame seeds"?

še-sa, Akk. *laptum* "roasted barley," in measures of dry capacity. See *CAD* L pp. 96f.; *AHWB* p. 526 (under *lābtu(m)*).
Pre-Sargonic nos. 22, 23, and 144

zíd, Akk. *qēmum* "flour," in measures of dry capacity. See *AHWB* p. 913.
Fara no. 129: 1(ul) 1(bán) zíd ninda kú "flour for bread-eating"
Pre-Sargonic no. 138 (Price)

zíd-ba "flour allotment(?)," in measures of dry capacity.
Sargonic no. 175: 2(bán) zíd-ba (Price)
The meaning of zíd-ba in this context is uncertain. Krecher, *ZA* 63 (1974) p. 217, speculated that -ba of zíd-ba means "verteilt," and connected it with níg-ba "Zuweisung." Compare also še-ba above.

zíz, Akk. *kunāšum* "emmer wheat," in measures of dry capacity. See *CAD* K pp. 536ff.; *AHWB* p. 506.
Fara no. 20 (Price)
Pre-Sargonic no. 142

11.3. *Fruits and Vegetables*

ga-raš^{SAR}, Akk. *karašum* "leek," in sa (bundle). See *CAD* K pp. 212f.; *AHWB* p. 448.
Pre-Sargonic nos. 22, 23, and 144

lu^{SAR}, Akk. *laptum* "turnip," in sa (bundle). See *CAD* L p. 96; *AHWB* p. 537.
Pre-Sargonic nos. 22 and 144
The form lu^{SAR} is an abbreviated writing for lu-úb^{SAR}. For the latter spelling, see *CAD* L p. 96 (under the lexical section of *laptu*). The spelling lu^{SAR} also occurs in the Sargonic texts *ITT* 2/2, 4381:2; *PBS* 9, 56 i 3′, vi 3′, 75 iv 1′, 87 iii 5′, etc. Compare also the spelling lú-úb^{SAR} of lexical sources (*CAD* L p. 96).

sum-⌈gu⌉ (meaning unknown), in units.
Pre-Sargonic no. 23
This commodity is either a vegetable or, assuming that gu stands here for *qûm* "string," onions (sum) measured in strings.

sum-sikil, Akk. *šušikillum* "garlic," in sa (bundle). See Gelb, *AS* 16 p. 57.
Pre-Sargonic no. 22

zú-lum, Akk. *suluppum* "dates," in measures of dry capacity. See *AHWB* p. 1057; *CAD* S pp. 373–77.
Pre-Sargonic no. 19a
Sargonic no. 172
Sargonic nos. 168, 174, and 191 (all Price)

11.4. *Liquids*

Though the following commodities are listed as "liquids," the exact nature of their consistencies is not known, for the same measures (silà, etc.) are used both for liquids and solids.

ga, Akk. *šizbum* "milk," in measures of liquid capacity. See *AHWB* pp. 1253f.
Pre-Sargonic no. 19b (in dug)

gará, Akk. *lišdum* (*lildum*) "cream," in units. See *AHWB* p. 552; *CAD* L p. 215.
Pre-Sargonic no. 19b

geštin, Akk. *karānum* "wine," in measures of liquid capacity. See *AHWB* pp. 446f.; *CAD* K pp. 202–06.
Pre-Sargonic no. 19b (in dug)

ì, Akk. *šamnum* "animal oil/fat," in measures of liquid capacity. See *AHWB* pp. 1157f.
Fara no. 13 (Price?; in dug [wr. dug+ì])
Fara nos. 14, 15 (in silà)
Fara (*passim* in nos. 100–136; in silà [*passim*] and in šakan [no. 132])
Fara no. 134 (Price; in silà)
Pre-Sargonic no. 19a (in dug)
Pre-Sargonic nos. 22, 23, and 144 (in šakan)
Pre-Sargonic nos. 36, 37, 140, and 143 (in silà)
Sargonic nos. 40, 41, and 237 (in silà)
Sargonic no. 175: 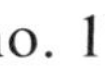 Ì SILÀ (Price)
Sargonic no. 189 (Price; in silà)
The writing 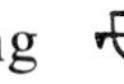 Ì SILÀ, attested in no. 175, is to be interpreted as ½ silà ì, as in 2½ ì-KAL silà (*MAD* 4, 70:1), where silà is also written following the sign for oil and the numeral likewise represents ½, and not 1(bán) (note that in the following line the same number clearly stands for ½ shekel of silver). In nos. 14 and 15, ì alternates with ì-udu "sheep oil," and in no. 143, with ì-šáḫ "pig oil, lard."

Ì.DÙG.GA "sweet, perfumed oil," in measures of liquid capacity.
Sargonic no. 38 (in DUG)

ì-ir "scented, perfumed oil," in measures of liquid capacity.
Pre-Sargonic(?) no. 46 (in silà?)
For ir, Akk. *erī/ēšum* "smell, scent, fragrance," see *CAD* E pp. 280f.; *AHWB* p. 242. In the Pre-Sargonic texts from Lagash, this commodity is written ì-ir-a; see Deimel, *Or.* 21 (1926) p. 11.

ì-nun, Akk. *ḫimētum* "ghee, butter," in measures of liquid capacity.
See *CAD* Ḫ pp. 189f.; *AHWB* p. 346.
Fara nos. 104 and 130 (in silà)
Pre-Sargonic no. 19a (in dug)
Pre-Sargonic no. 145 (in silà)
Pre-Sargonic no. 149 (Price; in silà)
Sargonic no. 50 (in GÍN?)

ì-sag, Akk. *šamnum rēštum* "first-quality oil," in measures of liquid capacity. See *AHWB* pp. 972, 1157.
Pre-Sargonic no. 23 rev. ix 33 (in silà)

ì-šáḫ, "pig oil/fat," in measures of liquid/dry capacity.
Pre-Sargonic nos. 36, 140, 142, and 143 (in silà)
Sargonic no. 38 (in DUG)
Sargonic nos. 165 and 171 (in silà)
Sargonic nos. 168 and 182a Q (Price; in silà)
Sargonic no. 189 (Price?; in silà)
In no. 143, ì-šáḫ alternates with ì "animal oil/ fat."

ì-udu, "sheep oil/fat," in umbin? (most probably a container of the capacity of 2 silà, see note to no. 14 i 7).
Fara nos. 14 and 15
Sargonic no. 182a I, J (Price and AP)
Alternates with ì "animal oil/fat," (in silà) in nos. 14 and 15.

kas, Akk. *šikārum* "beer," in measures of liquid capacity. See *AHWB* pp. 1232f.
Pre-Sargonic nos. 137, 139, 140, 143, 145, 146, and 148 (in dug)
Pre-Sargonic no. 147: 1 dug-NIGÍN.NIGÍN kas "1 jar (of the capacity of 1) NIGÍN.NIGÍN of beer"
Pre-Sargonic no. 149 (Price; in sá-dug$_4$)
Pre-Sargonic no. 151 (Price; in dug)
Compare also še šám kaš (under še above).

kas-gi$_6$ "dark beer," in measures of liquid capacity. See Deimel, *Or.* 22 (1928) pp. 63ff.
Pre-Sargonic no. 141 (in dug)

NIGÍN+ḪA.A (a type of liquid), in measures of liquid capacity.
Fara (*passim* in nos. 100–136; in kúr)
Since NIGÍN+ḪA.A is measured in kúr, it must denote some kind of liquid. Compare also under tu$_7$ "soup" below.

tu$_7$, Akk. *ummarum* "soup," in measures of liquid capacity. See *AHWB* p. 1414.
Fara (*passim* in nos. 100–136; in kúr)
Pre-Sargonic nos. 22, 23, and 144 (in silà)
Pre-Sargonic (*passim* in nos. 137–56; in silà)
This commodity is written in the Fara texts with the sign ḪI+AŠ, and in the Pre-Sargonic texts, with the sign ḪI+BAD (= KAM). Since it is measured in either kúr or silà, we can assume that it represents a liquid of some sort. Most likely, ḪI+AŠ and ḪI+BAD have here the reading tu$_7$, which corresponds to the Akkadian *ummarum* "soup." See *MSL* 3 p. 221 G$_7$ ii 1′: [tu-ú] [ḪI+BAD] = [*um-m*]*a-rum* (based on Proto-Ea 371: tu-ú ḪI+BAD).

11.5. *Wool and Cloths (Garments)*

^{TÚG}BAL (a type of cloth), in units.
Sargonic no. 45
This type of cloth is also attested in the Sargonic texts *FM* 35:11; *ITT* 1, 1080:6; 5, 6674:2′. Note also TÚG.BAL NAR.E? (*BIN* 8, 286:14) and TÚG. BAL SIG$_5$ (*ITT* 2/2 p. 35 no. 4629).

bar-dul$_5$, Akk. *kusītum* (a type of elaborate cloth), in units. See *CAD* K pp. 585ff.; *AHWB* p. 514; *MAD* 3 p. 152.
Pre-Sargonic no. 140
Sargonic no. 176 (Price)
Compare bar-dul$_5$ gíd-da below.

bar-dul$_5$ gíd-da, "long bar-dul$_5$ cloth," in units.
Pre-Sargonic nos. 141 and 143
Sargonic no. 166
Sargonic no. 182a CC (Price)
Compare bar-dul$_5$ above.

bar-si, Akk. *parš/sīgum* "band, headband," in units. See *AHWB* p. 836; *MAD* 3 p. 218.
Pre-Sargonic no. 141
Note that in the Sargonic text *FM* 7:8, this piece of apparel is written TÚG.BAR.SIG (with the qualification GAL). Compare bar-síg^{TÚG} below.

bar-síg^{TÚG} (a type of cloth), in units.
Sargonic no. 171
According to Edzard, *SRU* p. 85, bar-síg^{TÚG} is a variant spelling of bar-si.

gada, Akk. *kitûm* "linen (cloth)," in units. See *CAD* K pp. 473ff.; *AHWB* p. 495.
Pre-Sargonic no. 19a

ḫa-la-um^{TÚG} (*ḫalûm*) (a type of cloth), in units. See *CAD* Ḫ pp. 53f.; *AHWB* p. 314; *MAD* 3 p. 127.
Sargonic no. 237

^{TÚG}ÍB.DÙ, ÍB.BA.DÙ^{TÚG}, "belt," in units.
Fara nos. 114 and 125 (^{TÚG}ÍB.DÙ)
Pre-Sargonic App. to no. 32 (ÍB.DÙ^{TÚG})
Sargonic no. 165 (ÍB.BA.DÙ^{TÚG})
This word is probably to be interpreted as íb(-ba)-dù /ib-a-du/ "loin-band," lit. "loin-binding (cloth)," a construction which may be parallel to ŠÀ.GA.DÙ /šag-a-du/ "waist-band, girdle." See Steinkeller, *Or.* n.s. 51 (1982) p. 362.

^{TÚG}ME.GÁL, ^{TÚG}ME.A.GÁL (a type of cloth), in units.
Fara nos. 108, 109, 117, 119, 122, 123, 126, 127, 130, and 131 (all ^{TÚG}ME.GÁL)
Fara nos. 102, 110, and 113 (all ^{TÚG}ME.A.GÁL)
Probably to be read ^{TÚG}me-gál(-a) or ^{TÚG}gál-me(-a).

NI.TÚG (a type of cloth), in units.
Pre-Sargonic App. to no. 32
Sargonic no. 182a J
Occurs also in *TMH* 5, 46 ii 5; *BIN* 8, 30:2; *Fara* 2, 64 viii 11; *MAD* 1, 169:4, 187:21 (in the last two examples, written TÚG.NI).

níg-bar-3^{TÚG} (a type of cloth), in units.
Pre-Sargonic App. to no. 32

níg-lal-gaba^{TÚG} "chestband," in units.
Pre-Sargonic App. to no. 32
Found also in *BIN* 8, 30:4; *MAD* 1, 169 i 8. Compare also ^{TÚG}níg-lal-gaba-a in *MSL* 10 p. 147 l. 93.

níg-lal-sag, níg-sag-lal, níg-sag-lal-SAL "headband," in units.
Fara no. 127 (níg-sag-lal)
Pre-Sargonic no. 21 (Price; níg-lal-sag)
Pre-Sargonic App. to no. 32 (níg-lal-sag^{TÚG})
Pre-Sargonic nos. 141, 142, and 143 (níg-sag-lal-SAL)
Pre-Sargonic no. 140 (níg-sag⟨-lal⟩-SAL)
Note that Waetzoldt, *UNT* p. 118, reads this word ^{túg}nì-sag-LÁxMÍ. However, this reading is unlikely since the term appears to be composed of níg-lal "band" plus sag "head," parallel to níg-lal-gaba "chestband," cited above. SAL is here a qualification of the headband, probably meaning "fine," and not necessarily meaning "female," as suggested by Edzard, *SRU* p. 70.

^{TÚG}níg-lám, níg-lám^{TÚG}, níg-lám, Akk. *lam(a)ḫuššûm* (a type of cloth), in units or in (ma-na). See *CAD* L pp. 58f.; *AHWB* p. 532.
Fara no. 13 (Price?; in (ma-na); níg-lám^{TÚG})
Fara no. 110 (^{TÚG}níg-lám)
Pre-Sargonic no. 19a (níg-lám)
Pre-Sargonic no. 145 (níg-lám)
Compare ^{TÚG}níg-lám gíd-da below.

^{TÚG}níg-lám gíd-da "long níg-lám cloth," in units.
Pre-Sargonic no. 138 (Price and AP)
Compare níg-lám above.

níg-sag-kéš "headband," in units
Fara no. 125
Pre-Sargonic App. to no. 32

síg, Akk. *šipātum* "wool," in ma-na.
Fara no. 13 (Price?)
Fara nos. 14 and 15
Fara (*passim* in nos. 100–136): x ma-na síg túg "x pounds of wool (as an equivalent of) cloth." Compare also x ma-na urudu túg under urudu below.
Pre-Sargonic nos. 32, 33, 37, 46, 137, 139, 140, 141, 143, and 145
Pre-Sargonic no. 138 (Price)
Pre-Sargonic no. 21 (Price and AP)
Sargonic nos. 40, 41, 49?, 165, 227, and 237
Sargonic no. 44 (Price)
Sargonic no. 189 (Price?)

síg-bar-udu "fleece of a sheep," in units. See Waetzoldt, *UNT* p. 39.
Pre-Sargonic nos. 22, 23, and 144

síg-bar-udu-bar "fleece of a sheep (growing) a (new) fleece(?)"
Pre-Sargonic no. 22
Probably an abbreviation for síg-bar udu-bar-mú. For udu-bar-mú "sheep growing a (new) fleece,"

see Waetzoldt, *UNT* p. 39. For bar "fleece," see under u_8 and udu below.

SÍG.GAN (a fixed quantity of wool), in units. See chapter 9 under nos. 43 and 44.
Sargonic nos. 43 and 44

SÍG.GI_6 "black wool," in GÚ.
Pre-Sargonic no. 37

síg-ŠÀ.ŠÈ (a type of wool), in ma-na.
Pre-Sargonic no. 23 (Price)
Possibly the same term as síg-šà-síg "Schussfaden," discussed by Waetzoldt, *UNT* p. 126.

SÍG.UDU "sheep wool," in GÚ.
Sargonic no. 235 (Price)

ŠÀ.GA.DÙ^{TÚG}, Akk. *šakattûm* "girdle," in units. See *AHWB* p. 1139; *MAD* 3 p. 265.
Sargonic no. 227
Written ŠÀ.GA.DU in *ARM* 8, 11:4 and *passim* (OB). This cloth apparently appears as TÚG.ŠÀ. GA.TUM in Hittite texts, and as *sa-ga-tù* and ^{TÚG}*sa-ga-te* in Assyrian texts (see A. Goetze in *Sommer Festschrift* pp. 54f.). For the formation, see under ^{TÚG}ÍB.DÙ above.

^{TÚG}šu-ni-ra (a type of cloth), in units.
Sargonic no. 168 (Price)
For šu-nir "emblem" in connection with garments, see Waetzoldt, *UNT* p. 30 and n. 243.

TÚG, Akk. *ṣubātum* "cloth," in units.
Fara no. 30b

TÚG.A.AL (a type of cloth), in units.
Pre-Sargonic App. to no. 32

TÚG.A.SU (= aktum), A.SU.TÚG, SU.A.TÚG, TÚG. SU.A, Akk. *ṣapšum* (a type of cloth), in units. See *CAD* Ṣ p. 97; *AHWB* p. 1082.
Fara nos. 103, 121, and 125 (TÚG.A.SU)
Fara no. 134 (Price; TÚG.A.SU)
Pre-Sargonic no. 21 (Price; TÚG.SU.A)
Pre-Sargonic nos. 32 and 33 (SU.A.TÚG)
Pre-Sargonic App. to no. 32 (A.SU.TÚG)
Pre-Sargonic no. 36 (TÚG.A.SU)
Sargonic nos. 165, 182, and 182a J (A.SU.TÚG)
Sargonic no. 237 (TÚG.A.SU)
Sargonic no. 172 (Price; SU.A.TÚG)
According to Sollberger, *JCS* 10 (1956) p. 14 n. 14, aktum may have been an Akkadian loanword, which was later lost by Akkadian and came to be considered a Sumerian word.

TÚG.DÙL.GARÁ?.SÁR+DIŠ (a type of cloth), in units.
Pre-Sargonic App. to no. 32

túg ki-sì-ga bala "funerary(?) cloth"
Sargonic no. 182a A (Price)

TÚG.ŠU.DU_7.A.BAL (a type of cloth), in units.
Sargonic no. 40
The name of this cloth is probably ^{TÚG}šu-du_7-a, and bal is an additional qualification, as suggested by the occurrence of ^{TÚG}šu-du_7-a é-ba-an in *RTC* 19 iii 8 (Pre-Sargonic).

TÚG.ŠU.SÈ.GA, TÚG.ŠU.ZA.GA (a type of cloth), in units.
Sargonic no. 40 (TÚG.ŠU.SÈ.GA)
Sargonic no. 41 (TÚG.ŠU.ZA.GA)

TÚG.TUM.GUNU (a type of cloth), in units.
Sargonic no. 240
This cloth is also attested in the Sargonic texts *ITT* 1, 1091:7; *MVNS* 3, 74:5; *BIN* 8, 290:4 (with the qualification ú), 7 (*gada*); *BE* 1, 11:7 (*é-dam-mu*), 8 (*ḫi-šè-lu-ḫi-na*), 9 (*é-dam-m⟨u⟩* LIBIR).
See also Gelb, *Friedrich Festschrift* p. 191.

11.6. *Metals*

kug, Akk. *kaspum* "silver," in gín and ma-na.
Fara nos. 14 and 15 (both Price)
Fara (*passim* in nos. 100–136; Price and AP)
Pre-Sargonic no. 141
Pre-Sargonic nos. 27, 30, 47, 137, 138, 143, 146, 151, 152, 153, and 155 (all Price)
Pre-Sargonic no. 29 (Price?)
Sargonic nos. 164, 165, 166, 167, 169, 171, 172, 173, 174, 175, 176, 178, 179, 180, 181, 182a, 183, 184, 185, 186, 187, 188, 189, 191, 193, 194, 204, 206, 209, 210, 211, 212, 214, 223, 224, and 225 (all Price)
Sargonic no. 207 (Price and AP)
Ur III nos. 257, 261, 268, 270, 286, 289, 296, and 312 (all Price)

kug-babbar, Akk. *kaspum* "silver," in gín and ma-na.
Fara no. 16 (Price and AP)
Pre-Sargonic nos. 30a, 32, and 34 (all Price)
Pre-Sargonic no. 36 (Price and AP)
Sargonic nos. 42, 44, 157, 158, 159, 160, 161, 162, 163, 195, 197, 198, 199, 200, 201, 202, 203, 208, 215, 216, 217, 218, 219, 220, 221, 222, 228, 230, 233, 234, 235, 236, 238, 240, and 241 (all Price)
Sargonic no. 45 (Price?)
Sargonic nos. 41, 43, 227, and 237 (Price and AP)
Ur III (*passim* in nos. 247–370; all Price)

kug-luḫ-ḫa, Akk. *kaspum mesûm* "washed, purified silver," in gín and ma-na. See *CAD* M/2 p. 30 (under the lexical section of *mesû*); *AHWB* p. 647 (under *mesû*).
Fara (*passim* in nos. 100–136; Price and AP)
Pre-Sargonic nos. 141, 142, 149, 150, and 155 (all Price)
Pre-Sargonic no. 139 (Price and AP)

kug-UD.UD "white (purified) silver," in gín and ma-na.
Ur III nos. 274a, 320, and 344 (all Price)
Since kug-UD.UD occurs only in the Ur III period, the complimentary distribution favors the identification with kug-luḫ-ḫa of earlier periods and its translation as "purified or white silver" (Akk. *kaspum mesûm* / *ṣarpum* or *kaspum peṣûm*). Compare also KUG.BABBAR *el-lum* "pure silver," found in *MAD* 1, 303:1. Alternatively, kug-UD.UD could be analyzed as an archaic spelling kug-bar_6-bar_6 (for kug-babbar).

níg-urudu-babbar (meaning unknown), in ma-na.
Pre-Sargonic no. 21 (Price)

urudu, Akk. *werûm* "copper," in ma-na. See *CAD* E pp. 321ff. (under *erû*); *AHWB* pp. 1495f.
Fara (*passim* in nos. 100–136; Price and AP)
Fara nos. 20 and 25 (both Price)
Fara no. 17 (Price)
Fara (*passim* in nos. 100–136): x ma-na urudu túg "x pounds of copper (as an equivalent of) cloth," parallel to x ma-na síg túg (under síg).
Fara no. 125 (Price; written urudu$^{\text{ru12-da}}$)
Pre-Sargonic no. 31 (Price)
Sargonic nos. 45 and 50
Sargonic no. 182a A (Price)

UD.KA.BAR (= zabar), Akk. *siparrum* "bronze," in ma-na. See *CAD* S pp. 296ff.; *AHWB* p. 1048.
Sargonic no. 38
Compare also the writing KA+UD.BAR with [X]? in section 11.7 below.

11.7. *Metal, Stone, and Wooden Objects*

ad-tab za-gìn, Akk. *miḫṣu* "decorative collar," made of lapis lazuli, in units. See *CAD* M/2 p. 62.
Pre-Sargonic App. to no. 32

BA.AN, BA.AN ŠE (a container), in units.
Sargonic nos. 43 and 227 (BA.AN)
Sargonic no. 44 (BA.AN ŠE)
Compare also the following occurrences: ba-an kaš (*TSŠ* 515 i 8, and similarly 604 i 1); 2 ba-an 5 silà (Pinches, *BTBC* 89 ii 18; Reisner, *TUT* 254:1); 1 ^{URUDU}ba-an 5 silà (*UET* 3, 739:6′); 3 ^{GIŠ}ba-an (Hussey, *Bulletin of the Buffalo Society of Natural Sciences* 11/2 [1915] p. 125 no. 2:35). Oppenheim, *Eames Coll.* p. 10 n. 28, links the Sumerian spelling with the Akkadian ^{GIŠ}*ba-an-nu-um*. More plausible is the connection with the Akkadian *pānum*, translated as "ein Korb" in *AHWB* p. 822.

^{URUDU}*ba-da-ru-um* (*patarrum*) UD.KA.BAR (a type of weapon, in bronze), in units. See *AHWB* p. 848; *MAD* 3 p. 220.
Sargonic no. 40

^{GIŠ}DU.DA URUDU, Akk. *dūdum* "kettle," in units. See *CAD* D p. 170; *AHWB* p. 174; *MAD* 3 p. 105.
Sargonic no. 237

esir$_x$(LAK-173) kug "silver sandals," in units.
Pre-Sargonic App. to no. 32
For the reading esir$_x$ of LAK-173, see Steinkeller, *AOF* 28 (1981/82) pp. 140f.

gi$_4$-gi$_4$-lum kug (a piece of jewelry, made of silver), in units.
Pre-Sargonic App. to no. 32
Gelb, *MAD* 3 p. 117, suggested that gi$_4$-gi$_4$ is to be read gil$_x$ or kil$_x$, and reconstructed the word as *gillum*. However, this reading cannot be proved at present. Other possible reading would be *gigillum* or *gikillum*; cf. the fruit *gikillu* (*gigillu*), listed in *CAD* G p. 71.

gíd-da kug "silver(-headed) spear?," in units.
Pre-Sargonic App. to no. 32
Perhaps the same as giš-gíd-da, Akk. *ariktum* "spear." See *CAD* A/2 p. 267; *AHWB* p. 68.

^{GIŠ}GIGIR, Akk. *narkabtum* "chariot," in units. See *CAD* N/1 pp. 353–59; *AHWB* p. 747.
Sargonic no. 49

^{GIŠ}gigir gam-ma (a type of chariot), in units.
Pre-Sargonic App. to no. 32

^{GIŠ}GIGIR.NÍG.ŠU (a type of chariot), in units.
Sargonic no. 40
For the type of chariot or wagon called níg-šu, equated with *narkabtum* "chariot" in lexical texts, see Civil, *JAOS* 88 (1968) p. 13 and n. 56.

gír kug, Akk. *paṭrum* "silver dagger," in units. See *AHWB* p. 848.
Pre-Sargonic App. to no. 32

ḫa-zi^{URUDU}, ^{URUDU}ḪA.ZI UD.KA.BAR, *ḫa-zi-*[*núm*]?, Akk. *ḫaṣṣinnum* "axe," in units. See *CAD* Ḫ pp. 133ff.; *AHWB* p. 332; *MAD* 3 pp. 134f.
Pre-Sargonic App. to no. 32 (ḫa-zi^{URUDU})
Sargonic no. 40 (^{URUDU}ḪA.ZI UD.KA.BAR)
Sargonic no. 43 (*ḫa-zi-*[*núm*]?)

IŠ.DÈ ^{GIŠ}taskarin (a wooden object), in units.
Pre-Sargonic App. to no. 32
Possibly a piece of furniture ("chair?").

ki-li-lum (*kilīlum*) KUG.BABBAR "silver wreath, head-band," in units.
See *CAD* K p. 358; *AHWB* p. 476; *MAD* 3 p. 146.
Sargonic no. 40.

MAŠ.DA.LÚ kug (meaning unknown), in units.
Pre-Sargonic App. to no. 32

^{URUDU}*maš-sa-tum* (*maššatum*) (a type of weapon), in units. See *CAD* M/1 p. 389; *AHWB* p. 629.
Sargonic no. 40

men, Akk. *agûm* "crown," in units. See *CAD* A/1 pp. 153ff.; *AHWB* p. 16.
Pre-Sargonic App. no. 32

^{URUDU}*na-ap-la-aq-tum* (*naplaqtum*) UD.KA.BAR (a type of weapon), in units. See *CAD* N/1 p. 305; *AHWB* p. 739.
Sargonic no. 40

nàd ^{GIŠ}taskarin, Akk. *eršum* "bed," in units. See *CAD* E pp. 315–18; *AHWB* p. 246.
Pre-Sargonic App. to no. 32

PI (= geštug) "earring," in units or in gín. An abbreviation of níg-geštug.
Fara no. 127: 1 gín PI
Pre-Sargonic App. to no. 32: 1 é-ba PI kug "1 pair of silver earrings"
Sargonic no. 38: 1 GÍN PI KUG.GI
PI is also attested in the Sargonic text *PBS* 9, 45:2 (1 gín PI kug). For níg-geštug, see Limet, *Métal* p. 223.

$SI_4.SI_4$ (meaning unknown), in units.
Sargonic no. 38

su-ga-nu (*šukānum*) KUG.BABBAR *maš-ga-na-at* "(precious object) overlaid with silver," in units. See *AHWB* p. 1262.
Sargonic no. 40
For this meaning of *šukānum*, compare W. G. Lambert, *BWL* p. 294.

ŠÀ.DAḪ (meaning unknown), in units.
Pre-Sargonic App. to no. 32

uri^{URUDU} (a metal container), in units.
Sargonic no. 181 (Price)
See Limet, *Métal* p. 233.

UD.KA.BAR (= zabar) kug(-luḫ), Akk. *mušālum*, "silver mirror," in units. See *CAD* M/2 pp. 256f.; *AHWB* p. 681.
Pre-Sargonic App. to no. 32

KA+UD.BAR (= zabar) [(X)] (an object), in units.
Sargonic no. 38: To be interpreted as either "(object) of bronze" or "mirror." Compare UD.KA.BAR above.

[. . .]-KU (an object), in units.
Pre-Sargonic no. 145: [. . .]-KU ki-lal-bi 4 ma-na

11.8. *Animals*

áb, Akk. *lītum*, *littum* "cow," in units. See *CAD* L pp. 217ff.; *AHWB* pp. 557f.
Sargonic no. 38 (Price)
Sargonic no. 49 (AP?)
Ur III no. 325 (Price)

anše, Akk. *imērum* "donkey," in teams (erín). See *CAD* I/J pp. 110–14; *AHWB* pp. 375f.
Pre-Sargonic App. to no. 32

ANŠE.BAR.AN (= kungá) "mule," in teams (ERÍN).
Sargonic no. 40

ANŠE.SAL (= emè), Akk. *atānum* "she-ass," in units. See *CAD* A/2 pp. 481ff.; *AHWB* p. 86.
Sargonic no. 181

BAL+U "male goat," in units.
Fara no. 20 (Price)
For the meaning, see note to no. 20 iii 2.

gud, Akk. *alpum* "bull, ox," in units. See *CAD* A/1 pp. 364–72; *AHWB* p. 38.
Fara no. 13 (Price?)
Sargonic no. 38 (Price)

ku_6-dar-ra "dried fish," lit.: "a fish split (for drying)," in units.
Pre-Sargonic nos. 22, 23, 141, and 144
The meaning of dar is here "to split, to halve" (Akk. *ḫepûm*, *letûm*). Compare Enūma eliš IV 137: *iḫpīšima kīma nūn mašṭê ana* 2-*šu* "he split her into two (parts) like a fish (split for) drying."

ku_6-KU (a type of fish), in units of ḫubur-containers.
Pre-Sargonic no. 149: 1 ḫubur ku_6-KU (transliteration only; Price)

máš, Akk. *puḫādum* "goat," in units. See *AHWB* p. 875.
Fara no. 127a

máš-bar-du_8 (a type of goat), in units.
Sargonic no. 166 (Price)
The term máš-bar-du_8-a is also attested in the Sargonic text *ITT* 2/2 p. 39 no. 4697.

SAL.ÁŠ.GÀR (= ^{SAL}áš-gàr), Akk. *unīqum* "female kid," in units. See *AHWB* pp. 1420f.
Sargonic no. 166 (Price; AŠ.SAL.GÀR)
The spelling ÁŠ.SAL.GÀR is also attested in the Sargonic text *TMH* 5, 163 i 4.

šáḫ-ŠE (= šáḫ-niga) "barley-fed pig," in units.
Fara no. 20 (Price)
For šáḫ, Akk. *šaḫûm* "pig, hog," see *AHWB* p. 1133.

šáḫ-ú "'grass'-fed pig," in units.
Sargonic no. 189 (Price)

u_8, Akk. *immertum*, *laḫrum* "ewe," in units. See *CAD* I/J pp. 128f.; L pp. 42ff.; *AHWB* pp. 378 and 528.
Sargonic no. 189 (Price?)

u_8-bar-gál-la "unshorn ewe," lit.: "ewe with (its) fleece on," in units.
Ur III no. 362 (Price)
For bar-gál-la "with fleece," and the related expressions bar-su-ga "without fleece" and bar-mú "growing (new) fleece," see Waetzoldt, *UNT* p. 39. Compare udu-bar-gál "unshorn sheep" and udu-nita-bar-gál-la "unshorn ram" below.

udu, Akk. *immerum* (*emmerum*) "sheep," in units. See *CAD* I/J pp. 129–34; *AHWB* p. 378.
Pre-Sargonic no. 19b
Pre-Sargonic no. 23
Sargonic nos. 38 and 190 (Price)

udu-bar-gál "unshorn sheep," lit. "sheep with (its) fleece on," in units.
Sargonic no. 166 (Price)
Compare u_8-bar-gál-la "unshorn ewe" and udu-nita-bar-gál-la "unshorn ram."

udu-nita "ram," in units.
Sargonic nos. 182a A and 191 (both Price)

udu-nita-bar-gál-la "unshorn ram," lit. "ram with (its) fleece on," in units.
Sargonic no. 173 (Price)
Compare u_8-bar-gál-la "unshorn ewe" and udu-bar-gál "unshorn sheep."

11.9. *Human Beings*

SAG.NITA "male head (= slave)," in units.
Sargonic no. 40

SAG.SAL "female head (= slave woman)," in units.
Sargonic no. 40

DUMU.SAL, Akk. *ṣiḫḫirtum* "girl," in units.
Sargonic no. 40

11.10. *Miscellaneous*

gán še-mú-a "barley-producing field," in iku.
Pre-Sargonic no. 149: 1(iku) gán še-mú-a (Price)

iš-gán (še) (meaning uncertain), in measures of dry capacity (NI-ga).
Fara nos. 14 and 15
For this commodity, see note to no. 14 i 9.

ŠU.KEŠDA (meaning unknown), in units.
Pre-Sargonic nos. 22, 23, and 144

In addition, nos. 19a and 19b (both Pre-Sargonic, Lagash) list a number of commodities, the meanings of which are uncertain. The interpretation of these items is particularly difficult in no. 19b, where some of the entries may in fact be personal names. See the following listing:

AN.SÁR+AŠ, in units.
Pre-Sargonic no. 19a
ÉŠ, in units.
Pre-Sargonic no. 19b
ÉŠ MÁ?, in units.
Pre-Sargonic no. 19b
ÉŠ MÁ?.GÍD, in units.
Pre-Sargonic no. 19b
GAM.ERIN?, in units.
Pre-Sargonic no. 19a
GI.GIŠ.INNIN, in units.
Pre-Sargonic no. 19b
GIŠ.LAL.LU, in units.
Pre-Sargonic no. 19b
NUN.IR.LAL.A, in units.
Pre-Sargonic no. 19a
SUM.[T]I.KI, in units.
Pre-Sargonic no. 19b
SUM.[X].KI, in units.
Pre-Sargonic no. 19b
X, in šakan.
Pre-Sargonic no. 19a

CHAPTER 12

LIST OF AKKADIAN AND SUMERIAN WORDS DISCUSSED

1. *Akkadian*

aḫāzum	232
akālum	227, 230
A-ki	150
annūtum	248
ap-lu	110
arāmum	241
ar(r)ugimānē rašājum	248
áš-dè	91–92
áš-ti	161
atru	223–24
attarum	224
awatam nukkurum	246
bakrum/bukrum	140
bar-ga-ad	150
be-lu GÁN	227
dabābum	240
daddarum	115
dūdum	296
edēšum	246
egûm	248
enûm	244
gamārum	72
gamrum	217
ḫalûm	294
ḫaṣṣinnum	296
iškinū	220–22, 224–25
išpikū	221
ištēniš	244
Izubîtum	119
kilīlum	296
kiškattûm	140
kuānum	236
kudurru	1–2, 21, 24
kullum	247
laqāʾum	232
maḫārum	227, 229–30
maššatum	296
mitḫāriš	244
mubbalkitum	247
muqippum	236
mu-za-zu	235
nadānum	229, 232
nakārum	110, 246
naparkudum	150
naparkûm	248
naplaqtum	296
nasākum	64
našāqum	105
nubattu	43
pānum	115
paqārum	246
patarrum	41–42, 296
pitiqtum	241
qiāpum	236
raʾāmum	72
ragāmum	246
rēʾûm	99
saḫārum	99
sapāḫum	64
sikkatum	23–24, 241
sissiktam batāqum	225
sulumḫû	64
šaʾāmum	231–32
šadādum	209, 232, 242
šadjum	150
šakānum	242
šaqālum	229
šîbtum	234–35
šîbum	234–35
šiddatum	209
šimtum	243
šiʾmū/šîmū	217
šukānum	297
tuārum	244
ù	104
uruḫḫum	95
zilul(l)ûm	99

2. *Sumerian*

a . . . dé	242
A.ḪA = ḪA.RAD	41
⌜A⌝?.SAR.RA?	46
a . . . sì	242
A.SU.TÚG	295
A.UŠ(.TA)	72
ABxÁŠ	234–35
ad-tab	296
adda	150
$^{a-da}$adda(LÚ.GUNU+ÚŠ)	150

AG.EN.NAM 67
ág 229
AN.RU 104
(AN.)TAR 225
Anzud$_x$(AN.IM.MI.MUŠEN) 63
Anzud$_x$(AN.MI.MUŠEN) 63
arád 102
asál 100
asal$_x$(RÉC-65.A) 110
Áš-DI^{KI} 115
as$_7$(SÁR+DIŠ) 104
ATU-132 28
ATU-139 28
ba 229
BA.AN (ŠE) 284, 296
ba-dar 41–42
BA.DAR 42
BA.NAM 42
BAḪÁR 55
^{TÚG}BAL 294
BAL+U = LAK-20 72, 297
bala 246
BAN 55
banšur$_x$(ASARI) 291
BAPPIR 291
bar-dul$_5$ 294
bar-si 294
bar-síg^{TÚG} 294
BARAG 54–55
BE.SUG 67
BUR 115
BUR.LA.ŠIR 38–39
bùr-*gunû* 71–72
burʾu 45–46, 67, 71–72
dab$_4$(DUB) 113
dam-gàr 235, 239
dar 297
DARA$_4$ 54
DILMUN 109
dím 46
DIN.SILÀ 28
dirig 223–24
^{GIŠ}DU.DA 296
dù 247
du$_8$ 102
DUB 113
^{d}DUB-an 113
dub-sar 238
dub-sar-gán 237–38
DUG+DÙG 33
DUG+Ì 33
DUG+Ì+vertical-GIŠ.X 42
DUG+KAG 34
DUG.RU 80
dug-silà 28–29
DUG.SILÀ 28–29, 31
DUMU.DUMU 11, 93, 104
dumu-gán 227
DUMU.SAG 140
DÚR/TUŠ 55
dúr . . . gar 221
durun$_x$(TUŠ.TUŠ) 55
E-ga-rin 74
é 223
É.BAḪÁR.NUNUZ 64
é-dù 215, 223
é-dù-a 215
É-dúr-BAḪÁR- . . . 63–64
É-dúr-BAḪÁR.NUN.ZA 64
é-kas 99
é-kas$_4$ 99
é Mug-si 102
é-ta . . . è 55, 240
É.ZA.NUN.BAḪÁR 64
è 231
EDIN 55, 115
EN.A 42
EN.ŠÀ 42
engar 237–38
engar èš 40
engar ki gu[b] 88
ENGAR.UŠ 237–38
engar zag/ki durun-durun 238
ERÍN+X 106
esir$_x$(LAK-173) 296
ÉŠ.A 44
ÉŠ.GÍD SI.SÁ 80, 94, 113, 215
ÉŠ MÁ?.GÍD 69
éš šám-ma-ta 26, 80, 215
èš 40
gá-la . . . dag 248
gáb-gi 236
gal-nigir 237
GAL.TE 74
galla-gal 74
GAM.GAM 55
gán 213
GÁN GAR 70
GÁN.NINDÁ 214
GÁN ŠÁM 91
gán še-mú-a 298
gar 229
GAR-en$_5$-si 102–3
GAR.GU.SUR(.NUN) 72
GÁR 55
gemé 216
geštug 296
gi-(n) 236, 248
gi$_4$ 231, 244–46
gi$_4$-gi$_4$-lum 296
GIBIL 246
gíd-da 296
^{GIŠ}gigir gam-ma 296
^{GIŠ}GIGIR.NÍG.ŠU 296
GÍR 110
GÍR-gal 55
GÍR-*gunû*-GAL 55
GÍR.SU.ME 67
GIŠ.ERÍN = IGI+LAK-527 105
giš-gan(-na) . . . bala 242–43

giš-gi An-tum 38–39
giš-gíd-da 296
giš-gub-ba 215
GIŠ.KIN.TI 140
GIŠ.UB.U$_8$.SAL(.A) 43
gišimmar 215
GIŠIMMAR 110
^{d}Gu-nu-ra 55
GU.SUR.NUN 72, 237–38
gúg 291
GÚG 54
gunû-LÚ-*šeššig*(= rin$_x$)-na-ra 215
gur(-maḫ) 72
ḪA.RAD = A.ḪA 41
ḪA.RAD.ÚR 40–41
ḪA.RAD.ÚR = Urum 41
ḪA.ÚR 40
ḫa-zi^{URUDU} 296
ḪI.ÚŠ 110
ḪU.TUŠ.BU-rúm 74
ì . . . ag 241
Ì.DÙG.GA 293
ì-ir 293
ì-sag 293
ì-šáḫ 293
ì-udu 293
Ì.ZAG 225–26, 242
IB 102
ÍB.BA.DÙ^{TÚG} 294
^{TÚG}ÍB.DÙ 294
ÍD.ZUBI 119
IGI.GAR? 68
IGI+LAK-527 105
igi-nu-du$_8$ 216
im-dù-a 241
IN 54
inim-bi . . . dug$_4$ 240
inim-bi é-ta . . . è 240
inim-bi . . . til 239–40
inim . . . gál 247
inim . . . gar 246–47
inim . . . gi-(n) 247–48
inim . . . kúr 246
INNIN.ÙḪ 95
ìr 102
^{d}Irḫan$_x$(MUŠ) 150
^{d}Irra$_x$(KIŠ) 150
isin$_x$(IN) 54
IŠ.DÈ 296
iš-gán 220–22, 224–25
iš-gán (še) 54, 221, 298
Izubi 119
KA+GAR 66
kag 23–24, 241
kag . . . dù 240–41
kalag 291
KAR.LAGAB 38
ki-a . . . tuš 235
ki . . . gar 221
ki-^{GIŠ}sur$_x$(ERÍN)-ra 88, 249
KI.UD 215
KIB 107
^{GIŠ}kiri$_6$ 215
$^{\text{ki GIŠ}}$kiri$_6$ 215
KISAL 35
^{d}KIŠ 150
kú 230
KÚ 66, 104
ku$_6$-dar-ra 297
ku$_6$-KU 297
kug 217
kug-babbar 217
kug-bar$_6$-bar$_6$ 295
kug-bi šu . . . si 239
kug-bi-ta . . . è 239
kug(-bi)-ta . . . til 239
kug-dím 239
KUG.KUG è 248–49
KUG.KUG è TUR.TUR è 248
kug-luḫ-ḫa 295
KUG.NA 42
kug-ta . . . è 239
kug-UD.UD 295
laḫ$_4$ 231
LAK-7 55
LAK-20 72
LAK-173 296
LAK-175 34, 67
LAK-180 55
LAK-245 150
LAK-246 150
LAK-247 150
LAK-269 28
LAK-278 107
LAK-289 54
LAK-397 55
LAK-483 54
LAK-514 109
LAK-636 28
LAK-644 28
LAK-647 113
LAK-742 55
LAK-747 55
LAK-790 54
LAK-798 67
LAK-813 67
lal 229
LÀL 33–34
LÀL+vertical-GIŠ 33–34
lu^{SAR} 292
lu-úb^{SAR} 292
LÚ GÁN 91, 105
lú-gán-gíd-da 238
lú-gi-na-ab-túm 236
lú-giš-rín-dab$_5$-ba 238
LÚ.GUNU+ÚŠ 150
lú-inim-gi-na 236
lú-inim-ma 233–34
lú-ki-inim-ma 233–34
(lú-)kug-lal(-a) 238–39

LÚ.NA.ME 109
lú-níg-šám-ag 228
lú-níg-šám-kú 227
lú-Object of Sale-šám-a 228
lú-šám-ag 228
lú-šám-kú 227
lú-še-ág 238
LÚ.ŠEŠ.EN 227–28
lugal 227
^{d}Lugal-^{GIŠ}asál 110
^{d}Lugal-^{GIŠ}asal$_{x}$(RÉC-65.A) 110
^{d}LUGAL-bar-ga-ad 150
lugal [é] 227
lugal gán(-kam) 70, 227
LUL 107
lus$_{x}$(LUL) 107
MA.GÍD 38
ma-ta 102
MÁ? 69
MAŠ.DA.LÚ 296
maš-ga-na-sag 89
máš-bar-du$_{8}$ 297
^{TÚG}ME(.A).GÁL 294
ME.KA 67
mu$_{6}$-sùb 99
MUNSUB 225
MUNSUB(.AN).TAR 225–26
^{mu6}munsùb 99
munsub$_{x}$(PA.USAN) 99
^{d}MUŠ 150
^{d}MUŠ.DIN.DÚB.BU 150
^{d}MUŠ.DIN.TIR.BALAG 150
nam-kud 45
NAM.KUD 109
Nanna$_{x}$(ŠEŠ)^{na} 38
ne-me 248
ne-sag 140
ne-sùb 105
NI.TÚG 294
níg-ba 224–26
níg-bar-3^{TÚG} 294
níg-dirig 222–24
NÍG.DÚR.GAR 220–22, 224–25
NÍG.GU.SUR 72
NÍG.KI.GAR 220–22, 224–25
níg-lal-gaba^{TÚG} 294
níg-lal-sag 294
^{TÚG}níg-lám 294
NÍG.LÁM.TÚG 42, 48
níg-sag-lal 294
níg-sag-lal-SAL 294
níg-šám 217
(níg-)šám . . . til 239
níg-šu 296
NÍG.TUŠ.GAR = NÍG.DÚR.GAR 220–22, 224–25
níg-urudu-babbar 295
NIGIDA 115
NIGÍN+ḪA.A 293
nigir 238, 241
nigir-sila 237
nigir-uru 238, 241
Nin-GÍR.ḪA.RAD 41
ninda 291
ninda-banšur 291
ninda-bappir 291
ninda-durun$_{x}$(TUŠ.TUŠ)-na 292
ninda-ì 291
ninda-ì-dé-a 291
ninda-kalag 291
ninda-KU.KU-na 55, 292
ninda-sag 292
ninda-silà 292
ninda-še 292
ninda 1(ul) 291
ninda 2(ul) 291
NINDÁ 34
^{nun}nunuz$_{x}$(ZA) 64
PA.URU 99
PA.USAN 99
PÉŠ 140, 150
PI 296
RÉC-65 110
RÉC-164 28
RÉC-171 107
RÉC-265 55
RÉC-349.A.TU 102
RÉC-380 28
RÉC-382 28
RÉC-463 54
sag-du$_{5}$ 237–38
SAG.NINDA 292
sag-nita 216
sag-SAL 216
ság . . . dug$_{4}$/di 64
sàg-nu-di 64
SAG$_{7}$.DI 64
^{sá}sag$_{7}$-nu-di 64
SAL.ABxÁŠ 234–35
SAL.U$_{8}$.DI 43
^{d}Samàn(NUN.ŠE.ÉŠ.BU) 74
SAR.LAK-175 67
SÁR+DIŠ 104
SI 224
SI.A 105
si-(g) 223
sì 242
SI$_{4}$.SI$_{4}$ 115, 297
síg-bar-udu 294
síg-bar-udu-bar 294
SÍG.BU/SUD 64
SÍG.GAN 284, 295
síg-ŠÀ.ŠÈ 295
SIG$_{5}$ 105
SILÀ-*gunû*.DUG 28
simug 239
^{d}Sud-da 63
suluḫu 64
sum 229, 232, 240
sum-⌜gu⌝ 292

SUR 292
sur_x(GIŠERÍN) 88, 151
ŠA.DUG 28
ŠÀ.DAḪ 297
ŠÀ.GA.DU 295
ŠÀ.GA.DÙTÚG 295
$šaga_x$(LAK-175) 34, 67
šáḫ-niga 297
šáḫ-ú 297
šám 217, 231–32, 240
ŠÁM 34
ŠÁM+A 217
ŠÁM+ÀM 217
še-ba 292
ŠE.BAR.GI_4.TA 69
še DU 69
še-ḪAR 292
ŠE.NI.KID.NI 113, 292
še-sa 292
$ŠEG_9$-daKI 150
ŠEŠ *be-lu* GÁN 227
šeš-gán 227
ŠEŠ+IB 72
ŠEŠ.KI 37
ŠITA.dINNIN 95
ŠITA KUR.ZA_x(LAK-813) 67
$šita_4$(U+KÍD) 55
TÚGšu-du_7-a 295
ŠU.KEŠDA 281, 298
TÚGšu-ni-ra 295
šu-nir 295
šu . . . si 229, 239
šu . . . ti 229–30
TAG_4.ALAM 69
TE.GAL 74
téš-bi/ba 244
til-la 217
dTIR 48
tiru 74
tu_7 293
TÚG.A.SU 295
TÚG.DÙL.GARÁ?.SÁR+DIŠ 295
túg ki-sì-ga bala 295
TÚG.ŠU.DU_7.A.BAL 295
TÚG.ŠU.SÈ.GA 295
TÚG.ŠU.ZA.GA 295
TÚG.TUM.GUNU 295
túm 230–31
U+É 55
u_8-bar-gál-la 297
U_8.SAL 43
u_8-salsá 43
u_9(EZEN+AN) 107
ud(-ba) 219, 249
UD.GUG 38
UD.LU 38
udu-nita-bar-gál-la 297
ugula-ukkin 44
ÙḪ.INNIN 95
UKKIN 44
UM 150
um-me 48
um-mi-a lú-é-éš-gar 237
umbin? 54, 160
UMBIN 54
ÚR+GAR 54
d$Urhan_x$(MUŠ) 150
uriURUDU 297
URI 113
uru-sag 89
urudu$^{ru_{12}\text{-}da}$ 296
uruḫ(ÙḪ.INNIN) 95
Urum = ḪA.RAD.ÚR 41
USAN 105
UŠ.BUR.TÚG 42
ušùr(LÁL+LAGAB) 80
ušùr-da-gi_4-a 235
ZA_x(LAK-813) 67
zabar 296–97
zag 241
ZAG 106
zag . . . šuš 243
zíd-ba 292
zilulu(PA.GIŠGAL) 99
X.EDINKI 115